The Georgia Studies Book

Our State and the Nation

The Georgia Studies Book
Our State and the Nation

Edwin L. Jackson
Senior Author

Mary E. Stakes
Associate Senior Author

Lawrence R. Hepburn

Mary A. Hepburn

Carl Vinson Institute of Government
The University of Georgia

22 USA

January 2, 1788
Georgia

Other textbooks published by the
Carl Vinson Institute of Government

State Government in Georgia
Local Government in Georgia
An Introduction to Law in Georgia

THE GEORGIA STUDIES BOOK: OUR STATE AND THE NATION

Editor: *Emily Honigberg*

Design and production supervision: *Reid McCallister*
  Design: *Mary Porter*
  Computer graphics and design: *Jessica Mendelson*

Editorial staff: *Inge Whittle, Jayne Plymale*
  Proofreading: *Charlotte Eberhard, Dorothy Paul*

Digital composition: *Lisa Carson*
  Word processing: *Brenda Keen*

03 02 01 00 99 98   10 9 8 7 6 5 4 3 2 1

Library of Congress Cataloging-in-Publication Data

The Georgia studies book : our state and the nation / Edwin L. Jackson, senior
  author . . . [et al.].
        p.   cm.
    Includes index.
    Summary: A textbook that introduces the history, geography, and politics of Georgia.
    ISBN 0-89854-192-1
    1. Georgia—Juvenile literature. [1. Georgia.]   I. Jackson, Edwin L.
II. Carl Vinson Institute of Government.
F286.3.G463   1998
975.8—dc21   98-6892
                                                                           CIP
                                                                           AC

Foreword

Welcome to the new edition of *The Georgia Studies Book*. It now has a subtitle, *Our State and the Nation*, to reflect a greater emphasis on Georgia's story in the context of American history and government.

The Institute began publishing textbooks back in the early 1970s, when teachers asked us for materials to help them teach about Georgia government and history. As interest in these subjects grew, we responded to the need for textbooks that are accurate, up-to-date, inclusive, readable, and interesting to Georgia students. We always make sure that they meet all the current curriculum requirements set by the Georgia Department of Education.

The authors, who are all veteran faculty members at the Institute, have been teaching, researching, and writing about Georgia for many years. The printed and electronic materials they create and the workshops they teach are familiar to many people across the state—in the schools, in the government, and in the community.

We are especially proud to publish this colorful new edition of *The Georgia Studies Book* and trust that its contents help today's students become tomorrow's informed citizens.

Henry M. Huckaby
Director
Carl Vinson Institute of Government

Acknowledgments

Many Georgians contributed to the preparation of the current and previous editions of this textbook. Among them are the following, whose guidance and assistance are gratefully acknowledged.

Reviewers (1st ed.): University of Georgia faculty—Mark Williams, Anthropology Department; Robert Pratt, Phinizy Spalding, Charles Wynes, History Department; James Kundell, Institute of Government; Lief Carter, Political Science Department. (2d ed.): University of Georgia faculty—Anna Boling, Betty Clements, Michael Thurmond, Institute of Government. Other institutions—John Worth, Fernbank Science Center; Tom Scott, Department of History, Mercer University.

Others at the University of Georgia who leant their expertise: legal research—Betty Clements, Institute of Government, and Paul Hardy, Institute of Community and Area Development; statistical data, Haoran Lu, and historical data, Charly Pou (both Institute of Government).

Over the years, many Georgia educators have provided us with teacher reviews, helpful ideas, and insights. Their knowledge and their experience in the classroom have been invaluable in planning and creating this textbook.

Valuable assistance was provided by the Atlanta History Center, Library Archives; Georgia Department of Archives and History; High Museum of Art; Office of the Governor; Office of the Secretary of State; University of Georgia Libraries: Hargrett Rare Book and Manuscript Library, Photographic Services.

Rebecca McCarthy wrote the "Georgians in History" special features.

Photo and text credits on page 497.

Contents

Maps

See Appendix for current Georgia, U.S., and world maps.

Charts, Tables, and Diagrams

UNIT 1

1526	1732	1736	1766	1777	1783	1800	1829	1838	1860	1868
First European settlement in Georgia	Georgia colony created to extend from the Atlantic Ocean to the Pacific Ocean	Augusta becomes the first settlement on Georgia's Fall Line	Georgia clay shipped to Wedgwood pottery factory in England	First eight counties in Georgia are created	Georgia's western boundary is fixed at the Mississippi River	Georgia's population of 162,686 almost doubles the results of the 1790 census	Georgia's Gold Rush begins	Removal of last Cherokees from Georgia	State population surpasses 1 million	Georgia capital moved to Atlanta

Setting the Stage

1887	1893	1900	1919	1940	1952	1957	1967	1972	1996	1998
Bauxite production begins in Georgia	Georgia's most deadly hurricane hits Savannah	State population exceeds 2 million	Lincoln Memorial statue of Georgia marble completed	Record set for coldest temperature in Georgia, −17°F	Record set for highest temperature in Georgia, 112°F	Lake Lanier, one of Georgia's most popular lakes, created	All of Georgia placed in Eastern Time Zone	Cumberland Island National Seashore established	Over 5 million spectators attend Summer Olympic Games in Atlanta	El Niño weather phenomenon causes flooding in southwest Georgia

Coming Up Next!
- What is geography?
- A look at Georgia's location
- Regions of the world

Let's Talk Geography

To understand Georgia, you need to know something about its geography. For instance, did you know that—

- England believed that Georgia could produce silk?
- oranges, grapefruit, and bananas don't grow in Georgia?
- the Blue Ridge Mountains affected the early settlement of Georgia?
- most drinking water in north Georgia comes from rivers and lakes, rather than from wells?
- Georgia's population is growing at a much faster rate than most states?

Georgia's past, present, and future cannot be explained without a knowledge of everything around us. That is why we need geography.

What Is Geography?

The term **geography** comes from two Greek words—"ge" for *earth* and "graphia" for *write about*. Geographers study physical and cultural features on or near the earth's surface. **Physical features** are those that occur naturally, such as mountains, rivers, and oceans. **Cultural features** are those created by people, such as boundaries, towns, and roads. Geographers also look at living things—plants, animals, and people. They want to know how people shape and are shaped by their **environment**—all the things that surround us.

Geography, then, is the study of the earth in a way that shows the relationship between humans and their environment. That makes geography a story of people, places, and relationships.

Geographers have named the imaginary grid of lines covering the earth "latitude" and "longitude." Using these lines, we can pinpoint the exact location of any place on the earth's surface. All we must know are two things: (1) How far north or south it is from the Equator, and (2) How far east or west it is from Greenwich, England. You will soon find out why these two sites are important to location.

By remembering this, you will discover that many events in Georgia history did not just happen by chance. Rather, they involved people reacting to their physical surroundings. Geography is a tool that will help you interpret the past, understand the present, and prepare for the future.

What You Need to Know about Geography

When geographers tell us about the earth, they often use five basic themes of geography:

1. **Location**: where places are located on the earth's surface
2. **Place**: physical and human characteristics of places
3. **Relationships**: interaction of people and environment
4. **Movement**: movement and interaction of people
5. **Regions**: areas with similar characteristics

In the following pages, you will be introduced to these concepts and to some important skills of geography. In later chapters, these concepts and skills will be applied to show the many ways geography has influenced Georgia. As you read, keep in mind: *people, places,* and *relationships.* That's what geography is all about! ▶

A Look at Georgia's Location

If you were writing to a pen pal in another country, how would you describe Georgia's location? There are many ways it can be done. If you have ever given directions, you are already familiar with some of them.

▶ **Locating the Main Ideas**

1. Define: geography, physical feature, cultural feature, environment
2. Explain why geography is about people, places, and relationships.
3. How does the study of geography relate to Georgia history?

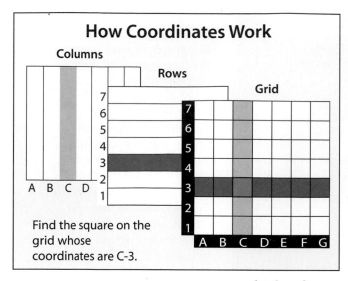

How Coordinates Work

Columns

Rows

Grid

Find the square on the grid whose coordinates are C-3.

Relative Location

Relative location refers to the position of one place in relation to another. For instance, Savannah is nearer the ocean than is Columbus. A good way to express relative location is by using **cardinal** and **intermediate** directions. Cardinal directions are the four main direction points on a compass—north, south, east, and west. Intermediate directions are the halfway points between cardinal directions, such as NE (northeast) or SW (southwest).

Absolute Location

A second type of location is **absolute location**, which refers to the exact spot on the earth's surface where a place is found. Unlike relative location, each place on earth has only one absolute location. Each place's location is unique, that is, different from that of every other place.

Geographers long ago invented a **grid**—or network—of invisible lines to cover the globe and help them locate places. If you have ever drawn a graph, you are familiar with the grid. It is a set of horizontal rows and vertical columns. Placing a series of rows over a series of columns makes a grid. The point where a row and column cross is known as an *intersection*. The letters or numbers that identify this point are called the **coordinates** of the intersection.

The imaginary grid of lines used to determine absolute location consists of *latitude* and *longitude*. You'll find out more about these two terms shortly.

Using Circle Measurements

The grid formed by latitude and longitude is special because the earth is round, like a circle. Ancient mathematicians developed a system for dividing a circle into 360 small, equal divisions called **degrees**. One degree—written as 1°—equals $1/360$ of a full circle. Degrees are further divided into smaller units called **minutes**. Just as an hour has 60 minutes, 1 degree has 60 minutes (written 1° = 60′). Minutes are divided into the smallest parts of a circle, called **seconds** (written as 1′ = 60″).

Degrees, minutes, and seconds allow us to identify the exact location of any place on the edge of a circle. Since there are 360 degrees in a circle, and 60 minutes in each degree, and 60 seconds in each minute, we can divide a circle into over 1 million different parts ($360 \times 60 \times 60 = 1,296,000$). Because we usually don't need to be that exact, you will sometimes see minutes and seconds rounded off. Remember, there are 60—not 100—parts to each degree and minute. For instance, 33°28′47″ would be rounded off to the nearest minute—33°29′.

▶ Locating the Main Ideas

1. Define: relative location, cardinal direction, intermediate direction, absolute location, grid, coordinate, degree, minute, second, sphere

2. Describe Georgia's relative location to its border states.

3. Explain why your street address is one type of absolute location.

4. Draw a grid with five rows and five columns. Label the rows using numbers. Label the columns using letters. Mark points at two different intersections, and give the coordinates for both points.

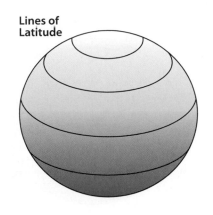

Lines of Latitude

Although the earth is round, it is not just a circle. It is a round body called a **sphere**. Every point on its surface is the same distance from its center. This makes it possible to measure the earth in degrees, just like a circle. ◀

Using Latitude to Find North and South

Latitude lines are used to determine location north and south from the **Equator**, an imaginary line that circles the earth at its widest part.

To calculate latitude, four reference points on earth are used. At the opposite ends of the earth are two geographic points—the North Pole and the South Pole. They are the opposite ends of an imaginary line called the earth's **axis**, around which our planet turns. Halfway between the two poles lies another imaginary line which divides the world in two. This is the Equator. The fourth reference point is the center of the earth.

The drawing on this page shows how latitude is measured. The starting point for measuring latitude—0°—is the Equator. The angle made if one line is drawn from the center of the earth to the Equator and another line from the center of the earth to the North Pole is 90°—a right angle. The same is true with the South Pole—another 90 degree angle. Therefore, the latitude of each pole is said to be 90°. The North Pole's latitude is 90 degrees *north*—stated as 90°N. The latitude of the South Pole is 90 degrees *south*, or 90°S. Because of this, the latitude of any location on earth must be between 0 and 90 degrees north, or between 0 and 90 degrees south, depending upon whether it is north or south of the Equator. The Equator thus divides the earth into two halves, known as **hemispheres**. The northern half is called the Northern Hemisphere, and the southern half is the Southern Hemisphere. If you look at a world map or globe, you can see that Georgia is located in the Northern Hemisphere.

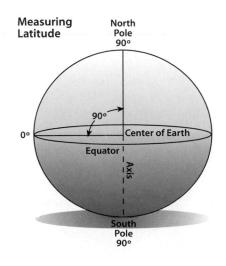

Northern Hemisphere

0° Equator 0°

Southern Hemisphere

Lines of latitude are sometimes called **parallels**. That is because *latitude* lines are *parallel*—they never cross, always remaining the same distance from each other. So, the "35th parallel" is the line that circles the globe marking 35 degrees of latitude.

The average distance between degrees of latitude is 69.06 miles. Minutes are just over one mile apart (6,077 feet), and seconds are 101 feet apart.

But latitude is only one-half of geography's grid system for determining location on earth. For example, Atlanta, Georgia's state capital, is situated at 33°45′N. But so are Ragland, Alabama; West Point, Mississippi; and many other places in the United States. In fact, 33°45′ crosses Lebanon, Iraq, Iran, Afghanistan, China, Japan, and several other countries of the world. What piece of information is missing? Latitude allows us to find location north and south of the Equator, but it doesn't help us on east and west. That's the story of longitude.

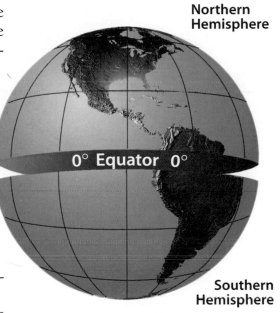

Measuring Latitude

North Pole 90°

90°

0°

Center of Earth

Equator

Axis

South Pole 90°

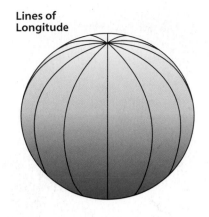

Lines of Longitude

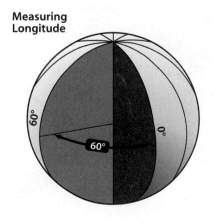

International Date Line (180°)

Eastern Hemisphere

Prime Meridian (0°)

Western Hemisphere

Measuring Longitude

60°

60°

0°

Using Longitude to Find East and West

Long ago, ocean navigators learned to use latitude to determine north and south. Halfway between the poles was a natural reference point for dividing north from south—the Equator. At night, they used the North Star to find north. But, measuring east and west was not as easy.

The term for measuring east and west location is **longitude**. Just like latitude, longitude is measured in degrees. The degrees represent the angle between two lines from the center of the earth—one to 0° longitude and the other to the place you are trying to locate. But where should 0° longitude be located? Unlike latitude, which has the Equator, there is no natural point on earth to separate east and west. Zero degrees longitude could be anywhere.

For centuries, each nation was free to decide how it wanted to measure east and west. A common practice for **cartographers**—map makers—was to select their own nation's capital city or a major port as 0° longitude. You can imagine how confusing this must have been.

The problem was finally solved in 1884, at an international meeting in Washington, D.C. There, an agreement was made that Greenwich, England, just outside London, would be 0°—the beginning point of world longitude. Greenwich was chosen for several reasons. Atop a hill in Greenwich stood the Royal Observatory. For some time, detailed navigation tables had been prepared here, with the observatory serving as 0° longitude. Also, at that time Britain was the world's leading sea power, and it made sense to follow its lead.

From the Royal Observatory, a line was extended to the North and South poles. This was the first of 360 north-to-south lines connecting the two poles. They were called **meridians**. Because Greenwich's meridian marked the point from which all other longitude was measured, it was named the **Prime Meridian**.

The Prime Meridian marks the dividing point between the Western Hemisphere and the Eastern Hemisphere. Because the earth is a sphere, a second dividing point is needed halfway on the other side of the world. That point is longitude 180°—half of 360°. The 180th meridian not only divides east from west. It also marks the beginning point for counting time and dates on earth and is known as the **International Date Line**. If you trace the Prime Meridian up to the North Pole, you will notice that it simply changes its name to International Date Line on the other side of the pole. Observe that 0° and 180° form one continuous line dividing the earth into eastern and western hemispheres.

To identify other longitudes, you must indicate whether they are east or west of Greenwich. The 81st meridian in the Western Hemisphere—which crosses through Savannah, Georgia—would be shown as 81°W. In the Eastern Hemisphere, 81 degrees of longitude would be indicated 81°E.

Notice that unlike parallels of latitude which never cross, meridians of longitude *converge*—or meet—at the two poles. Distance between meridians is greatest at the Equator—69.17 miles. At Georgia's southern border, meridians are 59.7 miles apart. By the time they reach the northern border, they've narrowed by another three full miles.

Longitude's Special Function

One special way longitude affects each of us is in telling time. A day consists of 24 hours—the length of time the earth takes to complete rotation on its axis. There are 360 degrees of longitude, and it takes one hour for the earth to rotate 15 degrees (360° divided by 24 hours = 15° per hour). The world has been divided into 24 **time zones**, about 15 degrees apart. These zones don't always follow every 15th meridian. A state, province, or country may want all of its people following the same time. However, larger countries like the United States, the Soviet Union, Canada, and Australia have no choice but to divide into different time periods.

The United States has a total of six different time zones. Four zones are shown below. Georgia is situated in the Eastern Time Zone. As you go west, you turn your clock back one hour as you enter each new time zone. As you travel east, you advance your clock ahead one hour for each zone.

To give you an idea how time works, on July 1, when it is 12 noon in Greenwich, England, it will be 7:00 a.m. in Macon, Georgia, and 4:00 a.m. in Los Angeles, California. Heading east from Greenwich, however, you turn the clock ahead one hour every 15 degrees, until you reach the International Date Line. At that point—180°—the clock will have just hit midnight, the dawn of a new day—July 2.

The Prime Meridian at the Royal Observatory in Greenwich, England, is a popular site for tourists. Here you can stand with one foot in the Western Hemisphere and the other in the Eastern Hemisphere.

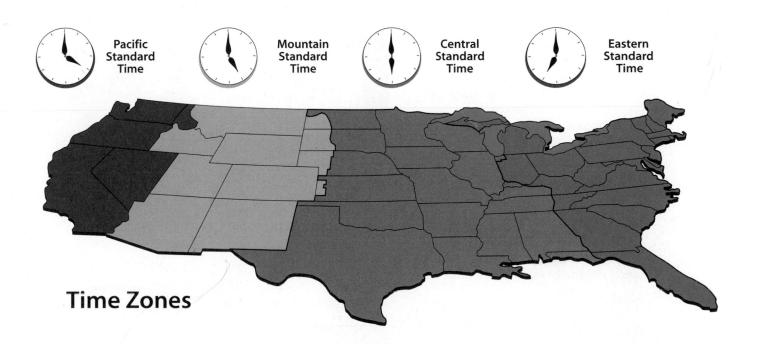

Pacific Standard Time   Mountain Standard Time   Central Standard Time   Eastern Standard Time

Time Zones

Understanding Maps

A map is a drawing of all or a portion of the earth's surface. There are many types of maps, but generally maps fall into the four categories shown below. However, it is possible for a particular map to include a combination of categories. For instance, a highway map may also show the political boundaries of cities and counties.

A **physical relief** map, sometimes called a *physiographic map*, shows land formations such as mountains, hills, rivers, and lakes. Also, different colors are often used to show elevation. Physical relief maps show how an area would look on a clear day when viewed from high above the earth's surface.

A **political map** shows the boundaries of political regions, such as school or election districts, cities, counties, states, and nations. The map to the left shows the boundaries of Georgia's counties.

A **highway map** shows major roads and highways identified by number and type (such as I-75, U.S. 78, Ga. 53). A highway map also shows the location of cities and towns, major rivers and lakes, and certain cultural features (such as military bases and state parks).

A **thematic map** (sometimes called a *data map*) shows information based on a theme or topic. The theme can be population, crops, occupation, finances, or whatever you choose to show. Because our government collects data on a county-by-county basis, thematic maps often include county outlines. The map at right shows where peanuts are grown in Georgia.

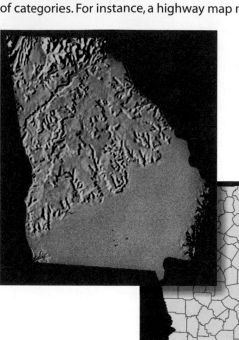

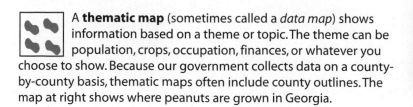

Peanut
Production
in Georgia
(1995)

= 5 million pounds of peanuts

Reading Maps

A. **TITLE.** A map should have a title that identifies the subject of the map.

B. **GRID.** The map grid helps you to locate places. A map will usually have an index that identifies place locations by grid coordinates, such as C-4 or A-12. The grid lines generally aren't drawn on the map. The numbers and letters of the rows and columns are written in the margins. To locate places, you must *mentally* connect the grid coordinates and look in the square they form. Not all maps use letters and numbers on a grid. Some use degrees of longitude and latitude—but it all works the same.

C. **SCALE.** A map is a drawing of an actual area. Maps are drawn "to scale," which means there is a relationship between distances on the map and real distances. A map **scale** allows you to measure distances on a map to determine the actual distance between places.

The *graphic scale*, which looks like a small ruler, is the most common type of map scale. The "ruler" is divided into units of measurement, typically miles or kilometers, so you can see how far apart two places on the map actually are. There are other ways to express scale.

A *verbal* or *word scale* is a simple statement of distance, such as "one inch equals ten miles." A *fraction scale* shows distance as a fraction or ratio, such as 1:500,000. If the map is based on inches, 1 inch on the map would equal 500,000 inches (about eight miles) on earth.

D. **LEGEND** or **KEY.** The map **legend**—or **key**—explains the symbols used on the map. The symbols may be small pictures, like a track to represent a railroad or a tree to represent a park. Dots of different sizes usually represent cities of varying populations—the larger the dot, the greater the population. Color is another kind of symbol on a map. Rivers are frequently drawn in blue, while forest areas are shaded green.

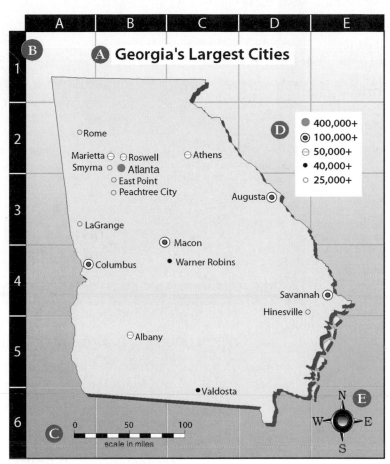

Source: U.S. Census Bureau, 1996 estimates

E. **DIRECTION.** A drawing of a **compass** showing the cardinal directions, or an arrow pointing north, should appear somewhere on the map. This symbol is important because the top of the page is not always true north.

Practice Your Skills

1. Define: map, scale, legend, key, compass
2. What is the title of the map on this page?
3. What are the coordinates of Augusta? of Columbus?
4. Rewrite the map scale as a word scale.
5. What information is given in the map legend? How many cities have a population in the category over 50,000? over 100,000? over 400,000?
6. Using the compass on this map, are the top of the page and true north the same?

*Latitude and longitude are **used** to form one or more boundaries of almost every state.*

Using Latitude and Longitude

Latitude and longitude are important because they provide a system for determining exact locations. They are important for other reasons, too. Look at the map of the United States and observe the lines of latitude and longitude and many of the state boundaries. A number of states—including Georgia—use latitude or longitude for one or more of their boundaries. Except for New Jersey and Hawaii, every state has one or more of its boundaries based on latitude, longitude, or both. Notice how this is especially true of the western states, which were settled last.

Why were latitude and longitude used so often in America for political boundaries? When England began creating new colonies in America, little was known about the geography of the country. Rather than worry about rivers and mountain ranges, the British government found it convenient to "colonize by latitude."

Knowledge of latitude and longitude is important in many ways. Pilots, navigators, surveyors, and military personnel use the network of invisible grids daily to locate places on earth. So do weather forecasters, geologists, cartographers, hikers, and others. ◀

Regions of the World: Where Does Georgia Fit In?

Appalachia, the South, Coastal Plain, and Metropolitan Atlanta—what do these terms have in common? Each is a **region** of the earth.

▶ **Locating the Main Ideas**

1. Define: latitude, Equator, axis, hemisphere, parallels, longitude, cartographer, meridian, Prime Meridian, International Date Line, time zone

2. What are the four reference points needed to calculate latitude?

3. What is the starting point for measuring latitude? longitude?

4. What directions does latitude measure? longitude?

5. How have latitude and longitude been important in U.S. history?

Region is a term geographers use to describe an area of the earth that is alike in ways that make it distinct from other areas of the earth.

Where are Appalachia, the South, Coastal Plain, and Metropolitan Atlanta located? These regions are probably not marked on a map. That's because a region does not have exact boundaries. The concept of region is somewhat like the idea of hot and cold. Although we can measure temperature with a thermometer, where is the exact boundary between "hot" and "cold"?

Although geographers may have difficulty identifying the exact boundaries of a region, they usually can agree on its general location. In some cases, to make their work easier, they will use existing political boundaries—such as county or state lines—to mark off a region.

An example of a region you may be familiar with is your local neighborhood. If you were to ask the people living around you about the boundaries of your neighborhood, you would probably get different responses. But, even if they couldn't agree, you would still have a pretty good idea about the area that makes up your neighborhood. You would know what it's like to live there and how it's similar to or different from other neighborhoods.

The key to a region is *shared characteristics* that make that area unique—different from other areas. A region can be any size—from classroom to community to continent to hemisphere—and may have many or few things in common. But to be called a region, it must have a set of distinct features.

Geographic Regions

There are hundreds of ways to classify the earth into regions. Any place on earth can be part of many different regions. These regions, however, do not have official boundaries set by government. They are called regions because of similarities found within them. These similarities may be *physical* in nature—such as location, soil, terrain, elevation, climate, and vegetation. Or, they may be *cultural* in nature, such as race, language, history, and standard of living. When a region is identified on the basis of physical or cultural features, we call it a **geographic region**. Let's look at several types of geographic regions of which Georgia is a part.

One type of geographic region is that based on *absolute location* on the globe. This involves using latitude and longitude to determine a region's exact location on the earth. Examples of this include dividing the world into hemispheres and time zones.

Another type of geographic region is based on *continental location*. Georgia is located on the continent of North America. The part of North America south of Mexico is commonly called *Central America*. The region from Mexico southward to the tip of South America is known as *Latin America*.

Census Regions of the United States.

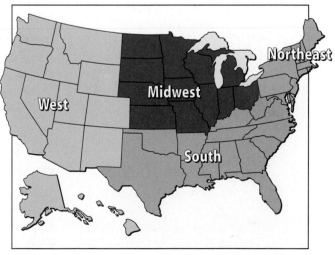

Regions may also be defined according to their *relative location*, which simply means the location of one area in relation to another. A good example of this is the division of the United States into the North, South, East, and West.

The South

In 1763, Charles Mason and Jeremiah Dixon were called upon to survey the boundary between Pennsylvania and Maryland to settle a disagreement. The results of that survey became known as the Mason and Dixon Line. Later, after Pennsylvania and other northern states outlawed slavery, this line became the dividing line on the East Coast between slave and free states. To many, the Mason-Dixon Line separated the "South" from the "North."

In 1861, 11 slave states broke away from the Union and formed the Confederate States of America (see page 189). These states are considered part of the South. Some geographers enlarge the South to include Maryland and Kentucky. The U.S. Census Bureau defines the South as also including West Virginia, Oklahoma, and even Delaware. Whatever definition is used, Georgia is always listed as part of the South.

The Deep South

Another regional term you will sometimes see is "Deep South." While the term involves relative location, it also refers to the heart of the old Confederacy. It was a region that was rural, poor, and dependent upon agriculture—particularly cotton. States in the Deep South had much in common. Usually included as part of the historic "Deep South" are South Carolina, Georgia, Florida, Alabama, Mississippi, Louisiana, and sometimes Arkansas and North Carolina.

The Southeast

Georgia is also part of a region known as the "Southeast." There is no official list of which states make up the southeastern United States, but Georgia is always included. In many ways, Georgia has more in common with neighboring states of the Southeast than with such southern states as Texas and Maryland, or with such eastern states as Maine and New York.

The Sun Belt

During the 1980s, a new regional term came into use: "Sun Belt." This term applies to a band across America of southern and western states whose warm climates have attracted Northerners to move there. The Sun Belt has no exact boundary, but 37°N is about where it begins. The states most commonly associated with Sun Belt growth are Florida, North Carolina, Georgia, Texas, Arizona, and California.

Political Regions

In addition to regions based on location, there are other types of regions important to Georgia. A **political region** is an area of land that has legal boundaries and has its own government. The best examples of this type of region are your city, county, state, and nation.

People living in a political region have many things in common. For example, the laws, traditions, and beliefs in Georgia about what services government should provide are different from those in Massachusetts, California, or even neighboring Florida. Likewise, life in rural Echols or Quitman counties is different from life in urban counties, such as Fulton or DeKalb.

Population Regions

Georgia is one of the fastest growing states in the nation, in terms of population. Because of this rapid growth, our state faces many tough challenges. For example, growth can bring needed jobs to a community, but it can also create serious traffic and pollution problems. To think about population, some special terms are important to know.

The U.S. Census Bureau uses three terms to describe nonpolitical regions on the basis of population. These terms are *urban, rural,* and *suburban.* They refer to both the population (number of people living in a region) and the **population density** (how many people live in a square mile.)

Urban Areas

The term "urban" comes from the Latin word for city, "urbs." Even though the terms urban and city are related, they don't mean exactly the same thing. The term *city* describes a politically defined area. The terms *urban* and *urban area* describe areas based on population.

The Census Bureau defines **urban** as (1) any city with a population of at least 2,500, or (2) any urbanized area of at least 50,000 residents. An **urbanized area** includes a central space together with a densely settled *urban fringe* next to it. It must have a combined population of at least 50,000. The "central space" may be a city, but not necessarily. An urban fringe is an area with at least 1,000 people per square mile.

Suburban is a word used to describe the heavily populated residential areas around cities. Suburb comes from a Latin word meaning "near the city." Sometimes suburbs are called bedroom communities because residents sleep there at night, but in the day they **commute** (travel back and forth) to work or shop in the city.

Political Regions

City
County
State
Nation

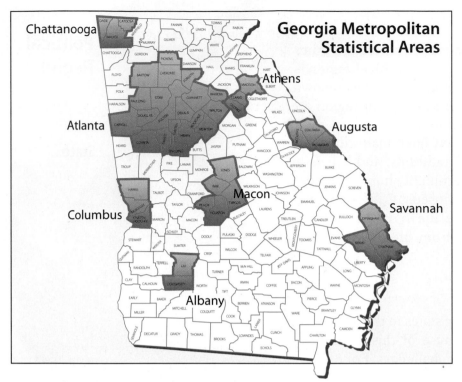

Georgia Metropolitan Statistical Areas

Chattanooga
Athens
Atlanta
Augusta
Columbus
Macon
Savannah
Albany

Rural Areas

When you think of rural Georgia, you probably think of farms or forests. But you can find rural areas within 20 miles of downtown Atlanta! What makes an area rural? The Census Bureau says that any place not meeting the definition of urban or urbanized area is considered **rural**. This means that any Georgia town or community with fewer than 2,500 residents is classified as rural. Likewise, any area outside a city with fewer than 1,000 people per square mile would be considered rural.

Metro Areas

One special type of population area is called a **Metropolitan Statistical Area (MSA)**. TV news shows sometimes refer to "**metropolitan** Atlanta." The term refers to the city of Atlanta, plus the large, populated area surrounding it.

Many federal grant programs (such as housing, crime-fighting, and transportation) apply only to MSAs. These areas receive money to help solve problems related to their dense population. An area can be designated an official MSA if it has (1) a central city with 50,000 or more residents, or (2) a total population of at least 100,000 that includes an urbanized area of at least 50,000.

The federal government has guidelines to decide what counties to include in a metro area. MSAs always consist of entire counties—even though some portions of outlying counties may actually be rural in nature. That results in some outlying counties being officially classified by the federal government as both rural and metropolitan.

In 1993, the federal government designated eight metropolitan areas in Georgia. Officially, these eight metro areas are known as MSAs. The Atlanta MSA is by far the largest in population as well as in geographic size. It has 20 counties and half the population of the entire state. Today, 68 percent of all Georgians—that's two out of three—live in a metropolitan region. These regions are growing faster than Georgia's non-metro regions. Since the 1980s, 8 out of every 10 new Georgia residents settled in one of the state's metropolitan areas—most often Atlanta. ◀

▶ **Locating the Main Ideas**

1. Define: region, geographic region, political region, population density, urban, urbanized area, suburban, commute, rural, Metropolitan Statistical Area, metropolitan

2. Identify: Mason and Dixon Line, the South, the Southeast, Sun Belt

3. Explain the statement, "people create political regions."

CHAPTER ACTIVITIES

Reviewing the Main Ideas

1. What are the five basic themes of geography?

2. If you place a compass on top of the circle shown on page 4 so north is at 270°, what are the degrees for the remaining cardinal and intermediate directions?

3. The earth can be divided into four hemispheres. What are they? Name the dividing lines for each of the two sets.

4. Why was Greenwich, England, chosen as 0° longitude?

5. If you watch a two-hour movie, how many degrees will the earth have rotated during the movie?

6. Name the regions of the world in which you live: (a) two hemispheres, (b) continent, (c) nation, (d) three other regions.

7. Why are latitude lines also called parallels?

8. Why is it possible to live in more than one region?

9. What two things must a political region have?

10. Using the map on page 14, decide if you live inside or outside a Metropolitan Statistical Area. If you live inside an MSA, what is the central city? If you live outside an MSA, which MSA do you live nearest?

Give It Some Extra Thought

1. **Identifying Features**. Name two physical features and two cultural features you can find in your community.

2. **Making Community Connections**. What kinds of shared characteristics can you identify that make your community a distinct region?

Sharpen Your Skills

1. **Reading a Map**. Use the Georgia highway map (page 454) to answer the following questions.

a. List five physical or natural features as they are named on the map. Do the same for five cultural features.

b. Using cardinal and intermediate directions, describe the location of the city of Macon in relation to the city of Columbus; the location of Athens to Savannah; the location of Waycross to Albany.

c. Give the grid coordinates for Bainbridge, Augusta, Gainesville, and Dublin.

d. Rewrite the map scale in words.

e. What symbols are used in the legend for a U.S. highway, a county seat, a military base, and the state capital?

2. **Using an Atlas**. Make a list of the different kinds of atlases available in your library or media center. Briefly describe the kinds of maps in each. Using the index of the atlas, locate a historical map that relates to Georgia history and describe what the map shows. (Hint: National Geographic's *Historical Atlas of the United States* and the University of Georgia's *The Atlas of Georgia* are good sources for historical maps.)

Going Further

1. **Using a Globe**. Find the approximate location of your city on a globe. Locate the longitude of your city by holding a piece of string so it crosses your city and the north and south poles. Name the countries the string touches. Next, circle the globe with the string as a latitude line, again going through your city. What continents does it touch?

2. **Inferring from a Globe**. Using a string as a latitude line on the globe, see if you can determine why England believed Georgia could produce silk.

Coming Up Next!
- The physical geography of Georgia
- Georgia's natural resources

The Land of Georgia

Georgia is a large state. Including land and water area, it takes in approximately 58,900 square miles. That's larger than many countries of the world. At the points of greatest distance between borders, Georgia is 300 miles from north to south and 250 miles east to west. It is the largest state east of the Mississippi River.

When Britain created Georgia in 1732, its boundaries were much different. Then, the colony consisted of all the land between the Savannah and Altamaha rivers, westward all the way to the Pacific Ocean! Later, the Mississippi River became Georgia's western boundary. There were other changes, but by 1802, Georgia looked much as it does today.

The Physical Geography of Georgia

Georgia Landforms

Look out your window. Is the land around you flat or hilly? In the distance, can you see tall hills, or maybe even mountains? Depending on where you live, the surface features of Georgia can be quite different. Near the coast, you will see flatlands. In north Georgia, you will see ridges, valleys, and mountains. Nature has produced a wide range of land formations (or **landforms**, for short) in Georgia.

Why does Georgia have this variety of landforms? The ocean once covered the southern half of Georgia and wore away most land formations. To the north, the land was shaped by forces beneath the earth's surface and by water erosion. Today, **erosion**—the wearing away of soil and rock by natural forces, primarily water—is the main natural force affecting Georgia land formations.

Waterfall near Vogel State Park.

Mountains, Hills, and Plains

If you want to visit the highest point in Georgia, you will have to go to north Georgia. There, in the Blue Ridge Mountains, is Brasstown Bald, the tallest mountain in the state. On top of the mountain is this sign:

BRASSTOWN BALD,
The Highest Point in Georgia—4,784 ft.

However, if you could measure Brasstown Bald, you would find it is only 2,864 feet high from base to top. This difference can be explained because geographers have two ways of telling how high, or tall, a land formation is.

The most common measurement is **elevation**, which is height above sea level. The sign on top of Brasstown Bald giving the height of 4,784 feet refers to its elevation above the Atlantic Ocean, which is almost 300 miles away. Even though the mountain is far from the ocean, elevation is important for several reasons. First, temperature generally is related to elevation, dropping an average 3.3°F for each 1,000 feet above sea level. Higher elevations mean milder summers, colder winters, and shorter growing seasons. This directly affects the plant life and the type of crops that can be grown.

Elevation can also influence the amount and form of **precipitation**—water falling to the earth, such as rain and snow. The first tall mountains in the path of moist, warm air currents off an ocean will likely have high rainfall patterns in spring and summer. They will have frequent snowfalls in winter.

Elevation also affects how rivers are formed and how they flow. Because of greater rainfall in higher elevations, some of Georgia's

In north Georgia's Blue Ridge Mountains, many rivers have been dammed to create lakes.

Georgia's tallest mountain, Brasstown Bald, rises 4,784 feet above sea level.

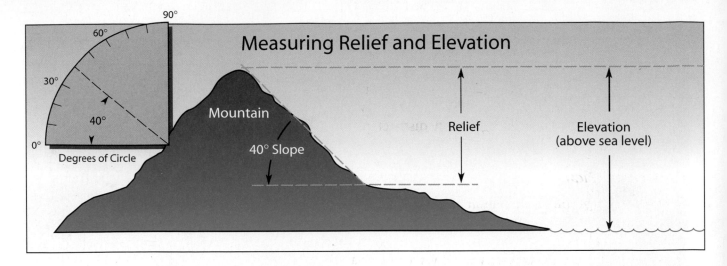

Measuring Relief and Elevation

major rivers begin here. Most of the rainfall in the mountains either runs off directly into streams, or is absorbed into the ground and then feeds countless springs. These springs are the source of mountain streams, which are pulled by gravity to lower elevations where they join with others to form rivers.

Related to elevation is **relief**, a term for the difference in elevation within a landform (such as the height of a mountain from its base to its peak) or between neighboring landforms. In the case of Brasstown Bald, from base to top, its relief is 2,864 feet. Stone Mountain, rising over 825 feet from the earth's surface, is another example of high relief.

Slope refers to the steepness of a landform and is measured in degrees of a circle. Land with absolutely no incline (0°) is "flat"—or horizontal. A 90° slope would be vertical—or straight up and down —like the edge of a building.

Portions of Georgia near the ocean have practically no slope. Most of the southern half of the state has low relief and flat to gentle slopes. In the northern half of the state you will see a variety of reliefs and slopes—from near flatlands to steep slopes. For the most part, this is an area of rolling hills. Extreme north Georgia, however, has a variety of landforms, including mountains and valleys. ◄

Physiographic Regions

Within the United States, geographers have identified more than 30 natural regions. These regions, called **physiographic provinces**, are based on similarities in land formations, elevation, rocks and minerals, soil, and other characteristics. Georgia is crossed by five provinces: (1) Coastal Plain, (2) Piedmont, (3) Blue Ridge, (4) Ridge and Valley, and (5) Appalachian Plateaus (or Plateau).

These provinces formed at different times and for different reasons. The outer layers of the earth consist of plates that move. When one plate collides with another, the earth's crust near the collision can fold and wrinkle—creating hills and mountains. Geologists believe that this is how the Appalachian Mountain chain that stretches along the eastern coast of North America was formed.

▶ **Locating the Main Ideas**

1. Define: landform, erosion, elevation, precipitation, relief, slope

2. The relief of Brasstown Bald is greater than the rise in elevation from sea level to its base. True or false?

3. Geographers use two ways to tell the height of a land formation. Explain the difference between the two.

4. How are the formation and flow of rivers affected by elevation?

Originally, these mountains were as tall or taller than any mountains on earth today, but over time wind, rain, and ice would erode their jagged peaks. Later, rising sea levels brought the ocean far inland. Slowly, the water retreated, leaving Georgia with distinct physiographic provinces.

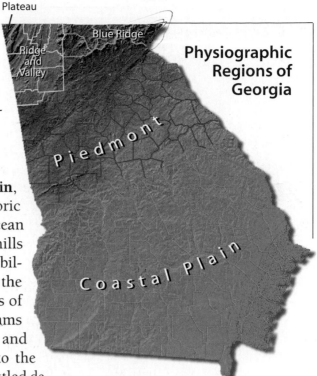

Physiographic Regions of Georgia

Georgia has five distinct physiographic provinces. In which region do you live?

The Coastal Plain

Georgia's largest physical region is the **Coastal Plain**, which covers about 60 percent of the state. In a prehistoric time, this area was entirely covered by ocean. As the ocean shoreline advanced inland, waves slowly wore away hills and other land formations in their path. As time passed, billions of seashells and other remains of ocean life sank to the sea floor. Tightly packed, they eventually became beds of a soft rock called limestone. Over time, rivers and streams deposited into the ocean large amounts of soil, clay, and rock that had eroded from the hills and mountains to the north. As a result, thousands of feet of **sediment**—or settled deposits—covered the ocean floor.

Eventually, the ocean retreated, leaving a vast area of limestone, clay, sand, and other sedimentary deposits. This region is known as the Coastal Plain. It extends along the Atlantic and Gulf coasts from Massachusetts to Mexico, inland up to 200 miles.

Along the eastern states, the Coastal Plain's interior boundary is marked by the **Fall Line**. This line is actually a **zone** or region several miles across. It marks the prehistoric ocean's shoreline. Land north of the line is higher in elevation than to the south, causing rivers to pick up speed as they travel—or fall—through this zone. South of the Fall Line, the ground is soft and sandy. Rivers widen, deepen, and move more slowly, making navigation by large boats possible. Later, you will learn how the Fall Line's importance to river navigation and water power influenced Georgia history.

The Coastal Plain is relatively flat, with low relief and flat to gentle slopes. With no steep hills or rock near the surface, rivers entering the Coastal Plain from the north flow slowly, develop wider banks, and take a winding path. By the time they reach the coasts, many of these rivers—such as the Altamaha and Savannah—have become much wider.

Along Georgia's coast, the land is low-lying. For about 75 miles inland, the soil typically consists of sand and clay, and is not very fertile. In general, the land is poorly drained, and swampy areas are common. Early settlers discovered that little would grow here except pine trees and brush, and they gave the name "Pine Barrens" to the region. Even today, this part of the state remains poorly suited for agriculture. The land is used mainly for pasture and growing pine trees for timber, pulp, turpentine, and other products.

Large areas of Georgia's coastal plain are well suited for agriculture.

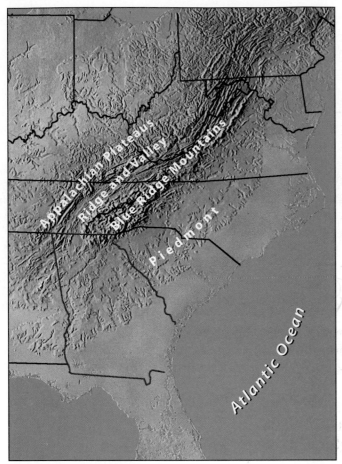

Four of the physiographic regions that stretch into Georgia form a vast area of the eastern U.S. known as the Appalachian Highlands.

Further inland, the Coastal Plain slowly rises in elevation, but seldom more than 500 feet above sea level. The well-drained soil consists of sand, clay, and other materials. This land is well suited for agriculture.

The Piedmont

Georgia's second largest physiographic province is the **Piedmont**, a French word for "foot of the mountains." This hilly region makes up about 30 percent of the state, and lies between the Fall Line and the mountain regions of north Georgia. Along its southern boundary, the Piedmont sits about 500 feet above sea level, but elevations range up to 1,700 feet at the southern edge of the Blue Ridge Mountains. The region consists mainly of rolling hills, with many valleys. In some areas, however, the hills are quite tall and almost appear to be mountains. Both hardwood and pine trees are found here.

The land is generally well drained and will support such crops as cotton, soybeans, and wheat.

In the Piedmont, large areas of solid rock are found just beneath the earth's surface. This is called **bedrock**, and consists of such stone as granite, gneiss (pronounced "nice"), and marble. Unlike the sedimentary rock of the Coastal Plain, Piedmont bedrock generally is very hard. Because of this, it is common to see large areas of exposed bedrock where the soil has been washed away. Other evidence of bedrock can be seen in river beds and along highways.

Numerous streams and rivers cross the Piedmont, generally flowing from north to south. Because of the bedrock, streams tend to have shallow beds, with narrow banks. Exposed rocks create frequent rapids, making navigation impossible for large boats.

Georgia's Piedmont is an area of rolling hills.

Blue Ridge

In terms of scenic beauty, Georgia's most striking physiographic province is the **Blue Ridge**. Here are found the Blue Ridge Mountains, the highest in the Appalachian Highlands. This range stretches from northeast Georgia to southern Pennsylvania, and contains the highest point east of the Mississippi River (North Carolina's 6,684-foot Mt. Mitchell). Georgia's highest mountain —Brasstown Bald, 4,784 feet above sea level —is located in the Blue Ridge province. Nearby, Springer Mountain (3,782 feet) marks the beginning of the Appalachian Trail, a hiker's path traveling 2,158 miles through the Appalachian Highlands to Maine.

The dramatic relief of Georgia's Blue Ridge Mountains can be seen in this view from atop Brasstown Bald.

The height of the Blue Ridge Mountains cools the warm, moist air currents off the Gulf of Mexico, producing great amounts of rainfall in most years. As a result, numerous rivers—such as the Chattahoochee and Savannah—begin here.

The Blue Ridge accounts for less than 1 percent of Georgia's prime farmland. Because of mountains and valleys, farms tend to be small. Steep slopes and high rainfall also contribute to the highest erosion rate in Georgia.

High elevation also affects agriculture in the Blue Ridge. The growing season—the period between the last frost of spring and the first frost of fall—varies from 210 days along the southern boundary to 180 days in the area of highest elevation. Apples, corn, and other vegetables are suitable to the climate. Hardwood timber, such as oak and hickory, does well in the mountains.

Ridge and Valley

Located due west of the Blue Ridge is the **Ridge and Valley** province, a region which stretches 1,200 miles from northern New York to central Alabama. The Ridge and Valley has long, parallel ridges overlooking wide, rolling valleys. From the valley floor, the ridges appear to be mountains, but really the highest has a relief of only 700 feet from top to base. Elevations within the region range from 700 to 1,600 feet above sea level.

The Ridge and Valley province is nestled between the Blue Ridge, Piedmont, and Plateau provinces. Unlike the provinces to the south and east, which consist of hard bedrock, the Ridge and Valley consists of softer sedimentary rock. The ridges are composed of sandstone, while the valley floors were formed from limestone, shale, and other sedimentary deposits.

Today, the sandstone ridges are forest-covered. Valley floors are used for farming and pasture. With an average growing season of

210 to 220 days, a variety of crops can be grown here, including corn, soybeans, wheat, and cotton. The soil is moderately suited for agriculture and accounts for 4 percent of Georgia's prime farmland. Much of the land is used for pasture and harvesting hardwood and pine timber.

Plateau

Georgia's smallest physiographic province is the **Appalachian Plateaus**, more commonly called the **Plateau**. A plateau is an area of flat or gently sloping land with a high relief over neighboring valleys and low-lying areas. Stretching from New York to Alabama are a series of plateaus along the western edge of the Appalachian Highlands. The southernmost of these—the Cumberland Plateau—includes about 300 square miles of the northwest corner of Georgia. Here you will find two flat-top features—Sand Mountain and the famous Lookout Mountain—separated by a deep and narrow valley. Off Lookout Mountain to the east is the thumb-like Pigeon Mountain.

The Plateau province consists of sedimentary rock, principally sandstone, shale, and limestone. Land here is primarily used for hardwood forest and pasture, although a small amount of corn and soybeans is grown. This area marks the only known source of coal in Georgia. ◀

▶ Locating the Main Ideas

1. Define: physiographic province, Coastal Plain, sediment, Fall Line, zone, Piedmont, bedrock, Blue Ridge, Ridge and Valley, Appalachian Plateaus, Plateau

2. How many physiographic regions are there in the United States? in Georgia?

3. How was the Fall Line created?

4. Why do many Georgia rivers begin in the Blue Ridge province?

(Top) The Ridge and Valley province is a region of long, roughly parallel ridges separated by wide valleys.

(Right) The Plateau is the smallest of Georgia's physical regions. It consists of two long plateaus—Lookout Mountain and Sand Mountain—separated by Lookout Valley.

Georgia's Coast

Sandy beaches, coastal wildlife, seafood restaurants, seaside rooms, and historic sites make Georgia's coast a popular place to visit. Here, you'll find vacation sites on the Atlantic Ocean, such as Tybee Beach, St. Simons Island, and Jekyll Island. This is also the area first settled by British colonists in the 1730s.

Georgia's coast is not particularly long. In a small plane, you can fly from one end to the other in about 45 minutes —a distance of less than 100

Georgia's sandy beaches are a part of the state's largest province—the Coastal Plain—that stretches from the Fall Line on the north to the Atlantic Ocean and Florida on the south.

miles. This flight, however, would not follow one long seashore. Instead, you would see a strange, irregular, yet beautiful scene below. Unlike California and Florida, Georgia's coast is not a continuous beach where sea abruptly meets dry land. Rather, it is a region consisting of (1) swamps, (2) rivers and streams, (3) **estuaries** (the area around a river's mouth where fresh and salt water mix), (4) numerous small islands in these estuaries, and (5) a chain of large coastal islands facing the ocean. Only on the seaward side of these outer islands will you find stretches of real beach.

There's another thing you should know about Georgia's coast. Because of **tides**—the daily rise and fall of the ocean—the point where sea touches land is constantly rising or falling. At low tide, sea level is down and Georgia rivers are free to flow out to sea. At high tide, however, the ocean's height is up by six or seven feet. Seawater now rushes in, forcing rivers and streams to reverse their flow and carry a mixture of salt and fresh water inland for a distance of 10 miles or more. In the process, coastal rivers—also called tidal rivers—spill over their banks and flood low-lying areas, thus creating saltwater marshes. These marshes are one of the most important features of the coast.

Coastal Wetlands

A **wetland** is any area of low-lying land covered by water all or part of the time and in which special types of plant and animal life are found. Georgia has large areas of wetlands—ranking fourth in the nation in total number of acres. Many freshwater wetlands are found south of the Fall Line—particularly along rivers and streams and near the coast. The largest freshwater wetland in the state is the famous Okefenokee Swamp, located south of Waycross along the Florida border.

The Okefenokee Swamp is the largest freshwater wetland in Georgia. Located near the Florida line, the swamp takes its name from the Indian word for "trembling earth."

Along Georgia's coast are 400,000 acres of saltwater wetlands, commonly called **marshes**. Twice each day, Atlantic tides flood coastal rivers, streams, and estuaries. For several hours at a time, nearby land—actually mud—is covered with salt water. As a result, little vegetation can survive, except for saltmarsh grass, cordgrass, and a few other plants. Amazingly, a complex and rich **ecosystem** is supported by the marshes. The salt marshes teem with life.

Acre for acre, they are far more productive than the most fertile farmland. The reason marshlands are so productive is that minerals and other nutrients are deposited there by freshwater rivers and streams, as well as by tides. These fertilize marsh plant life and cause a **food chain** (a term for "eat and be eaten") to begin. A variety of life is attracted, including insects, birds, wildlife, and—most important of all—fish, shrimp, and crabs. Here they find food, as well as a nursery to safely raise their young. Because of Georgia's marshes, an important seafood industry has developed along the coast.

Coastal marshes serve other valuable functions. They serve as buffers for storms. They filter out many pollutants from the Savannah, Ogeechee, Altamaha, and other rivers before they discharge into the Atlantic. And, as any traveler driving along Interstate 95 or U.S. 17 can see, these marshes are a delight to view. Here you will see marsh grass swaying in the wind, egrets and other large wading birds, fiddler crabs, and other wildlife. More than a century ago, the beauty of Glynn County's tidal wetlands so impressed poet Sidney Lanier that he wrote "The Marshes of Glynn," his most famous work.

Barrier Islands

Several miles off Georgia's mainland lies a chain of sea islands. Geographers call these **barrier islands** because they form a barrier, or wall, blocking ocean waves and wind from directly hitting the mainland.

Georgia's offshore islands are frequently called the "Golden Isles," a name given by early explorers expecting to find gold there. None was, but the name stuck. In the late 1800s, the title "Golden Isles" took on new meaning as millionaires from the North began buying these islands and building expensive winter homes there. Today, most of Georgia's sea islands are protected by state or federal authorities. Many have been reserved as national wildlife refuges and wildernesses, and one—Cumberland—is now a national seashore. These designations help protect the islands and their animal and plant life from human injury and destruction.

Large areas of Georgia's barrier islands barely rise above the sea and thus exist as marshlands because of the daily tides. Also, most are crisscrossed with rivers and streams. Viewed from the air, one large island actually appears to be several small connected islands.

Georgia's beaches are found on the seaward side of the outer islands. The most visited beaches are on the islands of Tybee, St.

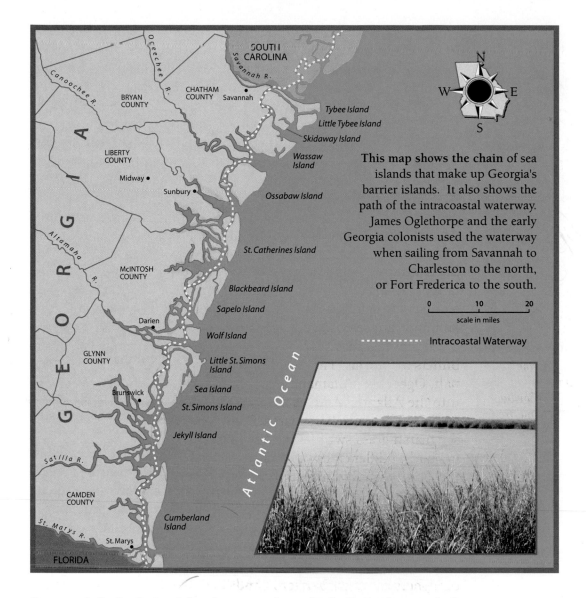

This map shows the chain of sea islands that make up Georgia's barrier islands. It also shows the path of the intracoastal waterway. James Oglethorpe and the early Georgia colonists used the waterway when sailing from Savannah to Charleston to the north, or Fort Frederica to the south.

Simons (of which Sea Island is a part), and Jekyll. Bridges and elevated highways (causeways) connect these three islands with the mainland, allowing visits by car. Access to other barrier islands is by boat or helicopter only.

While driving to or from Tybee, St. Simons, or Jekyll islands, you may have to stop and wait while a drawbridge is raised to allow a boat to pass. This marks the famous **Atlantic Intracoastal Waterway**, a 1,000-mile inland water highway stretching from New York to Miami. Located between the barrier islands and the mainland, this channel allows fishing boats, pleasure craft, and shippers to travel up and down the coast protected from direct ocean winds, waves, and currents.

Continental Shelf

Have you ever wondered how deep the ocean is off Georgia or why you can walk far out from shore before the water gets up to your head? On the East Coast, the ocean floor drops very gradually. For the first 70 or 80 miles off Georgia's coast, the drop is about two feet

▶ **Locating the Main Ideas**

1. Define: estuary, tide, wetland, marsh, ecosystem, food chain, barrier island, Atlantic Intracoastal Waterway, continental shelf, Gulf Stream

2. List the five features that make up Georgia's coastal zone.

3. How are Georgia's marshes important to humans and animal life?

4. What are two reasons why Georgia's barrier islands are called the "Golden Isles"?

for each mile away from shore. After that, however, the bed drops more sharply. If the ocean were drained, the floor from the shore to this drop-off would resemble a large, flat ledge—or shelf—attached to North America. Actually, this is the submerged part of the North American continent, and thus is called the **continental shelf**.

The continental shelf influences the path of the **Gulf Stream**. This is a current of warm ocean water flowing from the Gulf of Mexico up through the straits of Florida. It continues northward along the east coast of North America, and then in a northeasterly direction across the Atlantic Ocean. The Gulf Stream stays in the deeper waters beyond the continental shelf. ◀

Georgia's Natural Resources

Water Resources

Since the late 1970s, Georgia has been one of the fastest growing states in the nation. However, most of this growth has taken place north of the Fall Line, where over 70 percent of all Georgians live. The fastest growing region is the Piedmont. Three out of every five Georgians live there, but it has no major underground sources of water.

To help meet the growing demand for water in north Georgia, state, federal, and local officials have devised a plan. It calls for building regional **reservoirs**—large artificial lakes—as well as some smaller lakes. But there are many problems to face, such as where to build new reservoirs, how to protect valuable wetlands, and who is going to pay.

South of the Fall Line, water resources are affected by the make-up of the earth beneath the surface. Here, sedimentary beds of sand and porous rock such as limestone can store vast supplies of underground water, called **groundwater**. Pores—tiny spaces—in the sand and rock allow liquid to pass through it. Water-saturated layers of the earth are called **aquifers**. How does water get into an aquifer? If the aquifer is near the earth's surface, its water comes mainly from rainfall.

There are two types of aquifers. One is found near the earth's surface. It extends from the **water table**—the upper limit of water-saturated soil—down to the first dense, non-porous layer of earth. To obtain well water from this

This map shows the Gulf Stream and the continental shelf off the southeastern United States. About 450 miles east of Georgia's southern boundary is one of the deepest points in the Atlantic Ocean.

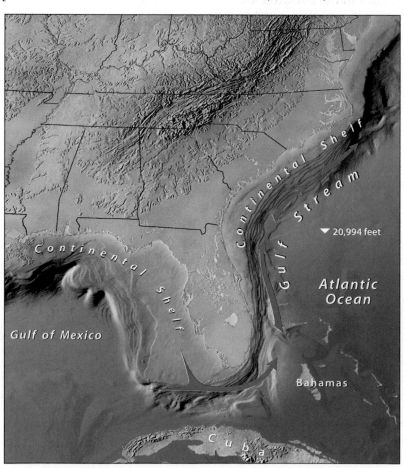

aquifer, an electric pump must be used to bring the water to the surface. A second and deeper type of aquifer is found in some parts of Georgia. This is the **artesian aquifer**. It is a porous layer of earth located between two denser layers. With nowhere to escape, water trapped in an artesian aquifer is under pressure. If a well is drilled into the aquifer, water will rise, perhaps even reaching the surface without the need for a pump.

South of the Fall Line, water for cities, irrigation, and other uses comes primarily from groundwater in artesian aquifers. North of the Fall Line, however, the earth is different. Instead of a porous soil, the surface has more clay and rock, which is less able to absorb rainfall. Because the surface is hilly, water runs off it, and less sinks into the ground than if the land were flat. Here, the geology of the subsurface is much different from the Coastal Plain. Except for northwest Georgia, there are few aquifers north of the Fall Line, and groundwater is limited. Bedrock beneath the surface further prevents large amounts of water from collecting underground. Thus, most north Georgia cities and industries must depend on **surface water**—that is, water flowing in rivers and streams, or stored in ponds and lakes.

Areas of the state with large amounts of groundwater do not depend on rivers and lakes for their water supply. Parts of the state lacking groundwater, however, must depend on surface water. A problem with river water is that rainfall declines in the summer and fall. If river levels get too low, cities have to restrict water use. They may put a ban on watering lawns or washing cars. No one can control rainfall, so we have to store water in reservoirs and use it wisely.

Georgia Rivers and Streams

Georgia is fortunate to have 20,000 miles of rivers and streams. Rivers determined Georgia's original boundaries and affected the location of its settlements.

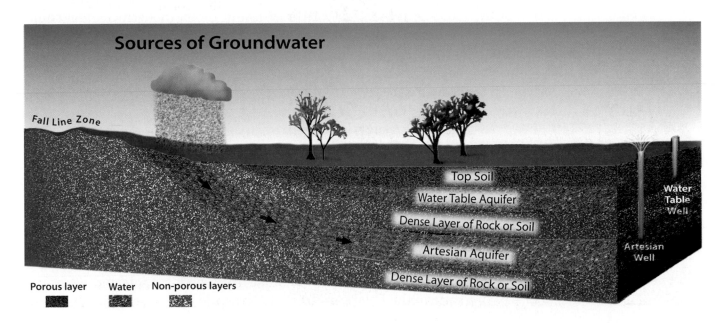

Sources of Groundwater

Fall Line Zone

Top Soil
Water Table Aquifer
Dense Layer of Rock or Soil
Artesian Aquifer
Dense Layer of Rock or Soil

Water Table Well

Artesian Well

Porous layer   Water   Non-porous layers

The Oconee River.

With few exceptions, Georgia rivers generally flow from north to south. Why? Because of the drop in surface elevation from north to south. Georgia as a whole slopes toward the southeast. Rivers and streams are pulled toward the sea, much like water flowing down a giant water slide.

Characteristics of Georgia Rivers

North of the Fall Line, rivers and streams tend to have different characteristics from those to the south. Because of frequent rock beds, rivers here are more shallow and narrow. Exposed rocks, uneven riverbeds, and the drop in elevation cause numerous rapids and waterfalls. The tumbling waters appear white. Attempting to "run" these rapids by raft or canoe is a popular sport, and Georgia is noted for its exciting—and dangerous—whitewater rivers.

Along some streams, you will find occasional **shoals**—shallow areas where the river bottom consists of sand or layers of rock. Because they marked convenient places to cross the rivers, shoals frequently attracted settlements. One such community that survives today is North High Shoals, on the Apalachee River.

As rivers from the north approach the Fall Line zone, the slope of the surface drops fairly quickly. The water picks up speed, providing a force to power mills and machinery. This water power was an important factor in settlement along Fall Line river sites.

Georgia Lakes

Every summer, millions of visitors head to Georgia's lakes to boat, ski, swim, fish, picnic, or simply relax. Four out of every five Georgians live within 40 miles of a major freshwater lake. But this hasn't always been true. Early in this century, the only lakes in Georgia were ponds and, in south Georgia, water-filled hollow places in the ground known as sinkholes. Every one of our 28 major reservoirs has been built since 1910. Without them, modern Georgia could not have developed as it did.

The lake-building era in Georgia began with the arrival of the age of electricity. Georgians built dams in order to convert flowing river water into electricity. In the process, many reservoirs were created. Dams and reservoirs serve other purposes as well. They prevent floods, supply water to nearby cities, and provide downstream navigation. They are important to fish and wildlife conservation and to recreation.

Rocks and Minerals

Rocks and minerals are a part of Georgia history. Before the coming of the Europeans, the natives chipped quartz and other stones into arrow- and spearheads. They shaped stone into tools and used clays to make pottery. Of course, the search for gold and silver was one of the chief reasons that Hernando de Soto explored Georgia in 1540. Almost three centuries later, the discovery of gold in Cherokee territory led to the nation's first gold rush, and hastened the removal of the Indians.

Before the American Revolution, Georgia's kaolin was shipped to England to make Wedgwood pottery. Today, Georgia is the world's leading producer of this mineral. Kaolin is used in many products, including the strong and glossy paper you see in some magazines and books, and in paints.

Georgia marble was first used in 1838. Today, Georgia ranks first in the nation in marble production. The world's largest open pit quarry is at Tate in Pickens County. Marble in crushed form is used for agricultural lime and as a filler for such products as toothpaste and gum. Marble is also popular for cemetery headstones and monuments. One of the most famous statues in the world, the Lincoln Memorial in Washington, D.C., is made from Georgia marble.

Georgia also ranks first in the nation in granite production. Although granite is popular for headstones, monuments, and buildings, it is mainly used in crushed form. One mile of four-lane highway may consist of over 40,000 tons of crushed granite. Elbert County is known as the granite capital of the world.

Other important rocks and minerals mined in Georgia include limestone, fuller's earth, mica, bauxite, barite, phosphate, feldspar, and over a dozen more.

Although rich in a variety of rocks and minerals, Georgia is lacking in energy-related resources. The only supplies of coal are in the extreme northwest corner of the state. To date, more than 200 wells have been drilled in exploring for oil or natural gas, but none were successful. ▶

Milky quartz.

Georgia's Weather and Climate

What's the weather like in Georgia today? Your answer will probably tell whether it's hot or cold, cloudy or sunny, rainy or dry, and windy or calm. Georgia is such a large state that the weather can be quite different, depending on where you happen to be.

Weather refers to conditions in the atmosphere—the air, clouds, and gasses around the earth—on any given day. **Climate**, on the other hand, refers to the average weather conditions over time—at least 25 to 30 years. Weather affects whether we go to the beach today or tomorrow. Climate determines what kind of crops a farmer will plant.

Climate was important to the creation of Georgia in 1732. Because Georgia lay at the same latitude as China, India, Persia, and Palestine, England's leaders believed the colony could become its new source of crops grown in those lands. They expected the colonies to produce wine, silk, rice, tea, olives, oranges, cotton, and indigo. As it turned out, some of the desired crops fared well in Georgia. Others—such as grapes for wine—were not suited to the humidity and diseases of the coastal climate.

▶ **Locating the Main Ideas**

1. Define: reservoir, groundwater, aquifer, water table, artesian aquifer, surface water, shoals
2. Where do most Georgians south of the Fall Line get their drinking water? North of the Fall Line, where does most drinking water come from?
3. List five reasons for building a reservoir.
4. How are granite and marble important to Georgia?

Georgia's climate is mainly determined by geographic location. It is near the Atlantic Ocean, the Gulf of Mexico, and the eastern edge of the continent. These factors, combined with Georgia's closeness to the Equator, result in a climate of hot summers, mild winters, and, in most years, abundant rainfall throughout most of the state.

Climate and Georgia's Development

Georgia's moderate temperatures have helped the state to grow and develop. The cool summers in the north Georgia mountains have attracted many new residents to this area. Dotting the slopes and ridges of the Blue Ridge Mountains are vacation and retirement homes. High elevations have even made a snow ski resort possible at Sky Valley, in the extreme northeastern corner of the state.

For the rest of the state, mild winters have contributed to a continuing population migration into Georgia. Mild winters have also helped attract the military. To date, a total of 11 army, air force, navy, and marine bases and installations have been built in Georgia. The latest is the Kings Bay submarine facility in Camden County. A warm climate means that outdoor training, flights, and other military operations can go on year-round.

Precipitation

Have you ever wondered how water gets into clouds, or what happens to rain after it hits the ground? The answer to these and many other questions involves the **water cycle**. This refers to the journey of water from ocean to rainfall, its use and reuse on land, and then its return to the sea.

In most years, Georgia receives abundant rainfall, snow, and other forms of precipitation—an average of 50 inches annually. Depending on where you live, you may get more or less rainfall than the state average. The annual rate varies from about 80 inches in Rabun County in extreme northeast Georgia to half that amount in the Augusta area.

Georgia's nearness to the ocean helps account for a usually abundant precipitation. The Gulf of Mexico is responsible for this blessing. That is because most winds and weather patterns affecting Georgia come from the west and southwest. As warm Gulf water evaporates, moisture rises and is blown to the northeast. Pushed over the Blue Ridge Mountains, the air cools, resulting in frequent rains. Precipitation also occurs as warm Gulf air meets colder air currents flowing down from Canada.

Hurricanes

Because of the shape of the southeastern coast, Georgia is less exposed to the full impact of hurricanes than either Florida or the Carolinas. The wide expanse of the continental shelf off Georgia's coast also helps influence most hurricane storms to move north-

Downtown Augusta, 1908. Such flooding was a common occurrence in river cities before the building of dams and levees.

ward. But a direct hit along Georgia's barrier islands is possible. Today, satellite tracking of hurricanes allows forecasters to predict where and when a storm may hit land, thus allowing time to evacuate residents. Hurricanes develop on warm ocean water, and are most likely to occur in September, and least likely in April.

Tornadoes

Tornadoes are violent whirlwinds that can develop when a cold front moves rapidly into an area of warm, moist air, resulting in severe thunderstorms. Winds may reach over 200 miles an hour, and destruction can be severe in their path. These damaging wind funnels strike Georgia an average of 19 times a year. Tornadoes are most likely to strike in April, and least likely in October. ▶

Air and Ocean Currents

When early explorers sailed to the New World on their voyages of discovery, they were risking their lives. Maps and navigation instruments were primitive, and once on the high seas, ship captains were at the mercy of the weather. In time, however, they learned to use wind and ocean currents to speed their long journeys across the Atlantic. A **current** is a continuous movement or flow of a large body of air or water along a particular path.

What causes air and water to travel great distances as currents? The main cause is the uneven heating of the earth by the sun. The sun strikes the earth most directly at the Equator, and least directly at the poles. This means that air, water, and land temperatures are hottest along the Equator, and coolest in the polar regions.

Air Currents

Have you ever wondered why cool breezes flow in off the ocean, or why chilling winds are so common during winter months? Winds, or air currents, occur because air tends to flow from cooler places, such as the ocean, to warmer places, such as land.

As air is warmed, it expands and rises. The opposite occurs as air cools—it contracts and sinks. Because warm air is lighter, it exerts less pressure on the earth's surface. In contrast, cooler air is heavier, producing greater pressure. Around the earth, air is always flowing from areas of high pressure to those of low pressure in order to balance our atmosphere. This constant shifting creates air currents on land and sea.

Early ship captains did not know what caused sea winds, but they soon realized how important they were to sailing across the Atlantic. As merchants and traders replaced explorers, the winds came to be known as the **trade winds**.

The trade winds helped in sailing from Europe to America. But what about getting back? Between latitude 35°N and 60°N, cold high pressure from the polar region influences a pattern of winds that blow from the west to the northeast. These air currents, called

▶ **Locating the Main Ideas**

1. Define: weather, climate, water cycle
2. Why did England's leaders think the Georgia colony could produce wine, silk, rice, tea, olives, oranges, cotton, and indigo?
3. How has Georgia's climate contributed to its growth?
4. How does the Gulf of Mexico help account for Georgia's abundant precipitation?

Lanier Elementary School was severely damaged when a tornado swept through Hall County in 1998.

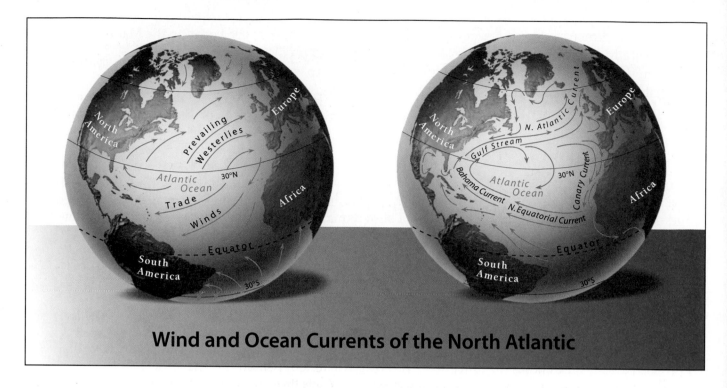

Wind and Ocean Currents of the North Atlantic

prevailing westerlies, helped carry sailing ships from America back to Europe.

One other air current which you should know about is the **jet stream**—since it sometimes brings very cold weather into Georgia. This is a "river" of air found between 30,000 and 40,000 feet above sea level, flowing at speeds of 100 to 300 miles per hour. This current follows an irregular pattern around the earth, sometimes bringing polar air in from the northwest and influencing weather in the United States. This current was named because pilots of high-flying jet aircraft found that they could cut flying time and fuel use by riding with this current.

Ocean Currents

Similar to air currents are the movements of water masses in the ocean. Near the surface, these tend to follow the general path of air currents. They result from wind action and the uneven heating of the world's oceans by the sun.

One of the most famous ocean currents in the world is the Gulf Stream. It originates in the Caribbean Sea and Gulf of Mexico and travels up through the straits of Florida and along the East Coast. Then it flows across the north Atlantic, breaking up south of Greenland. This warm water current helps keep the southeastern climate mild during winter. The Gulf Stream aided early travel and trade between Europe and the Western Hemisphere. The first to use it were the Spanish explorers returning to Spain aboard great ships loaded with gold, silver, and other treasure from Central and South America. Later, the current cut travel time on the voyage from the American colonies eastward to England. ◄

> ▶ **Locating the Main Ideas**
>
> 1. Define: current, trade winds, prevailing westerlies, jet stream
> 2. What are the causes of air and water currents?
> 3. How did ocean currents affect European exploration and trade with the New World?

CHAPTER ACTIVITIES

Reviewing the Main Ideas

1. How does Georgia's physical geography affect agriculture?
2. Why is erosion more severe in north Georgia than in other areas of the state?
3. Explain why the physical geography of north Georgia has more in common with the western Carolinas than with south Georgia.
4. Why is it possible to find fossilized shark's teeth in places as far away from the ocean as Macon?
5. Why are long droughts more likely to cause water shortages north of the Fall Line than south?
6. List some important functions that Georgia's saltwater marshes serve.
7. How does the continental shelf help protect Georgia's coast from hurricanes?
8. Explain why Georgia's coastal islands are called barrier islands.
9. Geographic features can shape history. How did gold do that for Georgia?
10. Identify a geographical factor that helps influence Georgia's climate.

Give It Some Extra Thought

1. **Inferring.** Georgia's population continues to grow at a fast pace. Discuss two features of our state's geography that might account for this.
2. **Generalizing.** If you started in Miami, Florida, and moved north along the eastern seaboard, what landforms would you expect to find? In your trip north, what difference in climate would the changing latitude make?
3. **Explaining.** Explain what this phrase from a bumper sticker means, "No wetlands, no seafood."

Sharpen Your Skills

1. **Mapping Information.** On an outline map of the state, draw in the five physiographic regions of Georgia. Label each region and the Fall Line. Identify the location of your hometown. Label the Atlantic Ocean on your map.
2. **Mileage Report.** Using a state highway map, decide which river you are closest to and choose another town located near the river. List the route numbers of the highways you would have to use to go from your town to the one you chose. Use the map scale and estimate the distance you would travel.
3. **Map Interpretation.** Using the map of "Wind and Ocean Currents of the North Atlantic" (page 32), describe the trip of an explorer from Spain to the Western Hemisphere and back home again. Include three things in your description: the names of the currents the explorer would have used, the direction in which the currents flow, and the continents the Spaniard might be able to explore.

Going Further

1. **Using Many Sources of Information.** Find more information about Georgia's rocks and minerals by using *The Atlas of Georgia*, encyclopedias, almanacs, and science books. Choose one rock or mineral and write a report about it. Tell where it is found in the state, what it is used for, and how much is produced. How does its production in Georgia compare to its production in other states or countries?

Spelunkers are people who enjoy exploring and studying caves such as this one—Johnson Crook Cave in northwest Georgia.

GEORGIA EVENTS

	People arrive in the Southeast						Pottery first made in North America (near Augusta)					John Cabot explores North American coast, possibly as far south as Florida

B.C. 12,000	10,000	8000	4000	2500	2000	1000	A.D.	1000	1492	1498
People first arrive in North America	Paleo-Indian period begins; animals domesticated in Near East	Archaic period begins; agriculture appears in Near East	Civilization develops in Near East; beginning of recorded history	Egyptians build Great Pyramid at Giza		Woodland period begins	Birth of Christ	Mississippian period begins; Leif Ericson explores Newfoundland	Columbus lands in West Indies	

EVENTS ELSEWHERE

Before It Was Georgia

		Ayllón colony briefly settles on Georgia coast	DeSoto expedition first to explore Georgia's interior		Spanish missionaries first arrive in Guale [Georgia]	Juanillo rebellion				Spain withdraws from Guale	Sir Robert Montgomery proposes to settle "Azilia" [Georgia] for Britain
1513	**1526**		**1540**	**1565**	**1566**	**1597**	**1607**	**1619**	**1663**	**1690**	**1717**
Ponce de León becomes first European to land on North American mainland		Potatoes from the Americas introduced as food into Europe	Spanish destroy French Fort Caroline, build St. Augustine				Jamestown, Virginia, becomes England's first permanent settle-ment in America	West Africans brought to Virginia	King Charles II creates colony of Carolina		

3

Coming Up Next!
- Why study history?
- How to do history
- The dating game

Diary

Recollections

It Really Happened

Oglethorpe

Memoirs

Biography

Family Bible

CIVIL WAR

Encyclopedia

Geography

Photo Album

Let's Talk History

What will life be like in Georgia in the twenty-first century? What does the future hold for you? The answers will depend in part on your knowledge of history.

Why Study History?

Imagine what life would be like if you lost your memory. You couldn't remember your friends, what you like to eat, or even your favorite songs. Life would be awful! You need your memory for everything you do. Making sense of the past helps you make decisions about today and tomorrow.

Besides having your own private memory, you also share memories of the past with others. You live around other people in your family, your community, your state, your nation, and your world. Just as each of us has a personal past, together we have a collective past. The record of this past is called **history**.

We need to be aware of history because we cannot possibly experience everything in life firsthand. We must rely on what others observed and remembered to increase our understanding of events. Not everyone can be the president, but we can read Jimmy Carter's memoirs and learn what it was like to be president. We can't travel back in time and be Georgia colonists, but we can read their accounts to know what challenges they faced.

History helps us better understand today by showing how we got here. It tells us the effects of decisions others made, and how life changed from one generation to the next. Many lessons can be learned from history, and some of them can help us avoid repeating errors of the past. ▶

How to Do History

To understand present conditions in Georgia, the United States, and the world, we have to know something about the past. How did Atlanta become an international city? Why has Georgia's farm population decreased? Why is Georgia one of the fastest growing states in the nation? Why does Georgia have a large African-American population? None of these questions can be fully answered without knowing about the past.

Persons whose job it is to find out what happened in the past are called **historians**. They may study what happened to a group of people (such as the Cherokee Indians), a geographic location (such as Savannah), or a part of culture (such as plantation life). Whatever the topic, historians do their work by asking questions and using many sources of information.

Starting with Questions

The study of history begins with questions concerning an event, place, or group. What caused the first settlers to come to Georgia? Why is Atlanta the capital of Georgia? Why were the Native Americans forced out of the state?

From what historians already know about such things, they form **hypotheses**, or preliminary conclusions, to the questions. One historian may think the settlers were seeking religious freedom. Another may think they left England because they were in debt.

To test the accuracy of their hypotheses, historians have to gather evidence. There are many sources of information to which historians may turn for evidence.

Sources of Information

Historians primarily rely on two kinds of information: primary sources and secondary sources.

Primary sources are firsthand or original accounts of historical events. Examples of written primary sources are letters, diaries, speeches, autobiographies, newspaper reports, government documents, and business records. Other kinds of primary sources are oral accounts by persons who recall an event, and physical remains such as buildings, tools, clothing, art, and even grave markers. Old photos are also primary sources. In general, primary sources date closely in time to the event under study.

Secondary sources are accounts of historical events written by people who did not personally witness the event. They result from historical research of primary sources and often are far removed in time from the events they describe. Secondary sources such as biographies, textbooks, maps, encyclopedias, and other reference books are useful for getting background information on a topic. Secondary sources would not be possible if people living at the time of an event had not recorded what they had seen, heard, and read.

▶ **Locating the Main Ideas**

1. Define: history
2. Give the title of a nonfiction book you have read. In one sentence, describe how the book let you learn about an experience you have not had.
3. How can history help you make wise decisions about the future?

This marble statue of Clio can be seen in the U.S. Capitol in Washington, D.C. The Greek goddess of history is represented traveling in the chariot of time, flying above the earth. As she observes human affairs, she records important events in her book of history. What is the significance of having this statue in the Capitol?

Copy of a handwritten receipt for Georgia's electoral votes in the 1792 presidential election. What questions could you ask about this document?

Using Primary Sources

One of the historian's most important tasks is criticizing, or questioning, the sources. Is the source real or a forgery? Who wrote it? Was he or she an actual eyewitness to the event under study? If so, what was the witness's **frame of reference**? A person's views of an event can be influenced by his or her social group, religion, occupation, and political attitudes. These characteristics make up the witness's frame of reference. For example, if you and your grandparents went to a rock concert, it is likely that their description of the event would be different from yours. The more historians know about *why* a particular source came to be written, the better they can judge the value of the information it contains.

Analyzing and Evaluating Information

Finally, historians have to decide what really happened and why. For example, why was the colony of Georgia created? Why did the Civil War occur? Answering these questions involves pulling together pieces of evidence from many different sources. They have to weigh each piece and decide which is most reliable.

Sometimes, one event appears to cause, or lead to, another. Historians call such a relationship **cause and effect**. More often, however, historical events are much more complex, with not just one but several causes. Most big happenings—such as the settling of the New World or the outbreak of the Civil War—occurred because of many reasons. This principle is called **multiple causation**.

Now it is time to make **generalizations**, or broad conclusions, about what happened. Actually, the historian is answering questions asked at the start of the research. These answers may be quite different from the original hypotheses, or preliminary conclusions. Perhaps the historian will conclude that the first settlers came to Georgia for several reasons: to make a fortune, to escape persecution, and to get away from bad economic conditions.

As a final step, historians describe in writing what they have found. In doing this, they are creating new secondary sources. Historians try to be objective and not influenced by their personal feelings. Whether or not they like what they find, historians try to be guided only by the evidence. As other historians turn up new evidence about the same past event, they may describe things differently. In that case, the story of the past may change. ◀

▶ **Locating the Main Ideas**

1. Define: historian, hypothesis, primary source, secondary source, frame of reference, cause and effect, multiple causation, generalization

2. Is this book a primary or secondary source? Explain. Is a diary a primary or secondary source? Explain.

3. Why do you think that the work of a historian usually results in the creation of new secondary sources?

The Dating Game

Understanding dates and time relationships is an important part of studying history. In fact, history is *full* of dates. It's hard to write about history without telling *when* things happened.

Is knowing dates important? It depends. Several dates in Georgia history—such as its first settlement in 1733—are so important to our state that they should be remembered. Most dates, however, have little meaning by themselves. What is more important is knowing when one event occurred *in relation to others*.

Knowing the order in which a series of events occurred, the **chronology**, often can help you better understand a historical event.

Using a Time Line

A special chart that historians use to keep track of events is a **time line**. It shows at a glance the chronology or time order of events. Each unit in this book has a time line to help you discover the relationship of historical events. These time lines include important Georgia events as well as some major events occurring elsewhere in the nation and the world.

By examining a time line, you may be able to form some hypotheses about why important historical events occurred.

B.C. and A.D.

Sometimes a date has the letters B.C. after it, or the letters A.D. in front or after it. These are abbreviations used in the Christian system for counting time, using the birth of Christ as a starting point. B.C. stands for *before Christ*, while A.D. is the abbreviation for *anno Domini*, which means "in the year of our Lord." These notations identify a date as occurring either before or after the birth of Christ. When no abbreviation is used with a date, it is understood to be an A.D. date.

Expressions of Time

In addition to dates, there are other ways historians express time. Some are general terms which refer to when something happened in relation to today. *Past, previous,* and *former* describe events that have already happened. *Present, current,* and *contemporary* are terms to describe today, while *future* means events that have not yet occurred. The terms *ante-* and *pre-* are prefixes which mean before. Thus, antebellum or pre–Civil War refer to the period before the Civil War. *Post-* is a prefix which means after. Therefore, post–Civil War means after the war. The word *circa* means around, as in circa or ca.1900 (around 1900).

Time expressions that refer to the frequency of events include *periodically* (from time to time), *quarterly* (four times a year), and *annually* (once a year). *Biannual* means twice a year, but *biennial* means once every two years. The terms *era* and *period* are similar

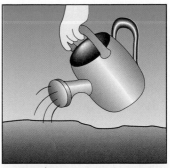

From top to bottom, is the chronology of the events correct?

Significant Anniversaries

100th	Centennial
150th	Sesquicentennial
200th	Bicentennial
250th	Semiquincentenary
300th	Tercentenary
400th	Quadricentenary
500th	Quincentenary
1,000th	Millennium

▶ **Locating the Main Ideas**

1. Define: chronology, time line, B.C., A.D., decade, century, centennial, bicentennial
2. Why would knowing when one event occurred in relation to others be important in studying history?
3. Describe the Christian system for counting time.

and refer to a span of time remembered for unique features or events.

Decades and Centuries

Two specific periods of time with special names are **decade**, a period of 10 years, and **century**, a period of 100 years. A decade can refer to any 10-year period, such as 1975–1985. More commonly, however, decades begin in a year ending in 0, such as "the decade of the 1990s." Because of the way years are calculated with the Christian calendar, centuries can be a little tricky. Based around the birth of Christ, the system goes from 1 B.C. to A.D. 1. The first century began in the year A.D. 1. This means the year A.D. 150 fell in the second century and not the first. Thus, the 1800s made up the 19th century, while the 16th century refers to the 1500s.

Commemorating Historical Events

Just as you celebrate your birthday each year, citizens commemorate many historical events on the day on which they occurred. That date is called an anniversary. Some events, such as the Fourth of July, are celebrated annually. There are special anniversaries to mark longer periods of time like 100 or 200 years. Have you noticed a **centennial** or **bicentennial** celebration of anything lately? The largest anniversary of all is the millennium—but most people never get to celebrate that event—as it only occurs once every thousand years. ◀

In 1986, Lt. Gov. Zell Miller participated in Louisville's bicentennial by helping to reenact the burning of the infamous Yazoo Act (see pp. 127-28). Miller, portraying Gov. Jared Irwin, read from a proclamation ordering that "fire be drawn down from heaven" to burn the condemned documents. Note the magnifying glass used to focus the sun's rays to start the fire.

CHAPTER ACTIVITIES

Reviewing the Main Ideas

1. Historians work in an orderly and careful manner to find out about the past. Put the steps listed here in the order in which a historian would do them.

   draw conclusions from evidence

   make a hypothesis

   report conclusions objectively

   decide on a question to study

   evaluate evidence and use the most reliable sources

2. When would a primary source most likely be produced? Name a primary source that you have created.

3. Identify each of these sources about the Civil War (1861–65) as either primary or secondary.

   a. Novel: Margaret Mitchell, *Gone with the Wind,* 1936.

   b. Proclamation: Gov. Joseph Brown, July 9, 1864.

   c. Biography: John P. Dyer, *Fightin' Joe Wheeler,* 1941.

   d. Letter: Confederate soldier to wife, 1862.

   e. Photograph: Fortifications on Peachtree Road, 1864.

   f. Story: Joel Chandler Harris, "A Baby in the Siege," in *Tales of the Home Folks in Peace and War,* 1898.

4. List four factors that might influence your frame of reference.

5. List three events that might happen at your school as a "cause" and describe the effect. Follow the example given.

CAUSE	EFFECT
the lunch bell rings	students go to the lunchroom

6. Important events or problems usually have a number of causes. For example, identify three possible reasons for the following.

   AN AFTER-SCHOOL JOB. Traci got a job after school because—

   1. *she wanted something to do.*
   2.
   3.
   4.

A DISCIPLINE PROBLEM. Joshua is often late for school because—

1. *school bores him.*
2.
3.
4.

7. Using a dictionary or thesaurus, look up the words *past, present,* and *future* and for each word give a synonym or phrase that is different from the ones used in the text.

Sharpen Your Skills

1. **Evaluating Information.** Think like a historian and be a smart consumer. Review the steps you put in order in question 1 and imagine you want to buy a used car. Write down three questions you would ask its owner and why you would want to know the answers before buying the car. Explain why the frame of reference of a mechanic who worked on the car would be different from the owner's. How would you decide whether the information from the mechanic was reliable? How would you decide about information from the car owner?

2. **Time Line.** Draw a time line that begins with the year you were born and ends with this year. On one side of the time line include events in your life such as the births of brothers or sisters, when you started school, or when you moved to a different house. On the other side of the line, put events that occurred in the state or the nation. If possible, extend the line to include the lives of your parents and grandparents.

3. **Primary and Secondary Sources.** Locate a primary source and a secondary source in your classroom, media center, or home. Identify each source and explain *what* makes it a primary or secondary source.

Coming Up Next!
• Unearthing clues to Georgia's prehistoric past
• Georgia's first inhabitants

Georgia's Prehistoric Past

What does the word "prehistoric" bring to mind? Dinosaurs, woolly mammoths, or cavemen with spears and clubs? **Prehistory**—which means "before history"—simply refers to that period of the past before written records were kept. This could go as far back as the beginning of time. In this book, however, we will look at the prehistoric past only during the period in which humans have inhabited Georgia.

The date the prehistoric era ended can be different from place to place and people to people. For example, Georgia's prehistory ended earlier than in California or Michigan, but later than in England or China. The key is to find out when people first kept written records about their culture. The answers will differ around the world.

Writing appears to have developed first in Africa along the Nile River. There, messages have been found carved or drawn on stone from as early as 5000 or 6000 B.C. Later, the Egyptians developed **hieroglyphics**—a form of early writing that used symbols and images. Once they invented the calendar, a process for making paper, and pen and ink, the Egyptians began recording the story of their culture. Egypt's prehistory, thus, ended thousands of years ago.

In contrast, Georgia's prehistoric period did not end until 460 years ago. Native Americans had lived here for thousands of years but had not developed a written language. Without writing, they could not permanently record the story of their past. Prehistoric jewelry, arrowheads, tools, pottery, and other evidence have been unearthed, but these early Indians left nothing in writing to tell us about their culture.

Giant Sloth.

In 1540, Spanish explorer Hernando de Soto and a party of 600 adventurers became the first Europeans to write eyewitness accounts about the Indians they saw. One even drew a map so others could learn of their discovery. For the first time, written information was recorded about Georgia. That is why we consider 1540 as the end of Georgia's prehistoric era and the beginning of its historic period.

Artist's idea of a mastodon being hunted by prehistoric Indians. Mastodons once lived in Georgia.

Unearthing Clues to Georgia's Prehistoric Past

How is it possible to learn about Georgia's prehistoric Indians if they left no books, letters, or written records? The answer is that these early inhabitants left behind other types of evidence about their lifestyle. Scientists known as **archaeologists** learn about previous societies by looking for clues in the physical evidence they left behind. Archaeologists look for two types of evidence: (1) **artifacts** (objects made or shaped by humans, such as arrowheads, tools, pottery, and jewelry), and (2) **ecofacts** (natural objects such as bones, teeth, skulls, and shells). Archaeologists use the term "ecofact" to refer to remains of living matter, such as grain, shells, and bone, that have *not* been shaped by humans. Both are important to unlocking the secrets of the past.

Artifacts and other remains provide clues to the **culture**, or way of life, of societies that vanished long ago. It's like working on a jigsaw puzzle. Too bad that archaeologists are never able to find all the pieces they need. Normally, the most durable materials—like stone, metal, and bone—can survive for hundreds or thousands of years.

A carved shell ornament, known as a gorget, from the Mississippian period. It could be worn around the neck. The carving is of a water spider with a circle and cross on her back representing sacred fire.

Yet, even from a few pieces of evidence, much can be learned about the lives of people who lived long ago. This is because archaeologists look for evidence in a scientific manner. When they dig for objects like clay pots and arrowheads, they aren't looking for souvenirs. They're digging for *information*.

Like the historian, the archaeologist starts with questions. Both might ask, "What kind of food did a particular people eat, and how did they prepare it?" To find the answer, the historian could read descriptions of meals in diaries or printed in recipe books at the time. The archaeologist looking at prehistoric societies, however, would have to find other sources. The answer would come from examining human bones or from clues in the ashes and garbage pits of ancient settlements.

Field Work

The task of getting information from artifacts and ecofacts begins in the field. The field location where an archaeological team works is called a **site**. It may be an abandoned village, burial ground, or earthen mound used centuries ago. Sometimes, archaeologists are able to predict the general area where a settlement was likely, such as near a river. Then they conduct a series of test digs to look for evidence of an Indian village. In other cases, a site is discovered by chance, as when a farmer plowing a field uncovers scattered **projectile points** (spear- and arrowheads), pottery **sherds** (bits of broken pottery), and other artifacts.

Before **excavating** (digging to expose a site), the team will carefully measure the site and mark it into a pattern of squares called a grid. Each square is numbered so the team can record exactly where an object is found. By knowing the exact location of an object, an archaeologist can determine its **context**—that is, how it relates to its surroundings at a site.

A team of archaeologists excavate a north Georgia site.

Knowing the context is important, since one artifact can be related to other pieces of information. For instance, a necklace found in a burial pit tells an archaeologist more than a necklace found alone in a plowed field. A necklace uncovered in a burial site tells something about the person, burial customs, and perhaps religion and belief in life after death.

An archaeological excavation may involve dozens of people and go on for several years. Because archaeologists want to collect reliable information, their work has to follow strict procedures. Artifacts such as pottery are fragile. If they are destroyed

At a laboratory sorting table, archaeologists study artifacts—such as these Mississippian period pot sherds—to learn more about cultures of the past.

through carelessness or ignorance, the information they contain is lost forever.

Shovels for digging and wire screens to sift each shovelful of soil for artifacts are basic tools at an excavation. As digging goes on through lower levels of soil, smaller tools (such as trowels, ice picks, and brushes) may be necessary to recover some objects without breaking them. A tape measure is needed for recording precise locations of each artifact. Archaeologists take many pictures and fill notebooks with written comments and sketches as they work.

A site map is drawn to show the location of key features of an excavation. This map often reveals something about life at the site hundreds or thousands of years ago. For example, **postmolds**—stains in the soil left from decayed wooden posts—may reveal the outline of a house. Artifacts found inside the outline can give a clue to the work done by the people who lived there.

Every sherd, tool, and other piece of evidence found at a site can be a useful source of information. Even ecofacts, such as bones and shells, serve as evidence of what materials were available and how they were used long ago.

Laboratory Work

When an excavation is finished, the archaeologist's work shifts to the laboratory. That's where the pieces of the jigsaw puzzle are put together. Researchers begin by cleaning, sorting, and identifying evidence collected in the field.

Laboratory work is slow and painstaking. On a given project, archaeologists may spend more time in the lab than in the field. There are hundreds of questions to be answered. What is this object? How was it used? What is it made of? How was it made? Who was its likely owner? Is it similar to objects from other sites?

Depending on the object, there are several different methods to determine the age of some artifacts. **Carbon 14 dating** is one technique frequently used to find the age of

Mississippian Period bowl and jar fragments, being reconstructed.

▶ **Locating the Main Ideas**

1. Define: prehistory, hieroglyphics, archaeologist, artifact, ecofact, culture, site, projectile points, sherds, excavate, context, postmolds, carbon 14 dating, organic

2. What did humans have to invent or develop to end their prehistory period?

3. Why could archaeology be called "the science of rubbish?"

4. Explain why the archaeologist must use pieces of a culture to draw conclusions about past societies.

plant or animal matter. Carbon 14 is a radioactive element found in all living matter. It begins to disintegrate—or break down—at a steady rate once a plant or animal dies. By determining the amount of carbon 14 in the remains of something that once was alive, scientists can measure its age. The less carbon 14 found, the older the object.

Carbon 14 can be used to date the remains of objects thousands of years old, with an accuracy within 200 years of the actual age! But, carbon 14 can only be used with evidence composed of **organic** (plant or animal) matter. How could an artifact made of inorganic matter like stone or clay be dated? By knowing its context. Let's say an archaeologist on a dig finds a stone ax head in a fire pit. A carbon 14 dating lab reveals that the charcoal in the fire pit is about 2,500 years old, but the lab cannot give a date on the ax head because it is not organic. However, by knowing the context of the ax head—that is, it was found in the fire pit—the archaeologist may assume it came from the same time period. To confirm this, the ax head's style would be checked against other ax heads already identified from this time period.

The final and most important stage in the archaeologist's work is to report to others what has been found. Into this report will go the archaeologist's own findings and comparisons with discoveries by other archaeologists at other sites. Perhaps the report will draw some conclusions about the behavior of people whose way of life vanished long ago. ◀

Georgia's First Inhabitants

Who were the first humans to live in the land we call Georgia? When did they arrive? Where was their original home? Why did they come? What kind of wild animals did they find here? What did these early people eat? What did they wear? Where did they live? This section is about the first people to settle in Georgia—the prehistoric Native Americans.

Humans Arrive in North America

Sometime in the not-too-distant past—perhaps as recently as 12,000 years ago—humans first reached North America. Where did America's first colonists come from, and how did they get here? Not from Europe by boat, as you might imagine. Instead, they came on foot from Asia. Look at a map or globe and you will see that Asia and North America are separated by an ocean. How, then, was it possible to *walk* to our continent? The first humans arrived long ago during a geological period known as the **Ice Age**. Cold temperatures caused a great deal of the earth's water to freeze into glaciers and polar ice. As a result, ocean levels were as much as 300 feet lower than today. One land mass exposed during the Ice Age was **Beringia**—the land between present-day Alaska and Siberia.

The exposure of the land mass called Beringia created a "bridge" to North America from Siberia.

Beringia

Beringia served as a "land bridge" because it allowed passage from one continent to another. Scientists estimate it was as wide as 1,300 miles, or four times the length of Georgia! Later, as global temperatures rose, the world's great ice fields melted, causing the sea to rise. Today, Beringia is covered by the ocean, and the area is known as the Bering Strait.

The **migration**—or movement—of people from Asia into North America was not planned. The first migrants were **nomads**—or wanderers—in search of food. Without maps, they had no idea where they were going. Perhaps while following a herd of game, the first of many bands eventually crossed Beringia into North America. Others followed, and slowly the new inhabitants pushed southward, where the climate was warmer and food more abundant. Here, they found woolly mammoths, mastodons, great ground sloths, giant bison, musk ox, moose, bear, sheep, antelope, and a variety of other game. From these bands of Asian nomads descended all Native Americans—or "Indians"—in both North and South America.

By 10,000 B.C., the first humans had arrived in the Southeast. We divide the next 11,700 years of Georgia prehistory into four cultural periods—sometimes called **traditions**—that developed among Native Americans: (1) Paleo, (2) Archaic, (3) Woodland, and (4) Mississippian. ▶

Paleo-Indian Period (10,000 to 8000 B.C.)

The first 2,000 years of Indian life in the Southeast is called the **Paleo-Indian** period. (The word "paleo" means "ancient.") These natives lived in small **bands**, or groups, of 20 or so adults and children. Paleo-Indians depended on wild animals—or game—for food, clothing, and even many tools. Their diet consisted mainly of meat from giant bison, mastodons, giant sloths, and other large mammals—most of which are now extinct. They also ate small game, berries, and wild fruits and vegetables.

On the move in search of food, the early Indians never stayed in one place for long. Usually, they camped out in the open. To protect against cold and wind, they might dig pits or build shelters covered with bark, brush, or animal hides, but we have no evidence of permanent settlements.

Paleo-Indians faced a hard life. Few lived to be older than 30 or 40, and many children died before their first birthday. Yet, helped by a moderate climate, the Indians were able to turn to nature for all their needs. The animals they hunted provided food, bone and antler for tools, leather for shoes and clothing, hide for blankets and shelter, and fur for coats. They knew which type of rock to use for making knives, spearheads, ax heads, and tools. Small tree trunks and cane were good for spear shafts, ax and tool handles, and poles for shelters. Today, it is hard to imagine living totally off of nature—but Georgia's early Indians did.

▶ **Locating the Main Ideas**

1. Define: Ice Age, Beringia, migration, nomads, tradition
2. Identify: Bering Strait, Native Americans
3. Explain what happened to Siberia and Alaska during the Ice Age.
4. Why do scientists think that the first prehistoric people came to North America?

Small bands of Paleo-Indians moved southward into North America, eventually reaching the Southeast. These were Georgia's first human inhabitants.

Among the many Paleo artifacts uncovered at former campsites are large, distinctive spearheads known as "Clovis" points. Clovis points have been found all over North America, including Georgia, and even in South America. These points were used on heavy spears, which were used for jabbing more than throwing. The bow and arrow had not yet been invented, and hunters had to get very close to their prey before making a kill with a spear. In time, Paleo-Indians may have developed the spear-throwing device known as the **atlatl**. Clovis points have been found with the bones of a variety of extinct mammals, including mammoths and mastodons, suggesting the Paleo-Indians were brave and skillful hunters.

What else do we know about this culture? Few items have survived—or at least been uncovered so far—other than tool and weapon artifacts. One rare discovery, two Paleo-Indian skeletons buried with artifacts and covered with red powder, suggests the existence of burial customs. Perhaps they believed that the dead could carry these into an afterlife.

Archaic Period (8000 to 1000 B.C.)

Around 8000 B.C., the culture of Georgia's Indians began to change, making way for a new tradition known as the Archaic Period. During the next 7,000 years, **Archaic Indians** adapted to a warming climate and the disappearance of big game, such as the mammoth and the giant sloth. They became dependent on a combination of hunting, fishing, and gathering. Deer, bear, small game (such as rabbit and squirrel), fish, berries, nuts, and wild fruits and vegetables were their main sources of food. Great heaps of shellfish and oyster shells discarded by the Indians have been found near the coast and in the interior. These heaps are called **middens**. One shell midden on Stallings Island, located in the Savannah River near Augusta, is 500 feet wide, 1,500 feet long, and 6 to 12 feet deep. A garbage pile this size indicates that the Indians returned year after year. At first, Archaic Indians continued living as nomads, traveling much of the time in search of food. Gradually, this changed. Archaic Indians learned to use the resources around them in new ways. Their diet had more variety, and they no longer depended heavily on large game. They used a wider variety of tools and weapons that changed the way they hunted, saving them time and effort.

The atlatl made it possible for spears to be thrown much farther and with greater accuracy—the same way a baseball bat or golf club enables the user to hit the ball farther and with more precision.

Projectile Points. *What we commonly call "arrowheads," archaeologists call projectile points. Many times what looks like an arrowhead is actually a spear point, or even a knife. In this photo, only the Woodland and Mississippian points are true arrowheads.*

Labels within the image:

Late Archaic
3000 B.C. - 1000 B.C.

Mississippian
900 A.D. - 1540 A.D.

Woodland
500 B.C. -
900 B.C.

Early Paleo-Indian
10,000 B.C.
Clovis Point

Late
Paleo-Indian
9000 B.C.

Early Archaic
7500 B.C.   6000 B.C.

Middle Archaic
5000 B.C.   4000 B.C.

One such tool, the atlatl, came into wide use. The atlatl is a wooden shaft about 2 feet long with a bone or antler hook on one end in which a spear can be placed. The atlatl serves as an extension of a hunter's arm and allows a spear to be thrown farther and harder than with the arm alone.

Archaic Indians hunted many animals, including bear, fox, raccoon, opossum, squirrel, and turkey, but deer was their favorite game animal. The Indians learned to burn small areas of the forest to improve their hunting. The bushes and plants that grew back in the cleared areas attracted deer and other game.

With less time required for hunting, the Indians had more time for other activities. Archaic Indians learned how to polish stone and crafted many useful as well as decorative items from stone and bone. At the end of the Archaic period, they found out how to make clay pottery—a discovery that changed the way they prepared their food.

The oldest evidence of pottery in North America, dating to about 2500 B.C., has also been found on Stallings Island. This early pottery was made of clay, mixed with fibers of Spanish moss, grass, or roots to keep it from cracking during firing. With pottery, Indians were able to cook their food with water or oil. It is also evidence that life was becoming more settled. After all, pottery couldn't easily be carried long distances without being broken.

Archaic Indians surely had some type of religious beliefs. Proper burial of the dead seems to have become important. Tools, weapons, and body ornaments found in some burial pits suggest a belief in life after death. ▶

▶ **Locating the Main Ideas**

1. Define: Paleo-Indians, bands, atlatl, Archaic Indians, midden
2. Why is it unlikely that Paleo-Indians built permanent homes?
3. Explain how the development of the atlatl and pottery changed the way Archaic Indians lived.

Woodland Period (1000 B.C. to A.D. 1000)

By about 1000 B.C., a new Indian tradition was emerging. During this period, **Woodland Indians** throughout the Southeast built thousands of earthen mounds, many of which remain today. Kolomoki Mounds, located near Blakely in Early County, were built during this period. The mounds varied in size, shape, and usage. Some were only a few feet high, while others were enormous. Some were round, and others flat on top. Through excavations, archaeologists have discovered that there were many different types of these earthen structures. Some were burial mounds and some were flat-topped, perhaps for ceremonial activities. The Indians even made mounds in the shapes of animals. In Georgia, Rock Eagle is a well-known **effigy** mound from this tradition.

Like their Archaic ancestors, Woodland Indians were at home in the forest. For hunting, they developed a new weapon, the bow and arrow. The arrowheads were much smaller than the spear points used earlier. Even more important was the development of agriculture.

Woodland Indians began to save seeds in the fall for spring planting in cleared forest areas. Nuts became more important in their diet, and they dug underground pits to store nuts and seeds. Corn, squash, and bottle gourd from what is now Mexico were other, less important, plant species used by the Indians.

These practices helped increase the food supply. The population grew, smaller groups joined together to form tribes, and villages began to appear. The Indians became more settled, and archaeologists have discovered traces of sturdy houses, built to stand longer than the earlier Indian shelters.

During this time, the use of pottery became widespread throughout the Southeast. Instead of plant fibers, pottery makers began using crushed rock with the clay. Designs were stamped on the pots,

(left) Numerous Indian mounds were found throughout the Southeast. Identified are four Georgia mounds that can be visited.

(right) Rock Eagle, located just north of Eatonton, Georgia, is an example of an effigy mound built during the Woodland Period, circa A.D. 200.

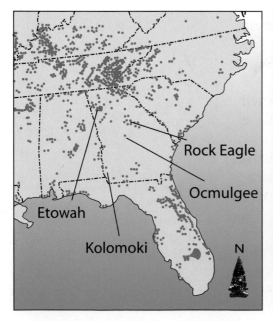

or the surface was engraved with a stick. Each region had its own special designs.

There is evidence that Woodland Indians traded throughout what is now the eastern United States. Artifacts have been found in Georgia made of copper from as far away as the Great Lakes.

This evidence also reveals that Georgia's Indians may have shared religious ideas with other Indians of the eastern woodlands. Their burial mounds, made of earth and stone, often contained jewelry, pottery figurines of humans and animals, and other ceremonial objects.

Here is an artist's idea of the great Mississippian mound complex of Cahokia. Though much smaller, Georgia's mound village at Etowah would have been similar in appearance.

Mississippian Period (A.D. 1000 to 1600)

Between A.D. 700 and 900, a new cultural tradition developed along the Mississippi River, later spreading to other areas in the Southeast. The **Mississippian Indians** preferred places that offered (1) rich bottomlands by rivers, (2) long moist growing seasons, and (3) good deer and turkey hunting. This tradition is named for the area where it first began.

Wild foods remained important to the Indians of the Mississippian period, but they also had come to rely more on agriculture, particularly corn. In addition, these Indians grew beans. Harvested crops were stored in community storehouses, giving the tribe a constant food supply.

Agriculture supported a larger population. It enabled the Mississippian people to live in large permanent settlements. A Mississippian settlement was usually protected by a wooden **palisade** (a wall made of tall posts) and a **moat** (a wide ditch) outside the palisade. Within the safety of the walls, many structures of wood and clay (known as **wattle and daub** houses) were built by the people to live in.

A new, more complicated social and political organization developed, called a **chiefdom**. It might include only a few villages, or ex-

Until the arrival of European traders, the bow and arrow was the Mississippian Indian's main weapon for hunting and battle.

A Mississippian village along the Savannah River in an area that is now Elbert County. What evidence is there that this was a permanent settlement?

tend over a wide area and many villages. At the top, a priest-chief ruled, perhaps over several villages. This job was handed down through the ruling family.

Mississippian Indians built large flat-topped mounds with temples and other buildings for ceremonies at the top. Inside and at the base of mounds were burial places. Buried with the dead were food, tools, ornaments, and ceremonial objects of wood, copper, seashell, and stone. Etowah and Ocmulgee are the best known Mississippian mound sites in Georgia.

Indian culture reached a high point during the Mississippian period. Evidence recovered from the many sites of the period tells us more about these people than we know about any of their ancestors. We know that Indian traders regularly traveled along waterways and forest trails between settlements such as Etowah (near Cartersville) and Ocmulgee (near Macon). Artifacts unearthed from burials show the high artistic level of the people. We even know what games they played, and that they smoked tobacco and decorated themselves with jewelry, feathers, and tattooing. We know their lives were full of ceremony and that they had special places to conduct ceremonies.

It was the Mississippian Indian culture that Hernando de Soto encountered in his exploration through Georgia in 1540. In a very short time, the societies of mound builders and chiefdoms vanished, as Europeans brought death in the form of diseases and steel weapons. The lives of Georgia's Indians were changed forever. But there were survivors, and from these would come such Indian societies as the Creek and the Cherokee. ◀

▶ **Locating the Main Ideas**

1. Define: Woodland Indians, effigy, Mississippian Indians, palisade, moat, wattle and daub, chiefdom

2. Identify: Rock Eagle, Etowah Mounds, Ocmulgee Mounds

3. Describe the different types of mounds Woodland Indians built and their uses.

4. How did the practice of farming encourage the development of permanent settlements by the Mississippian Indians?

CHAPTER ACTIVITIES

Reviewing the Main Ideas

1. What is the difference between history and prehistory?
2. Explain why knowing the context of an artifact can be as important as the artifact.
3. Explain this sentence: The steps that historians and archaeologists take to do their work are similar, but the way they gather evidence is very different.
4. What types of artifacts and ecofacts are being left by our society today for future archaeologists to interpret?
5. Why would the discovery of artifacts in a burial pit suggest Indians were concerned with life after death?

Give It Some Extra Thought

1. **Organizing Information.** Organize information by listing what each Indian tradition had or used in each of the following categories:
   a. weapons available
   b. food sources (animals and crops)
   c. shelters built
   d. evidence of religion

2. **Drawing Conclusions about Changes over Time.** Use the information on your list to write a paragraph describing the changes in prehistoric Indian life over tlme. Write an ending sentence for your paragraph that draws a conclusion about the development of the Indian culture over a long period of time.

Etowah Indian mounds in Cartersville.

Sharpen Your Skills

1. **Using the Map Scale.** Using the scale on a map of the United States, locate two cities that are approximately 1,300 miles apart in order to "see" how wide the land bridge between Siberia and the North American continent was. Write down the names of the two cities and the mileage between them.

2. **Cause and Effect.** Decide what effect the following events had on the culture of prehistoric Indians, and write your answers.
   a. invention of the bow and arrow
   b. invention of pottery
   c. contact with Europeans
   d. development of agriculture
   e. trading with other tribes

3. **Using Maps to Explain.** Discover how far away the Woodland Indians traded objects. On a U.S. map, using Macon as the Georgia starting point, write down the distance to the following cities around the Great Lakes: Chicago, Illinois; Duluth, Minnesota; and Detroit, Michigan. Do you think the Woodland Indians actually traveled that far to trade?

Going Further

1. **Analyze the Artifact.** Visit a museum, historic site, or other location that has a display of Indian artifacts. In a report to the class, describe the artifacts you saw and name the Indian tradition that produced it. You may want to include sketches of the artifacts in your report.

Mississippian Period incised bowl, circa 1500. Found at Ocmulgee Mounds.

5

Coming Up Next!
- The age of discovery
- Spain comes to the Southeast
- England comes to North America

Europe Discovers the New World

The first European to set foot on North America was a Viking explorer named Leif Ericson. Around the year 1000, he sailed from Greenland, probably landing along the coast of Newfoundland, Canada. The Vikings settled there briefly, but left the new continent and returned to Greenland. In time, the story of Ericson's discovery became a well-known Viking legend.

The Age of Discovery

By the fifteenth century, the future of Georgia and its native people was being shaped by events taking place thousands of miles away. Far across the Atlantic, Europe's great "Age of Discovery" was about to begin. Thereafter, for almost three centuries, European nations would challenge each other for rights to the Western Hemisphere.

In the beginning, Europe was not interested in North or South America. The truth is, neither continent was known to exist. Rather, Europeans believed the world consisted of only three continents—Europe, Africa, and Asia—plus scattered islands in the ocean.

Europeans were really interested in the **Far East**, a region of southeastern Asia that included India, China, and Japan. This area, also known as the **Indies**, was the source of goods highly prized in Europe, such as silk, spices, tea, and gems. Muslim traders in western Asia, however, controlled the land and sea routes over which these goods were supplied to the west. The Age of Discovery began because European nations wanted their own direct access to the Far Eastern trade.

Portugal took an early lead in this race, exploring the western coast of Africa southward in search of an eastern route to the Indies. By now, most European geographers recognized that the earth was

round. If this were true, would it be possible to find a shorter route to the Far East by sailing west? "Yes!" said Italian-born explorer, Christopher Columbus, believing that to the west, only ocean separated Europe from the Indies. Little did he know that two vast continents—North and South America—lay as great barriers to the Indies.

Columbus tried to get support for a voyage westward across the Atlantic Ocean. King John of Portugal turned him down, preferring to seek an eastern route. Columbus turned to Spain, and finally convinced King Ferdinand and Queen Isabella to finance his great exploration. Columbus was instructed to discover and conquer any islands or continents he should find on behalf of Spain.

Columbus Discovers the New World

You can imagine the relief felt by the crews of the *Nina, Pinta,* and *Santa Maria* on the morning of October 12, 1492. After six weeks at sea, they finally sighted land. The land turned out to be an island, which Columbus claimed for Ferdinand and Isabella. In the weeks that followed, other islands were discovered and claimed. Convinced that these were part of the Indies, Columbus called the dark-skinned natives living on the islands "Indians." It was a term Europeans came to apply to all natives in this newly discovered world.

On October 12, 1492, Christopher Columbus landed with his party on the Caribbean Island of San Salvador. Columbus believed he had reached islands on the eastern edge of the Indies—the east Indies. However, as later explorers would discover, these weren't the Indies at all. Soon, Europeans began calling these islands the West Indies to distinguish them from those in the Far East.

Coat of arms of Ferdinand and Isabella.

For several months, Columbus explored the islands of the Caribbean Sea. He was disappointed to find no silk, spices, or riches, except for native jewelry. But he remained convinced that this was the Indies. Columbus returned to Spain with the great news that a westward route had been found.

Three other explorations would follow. Until his death, Columbus believed he had reached the Far East. Others, however, soon realized that the continents and islands being discovered were part of a world previously unknown to Europeans. Accompanying one expedition was Amerigo Vespucci, an Italian businessman. Vespucci was convinced that a new continent had been found and called the region a **New World**. The term became popular in Europe, although in 1507 a Swiss mapmaker applied a different name to this area of the world. For some unknown reason, he named it after Amerigo Vespucci. Soon, other explorers discovered that "America" was not just one continent but two.

Spain Claims the New World

Although Columbus had found no riches, Spanish claims in the New World worried Portugal. Portugal had been searching for an eastern sea route to the Far East. By sailing west, Columbus had appeared to achieve in one voyage what Portugal had failed to accomplish in nearly a century. Spain was now an active rival for access to the Far East. Portugal also feared that Spain might threaten its shipping lanes around Africa. Because both Spain and Portugal were Catholic nations, Pope Alexander VI, head of that church, feared the two countries would become enemies. Therefore, in 1493 he issued a decree dividing rights to the New World between Spain and Portugal.

According to Pope Alexander, at a point nearly 400 miles to the west of the Azores Islands, a line would be drawn north and south to the two poles. This line was known as the **Line of Demarcation**. All lands east of this line could be claimed by Portugal, while lands to the west—including what today is Georgia—went to Spain.

Portugal, however, was not happy. The Portuguese believed the Line of Demarcation favored Spain. Portugal called upon Spain to negotiate a new line. The next year, the two nations signed the Treaty of Tordesillas (pronounced Tor-da-see-yus), which shifted the line 700 miles further to the west. Portugal's shipping interests around Africa were better protected—but new land was another matter. Although no one knew it at the time, Portugal received rights to only one territory in the New World—a South American land it would one day name Brazil.

English Claims in the New World

Other European nations refused to accept Spain and Portugal's division of the Americas between themselves. England and France prepared to make their own explorations.

A 16th century navigator's compass.

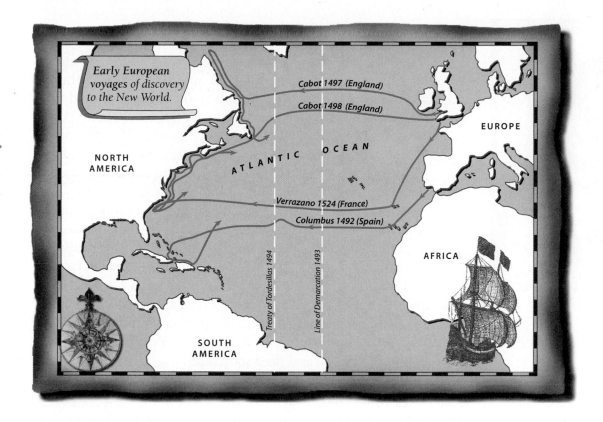

Early European voyages of discovery to the New World.

Cabot 1497 (England)
Cabot 1498 (England)
Verrazano 1524 (France)
Columbus 1492 (Spain)

NORTH AMERICA
ATLANTIC OCEAN
EUROPE
AFRICA
SOUTH AMERICA

Treaty of Tordesillas 1494
Line of Demarcation 1493

Within four years of Columbus's first voyage, English merchants were anxious to have access to the New World. In 1497, John Cabot sailed from England to the northeastern coast of North America. The following year, Cabot began a second exploration, possibly sailing as far south as the Carolinas, Georgia, or even northern Florida. England later claimed North America's eastern seaboard for itself, arguing that Cabot's voyage gave England the rights to it.

England ignored the pope's decree that North America belonged to Spain. England also rejected the Treaty of Tordesillas as a basis for Spanish rights to the New World. Spain replied with a third defense: the right of first discovery. According to this theory, a country could claim those lands its explorers found first.

In the race to discover as much land as possible, Spain financed more than 80 voyages to the New World during the 12 years after Columbus's first voyage.

How much land could an explorer claim, and for how long? European nations could not agree, so England proposed another standard: any first discovery claims had to be followed by actual occupation. It was not enough to plant a flag on the beach. To enforce a claim, settlers and soldiers from the explorer's country must follow and **colonize**—or occupy and control—the land.

On one point, however, all European powers agreed. New World claims did not require permission from Native Americans. Catholic and Protestant rulers alike believed they had a legal right to occupy any land not already colonized by another power. They also felt a moral duty to convert the natives to Christianity. ▶

▶ **Locating the Main Ideas**

1. Define: Far East, Indies, New World, Line of Demarcation, colonize

2. Identify: Leif Ericson, Pope Alexander VI, Treaty of Tordesillas

3. Why were Native Americans called "Indians"?

4. Why is Portuguese the official language of Brazil?

Spain Comes to the Southeast

In the New World, Spain hoped to convert the natives, expand its empire, and discover new riches—God, glory, and gold (although not always in that order). At first, the Spanish concentrated their efforts on the West Indies, Central America, and northern South America. But soon came stories of the fabled cities of gold to the north.

The first Spanish explorer to set foot on the soil of what today is the United States was Juan Ponce de León. He came in search of riches, adventure, and a legendary fountain of youth located somewhere north of Cuba. In April 1513, Ponce de León came ashore on what he thought was a large island. Actually, it was the Florida coast near the future site of St. Augustine. Because he arrived during the religious holiday Pasqua Florida, he named his discovery "Isla Florida" (Island of Flowers), later shortened to **La Florida**. Eight years later, Ponce de León returned to Florida's west coast, now intending to begin a permanent settlement. Hostile Indians attacked his force, and many Spaniards were killed. Ponce de León was wounded in this battle and died soon after.

Despite the dangers, other Spanish explorers came. Spain wanted to see the settlement of La Florida, an area that includes what today is Florida, Georgia, South Carolina, Alabama, and Mississippi.

First European Settlement in North America

Until recently, Georgia history books named Hernando de Soto as the first European to set foot in Georgia. But, in the early 1990s,

Juan Ponce de León.

Artist's conception of Ayllón's colonists building San Miguel de Gualdape—the first Spanish settlement in North America.

researchers found evidence that other Europeans had come here earlier. Not only that, but many historians now believe that the first European settlement in North America since the Vikings occurred along the coast of Georgia. They think that happened 14 years before de Soto's expedition through Georgia in 1540.

In 1504, a young Spanish lawyer named Lucas Vázquez de Ayllón was appointed to a judgeship on the Caribbean island of Hispaniola. He became an owner of a sugar cane plantation that was worked by Indian slaves. Many of the slaves died from disease and other reasons, and Ayllón and other planters began looking to the north for more Indians to enslave. One expedition to capture new slaves, financed by Ayllón, landed on the coast of what is present-day South Carolina. Based on reports about the land, Ayllón asked for and received permission from the king of Spain to explore and colonize La Florida.

In July 1526, Ayllón sailed from Hispaniola with 600 Spanish settlers. Aboard were men, women, and children, among them many Africans (whose number included slaves and perhaps some free blacks who were skilled laborers). Their destination was the mainland of North America. Their objective was not gold or silver but rather to settle the land granted by the king. If successful, Ayllón's colony would be Spain's first settlement on the North American mainland.

Ayllón's fleet landed on the Carolina coast in August, too late in the year to plant crops. He hoped to find friendly Indians who not only would allow them to settle but would provide the colonists with food until they could grow their own crops. Failing to find Indians, Ayllón's colonists sailed southward in September. Near the mouth of a river in what is today McIntosh County, Georgia, they found Indians nearby. On September 29, 1526, they unloaded their personal belongings, tools, and livestock and began construction of the new settlement of San Miguel de Gualdape.

As it turned out, however, the colony was doomed. Cold weather came unusually early that year. Just 10 days after their arrival, Ayllón died. Illness and death followed for others in the settlement. Fear set in over lack of food and shelter, and a revolt broke out among the colonists. The African slaves rebelled—the first case of a slave revolt in America—and the Indians rose up against the Spanish colonists.

Soon, San Miguel de Gualdape was abandoned, and the survivors set sail for Hispaniola. Only 150 of the colonists are known to have made it back to the island alive.

Hernando de Soto Explores Georgia

In 1537, Hernando de Soto decided he would succeed where Ayllón had failed. Using gold and silver from his conquests in Peru, de Soto asked the king of Spain for permission to colonize La Florida. The king agreed, giving him 18 months to explore an area 600 miles

More than gold changed hands....

Take to the New World:
wheat
oranges
sugar cane
horses
cows
pigs
chickens

Bring back to Spain:
corn
potatoes
tomatoes
pineapple
tobacco

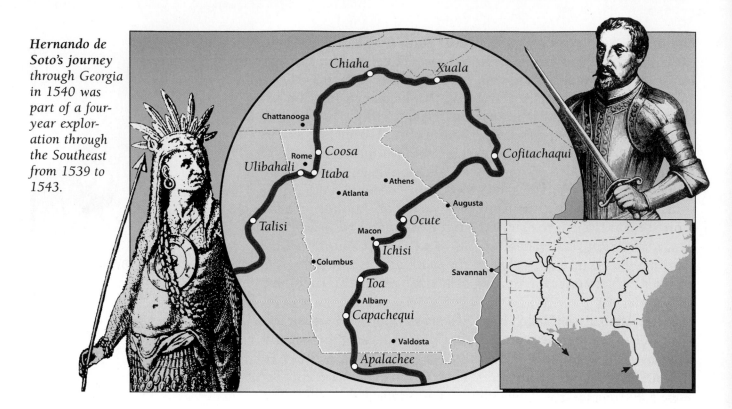

Hernando de Soto's journey through Georgia in 1540 was part of a four-year exploration through the Southeast from 1539 to 1543.

inland from the Florida coast. De Soto was to look for riches and conquer hostile Indians there. In return, he would be given a title, land, and a portion of the colony's profits.

In 1538, de Soto and 600 followers sailed from Spain to Cuba, where they spent most of a year preparing for their expedition. In 1539, they sailed for the North American mainland, landing on Florida's western coast. After spending the winter near present-day Tallahassee, they headed north, crossing into Georgia in March 1540. On this journey, the Spanish encountered the Indian chiefdoms of the Mississippian period.

De Soto's route through the Southeast quickly became a journey of death and disappointment. Food was a continual problem, and de Soto often seized stored food supplies from the Indians. Meat was in such short supply that the expedition reportedly even ate the dogs in some Indian villages. The four-year search turned up practically no gold or silver. Almost half of the expedition—including de Soto himself—died from disease, exposure, Indian attacks, or other causes.

More tragic was the fate of the Indians of the Southeast. The natives had never seen guns, steel swords, metal armor, and horses. They had only weapons of stone and wood and were often unable to defend themselves successfully. Many were killed in battle, tortured and murdered by the Spanish, or forced into slavery. Worst of all, they were exposed for the first time to European diseases against which they had little resistance, such as measles and chicken pox. Smallpox, which spread rapidly throughout the Southeast, killed about one in three Indians. In just a matter of years, chiefdoms were abandoned and entire villages stood vacant.

During the two centuries following the discovery of the New World, over 90 percent of the native population vanished. As a result, the Spanish began importing black slaves from western Africa to work the fields and mines of the Caribbean islands. For the few Indians who survived, life was forever changed. Their descendants would later emerge as the Cherokee, Creek, and other native tribes and nations.

French Claims in the Southeast

France had been the third European power to enter the race for North America. In 1524, only three years after Ponce de León's death, Giovanni de Verrazano sailed from France. Like Columbus, Verrazano believed that he could sail westward from Europe to Asia. Instead, he found his way blocked by North America. He first came ashore on the Carolina coast, or possibly even as far south as Georgia or Florida. From there, he sailed up North America's east coast to Nova Scotia before returning home. France later used Verrazano's exploration as the basis for its claim to much of North America, including the Southeast.

By 1562, France was ready to join Spain in the New World. Jean Ribault (pronounced Jahn Re-bow) and a band of 150 **Huguenots** (French Protestants) landed on Florida's coast and sailed northward looking for a place to settle. Just north of present-day Savannah, Ribault discovered a protected inlet, which he named Port Royal. Here the French constructed Charles Fort, the first European fort on the North American mainland. Famine and other hardships, however, forced them to abandon the settlement.

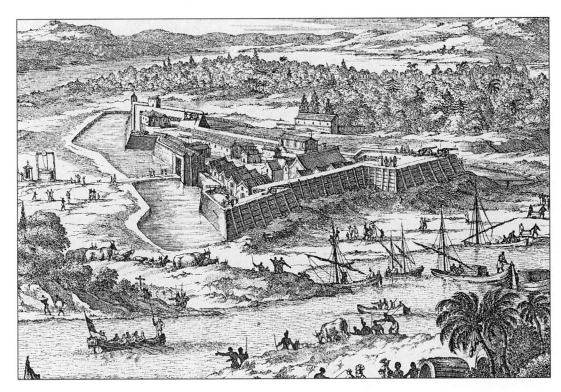

French Fort Caroline.

Two years later, a second group of Huguenots arrived in Spanish Florida. There, at the mouth of the St. Johns River, they built Fort Caroline. Catholic Spain was outraged. Not only were these French Protestants building forts and settling on Spanish soil, they were even raiding Spanish ships. Spain now moved quickly to push the Huguenots out.

In 1565, Pedro Menéndez and a large force of soldiers and colonists sailed from Spain. Their orders were to drive the French out and begin colonizing La Florida. They quickly carried out their orders. After landing on the coast of Florida, Menéndez proceeded to the St. Johns River for a surprise raid on Fort Caroline. The Spanish captured Fort Caroline and then executed its French Huguenot defenders.

Spanish Settlements in La Florida

Menéndez founded St. Augustine, Spain's first successful settlement on the North American continent. Located on the Atlantic coast, St. Augustine soon became an important military and political base for La Florida. It was also well situated to protect Spanish treasure ships using the Gulf Stream to speed their return home. Spanish ships loaded with New World gold and silver were tempting prizes for pirates or raiders hiding along the East Coast. Because St. Augustine is close to the Gulf Stream, Spanish crews could patrol the waters off Florida's coast, thus giving some protection along this passageway.

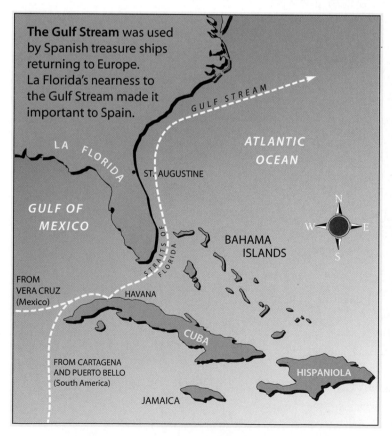

The Gulf Stream was used by Spanish treasure ships returning to Europe. La Florida's nearness to the Gulf Stream made it important to Spain.

Spanish Missions in La Florida

In an attempt to transform La Florida's Indians into Christian subjects of the King, Spain proceeded to build Catholic **missions**—church outposts—along the Atlantic and Gulf coasts. Church missionaries, known as **friars**, lived and worked with the Indians at these outposts. Sometimes, a few soldiers were assigned to a mission, for protection.

Missions—not forts—were the key to Spain's plan to prepare the Southeast for colonization. A mission was usually built at the village of an important local chief. Here the Indians could be instructed in religion and social behavior. The young would be taught to read and write, while adults learned of new crops and farming methods. The missions also provided a place for trading between Indians and Spanish colonists.

For purposes of missionary work, Georgia's coast was divided into two Spanish provinces. **Guale** (pronounced Wal-lee) was in the north, and **Mocama** was in the south. Guale consisted of the coastal area between the Savannah and Altamaha rivers. Mocama included the area between the Altamaha and St. Marys rivers.

Within a century from the founding of St. Augustine, 38 Spanish missions were in operation in La Florida, providing contact with some 25,000 Indians. But the work of the missionaries was not always welcomed by these Native Americans. Several friars lost their lives because of Indian uprisings.

Guale and Mocama

Soon after the founding of St. Augustine, Pedro Menéndez began a search for sites to build missions. In early 1566, he traveled up the Atlantic coast. Leaving a **garrison** (unit) of Spanish soldiers on Cumberland Island, he visited the main chief of the Guale Indians on St. Catherines Island. Here, Menéndez erected a cross and conducted four days of religious instruction for the Indians.

Father Antonio Sedeno and Brother Domingo Baez were assigned to St. Catherines Island. Here they began the mission known as Santa Catalina de Guale. Baez died of malaria before the year's end, while Sedeno stayed for 16 months. During this time, only seven Indians were converted, four of them children. Missionary work came to a standstill.

In the 1580s, a new round of missionary work began in Mocama. A decade later, Spanish missionaries became active along the Georgia coast in Guale.

Juanillo Rebellion

In 1597, an event occurred that threatened the future of the Spanish missions. Don Juanillo, a Guale Indian, was next in line to become chief. The young Juanillo, however, had two wives—a practice local missionaries had tried in vain to change. Now, he was about to become chief. Taking a bold step, one of the friars declared Juanillo unfit to be chief and named another tribal member as the next leader.

Juanillo was furious. By what right did Spanish friars have the power to say who should be chief? Juanillo assembled a small band of Indians to kill the friar who had denied him his chiefdom.

After the murder, Juanillo called for other chiefs in Guale to revolt against the Spanish missionaries. The unarmed priests could do nothing, and one by one, the missions fell. Finally, on Cumberland Island, Mocama Indians who supported the Spanish turned back the uprising. The Juanillo Rebellion ended, but not before five missionaries were executed.

Later, the missions would again become active. Recent excavations on St. Catherines Island, have uncovered a mission graveyard with the remains of over 400 Native Americans. Religious artifacts buried with the bodies suggest Catholic influence on these coastal Indians. ◀

England Comes to North America

During the sixteenth century, Spain grew richer and more powerful because of its dominance in the New World. England was concerned about its future and determined to enjoy a share of the New World trade. When Spain refused to share, English sea captains began raiding Spanish ships and settlements in the Americas. In 1586, Sir Francis Drake attacked and burned St. Augustine, the main city in La Florida. The conflict continued for almost 20 years. Finally, in 1604, the two powers signed a peace treaty. Now, England was ready to claim its share of North America.

Using Cabot's 1497 and 1498 explorations to justify English rights in the New World, King James I prepared a plan to establish **colonies**—territories on foreign soil that it controlled and settled. In 1606, he issued a **charter** (a legal document signed by the king) to some merchants for a new colony in America. These merchants were known as the Virginia Company.

In January 1607, three small ships sailed from England with Virginia's first settlers. Once in the new land, the leaders selected an inland site on the James River for the colony's first settlement. Named in honor of the king, James Town (later combined as Jamestown) became England's first permanent settlement in America. Within a hundred years, England had colonized most of the eastern coast of North America.

▶ **Locating the Main Ideas**

1. Define: La Florida, Huguenots, mission, friar, Guale, Mocama, garrison

2. Identify: Juan Ponce de León, Lucas Vázquez de Ayllón, Hernando de Soto, Jean Ribault, Pedro Menéndez, Santa Catalina de Guale

3. What was the most tragic result of Hernando de Soto's contact with the Indians?

4. What were the reasons why France's two colonies failed?

England had many reasons for wanting colonies in North America. Foremost was the desire to compete with other countries for power and glory. By being the first to establish permanent colonies, England would win out over rival countries in controlling land areas in North America.

Economic gain was another reason. Colonies in North America had the potential to provide resources that would benefit England economically. During the 1600s, a policy known as **mercantilism** was practiced by England. Mercantilism was a trade policy designed to make a nation as self-sufficient and wealthy as possible. The idea was for England to sell more to other countries than it had to buy from abroad. But the small island nation simply did not have the needed natural resources to sustain its economy. Also, because of its latitude and climate, many crops—such as cotton, tobacco, oranges, grapes, and spices—could not be grown at home.

For mercantilism to work, England had to find new sources of needed goods and raw materials. This would only be possible if England had its own colonies. The vast continent of North America held the most promise as a new source of food crops, tobacco, and raw materials for England. Colonies would also serve as a valuable market for English goods.

Although Virginia, England's first American colony, had a poor beginning, it proved mercantilism could work. The key was introduction of sweet tobacco from the West Indies and South America. Prized in Europe, the plant grew well in Virginia and fit perfectly into England's mercantile scheme. Virginia's success with tobacco encouraged other English colonies to follow its lead. Trading companies and wealthy persons were an important force in English colonization of North America.

The idea of colonies in North America appealed to England's upper class for still another reason. They believed their country was overpopulated with poor, homeless, and unemployed people who survived by begging or criminal activity. New colonies could provide a home for the poor and give them hope for a better life.

Finally, new colonies could serve as a home for religious groups seeking to practice their faith without discrimination. In England a group known as **Puritans** were speaking out against the Church of England. They opposed many of its practices and beliefs. Some Puritans only wanted to reform—or change—the Church of England. Others, known as Separatists, wanted to break away and create a new church.

In 1617 one group of Separatists requested permission to immigrate to America. Three years later, the *Mayflower* sailed from England with 101 colonists known as the **Pilgrims**. Not all came to America for religious reasons. Landing near Cape Cod, the Pilgrims began the Plymouth settlement, which eventually became part of the Massachusetts Bay Colony.

Britain's American Colonies: Mercantilism in Action

Exported by Colonies
fish, whale oil, furs, lumber, rum, corn, wheat, meat, iron, rice, tobacco, hides, indigo, silk, naval stores*

Imported by Colonies
goods manufactured in Great Britain, including cloth, glass, tools, china, furniture, weapons, gunpowder, and metalware; tea, wine, sugar, and molasses from other colonies around the world

*naval stores included tar, pitch, resin, and other products for sealing wooden sailing ships

Types of Colonies

In most cases, a new colony was created following an appeal to the king by a person, group, or company. The appeal was usually based on a combination of reasons, such as defense, trade, and religion. No matter what its purpose, creation of a new colony required a formal charter from the king. In many ways, the charter served as a constitution for the colony, describing its form of government. In some cases, charters were given to friends of the king, and in one case—Pennsylvania—the charter was issued to repay a debt owed by the king.

England's American colonies took one of three forms. One type of colony was the **corporate colony**. The king gave a grant of land to a corporation to settle a new colony in America. Most often the corporation was a **joint-stock company**. The company assumed all costs for the colony through the sale of stock to investors in England. In return, profits from colonial trade, the sale of land, and other sources went back to the company and its stockholders. Virginia—England's first colony in North America—was founded by a joint-stock company.

A second type of colony in America was the **proprietary colony**. This was a colony where the king issued a charter granting ownership of a colony to a person or group. The owner then had full rights to govern and distribute land in the new colony. Pennsylvania, established as a safe place for Quakers, was a proprietary colony.

The third type of colony was the **royal colony**. This was a colony operated directly by the English government through a royal governor appointed by the king. No American colonies started out this way, but by the end of the colonial period most had become royal colonies.

The colony of Carolina, chartered in 1663, had its boundaries extended by King Charles II in 1665. Much of this land, however, was already claimed by Spain as its colony of Florida.

England Creates Carolina

At first, England focused its efforts on colonies north of Virginia. Then, in 1663, King Charles II issued a charter for England's sixth American colony. Located south of Virginia, it would be named "Carolina."

The 36th parallel was selected as Carolina's northern boundary, and the 31st as its southern. England was now asserting a claim to most of Spanish Guale and Mocama. Two years later, King Charles claimed even more. He announced that Carolina's southern boundary actually was the 29th parallel —a latitude some 60 miles to the south of the Spanish fortress at St. Augustine. King Charles said that because John Cabot in 1498 had sailed as far south as the 29th parallel, England was entitled to this area. He also slightly extended the northern boundary to 36°30'.

The British began settling the new Carolina colony. In 1670, the new settlement of Charles Town (later Charleston) quickly drew the anger of Spanish officials at St. Augustine. They correctly guessed that Charles Town would become a base for English efforts to gain control of Guale and Mocama. They could see that England intended to take over the entire Southeast. Carolina traders soon developed an active business with the Indians to the south of the Savannah River. They exchanged firearms, tools, clothing, and other items for deerskins and furs.

The 1715 Yamasee Revolt made clear the need for a buffer colony to protect South Carolina.

In 1680, English officers led a party of 300 Indian allies in a raid on Santa Catalina de Guale, the Spanish mission on St. Catherines Island. Though vastly outnumbered, the mission's defenders bravely turned back the attack. Fearing another attempt, however, the Spanish abandoned the outpost and retreated to Sapelo Island. They continued missionary work there for four years and then retreated to St. Augustine. By 1685, Spain had withdrawn entirely from coastal Georgia. However, for 60 more years, Spain continued to claim the provinces of Guale and Mocama.

Meanwhile, the French claimed much of North America, from the St. Lawrence River to the Great Lakes and down the Mississippi all the way to the Gulf of Mexico. In the Southeast, they were quietly extending their influence along the Gulf Coast, with an eye toward reaching the Atlantic Ocean. Thus, at the turn of the century, in 1700, all the conflicting claims to land caused some to call the region south of Carolina's frontier "the debatable land."

In 1712, Carolina was divided into a southern and a northern province. Three years later, South Carolina was rocked by a Yamasee Indian revolt. Many settlers along the frontier were killed before the revolt was put down. The Yamasees fled southward to Florida. Now, more than ever, England worried about protecting Carolina's southern frontier.

A New Colony South of the Savannah River

The first serious proposal to colonize the area south of the Savannah River for England came in 1717. Sir Robert Montgomery proposed that he be allowed—at his own expense—to settle the land between the Savannah and Altamaha rivers. He called the land "the most delightful country of the universe."

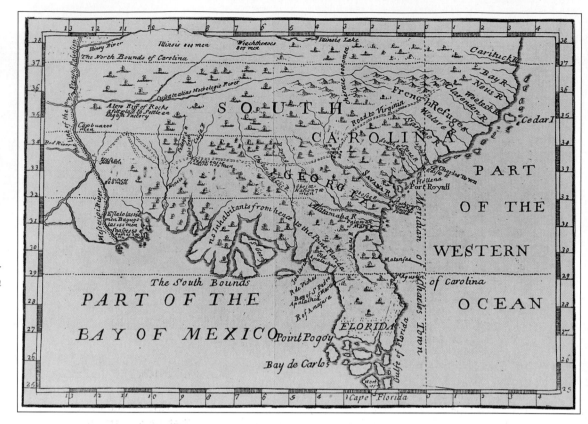

This 1733 map shows the boundaries of Georgia: from the mouth of the Savannah and Altamaha rivers upstream to the headwaters, then westward to the Pacific Ocean. Because it was drawn before the first colonist's arrival, the settlement of Savannah was not shown. Notice how Georgia divided South Carolina into two parts.

Montgomery proposed to name the settlement Azilia. His dream was to produce silk, wine, and other products for England. Azilia's main purpose, however, would be as a **buffer** to protect South Carolina from Spanish, French, and Indian attacks. Montgomery, however, was unable to raise money or enlist colonists for his venture. Plans for a buffer colony were postponed.

Then, in 1720, John Barnwell, a Carolina trapper, called on Britain to build a series of small forts at various sites to the south and west of Carolina's frontier. Government officials agreed. The first outpost would be built near the mouth of the Altamaha River. When construction of Fort King George began in 1721, Spain immediately protested. Other factors, however, spelled doom for the fort. Sickness, climate, and biting insects contributed to an unhappy garrison, and in 1727 the post was abandoned.

Other proposals soon followed, including one in 1724 by Jean Pierre Purry of Switzerland. Although his proposal failed, his idea for naming the new colony would survive. In recognition of England's king, Purry suggested two names for the new colony. "Georgine" was one. His other choice was "Georgia."

Even though these early attempts were unsuccessful, interest in starting a new colony continued to develop in England. A member of Britain's Parliament, James Oglethorpe, had become well known for his work on prison reform, particularly in freeing people in jail for not paying their debts. By 1732, he and his supporters had convinced King George II to approve a new English colony south of the Savannah River. That colony would be Georgia. ◀

▶ **Locating the Main Ideas**

1. Define: colony, charter, mercantilism, Puritans, Pilgrims, corporate colony, joint-stock company, proprietary colony, royal colony, buffer

2. Identify: St. Augustine, Jamestown, *Mayflower*, Charles Town, "the debatable land," Azilia, Fort King George, Jean Pierre Purry

3. What three European countries wanted to colonize the Southeast? From what direction was each country moving into the Southeast?

CHAPTER ACTIVITIES

Reviewing the Main Ideas

1. The fifteenth century in Europe has been called the "Age of Discovery." What was being discovered? What are the dates of the fifteenth century in years?

2. How were Muslim traders indirectly responsible for the discovery of the New World?

3. Explain Spain's theory of "first discovery." What was England's response?

4. How much say did Native Americans have in the claiming of their territory by foreign powers?

5. Explain the following statement: The time of year of the Ayllón expedition contributed to its failure.

6. How did St. Augustine's geographic location help Spain protect its treasure ships along the Florida coast?

7. What goal did Spain hope to achieve by setting up missions along the southeastern coast of North America? Did Spain achieve its goal?

8. According to the theory of mercantilism, why did England need colonies in the New World?

9. How did the settlement of Charles Town give the English the opportunity to further colonize the Southeast?

10. What do Sir Robert Montgomery, Jean Pierre Purry, and John Barnwell have in common?

Give It Some Extra Thought

1. **Collecting Evidence.** "Spain was more interested in finding riches than it was in colonizing North America." Use evidence given in this chapter to support or disprove the statement.

Sharpen Your Skills

1. **Using a Globe.** During the Age of Discovery, explorers relied on air and ocean currents as they traveled. Review the air and ocean current section in Chapter 2 and the maps in this chapter showing the routes of explorers. Choose one explorer and, using a globe, trace the route he used and explain how the currents aided him. Name the land areas the explorer may have touched in his travels.

2. **Using Maps.** Use a map of the southeastern United States and identify the following.

Hernando de Soto was one of many Spanish explorers to visit Georgia in the 16th century.

a. The Huguenots settled in Florida at the mouth of the St. Johns River. What present-day city is located here?

b. In 1663, King Charles II set 36° N and 31° N as the boundaries for the colony of Carolina. Locate the area between these two parallels and name the present-day states bordering the Atlantic Ocean that were part of the original colony. What states, bordering the Atlantic, were added when Charles later extended the southern boundary of Carolina to 29° N?

3. **Reading Old Maps.** Review the "Map Reading" activity on page 9. Which parts of a map (title, grid, legend, scale, and compass) are on the 1733 map of Georgia on page 68? What city did the cartographer use as 0° longitude? (Hint: What is another name for lines of longitude?) What do the numbers in the map margins represent?

Going Further

1. **Making a Chart.** Make a classroom chart of "Explorers of the New World." Include the following headings on the chart. *Explorer's Name, Country Represented, Date, Territory Discovered or Explored, Results.* You may want to use additional sources to add details to your chart.

2. **Think Creatively.** America was named for Amerigo Vespucci. Using the names of other explorers, suggest different names for the country. Likewise, Georgia was named for King George II although it was earlier known as La Florida and could have been called Azilia. Propose other names for the Georgia colony that are related to early explorers and events in its history.

GEORGIA EVENTS

King George II signs charter establishing colony of Georgia	Oglethorpe and first Georgia colonists arrive at Yamacraw Bluff	German Salzburgers arrive in Georgia	Oglethorpe and new colonists build Fort Frederica on St. Simons Island	Construction of Fort Augusta begins	Chief Tomochichi dies	Oglethorpe's forces defeat Spanish at Battle of Bloody Marsh	Oglethorpe promoted to rank of general, returns to England		Trustees give up charter; Georgia becomes a royal colony	Capt. John Reynolds arrives as Georgia's first royal governor
1732	**1733**	**1734**	**1736**	**1737**	**1739**	**1742**	**1743**	**1750**	**1752**	**1754**
George Washington born in Virginia				Oglethorpe leaves England with 600 soldiers to defend Fort Frederica	Britain declares war on Spain			In London, Trustees vote to allow slavery in Georgia	Britain adopts Gregorian calendar	French and Indian War begins

EVENTS ELSEWHERE

Colonial Georgia

1732–1776

Georgia's first slave code enacted	James Wright becomes governor of Georgia	First newspaper, *Georgia Gazette,* established in Georgia	Georgia's southern boundary defined		Georgians begin choosing sides, becoming Whigs or Tories		Creeks and Cherokees cede lands later called Wilkes County	Georgians split, send no delegates to Continental Congress	Royal government in Georgia loses power
1755	**1761**	**1763**	**1764**	**1765**	**1767**	**1770**	**1773**	**1774**	**1775**
		French and Indian War ends; Britain gives up claims west of Mississippi River	New colonies of East and West Florida created	American colonies protest Stamp Act	Colonists begin boycott of British goods	Boston Massacre	Boston Tea Party	Intolerable Acts; First Continental Congress agrees not to trade with Britain	American Revolution begins

6

Coming Up Next!
- Georgia is created
- Georgia as a trustee colony
- Georgia becomes a royal colony

The Founding of Georgia

In the year 1696, Eleanor and Theophilus Oglethorpe celebrated Christmas in England with their new baby son, James Edward Oglethorpe. The last of 10 children, James would prove to be the most famous of the Oglethorpes of Surrey County, England.

At age 25, James Oglethorpe was elected to **Parliament**, the national legislature of Great Britain.* There, he learned about the many problems facing his country. The British were having hard times at home, especially in their cities and towns. There were not enough jobs, and many people were in debt. Those who couldn't pay their debts were often thrown into prison. As a result, London's jails were overcrowded with thousands of unfortunate debtors.

Convinced that something had to be done, Oglethorpe became a leader in Parliament for prison reform. As a result of his work with a jails committee, many debtors were released from prison. They joined other homeless, hungry people in London who could not find work.

---

*In 1707, England and Scotland united to form Great Britain. The agreement allowed each country to keep its name and boundaries, but the national government would be called "British"—not "English."

King George II issued Georgia's charter in 1732.

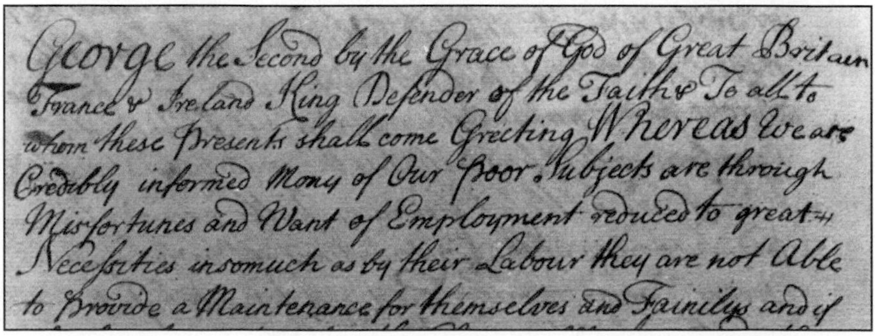

George the Second by the Grace of God of Great Britain France & Ireland King Defender of the Faith & To all to whom these Presents shall come Greeting Whereas We are Credibly informed Many of Our Poor Subjects are through Misfortunes and Want of Employment reduced to great Necessities insomuch as by their Labour they are not Able to Provide a Maintenance for themselves and Families and if

Wanting to help even more, Oglethorpe met with John Percival, an influential member of Parliament who had served on the jails committee. Why not ask the king for a new colony in America and allow released debtors and other unfortunate poor to be sent there on charity? Percival agreed, so they asked King George II for a grant of land south of the Carolina frontier. In his honor, they proposed that it be called Georgia.

Georgia Is Created

On June 20, 1732, Georgia received its official charter. This important legal document, issued by the British government, specified the colony's boundaries, its form of government, the powers of its officials, and the rights of its settlers.

According to its charter, Georgia had three purposes:

1. *Charity:* To help relieve poverty and unemployment in Britain. Georgia was seen as a home for the "worthy poor"—particularly those crowding the streets of London.

2. *Economics:* To increase Britain's trade and wealth. Georgia would fit neatly into the mercantile system, providing needed agricultural products while serving as a valuable market for British goods.

3. *Defense:* To provide South Carolina with a buffer against Indian attacks. Although the charter did not refer to the threat of Spanish or French forces, its backers clearly saw Georgia as a buffer against that threat.

In order to receive decent treatment, jailed debtors in England had to pay for room, board, and special privileges.

Though not stated in the charter, *religion* was a fourth reason for Georgia's creation. England saw the new American colony as a home for Protestants being persecuted in Europe.

European nations commonly had an official state religion. The Anglican Church, a Protestant body, was the Church of England. For Spain and France, the official church was Roman Catholic. Unfortunately, Catholics and Protestants had problems getting along with each other, and religious differences in Europe carried over to the New World.

Georgia's charter did not impose an official church for the colony, and persons coming to Georgia would be free to worship as they pleased. The charter's guarantee of freedom of religion, however, specifically excluded Catholics because of the threat of Spanish (and Catholic) Florida to the south.

English concerns about Catholic Florida were further heightened because Florida had a policy of giving freedom to any English slave

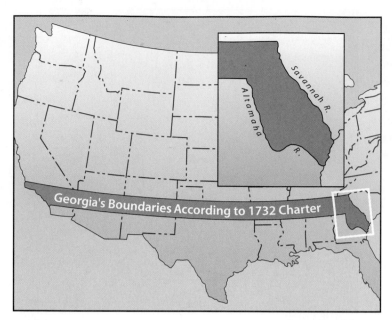

Georgia's Boundaries According to 1732 Charter

If Georgia included all the land assigned to it when chartered in 1732, the city of Los Angeles would be our state's largest city. Name the present-day states that would be part of Georgia.

who would convert to Catholicism. Some South Carolina slaves did escape, converted, and became Spanish subjects. Thus, white Carolina colonists were happy to see a new English colony to their south. Maybe this would stem the number of slaves escaping to Florida. Also, Georgia's existence would make it more difficult for former slaves living in Florida to return and spark a slave rebellion.

Georgia's Boundaries

At the time of Georgia's creation, South Carolina had no settlements south of the Savannah River. Thus, that river was selected as Georgia's northern boundary. The Altamaha River—the largest river on Georgia's coast—would be its southern border. At the head of each river, a line would be drawn due west to the Pacific Ocean. On paper, Georgia stretched across the entire continent of North America.

Spain and France protested Britain's attempt to colonize an area that they also claimed. Britain, however, pointed out that Spain long ago had withdrawn its missionaries and soldiers from the region. For the time being, neither Spain nor France was in a military position to challenge the new colony of Georgia. ◀

Georgia as a Trustee Colony

For the first two decades, the new colony of Georgia was unlike any other American colony. Clearly, it was not a joint-stock colony like Virginia. Nor was it a royal colony like South Carolina. In some ways it was like a proprietary colony—but no one owned Georgia. Rather, Georgia was England's only colony in America to be governed by **trustees**. It was a trustee colony.

Georgia's Charter of 1732 named James Oglethorpe and 20 other British gentlemen interested in charity as trustees. They would be responsible for managing Georgia for the next 21 years. The word "trustee" refers to someone placed in an official position of trust to act on behalf of someone else. Trustees are not supposed to benefit personally from decisions they make. Instead, they should act in the best interests of those for whom they are responsible. To assure that the trustees would not act out of self-interest, Georgia's charter prohibited several activities. Trustees could not receive a salary, own land in the colony, or hold public office in Georgia. They accepted this trust and adopted an official motto, "Not for ourselves but others."

Georgia was to be a great social experiment. The trustees wanted to avoid the conditions that led to poverty and other problems in England. They believed Georgia could become a model society. The

▶ **Locating the Main Ideas**

1. Define: Parliament
2. Identify: John Percival, King George II, Georgia's Charter of 1732
3. What events led Oglethorpe to propose the creation of a new colony?
4. What four things did Georgia's charter specify?
5. Which religious group was specifically excluded from coming to the new colony of Georgia? Why?

key would be (1) strict rules on land and work, and (2) carefully selected colonists.

The first task facing the trustees was to raise money to send colonists to Georgia and to pay for the food and tools they would need once there. Throughout the summer and fall of 1732, sermons, pamphlets, speeches, and newspapers carried appeals for contributions. Soon, enough money had been donated to send Georgia's first shipload of colonists.

Deciding who would go was the trustees' next problem. Newspaper announcements about the chance to go to Georgia brought many applications. From these, the trustees had to decide which to send "on charity." They looked for hardworking people who were down on their luck *and* who had the skills to make the colony a success.

Eventually, 35 families were selected. Not a single debtor released from prison was among them. Instead, the list included farmers, carpenters, tailors, bakers, merchants, and those with other skills and trades.

Families going on charity received more than free passage to Georgia. Once there, they would receive land on which to live and work. They would be given weapons, tools for building and farming, seed, and food to support them until the first harvest came in. In return, the colonists had to clear lands, raise crops, build houses and public structures, and follow the trustees' rules.

The First Colonists Sail to Georgia

In late November 1732, James Oglethorpe and 114 settlers sailed from England on the ship *Anne*. Fifty-seven days later, the *Anne* sailed into Charles Town harbor where Oglethorpe conferred with South Carolina officials about the new colony. The Carolinians promised to support Georgia in any way possible.

The next day, the colonists sailed southward to Port Royal, Carolina's southernmost outpost. While Georgia's settlers recovered from their voyage, Oglethorpe and some Carolina rangers sailed south to explore the Savannah River, Georgia's northern boundary.

About 18 miles upriver from the ocean, Oglethorpe found a large flat area, ideal for a settlement. Just upstream was a small village of Yamacraws, a branch of the Creek Indians. Nearby, John Musgrove, a Carolina trader, and his wife Mary operated a trading post. Mary's father was a white trader and her mother was a Creek. The Musgroves told Oglethorpe the area he wanted to settle was known as

This fanciful view of life in Georgia appeared in a 1733 pamphlet published by the trustees to encourage support for the colony. How does the artist show Georgia as a model society? What evidence is there that the artist had never been to coastal Georgia?

Georgia Trustee's Seal 1733–52.

In addition to allowing Georgia colonists to settle on Yamacraw lands, Chief Tomochichi became a close friend and ally of James Oglethorpe.

Yamacraw Bluff. Permission to settle there would have to come from Tomochichi, chief of the Yamacraws.

The chief spoke little English, so John Musgrove translated during the talks between Oglethorpe and Tomochichi. Why would the Yamacraw leader even consider giving up his people's land to the English? By this time, his small tribe had come to depend on English goods, for which they traded deerskins and furs. Too much hunting in the past, however, left few game animals in the area. Not being farmers, the natives had little use for the land at Yamacraw Bluff. Tomochichi concluded that a nearby English settlement might improve life for his poor village. He announced his decision: the English were welcome.

Oglethorpe returned to Port Royal with the exciting news. Quickly the colonists prepared for the final leg of their long journey. On February 12, 1733—a day we now celebrate as Georgia Day —the colonists arrived at Yamacraw Bluff. Most people consider this to be the date of Georgia's **founding** (or creation), even though the colony was legally created in 1732, the year Georgia's charter was issued.

Georgia's First Settlement

Living in tents, the colonists began building Georgia's first settlement, named Savannah for the nearby river. They started by clearing the pine forest atop Yamacraw Bluff.

Using only hand tools, they cut down trees and sawed them into lumber for houses and buildings. Tree stumps and roots had to be removed from the ground. The work was hard, and even with everyone pitching in, Oglethorpe needed to hire some black sawyers from Charles Town to help out.

The town of Savannah was laid out using a special plan designed in London. Open spaces called "squares" were one of its main features. Each public square was to be a kind of neighborhood center. Facing each square were four special lots set aside for public buildings. Around each square were 40 house lots, each 60 by 90 feet, organized into 4 groups of 10.

Just as Savannah was beginning to take shape, a crisis occurred. The colonists, who got their drinking water from the river, started coming down with dysentary and other diseases. In April, their only doctor died. During the next 10 months, death came to one out of every four colonists.

Fortunately, the problem improved once a town well was dug. Soon, with the arrival of new colonists, Savannah began to recover. Among the first was a group of 40 Jews who had been displaced from Portugal and Spain. Among their number was a doctor, who performed valuable services to the colony. Other immigrants included Italian silk producers, Lutheran Salzburgers, Germans, Swiss, and other nationalities. These were in addition to the English who came on charity or paid their own way.

By the end of its first 12 months, Savannah had more than 50 houses, as well as several public buildings. Oglethorpe, however, continued to live in his tent, insisting that all colonists be housed first.

Georgia's founder spent nearly every minute of the day tending to the affairs of the colonists. A visitor from South Carolina observed:

Savannah, 1734. One year after Savannah's founding, Oglethorpe's town plan was taking shape. On the left, note the house lots, open square, and three completed public buildings.

> He is extremely well beloved by all his people; the general title they give him is Father. If any of them is sick, he immediately visits them, and takes a great deal of care of them. If any difference arises, he is the person that decides it....He keeps a strict discipline; I never saw one swear, all the time I was there. He does not allow them rum, but in lieu [instead] gives them English beer. It is surprising to see how cheerfully the men go to work, considering they have not been bred to it. There are no idlers there; even the boys and girls do their parts. [From a letter in the *South Carolina Gazette*, Charles Town, March 22, 1733.] ▶

Growing Pains

Life was hard, and some colonists began to grumble. In summer, Savannah was not the paradise they had expected. There were frequent and sometimes very heavy rains. Also, they were not used to the insects, humidity, and heat of coastal Georgia.

Georgia colonists complained the most, however, about three of the trustees' regulations: (1) restrictions on land ownership and inheritance, (2) a ban on slavery, and (3) prohibitions on rum and other hard liquors.

▶ **Locating the Main Ideas**

1. Define: trustees, founding
2. Identify: Yamacraw Bluff, John and Mary Musgrove, Tomochichi, Georgia Day, public squares
3. How did the trustees intend to make Georgia a model society?
4. Why did Tomochichi allow the English to settle on Yamacraw Bluff?

The Founding of Georgia / 77

Tomochichi

He had no formal education, no bodyguards or chauffeurs, and no special training. Yet, a Native American tribal chief, Tomochichi, easily qualifies as Georgia's first ambassador. Without his diplomatic skills and influence, the settling of the state by Europeans would have been much more difficult and dangerous.

Born around 1650, Tomochichi commanded a Yamacraw tribe that had been banished to the Georgia coast by the lower Creeks. They relocated in what is today Savannah, along Musgrove Creek Canal. In this Yamacraw village in 1733, James Oglethorpe met Tomochichi—dignified and physically impressive, standing six feet tall.

The elderly Tomochichi allowed Oglethorpe to settle on Yamacraw Bluff, and the two became close friends. The next year, Tomochichi helped assemble representatives of major Creek tribes. He convinced them to sign a treaty giving English colonists the land between the Savannah and Altamaha rivers, as far upstream as the tide flowed. The treaty also set trade agreements between the two sides and restored Tomochichi's position as a respected leader among the Creeks.

Oglethorpe repaid these efforts by taking Tomochichi, some of his relatives, and other chiefs to

Tomochichi and his nephew, Tooanahowi.

England in 1734. There Oglethorpe asked for further support for the struggling Georgia colony. So impressed was King George with Tomochichi's bearing and eloquence that he gave the visitors money and showered them with gifts.

With conflict between the colonists and the Spanish becoming more likely, Tomochichi helped set up a meeting between Oglethorpe and major Native American chiefs. His goal was to obtain a collective promise of neutrality. They reached this agreement in the lower Creek capital of Coweta Town, a site near what is today Columbus. When fighting did erupt a few years later, Tomochichi's heir and nephew, Tooanahowi, served with Oglethorpe in the Battle of Bloody Marsh in 1742.

In 1739, Tomochichi died in Yamacraw Village at an advanced age (some say just shy of his 90th birthday). When Oglethorpe learned of the chief's death, he rushed from Augusta to Savannah, arranging for a full military funeral. In keeping with Creek tradition, Tomochichi was buried with some of his possessions, including a silver snuffbox from England, and his graveside was marked with a stone mound.

The trustees wanted to prevent the development of a rich upper class. Therefore, land ownership was limited. Each male adult who came on charity received a town lot for a house plus 50 acres of land (45 acres in the country and 5 at the edge of town). Colonists who paid their own way got 50 acres, plus 50 acres for each servant they brought, up to 500 acres.

In some cases, the land was poorly drained and not suited for growing crops. But the trustees refused to issue new land grants in these cases. Also, colonists were prohibited from selling or leasing their land. If a colonist left Georgia, his land went back to the trustees.

The most unpopular land policy, however, concerned inheritance. The trustees wanted to make sure that each land grant had an adult male trained to protect it, with firearms if necessary. Therefore, the trustees provided that land could only be passed on to a male heir. If a man died without a son to take his place, the land was to be returned to the trustees and distributed to another family.

Another policy opposed by many colonists was the trustees' ban on slavery. Some trustees, including Oglethorpe, were against the practice. But others argued that slavery was allowed in every other American colony, and it was unfair not to allow slaves in Georgia.

The trustees' third unpopular policy was a prohibition on rum and other types of hard liquor. Colonists could drink English beer and wine, but not other alcoholic drinks. Many colonists, however, ignored the ban.

Oglethorpe faced a tough problem. When he enforced the trustees' regulations, the colonists complained. But if he relaxed the rules, the trustees objected. Eventually, trustee policies on land and slaves were repealed.

Building Forts

In the summer of 1734, James Oglethorpe returned to England to brief the trustees on Georgia's status. With him was Tomochichi, the chief's nephew Tooanahowi, and a delegation of Creeks. Their strange appearance created quite a stir in London. The Creeks pledged their friendship to the trustees, and they met the king and queen before returning to Georgia.

While in England, Oglethorpe and the other trustees asked Parliament for government funding of their colony. No longer was there talk about charity for the needy. Now, Georgia's importance as a military buffer against the French and Spanish and their Indian allies was stressed. Parliament agreed to provide funds to build forts along Georgia's southern border.

To build Georgia's first fort, the trustees sent 150 Scottish Highlanders to Georgia's southern boundary. At Darien, just north of the mouth of the Altamaha River, they built a small fort and settlement.

In December 1735, Oglethorpe and 257 new Georgia colonists sailed from England with instructions to build a second fort. Their destination was St. Simons Island, just south of the Altamaha's

Ruins of Fort Frederica, St. Simons Island. The fort guarded the inland waterway used for travel along the coast.

mouth. Arriving in February, Oglethorpe laid out the town and fort of Frederica, which in time grew to house Britain's largest military base in America.

While work was under way on Frederica, Oglethorpe and Tomochichi sailed to the south. During this trip, additional sites were selected for British forts as far south as the St. Johns River.

Naturally, the Spanish were upset at British forts being built on land they still claimed. Later that year, Oglethorpe and the Spanish governor of Florida, Moral de Sanchez, worked out a temporary treaty. But how long could they keep the peace? ◀

Indian Relations

Oglethorpe brought instructions from the British government on another matter: keeping the friendship of Georgia's Native Americans. Georgia needed Indian trade, and if war broke out with the Spanish, it would be critical to have them as allies. But this friendship was threatened because colonial traders—many from South Carolina—were cheating the Indians.

The trustees had another concern—traders were supplying rum to the Indians. They directed Oglethorpe to regulate the Indian trade. Any person wanting to trade with Georgia's natives would have to get a license, pay a fee, and agree to follow certain rules. So that Indians would be treated fairly, an official exchange rate for animal skins and other trade items was established.

Much of the Indian trade took place in Georgia's **backcountry** (or **upcountry**)—the unsettled area far inland from the coast. To better control this trade, Oglethorpe in 1736 ordered that Fort Augusta be built on the Savannah River.

War with Spain

As relations between Britain and Spain grew worse, Georgians feared a possible Spanish invasion. In November 1736, Oglethorpe left Georgia to return to England. There, he appealed to Parliament for money to fund the colony for another year. He warned high officials that a Spanish invasion was likely. Without British soldiers to defend Georgia, the colony would fall.

By the fall of 1737, it seemed that Oglethorpe was right. Rumors in London told of a large military force being sent to Cuba by Spain. In Europe, relations between Britain and Spain were getting worse. It was now time to act.

In October, King George II gave Oglethorpe the rank of colonel in the British army. The king authorized him to raise a regiment of 600 soldiers for Georgia. At the same time, Oglethorpe was placed in charge of all British forces in Georgia and South Carolina. He immediately began recruiting soldiers and by spring of 1738 was ready to sail to Georgia. Most of the soldiers were sent to Fort Frederica.

▶ **Locating the Main Ideas**

1. Identify: Fort Frederica

2. What summertime conditions caused problems for the new colonists in Georgia?

3. Why did the trustees put restrictions on the number of acres of land a colonist could own?

4. After Oglethorpe's trip to England in 1734, how did the purpose of the colony change?

In 1739, Britain declared war on Spain—a war that surely would spill over to America. Rather than wait to be invaded, Oglethorpe took action. He prepared to invade Florida and destroy the Spanish fortress at St. Augustine.

In the spring of 1740, Oglethorpe led an invasion force south into Florida. Just north of St. Augustine they came upon two Spanish forts. The English captured the first one, Fort Diego, in what would prove to be their only victory. The second was Fort Mose, home of the Black Militia—a unit of Carolina slaves who had escaped to freedom in Spanish Florida. Outnumbered by the invasion force, Fort Mose's defenders had fallen back to the main fort in St. Augustine. Oglethorpe marched on to St. Augustine to begin a siege of the fortress. Part of his force made Fort Mose their quarters during the siege. In a dawn attack, 300 Spanish soldiers, including members of the Black Militia, crept out of the main fort at St. Augustine and struck the British soldiers in Fort Mose. When the smoke cleared, 68 of Oglethorpe's men were dead and another 34 taken prisoner—the worst loss of the entire campaign. Discouraged by this loss and the inability to take the main fort, Oglethorpe ordered his troops back to St. Simons Island.

Two years passed. Then, late in June 1742, a fleet carrying several thousand Spanish soldiers appeared on the ocean's horizon. Georgia's defenders were badly outnumbered and pulled back to Fort Frederica. It appeared that the island would fall.

On July 7, an important event in Georgia history took place. Advancing from the south, a Spanish force approached within a mile of Fort Frederica. A patrol of Oglethorpe's rangers opened fire from the woods, catching the enemy by surprise. The Spanish turned back, and the rangers rushed to Frederica to warn Oglethorpe. Oglethorpe hastily assembled a small force of soldiers and led them in hot pursuit of the Spanish.

Reenactment of the Battle of Bloody Marsh.

Several miles to the south, at the edge of a marsh, the dirt road narrowed to a foot path. Here, Oglethorpe positioned his troops behind bushes and trees to defend the trail and then rode back to check on Frederica.

Meanwhile, the Spanish reappeared at the marsh. Oglethorpe's hidden troops opened fire. A brief, but fierce, battle followed. From a distance, Oglethorpe could hear the gunfire. Though riding desperately, by the time he arrived the Battle of Bloody Marsh was over.

Several days later, the Spanish were turned back again, this time in an at-

General James Oglethorpe sailed to England in 1743, never returning to the colony he founded.

tempt to capture Fort Frederica by sea. Discouraged, the invasion force withdrew to the safety of St. Augustine. Georgia had been saved. In recognition of the victory, King George promoted Oglethorpe to the rank of general.

In 1743, General Oglethorpe returned to England. As it turned out, he never again set foot on Georgia soil. After being paid by Parliament for most of the personal funds he had spent on the colony, the general, now almost 48 years old, met Elizabeth Wright. Shortly thereafter, they married. Oglethorpe continued as a member of Parliament for another decade, but his activities on the board of trustees declined. He watched with sadness as the remaining trustees abandoned the principles which had made Georgia unique.

The Colony Declines

After Oglethorpe left, the future of Georgia looked bleak. Many colonists gave up and returned to England, or went to other colonies. The colony wasn't producing much, so its export business was poor. The trustees' officers in Savannah worked hard to keep things going, but crop failures and discontent among the colonists made it difficult.

Gradually, the trustees relaxed their restrictions on land ownership and inheritance. Finally, in 1750, they dropped their prohibition on slavery. In 1752, the trustees transferred control of the colony to the British government. After two decades, the great experiment was over. Henceforth, Georgia would become more like the other American colonies. ◀

Georgia Becomes a Royal Colony

In 1752, Georgia became a royal colony under the direct control of the British government. The colonists were delighted, although two years would pass before the changeover was completed.

In 1754, Captain John Reynolds sailed from England to become Georgia's first royal governor. As the king's representative as well as the chief executive officer of the colony, Reynolds had the most important office in Georgia's new government. Like the other royal colonies, Georgia would have its own legislature. An appointed upper house would advise the governor. An elected lower house—the Commons House of Assembly—would give Georgia colonists their first chance at self-government. It was a limited voice, however. Only white males owning at least 50 acres of land could vote in Assembly elections. To serve in that body, a member had to own at least 500 acres. Laws enacted by the Assembly could be vetoed by the royal governor or by the king back in London. Still, colonists had more of a voice than was ever possible under the trustees.

Reynolds proved to be neither popular nor effective and was replaced after two years. His replacement, Henry Ellis, was commit-

▶ Locating the Main Ideas

1. Define: backcountry, upcountry
2. Identify: Fort Mose, Battle of Bloody Marsh, Elizabeth Wright
3. Why did the trustees want Oglethorpe to regulate the Indian trade?

ted to strengthening Georgia's defenses, increasing its population, and improving its economy.

In 1758, the royal Assembly declared the Anglican Church (the Church of England) the official church of Georgia. Lawmakers divided the colony into eight religious districts known as **parishes**. In each parish, residents voted for church wardens and paid taxes to support the church and to help the poor. The parishes served other purposes as well, including certain political functions. In a way, these were Georgia's first counties.

Ellis was an improvement over Reynolds, but he was not happy serving as Georgia's governor. He couldn't stand the summer heat, so after only three years in office, he was granted permission to return to England.

Georgia's third—and final—royal governor proved to be its ablest. Sir James Wright was genuinely concerned about the colonists, and served the people well for almost two decades.

Sir James Wright, the most popular and effective of Georgia's three royal governors.

The French and Indian War

In 1754, the same year that Governor Reynolds arrived in Georgia, Great Britain and France went to war over their world empires. The war began in North America. Because many Indians fought on the side of France, American colonists, who fought with the British, called it the **French and Indian War**. On the frontier, the fighting was savage, with scalpings and other cruelties. Fortunately for Georgia, most of the fighting took place far to the north.

Soon, the war had spread to Europe, and eventually even to India. Throughout most of the fighting, Spain stayed out of the conflict. However, late in the war, Spain joined France as an ally, but much too late to affect the outcome. In so doing, Spain made a costly mistake.

In 1762, France and Spain asked for peace. In the Treaty of Paris of 1763, Britain demanded that the two countries give up great portions of their claims to land in North America. France gave up its claims to Canada and all territory east of the Mississippi River, except New Orleans. The price of defeat for Spain was the loss of Florida.

One provision of the Treaty of Paris affected Georgia. Until then, Britain claimed that several of its colonies extended all the way to the Pacific Ocean. In the new peace treaty, however, Britain gave up all claims west of the Mississippi River. Thus, in 1763, the Mississippi became Georgia's western boundary.

The Proclamation of 1763

With the end of the war, Great Britain found itself with a huge empire in North America. What should it do with its new possessions —create new colonies? Now that the war was over, there was also the matter of Indian uprisings over whites settling on their lands.

In 1764, a royal commission set East and West Florida as Georgia's southern boundary. What other present-day states were part of Georgia in 1764?

Also, defending the American colonies had been expensive to the British taxpayers. How could a greater share of these costs be shifted to the American colonists themselves?

That fall, King George III issued the **Proclamation of 1763**. In this document, Britain announced it was creating four new North American colonies—Quebec (in Canada), Grenada (in the Caribbean), East Florida, and West Florida. Georgia's southern boundary was extended to the St. Marys River. The Proclamation of 1763 reserved all lands west of the Appalachian Mountains for the Indians.

The next year, Georgia's boundaries were changed to include all land north of West Florida and East Florida. As you can see on the map, Alabama and Mississippi were once part of Georgia.

The Colony Prospers

The end of the French and Indian War became a time of growth in Georgia. The Spanish and French were no longer a threat to the colony. After the war, the Creeks ceded more than 2 million acres of land to Georgia. Quickly, Georgia began surveying its new territory.

The land could have been offered for sale, but Georgia decided it would be easier to attract new colonists by giving the land away. A plan known as the **headright system** was adopted. Under it, the head of each family was given a "right" to 100 acres, plus 50 acres for each additional family member, indentured servant, or slave. The only costs to the family were small surveying and recording fees.

New settlers began to rush to Georgia for the free land. Some came from Europe, but many migrated from other colonies. The Appalachian Mountains formed a natural barrier preventing eastern farmers from migrating due west. Anyway, Britain had reserved the land west of the Appalachians for the Indians. Thus, geography and government policy encouraged colonists in search of new land to go southward into Georgia.

By boat, horseback, wagon, or foot, thousands of new settlers came to Georgia after the French and Indian War. Some brought slaves with them, and in a few years almost half of Georgia's inhabitants were black. By 1766, Georgia had 10,000 white settlers and 8,000 black. In another 10 years, there were 50,000 colonists, about half of them from Africa. At the same time, new lands were opened for settlement. The colony was gaining a new life. ◄

▶ **Locating the Main Ideas**

1. Define: parish, French and Indian War, Proclamation of 1763, headright system

2. Identify: John Reynolds, Henry Ellis, James Wright

3. What were the qualifications for voting in Assembly elections? for serving as a member?

4. Under the terms of the Treaty of Paris of 1763, what territory did France give to Britain? What did Spain give to Britain?

CHAPTER ACTIVITIES

Reviewing the Main Ideas

1. Explain how the new colony of Georgia was supposed to relieve the problems of unemployment and poverty in England.

2. List the three purposes for the founding of Georgia stated in its charter.

3. What did the charter prohibit the trustees from doing so they could not profit from the Georgia colony?

4. Review the list of occupations of the first 35 families selected to come to Georgia and write down five additional occupations that would be useful in starting a new colony.

5. Give evidence to support this statement: In allowing the English colonists to settle Yamacraw Bluff, Tomochichi was thinking about the good of his people.

6. Reread the letter from the *South Carolina Gazette* describing Oglethorpe. What was surprising to the writer of the letter? What does he mean when he writes, "There are no idlers there"?

7. List three things Oglethorpe did to regulate the Indian trade.

8. Why did the trustees turn control of Georgia over to the British government?

9. In what way did colonists participate in governing themselves after Georgia became a royal colony?

10. Why did Georgia begin to prosper after the French and Indian War?

Give It Some Extra Thought

1. **Analyzing Values and Beliefs**. Explain what the motto of the trustees, "Not for ourselves but others," means. List three words or phrases that might describe the trustees as they lived up to their motto.

2. **Analyze the Change**. Georgia's original charter contained three purposes. When the trustees turned control of the colony over to the British government, which one of the three purposes was no longer emphasized? In your opinion, were the trustees successful in developing a model society in Georgia?

Sharpen Your Skills

1. **Interpreting Visual Evidence**. Locate the following items on the town plan of Savannah: (a) the stairs on the bluff, (b) the crane for unloading ships, (c) Oglethorpe's tent, (d) the palisades, (e) the battery of cannon, (f) four public squares. What evidence is there that Savannah was a planned city? What evidence shows that Savannah's colonists were concerned about military defense? Why do you think Oglethorpe chose to live in a tent instead of a house?

Going Further

1. **Persuasive Writing**. Write a newspaper ad the trustees could use to attract the kind of colonists they wanted to settle in Georgia. Post your ad on the bulletin board.

2. **Planning an Event**. The visit of Tomochichi and the other Creek Indians to London in 1734 was a real "media event." Imagine that Oglethorpe was taking the Indians to London today. You be the media event coordinator and plan the day's activities for the group. Your goal is to impress the people of London and raise money for the Georgia colony. You may want to schedule television appearances and set up appointments with important people as part of your plan.

Regulated Prices of Goods in the Indian Trade

Items	Pounds of Leather
1 blanket	8
1 white shirt	3
1 trading gun	16
hoes	3-4
saddles	20-60

A dollar is sometimes called a buck. How do you think that term developed?

Coming Up Next!

- Regional differences among American colonies
- The Ebenezer community
- Africans come to America
- Georgia society and culture

7

Life of the People in Colonial Georgia

Georgia had much in common with the other American colonies. The great majority of colonists had immigrated from England, which meant they shared a common language and culture. All colonies were expected to provide England with raw goods (such as food, tobacco, lumber, naval stores, and deer hides) and in turn purchase finished products made in the mother country. Yet, long before the founding of Georgia, it was clear that even though they were similar in some ways, the American colonies had many differences.

Regional Differences among American Colonies

By the late 1600s, England's American colonies were developing along three regional patterns—New England, Middle Atlantic, and Southern. Each region had distinct economic, social, and political characteristics.

New England Colonies

In the New England colonies of New Hampshire, Massachusetts Bay, Rhode Island, and Connecticut, agriculture was limited by the cold climate, short growing season, and rocky, hilly land. Farms were small and crops were grown primarily for

A coppersmith's workshop.

86

family use, and there was very little demand for slaves to work the fields. However, slaves were sometimes used as household servants, laborers, and skilled and semi-skilled workers. Natural harbors along the coast promoted a growing fishing industry and sea trade, both of which led in turn to shipbuilding. New Englanders also made their living as skilled blacksmiths, coopers (barrel makers), silversmiths, and furniture makers.

Because farms were small and church life important, colonists tended to settle close to one another. Mostly, people settled in small towns, but there were several major port cities, including Boston (the largest), Providence, and Newport. New England became the most urbanized of the colonial regions. Most New England colonies had been founded for religious reasons, so the ability to read the Bible was important. All but one of the New England colonies had school laws in place by 1671. New Englanders were almost exclusively of English background.

Middle Atlantic Colonies

The Middle Atlantic colonies of New York, New Jersey, Delaware, and Pennsylvania were the most diverse in terms of people, religion, and economy. A temperate climate provided a longer growing season than in New England. Gently rolling land and fertile soil allowed farmers to raise a variety of crops—such as wheat, oats, and corn. Enough food was grown to permit selling surplus crops. Some colonists became interested in slave labor to work the land for profit.

While agriculture was the main economic activity in the Middle Atlantic colonies, the presence of rich iron ore deposits and other minerals led to the development of mining and mineral processing. Abundant forest land also provided a source of timber for shipbuilding and the production of barrels and large covered wagons known as Conestoga wagons. As a result of the diverse natural resources, a combination of rural farm areas, small towns, and cities developed. Philadelphia and New York were the largest cities not only in the Middle Atlantic colonies but in all of the American colonies. There were no requirements for public schooling in the Middle Atlantic colonies, and formal education was left to private tutors or church schools. Colonists in this region were primarily of English background, though there were many whose heritage was Dutch, German, and Scots-Irish.

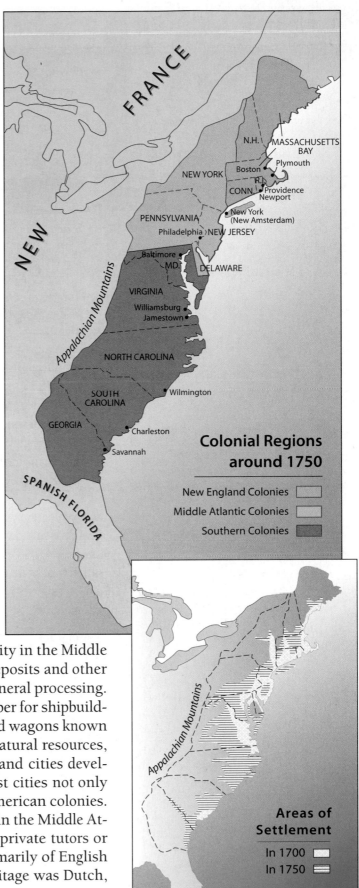

Colonial Regions around 1750

New England Colonies

Middle Atlantic Colonies

Southern Colonies

Areas of Settlement

In 1700

In 1750

Southern Colonies

The warm climate, rich soil, and vast areas of the Coastal Plain in the Southern colonies of Virginia, Maryland, North Carolina, South Carolina, and Georgia led to an agricultural economy. As in the Middle Atlantic colonies, there were numerous small farms —but the thing that made Southern colonies different was the **plantation**. A plantation is a large-scale farm operation that requires many workers doing the same task at the same time. Although some crops may be grown in order to feed workers and animals, plantations exist only where they can produce a cash crop for which there is high and continuing demand. In Virginia and Maryland, that crop was tobacco. In South Carolina and Georgia, the crops were rice and indigo (a pea-like plant that produces a deep blue dye for coloring cotton and wool).

Geography and climate were responsible for the different types of plantations. Virginia and Maryland colonists lived inland from the ocean, where the fertile and dry soil was ideal for growing tobacco. In South Carolina and Georgia, however, most colonists lived near the coast, a region of hot and humid weather, frequent rainfall, and poor soil. Conditions were perfect for rice plantations. By building low dirt walls with floodgates along the banks of tidal rivers, rice fields could be flooded when the tide came in. Rice thrives in water. On nearby dry land, many rice planters also grew indigo.

Plantation agriculture depended on cheap labor, and workers had to toil long hours in the summer heat. Plantation owners found it to their advantage to purchase slaves for this work.

Because the economy was so tied to agriculture, few towns and cities developed in the Southern colonies. Charleston was the only major southern city during the entire colonial era. There were few schools and no educational requirements in the southern colonies. Children of the well-to-do were either taught at home by tutors or sent to private schools. Most children, however, received little or no education. In terms of national background, people in the Southern colonies were primarily of English, African, and Scots-Irish heritage.

Life in Georgia

European immigrants arriving in Georgia found a place they could not have imagined. It was unlike anything they knew back home. Here was a wilderness made unpleasant by summer heat and fierce biting insects. The settlers found strange plants, and even stranger animals—such as the alligator, cougar, opossum, buffalo, pelican, raccoon, and rattlesnake.

For many settlers, their European backgrounds did not serve them well in the new land. Thousands died, and many others gave up and left for other colonies or returned to Europe. Others, however, learned to adapt and survive, and sometimes even to prosper in Georgia.

For the most part, Georgia settlers developed an *agrarian culture* —one centered around farming. Communities were usually small and far apart. For most people, life was simple: survival was the aim and hard work the rule. Gradually, the clothes they wore, the foods they ate, the methods used to farm, and the materials used to build changed from what they had known in Europe. By the end of the colonial period, life in Georgia would be quite different from that in 1733 when the first English settlers arrived.

As Georgia society grew, it came to include people from many countries. Within several years of its founding, the colony was home to immigrants from many lands. People came to Georgia from England, Scotland, Wales, Ireland, Germany, Italy, Portugal, Switzerland, and France. Many religions were represented, including Anglicans (Church of England), Jews, Lutherans, Moravians, Baptists, and Presbyterians. These newcomers brought differing beliefs and values, which they adapted to Georgia's environment. ▶

▶ **Locating the Main Ideas**

1. Define: plantation
2. Why did the New England colonies emphasize education and schools?
3. Which region had the largest two cities in the colonies? Name them and the colony in which each was located.
4. What crops were commonly grown on plantations in the Southern colonies?
5. What are some of the things the first Georgia colonists had to adapt to?

The Ebenezer Community

In 1734, a group of German-speaking settlers arrived in Savannah. They were known as Salzburgers because they came from Salzburg (a city in present-day Austria). Back home, these Lutheran Protestants had been persecuted because of their religious beliefs. So they fled to England, where the trustees raised funds to send them on to Georgia. Here the Salzburgers received land and provisions. They became Georgia residents with the same rights and responsibilities as British colonists.

Their settlement, about 25 miles upriver (northwest) from Savannah, was named Ebenezer. Oglethorpe laid out Ebenezer and sent workers from Savannah to help the Salzburgers clear the land and put up temporary shelters. Ebenezer grew quickly to almost 200 people, but things did not go well for the settlers. Their location was too far from the river to use it for commerce. The land was swampy and the soil poor. In 1736, the Salzburgers asked Oglethorpe for a better location. A spot known as Red Bluff, where Ebenezer Creek met the Savannah River, became New Ebenezer. At Old Ebenezer nothing remained but a cow pen.

Jerusalem Church at the site of Ebenezer is the oldest colonial public building in Georgia.

John Martin Boltzius was the Salzburgers' pastor, community leader, teacher, and spokesman from their arrival in 1734 until his death in 1765. During those years, Pastor Boltzius kept a daily diary of happenings at Ebenezer. He sent detailed reports on the community back to the Lutheran Church in Germany and wrote many letters to the trustees. Excerpts from his writings appear below.

May 28, 1735 (Ebenezer)—Mr. Causton (government storekeeper in Savannah) has sent several bushels of rice for planting. He desires that the Salzburgers should clear some swampy and wet places and try this seed.

The people intend to be obedient and start with this tomorrow.

November 22, 1735—The rice which has been planted by the Salzburgers in communal labor as an experiment did not do very well because there was no rain for too long a period. But we see that planting it does not require much more labor than is required for other fruits of the land. It is said that the hardest labor is required in threshing the rice to separate it from its hulls. Only Negro slaves are used to perform this labor in Carolina.

February 17, 1736—I wish that Mr. Oglethorpe were here to see our garden, which has again been nearly half under water since the recent rainy weather. Then he would be able to comprehend what was recently told him.

We still hope that the Salzburgers will enjoy the rights and liberties of Englishmen as free colonists. It appears to me and to others that the Salzburgers are a thorn in the eyes of the Englishmen, who would like to assign them land that no one else wants.

February 27, 1736—At the end of the sermon, I had to apply the discipline of the church, in the presence of the congregation, against Ruprecht Zittrauer who had offended the congregation last Wednesday by getting drunk once again.

April 17, 1736 (New Ebenezer)—Most of the people are already living here now. Only a few women and children will stay at Old Ebenezer to watch out for the seeds planted there and wait on the sick. Everyone seems pleased with living here, and the air seems healthier than there.

July 27, 1737—The heat is so great that we can hold school only in the morning with the few children who are still well.

July 28, 1737—A man told me that his corn was so badly blighted [ruined] by the worms that he had little hope of a good harvest, if God were not to prevent further damage. He was quite composed, however, and trusted in the Lord.

The boat returned to Savannah today to buy a few more kegs of flour, and we intend to contribute money from the poor box to those who cannot afford it.

July 30, 1737—Paul Lemmenhofer was very fatigued for a long time and could find no rest day or night. Although his condition seemed improved this morning, he died suddenly and against all expectations.

Of the congregation who have been with us from the beginning, 31 adults and 24 children have died; among the living are 89 adults and 43 children.

August 9, 1737—Our poor people are about to lose most of their fowl and other small livestock. They cannot give them much feed at home and therefore let both chickens and hogs run free so they may find food in the swamps and bushes. There they are preyed upon by bears, crocodiles and a certain type of large wild cat.

August 14, 1737—While most in our community suffer from weakness caused by the fever, this does not prevent them from listening to the Lord's word. They attend the sermon; and, when the fever strikes them, they simply leave, which is otherwise rare in our meetings.

March 16, 1738—Some Indians have come to our place again with their wives and children and are bringing pieces of meat for rice. One of them brought an entire deer for the orphanage.

Interpreting the Source

1. Describe the role of Pastor Boltzius in the Ebenezer community.

2. What evidence in the diary shows that the Salzburgers watched after one another? Give specific examples.

Disease and hardship followed the Salzburgers. So many adults had died by 1737 that an orphanage had to be built for their children.

Ebenezer was a religious community. The minister, John Martin Boltzius, was the leader, and each settler had to follow strict church regulations. Residents worked according to a set plan that required them to support the church and its school and orphanage with their labor. No hard liquor, dancing, gambling, or other frivolous activities were allowed. The minister watched over the people. Those misbehaving were punished according to church rules.

After a difficult start, the Salzburgers began to prosper. They produced and sold lumber, rice, beef, and pork. Eventually, Ebenezer led all Georgia communities in producing silk and grew the first cotton in Georgia.

For many years, the Salzburgers' German language and close-knit society kept them separate from other Georgians. As they began speaking English and became involved in the life of the colony, they became more like other Georgians. One Salzburger, a school-teacher named John Adam Treutlen, became the first person to bear the title "governor" of Georgia. ▶

Life cycle of the silkworm.

Africans Come to America

The first African to come to the Americas is believed to be Juan Canaries (pronounced kah-NAHR-eez), a free black crew member on Columbus's first voyage to the New World in 1492. If Canaries indeed sailed with Columbus, it should come as no surprise. We now know that Africans probably participated in most Spanish explorations and military expeditions to America.

Why were Africans sailing to America on Spanish ships? Africans had lived in Spain for over 700 years before Columbus's voyage to the New World. They came as slaves with Islamic forces who invaded Spain in the eighth century. Later, Spanish and other European traders brought in new slaves. They did this by finding African rulers willing to sell captured Africans in return for guns, rum, and other goods.

Actually, slavery had existed around the world for thousands of years. The pyramids in Egypt were built using slave labor. Making slaves of enemies captured in battle—and often of their women and children—was a common practice around the world.

Being a slave meant you lost your freedom and were forced to work for someone who owned you—your "master." Slavery was not the same thing in all societies. In some places, slaves were freed after several years and became regular citizens. In other societies, however, slavery could last a lifetime.

Many of the African slaves in Spain were household servants for their masters. Others worked in Spanish port cities as laborers, artisans, or skilled workers in a variety of trades—including shipbuild-

▶ **Locating the Main Ideas**

1. Why did the Salzburgers come to Georgia?
2. Why were the Salzburgers unhappy with their location at Old Ebenezer?

ing. Some slaves worked as crew members aboard sailing vessels based at these ports.

By law and tradition, slaves living in Spain were entitled to more rights and protections than slaves in most other countries. Many were able to purchase their freedom, so it is not surprising that the crews of Spanish ships included one or more free Africans. Also, many of the adventurers in Spanish expeditions to the New World brought their personal servants with them. As a result, Africans—both free and slave—were frequently aboard Spanish ships and took part in land expeditions.

Africans Accompany Spanish Explorers

The first Africans known to visit the North American mainland were among Lucas Vázquez de Ayllón's 600 colonists who landed on Georgia's coast in 1526. Most were slaves, but some may have been free Africans. There is no record of how many came with Ayllón. Likely, some were laborers brought to clear the land and build the settlement. Others may have been skilled workers, artisans, and personal servants—all of whom would be needed in the new colony.

Shortly after arriving, Ayllón died. Facing starvation during the winter ahead, one group of colonists tried to seize the ships and return home. The mutiny was put down, but the surviving colonists soon decided to abandon the settlement. In the meantime, however, the African slaves staged a revolt of their own, escaping to live with the Guale Indians. Thus, the first slave rebellion in American history took place in the Ayllón settlement along Georgia's coast.

The next time Africans came to Georgia was in 1540 as part of de Soto's exploration of the Southeast. Many of the Spaniards in the 600-member expedition brought their personal slaves. Some of the slaves escaped to live with the Indians. Johan Biscayan and a man named Gomez were two such Africans. Another African known as Robles was disabled and left behind at the Indian town of Coosa in present-day Gordon County. Free Africans also were part of de Soto's party, including a man named Bernaldo who stayed with the expedition the entire four years.

Spain's first permanent settlement in North America was St. Augustine, established on the northern coast of Florida in 1565. As many as 50 African slaves accompanied the first colonists. Upon arriving, they cut down trees, sawed the trunks into lumber, cleared the land for planting, built ships, and helped construct a fort, church, and other structures. Some Africans were trained as soldiers to help staff Spain's chain of military garrisons from St. Augustine northward along the coast of Georgia and beyond. After 1685 and Spain's withdrawal from Georgia, Spanish officials in Florida openly encouraged slaves in England's Carolina colony to escape. They offered freedom and land to all who converted to Catholicism. Many slaves risked their lives escaping to Florida. Once there, some eventually formed a Spanish military unit known as the Black Militia.

A member of the Black Militia.

What was it like to be brought to America as a slave? As slaves were seldom allowed to learn to read and write, there are very few firsthand accounts by slaves. One that does exist, however, is by Olaudah Equiano.

Olaudah Equiano was born in 1745 in the Kingdom of Benin in west Africa. At age 11, he was captured, sold to slave traders, and taken to the West Indies. From there he was taken to America.

Equiano was renamed Gustavus Vassa by his master. Unlike most slaves, Equiano learned to read and write and was eventually given his freedom. Later, he moved to England where he was active in anti-slavery efforts.

The following account is taken from Equiano's autobiography, published in 1791.

The first thing I saw when I got to the coast was the sea and a slave ship waiting for its cargo. These filled me with much astonishment and terror.

When I was carried on board, I looked around and saw a large furnace boiling and many black people chained together. I no longer doubted my fate.

I was soon put down under the decks. There with the terrible stench and crying, I became so sick and low that I was not able to eat. I wished for death to relieve me. Soon two white men offered me food. When I refused to eat, one of them held me by the hands. My feet were tied and I was severely whipped....

In a little time, I found some people from my own nation among those who were chained. I asked them what was to be done with us. They told me that we were to be taken to the white people's country to work for them....

The closeness of the hold, the heat of the climate, so crowded was it that each person scarcely had room to turn...it almost suffocated us. This brought on sickness and many died. I became so low I was put on deck.

One day two of my country men who were chained together jumped into the sea. They preferred death to a life of such misery. Then another followed their example. I believe that many more would have done the same if they had not been prevented by the ship's crew. Two of the wretches were drowned, but they got the other and flogged him unmercifully for attempting to prefer death to slavery.

Finally, we came in sight of land.... Many merchants and planters came on board. They put us into separate groups and examined us with great attention. We thought we would be eaten by these ugly men....

Soon we were taken to the land where we were led immediately to the merchant's yard. There we were penned up together like sheep without regard to sex or age.

In a few days, we were sold. On a signal, the buyers rush into the yard where the slaves are kept. They choose those they like best. The noise and clamor which accompany this, and the eagerness in the faces of the buyers, serve to increase the fear of the terrified slaves. In this manner, relatives and friends are separated, most of them never to see each other again....

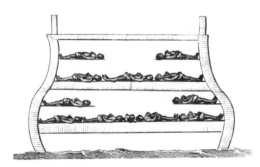

Interpreting the Source

1. Why are there so few existing primary sources written by slaves?

2. Why do you think Equiano's master renamed him?

3. What did Equiano write that tells you that not all the Africans on the ship were from the same place?

4. How did the Africans resist slavery while they were on the ship?

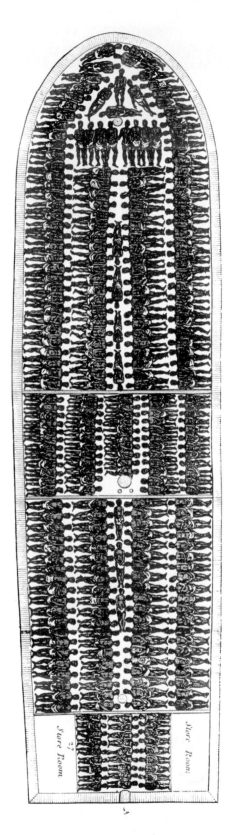

Slave ships were designed to squeeze as many Africans aboard as possible. Confinement, heat, and lack of sanitation killed thousands before they reached America.

In 1738, Florida's governor, Manuel de Montiano, granted the Black Militia land north of St. Augustine, where members of the unit built and garrisoned Fort Mose. Thus, Florida began a tradition of serving as a sanctuary for escaped slaves.

Slavery in the American Colonies

The introduction of Africans to the English colonies in America occurred in Virginia. In 1619, a Dutch ship captain stopped at Jamestown in need of provisions. On board were 20 West Africans, whom he offered to exchange for the goods he needed. Because the Africans had been Christianized, English law at the time did not allow them to be sold as slaves. Instead they became servants. But Virginia plantation owners wanted more than servants. They wanted slaves to work long, hard hours in the tobacco fields.

How did slavery become legal in America? In 1640, a Virginia judge sentenced an indentured African servant to life enslavement as punishment for running away. Then, a 1662 law provided that an African baby born in Virginia had the status—free or slave—of its mother. Finally, in 1705, a Virginia law designated slaves as real property that could be inherited as part of an owner's estate.

Importing African slaves to work on tobacco plantations quickly became common in Virginia. But England's other colonies needed workers, too. There was far more work to be done—clearing the land, farming, lumbering, and building—than workers to do it.

To meet the need for cheap labor, some landowners used **indentured servants**. These were immigrants—usually poor, white, and young—who agreed to work as servants for anyone paying their way to the colonies. Their indenture (or contract) required four to seven years of work, after which the servant became a free person with all the rights of the other colonists.

But indentured servants didn't always satisfy their masters, particularly in the fields. They refused to do certain kinds of hard work. Moreover, they often ran away before their indenture was worked off.

Many landowners preferred using African slaves to work their plantations because they worked harder and did not have to be replaced every few years. Also, landowners felt slaves were less likely to run away since they could be easily recognized by the color of their skin.

As the demand for slaves increased, traders in both England and America took advantage of the situation. In 1672, England chartered the Royal African Company to supply slaves from Africa to her colonies in North America and the West Indies. The plan called for using English traders to ship English goods to Africa to exchange for slaves. The new cargo of slaves was then shipped to the Caribbean. There, the slaves were sold to sugarcane plantation owners in exchange for sugar and molasses. The new cargo was then shipped back to England or taken to the American colonies. Money from the sale of sugar and molasses in America would be used to purchase tobacco, rice, indigo, fish, timber, tar (and other naval stores), animal skins, and other raw materials for shipment to England. The plan also called for English ships taking some African slaves directly to the American colonies. Only a small percentage of newly enslaved Africans came in this manner.

Before long, shipowners and sea captains in the American colonies got involved. American slave traders were shipping New England rum to Africa, where it was exchanged for slaves to be sold in the American colonies. Far more common, however, was a system known as the **triangular trade**. New England rum was shipped directly to Africa, where it was sold for payment in newly captured slaves, who were taken to the West Indies and sold to sugarcane planters. Money from the sale of slaves was used to purchase a cargo of sugar and molasses that was taken and sold to New England distilleries to be used in making more rum.

Most newly captured African slaves did not end up in the American colonies. During the 1700s, just under 400,000 Africans were shipped to the American colonies. That's a large number, but only a small portion (6 percent) of the total slave traffic. The most frequent destinations were Brazil (3,600,000), British colonies in the West Indies (1,700,000), French colonies in the Atlantic (1,600,000), and Mexico (1,500,000). More than 9 out of 10 African slaves were destined to work the sugar plantations or mines of South America, the Caribbean, or Mexico.

By 1800, as many as 20 million slaves captured along the western coast of Africa had been shipped to the Americas. Most came from what today are the countries of Senegal, The Gambia, Sierra Leone, Ghana, Togo, Benin, Nigeria, and Angola.

Cutting sugar cane.

Slavery in Georgia

The trustees had intended that there be no slavery in Georgia, and Oglethorpe vigorously opposed any attempts to bring in slaves. However, in December 1738, a group of Savannah colonists known as "Malcontents" petitioned the trustees to allow slaves in Georgia. They argued that they could never raise enough products for export without help. How could they compete with the Carolinians who had slave labor? Besides, the Georgia climate was too hot for white farm workers. Rice, they said, could be raised only by black workers.

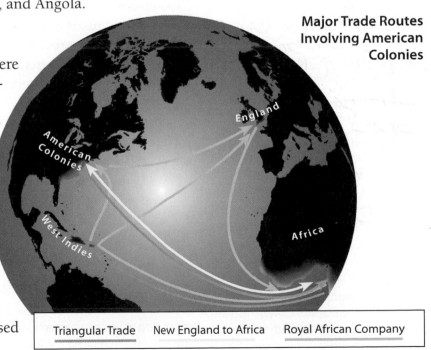

Major Trade Routes Involving American Colonies

England

American Colonies

West Indies

Africa

Triangular Trade   New England to Africa   Royal African Company

Other Georgians objected to slavery. In January 1739, Scottish settlers at Darien asked the trustees to keep their ban on slavery. They argued that having slaves would take away the white settlers' will to work hard. Moreover, said the Scots,

> It is shocking to human nature, that any race of mankind… should be sentenced to perpetual slavery;…freedom to them must be as dear as to us.

The Salzburgers, too, spoke out against slavery. The idea that white workers couldn't raise rice was ridiculous. They themselves had already done so.

The trustees rejected the Savannah petition, but slaves were brought in anyway. Some planters "rented" slaves from their Carolina owners or sneaked them in to work in their fields. The slavery faction grew. Finally, in 1750, the trustees gave in.

Once slavery was permitted, many more Africans were brought from South Carolina, other colonies, and the West Indies. In 1752 alone, more than 1,000 slaves were brought to Georgia. Eventually, many opponents of slavery accepted it. Even the Salzburgers at Ebenezer had slaves. By 1773, the colony had about 15,000 black slaves, almost as many people as the 18,000 whites.

Slave Codes

The growing number of slaves in the colony resulted in laws known as **slave codes** to govern their behavior and regulate their treatment. Slave codes were passed by the colonial assembly in 1755 and 1770. Provisions from the 1770 code reveal something of the legal position of Georgia's slave population. The 1770 Slave Code provided that

- the offspring of slaves were to remain absolute slaves and to be the personal property of their owners;
- slaves could not travel outside the town or plantation limits without a ticket signed by a responsible person. If slaves were found without a ticket or not in the company of a white person, punishment was a whipping on the bare back not exceeding 20 lashes;
- if a slave struck a white person, the slave would suffer after trial and conviction any punishment the justice thought fit, not extending to life or limb. For the second offense, the punishment was death;
- any person employing a slave on the Lord's Day (Sunday), except in work of absolute necessity, must forfeit 10 shillings;
- anyone teaching a slave to write or read would forfeit a sum of 20 pounds.

In some instances the code offered slaves some protection. The overall intent, however, was to make sure slaves were kept in their place. ◀

▶ **Locating the Main Ideas**

1. Define: indentured servant, triangular trade, slave code
2. Why was it possible to find both free and enslaved Africans aboard Spanish expedition ships going to the New World?
3. How did Florida become a haven for escaped slaves?
4. How was being a slave different from being an indentured servant? How was it similar?
5. In which countries or areas of the Western Hemisphere were most African slaves destined to work during the 1700s?

Tidal rivers along Georgia's coast allowed the regular flooding of fields necessary for rice cultivation.

Georgia Society and Culture

During the early years, life in Georgia had been fairly simple. The model society the trustees planned allowed for few social differences. All settlers were expected to be hardworking "common folk." Each family would have the same amount of land and the same kind of life.

Forty years later, however, it was quite different. By 1773, Georgia was a colony of 33,000 people, about half of them black slaves. With many slaves working on great rice plantations, some planters became very wealthy. For example, Sir James Wright, Georgia's royal governor, owned 11 plantations with about 26,000 acres and 525 slaves. As some colonists began to prosper, social classes developed.

Life in Savannah

By 1773, Savannah had become a busy seaport of the British Empire. Prosperity brought change to Savannah society. In 1733, colonists had to work with their own hands just to survive. Forty years later, many had the help of hired laborers, indentured servants, or slaves. Savannah residents could also turn to many kinds of specialists for the things they needed. There were shoemakers, tailors, cabinetmakers, coopers, blacksmiths, gunsmiths, masons, saddlers, wheelwrights, sailmakers, mechanics, and even artists. The city also had millers, bakers, and butchers. As the colony's capital, Savannah had the services of trained professionals, such as lawyers, doctors, clergymen, and teachers.

So, by 1773, Savannah had several distinct groups. The structure of its society may be likened to a ladder. Depending on their ability and ambition, men might move up (or down) the ladder. There was little opportunity for a woman to be independent. Her position in society was tied to her husband's. Blacks, however, except for a

Colonial Social Ladder

Plantation Owners, Merchants

Lawyers, Doctors, Clergymen

Owners of Small Farms, Artisans

Laborers

Indentured Servants

Africans

America's social system was similar to that of Europe. However, in America, it was easier to move up the ladder.

few freedmen, were locked into the lowest position as slaves.

The small group of wealthy rice planters and shipping merchants at the top of the ladder provided most of the colony's leaders. Other men who owned property had a smaller voice in the colony's affairs. They included the professionals; owners of small farms and businesses; **artisans** (people skilled in a craft, such as woodworkers, tailors, or silversmiths), and mechanics.

Laborers, indentured servants, and slaves had no such voice. For the lower ranks, life in Savannah varied little from one day to the next. It was mostly work.

Those higher up the ladder, though, had time for social activities. Public celebrations and military ceremonies, as well as weddings and funerals, were big events. The biggest event was the annual celebration of the king's birthday. Dances, picnics, and other social events were highlights of Savannah social life.

Some of Savannah's men belonged to social clubs and fraternities. Clubs sometimes had political or civic interests in addition to social ones.

Savannah had several taverns or public houses. Drinking and gambling were popular, but these places served another purpose in colonial Georgia. They provided a place for people to meet and exchange the news of the day.

Those who could read obtained books from booksellers and libraries. In 1763, they could also buy Savannah's first newspaper, the *Georgia Gazette*.

Life in the Backcountry

Even though Savannah was the heart of the colony, by the 1760s Georgia's real growth was in the frontier area known as the backcountry. Augusta was the one area in the colony to grow steadily. It began in 1736 as a station used by Indian traders on their way into Creek and Cherokee country. Later, as settlers moved into Georgia from Virginia and the Carolinas, Augusta became the gateway to the backcountry. It was the unofficial capital of Georgia's frontier.

In contrast to life in Savannah, living on the frontier was rowdy, rugged, and simple. The self-reliance necessary to live on the frontier created a Georgian with an outlook different from that of Georgians who lived on the coast. Backcountry settlers had to rely on their own skills to get by. There were few rules, and people didn't like government to interfere in their lives.

The new settlers were primarily small-scale farmers. They arrived in carts or wagons, using the trading paths and Indian trails that crisscrossed the backcountry. A family's belongings might include simple tools, guns, a spinning wheel, and kitchen items such as churns, iron pots, and dippers. The settlers cut down trees and cleared the land. Men and boys spent their days tending the crops, building or repairing farm buildings, or hunting for food. Women tended the garden, cared for the children, prepared meals, and sewed the family's clothes.

Dances, shooting matches, and horse races were some of the few recreational events on the frontier. But settlers often used their work gatherings—such as corn shuckings, barn raisings, and quilting bees—as social events.

On the frontier, women made essential contributions to the survival of most families.

Education

Neither the trustees nor the royal government established a school system in Georgia. As in other American colonies, children were taught mainly by their parents. A boy learned a trade or how to farm from his father. A girl learned from her mother how to manage a household. Sometimes, boys who were orphans or from poor families would be "bound out" to a skilled mechanic or artisan to learn a trade. Girls might be bound out to a family to learn household skills.

From time to time, schools were set up in Savannah, but only one, Bethesda Orphan House, lasted very long. Schoolmasters were often clergymen, and religion was taught along with reading, writing, and arithmetic. The larger plantations often had tutors for the planters' children. Most children in colonial Georgia, however, never went to school.

Religion

Georgia's trustees had been concerned about the religious life of the settlers. Hundreds of Bibles, prayer books, and other religious works were sent with the first group of colonists. The trustees also sent clergymen to the colony.

In Great Britain, the Anglican Church raised money for the new colony. Most of the settlers who came with Oglethorpe were Anglicans. However, other religious groups (except Roman Catholics) were welcome to settle. [Only after the American Revolution were Catholics allowed to settle in Georgia. They built their first church in Wilkes County in 1796.] The first Jewish families arrived in Savannah in 1733. One Jewish immigrant, Dr. Samuel Nunes, was noted for treating the illnesses and diseases the first colonists faced. Abraham De Lyon, an experienced winemaker, brought skills the trustees hoped to use in the colony. Also among the Jewish settlers were many young men who joined Oglethorpe's regiment to defend the colony.

The First African Baptist Church in Savannah is one of the oldest black congregations in America. Andrew Bryan was its first pastor. The church grew out of a congregation begun in 1777 by George Liele, a freed slave.

The new colony also attracted Anglican clergymen. Two of them, John and Charles Wesley, came in 1736 to minister to the colonists and to convert the Indians to Christianity. Charles also served as Oglethorpe's secretary. His brother, John, conducted religious instruction for children every Sunday—one of the earliest known "Sunday Schools." John later became known as the founder of Methodism.

George Whitefield, another Anglican clergyman to come to the colony, established Bethesda Orphan House. Whitefield traveled throughout the colonies and made several trips to England preaching the "great awakening" of religion. At the time of his death in 1770, Whitefield was one of the best known colonial clergymen. Phillis Wheatley, a 17-year-old slave and poet in Boston, honored him with "An Elegiac Poem, on the Death of that Celebrated Divine...George Whitefield." Her poem received widespread acclaim.

When Georgia became a royal colony, interest in religion continued. The royal governor was required to see that the Sabbath was properly observed. In 1758, the colonial assembly passed an act making the Church of England the colony's official church. All Georgians were taxed to support the church but remained free to worship as they chose.

By the end of the colonial period, several different religious groups had churches in Savannah. Elsewhere in the colony, religion's place in everyday life varied greatly. In Ebenezer, the church was the center of the community life. In the backcountry, except for Augusta which had an Anglican church, religion barely existed. That would change with the arrival of Baptist and Methodist missionaries about the time of the Revolutionary War. ◄

▶ Locating the Main Ideas

1. Define: artisan

2. Identify: Samuel Nunes, Abraham De Lyon, John and Charles Wesley, George Whitefield, Phillis Wheatley

3. Why did different social classes develop in Savannah? Why were social classes less likely to develop on Georgia's frontier?

4. Why were taverns useful for keeping up with the news in colonial Georgia?

5. In what ways could children get an education in colonial Georgia?

CHAPTER ACTIVITIES

Reviewing the Main Ideas

1. Explain how geography helped to create regional differences among the American colonies.
2. Give evidence to show that the church played a large role in the lives of the Ebenezer Salzburgers.
3. What country first brought Africans to North America? What tasks did they perform?
4. According to the Royal African Company's plan, what was traded at each of the following ports of call in Africa? the West Indies? North America? England?
5. Why were slave codes passed? In the excerpts from the 1770 Slave Code, which one offers the slave some protection from constant work?
6. Why was loss of life among captured Africans a frequent occurrence on slave ships to America?
7. How did distinctions among social classes come about in Georgia?
8. What kinds of social activities were available in colonial Savannah? on the frontier?
9. Were education and religion the same for all colonists?
10. Why did backcountry settlers develop an outlook on government different from coastal residents?

Give It Some Extra Thought

1. **Making Comparisons**. Identify the differences in each colonial region in the following categories: (1) climate, (2) agriculture, (3) types of towns and cities, and (4) ethnic background.
2. **Recognizing Differing Positions**. List the arguments made for and against allowing slavery in colonial Georgia. Identify the people making the arguments.

Sharpen Your Skills

1. **Time Line**. Create a time line to cover events in the lives of the Salzburgers in the Ebenezer community. There is information about the Salzburgers in this chapter covering the time span from 1734 to 1777. Some years may have more than one event.
2. **Identifying Facts and Opinions**. Use the diary of Pastor Boltzius and identify three fact statements and three opinion statements.
3. **Interpreting a Cartoon**. What aspect of life changed greatly during the colonial years? What are some of the reasons for the change? Can you think of another title for the cartoon?

Going Further

1. **Map Study**. Locate the cities of Athens, Berlin, Dublin, Oxford, Rome, and Vienna on a state highway map. Give the grid coordinates for each city. Use a world atlas or a gazetteer (geographical dictionary) and list the names of other countries where you can find these cities. On your list, circle the names of the countries from which immigrants came to settle in colonial Georgia.

Changing colonial lifestyle.

UNIT 4

8 **The American Revolution and Georgia Statehood**

9 **Growth and Prosperity**

10 **Conflict Over Indian Lands**

GEORGIA EVENTS

Governor Wright flees Georgia; Whig government adopts temporary constitution	Georgia adopts first state constitution; parishes replaced by counties	British capture Savannah; Governor Wright returns	Royal government re-established; Battle of Kettle Creek; Count Pulaski killed	Whigs recapture Augusta		University of Georgia chartered by General Assembly	Georgia resolves boundary dispute with South Carolina	Georgia ratifies U.S. Constitution	Georgia adopts new state constitution	Eli Whitney invents cotton gin
1776	**1777**	**1778**	**1779**	**1781**	**1783**	**1785**	**1787**	**1788**	**1789**	**1793**
Lyman Hall, George Walton, and Button Gwinnett sign Declaration of Independence		France joins fight against British		British surrender to General Washington at Yorktown; Articles of Confederation ratified	Treaty of Paris ends American Revolution	James Oglethorpe dies at age 89 in England	New U.S. Constitution proposed; Northwest Territory created		New U.S. Constitution goes into effect	

EVENTS ELSEWHERE

The Pioneer Spirit
1776–1840

1795	Yazoo Land Fraud
	Spain gives up claim to Georgia's western territories
1802	Georgia cedes western territories to United States
1803	Louisiana Purchase
1805	First land lottery held in Georgia
1807	Milledgeville becomes state capital
	Fulton develops steamboat
1820	Missouri Compromise
1825	Chief William McIntosh killed for signing Creek cession treaty
	Mexico opens Texas to American settlers
1827	Last Creeks leave Georgia; Cherokees draft national constitution
1828	Gold discovered near Dahlonega; Cherokee Phoenix begins publication
	Andrew Jackson elected U.S. president
1836	Georgia legislature creates W & A Railroad
	Texas declares independence from Mexico
1838	Cherokees forcibly removed to Oklahoma on the "Trail of Tears"
	"Underground Railroad" becomes active

The American Revolution and Georgia Statehood

After the French and Indian War, the American colonies prospered. Still, colonists were growing restless under British rule. In particular, they didn't like the way the mercantile system forced them to trade only with Great Britain. More and more, Americans wanted freedom to make or grow whatever they wished and to sell to whomever they pleased. A few colonists began ignoring British laws and carried on **smuggling** (illegal trade) with French, Dutch, and Spanish merchants.

Taxes were another major source of conflict between Britain and the American colonists. While fighting the French and Indian War, Britain had gone heavily into debt. To help pay off this debt and run its empire, Parliament passed a series of tax laws. Some of these laws, such as the Sugar Act (1764) and the Townshend Act (1767), placed **duties** (taxes on imports) on products coming into the colonies. Incoming goods that were taxed included sugar, coffee, tea, wine, paper, lead, glass, and paint. The Stamp Act (1765), which required that all printed paper used in the colonies bear a tax stamp purchased from the government, was strongly opposed.

American colonists protested loudly to Parliament. At home, they began to take action to show their discontent. Groups such as the Sons of Liberty were formed to stir people to action. Some colonists **boycotted** (refused to buy) goods that were taxed and instead smuggled non-British goods into the colonies. Sometimes, officials trying to collect the new taxes were met with threats and even attacks.

Parliament finally backed down and repealed most of these unpopular taxes. But by then, an anti-British attitude had formed in the minds of many colonists.

The Clash of British and American Ideas

The views of American colonists on government and economics were influenced by several important ideas they brought from Britain.

One of these ideas was the concept of *consent of the governed*. This means that government should rule only so long as its citizens consent (or agree) to be governed. If the people become unhappy with their government, or it no longer can protect them, that government loses its right to govern. If it refuses to step down, the people have the right to rebel.

Related to the idea of consent is that of *representative government*. This means that people have the right to elect persons to represent them and make political decisions that affect their lives. These elected representatives must be able to assemble in legislative bodies to make laws and set taxes.

A third idea colonists brought from Britain was the concept of *limited government*. This means that the power of government is limited by "natural law." The theory of **natural law** says that people have *natural rights*—which come from God or nature—that government cannot take away. The most basic of these are life, liberty, and property.

In addition, American colonists had developed their own ideas about self-government. They held town meetings to handle local problems, such as building roads. They had colonial legislatures to make laws on such matters as taxes and maintaining a **militia** (a unit of citizen soldiers). From these experiences, Americans came to believe that only their own elected representatives should pass laws and set taxes in the colonies.

Resentment and Conflict

Many Americans resented Britain's effort to impose new laws and taxes on the colonies. First, taxes passed by Parliament (for whose members Americans could not vote) violated the colonists' right to be taxed only by their own elected representatives. Second, Americans were supposed to enjoy the rights of British citizens, but often their legal rights were ignored. For instance, some British laws permitted government officers to search homes without a specific search warrant. Persons accused of smuggling could be brought before military courts with no rights to trial by jury.

Events Leading to War	
1763	French and Indian War leaves Britain with large debt from defending American colonies
1764	Sugar Act: tax on sugar, molasses, coffee, indigo, and wine to raise money for Britain
1765	Stamp Act: requires tax stamp on all printed items and documents. Quartering Act: requires colonists to house British soldiers and provide certain supplies
1767	Townshend Acts: tax on glass, lead, paper, paints, and tea
1770	**March:** Boston Massacre **April:** Townshend Acts repealed
1772	Colonists establish Committees of Correspondence to communicate with other colonies
1773	**May:** Tea Act: tax on tea **December:** Boston Tea Party
1774	First Continental Congress meets; all colonies present except Georgia

The Boston Massacre. On March 5, 1770, British troops fired on a crowd of colonists. Among the first men killed in the American Revolution was Crispus Attucks, a former slave. Paul Revere, a patriot and a silversmith, engraved this drawing on copper so it could be reprinted. The picture helped arouse anti-British feelings throughout the colonies.

As public protests and violence against government officials grew, Britain sent more troops to enforce the unpopular laws. Sometimes, Parliament required colonial legislatures to come up with the money for housing soldiers in inns, taverns, and other locations. This only added to the trouble.

American anger at British policies was greatest in the northern colonies. Soldiers were booed in the streets, and sometimes eggs or snowballs were thrown at them. In 1770, one skirmish got out of hand. Several British soldiers, attacked by a crowd, were rescued by fellow troops. As the crowd pressed around them, the soldiers panicked and opened fire. Five people fell dead, and six were wounded. Soon, word of the "Boston Massacre" spread across the colonies, carrying with it the flame of American discontent.

The Final Straw

In 1773, Parliament passed the Tea Act, which gave one British company a **monopoly**—or exclusive right—to sell tea to America. Tea was a very popular drink, but many colonists refused to buy the company's tea, even though it was priced cheaply. They felt it was being forced on them by Britain. Meanwhile, some colonial merchants who had been illegally importing Dutch tea felt the new monopoly would threaten their businesses. On the night of December 16, 1773, members of the Sons of Liberty dumped several shiploads of British tea into the Boston harbor. In other ports, tea was also dumped overboard or burned.

To punish Massachusetts and control the colonies, Parliament passed several harsh measures. These included (1) closing the port

1775: The Crisis Deepens	
April:	Battles at Lexington and Concord
May:	Second Continental Congress meets, decides to draft Declaration of Independence
June:	George Washington appointed head of Continental Army
June:	Battle of Bunker Hill and Breed's Hill
August:	King George III declares American colonies to be in rebellion

of Boston until the tea was paid for, (2) not allowing the people of Massachusetts to elect their own officials or hold town meetings, and (3) requiring the people in all the colonies to feed and house British soldiers.

These "intolerable acts," as they were called by the colonists, only increased opposition to Britain. Patriots in each colony joined in protest. A Continental Congress, with delegates from all colonies except Georgia, met in Philadelphia and agreed to boycott all British goods. In incidents around the colonies, government officials were attacked or run out of town. British goods were burned, and persons openly loyal to Britain were tarred and feathered (smeared with tar and covered with feathers as a punishment). Britain sent more troops to the colonies to control the situation.

Finally, on April 19, 1775, Massachusetts "minutemen" and British troops battled at Lexington and Concord. It was, as later described, "the shot heard 'round the world."

News of the battles spread quickly throughout the colonies. Colonial assemblies voted to raise militias to defend themselves against the British. The war for American independence had begun.

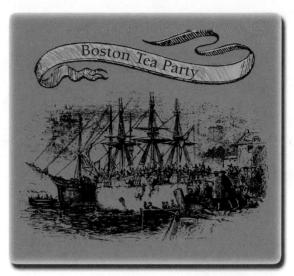

Encouraged by such patriots as Samuel Adams, the Sons of Liberty boarded British ships and dumped 15,000 pounds of tea into the Boston harbor.

Georgia Chooses Sides

Georgia was much younger than the other American colonies and didn't have a long history of self-government. Also, along the coast a number of Georgians had become wealthy from trade with Great Britain. Under the royal governor, Sir James Wright, the colony had grown and prospered. Thus, when northern colonies began pushing for freedom from Britain, Georgia was not quick to join in.

Loyalty to Great Britain was strongest in coastal Georgia. Far inland, backcountry Georgians were far more likely to want independence. However, even in coastal Georgia, support of the mother country began to weaken. Georgians soon began to take sides. As in the other colonies, anti-British Georgians were known as **Whigs**, and later as "patriots." Supporters of Britain were called **Tories** or "loyalists." ▶

The Independence Movement in Georgia

In 1775, the battles at Lexington and Concord in Massachusetts signaled the beginning of the American Revolution. In Savannah, patriots greeted the news with great excitement. They openly defied Georgia's royal government. They raided the colony's gunpowder storehouse and disrupted Governor Wright's celebration of the king's birthday. Amid much confusion, the royal government began to fall apart.

Royal Government Comes to an End

In July 1775, a "Provincial Congress" of delegates from Georgia's parishes met in Savannah. The delegates voted to join the other

▶ Locating the Main Ideas

1. Define: smuggling, duties, boycott, natural law, militia, monopoly, Whig, Tory

2. Identify: Sons of Liberty, Crispus Attucks, Paul Revere, representative government, Boston Massacre

3. In what ways did American colonists gain experience in self-government?

4. Why was the Georgia colony at first reluctant to join with the other colonies in gaining freedom from Britain?

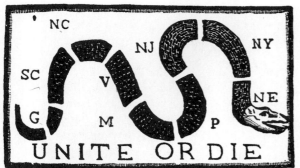

Ben Franklin drew a version of this cartoon in 1754 with the motto, "Join or Die." Do you think the cartoon was pro-British or anti-British?

colonies in a complete boycott of trade with Great Britain. The Whigs also set up a "Council of Safety" to enforce the boycott and to work with other colonies.

For a while, Georgia had *two* governments. Britain's royal government, headed by Sir James Wright, and the Whigs' provisional (temporary) government. The days of royal government, however, were numbered as anti-British sentiment built in Georgia.

Gradually, the Whigs took over Georgia's militia, removing Tory officers. They approved new taxes to finance Georgia's defense against British attack. They also took control of the courts and other government activities—such as handling Indian relations. Governor Wright was powerless. He watched as his royal authority crumbled.

In January 1776, Whig forces arrested Governor Wright, who managed to escape to the safety of a waiting British warship. This meant the end of the royal government, at least for the time being. Many Georgians still remained loyal to King George. Political control, however, now rested with Whig factions.

In April 1776, Georgia's Provincial Congress adopted a set of "Rules and Regulations" as a temporary constitution. In clear language, its **preamble** (introduction) proclaimed the concept of **popular sovereignty**—that government rests on the will of the people:

> This Congress, therefore, as the representatives of the people, with whom all power originates, and for whose benefit all government is intended…do declare, order, and direct that the following rules and regulations be adopted in this Province….

The Declaration of Independence

Meanwhile, Georgia had sent five delegates to the Second Continental Congress in Philadelphia. These colonial representatives had to decide what to do. Would it be war or peace? The delegates decided to prepare for both. They organized an army to be commanded by George Washington of Virginia. At the same time, they sent King George III a **petition** (a formal written request) stating their loyalty to him, but asking him to stop Britain's hostile actions against the colonies.

In London, King George refused to accept their petition. Instead, he declared the colonies in a state of rebellion. Parliament banned all trade with America.

American colonists remained divided, but the independence movement gained strength throughout the spring of 1776. Finally, in May, delegates to the Second Continental Congress voted to instruct each of the colonies to prepare for the end of British rule. Delegates debated how and when to announce a formal break from Great Britain.

On July 4, 1776, the Second Continental Congress took action, adopting the **Declaration of Independence**. All the delegates signed

The Americans Take a Stand

1776 **January:** Thomas Paine writes *Common Sense,* a political pamphlet urging independence and increasing "American" feelings

July 4: Declaration of Independence adopted

December: Washington wins a surprise victory at Trenton; morale is raised

1777 **January:** Washington wins at Princeton

October: British General Burgoyne surrenders to General Gates at Sarasota

November: Articles of Confederation drafted and sent to states for approval

1778 France becomes an American ally

John Adams, Roger Sherman, Robert Livingston, Thomas Jefferson, and Benjamin Franklin stand at the table presenting the Declaration of Independence to John Hancock, president of the Second Continental Congress. George Walton, the only Georgia delegate shown, is seated directly underneath the ribbon that is hanging from the flagpole on the wall.

the document, including Georgia's delegation—Button Gwinnett, Lyman Hall, and George Walton.

This revolutionary document, written mainly by Thomas Jefferson of Virginia, included the following ideas:

1. All men are created equal.
2. Everyone is born with certain rights that government cannot take away—namely life, liberty, and the pursuit of happiness.
3. Government gets its power from the people.
4. The people can do away with a government they no longer approve of.

The declaration ended with the bold proclamation that "these United Colonies are…Free and Independent States." All political connections between the new states and Great Britain were dissolved.

On paper at least, the 13 American colonies were now independent "states" united in their desire for freedom from Great Britain. At that time, **state** was another word for **nation**. Both terms referred to an independent country with its own government. Only later did "state" come to have an additional meaning in America as a level of government below that of the nation. ▶

Reaction in Georgia to the Declaration of Independence

Although signed on July 4, 1776, news of the Declaration of Independence did not reach Georgia for a month. In early August, the declaration was read publicly in Savannah. Patriots fired cannons and staged a mock funeral for King George III. Other Georgians, however, did not share in the celebration.

▶ **Locating the Main Ideas**

1. Define: preamble, popular sovereignty, petition, Declaration of Independence, state, nation
2. Identify: Button Gwinnett, Lyman Hall, George Walton, Thomas Jefferson
3. Why was it important to the rebelling Georgia colonists to include the concept of popular sovereignty in their temporary constitution?

Independence Hall in Philadelphia, *Pennsylvania. Delegates to the Continental Congress adopted the Declaration of Independence here on July 4, 1776.*

Differences with Britain sometimes caused a split within families. Typically, first-generation Georgians were loyalists, tied to England by tradition, friends and relatives, and strong memories of their mother country. Noble Jones and James Habersham, two of the earliest Georgia colonists, never wavered in their support of King George III and royal government. On the other hand, their Georgia-born children often joined in the fight for liberty. Noble Wimberly Jones and the three Habersham boys—James Jr., John, and Joseph—became political and military leaders in the Whig cause.

Some 1,500 Tories decided to leave Georgia. Some left for East and West Florida or went to British colonies in the Caribbean; some returned to Britain. Many loyalists, however, stayed to protect their property, but kept quiet about their feelings toward Britain.

Georgia's First Constitution

As a state, Georgia needed a more permanent form of government than the "Rules and Regulations." An election was called to select delegates to write a new constitution.

A **constitution** is the fundamental plan of operation for a government. As the highest level of law, it spells out what government can and cannot do. It sets up the different branches of government, identifies major offices in each branch, and says how each office is to be filled. A constitution may also spell out important rights and liberties of the people.

By February 1777, the convention had completed its work. The preamble to the new constitution recognized the important principle of popular sovereignty. The very first article of the new constitution, however, introduced a new principle—that of **separation of powers**:

> The legislative, executive, and judiciary departments shall be separate and distinct, so that neither exercise the powers properly belonging to the other.

Although Georgia's 1777 constitution appeared to create three independent branches of government, in reality the legislative branch was supreme. The constitution set up a **unicameral** (one-house) legislature. Unlike Georgia's state government today, there was not a second house acting as a safeguard against hastily passed laws. The legislature, called the House of Assembly, was given broad authority to enact laws. It also had power to appoint officials in the executive and judicial branches.

Because of their experience with royal governors under British rule, framers of Georgia's 1777 constitution severely weakened executive power in the new state government. For example, legislators elected the governor, who only had a one-year term and could not succeed himself in office. The governor could not veto legislation. In fact, just the opposite was true. The legislature elected 12 of its own members to serve as an executive council, with veto power over the governor. The power to grant pardons, traditionally an executive function, was placed in the hands of the legislature. This left the governor as chief executive in name only.

The constitution set up eight counties* to replace the colonial parishes. Each county would have its own officials, courthouse, schools, and militia. To settle disputes, each county had a court, called the superior court. The constitution stated how cases were to be tried.

Problems of the New State Government

In May 1777, the new constitution went into effect. The House of Assembly named John Adam Treutlen the first governor of the state. Georgia's political leaders, however, faced great difficulties. Thousands of people were still loyal to King George III and wanted to see the new government fail. Even more of a problem was a power struggle among different Whig groups.

Bitter feelings between members of a radical backcountry party and a conservative city party led to the death of one of Georgia's signers of the Declaration of Independence. In the 1700s, it was common for a gentleman to defend his honor to the death with sword or pistol. When conservative Lachlan McIntosh publicly called radical Button Gwinnett "a scoundrel and lying rascal," Gwinnett challenged him to a duel. On May 16, 1777, the rivals exchanged pistol shots outside Savannah. Both were wounded and Gwinnett died three days later.

Of course, the biggest difficulty facing the new government was war with Great Britain. ▶

War Comes to Georgia

The sparks that lit the American Revolution had come from the northern colonies. With British troops occupied there, Georgia was spared from battles during the early years of war. Still, there was no real peace at home. Only about one-third of the Georgians were Whigs. Another third were Tories, and the rest remained neutral, waiting to see what would happen. From 1776 to 1778, with the Whigs in control, some of the Tories were driven out of Georgia, their property taken over by the state. In addition to this fighting between Georgians, fights erupted between Georgia patriots and loyalists in East Florida. On three occasions, Georgia forces participated in failed attempts to capture the British garrison at St. Augustine.

Counting on the help of loyalists and Indian allies, Britain in 1778 decided to try to regain control of the Carolinas and Georgia. In December, a British army from New York reached Savannah. A

---

*Burke, Camden, Chatham, Effingham, Glynn, Liberty, Richmond, and Wilkes.

Events Look Bleak	
1777– 78	Washington and troops spend cold winter at Valley Forge; Baron von Steuben instructs soldiers in military drill
1778	Savannah recaptured by the British
1779	Royal governor returns to Georgia; Americans lay seige to Savannah; Count Pulaski killed

▶ **Locating the Main Ideas**

1. Define: constitution, separation of powers, unicameral

2. Identify: July 4, 1776, House of Assembly, John Adam Treutlen

3. Why were some Georgia families divided in their loyalty to Great Britain?

4. Why was Georgia's Constitution of 1777 written to give the legislative branch the most power?

The Liberty Bell in Philadelphia is said to have been rung on July 8, 1776, to celebrate the Declaration of Independence.

force of 700 patriots faced more than 2,000 British soldiers. The battle was over quickly. More than 100 of the American defenders were dead, and 450 captured. Georgia's Whig government barely escaped. British troops moved on to Sunbury, Augusta, and Ebenezer. By the end of January 1779, every important town in Georgia was in the hands of the British.

Meanwhile, Sir James Wright, who had fled in 1776, returned to Savannah to reestablish royal authority. Many loyalists came out of hiding to openly support British authority. Some wealthy coastal planters did take an oath of allegiance to the king, but the back-country farmers held out for independence.

Far inland from the coast, state leaders tried to carry on the fight, meeting wherever they could. The British and the Tories, however, kept them on the run.

Slaves Join the Fight

Prior to the American Revolution, almost half of Georgia's 33,000 inhabitants were black slaves. During the war some slaves, men such as Austin Dabney, fought with the patriots. However, far more earned their freedom by siding with the British. Why? Early in 1776, British commanders began offering freedom to any slave who would join their fight against the American colonists. Eventually, this offer was extended to include the family and relatives of each black recruit. For black slaves, it was not a matter of disloyalty. Rather, to them, freedom from slavery was more important than freedom from Great Britain.

In some cases, slaves helped the British not as soldiers but as spies or guides. In the December 1778 battle for Savannah, Quamino Dolly led a British invasion force through little-known swamp paths to bypass a patriot force. Because of his help, the British were able to attack the Americans from the rear and win a total victory, capturing Savannah.

After Savannah's capture, British-occupied areas of coastal Georgia became a haven for escaping slaves. By war's end, as many as 10,000 Georgia slaves had won freedom by siding with the British. After Americans won the revolution, some of the blacks who had fled to Georgia's coast were re-enslaved. However, many fled to Indian territories in extreme south Georgia and Florida. Some were evacuated to Canada or other British colonies in the Caribbean.

Battle of Kettle Creek

Early in 1779, at Kettle Creek in Wilkes County, Lt. Col. Elijah Clarke led a force of Georgia patriots in an attack against British loyalists. Aided by South Carolinians, the patriots scattered the Tories, killing their British commander.

Although the Battle of Kettle Creek didn't involve large armies, it was important to the patriot cause. The patriots gained badly needed arms, ammunition, and horses. Also, their victory won over

All Spirited
YOUNG MEN
Have now an opportunity of diftin-
guifhing themfelves, (His Majefty having been gracioufly pleafed to permit
a regiment to be raifed in this province, to affift in putting an end to
the prefent unhappy rebellion) by joining the
GEORGIA LOYALISTS,
COMMANDED BY
James Wright, Efq;
for TWO YEARS, or during the continuance of the faid REBELLION. They
may depend on receiving the beft of
treatment, enter into immediate pay,
and be well clothed. And on repairing to me in Savannah, fhall receive a
bounty of FIVE GUINEAS.
JAMES WRIGHT, Jun.

Kettle Creek 1779

Augusta 1780, 1781

Brier Creek 1779

Savannah 1778, 1779

Sunbury 1779

The Revolutionary War in Georgia

This 1779 recruitment poster advertises to raise an army of Georgia loyalists. What does the poster promise young men who join? Because Georgia was the southernmost colony, there were fewer battles here than in the more northern colonies.

many Georgians who had been lukewarm in their support of the war. Never again were the Tories able to gather a large force in the backcountry.

The Battle of Kettle Creek was fought between Americans—patriots and loyalists. In fact, the Revolutionary War in Georgia was in some ways like a civil war. Frequently, neighbor fought neighbor. Sometimes families, and even whole communities, were split down the middle.

Siege of Savannah

During the fall of 1779, patriots—aided by France, which had joined the American side—tried desperately to retake Savannah. An American army and a French fleet laid siege to the city for three weeks. After a fierce bombardment, the Americans attempted to take the city by storm. In a daring cavalry charge, Count Casimir Pulaski, a Polish nobleman who had come to America to help the patriots, was killed. The attack failed.

In the end, the British were able to hold Savannah and lost only 150 men. The Americans and their allies had 1,000 men killed or wounded and gained nothing.

The End of the War

During 1780, the British controlled most of Georgia. It was the only one of the 13 former colonies in which the king's government was

▶ **Locating the Main Ideas**

1. Identify: Elijah Clarke, Casimir Pulaski, Treaty of Paris (1783)
2. Give reasons why the British may have decided Georgia was a good target for them to recapture.
3. What was the importance of the Battle of Kettle Creek?

restored. However, the Whigs and the Tories continued their bitter fighting in the backcountry. Families were driven from their lands, their homes burned, their livestock killed, and their crops destroyed.

In 1781, the Whigs recaptured Augusta. Meanwhile a large British army surrendered to General Washington at Yorktown, Virginia. For all practical purposes, this marked the end of the American Revolution. However, it took awhile for the British to withdraw their troops. In the spring of 1782, the Tories and the British troops gave up Georgia. As the American troops marched joyfully into Savannah, more than 2,000 Tories and their slaves left the state. All of Georgia was once again under control of its own government.

The American Revolution ended with the signing of the Treaty of Paris in 1783. Georgia, along with the other former colonies, was now a free and independent state. However, all its troubles were not over.

During the revolution, Spain had joined the struggle and seized West Florida from the British. As part of the peace treaty, Britain had to return East and West Florida to Spain. But the United States disagreed with Spain over the northern boundary of West Florida. For the next 12 years, ownership of a sizeable area of Georgia's western land was in dispute.

Unfriendly Indians, some of whom had taken the British side in the war, posed a threat along Georgia's frontier. Georgia now faced some of the same problems as before the war. This time, however, the problems would be handled by a state, not a colony. ◀

Building a New Nation

The transition from 13 separate colonies to a union—first as colonies, then as states—involved many actions and spanned more than a decade in time. Some date the official birth of the union to September 1774, when delegates from every colony but Georgia assembled in Philadelphia for the First Continental Congress. However, other than pass resolutions and agreements, this body could take no official action.

In April 1775, the movement towards union received a big boost when British forces collided with American militiamen at Lexington and Concord—the first battles of the American Revolution. Another important step toward union came the next month when the Second Continental Congress convened in Philadelphia. This Congress became the acting government for the American colonies. On June 15, 1775, it named George Washington as commander in chief of the Continental Army. Two days later, American forces repelled three British assaults at the Battle of Bunker Hill (actually fought on Breed's Hill) before running out of gunpowder and being forced to retreat.

George Washington.

In 1776, the Second Continental Congress took a major step toward creating a new nation when it adopted the Declaration of Independence. But, the Declaration was unclear about how that nation would be formed. Were the colonies now independent "united States," or were they a single nation known as the "United States"? Whatever the answer, from that point, the Second Continental Congress was clearly the national government for the former colonies.

With war under way, many delegates felt the Continental Congress needed some form of legal authority if British forces were to be defeated. In November 1777, delegates adopted a formal basis for union—the **Articles of Confederation**. This document was then sent to each of the states for approval, a process that was finally completed on March 1, 1781. It strengthened the union of the American states and served as the first constitution for the new nation.

The Articles created a new union of states, but it was a weak union. Even though they were at war, most Americans feared a strong central government—even one of their own creation. Also, a number of Americans felt a stronger allegiance to their state than to some new national union of states.

The Articles created a national government with only one branch, a unicameral legislature. The Confederation Congress had few powers to govern the nation. For instance, it could not **levy** (impose) taxes or regulate trade between the states. There was no president to carry out the laws, nor any court system to handle grievances.

Under the Articles, each state had an equal vote in Congress, regardless of size or population. In effect, the United States was a **confederation**, or partnership, of independent, equal states. A few powers had been delegated to a weak central government, but most power remained with the states.

After the American Revolution, the 13 states faced the challenge of forging a stronger nation. Across the country, the economy was shaky. In some places, business was almost at a standstill. State governments discouraged trade by taxing the products of other states. Some of them issued nearly worthless paper money that many merchants refused to accept.

In 1786, the state of Massachusetts levied taxes to pay the war debt. The following year, led by Daniel Shays, disgruntled citizens rebelled. Shays' Rebellion was quickly put down by the state militia, but it caused alarm throughout the country. Other states argued over boundaries and the control of navigation and shipping on interstate rivers. Political leaders now realized that a stronger central government was needed.

In May 1787, delegates from every state except Rhode Island met in Philadelphia, Pennsylvania, to tackle a big problem—how to

Turning Point	
1780	General Cornwallis captures Charleston, moves north losing battles at Kings Mountain, Cowpens, Guilford Court House
1781	**October 18:** British under Cornwallis surrender at Yorktown, Virginia, while the British army band plays, "The World Turned Upside Down"
1783	Treaty of Paris signed, officially ending the war

During the war, few records were kept. The heroic deeds of the patriots, however, spread by word of mouth. Years later, people still talked about them. During the 1800s, people wrote down different versions of these stories.

The stories presented here are adapted from versions published in 1854. Because the persons writing them down did not witness the events, these are secondary, not primary, sources. Although they are a blend of fact and fiction, they give us a look into the lives of the backcountry patriots.

Aunt Nancy Hart

The Rev. Mr. Snead of Baldwin County, a connection of the Hart family, says he remembers Aunt Nancy, as she was usually called. He describes her as being about six feet high, very muscular, and erect in her gait [walk].

Among the stories about her is the following from Mrs. Ellet's "Women of the Revolution":

On an excursion from the British camp at Augusta, a party of Tories penetrated the interior. They savagely murdered Colonel John Dooly in bed in his own house. They then proceeded up the country to commit further outrages. On their way, five of them crossed the Broad River to pay a visit to their old acquaintance, Nancy Hart.

On reaching her cabin, they entered it unceremoniously, receiving from her no welcome but a scowl. They ordered her to give them something to eat. She replied, "I never feed King's men if I can help it. The villains have put it out of my power to feed even my own family and friends. They have stolen and killed all my poultry and pigs, except that one old gobbler you see in the yard."

"Well, and that you shall cook for us," said one, who appeared to be the head of the party. Raising his musket, he shot down the turkey and handed it to Mrs. Hart. She stormed and swore awhile—for Nancy occasionally swore. But, at last she agreed to cook it, assisted by her daughter, Sukey, who was some 10 or 12 years old. Nancy now seemed in a good humor, exchanging jests with the Tories. They invited her to partake of the liquor they had brought with them.

Before cleaning and cooking the turkey, Mrs. Hart sent Sukey to the spring, a short distance from the house, for water. At the spring was kept a conch shell. It was used as a crude trumpet by the family to give information, by means of various notes, to Mr. Hart, or his neighbors, who might be at work in a field. Mrs. Hart had directed Sukey to blow the conch in such a way as to inform her husband that Tories were in the cabin.

Later, after they had become merry over their jug, the Tories sat down to feast on the slaughtered gobbler. They had cautiously stacked their arms where they were within view and within reach. Mrs. Hart attended to her guests at the table and occasionally passed between them and their muskets. She had slipped out one of the pieces of pine chinking between the logs of the cabin. Then she put out of the house, through that space, two of the five guns.

She was detected in putting out the third. The men sprang to their feet. Quick as a thought, Mrs. Hart brought the gun she held to her shoulder and declared she would kill the first man who approached her. All were terror-struck. At length one of them made a motion to advance upon her. True to her threat, she fired. He fell dead upon the floor!

Instantly seizing another musket, she brought it to the position of readiness to fire again.

Sukey, who had returned from the spring, took up the remaining gun and announced, "Daddy and them will soon be here." This information increased the alarm of the Tories. They proposed a general rush.

No time was to be lost by the bold woman; she fired again, and brought down another Tory. Sukey had the other musket in readiness. Her mother took it, and positioning herself in the doorway, called upon the party to surrender.

Her husband and his neighbors came up to the door. They were about to shoot down the Tories. Mrs. Hart stopped them, saying they had surrendered to her. She swore that "shooting was too good for them." The dead man was dragged out of the house. The wounded Tory and the others were bound, taken out, and hanged.

The tree upon which they were hanged was pointed out, in 1838, by a person who lived in those bloody times. This person also showed the spot once occupied by Mrs. Hart's cabin, with the remark, "Poor Nancy—she was a honey of a patriot, but the devil of a wife."

Austin Dabney

The following account of Austin Dabney, a remarkable "free man of color," was given by Governor Gilmer:

In the beginning of the revolutionary conflict, a man by the name of Aycock moved to Wilkes County. He brought with him a mulatto boy, named Austin, who passed as Aycock's slave.

As the conflict in that area became bitter, Aycock was called on to join the fight. He wasn't much of a fighter, though, and offered the mulatto boy as a substitute. The patriots objected, saying that a slave could not be a soldier. Thereupon, Aycock admitted that the mulatto boy was born free. Austin was then accepted into service, and the captain to whose company he was attached added Dabney to his name.

Dabney proved himself a good soldier in many a skirmish with the British and Tories. He fought under Colonel John Dooly and was with Colonel Elijah Clarke in the battle at Kettle Creek. At Kettle Creek, he was severely wounded by a rifleball passing through his thigh. He was taken into the house of a Mr. Harris, where he was kindly cared for until he recovered. The wound made him a cripple for life. Dabney was unable to do further military duty and afterwards labored for Harris and his family.

After the war, when prosperous times came again, Austin Dabney acquired property. Later, he moved to Madison County, carrying with him his benefactor and family. Here he became noted for his fondness for horseracing and he betted to the extent of his means. His means were aided by a pension, which he received from the United States on account of his injury.

In the distribution of the public lands by lottery among the people of Georgia, the legislature gave Dabney some land in the county of Walton. At the election for members of the legislature the year after, the County of Madison was divided. They voted according to whether the candidates were for Dabney or against him. People were incensed that a mulatto should receive a gift of land. Some felt such gifts belonged to the white freemen of Georgia.

Dabney soon after moved to the land given him by the state, and carried with him the Harris family. He continued to labor for them and contributed whatever he made to their support, except what he needed for his own clothing and food. He sent the eldest son of Harris to Franklin College, and afterwards supported him while he studied law. When Harris was undergoing his examination, Austin waited outside. When his young friend was sworn in, he burst into a flood of tears. Upon his death, Austin Dabney left the Harris family all his property.

Interpreting the Source

1. What is likely to happen to stories of heroic people as they are told and retold over time? Do you think it has happened in these stories?

2. How did Mrs. Hart warn her husband of the presence of Tories?

3. How did Mr. Dabney repay the Harris family for taking care of him after he was wounded in the Battle of Kettle Creek?

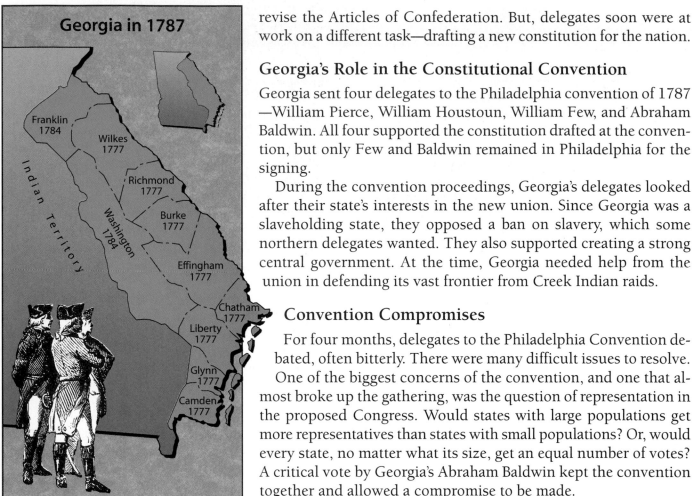

Georgia in 1787

Franklin 1784
Wilkes 1777
Indian Territory
Richmond 1777
Washington 1784
Burke 1777
Effingham 1777
Chatham 1777
Liberty 1777
Glynn 1777
Camden 1777

▶ **Locating the Main Ideas**

1. Define: Articles of Confederation, levy, confederation, federal, legislative, executive, judicial, checks and balances

2. Why were Americans interested in creating a weak union of states under the Articles of Confederation?

3. List three problems that made political leaders realize a strong central government was needed for the new nation.

4. Why did delegates to the constitutional convention divide the new government into three separate branches?

revise the Articles of Confederation. But, delegates soon were at work on a different task—drafting a new constitution for the nation.

Georgia's Role in the Constitutional Convention

Georgia sent four delegates to the Philadelphia convention of 1787 —William Pierce, William Houstoun, William Few, and Abraham Baldwin. All four supported the constitution drafted at the convention, but only Few and Baldwin remained in Philadelphia for the signing.

During the convention proceedings, Georgia's delegates looked after their state's interests in the new union. Since Georgia was a slaveholding state, they opposed a ban on slavery, which some northern delegates wanted. They also supported creating a strong central government. At the time, Georgia needed help from the union in defending its vast frontier from Creek Indian raids.

Convention Compromises

For four months, delegates to the Philadelphia Convention debated, often bitterly. There were many difficult issues to resolve.

One of the biggest concerns of the convention, and one that almost broke up the gathering, was the question of representation in the proposed Congress. Would states with large populations get more representatives than states with small populations? Or, would every state, no matter what its size, get an equal number of votes? A critical vote by Georgia's Abraham Baldwin kept the convention together and allowed a compromise to be made.

Among the other issues decided by delegates was the division of power between states and the national government. Under the new Constitution, state and national governments would function side by side, each with certain powers spelled out, in what is called a **federal** system. In some areas—such as defense, interstate commerce, and foreign relations—the national government would be supreme. In other areas—such as roads and taxes—both states and the central government would have powers to act. Finally, on a great number of issues, states would be free to act without national interference.

To prevent the national government from growing too powerful, the delegates at Philadelphia divided its powers among three separate branches. They created a **legislative** branch to make the laws, an **executive** branch to carry out the laws, and a **judicial** branch to interpret the laws and settle legal disputes. Into the new constitution was built a plan of **checks and balances** to prevent any of the branches from overpowering the others. Each branch had certain powers to *check* the others to keep a *balance* of power. ◀

Georgia Ratifies the Constitution

On September 17, 1787, convention delegates gave their final approval to the new constitution. One final step remained for the new

Abraham Baldwin: A Georgian and the Great Compromise

The debate over equal representation in Congress came to a head on July 2, 1787. Both sides were dug in, and delegates from the smaller states were determined to leave the convention if they didn't get equal representation. The roll was called. Georgia voted last. When its turn came, the issue was tied. Georgia's delegation, now down to Baldwin and Houstoun, could break the tie. Houstoun voted with the large states. To many people's surprise, Baldwin voted with the small states.

By splitting Georgia's vote, the question remained a tie. The convention had no choice but to turn the matter over to a committee. By his action, Baldwin gave the delegates a chance to fashion what has been called the Great Compromise.

Delegates agreed that Congress would consist of *two* houses—a House of Representatives and a Senate. In the House, states would be represented according to their population. In the Senate, each state would have two senators without regard for the size of its population.

---

constitution to go into effect: **ratification** (formal approval) by nine states.

Despite all the problems with the Articles of Confederation, not all Americans supported the proposed constitution. Some thought that the national government was too powerful. They also worried that the constitution contained no list of rights and liberties protected from government interference.

Most Georgians welcomed the idea of a stronger national government. They needed the help and protection a strong national government could provide in defending the frontier against the Indian population. Also, there were promises that a **bill of rights** would be added once the constitution was ratified. That, along with compromises in the Constitution, would keep the national government from becoming too strong and not protecting individual liberties.

On January 2, 1788, Georgia became the fourth state to ratify the Constitution of the United States, following Delaware, Pennsylvania, and New Jersey. A year later, the new national government took over, and George Washington was elected as the first president of the United States.

State Government

In 1789, Georgia adopted a new state constitution, one more in line with the new national constitution. Like the national Congress, the Georgia legislature would now be **bicameral** (or two-house), with a Senate and a House of Representatives.

As in the 1777 constitution, Georgia's state government would have three branches. But unlike the federal government, the branches

Key Constitutional Compromises

	PROBLEM	SOLUTION
The Great Compromise (also called the Connecticut Compromise because it was proposed by Roger Sherman of Connecticut)	In the legislative branch, states with large populations wanted representation based on population. States with small populations wanted equal representation.	Congress was created with a Senate (with two Senators per state) and a House of Representatives (with the number of representatives based on population).
The Three-Fifths Compromise	How to count the slaves for the purposes of taxation and representation in the House of Representatives?	Only three out of every five slaves were counted for taxation and representation.
The Commerce Compromise	Who would regulate trade with foreign nations and among the states? The South's economy depended on free trade.	Congress would regulate all trade. It could impose tariffs on imports only. The tariffs had to apply throughout the country.
The Slave Trade Compromise	As a result of the Commerce Compromise, Congress would regulate trade. Did that mean Congress could also prohibit the slave trade by law and tax slaves as imports?	Congress was prohibited from regulating the slave trade for 20 years (until 1808). During that time the import tax could not exceed $10.

were not balanced. Most real power rested with the legislature (known as the **General Assembly**). Legislators controlled raising and spending money; chose the governor, the judges, and other state officials; and even granted divorces.

The highest courts in the state were the **superior courts**. Superior court judges traveled a regular "circuit" from city to city by horseback or stagecoach. They handled the most serious cases in several counties. Each county had an **inferior court** for less serious cases, and each community had a justice of the peace court to handle minor matters.

Looking Ahead

By 1789, both Georgia and the nation had new constitutions. Georgia, one of the largest states in area, stretched across present-day Alabama and Mississippi to the Mississippi River. Included in this area were large numbers of Cherokee, Creek, Chickasaw, and other Native Americans. Yet, in terms of non-native population, Georgia was the smallest of the 13 states. Attracting new settlers would help protect Georgia's exposed frontier. It would also mean more population and voting strength in Congress. Because of this, Georgia's destiny depended on growth. ◀

▶ **Locating the Main Ideas**

1. Define: ratification, bill of rights, bicameral, General Assembly, superior court, inferior court

2. Why were Georgians in favor of the new Constitution and a stronger national government?

3. What was Georgia's population ranking among the 13 states? Why was population growth important to Georgia's future?

CHAPTER ACTIVITIES

Reviewing the Main Ideas

1. Explain how the mercantile system and taxes caused the colonists to develop anti-British attitudes.

2. Explain these ideas of government: (a) consent of the governed, (b) representative government, and (c) limited government.

3. In what ways did the colonists show their discontent with the actions taken by Parliament?

4. What was the purpose of the Declaration of Independence?

5. Why did Georgians write a state constitution in 1777? What did it replace?

6. What were some of the things Georgia Tories did after the Declaration of Independence was signed?

7. In what sense was the American Revolution (especially in Georgia) a civil war?

8. How did the Treaty of Paris (which ended the American Revolution) result in Georgia having a boundary dispute?

9. What was the Great Compromise made during the Constitutional Convention? What role did Abraham Baldwin play in that compromise?

10. What were the names of Georgia's legislative body and its two houses under the Constitution of 1789?

Monument at Minuteman National Historic Park in Concord, Massachusetts.

Give It Some Extra Thought

1. **Supporting Evidence.** When the colonists used the popular slogan, "no taxation without representation," what were they protesting?

2. **World Connections.** The first shot fired in the American Revolution in the battles of Lexington and Concord was known as "the shot heard 'round the world." What does that mean? What do you think America's fight for independence meant to the rest of the world? What do you think America symbolizes for people around the world today?

3. **Analyze Change over Time.** Before the American Revolution, the word *state* had a different meaning than after the U.S. Constitution was written. Analyze the change by giving the definition of state as used in the phrase, "that these United Colonies are...Free and Independent States," from the Declaration of Independence. Second, describe how the definition for state changed when states became part of the federal system created by the U.S. Constitution.

Sharpen Your Skills

1. **Identifying Problems.** Imagine life as a Tory in Georgia before and during the American Revolution. Describe how life would change. What are some of the problems a Tory would have?

2. **Taking the Opposite Point of View.** Think of yourself as a British citizen in London hearing about American colonists dumping tea in the Boston harbor. What would be your reaction to the news? Write down two statements you might make about the colonists.

Going Further

1. **Researching.** Use other sources and write a brief report on the addition of the Bill of Rights to the U.S. Constitution. Try to find out and include the following information in your report. Why wasn't it a part of the original constitution? Why was the addition of the Bill of Rights important to the ratification of the Constitution? When was it added to the Constitution?

Coming Up Next!

• Georgia's land area expands
• Government encourages economic growth

Growth and Prosperity

In the 50 years between 1790 and 1840, the population of Georgia quadrupled. A similar growth pattern occurred for the nation. The population grew from about 4 million residents in 1790 to more than 17 million in 1840.

Before the American Revolution, to preserve peace with the Native Americans, Britain had restricted settlement west of the Appalachian Mountains. Many colonists disobeyed this order and moved west anyway. But covered wagons could not be pulled over these mountains, so most settlers were forced southward along wagon roads into Virginia, the Carolinas, and Georgia.

Before long, an important geographical feature was discovered. Many years before the colonists came, the Native Americans had found a pass in the mountains that allowed them to travel east and west. English settlers named it the Cumberland Gap. After the revolution, the old Indian path through the gap was widened for use by covered wagons. Soon, settlers were using the route to travel westward into the rich lands that one day would become Kentucky and Tennessee.

After independence, most states with land claims west of the Appalachians turned them over to the national government for the creation of new states. North of the Ohio River was a large land area known as the Northwest Territory. In 1787, the Confederation Congress had agreed on a plan for dividing this area into states. Fifteen years later, Georgia gave up its western territories, from which Alabama and Mississippi would be created. But the largest land gain to the nation came in 1803 with the Louisiana Purchase, which almost doubled the land area of the United States. For $15 million—only about 3 cents per acre—France sold to Pres. Thomas Jefferson 828,000 square miles of land west of the Mississippi.

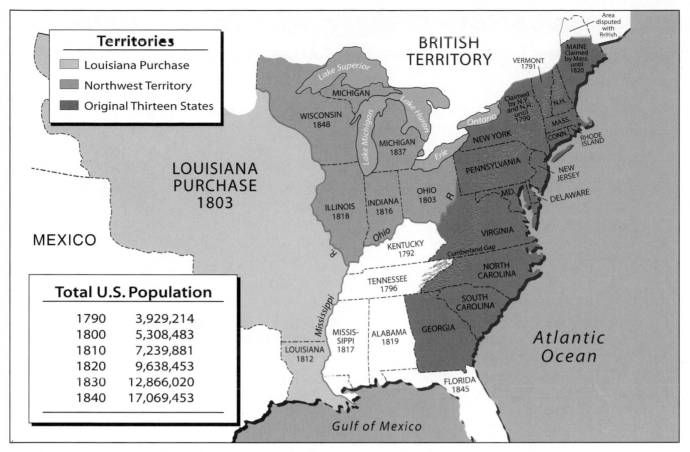

Territories

- Louisiana Purchase
- Northwest Territory
- Original Thirteen States

LOUISIANA PURCHASE 1803

MEXICO

Total U.S. Population	
1790	3,929,214
1800	5,308,483
1810	7,239,881
1820	9,638,453
1830	12,866,020
1840	17,069,453

BRITISH TERRITORY

Population movement in the early 1800s. How might an event, such as the Louisiana Purchase, and a natural feature, such as the Appalachians, influence migration?

People migrated westward for many reasons, but most came for cheap or free land. As thousands of settlers poured into the rich lands west of the Appalachians, the Indians fell back, hopelessly outnumbered.

During this period, technology advanced rapidly, changing the way Americans did things. Steamboats and railroads brought faster and cheaper transportation. New machines, such as those developed by Samuel Slater to make textiles (finished cloth), helped create the factory system. Other inventions made great changes in agriculture. Some of the most important ones were Eli Whitney's cotton gin, Henry Blair's corn harvester, and Cyrus McCormick's mechanical reaper. All these new developments affected Georgia in many ways.

Georgia's Land Area Expands

As first created by Britain in 1732, Georgia's boundaries extended from the Atlantic to the Pacific Ocean. Later, after the French and Indian War, the Mississippi River became Georgia's new western boundary. Despite this vast territory, the actual area open to settlement was much smaller. Creeks, Cherokees, and other Native Americans inhabited most of the land being claimed by Georgia.

The First Census

In 1790, the United States held its first **census**. Across America, government workers went door to door trying to count the population of each of the 13 states, as well as the territories of Kentucky, Vermont, and Maine. The Constitution required that every 10 years a census would be taken. This determined how many U.S. representatives each state would have in Congress.

In contrast to today, the early censuses asked very few questions. Still, they are important sources of information to tell us how quickly the states and nation grew in population after 1790.

How many students go to your school? What percentage of Georgians live on farms? What's the number of counties in Georgia? Information such as this—anything that can be *counted*—is called **quantitative data**. This term comes from the words *quantity* (which means "how many") and *data* (a term for "facts" or "information"). Thus, quantitative data is information that can be expressed in numbers.

Often, you will see numbers, dates, and other types of quantitative data expressed in tables, graphs, charts, and maps. A **table** is an arrangement of data in columns and rows. A **graph** is a picture of data shown as lines, bars, or circles. A **chart** is a general term that can refer to either tables or graphs.

Using Tables and Graphs

Simple examples of quantitative data can be written as a sentence. You can say, for instance, "In 1790, the population of Georgia was 82,548." But imagine if you wanted to compare the state population over a number of different decades. Or, what if you wanted to compare the growth of black and white populations over five decades? This is where tables and graphs come in handy.

Often, a graph can be used to show data from a table in visual form. Because it is a picture, a graph allows you to see relationships between different kinds of data in a table. Also, graphs can show changes over time. They can even help you predict events that might happen some time in the future.

Georgia Population by Race, 1790–1840

Year	White Population	Percent of Total	Black Population	Percent of Total	Total Population of Georgia
1790	52,886	64.1	29,662	35.9	82,548
1800	102,261	62.9	60,425	37.1	162,686
1810	145,414	57.6	107,019	42.4	252,433
1820	189,570	55.6	151,419	44.4	340,989
1830	296,806	57.4	220,017	42.6	516,823
1840	407,695	59.0	283,697	41.0	691,392

Types of Graphs

There are three basic types of graphs: circle graph, bar graph, and line graph. The type of graph used depends in part on the information to be shown. To illustrate, information from the above table is presented in each of the types of graphs on the next page.

Circle Graph (Pie Chart). A circle graph is useful for showing the distribution of parts that make up the whole. Because these parts are drawn as wedges, like pieces of pie, this graph is often called a pie chart. Usually, the parts on a pie chart are shown as percentages of the whole. The wedges are drawn in proportion to the percent they represent. For example, 50 percent would be drawn as half of the circle. Remember that a circle graph shows information about something at one point in time.

Distribution of Georgia's Population, 1790–1840

These thematic maps show the distribution of people (the data) in Georgia over a 50-year period. The blank area is Native American territory where no census was taken. By 1840, what area of the state shows the greatest concentration of people?

One dot equals 400 people

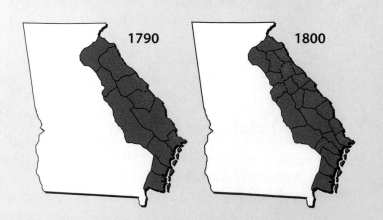

Circle Graph

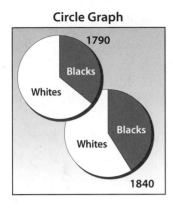

Bar Graph

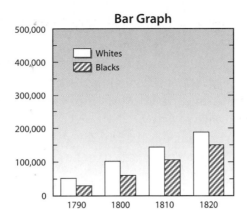

Line Graph

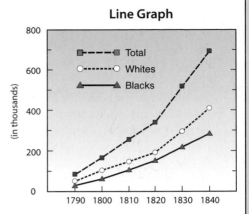

Bar Graph. Like a pie chart, a bar graph can be used to show data at one point in time. But it also can be used to compare data over time. Bar graphs can be drawn vertically or horizontally. The larger the number, the longer the bar.

Line Graph. The line graph is useful in presenting data over a period of time, making it possible to see changes and trends. Commonly, the horizontal axis—the line going across the page—represents time, typically years at regular intervals. The vertical axis—the line going up and down the page—measures the amount of what is being graphed. To save space, large numbers may be written without all the zeroes with a statement such as "in thousands." One advantage of a line graph is that several sets of data can be graphed together.

Practice Your Skills

1. Define: quantitative data, table, graph, chart

2. Use the table to find the decade in which the number of blacks and the number of whites in Georgia were most nearly equal.

3. Compare the two pie charts and make a generalization about what happened to the racial makeup of Georgia between 1790 and 1840.

4. On a piece of paper, copy the bar graph above and add the bars for 1830 and 1840.

5. Estimate, from the line graph, the total population of Georgia in 1810. Refer to the data in the table to see how close you were to the actual number.

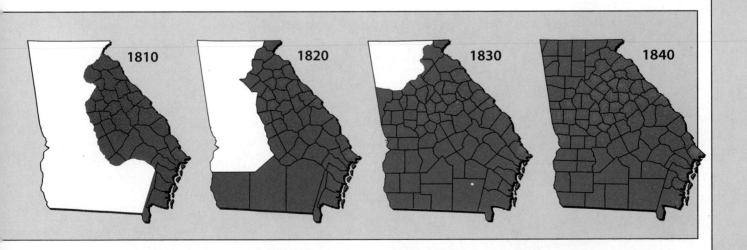

▶ **Locating the Main Ideas**

1. Define: census, cede
2. Give two reasons why colonists did not settle west of the Appalachian Mountains before the American Revolution.
3. What was Georgia's western boundary in 1732? at the end of the French and Indian War?
4. How would a larger population increase Georgia's strength in the national government?

In some cases, the Native Americans went heavily into debt from dealing with shrewd white traders. To settle these debts, the Creeks and Cherokees in 1773 gave up more than 2 million acres of land in the backcountry region. Surveyors marked off tracts of land and colonial officials distributed them.

After the American Revolution, state officials continued to encourage new settlers to come to Georgia. A growing population would mean more representatives in Congress, thus giving Georgia a greater influence in the national government. Also, new settlers would turn forests into farms, helping Georgia's agricultural economy to grow.

In the decades that followed, Georgia state government pressured the Native Americans to **cede** (give up) their land. Slowly, this goal was achieved. ◀

Distributing Public Land

Each time the Native Americans ceded land to the state, Georgia officials faced the question of how to distribute it. Selling the land would bring in money needed for roads, schools, and other public services. On the other hand, giving the land away would encourage more people to come to Georgia. State leaders decided to favor population growth.

At first, Georgia distributed land under the headright system. The head of a family was entitled to 200 acres of unclaimed land for himself, plus 50 acres for each member of his family. There was a limit of 1,000 acres per family. Veterans of the Revolutionary War were entitled to additional acres—ranging from 288 acres for privates to 1,955 acres for generals.

Each person receiving a grant of land was free to go out and claim the best vacant land available. Often, this was the land along a winding creek or river. Surviving **plats**—maps of land lots—show that headright lots often were a maze of irregular shapes.

Georgia's Capital Moves

From the colony's founding, Savannah had served as Georgia's capital. After the revolution, the General Assembly alternated meeting in Savannah and Augusta. But Georgia's real growth was taking place in the backcountry—not along the coast. By 1784, there was increasing concern that the capital not return to Savannah. Frontier settlers had found how convenient it was to have the capital in Augusta. In those days, many everyday matters had to be acted upon by the legislature. For example, state lawmakers had to approve all divorces, name changes, and permits to operate bridges. There were no trains, and other forms of transportation were slow, so it was important to live near the legislature's meeting site.

Georgia's capitals. How did the movement of Georgia's capital from city to city relate to where population growth was taking place?

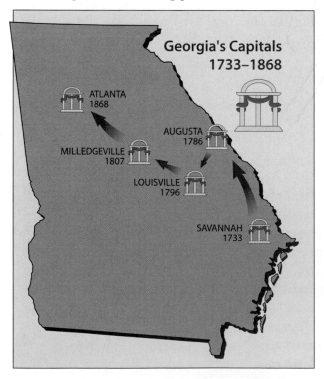

Georgia's Capitals
1733–1868

ATLANTA
1868

AUGUSTA
1786

MILLEDGEVILLE
1807

LOUISVILLE
1796

SAVANNAH
1733

According to tradition, lawmakers decided that no ordinary fire should be used to burn the Yazoo Act. Rather, a magnifying glass focused the sun's rays to start the fire. This symbolized "fire from heaven" destroying the unjust act.

So many people insisted that the capital stay in Augusta that in 1785 the General Assembly decided to hold all future meetings there. However, for many, even Augusta was too far east. So, the legislature appointed a commission to find a new capital site—one that would be centrally located and accessible to all Georgia residents.

In 1786, the General Assembly chose a site on the Ogeechee River as capital, and named it Louisville. After many delays, state government moved, in 1796, to the new two-story brick statehouse at Louisville.

After only a decade, there was pressure to move the state capital yet again. This time a site on the Oconee River to the west was selected. Here the town of Milledgeville was laid out and a new capitol building erected.

The Yazoo Land Fraud

During Augusta's decade as state capital, many events occurred. In 1785, lawmakers created the nation's first state-chartered institution of higher education—the University of Georgia. In 1788, Georgia ratified the U.S. Constitution. Three years later, the nation's new president, George Washington, visited Augusta. But an unfortunate event took place there in 1795. That was the year of the state's worst political scandal—the infamous **Yazoo Land Fraud**.

At that time, Georgia extended westward to the Mississippi River. State leaders wanted to open this vast expanse to white settlement, but the land was occupied by the Creeks, Cherokees, and other tribes. If the Native Americans could be persuaded to leave Georgia, a land rush would follow, making Georgia's population explode.

A land rush would also mean big profits as the land was sold. Businessmen formed several land companies and approached state officials about buying large portions of Georgia's western territories. These were **land speculators**.

Land speculation is the practice of buying land at a low price, holding it until the price rises, then selling it at a profit. It is a common and perfectly legal business practice. But it's another thing when done by government officials, who are supposed to act to benefit the public—not themselves.

In 1795, four private land companies bribed many members of the General Assembly to pass a law. This law allowed the companies to buy 35 million acres of Georgia's western lands extending to the Yazoo River. Much of what today is Alabama and Mississippi was sold to the companies at the incredible price of less than 2 cents per acre. The companies then made big profits by selling the land to the public. Millions of acres were sold—some to other land speculators, some to innocent citizens who planned to move to the frontier territories.

When Georgians learned of the Yazoo Land Fraud, they were outraged. Some of the dishonest legislators, fearing for their lives, fled the state. The next year, a newly elected legislature met at the new statehouse in Louisville and **repealed** (abolished) the law authorizing the Yazoo land sale. The legislature also directed that the Yazoo Act be publicly burned on the statehouse grounds and that all copies of the infamous legislation be destroyed.

After repealing the Yazoo Act, the legislature provided for refunding the money to those who had purchased Georgia's western lands. But many buyers weren't willing to give up their bargain. They went to court, and the Yazoo controversy eventually landed in the U.S. Supreme Court. The issue took years to resolve. It finally ended in 1814 when the federal government took over the contested territory and paid off the remaining Yazoo claims. ◀

Georgia Loses Its Western Territory

For a dozen years after the American Revolution, Spain and Georgia both claimed a large stretch of land between the Chattahoochee and Mississippi rivers. In a treaty with the United States in 1795, Spain finally gave up its claim. It was now unclear whether that land belonged to the United States or to Georgia. Congress, in 1798, decided that the area would be called the Mississippi Territory and that it would have its own government. This meant that the land would no longer be part of Georgia.

Georgia was unhappy with this action, but by now its leaders were tiring of the trouble caused by the western territories. They

▶ **Locating the Main Ideas**

1. Define: plat, Yazoo Land Fraud, land speculators, repeal

2. What were the advantages to the state in selling public land? What was the advantage in giving it away?

3. Why did the capital of Georgia move from Savannah to Augusta?

4. Explain how dishonest land speculators made a profit on the Yazoo Lands.

were tired of the lawsuits over the Yazoo Act's repeal, the questions over Native American rights, and the burden of protecting frontier settlements. These and other problems finally convinced state leaders, in 1802, to transfer the contested territories to the federal government. In return, the national government paid Georgia $1,250,000 and promised to remove all remaining Native Americans from the state.

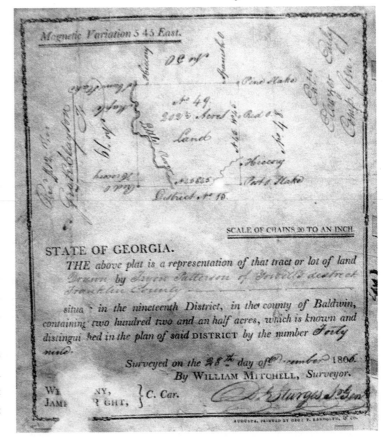

Georgia Acquires Indian Lands

After 1802, Georgia's boundaries were pretty much what they are today. Now, state lawmakers in Louisville wanted to gain control over all territory belonging to Georgia. This meant getting the Indians to cede their lands. Slowly but surely, the Indians moved out.

Georgia loses its western territories. By 1802, Georgia's boundaries looked much as they do today.

In 1802, fighting broke out between the Creeks and Georgians along the Oconee River. Since the American Revolution, the Oconee had served as the Creek boundary with Georgia. Many whites, however, wanted to settle west of that river and often tried to move onto Indian lands. In fact, in 1794, Gen. Elijah Clarke and a group of followers had tried to create an independent government on Creek Indian lands across the Oconee River. They built several forts in what they called the Trans-Oconee Republic before Georgia and federal troops were sent in, forcing them to leave.

Deed to land lot of 202½ acres in Baldwin County, drawn in the land lottery on December 28, 1806, by Irwin Patterson of Franklin County.

In June 1802, the Creeks signed a treaty at Fort Wilkinson ceding a stretch of land west of the Oconee River to Georgia. Three years later, another treaty gave up a large area of land as far west as the Ocmulgee River.

How would these newly acquired lands be distributed? Georgia abandoned the old headright system. Now, land would be equally distributed through a land lottery.

Land Lotteries

In 1803, Georgia changed its method of distributing public lands. No longer were large 1,000-acre land grants issued. Nor could land grant winners get to pick the location and shape of their lots.

Under the new system, surveyors divided as much of the land as possible into square lots. In general, these lots were smaller than under the headright system. This was designed to encourage a larger number of families to settle the frontier.

The lottery gave many people an opportunity to own land in Georgia.

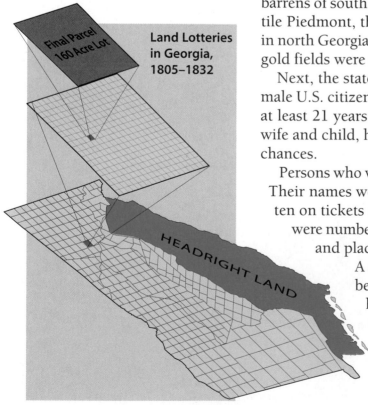

Final Parcel 160 Acre Lot

Land Lotteries in Georgia, 1805–1832

HEADRIGHT LAND

Lot size varied according to the quality of the land. In the pine barrens of south Georgia, lots were 490 acres each. In the more fertile Piedmont, they were 202$\frac{1}{2}$ acres each. Later, Cherokee lands in north Georgia were divided into 160-acre lots, though lots in the gold fields were as small as 40 acres.

Next, the state held a **lottery**—drawing for a prize. Every white male U.S. citizen who had lived in Georgia for 12 months and was at least 21 years old was allowed one draw or chance. If he had a wife and child, he got two chances. Widows and orphans also got chances.

Persons who wanted land would register at a county courthouse. Their names were sent to the state capital where they were written on tickets and placed in a barrel. Land lots to be given away were numbered. The number of each lot was written on a ticket and placed in another barrel.

A state official simultaneously drew names and numbers from the barrels. Those receiving land were known as "fortunate drawers." Except for a recording fee of $4 per 100 acres, the land was absolutely free. People who got land could farm it or sell it as they wished.

The first land lottery was held in 1805. During the next 28 years, five more lotteries were held. Under the lottery system, Georgia distributed about 30 million acres of land west of the Oconee River to more than 100,000 fortunate drawers. ▶

Government Encourages Economic Growth

As the Indians moved westward, Georgia slowly opened to settlement. As Georgia's population grew, so did its economy.

Several factors combined to encourage economic growth in Georgia. The invention of the cotton gin (see Chapter 11) was a major factor. The cotton gin made it faster and cheaper to get cotton ready for making cloth. Georgia's backcountry had the right soil and climate for growing cotton. Also, there was the plantation system based on slave labor—a profitable arrangement for landowners. People flocked to Georgia, hoping to get rich.

Government and Transportation

State government encouraged Georgia's growing prosperity. To have a strong economy, Georgia needed a better way to distribute goods and move people. Georgia government officials worked with business people to develop a transportation system. As people moved into unsettled areas, cities and towns developed. Georgia's government helped to plan some of those cities.

Waterways

Georgia's waterways served as important inland "highways" for transportation to and from the frontier. The Savannah River was the most important waterway linking the backcountry to the ocean port at Savannah. Where the Fall Line crosses that river, Augusta grew up to become Georgia's major inland city. From there, trading paths and dirt roads ran westward past frontier settlements into Indian lands.

After 1800, other important trade centers were built along the Fall Line. These were Milledgeville on the Oconee River, Macon on the Ocmulgee, and later, Columbus on the Chattahoochee.

Rectangular barges—sometimes called "Oconee boxes"—carried bales of cotton downriver to ocean ports for shipment to distant markets. But these barges had one big drawback —they could not return upstream against the current.

▶ **Locating the Main Ideas**

1. Define: lottery
2. What problems occurring in Georgia's western territories convinced officials to transfer land to the federal government?
3. What qualifications did a person need to participate in Georgia's land lottery?
4. Who were "fortunate drawers"?

Georgia rivers and Native American paths. For about 100 years, Georgians generally followed transportation routes first used by Native Americans. Why do you think trading paths generally ran east and west?

The Frontier Spirit. Most Georgia pioneers settled permanently on the lands they received, but some moved almost constantly, along with the frontier. This restless spirit is illustrated in the life of Gideon Lincecum, born in middle Georgia in 1793. Gideon's father moved his family from place to place in Georgia and the Carolinas seeking better opportunity and more elbow room. Inheriting this same spirit, Gideon moved west with the frontier to Mississippi and Texas. Along the way, he learned enough to be a surveyor, school teacher, Indian trader, physician, and planter. The following excerpt from his autobiography tells about events beginning in 1804.

Autobiography of Gideon Lincecum

1804. My father sold his cotton for a good price and made a visit to his sister in Clark[e] County, Ga. He was gone two or three weeks, and when he returned, he told my mother that he had purchased a tract of land with a good house on it, one mile from Athens, Ga. We were soon on the road again, returning to Georgia. In the course of a week we were in our new home. Father worked hard at his new place. He planted and raised a large crop of cotton; and as soon as it began to open, every one that could pick five pounds a day was forced into the cotton field. We succeeded in gathering the cotton by Christmas, and father took it to the gin and got the receipts for 4,643 pounds, for which he received five cents a pound.

1805. He again became restless, and selling his place, put his wagon in good repair, and set out on a third attempt to get to Tennessee. I was delighted that we were on the road. Being in my twelfth year, I was an expert with a bow and arrow, and could run far ahead, shooting and killing many birds in the course of a day.

Father hired a straggling old fellow to drive for us this trip, and we rolled on bravely until we came to the Saluda river. There was there a store and blacksmith shop, and we stopped until the smith nailed a pair of shoes on the outriding horse.

The arrival of steamboats in the 1820s solved this problem. The steam-powered, flat-bottomed boats provided a fast and efficient way to transport large quantities of cotton downstream. They could also return upstream with goods needed inland.

Although steamboats were privately owned businesses, state government passed laws and spent tax money to protect river transportation. It had to keep the channels free of fallen trees and sandbars, and prevent people from placing fish traps or other hazards to navigation in the rivers.

News of New York's Erie Canal encouraged Georgians to think about building canals. In 1825, the Board of Public Works looked into the possibility of a north-south canal to connect the Ocmulgee

Father and his teamster became somewhat intoxicated and got two bottles of whiskey to carry with them. The river was wide and swift, but shallow. We forded it and landed safely in South Carolina again. After going about five miles further, my father and the driver became more deeply intoxicated. The driver fell off the wagon and frightened the horses. They ran away and tore up the wagon, hurting all who were in it. My grandmother was very seriously wounded.

The family settled in South Carolina, never making it to Tennessee. The next year they moved back to Georgia and settled at a place one mile from where they lived before.

1807. The lands beyond the Oconee river had been obtained by the United States from the Muskogee [Creek] Indians. No one had moved into this new purchase. Father intended to settle there as soon as the Indians had completed the twelve months' hunting which had been by a stipulation in the treaty with the United States reserved to them.

Father entered my sister, brother, and me as day scholars in a little old log cabin, a mile and a half from our home, at the rate of $7 each per year. I was 14 years old, and it was the first school house I had ever seen. I began in the alphabet. There were some very small boys, seven years old, who could read....

When the Indians finished their year of hunting and retired from the new purchase my father took me with him to explore the country. He preferred the country on the Little River, selected a place and we returned home to make ready for the removal as soon as possible....

My father had been moving about so much that he was not entitled to a chance in the lottery—and the place he wanted on the Little River was drawn by a man who would not part with it. Father then found a place belonging to Thomas McLellon, with a double cabin on it. For this place he gave all the money he had, along with "Mammy Pat" and two of her children. It was situated in the woods on a beautiful clear running creek, in one mile of where Eatonton now stands.

The next year after we came there the county seat was laid off and named Eatonton. I was one of the chain carriers to survey the streets and lots though I was but fourteen years old.

Interpreting the Source

1. What were some personal qualities of Gideon Lincecum? of his father?
2. How much money did Mr. Lincecum make on the cotton he sold at Christmas in 1804?
3. What are some of the reasons why Gideon was just starting school at age 14?
4. What requirement kept Mr. Lincecum from being able to participate in the land lottery?

or Oconee rivers with the Tennessee River. The Tennessee flows into the Mississippi River. Lawmakers hoped a connecting canal would give Georgia products access to the ocean port of New Orleans and to new markets in the nation's interior.

The project, however, was soon dismissed. The mountains of north Georgia were too great a barrier for a northward-flowing canal.

Roads

The few navigable waterways in Georgia generally ran north to south. To get products to riverside docks and move east and west in Georgia, overland transportation was needed.

Driving the zero point stake for the southern terminus—or end—of the new W & A Railroad.

Back in 1775, the colonial government had passed Georgia's first road law. It required males between ages 16 and 60 to work on local roads at least 12 days a year. The new state government continued this method of building and maintaining roads—all of them dirt in those days. Many of the early roads merely followed old Native American trails, twisting and turning through the forests. Even the best road—from Savannah to Augusta—was so bad that it took a stagecoach two to four days to make the trip.

As the interior of Georgia began to fill up with people and farms, the need for more connecting roads grew. To build such roads, state government approved turnpike corporations. A **turnpike** was a private roadway built and maintained by a company. Travelers using the roads paid toll charges, from which the turnpike's owners hoped to make a profit. At certain points, "pikes"—long poles serving as gates across the road—blocked wagons and stagecoaches until the drivers paid the toll.

Similar corporations were approved to build bridges and run ferries across rivers. They earned their income by charging tolls and fees to travelers. ◄

Railroads

Even with improved rivers and roads, better and more dependable transportation was still needed. Cotton-marketing towns such as Athens and Forsyth were far from navigable rivers. Shipping cotton by wagon over rough dirt roads was slow and expensive. In periods of low rain, rivers sometimes became too shallow for riverboats.

The invention of the railroad boosted Georgia's development. Georgia's first railroads were private businesses. Building rail transportation was very expensive, and the companies were limited by how much money they could borrow from investors. Because of this, Georgia's General Assembly decided that the state should step in and become a partner in railroad building.

The Coming of the Railroad to Georgia

On Christmas Day of 1830, residents of Charleston, South Carolina, cheered as the small locomotive, *Best Friend of Charleston*, chugged off pulling two cars of passengers. This event marked the first regular train service in America.

▶ **Locating the Main Ideas**

1. Define: turnpike
2. Why did cities develop first along waterways?
3. How were roads built and maintained in Georgia's early days?

In 1833, the track was completed from Charleston to Hamburg, South Carolina, just across the river from Augusta. But Augusta officials would not allow the line to continue across the bridge into Georgia. After all, this would give Charleston merchants and shippers direct access to Georgia's rich cotton markets, bypassing Augusta and Savannah.

Georgia needed its own rail transportation. In December 1833, Georgia's General Assembly chartered two railroads. The Georgia Railroad Company was to build a railroad westward from Augusta to Madison, Eatonton, and Athens. The Central of Georgia Railroad was to extend from Savannah to Macon.

By 1838, track was completed from Augusta to Greensboro, and on to Madison and Athens three years later. The rail line from Savannah progressed more slowly, but it finally reached Macon in 1843.

Rail, river, and road development, 1830–1860. Only the main routes are shown.

Atlanta and the Railroad

In 1836, the General Assembly passed a law for building a state-owned railroad from the Chattahoochee River in DeKalb County, north through Cherokee country to Ross's Landing (Chattanooga) on the Tennessee River. Known as the Western and Atlantic (W & A) Railroad, this line would connect railroads from Augusta, Macon, Milledgeville, and Columbus with America's interior.

The next year, surveyors determined the 138-mile route of the W & A. They located its southern end a few miles southeast of the Chattahoochee River. There they drove a stake into the ground and marked it "Terminus" (meaning "end"). This was the beginning of what one day would be the city of Atlanta. At the other end of the line, another great city developed—Chattanooga, Tennessee.

Terminus began to grow as construction of the W & A Railroad began. On Christmas Eve 1842, a locomotive made the first run, from Terminus to Marietta.

In 1845, the Georgia Railroad arrived from Augusta. Terminus was renamed "Marthasville" in honor of the daughter of ex-governor Wilson Lumpkin, a strong backer of the W & A. A year later,

Georgia's W & A Railroad connected two sites that would become the cities of Atlanta and Chattanooga. Chattanooga is located along the Tennessee River, just north of Lookout Mountain.

the Macon and Western Railroad linked Marthasville with the Central of Georgia Railroad from Savannah.

By 1847, town population reached 400. It was no longer a frontier village, and the name "Marthasville" didn't seem like a good name for a big-time railroad center. The chief engineer of the Georgia Railroad suggested the name "Atlanta" (from "Atlantic" in the W & A's name). The inhabitants agreed, and the General Assembly made it official.

In 1853 a fourth line, the Atlanta and West Point, was completed, linking Georgia's rail system to Alabama. By 1860, Atlanta was a major railroad center of the Deep South. The main link between the Atlantic seaboard and the Middle West, it was nicknamed the "Gate City."

Government and Town Planning

After Georgia became a state, many new towns sprang up unplanned at crossroads, ferry landings, railroad stops, or other places where farmers gathered to trade. Other towns followed special developments in the state. For example, when the General Assembly in 1801 selected a site in northeast Georgia for the University of Georgia, it set the stage for the founding of Athens.

Still other urban places were purposely planned by state government. When the state surveyed former Indian territory for distribution to white settlers, it reserved specific land for towns. Specially appointed commissioners laid out streets, set aside lots for public buildings, and sold town lots to settlers.

Between 1803 and 1828, as the Creeks gave up their lands and moved west, state government planned three cities for the new areas of settlement. Milledgeville was a planned city built to serve as Georgia's state capital, and did so from 1807 to 1868. More important to the state's economy, Milledgeville, Macon, and Columbus, located at the Fall Line, were trade centers. From these points, agricultural products could be easily shipped downriver to ports on the coast. Also, goods could be brought upriver to these locations for distribution throughout the interior of the state.

The legislature's plans were not the same for all three cities. However, the plans show that the state's leaders wished them to be attractive, healthy places to live as well as successful commercial centers. State government's planning of Macon and dozens of other cities and towns helped bring orderly growth to rough frontier areas. This kind of orderly growth contributed to Georgia's economic prosperity in the early 1800s. ◀

▶ **Locating the Main Ideas**

1. Why did state officials want railroads built in Georgia? Why would state government get involved in the building of railroads?

2. What other names did Atlanta have? How did it get them?

3. Why was it important to locate cities on the Fall Line?

4. What was the purpose of planned cities on the frontier?

Reviewing the Main Ideas

1. What was the significance of the Cumberland Gap in the growth of America?
2. Explain how the Chattahoochee River came to be Georgia's western boundary.
3. Why was it important for the state capital to be centrally located? What kinds of business had to be transacted by the legislature?
4. Compare the headright and lottery systems of land distribution in regard to the size and shape of lots and how the boundaries of each lot were determined.
5. List two notable events that took place in Augusta while it was the state capital.
6. What was the reaction of Georgia citizens when they learned of the Yazoo Land Fraud? How did the newly elected legislature respond?
7. In 1802, what did the national government promise Georgia in return for the land between the Chattahoochee and Mississippi rivers?
8. How did the state's lottery system solve the problem of land speculation? Was it fair?
9. State government did not own and operate steamboats but helped their operation in other ways. Identify two of those ways.
10. What present-day cities developed at either end of the W & A rail line?

Give It Some Extra Thought

1. **Interpreting.** The 1833 act incorporating the Georgia Railroad Company gave the company "exclusive rights to transport people and goods over the railroads." Could any other company transport people or goods by rail?
2. **Summarizing.** What are some of the things state government did to promote economic prosperity? to make the state a better place to live in?

Sharpen Your Skills

1. **Using a Map.** Explain how geography prevented the building of a canal connecting central Georgia with the Tennessee River. Use a map that shows Georgia's physical features to illustrate your explanation.
2. **Create a Bar Graph.** Use the U.S. Bureau of the Census figures (pages 123-24) and make a bar graph comparing the population of Georgia to that of the United States from 1790 through 1840. Make a generalization comparing U.S. and Georgia population changes in that 50-year period.
3. **Putting Events in Sequence.** Make a time line of railroad events using the information about them on pages 134-36. Write a generalization about the development of railroads in the 30-year period from 1830 to 1860.

Going Further

1. **Doing Research.** Use your library to get information on Eli Whitney, Henry Blair, Cyrus McCormick, or Samuel Slater. Write a brief report on how that person's invention changed life in America.

Best Friend of Charleston, first regular service passenger train in America.

Conflict Over Indian Lands

No matter where you live in Georgia, the land around you was once the home and hunting ground of native tribes. At first, European settlers coming to America simply asked the natives to share some of their vast lands. Some Native Americans, like Tomochichi's Yamacraws, welcomed the white colonists, signing treaties of friendship and peace. Other tribes, however, refused to give up their land, even for a price. Still, boatload after boatload of European settlers set sail for America. The treasure they came searching for was not gold or silver. It was *land*—the tribal lands of America's native inhabitants.

Only 105 years after the arrival of the first English colonists, Georgia's native population was gone, its tribal lands totally in the hands of whites. How could this have happened?

Conflicting Views

Georgia's early boundaries were so far apart that people originally thought there was plenty of room for both whites and native tribes to live in peace. But cultural differences between the two threatened this prospect.

Differing ideas about land ownership caused the most trouble between the two races. For the native tribes, an individual could no more *own* land than own air or rivers. Rather, a person could manage the land and use it. Thus, a tribe might have the right to use certain hunting grounds, and other tribes would respect that claim. But once that tribe stopped using the grounds (perhaps by moving away), it lost its special right to it.

Creek Chief William McIntosh.

138

Creek log house, 1791. What evidence of influence by white settlers do you see? What native customs have been retained?

Whites, on the other hand, held European beliefs about land ownership. Like a house or furniture, land was something that could be bought, sold, and inherited. A landowner was entitled to exclusive rights to his possession.

During the colonial period, tribal lands in Georgia were protected by the British government. After the American Revolution, however, native rights slowly eroded. At first, the issue was one of Native Americans sharing their land. But soon, Georgians became intent on removing the native people from the state entirely. After the Louisiana Purchase in 1803, many whites came to believe that the Indians *should* move west. Twenty-five years later, Pres. Andrew Jackson announced that they *had* to move west.

Tribal Leaders

Except for some missionaries, there were few white defenders of native rights in Georgia. The best defense came from such Native American leaders as Alexander McGillivray, William McIntosh, John Ross, Elias Boudinot, and George Guess (better known as Sequoyah). Born to European men and their Native American wives, these men were fully accepted as members of their mothers' tribes. In tribal culture, descent was traced through the mother—not the father. White fathers sometimes sent their mixed-blood sons back east for an education. Later, many of these young men became tribal chiefs or other spokesmen. As Georgia's Native Americans attempted to understand white civilization, they turned to those who were educated and knew the ways of whites. Because of their need to live in two worlds, many of the famous Creek and Cherokee leaders had English as well as Indian names.

Location of Georgia's major Native American tribes before 1800.

Georgia's Native American Tribes

Before the 1800s, white settlement was permitted only in a tiny portion of Georgia's vast expanse. Holding onto their native lands were five major groups of Native Americans—the Creeks, Cherokees, Seminoles, Choctaws, and Chickasaws.*

By 1764, about 60,000 natives lived within Georgia's boundaries. At the same time, living on the lands ceded by the Native Americans along the Savannah River and coast were some 10,000 whites and 8,000 blacks.

Georgia's largest tribe was the Choctaw, which had about 25,000 adults and children. They lived in what today is south Mississippi. To the north of the Choctaws were about 2,000 Chickasaws. Neither tribe played an important role in Georgia history because their lands were far to the west of Georgia's frontier.

Controlling most of what today is Georgia and Alabama were some 17,000 Creeks. To the north of them lived more than 13,000 Cherokees. These two tribes held the lands adjoining Georgia's frontier settlements. A third tribe in Georgia was the Seminoles, a branch of the Lower Creeks that had moved into the region stretching from southwestern Georgia into northern Florida. The number of Seminoles in Georgia was small, and eventually they lived entirely in Florida. Thus, the story of conflict between the white settlers and the Native Americans in Georgia focuses on the Creeks, Seminoles, and Cherokees. ◀

The Creeks

The Creeks were not a single tribe or people, but rather a loose confederation (or association) of tribes and chiefdoms. Because most spoke a variation of the Muscogean language, the Creeks were sometimes referred to as Muscogees.

There were two distinct groups. The Upper Creeks lived in towns and villages in the northern half of Alabama. The Lower Creeks located their towns in western Georgia, southern Alabama, and northern Florida.** The remainder of Creek territory—including most of Georgia—was used for hunting.

The Upper and Lower Creeks were separate parts of the confederation. Another part of the confederation was a group of Lower Creeks in south Georgia and Florida known as Seminoles.

---

*These five tribes would later be known as the "Five Civilized Tribes" because they adopted many characteristics of white culture. They made this effort in the nineteenth century, thinking it would help them to hold onto their native lands.
**The Yamacraw Indians Oglethorpe encountered in 1733 were part of the Lower Creeks.

▶ **Locating the Main Ideas**

1. What did Native Americans have that Europeans wanted even more than gold or silver?

2. Explain the Indian view of land ownership. How did it differ from the European view of property ownership?

3. Why were the sons of Indian mothers and white fathers likely to be tribal chiefs?

4. Why don't the Choctaws and Chickasaws play as big a part in the story of Georgia history as the Seminoles, Creeks, and Cherokees?

The Creek confederation was organized around a political unit known as the chiefdom. This consisted of one or more towns or settlements, governed by a chief, known as a mico, and a tribal council. One of the mico's most important jobs was to represent his people when dealing with other chiefdoms or when conducting treaties with whites.

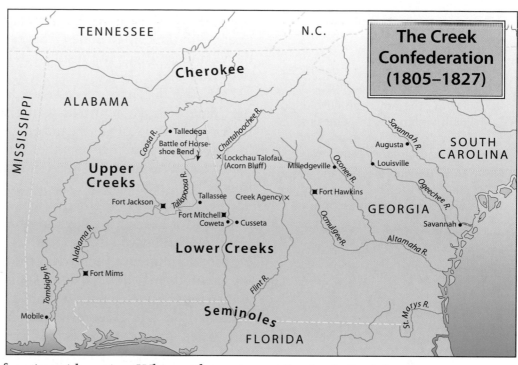

Conflicts between Creeks and Whites

During the Revolutionary War, some Creeks sided with the British, carrying on frontier raids against Whig settlements. After the war, white Georgians remembered this and demanded that the Creeks give up some of their land. What they wanted was the land between the Ogeechee and the Oconee rivers.

The Creeks were divided over what to do. The Lower Creeks agreed to turn over territory to the whites, but the Upper Creeks, led by chief Alexander McGillivray, refused.

Fighting between McGillivray's followers and white settlers on the border of the Creek nation almost became a full-scale war. Finally, in 1790, President Washington invited McGillivray to New York City, then the nation's capital. There the Creek leader was persuaded (and, perhaps, took money) to cede to Georgia lands between the Ogeechee and Oconee rivers. The 34-year-old chief died from an illness three years later. His dream of a strong Creek nation was dying, too.

After the Yazoo Land Fraud, Georgia turned over its western lands to the United States in 1802. In return, the state received $1,250,000 and the national government's promise to remove all Indians from the state *as soon as reasonably and peacefully possible.* (At the same time, the United States, in its treaties with the Indians, more or less promised to protect their lands from white take-over!)

In 1802, the U.S. government persuaded the Creeks to give up more land. For the first time, Georgia was able to expand west of the Oconee River. The next year, state lawmakers directed that a site be selected on the Oconee River for building a "permanent" state capital, to be named Milledgeville. The Creek **cession** (land given up or ceded) was then surveyed and distributed in Georgia's first land lottery.

The Creek Confederation was surrounded by other Native American tribes. The Chickasaws and Choctaws, not shown on this map, were in present-day Mississippi to the west of the Creeks.

▶ **Locating the Main Ideas**

1. Define: cession

2. Identify: mico, Alexander McGillivray, Benjamin Hawkins

3. During the American Revolution, with whom did the Creeks side? How did white Georgians later use this to their advantage?

4. How did the Yazoo Land Fraud help lead to the removal of the Creeks from Georgia?

The Creeks gave up an even larger area of land in 1805 in another treaty with the United States. This cession extended all the way to the Ocmulgee River and resulted in Georgia's second land lottery two years later.

Each time the Creeks ceded more land, they signed a treaty with the United States. In return for giving up land to Georgia, the Creeks received payments of money and other goods. Treaties also provided for settling disputes between the Creeks and whites.

In 1796, President Washington appointed Col. Benjamin Hawkins as U.S. Indian Agent. His job was to administer U.S. treaties and help promote peaceful relations with the Creeks. On the eastern bank of the Flint River (in present-day Crawford County), Hawkins established his headquarters—known as the Creek Agency. He tried to influence the lives of the Creeks, teaching them farming methods and homemaking skills. He helped keep the peace among the Creeks, a job made more difficult because of the constant pressure from white Georgians for more land. Eventually, these efforts failed when the Creeks took sides during the War of 1812. ◀

The War of 1812

In 1812 the United States went to war with Great Britain. The war was fought over a variety of issues. It was partly about U.S. shipping rights and partly about Americans' desire for land claimed by the British and their allies.

The Creeks were divided about whom to support. One group, mainly Lower Creeks, decided to stay friendly with the United States. The Upper Creeks, however, saw the War of 1812 as a chance to get their lands back. They were known as the Red Sticks, because red was the color associated with war.

Jay McGirt, a Muscogee descendant of the original Creeks of Georgia, lives in Oklahoma. He handcrafts authentic native clothing, such as that shown here.

Supplied with British arms, the Red Sticks launched a civil war against fellow Creeks who remained friendly to the United States. Soon, the Creek War spread to attacks against white settlers on the frontier. In 1813, more than 1,000 Red Sticks overran Fort Mims in southern Alabama, killing and scalping 500 people. Among those murdered were innocent white and mixed-blood families who had fled to the fort for safety.

The next year, an army under Gen. Andrew Jackson met the Red Sticks at Horseshoe Bend on the Tallapoosa River in eastern Alabama. Fighting with Jackson were many Cherokees, as well as a force of Lower Creeks led by Chief William McIntosh. Seeking revenge for the Fort Mims **massacre**, Jackson's forces killed about 700 Red Sticks before the day was over.

The Creek War continued, but it was now clear that the Red Sticks had lost. In August 1814, General Jackson called on all Creeks desiring peace to meet him at Fort Jackson in Alabama. Many friendly Creeks came, but only one Red Stick chief. Even though most of those present had been on his side, Jackson forced the Creeks to give up all their land in south Georgia and a large area in eastern Alabama.

Pressure on the Creeks Continues

After the war, the U.S. government encouraged Native Americans to go west to Arkansas and Oklahoma. Those not desiring to go could remain, but they could not continue as separate nations.

Some Creeks accepted the U.S. government's offer of free land to the west of the Mississippi River. Those who remained realized they had too few warriors to hold the land by force. The Creeks began to adopt more and more characteristics of white culture. Less time was spent on hunting and trading, and more on raising crops and livestock. Still, the Creeks were in possession of large portions of Georgia—land the state wanted for white settlement.

Pressured by Georgia's leaders, the U.S. government persuaded the Creeks to cede their lands westward to the Flint River in 1821. This wasn't enough. Georgians reminded the national government of its 1802 promise to remove *all* Indians from the state. The government in Washington tried to bargain with the Native Americans. Most Creeks, however, had decided not to yield any more land.

Chief McIntosh

The Lower Creek towns were led by William McIntosh, one of the five great chiefs of the nation. McIntosh, son of an Indian mother and a Scottish father, was first cousin to Georgia's governor, George McIntosh Troup. The Creek chief was a well-known warrior who had fought under General Jackson against other Creeks at Horseshoe Bend in 1814.

Governor Troup and representatives of the U.S. government believed they could work through Chief McIntosh to get the Creeks to sell their remaining lands. McIntosh is said to have received thousands of dollars for accepting the deal. However, he was unable to persuade other Creek leaders to agree.

Next, McIntosh, whom the Cherokees had made an honorary chief of *their* nation, tried to get the Cherokees to sell their lands. He offered some of the white man's money to Cherokee leader John Ross, who turned him down. The Cherokees warned the Creeks to watch their chief closely.

The warning came too late. On February 12, 1825, Chief McIntosh and a few followers signed a treaty ceding all Creek lands to the United States. As this was done without the support of the Creek people, McIntosh's days were numbered. Years before, the Creek National Council had passed a law condemning to death any chief who sold tribal lands without the council's approval.

Before dawn on May 1, 1825, Creek warriors surrounded Acorn Bluff, McIntosh's home in present-day Carroll County near the Chattahoochee River, and set it on fire. When the chief ran from the burning building, he was shot down and stabbed to death. Several of his followers were also killed.

Governor Troup demanded that the U.S. government honor the treaty signed by McIntosh and remove the Creeks at once. He also

In 1813, Gen. John Floyd and his Georgia militia joined Andrew Jackson in attacking Creeks at the Georgia border.

Born in a Creek village in eastern Alabama in 1804, Osceola joined the Seminoles in Florida. During the second Seminole War, he led his warriors in several successful battles against U.S. troops.

▶ **Locating the Main Ideas**

1. Define: massacre
2. Identify: Red Sticks, Andrew Jackson, William McIntosh, George M. Troup, Osceola
3. What two countries fought the War of 1812? Which side did the Upper Creeks help?
4. After the Creek War, under what condition could the Creeks remain in Georgia?
5. Why was the Seminoles' acceptance of runaway slaves threatening to white Georgians?

directed that the Creek lands be surveyed to prepare for distribution to white Georgians by lottery.

John Quincy Adams, president of the United States, thought the treaty might not be legal and would not enforce it. He threatened to arrest any surveyor found on the Creek lands. But when Governor Troup threatened war with the United States, President Adams backed down. He wanted to avoid any military showdown with Georgia.

So, by new treaties, the United States forced the Creeks to sell their remaining lands in Georgia. By the end of 1827, the Creeks were gone from Georgia. Most of them were removed to Oklahoma, where their descendants (known as Muscogees) still live today.

The Seminoles

Living in southwest Georgia and northern Florida, the Seminoles were a source of constant and grave concern to Georgians. They accepted escaped slaves from Georgia and South Carolina and allowed them to live on their lands in freedom. Sometimes runaway slaves lived together in "maroon camps" on Seminole land.* More often, however, escaped slaves were simply welcomed and lived as new members of the tribe. Intermarriages and close friendships were common, and Black Seminoles—as they were called—were fully accepted as tribal members. By encouraging this practice, the Seminoles threatened the existence of slavery.

White slave owners were angry that the Seminoles would not return their slaves. Making the situation worse, during the War of 1812, Great Britain had encouraged the Seminoles to harass Georgia and Alabama settlements. This led to increasing conflicts between the Seminoles and whites.

Finally, in 1817, American military forces crossed into Florida. U.S. military forces under Gen. Andrew Jackson were victorious in this action known as the First Seminole War. In 1819, Spain ceded Florida to the United States. The Seminoles were forced to move from south Georgia and north Florida to a reservation in central Florida. In 1830, Congress passed the Indian Removal Act, authorizing the removal of all southeastern tribes. The act required the consent of the Native Americans and offered compensation. Whether they consented or not, however, they were forced to move. Lands had been set aside west of the Mississippi River in Oklahoma and Arkansas.

The Seminoles resisted, and the Second Seminole War began. Under Osceola and other Seminole leaders, the war continued from 1835 to 1842. At great cost, the Americans won. As a result, except for 500 Seminoles who escaped to live in the Everglades, the entire Seminole nation was forced to move to Indian Territory in the west.

Next came the Cherokees. ◀

---

*Both the terms "Seminole" and "maroon" are derived from the Spanish word "cimarron," which means wild or runaway.

The Cherokees

The Cherokees lived in the southern ranges of the Appalachian Mountains, extending into four states—Tennessee, North Carolina, Georgia, and Alabama. Living in the mountains, they were out of the main path of white migration to the west. This allowed them to avoid removal longer than the Creeks.

Until the 1790s, the Cherokees frequently went to war—not only against whites but also Creeks. During the American Revolution, they sided with the British. After the war, Cherokee war parties continued their raids on frontier settlements and forts, particularly in Tennessee. In 1793, near the present site of Rome, Georgia, the Cherokees were defeated in their last major battle with American forces. The next year, the United States concluded a peace treaty with the Cherokees. It was the end of a long, bloody era of death and destruction on both sides. The next time the Cherokees took up arms, they sided with the United States during the Creek War of 1813 and 1814.

During the 1700s, the Cherokees, for the most part, lived in "towns" stretching along rivers and streams. Each town, and there were 80 or so, was an independent chiefdom. Only at the end of the century did the Cherokees move towards uniting their towns and people as a nation under a unified government.

The Cherokee nation, 1820–1838. Note that the boundaries of the Cherokee nation overlapped the boundaries of several states.

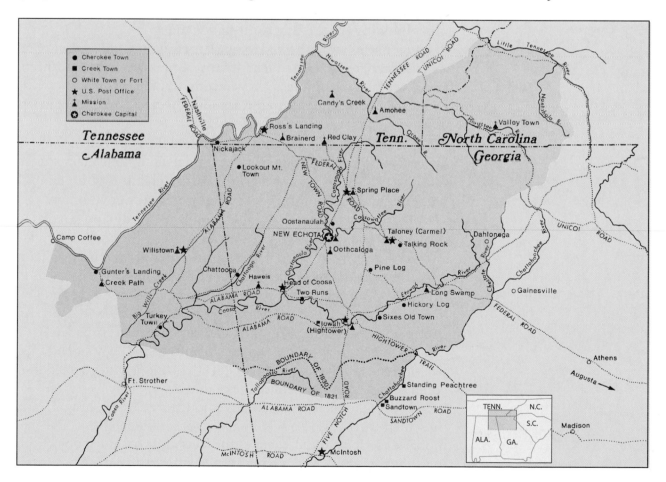

Sequoyah (George Guess), with a copy of the Cherokee syllabary. Although he used many letters of the English alphabet, he also created several unique symbols.

Progress and Setbacks in the Cherokee Nation

In the eyes of many white Americans, the Cherokees were the most "civilized" Indians. Whites considered the Cherokees to be advanced far beyond other tribal groups because they had adopted so much of the white culture.

In the early 1800s, white Americans learned that a Cherokee named Sequoyah [George Guess] was doing something that missionaries and other whites had been unable to do. He was writing and teaching others to write the Cherokee language.

The system taught by Sequoyah was a **syllabary**, not an alphabet. It was a set of written characters, or symbols, used to represent spoken syllables. Using the syllabary was a way to show that the Cherokees didn't need the white's written English.

In an attempt to save their homeland, the Cherokees joined together to form a nation that stretched across four states. New Echota, near present-day Calhoun, became the Cherokee capital. Here, in 1827, the Cherokees wrote a constitution for their nation. Patterned after the U.S. Constitution, it provided for legislative, executive, and judicial branches of government. The nation was divided into eight districts, and each sent elected representatives to the capital.

New Echota also served as the home of the *Cherokee Phoenix,* a bilingual (two language) newspaper. Its printing shop, along with other buildings of the time, still stands today.

Missionaries were allowed to operate churches and schools, and many Cherokees accepted Christianity. In many ways, the Cherokees lived just like whites. They lived in houses and made a living from farming or operating stores, mills, taverns, inns, and ferries. Some became lawyers and teachers.

Although the Cherokee government had the approval of the U.S. government, Georgia refused to recognize it. State leaders argued that the U.S. Constitution prohibited the creation of a "nation" within a state without the approval of that state's government.

In 1828, the Georgia General Assembly decided to put an end to the Cherokee nation. It passed an act extending the laws of the state and the authority of its courts over the Cherokee territory. Cherokee laws were declared "null and void"—that is, of no effect—as of June 1, 1830. The act also provided that no Indian, or descendant of an Indian, could be a witness against a white person in court. An Indian could not bring a lawsuit against a white person.

The Cherokees were outraged. After all, hadn't they signed treaties with the U.S. government? Hadn't the United States agreed they could set up their own government and laws?

In 1829, Cherokee representatives journeyed to Washington and presented their case, known as a Memorial, to Congress. The memorial was a formal statement of the facts and contained objections to actions by the U.S. government. (See pages 148-49.)

ᏣᎳᎩ ᏗᏟᏃᎮᎵ

CHEROKEE PHŒNIX.

VOL. I.   NEW ECHOTA, THURSDAY FEBRUARY 21, 1828.   NO. 1.

EDITED BY ELIAS BOUDINOTT.
PRINTED WEEKLY BY
ISAAC H. HARRIS,
FOR THE CHEROKEE NATION.

At $3.50 if paid in advance, $3 in six months, or $3.50 if paid at the end of the year.

To subscribers who can read only the Cherokee language the price will be $2.00 in advance, or $2,50 to be paid within the year.

Every subscription will be considered as continued unless subscribers give notice to the contrary before the commencement of a new year.

The Phenix will be printed on a Super Royal sheet, with type entirely new procur-

CONSTITUTION OF THE CHE-
ROKEE NATION,
Formed by a Convention of Delegates from the several Districts, at New E-chota, July 1827.

WE, THE REPRESENTATIVES of the people of the CHEROKEE NATION in Convention assembled, in order to establish justice, ensure tranquility, promote our common welfare, and secure to ourselves and our posterity the blessings of liberty; acknowledging with humility and gratitude the goodness of the sovereign Ruler of the Universe, in offering us an opportuni-

readmission. Moreover, the Legislature shall have power to adopt such laws and regulations, as its wisdom may deem expedient and proper, to prevent the citizens from monopolizing improvements with the view of speculation.

ARTICLE II.

Sec. 1. THE POWER of this Government shall be divided into three distinct departments;—the Legislative, the Executive, and the Judicial.

Sec. 2. No person or persons, belonging to one of these Departments, shall exercise any of the powers pro-

---

In March 1829, while Congress considered the Cherokees' request, Andrew Jackson took office as president of the United States. He asked Congress to pass an Indian removal bill, giving him more power in Indian matters.

Jackson also addressed the native people directly. His message, aimed specifically at the Creeks still in Alabama, let Georgia Cherokees know exactly where he stood. Speaking to the Creeks as his "red children," he told them to move to land in the west. Chief Speckled Snake's reply reveals that he no longer trusted President Jackson to keep his promises to native people. ▶

Discovery of Gold Brings Trouble to Cherokees

In 1828, gold nuggets were discovered in several creeks on the eastern boundary of the Cherokee nation. Then came word of gold mines near the present-day site of Dahlonega. The news spread quickly, and by 1829, America's first gold rush was under way. Thousands of gold seekers, many of them wild and lawless men, rushed into north Georgia. The Cherokees appealed to the national government for help. U.S. soldiers were sent in to drive the miners off Indian lands.

Rather than being pleased with the help of federal troops, Georgia officials were upset that the federal government was interfering in state affairs. As of June 1830, the state claimed there no longer was a Cherokee nation. Rather, all territory occupied by the Cherokees was now part of Georgia and subject to its laws. Georgia called on President Jackson to withdraw federal troops from the gold region. The president agreed to allow the state to handle the matter, and the soldiers were pulled out.

Georgia then directed any whites living in the Cherokee country to sign an oath pledging to uphold the laws of Georgia. This law was aimed not at gold miners but at Protestant missionaries living and working among the Cherokees. These missionaries opposed

The **Cherokee Phoenix** *newspaper. Three columns here are printed in English, while one column uses Sequoyah's syllabary. This first edition printed the new Cherokee constitution.*

▶ **Locating the Main Ideas**

1. Define: syllabary
2. Identify: Sequoyah, New Echota, *Cherokee Phoenix*, null and void
3. Why were the Cherokees able to remain in Georgia longer than the Creeks?
4. What reason did Georgia leaders give for refusing to recognize the Cherokee nation?

Conflict Over Indian Lands / 147

The Cherokees State Their Case...
The President Speaks...
The Indians Reply

Memorial

of John Ross and Others, Representatives of the Cherokee Nation of Indians, 20th Congress, 2d Session, March 3, 1829

...We...respectfully and solemnly protest, in behalf of the Cherokee nation, against the extension of the laws of Georgia over any part of our Territory, and appeal to the United States' Government for justice and protection.

The great Washington advised a plan and afforded aid for the general improvement of our

Indian Talk

From the President of the United States [Adapted from *Rural Cabinet,* May 30, 1829, Warrenton, Georgia]

Friends and Brothers—By permission of the Great Spirit above, and the voice of the people, I have been made President of the United States, and now speak to you as your Father and friend, and request you to listen. Your warriors have known me long. You know I love my white and red children, and always speak with a straight, and not with a forked tongue; that I have always told you the truth. I now speak to you, as my children, in the language of truth—Listen....

Where you now are, you and my white children are too near to each other to live in harmony and peace. Your game is destroyed, and many of your people will not work and till the earth. Beyond the great River Mississippi, where a part of your nation has gone, your Father has provided a country large enough for all of you, and he advises you to remove to it. There your white brothers will not trouble you; they will have no claim to the land, and you can live upon it, you and all your children, as long as the grass grows or the water runs, in peace and plenty. It will be yours forever. For the improvements in the country where you now live,

and for all the stock which you cannot take with you, your Father will pay a fair price....

Where you now live your white brothers have always claimed the land. The land beyond the Mississippi belongs to the President and to none else; and he will give it you forever....

Friends and Brothers, listen. This is a straight and good talk. It is for your nation's good, and your Father requests you to hear his counsel.

Signed, ANDREW JACKSON
March 23, 1829

nation, in agriculture, science, and government. President Jefferson followed the noble example, and concluded an address to our delegation, in language as follows: "I sincerely wish you may succeed in your laudable endeavors to save the remnant of your nation by adopting industrious occupations and a *Government of regular law. In this you may always rely on the counsel and assistance of the United States.*" This kind and generous policy to improve our condition has been blessed with the happiest results: our improvement has been without parallel in the history of all Indian nations. Agriculture is everywhere pursued, and the interests of our citizens are permanent in the soil. We have enjoyed the blessings of Christian instruction; and the advantages of education and merit are justly appreciated, a Government of regular law has been adopted, and the nation, under a continuance of the fostering care of the United States, will stand forth as a living testimony that all Indian nations are not doomed to the fate which has swept many from the face of the earth.

Under the parental protection of the United States, we have arrived at the present degree of improvement, and they are now to decide whether we shall continue as a people, or be abandoned to destruction.

In behalf, and under the authority of the Cherokee nation, this protest and memorial is respectfully submitted.

John Ross   Edward Gunter
R. Taylor   William S. Coody

Washington City, February 27, 1829.

Chief Speckled Snake Replies

[Speech made at council of Indian chiefs assembled to have President Jackson's talk read to them, from *Niles' Weekly Register*, June 20, 1829.]

Brothers! We have heard the talk of our great father; it is very kind. He says he loves his red children. *Brothers!* When the white man first came to these shores, the Muscogees gave him land, and kindled him a fire to make him comfortable; and when the pale faces of the south [the Spanish in Florida] made war on him, their young men drew the tomahawk, and protected his head from the scalping knife.

But when the white man had warmed himself before the Indian's fire, and filled himself with the Indian's hominy, he became very large; he stopped not for the mountain tops, and his feet covered the plains and the valleys. His hands grasped the eastern and western sea.

Then he became our great father. He loved his red children; but said, "You must move a little farther, lest I should by accident tread on you." With one foot he pushed the red man over the Oconee, and with the other he trampled down the graves of his fathers.

But our great father still loved his red children, and he soon made them another talk. He said much; but it all meant nothing, but "move a little farther; you are too near me." I have heard a great many talks from our great father, and they all began and ended the same.

Brothers! When he made us a talk on a former occasion, he said, "Get a little farther; go beyond the Oconee and the Oakmulgee; there is a pleasant country." He also said, "It shall be yours forever."

Now he says, "The land you live on is not yours; go beyond the Mississippi; there is game; there you may remain while the grass grows or the water runs."

Brothers! Will not our great father come there also? He loves his red children, and his tongue is not forked.

Interpreting the Source

Analyze the documents by answering the questions for each of the three documents.

1. Identify the author/speaker.

2. Identify the date.

3. Identify the intended audience.

4. Summarize two important points made by each author or speaker.

There's gold in them thar hills!

While stalking deer in the Lumpkin County woods, Benjamin Parks stumbled over a stone of an unusual color. Looking closely, he saw that the stone was gold. That same year, 1828, torrential thunderstorms plowed through the White County region, uprooting trees. Settlers were amazed to find gold nuggets in the roots of a fallen tree. Elsewhere, a glimmering, three-ounce chunk of gold was spotted sparkling in a mountain stream.

One report quickly followed another. The Cherokee hills of North Georgia held gold!

The discovery of gold and the arrival of thousands of miners would seal the fate of the Cherokees and the land they had lived on for generations. In 1838, the Cherokees were permanently removed from Georgia.

Georgia's efforts to take over native land, and urged the Cherokees to resist.

Several white missionaries refused to take Georgia's oath and were arrested. In 1831, they were tried, convicted, and sentenced to four years at hard labor in the Georgia prison at Milledgeville. When Georgia governor, George Gilmer, offered to pardon them, they refused. "After all, if we committed no crime, how could we be pardoned for it?" the missionaries asked.

The missionaries' situation gained national attention. Their case was carried to the U.S. Supreme Court. In 1832, Chief Justice John Marshall announced the Supreme Court's decision: Georgia laws did not apply in the Cherokee nation. The missionaries should be freed.

The Cherokees celebrated. They believed the decision meant that their laws and their nation would be saved. It was not to be.

Georgia's newly elected governor, Wilson Lumpkin, paid no attention to the Supreme Court. President Jackson, no friend of the Cherokees, sided with the state of Georgia. Said the president, "John Marshall has made his decision; now let him enforce it."

The Cherokees and Their Lands Divided

The Cherokee cause now was hopeless. In sadness, they watched as the state surveyed their land, preparing to distribute it to whites in a great land lottery in 1832. Ten counties were mapped out and Governor Lumpkin urged white settlers who had drawn land in the lottery to occupy it. Cherokee families were forced from their homes by the new owners.

Most of the Cherokees continued to resist. Early in 1834, in a statement to President Jackson, they even offered to give up their own government and some of their territory. They wanted only to stay as citizens of the United States. However, Jackson replied, "The only relief for the Cherokees is by removal to the West."

Like the Creeks earlier, the Cherokees were divided. Most followed Chief John Ross in resisting any move west. Another group followed the leadership of Major Ridge, his son John, and Elias Boudinot, the first editor of the *Cherokee Phoenix*. These men sincerely believed it was better for their people to move west.

In 1835, at New Echota, the Cherokee capital, the Ridge **faction** signed a treaty with the United States.* By this treaty, they agreed to give up their lands and move west in return for $5 million. The majority of the nation, led by John Ross, opposed this treaty.

Some Cherokees left for Arkansas across the Mississippi. Those who rejected the New Echota treaty stayed in Georgia. Within a few years, they were driven from their farms by white settlers. They continued to present their case in Washington, with no success.

Total Indian cessions in Georgia, 1733–1836.

The Trail of Tears

In 1838, U.S. Army troops, under Gen. Winfield Scott, rounded up the last 15,000 Cherokees in Georgia. Almost all the Cherokees resisted, and a few did escape to the mountains of western North Carolina.**

Although General Scott ordered his men to treat the Cherokees humanely, many did not. One Georgia soldier wrote many years

---

 *Major Ridge, John Ridge, and Elias Boudinot would later pay with their lives for their role in securing the Treaty of New Echota.

 **Eventually, they were allowed to live there in peace. Today, their descendants live on the Qualla Reservation, just outside Cherokee, North Carolina.

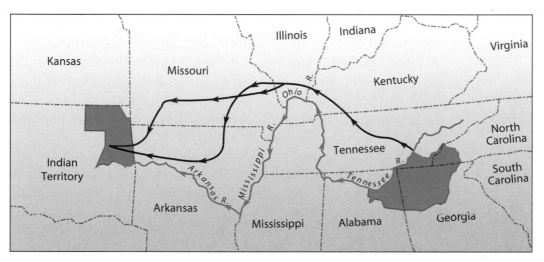

Routes of the Cherokee removal to Oklahoma.

Cherokee Forced Removal, 1838. Leaving behind everything they couldn't carry, the Cherokee people were forced off their historic homelands in the Southeast. Escorted by the U.S. Army, they left for Oklahoma. On the 800-mile journey in the dead of winter, thousands died from cold and disease. The Cherokee would forever remember this as their "Trail of Tears."

later, "I fought through the Civil War, and have seen men shot to pieces and slaughtered by thousands, but the Cherokee removal was the cruelest work I ever knew."

The last group of Cherokees left on November 4, 1838. A young Cherokee leader reported to Chief John Ross the following:

> We are now about to take our final leave and farewell to our native land, the country that the Great Spirit gave our fathers. It is with sorrow that we are forced by the authority of the white man to quit the scenes of our childhood. We bid farewell to the country which gave us birth, and to all that we hold dear.

The Cherokees were forced to march to the west on foot in the dead of winter. Exposed to bitter cold and disease, thousands of men, women, and children died. The Cherokees' suffering was so great that the route they took became forever known as "The Trail of Tears."

At last, total removal of Georgia's Indians was complete. Well, almost complete. In December 1838, the Georgia legislature granted full citizenship to 22 well-to-do Cherokee families of mixed blood. But to continue living on a piece of their land, these families had to buy it back from the fortunate drawers who had won it in the lottery. ◀

▶ **Locating the Main Ideas**

1. Define: faction
2. Identify: John Marshall, John Ross, Treaty of New Echota, Trail of Tears
3. Describe what happened in north Georgia when gold was discovered.
4. Did the Supreme Court rule in favor of the state of Georgia or the Cherokees in the case of the missionaries and the oath?
5. What did Major and John Ridge and Elias Boudinot believe the Cherokees in Georgia should do?

CHAPTER ACTIVITIES

Reviewing the Main Ideas

1. Compare the way Native Americans were treated by the British government during the colonial period to the way they were treated later by the government of the state of Georgia.

2. Why did President Washington appoint a U.S. Indian Agent for Georgia? Why was his job difficult?

3. How did Andrew Jackson reward the Lower Creeks for their assistance during the Creek War?

4. During the War of 1812 how did the British involve the Upper Creeks? the Seminoles?

5. Why was Chief William McIntosh killed by his own people?

6. Why was the development of a syllabary important for the Cherokee people?

7. Describe the government of the Cherokee nation established in 1827.

8. List rights the Georgia General Assembly took away from the Cherokees in 1828.

9. Why did Georgia officials object to U.S. troops protecting Cherokee lands from white gold miners?

10. What happened to the Cherokees who did not leave Georgia under the treaty of 1835 agreed to by Major and John Ridge and Elias Boudinot?

Give It Some Extra Thought

1. **Develop an Outline.** Use the chapter subheads to develop an outline of Georgia's conflict with the Indians under two major headings: I. The Creeks and II. The Cherokees.

2. **Recognizing Differing Positions.** At first the United States and Georgia took different positions toward the Cherokee government. What were they? How did the U.S. government's position change after Jackson became president?

Sharpen Your Skills

1. **Reading a Map.** Using the map of The Creek Confederation: (a) list the names of the Native American tribes; (b) list the names of the states; (c) use cardinal and intermediate directions to describe the relative location of each tribe within the state or states it inhabits; and (d) count the number of cities within Georgia's present-day boundaries.

2. **Map Study.** Use the map of the Cherokee nation, or the map key or legend, to answer the following questions.

Printing press at New Echota State Historic Site.

a. Into what present-day states did the Cherokee nation extend?

b. What are the names of three Cherokee towns, three Creek towns, a white town or fort within the boundaries of the Cherokee nation, the Cherokee capital, and a white mission in each of the four states occupied by the Cherokees?

3. **Understanding Other Viewpoints.** To understand others' points of view, write briefly how you would feel or what you would do if—

a. you were Georgia's governor and citizens were demanding that you get rid of Indians occupying the land they wanted.

b. you were a tribal leader who knew that, no matter what, you and your people eventually would have to leave your traditional lands.

c. you were an army officer who witnessed mistreatment and cruelty toward the Indians on "The Trail of Tears." Some of it was even ordered by your commanding officer.

Going Further

1. **Sequence of Events.** Copy the time line at the opening of the unit. Use information in this chapter to add dates and events in Creek and Cherokee history to the time line.

2. **Write a Headline.** Write a newspaper headline announcing the discovery of gold in Georgia. Write a headline that might have appeared in the *Cherokee Phoenix* the same day.

UNIT 5

GEORGIA EVENTS

1842	1845	1846	1847	1848	1850	1857	1859	1860	1861
Crawford Long first to conduct surgery using ether	Terminus renamed Marthasville	Marthasville linked to Savannah by railroad	Marthasville renamed Atlanta		Joseph E. Brown begins eight years as governor		General Assembly prohibits slaveowners from freeing slaves	Georgians call for secession	Georgia secedes from Union, joins Confederacy
Massachusetts limits child labor	Texas admitted as slave state	United States declares war on Mexico	Frederick Douglass publishes abolitionist newspaper	Gold discovered in California; Mexico cedes lands to United States	Compromise of 1850	Dred Scott decision	John Brown's raid at Harpers Ferry, Virginia	Abraham Lincoln elected president; southern states begin to secede	Confederacy formed; Confederate forces fire on Fort Sumter

EVENTS ELSEWHERE

A Divided Nation
1840–1876

Great Locomotive Chase; Union forces take Fort Pulaski	Battle of Chickamauga; Andersonville prison built	Battle of Atlanta; Sherman's March to the Sea	Reconstruction begins; new state constitution adopted; Thirteenth Amendment ratified		Georgia again under military occupation; blacks vote for first time	New state constitution adopted; Atlanta becomes state capital; Fourteenth Amendment ratified	Military rule returns to Georgia	Fifteenth Amendment ratified; federal troops withdraw; Georgia readmitted to Union	First statewide system of public schools opens
1862	**1863**	**1864**	**1865**	**1866**	**1867**	**1868**	**1869**	**1870**	**1871**
Lincoln issues Emancipation Proclamation	Battle of Gettysburg	Lincoln re-elected president; Grant takes command of Union armies	Confederate armies surrender; Lincoln assassinated	Ku Klux Klan founded in Tennessee		Ulysses Grant elected president	Congress bars Georgia delegation from being seated		Congress investigates KKK

11

Coming Up Next!
- Prosperity in antebellum Georgia
- Antebellum life
- Education, religion, and reform

Life of the People in Antebellum Society

Antebellum, a word that means *before the war,* has a special meaning in American history. It refers to the culture and lifestyle that developed in the South before the Civil War—a way of life quite different from anywhere else in the United States.

Prosperity in Antebellum Georgia

The antebellum period was a time for prosperity in Georgia. In 1790, it was one of the poorest states in the nation. By the 1850s, Georgia was doing so well that it was hailed as the "Empire State of the South."

What caused this change? The two factors most responsible for Georgia's growth were cotton and slavery. But there were other reasons for the state's progress. Georgia's government had encouraged a massive railroad-building program throughout the state, giving it one of the best systems in the Deep South. Other industries were growing too, such as textile mills, lumber yards, leather goods factories, metal works, and stone quarries.

Savannah, with more than 22,000 residents by 1860, was Georgia's largest city and most important industrial center. Its port connected Georgia planters, manufacturers, and merchants with the markets of the North and Europe. Other cities were prospering as well, especially the Fall Line cities of Columbus, Macon, and Augusta. The settlement of Atlanta came later, but it quickly grew as a rail center connecting Georgia to Chattanooga and other cities.

King Cotton Comes to Georgia

Cotton became an important crop in Georgia in the late 1700s. In 1786, sea island cotton from the Bahama Islands was introduced in

State capitol at Milledgeville.

A cotton plantation, with cotton gin and press (far right), planter's home (center), and slave quarters (far left).

Georgia. Sea island cotton—so named because it grew only on sea islands and along the coast—had long fibers and could be woven into soft, high-quality cloth.

Another type of cotton, a short-fiber variety, was a hardy plant that could be grown far inland. This short-fiber variety produced more cotton per acre than sea island cotton. But short-fiber cotton had a major drawback. Its seeds were so tightly entangled with the cotton fiber that it was a very slow process to remove the seeds by hand. The invention of the cotton gin in 1793 speeded up the process dramatically. Soon, cotton was "king" of the crops in Georgia.

Whitney's remarkable **cotton gin** made it possible to grow and process cotton far into the state's interior. All that was needed was well-drained top soil, a growing season of about 200 days without frost, 25 to 45 inches of rainfall each year, and a dry harvest season. These conditions were found in much of Georgia's Piedmont and Coastal Plain. A most suitable combination of soil and climate was present near the Fall Line.

Georgia's Fall Line region attracted cotton planters for another reason. The geography of this area created favorable conditions for industry. As rivers flowed southward through this zone, the water picked up speed. The moving water could then be used to power cotton gins, textile mills, and factories.

The arrival of steamboats in the 1820s provided Georgia planters a better way to transport large quantities of cotton to the ocean port at Savannah. By the 1840s, railroad construction gave planters another option. They no longer had to depend on river transportation. Using the rail lines, they could extend the cotton region far north of the Fall Line into Georgia's Piedmont.

Georgia's Largest Cities (1860)	
Savannah	22,292
Augusta	12,493
Columbus	9,621
Atlanta	9,554
Macon	8,247
Rome	4,010
Athens	3,848

Source: U.S. Census of 1860

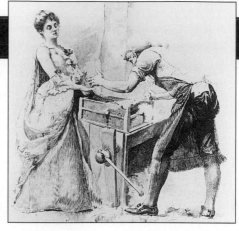

Catharine Greene and Eli Whitney.

The Invention of the Cotton Gin

In the fall of 1792, something happened that would change the future of short-fiber cotton, the future of the South, and indeed the future of the nation. Looking for a tutor for her children, Catharine Greene, widow of General Nathanael Greene, interviewed Eli Whitney, a graduate of Yale College. She was impressed with the 27-year-old New Englander and hired him to work at Mulberry Grove, her plantation just outside Savannah.

Whitney proved to be a man of many talents. One day, after hearing planters talk about the problem of separating cotton seed from the fiber, he began wondering if this could be done mechanically. In the spring of 1793, he completed a model of a special cotton "gin" (short for "engine").

Whitney's invention was a simple machine consisting basically of a roller with wire teeth. When turned by hand, the roller pulled the cotton from the seed, which dropped into a box. To everyone's delight, the gin proved it could do the work of 10 men. But, the wire teeth soon clogged with cotton lint. Mrs. Greene solved the problem, suggesting the teeth be cleaned with the stiff bristles of a fireplace brush. Whitney used her idea to perfect his gin. A row of brushes rotating in the opposite direction proved to be the solution for pulling cotton fiber from the teeth.

Whitney quickly patented his cotton gin. Unfortunately, its simple design was easily copied and Whitney was denied the profits he had expected. He went on to develop and patent a variety of other inventions—but none as famous as his cotton gin.

The success of Whitney's cotton gin lured many people into growing the white fiber plant. But growing cotton was labor intensive, requiring many hours of work. Field hands were needed to plant, hoe, and pick the crop. And it was all done by hand—there were no machines.

To make a profit, a planter needed a ready supply of cheap labor that would work long hours. Slavery filled that need, and cotton planters came to rely on it.

In 1790, only 1,000 bales were produced, mostly of the sea island variety. By 1840 production rose to over 400,000 bales of short-fiber cotton, and by 1860 to over 700,000 bales. ◀

Antebellum Life

Even today, mention of "antebellum Georgia" brings to mind visions of white-columned mansions, wealthy planters, hoop-skirted Southern belles, and cotton fields worked by loyal slaves.

This is the antebellum Georgia of Rhett Butler and Scarlett O'Hara in the famous novel, *Gone with the Wind*. There is evidence—such as the elegant antebellum homes that still stand throughout Georgia—that some people may have lived in such a storybook style. But, for most people—even successful planters—life was far different.

▶ **Locating the Main Ideas**

1. Define: antebellum, cotton gin
2. Identify: "Empire State of the South," King Cotton, sea island cotton, Eli Whitney
3. What were four reasons for Georgia's antebellum prosperity?
4. What geographical conditions were necessary to grow cotton? What special condition existed at the Fall Line that helped the cotton industry?
5. How did the cotton gin and the railroad make it possible for the cotton region to extend into Georgia's Piedmont?

Planters

The elite of Georgia society were the wealthy planters. Out of the nearly 600,000 white Georgians in 1860, fewer than 3,000 could be classified as **planters**. Planters were landholders who owned 20 or more field slaves. They made up the upper social class, along with bankers, lawyers, and merchants. These wealthy, educated people dominated the state's business and government.

Even though they were wealthy, many planters were short on cash. Most of their wealth was tied up in land and slaves, rather than in stocks and bank accounts. Thus, few could afford the costly mansions that many people think of when they imagine life in antebellum Georgia. A typical planter's house was a plain, unpainted, modestly furnished structure. Behind the main house stood the kitchen, smokehouse, barn, grain storeroom, and an outhouse. Farther away were the quarters for the overseer and slaves.

To be successful, a plantation had to be well managed. Planters stayed busy operating their plantations. Most used overseers or trusted slaves to direct the work in the fields. Many planters became community leaders, going on to serve in state government or Congress. The planter's wife supervised much of the day-to-day life on the plantation, which often involved the food, clothing, and health needs of the slaves.

Planters and their families enjoyed a comfortable life. At home there were barbecues and political gatherings to attend. Church activities kept families busy, too. Traveling abroad was a favorite pastime. Frequent visitors—both friends and relatives—sometimes stayed for weeks, and entertaining became a recreation the host and hostess could enjoy along with their guests. Plenty of food was available, and there was music and dancing along with the exchange of news and the latest gossip. Wealthy planters enjoyed outdoor

Occupations of White Georgians, 1860 (in categories totaling more than 2,000)	
Farmers	67,718
Farm Laborers	19,567
Laborers	11,272
Servants	5,337
Overseers	4,909
Clerks	3,626
Carpenters	3,219
Merchants	3,195
Planters	2,858
Factory Hands	2,454
Seamstresses	2,411
Teachers	2,123
Physicians	2,004

Loading cotton onto riverboats. A South Carolina visitor reported, "I arrived in Augusta; and when I saw the cotton wagons in Broadstreet, I whistled! but said nothing!!! But this was not all; there were more than a dozen tow boats in the river, with more than a thousand bales of cotton on each; and several steamboats with still more."

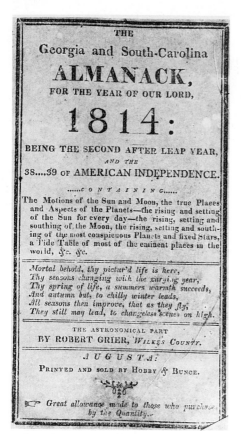

The almanac guided planting with its accurate weather forecasts. It also entertained and educated readers with its jokes, remedies for ailments (including love), recipes, and the names of public officials.

activities such as riding and hunting. Many prided themselves on maintaining libraries filled with classics. Their children, educated in private schools and academies close to home while young, often went elsewhere to finish their education. Sons were sent to colleges, often in the North, while daughters might attend one of the female seminaries (girls' schools) in the state.

Yeoman Farmers

Most white Georgians were middle-class farmers, sometimes called **yeoman farmers**. Owning land, usually less than 100 acres, gave these farmers a strong sense of independence and self-respect. Striving to improve their lives, many yeoman farmers were caught in a cycle of wanting more land and more slaves to produce more cotton to make more money.

As much land as the farmer could cultivate was devoted to cotton, which could readily be sold for cash. Cotton money bought supplies and food items that couldn't be grown at home (such as coffee and sugar) and paid debts and taxes.

For the most part, yeoman farmers grew what they ate, mainly corn, wheat, oats, sweet potatoes, peas, and beans. Chickens, pigs, and cows provided eggs, meat, and milk. The usual dwelling was a log cabin. **Dogtrot** cabins consisted of two connected one-room log structures. The connecting space was covered by the roof and had a floor. This open air breezeway was pleasant in mild or hot weather. Because the farmer's dogs enjoyed the space along with the people, the dwellings were called dogtrot cabins. Another house style that also took advantage of the cooling breezes was the modest frame cottage built a few feet above the ground. Furniture was homemade, as were most clothes, mattresses and quilts, and essential items such as soap. Cooking was done in a fireplace, which also heated the house. Women tended to the domestic chores of cooking, canning, gardening, making clothes, and raising children. Men farmed, supplied the family with meat, and kept the farm buildings repaired.

An agricultural-based economy demanded hard work, but work wasn't the only thing farm families did. They took time for recre-

As Georgia's frontier moved westward, yeoman farmers turned forests into cotton fields. Every able family member was expected to help.

ation such as shooting matches, barbecues, dancing, wrestling and fighting, hunting and fishing, quilting bees, and corn shuckings. The county courthouse was a popular place to meet and socialize.

Poor Whites

At the bottom of white society were the poor whites—those who owned no land and got by the best they could. About 1 in 10 white Georgians was poor. Although they lived all over the state, poor whites were concentrated in the pine barrens of south Georgia and in the mountain regions in the north. They often built crude dwellings on land they didn't own, keeping chickens and a few cattle or hogs. The men hunted and fished to provide meat for the family or to sell for a few extra dollars. Women might raise a little cotton and corn to sell for cash.

Eli Whitney's cotton gin.

Poor whites generally were looked down upon by the rest of society, including slaves. They were characterized as idle troublemakers with little ambition. A poor diet and diseases such as malaria and hookworm, which left victims drained of energy, accounted in part for their condition. Not helping was the fact that they were often illiterate.

Black Georgians

Held at the very lowest level of society were black Georgians, over 99 percent of whom were enslaved. The lives of slaves varied considerably, depending most on their owners and their work assignments.

For slaves who worked cotton, life could be very hard. During the busy season on large plantations, field hands were awakened while it was still dark and expected to dress, eat, and be at work by sunrise. After a midday break for lunch and rest, they returned to working the fields until the sun went down. The only exceptions to this routine were rainy weather, the winter months between seasons, and a few holiday occasions. Except in the busy season, most owners also gave their slaves Saturday afternoon and Sunday off as a time to rest, socialize, or attend church.

Blacks not only worked the fields of the South. Their jobs ranged from house servants, cooks, and nursemaids, to skilled artisans and factory workers. For these slaves, and for the very young and the elderly, life tended to be easier than that of the field hand.

Some owners were very cruel to their slaves, frequently using the whip for discipline. Others cared for their slaves and liked to think of them as members of an extended family. Most owners behaved somewhere between those two extremes. Because so much wealth was tied up in slaves, it was in an owner's best interest to keep them healthy and productive. Still, slaves—especially field hands—with backs scarred from whipping were a common sight in the South.

The cotton gin was used to remove seeds from the cotton lint. Carried in baskets to a cotton press, the lint was packed into bales weighing about 400 pounds each. Most ginning operations could process three or four bales of cotton in a day.

▶ **Locating the Main Ideas**

1. Define: planter, yeoman farmer, dogtrot
2. Identify: Gullah, trickster tales, Joel Chandler Harris
3. Why didn't all antebellum planters live in mansions?
4. How did poor whites make a living?
5. What problems did free blacks face in antebellum Georgia?

No matter how the master treated his slaves, or how easy or difficult the work, slavery was degrading for it deprived blacks of their freedom and fundamental human rights. Under Georgia law, slaves had no political or civil liberties. Though laws protected them against excessive discipline or murder by owners, these were hard to enforce, especially since slaves could not testify against whites in court. Nonetheless, many found ways to resist.

Because each slave was considered a separate piece of property, legal marriages between slaves were not recognized in antebellum Georgia. Many owners, however, allowed informal marriages. Slave families always ran the risk of being split up, and sometimes were. Most slaveholders had little available money in the bank. If an emergency arose, selling a slave was the quick—and sometimes only—way to raise cash.

In addition to almost half a million blacks who were slaves, about 3,500 free blacks were living in Georgia by the end of the antebellum era. Most had been granted freedom by their owners, though a few had managed to purchase their freedom. Free blacks usually lived in cities, where they had the best chance of earning a living. However, they faced a difficult situation. Free blacks with skilled jobs were criticized for taking jobs away from whites. Those unable to find jobs were accused of being lazy. Whites also worried that free blacks secretly were helping their enslaved brothers and sisters escape to freedom.

In an effort to control the free black population, state law required all free blacks to register in their county of residence. An 1819 report from Richmond County shows a total of 194 free black men, women, and children living there. Most of the women listed their occupations as sewing and washing. The men reported a wider variety of occupations, including steamboat pilot, barber, saddle maker, carpenter, and laborer.

Even though the white society held tight control over slaves and even free blacks, the black community made many contributions to southern life. West African traditions combined with southern lifestyles to create a unique black culture. Slaves living along the coast of Georgia and South Carolina created a new language, known as Gullah, that can still be heard today. The words of Gullah are English, but the way words are put together in sentences is African.

Skills such as woodcarving, basketmaking, and quilting were done in the African style but adapted to the materials available. Okra, black-eyed peas, and distinctive ways of cooking and flavoring foods became part of southern menus. Slaves told animal trickster tales learned in Africa to teach lessons of how cleverness can outwit a stronger opponent. Later those tales were recorded by Joel Chandler Harris as Uncle Remus and Brer Rabbit stories. Music in the form of spirituals, rhythm songs, and the development of the banjo were among other contributions of the black community in antebellum Georgia. ◀

SKILL ACTIVITY

Interpreting Data

Georgia's Slave Population

During the antebellum period, the number of slaves in Georgia increased greatly. By the end of that era, Georgia had a very large slave population, ranking only behind Virginia in total number. According to the U.S. Census of 1860, Georgia's population consisted of 591,588 whites (including 38 Indians), 462,198 slaves, and 3,500 free blacks. Almost half of the state's residents were of African descent.

Georgia's Slave Population

1790	29,264
1800	59,406
1810	105,218
1820	149,654
1830	217,531
1840	280,944
1850	381,682
1860	462,198

However, the majority of Georgians did not own slaves. The 1860 census counted 118,000 white families living in Georgia. Of these, only 41,084 families owned slaves. Two out of every three slaveholding families owned fewer than 10 slaves, and many only 1 or 2. Owning large numbers of slaves was the exception.

Slave Ownership in Georgia, 1860

Number of Slaveholding Families	Number of Slaves Owned
11,068	1-2
9,009	3-5
7,114	6-9
7,530	10-19
5,049	20-49
1,102	50-99
181	100-199
23	200-299
7	300-499
1	500+

Source: U.S. Census of 1860

Sharpen Your Skills

1. What percentage of white families in Georgia owned slaves in 1860?

2. How many cases were reported by the census bureau of a family owning 100 or more slaves?

3. Compare the slave population map with the cotton production map. What do the maps tell you about slavery and cotton production? In what areas of the state was slavery least important? Why? Where is the heaviest concentration of slaves found? Why?

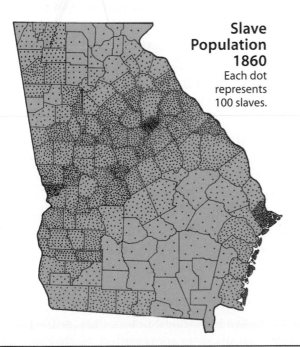

Slave Population 1860
Each dot represents 100 slaves.

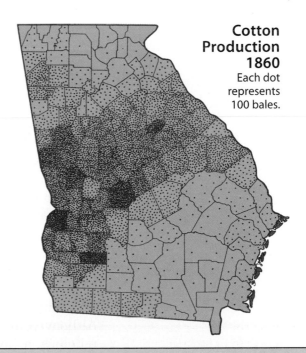

Cotton Production 1860
Each dot represents 100 bales.

Wesleyan College in Macon was one of the first women's colleges in America.

Education, Religion, and Reform

Education

Although Georgia's first constitution called for schools in each county, the legislature did not provide enough money to set up a true public school system for the whole state. At the same time, Georgians did not demand public schools for their children. Education, in the minds of antebellum Georgians, was best left for individuals, rather than government, to provide. The need for children to work in the fields, the wide distribution of the population, and the poor condition of roads tended to keep education a low priority.

In 1817, the legislature attempted to provide a few years of public education for needy children by creating a "poor school fund." Many Georgians, however, were too proud to let their children attend state-supported poor schools. In rural areas, farmers built one-room schools in old abandoned cotton fields and paid someone to teach. Unfortunately, most teachers in these "old field schools" were not very well qualified and children received only a very basic education. An effective statewide education system never really developed. As late as 1850, one out of five white adults in Georgia was illiterate. Throughout the antebellum period, the best educational opportunities went to children whose families could afford to send them to private schools and academies.

Higher education fared better in Georgia. In 1785, the General Assembly had chartered the University of Georgia—the nation's first state university. Classes did not begin until 1801, but soon the university at Athens was graduating men who would lead the state in business and politics. Women would not be permitted to enroll until 1918. The university added a school of law in 1859 under the guidance of Joseph Henry Lumpkin and Thomas R. R. Cobb.

The Medical College of Georgia was established in 1828 in Augusta. Formal training for doctors was just beginning. Epidemic diseases such as cholera and malaria were still uncontrolled. Other diseases, infections, and even pregnancy were a constant threat to the lives of Georgians.

Various religious denominations established and supported colleges in the state. Emory College in 1836 was Methodist supported; the Presbyterians set up Oglethorpe College in 1835; and in 1837, the Baptists established Mercer University.

One of the first women's colleges in the country was the Georgia Female College, later called Wesleyan Female College, in Macon. Classes began in 1839 and soon women were earning college degrees there.

Religion

Although not all Georgians in the period before the Civil War were religious, many denominations were represented. Early Protestant

A backcountry camp meeting could be an intense religious experience, with fiery preaching continuing for days.

denominations in the state included Presbyterian, Episcopalian, Lutheran, Moravian, and Baptist. A Jewish congregation in Savannah dated back to the colony's first year. Catholics had come to Georgia in 1796, most of them originally settling in Wilkes County.

In the early 1800s, a Protestant religious movement called the Great Revival swept the South. Through camp meetings and revivals, thousands of Georgians, both black and white, were attracted and converted. Church membership increased greatly and new churches were established—the majority of them Baptist or Methodist. At the beginning of the nineteenth century, many churches had preached equality and denounced slavery. By the 1830s, however, slavery was being defended more and more from the pulpit. Baptist and Methodist denominations eventually broke away from their northern counterparts over the issue.

Most slaves, if they attended church at all, did so with their masters. However, for many, religion meant secret and generally forbidden meetings in the slave quarters. There, they looked to the time when they would reach the promised land and be delivered from bondage.

During the antebellum period, separate black churches—primarily Baptist—were founded in some Georgia cities. The African Methodist Episcopal (AME) and African Methodist Episcopal Zion (AME Zion) denominations, first established in the North, were opposed to slavery. As such, their existence in the South was limited and their real growth didn't occur until after the Civil War.

Crawford W. Long

When you were younger, you may have had your tonsils removed and stayed overnight in a hospital, waking with a sore throat—but with no memories of the actual surgery. You experienced no pain during the operation because you were given a strong, pain-killing drug called an anesthetic. The first of these substances was ether, and its unique properties were demonstrated in 1842 by Georgia native Crawford W. Long.

Before Dr. Long's revolutionary discovery, surgery was a very painful and often hurried procedure. Patients sometimes drank large quantities of alcohol to dull the pain, and doctors rushed through their work while their patients were unconscious. People often passed out from pain and even died from shock. Ether, Dr. Long observed, allowed people to endure pain without realizing it—by numbing their senses and memory. Doctors could perform longer, more complicated operations, knowing their patients wouldn't wake suddenly.

Born in Danielsville in 1815, Dr. Long enjoyed a prosperous career as a surgeon, beginning with a practice in Jefferson, moving to Atlanta and finally relocating in Athens, where he died in 1878. His moment in medical history occurred in his Jefferson office, when he was only 26. After giving a patient a dose of ether, he removed two cysts from the patient's neck. When the man regained consciousness, Dr. Long learned his patient neither felt nor remembered any pain.

Being a humble man who considered himself a simple country doctor, Dr. Long did not publicize his findings and thus did not receive proper credit until some 30 years after his historic operation. Today, however, Crawford W. Long is honored as one of Georgia's most distinguished citizens.

Southern Reforms

During the antebellum period, Georgia and other southern states began to take a more humane approach in dealing with criminals and the needy. In 1816, the state enacted a new code of laws abolishing cruel punishments. No longer would white men be whipped or have their hands and heads locked in the pillory for crimes such as theft. In 1817, the state opened a penitentiary (so called because the prisoners locked up there would have time to repent for their crimes). The next year the state began to furnish prisoners in county jails with clothing, blankets, heat, and medical attention. Later in 1823, a law was passed that made it more difficult to put people in prison for not paying their debts.

The state also began taking care of its needy. An asylum for the insane was opened in 1842 at Milledgeville. Formerly, mentally ill and retarded persons were thrown in jail with criminals. Five years later, a school for deaf persons was opened at Cave Springs. In 1852, the state took over responsibility for helping blind persons at the Georgia Academy for the Blind in Macon.

By the end of the antebellum period, state government was slowly moving to a more active role in society. Earlier it had begun to promote economic development and transportation. Now, Georgia was working to improve the welfare of its people. ◄

▶ **Locating the Main Ideas**

1. Identify: old field schools, Crawford Long, Joseph Henry Lumpkin, T.R.R. Cobb, Wesleyan College
2. What conditions kept education a low priority in antebellum Georgia?
3. Why did the number of Methodist and Baptist churches in Georgia increase?
4. What were some of the reforms that brought about improvements in the way criminals were treated?

CHAPTER ACTIVITIES

Reviewing the Main Ideas

1. How did Georgia progress from one of the poorest states in the nation in 1790 to one of the more prosperous states by 1850?

2. Explain how the cotton gin brought about a revolution in Georgia agriculture.

3. Why was cotton a labor intensive crop in antebellum Georgia?

4. Even though antebellum planters were wealthy, why did they often have a shortage of cash in the bank?

5. Give two examples of how yeoman farmers were self-sufficient.

6. What conditions kept poor whites at the bottom of white society?

7. Describe some of the hardships faced by blacks under slavery.

8. Give three adjectives to describe each group within antebellum society: planters, yeoman farmers, poor whites, slaves, free blacks.

9. Why weren't public schools established as called for in Georgia's first constitution?

10. Why were the lives of Georgians endangered by diseases, infection, and even pregnancy?

Give It Some Extra Thought

1. **Identifying Results.** Explain the effect of the invention of the cotton gin on Georgia's economy.

2. **Apply What You Know.** What changes over the period 1800 to 1830 would cause southern churches to change their position from denouncing slavery to supporting it?

Sharpen Your Skills

1. **Comparing Population Data.** Use the map on page 9 and list in order, from largest to smallest, the 11 Georgia cities with 40,000+ or more inhabitants. Compare it to the 1860 city population list in this chapter. What city is on the 1860 list but not on your list? Do the three most populated cities in 1860 still rank as the three most populous after Atlanta in 1996? What cities are on the 1996 list that are not on the 1860 list?

2. **Relating Past to Present.** Review the table of occupations identified by the U.S. Census Bureau in 1860. Identify three occupations that you would likely not find on the census today and explain why.

Going Further

1. **Explaining.** Write a paragraph using the following topic sentence: "Slavery was like being in a jail with no walls."

2. **Relating Past to Present.** Look through a copy of a recent farmer's almanac and list three general topics covered in the almanac. Do you think the almanac has changed much since the days of the antebellum farmer? Do farmers today still use the almanac to decide when to plant and harvest their crops? Explain.

Liberty Hall, the plantation home of Alexander Stephens in Crawfordville, Taliaferro County. His plantation had over 1,000 acres and was worked by 30 slaves.

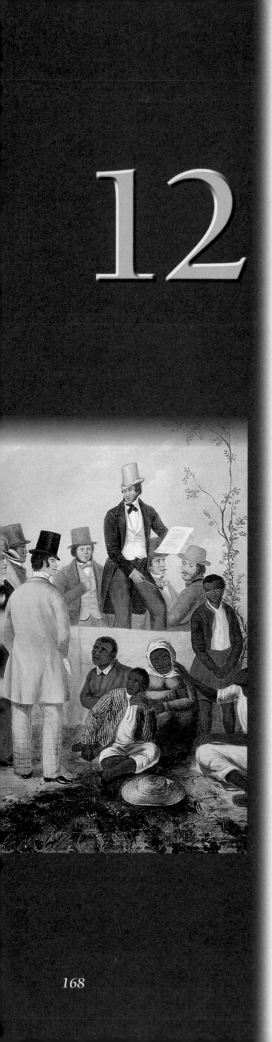

12

A Nation Comes Apart

By 1860, differences between the South and other parts of the nation were so great that the United States was on the verge of being torn apart. What was it that made Georgia and other southern states so different from the North and West? The obvious answer was slavery, but there were other things as well.

Economic Differences

In the early 1800s, both the northern and southern sections of the United States had mixed economies, that is, some agriculture and some industry. But because of its rocky soil and colder climate, the North could not rely heavily on farming. Increasingly, northern states turned to industry, especially after development of the steam engine and the factory system. The North had the advantage of swift rivers and waterfalls to power its mills and factories, and natural harbors for conducting foreign trade.

Meanwhile, the South's warmer climate and fertile topsoil encouraged an agrarian (agricultural) economy. Tobacco had been the first important crop. Corn, rice, indigo, and naval stores were among the cash crops well suited to the southern climate. In the 1790s, the invention of the cotton gin tied southerners even more closely to the land. Soon, cotton was "king," its value commanding respect at home and abroad.

Urban North, Rural South

In the North, the rise of an industrial economy led to the growth of cities. Families moving from farms to work in city factories found they could no longer be self-sufficient. In the city, there wasn't room for each family to have its own cows, pigs, sheep, and chickens for

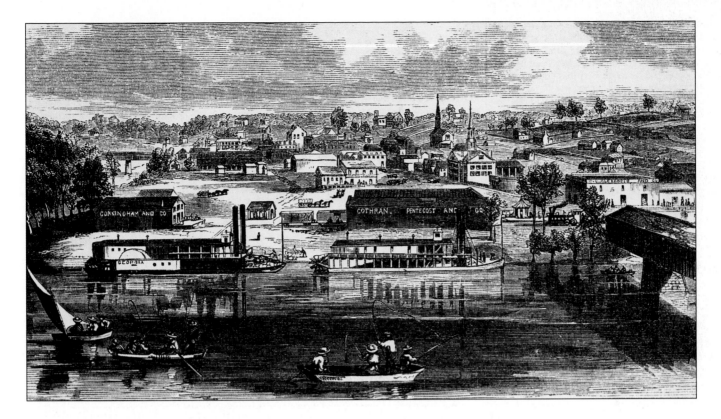

Rome, Georgia, 1856. As the county seat, Rome could claim a courthouse along with three churches, Odd Fellows and Masonic halls, schools, covered bridges, and numerous businesses.

food. Besides, neighbors would complain about the noise and smell. Nor could you cut down city trees for firewood. Urban residents, therefore, tended to be **interdependent**—that is, dependent on one another for various needs, such as food, shelter, and clothing. Meat came from a butcher, milk from a dairy, and coal or firewood from a dealer. In the developing cities of the North, people also came to expect more from government, such as police and fire protection.

The agricultural South, in contrast, had few factories and jobs to attract workers to cities. Most people lived in the country, where they provided for themselves—usually by farming, raising poultry and livestock, hunting, and fishing. For this reason, southerners tended to expect little in the way of services from government. Thus, people in the South were more isolated and independent than in the North. ▶

Growing Regional Differences

Because their economies were different, the North and the South were not affected by events in the same way. For example, a government policy or business boom might help one region and hurt the other.

By the 1820s and 1830s, political leaders in northern and southern states increasingly looked at issues in terms of how they affected their particular region—or section—rather than the nation as a whole. Placing sectional interests above national ones is called **sectionalism**.

▶ **Locating the Main Ideas**

1. Define: interdependent
2. What conditions caused the North to develop an economic base different from the South?
3. Why were northern cities larger and more populated than southern ones?

View of Utica, New York, around the 1850s. How is Utica different from Rome, Georgia?

Often, politicians made decisions more as northerners or southerners than as Americans. This sectional approach to national policy became evident in the issues of tariffs, states' rights, the settling of the West—but most of all, in the issue of slavery.

Tariffs

A **tariff** (also called a "duty") is a tax that one country places on goods imported from other countries. Tariffs can be an important source of government revenue. They also can be used to protect a nation's industries from foreign competition.

For example, a tariff on steam engines imported from Great Britain made them more expensive to sell in America. The tariff could be set so as to make British steam engines more expensive than American engines. If a British and an American engine were of similar quality, buyers would likely choose the cheaper one. A tariff thus allowed U.S. manufacturers to sell more goods and improve their profits.

To protect their industries against British competition, northern business leaders favored high protective tariffs. Southerners, however, did not. First, there were few industries in the South to protect. Second, southern planters and merchants had a healthy trade with Great Britain, and they didn't want to pay higher prices for British goods just to protect northern businesses. Third, American tariffs on cotton clothing imported from England meant higher prices, which cut demand. The result was that British manufacturers imported less cotton from the South. Finally, American tariffs caused other countries to place similar tariffs on American exports.

Moderate tariffs were one thing, but in 1828 Congress passed a huge increase for tariffs on imported goods. Four years later, Con-

The following **conversation** took place between Mrs. Lyell, an Englishwoman, and the landlady of a Milledgeville hotel. It was recorded by Charles Lyell, a geologist visiting Georgia in 1846.

Economics in Action– Two Views

COLGATE & CO. CASHMERE BOUQUET ☆ TOILET SOAP ☆

Interdependency   Self-Sufficiency

Among other inquiries, she said to my wife, "Do tell me how you make your soap in England."

Great was her surprise to hear that ladies in that country were in the habit of buying the article in shops, and would have been much puzzled if called upon to manufacture it for themselves. She looked upon this fine-lady system of purchasing every article at retail stores as very extravagant.

"That's the way they do in the north," said she, "though I never could understand where all their money comes from."

She then explained how economically she was able to supply herself with soap.

"First, there is the wood, which costs nothing but the trouble of felling the trees; and, after it has served for fuel, it yields the ashes, from which we get the potash. This is mixed with the fat of sixty hogs, which costs nothing, for what else could I do with all this fat at killing time? As for the labor, it is all done by my own people. I have nine maids, and they make almost every thing in the house, even to the caps I wear."

Interpreting the Source

1. How does Mrs. Lyell get her soap? How does the landlady get her soap?

2. What does the landlady think of the way Mrs. Lyell gets soap?

3. According to the landlady, who else gets soap the way Mrs. Lyell does?

4. Which woman, the landlady or Mrs. Lyell, is an example of an independent lifestyle? How?

gress lowered tariffs on some imports but raised them on others. Many Southerners were angry and complained bitterly that southern rights were being sacrificed to northern business interests. Feeling was so strong in the South that some politicians talked of ignoring the new laws.

Eventually, rates were lowered—but by the 1830s the tariff issue had become a major factor in the emergence of southern sectionalism.

States' Rights

Dispute over tariffs fueled another burning issue. Under our federal system of government, what rights and powers belonged to the states? The question of how much power the national government should have over the states had been debated during the Constitutional Convention of 1787. Everyone agreed that in ratifying the U.S. Constitution, the states delegated certain powers to the federal government. But, did the states retain all powers not specifically granted to the new national government? Americans differed on this question. They also differed on the question of whether states which voluntarily entered the federal union could voluntarily leave it.

John C. Calhoun, the senator from South Carolina, believed states could nullify federal laws.

The belief that states are **sovereign**—that is, subject to no higher power except for powers specifically granted to the national government in the U.S. Constitution—came to be known as **states' rights**. The term "states' rights" became widely used throughout the South in the early 1800s. Georgia even had a political party in the 1830s known as the State Rights Party.

Southerners generally favored the doctrine of states' rights, though that view was less popular in the mountain regions of Georgia, Tennessee, and the Carolinas. Some believed so strongly in states' rights that they argued states have the power of **nullification**—the right to determine if a law passed by Congress is constitutional or not. If a state believes that a federal law violates the U.S. Constitution, then it can declare such law "null and void" (without force) within that state.

In the North, there was much less support for states' rights. Most northern leaders opposed the theory of nullification, arguing that only the U.S. Supreme Court can declare a law unconstitutional.

The strongest support for nullification came from South Carolina. There, a special convention in 1832 went so far as to nullify the tariffs of 1828 and 1832 and discuss **secession**—withdrawing from the Union. Many Georgians wanted to join South Carolina but found themselves in a difficult position. Pres. Andrew Jackson, who was popular in Georgia because of his removal of the Cherokees, strongly opposed nullification. Also, at the same time, many Georgians—particularly in the mountain regions of the state—felt a strong desire to stay within the Union. So, Georgia backed away from nullification.

Another states' rights issue dividing the nation was disagreement over the nature of the Union. Many southern politicians argued that the U.S. Constitution was a compact, or agreement, among independent states. Just as states had voluntarily joined that compact, they could voluntarily leave, or **secede**, in order to protect their rights. Most northerners, on the other hand, argued that secession was illegal.

The West

Another point of sectional conflict was the United States' territories in the West. A **territory** was a frontier area that belonged to the United States but had not yet become a state. As the United States acquired vast areas of land, the North and South developed different ideas about the future of the new territories. Who should settle there? How quickly would they be developed? Under what conditions would they be admitted to the Union? As states, would they line up politically with the North or the South?

The western territories, with their rich prairie soils, good climate, and great rivers, were well suited to growing and transporting grain, corn, and other agricultural products. People from both the North and the South were eager to make use of the region.

Generally, southerners favored distributing western lands as cheaply as possible. This way, they could develop them quickly into large agricultural holdings like those in the South. Northerners preferred that the U.S. government sell the public lands at a good price in order to bring in revenue. Some northern factory owners feared losing workers if the West were made too attractive to settlers.

Northerners tended to favor the idea of developing the West, which included building roads and canals, at government expense. Southern leaders opposed such activities by the national government and didn't want to be taxed in any way to support them.

As the West grew, its inhabitants developed their own sectional views. Some of the settlers in the West were from the North and some from the South. Views of the settlers there were mixed. Their main differences were over the biggest question splitting North and South—slavery. ▶

▶ **Locating the Main Ideas**

1. Define: sectionalism, tariff, sovereign, states' rights, nullification, secession, secede, territory
2. Why did high protective tariffs hurt southerners more than northerners?
3. What was the southern justification for secession?
4. Why did northern factory owners favor making it more difficult for settlers to obtain land in the western territories?

Slavery Divides the Nation

Many issues divided the North and South. But no matter what the issue, slavery always entered in. Whether Americans argued about states' rights, the powers of the national government, or the future of the West, slavery was part of the debate.

Slavery had a long history in America—not just in the South. Every colony had allowed slavery, although officially the practice was banned in Georgia until 1749. Even though the Declaration of Independence proclaimed that "all men are created equal," it contained no prohibition on slaveholding. All of the 13 new states allowed the practice to continue.

In 1780, Pennsylvania and Massachusetts became the first states to **emancipate**, or free, their slaves. Four years later, Connecticut and Rhode Island took similar action. Soon, other northern states would follow. These were states with industry and small-scale farming, not plantation agriculture, as their economic base. Pro-slavery factions were not powerful in these states, and the arguments against slavery prevailed.

Emancipation by the States
1777 Vermont (prior to statehood)
1780 Pennsylvania and Massachusetts
1784 Connecticut and Rhode Island
1792 New Hampshire
1799 New York
1804 New Jersey

Westward Expansion of Slavery

After signing the new U.S. Constitution, both northern and southern states began thinking about the large, unsettled territory to the west of the Appalachian Mountains. One day, new states would be created from this territory. Would they be free states friendly to the North or slave states friendly to the South? For the next 73 years, this became a great debate dividing the Union.

In America, there was broad support for settlement of the frontier territories. The Constitution provided a procedure for Congress to create new states from these territories. Once admitted, a new state was on equal footing with the 13 original states. This meant

Using Primary Sources

In order to explain past events, historians must analyze and evaluate information available about the events. In the case of a primary source, the historian asks, "What is the frame of reference of the eyewitness? Are there differing interpretations of the same event? Is there enough information to form a conclusion or generalization?" Below are two primary sources, both written in the 1850s, discussing the issue of slavery. Read the sources, then use the historian's approach to analyze and evaluate the information.

Slave Life in Georgia

When **nearly 10 years old**, John Brown was separated from his mother and sold to a planter in Baldwin County, Georgia. He endured slavery for 30 years before escaping through the Underground Railroad, first to Canada and then to England. He dictated his memoirs to Louis Alexis Chamerovzow, secretary of the British and Foreign Anti-Slavery Society. He published a narrative of his life in 1855.

John Brown

When I think of all I have gone through, and of the millions of men, women, and children I have left behind me in slavery, I ask myself when this is all to end? and how it is to be ended?

Slavery is kept up entirely by those who make it profitable as a system of labor. Cruelty is inseparable from slavery, as a system of forced labor; for it is only by it, or through fear of it, that enough work is got out of slaves to make it profitable to keep them.

It is not true—so far as my experience goes—to say that the masters treat their slaves well, because it is their interest to do so. The cattle are better treated than we are. They have warm stables to lie down in; they are tended and regularly fed, and get plenty to eat; their owners know that if they overwork them they will die. But they never seem to know when we are overworked, or to care about it when they do know. If we fall off our work, they call us idle, and whip us up to their mark. They seem to act only on the principle that there are no bounds to human endurance.

Our huts are only of logs, with a flooring of mud. The wind and the rain come in, and the smoke will not go out. We are indifferently clad, being nearly naked half our time, and our doctor, when we are sick, is generally some old "Aunt" or "Uncle" who has "caught" a little experience from others; and that not of the best. Our food is insufficient, and of bad quality. If we did not steal, we could scarcely live.

I have heard long preachments from ministers of the Gospel to try and show that slavery is not a wrong system. Somehow, they could not fix it right to my mind, and they always seemed to me to have a hard time bringing it right to their own. I kept in my mind the death-bed scenes I have witnessed of slaveholders, who were cruel to their slaves, but when the dark hour came, could not leave the world without asking pardon of those they had ill-used. It is a common belief amongst us that all the masters die in an awful fright, for it is usual for the slaves to be called up on such occasions to say they forgive them for what they have done. So we come to think their minds must be dreadfully uneasy about holding slaves, and therefore there cannot be any good in it.

A Defense of Slavery

Thomas R.R. Cobb, a prominent lawyer in the 1850s, helped found Georgia's first law school at Athens. He was a leader in a move to have Georgia leave the Union and later wrote the Confederate States Constitution.

...[S]lave labor is the only effective, and therefore cheapest, labor which the Southern States can use in the production of their staples [major crops]. Experience, in the South, has shown this to be true in the building of railroads. Slave labor must be used successfully on uniform work, requiring physical strength without judgment or discretion. Wherever such work can be found in the Southern climate, slave labor is the cheapest that can be applied.

As a social relation negro slavery has its benefits ....That the slave is incorporated into and becomes a part of the family, that a tie is then formed between the master and slave, almost unknown in the relation of master and hireling [hired worker] ...that the old and infirm are thus cared for, and the young protected and reared, are indisputable facts. Interest joins with affection in promoting this unity of feeling.

To the negro, it insures food, fuel, and clothing, medical attention, and in most cases religious instruction. The young child is seldom removed from the parents' protection, and beyond doubt, the institution [slavery] prevents the separation of families, to an extent unknown among the laboring poor of the world. It provides him with a protector, whose interest and feeling combine in demanding such protection.

To the master, it gives a servant whose interests are identical with his own, who has indeed no other interest, except a few simple pleasures....

So long as climate and disease, and the profitable planting of cotton, rice, tobacco, and cane, make the negro the only laborer inhabiting our Southern savannas [grasslands] and prairies, just so long will he remain a slave to the white man....

Thomas R.R. Cobb

Practice Your Skills

1. **Frame of Reference.** Each individual's frame of reference is based on his or her experiences and beliefs. Identify the authors of each source and list information about the author that shapes his frame of reference. Given what you know about each person, do their views surprise you?

2. **Differing Interpretations of the Same Event.** A frame of reference may influence or bias the way an individual interprets events. Because frames of reference vary, interpretations of the same event may differ. Compare the interpretations of slave life that Brown and Cobb have by listing their views on food, health care, and clothing for slaves.

3. **Making Generalizations.** When historians have examined the sources and considered the biases of the authors, they are ready to make generalizations. Using just two sources, particularly where they represent opposing views, would not be enough on which to base a generalization. Would all planters agree with Cobb? Would all slaves agree with Brown? What types of historical information would help you make a valid generalization about slavery conditions in Georgia?

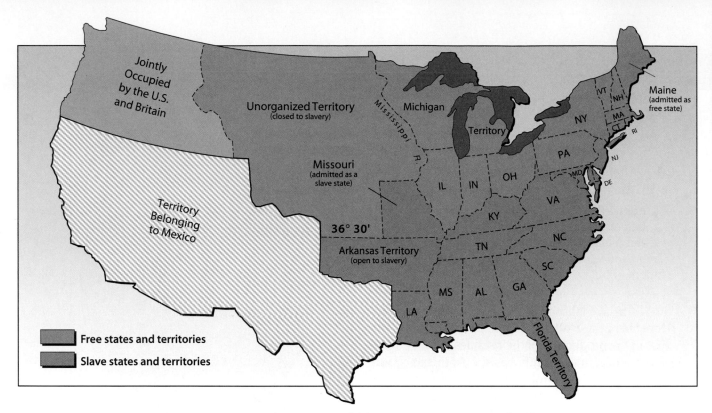

Jointly Occupied by the U.S. and Britain

Unorganized Territory (closed to slavery)

Michigan Territory

Mississippi R.

Missouri (admitted as a slave state)

Territory Belonging to Mexico

36° 30'

Arkansas Territory (open to slavery)

NY

PA

IL IN OH

VA

KY

TN

NC

SC

MS AL GA

LA

VT NH MA CT RI

NJ MD DE

Maine (admitted as free state)

Florida Territory

Free states and territories

Slave states and territories

The Compromise of 1820. What part of the Louisiana Territory (the far west was not yet part of the United States) was to be open to slavery? What part was closed to it?

each state would have two senators and at least one representative in the U.S. Congress. For Georgia and other southern states to maintain a balance of power in the national government, at least half of the number of new states would have to allow slavery.

At first, the North and South were able to agree on admitting new states while keeping a balance in Congress. When Alabama joined the Union in 1819, the count was 11 slave states and 11 free states. By then, most of America between the Atlantic Ocean and the Mississippi River was organized into states. The next question centered on the future of slavery in the area acquired in the Louisiana Purchase—the vast territory west of the Mississippi River purchased from France in 1803.

Missouri Compromise

No sooner had Alabama become a state than the Missouri Territory (part of the Louisiana Purchase) applied for admission to the Union —as a slave state. Northern congressmen immediately protested, since this would upset the balance between free and slave states. In fact, some northerners wanted to prohibit creation of *any* slave states west of the Mississippi.

In 1820, Congress agreed to a compromise. Maine would be admitted as a free state, and Missouri as a slave state. In the future, slavery would be prohibited north of latitude 36°30′. This had been the latitude picked by King Charles in 1665 as Carolina's northern boundary. Now, it also marked slavery's northern boundary in the western territories.

The South soon realized that the Compromise of 1820 threatened the balance between slave and free states. Unless additional territories in the West could be gained from Mexico, the only area in which to expand slavery was the Arkansas Territory. In contrast, a sizeable expanse of America lay north of 36°30' for creation of numerous free states.

Compromise of 1850

In the 1840s, as the United States gained territory as far as the Pacific Ocean, northerners and southerners fiercely debated the westward expansion of slavery. After Texas had won its independence from Mexico, many southerners moved there with their slaves. In 1845, Texas was admitted as a slave state.

The following year, the United States and Mexico were at war, a conflict ending two years later with an American victory. In defeat, Mexico agreed to cede the vast area between Texas and the Pacific Ocean—522,568 square miles—to the United States for $15 million.

A few years later, gold was discovered in California. "Forty-niners" (so called because of the 1849 gold rush) seeking their fortunes streamed into the territory, which then applied for admission to the Union.

In Georgia, state lawmakers talked of secession if California were allowed to join the ranks of free states. In Congress, however, Georgia's representatives favored moderation. A Georgian, Howell Cobb, was then speaker of the U.S. House of Representatives. Cobb and fellow Georgians Alexander Stephens and Robert Toombs helped win passage of a compromise offered by Sen. Henry Clay of Kentucky.

The Compromise of 1850. The expansion of U.S. boundaries to the Pacific Ocean reopened the debate over extending slavery into western territories.

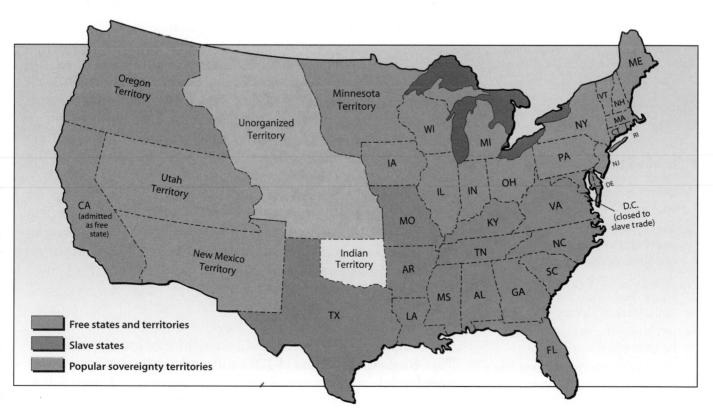

- Free states and territories
- Slave states
- Popular sovereignty territories

Georgian Howell Cobb served as speaker of the U.S. House of Representatives (1849–1850) and U.S. secretary of the treasury (1857–1860).

The Compromise of 1850 allowed California to enter the Union as a free state. In return, Congress enacted the Fugitive Slave Law, which required free states to return escaped slaves to their owners in southern states. Even more important, the old 36°30′ northern limit of slavery would not be used in the remaining territory gained from Mexico in 1848. In the future, residents of any part of this territory seeking statehood would vote on whether their new state would be slave or free. Because it allowed the people to decide, this was called "popular sovereignty."

The compromise was doomed, however, when Congress created the territories of Nebraska and Kansas in 1854. Voters of each territory would decide whether slavery would be permitted. But supporters of slavery and of **abolition** (making slavery illegal) both sought to use popular sovereignty to their advantage. National attention turned to Kansas. Thousands of slaveowners from the South and **abolitionists** (persons opposed to slavery) from free states rushed to settle and control the territory. So savage were their raids on each other's settlements that the area became known as "Bleeding Kansas."

Further dooming the Compromise of 1850 was growing opposition in the North to the new Fugitive Slave Law, which required free states to return runaway slaves to the South. In fact, the law promoted a growing abolitionist movement in the North.

Now, more than ever, the nation was divided over the institution of slavery. ◀

Slavery in Georgia

As cotton production grew in Georgia, so did the need for slaves. Cotton and slavery were so interrelated that a Scottish visitor to Georgia in 1844 reported, "Nothing was attended to but the rearing of cotton and slaves. The more cotton the more slaves and the more slaves the more cotton!"

As more and more land was given over to King Cotton, the price of slaves rose. In 1790, a planter had to pay $300 for a good field hand. By 1850, the price was over $1,000, and by 1860 it was up to $1,800. As Georgia planters sank most of their money into slaves, the calls of northern abolitionists for freeing all slaves in the United States sounded more threatening.

Early Anti-slavery Sentiment

Anti-slavery attitudes existed in Georgia since its founding in 1733. The Georgia Constitution of 1798 outlawed the introduction of any more foreign slaves into the state. Even after the development of

▶ **Locating the Main Ideas**

1. Define: emancipate, abolition, abolitionist
2. Identify: Missouri Compromise, Compromise of 1850, Howell Cobb, popular sovereignty, "Bleeding Kansas"
3. Why was it important that there was an equal number of slave and free states represented in Congress?
4. What was the importance of the latitude of 36°30′?
5. What state entered the Union as a result of the Compromise of 1850?

large cotton plantations, many Georgians hoped to find a practical way to get out of the practice of slavery. In 1817, an editorial of the *Georgia Journal* in Milledgeville (then the state capital) called for Georgia to gradually reduce slavery. Four years later, another editorial observed that no newspaper editor in the state would dare argue for slavery.

Some slaveowners made provision in their wills for their slaves to be freed after the owner's death. Concern about this practice led Georgia's legislature to pass a law, in 1801, that only it could free slaves living in Georgia. Whites wanting to free their slaves got around the new law in several ways. One was for an owner simply to allow his or her slaves to live as free blacks, and not go through the formal process of emancipation. Another was for an owner to accompany his slaves to a free state, and there grant them freedom. A freed slave, however, could not return to Georgia, as the state prohibited the entry of free blacks.

One of the most ambitious efforts to deal with the slavery problem was a colonization movement to return blacks to Africa. A leader in the movement was Paul Cuffe, a black shipping merchant in Massachusetts. Even with his substantial wealth, Cuffe experienced discrimination in the North. He eventually became convinced that blacks—whether slave or not—could only experience freedom in their native homeland, Africa. In 1816, at his own expense, Cuffe arranged passage for 38 American blacks to settle in Sierra Leone on the West African coast. But many other free blacks rejected this approach. Abolitionists also opposed the idea of black removal from the United States.

In late 1816, the American Colonization Society was formed. Among its leaders was a prominent Georgian, William H. Crawford, then U.S. secretary of the treasury. The society attracted supporters in both the North and South who were genuinely concerned about the plight and mistreatment of blacks in this country. It also attracted slaveholding politicians who hoped the colonization program would address problems regarding the future of free blacks in the South.

In 1820, 86 black pioneers, sponsored by the society, sailed from New York to create a colony on the coast of West Africa. The society named it Liberia (from the Latin word

Robert Toombs. As a U.S. senator, he worked hard to keep the union together. Later he would become one of the most zealous defenders of southern independence.

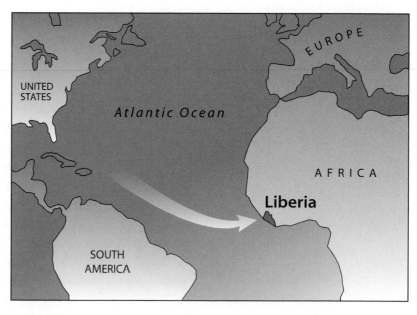

▶ **Locating the Main Ideas**

1. Identify: Paul Cuffe, William H. Crawford, Liberia, Richard and Emily Tubman, William Tubman

2. Why did slavery grow in importance in Georgia in the early 1800s?

3. How did Georgia slaveowners who wanted to free their slaves get around the state law forbidding them to do so?

4. What was the aim of the American Colonization Society?

liber, meaning free). Though the controversial program was slow to get under way, eventually 12,000 ex-slaves and other free blacks from America were sent to Liberia, which became an independent nation in 1847.

About one in ten of the Liberian colonists was from Georgia. In Augusta, at least 18 white owners paid for their slaves' passage to Africa. One of these was Richard Tubman, who died in 1836. Tubman left $10,000—a great deal of money in those days—to be used to free his slaves after his death. Tubman's wife, Emily, used the money to send 42 of the family slaves to Liberia. There, bearing the name of their former owners, the ex-slaves prospered and became leaders in the West African country. In 1944, William Tubman, grandson of an ex-slave from Augusta, Georgia, was elected president of the Republic of Liberia. ◀

Free Blacks in Georgia

Georgia's free black population posed a dilemma to white leaders. They had difficulty finding a place for free blacks. A successful free black population in the South made it harder for whites to justify continued enslavement of blacks. Free blacks also were suspected of helping runaway slaves to escape.

"Free persons of color" were not really free. Legally, they were considered wards of the state—much like orphans. Numerous state and local laws governed their occupations, movement, activities, and rights. In Georgia, free blacks were not considered citizens, and thus had no political rights. However, one right they did have was to own property, which could be passed to their descendants. Be-

cause of this, Georgia law required that every free black have a legal guardian. The role of the guardian was not to monitor a free black's daily life but to handle his or her legal matters such as administering a will or signing a contract.

Cities began passing laws to discourage the presence of free blacks. For example, Milledgeville, the state capital, prohibited free blacks from living within the city without a guardian. A free black moving to Atlanta had to pay $200 for permission to live in the city. In Augusta, a free black violating a city law could be sold into slavery.

In 1859, Georgia's legislature restricted slaveowners from providing in their wills for a slave's freedom in another state. Lawmakers also specified that any free black caught "wandering or strolling about, or leading an idle, immoral or profligate [extravagant] course of life, shall be deemed and considered a Vagrant." Punishment for a first offense was two years of slavery. A second offense brought a penalty of "perpetual slavery."

By the end of the antebellum period, the future for free blacks in Georgia was in grave doubt. As an Atlanta newspaper editorial noted:

> We are opposed to giving free negroes a residence in any and every Slaveholding state, believing as we do, that their presence in slave communities is hurtful to the good order of society, and fraught of great danger to our "peculiar institution"....
> —*Daily Intelligencer*, Jan. 9, 1860

Forces Line Up on Both Sides of the Slavery Issue

After 1830, many white Georgians—particularly planters and politicians—became more outspoken in their defense of slavery. Why?

Several factors strengthened support for slavery: (1) the growing importance of cotton made slaves more valuable; (2) in Virginia, a slave named Nat Turner led a slave revolt that aroused fear that similar uprisings would spread throughout the South; and (3) abolitionists, on the increase in the North, angered southerners by demanding the immediate freeing of all slaves.

In the 1830s, abolitionists organized anti-slavery groups, established anti-slavery newspapers, and raised money to wipe out slavery. They also set up an **Underground Railroad** to smuggle runaway slaves out of the southern states. It was not really a railroad but a network of people and places to shelter blacks as they escaped.

For slaves living in the northern half of Georgia, the Underground Railroad gave them a chance to escape to freedom in Canada. However, not all Georgia runaway slaves fled north. Those in the southern part of the state were more likely to head for Florida. Some escaped slaves eventually made it to the Everglades, where they lived with the Seminole Indians. Others attempted to stow away on ships destined for the Bahamas, where slavery was outlawed.

Some of the leading abolitionists were ex-slaves. Two such leaders were Frederick Douglass, who edited an abolitionist newspaper, and Harriet Tubman, who risked her life many times leading slaves along the Underground Railroad. Others were white ministers, authors, teachers, and merchants who felt that slavery was morally wrong—that it violated the Bible and the Declaration of Independence. The most famous abolitionist, a Bostonian named William Lloyd Garrison, carried on a crusade against slavery through his newspaper, the *Liberator*.

In the North, abolitionists were not highly popular at first. But in 1852, abolitionist Harriet Beecher Stowe wrote a novel, *Uncle Tom's Cabin,* about slave life in the South. The cruelties and suffer-

Harriet Tubman was one of the most famous "conductors" of the Underground Railroad. Making an estimated 19 trips to the South, she helped more than 300 slaves escape to freedom.

Frederick Douglass was a noted writer and lecturer. He spoke out against slavery and the death penalty, and supported equal rights for women and Native Americans.

ing portrayed in this book helped swing many northerners to the abolitionist side.

Southern whites reacted strongly to the abolitionists' attacks. They resented what they felt were false descriptions of slavery and southern life. They also objected to the open defiance of state and federal laws by abolitionists who helped slaves escape from their legal owners.

So outraged were Georgians by Garrison's attacks in the *Liberator* that the General Assembly passed a resolution providing a $5,000 reward for Garrison or any person circulating his newspaper in Georgia. In 1835, the General Assembly made conviction for circulating in Georgia any paper which might incite blacks to revolt punishable by death!

Resistance within Georgia

Attacks on slavery didn't just come from northern abolitionists. Slaves themselves resisted and fought against slavery.

The most extreme form of resistance was a slave revolt. Although a large-scale uprising never took place in Georgia, there was constant fear among whites that one was being planned. Reacting to that fear, Georgia legislators continually added more restrictive laws to the state's Slave Code. Slaves were prohibited from assembling without a white person being present. Slaves were not allowed to travel without a pass, learn to read or write, or work in a print shop. They were even prohibited from possessing drums (which whites feared could be used to send messages). Many laws in the Slave Code were intended to keep slaves from communicating or having an opportunity to gather and plan a revolt.

Blacks fought slavery in other ways, including murdering their overseers and setting fire to plantation buildings. When caught, however, the penalties were severe and quick.

It was not uncommon for newly enslaved Africans to commit suicide. Less extreme and far more common, however, was running away. Slaves fortunate enough to reach the Underground Railroad could escape to freedom.

Probably the most widespread resistance to slavery was at the workplace. Working slowly, doing just enough to get by, pretending sickness, damaging tools and property, and stealing were common ways slaves fought against the system.

The End Approaches

By the late 1850s the nation was divided, more than ever, on the future of slavery. U.S. Sen. William Seward foresaw an approaching conflict. He warned that "the United States must and will, sooner or later, become entirely a slave-holding nation, or entirely a free-labor nation." As it turned out, Seward was correct. ◀

▶ **Locating the Main Ideas**

1. Define: Underground Railroad

2. Identify: Frederick Douglass, Harriet Tubman, William Lloyd Garrison, *Uncle Tom's Cabin*

3. Why were free blacks a threat to white leaders in the South?

4. List four things abolitionists did to combat slavery.

CHAPTER ACTIVITIES

Reviewing the Main Ideas

1. Why would living in a city force residents to become interdependent? Why would city dwellers be more dependent on government than rural residents?

2. What does it mean to take "a sectional approach to national policy?"

3. Did settlers in the West support or oppose slavery?

4. How many states emancipated their slaves prior to the adoption of the U.S. Constitution? What characteristics did those states have in common?

5. How did the Mexican War bring the debate over slavery to the West?

6. Give examples of how city governments and the state government made it difficult for free blacks to live in Georgia.

7. What was the difference in the laws passed in 1801 and 1859 concerning slaveowners using their wills to free their slaves?

8. What is the "peculiar institution" the editor of the Atlanta *Daily Intelligencer* newspaper referred to in the January 9, 1860, editorial?

9. What three factors hardened support for slavery in the South after 1830?

10. Give three examples of how blacks fought against being enslaved. Discuss how effective you think those forms of resistance were.

Give It Some Extra Thought

1. **Making Regional Comparisons.** Explain how geography and economics were responsible for the development of different ways of living in the North and in the South.

2. **Drawing Conclusions.** What events made the slave John Brown conclude that deep down, many slaveowners had doubts about the morality of slavery?

3. **Put in Your Own Words.** It has been said of Harriet Tubman's work on the Underground Railroad that she never ran a train off the track and she never lost a passenger. What do you think that means?

Sharpen Your Skills

1. **Frame of Reference.** Compare the viewpoints of the North and the South, resulting from different frames of reference, on tariffs, states' rights, new states in the west, and slavery.

2. **Map Study.** Using a map of the 48 contiguous states in the United States today, extend the 36°30' latitude line from the Mississippi River to the Pacific Ocean. Write down the names of the states that would have become slave states if the Missouri Compromise had not been altered by the Compromise of 1850. Include a state even if only part of it crosses the compromise line.

Going Further

1. **Investigating.** From 1790 to 1860 the price of a slave had increased from $300 to $1,800. One reason was the increased demand for slaves to work the land. Read Article I, Section 9, Paragraph 1 in the U.S. Constitution and find another reason why slaves were becoming more costly. Using other sources, write a paragraph describing what happened to the slave trade in the United States after 1808.

2. **Write a Brief Biography.** Use other sources to write a brief report on one of the people mentioned in this chapter. Include a description of the person's contribution to political, economic, or cultural life in the antebellum period.

The Civil War

Between 1861 and 1865, this nation fought the deadliest war in its history. No war before or since has resulted in as many American dead and wounded. Rather than facing a foreign enemy in 1861, young American soldiers prepared to go into battle against each other. This conflict would not only split our nation; it would split states, communities, friends, and even families.

Causes of the War

What caused this terrible conflict we refer to as the Civil War?* The reasons are complex. Although slavery was a major issue leading to the war, it wasn't the only issue. In searching for answers, a useful approach is to think of two kinds of causes: fundamental and immediate.

Fundamental (or underlying) causes develop over a long time. The differences between North and South over economics, states' rights, and slavery grew over many years. These causes, presented in the previous chapter, led to the breakup of our nation in the 1860s.

Immediate causes come into being just before the major event itself occurs. Abolitionist John Brown's 1859 raid at Harpers Ferry in Virginia, Abraham Lincoln's election as president of the United States in 1860, and the secession of southern states all happened shortly before the war began. In this chapter, you will discover the series of events that led to the opening shots of the Civil War.

---

*This conflict has other names. At the time, northerners called it the "War of the Rebellion." In the South, it was often referred to as the "War for Southern Independence." Later, many southerners preferred to call it the "War Between the States." However, by far the most common name is the "Civil War."

Lincoln's Election

In 1854 the Republican party was born. Its founders were from the North, although its first candidate for president was Savannah-born John Fremont. Republicans favored protecting northern industry by taxing foreign goods imported to America. They supported free land in the West and opposed extending slavery into the western territories. A few were outright abolitionists.

By 1860, the North and South were deadlocked over the future of slavery in America. The national debate came to a boiling point in that year's presidential election. Representing the Republican party was Abraham Lincoln of Illinois. Lincoln had stated publicly that America could not continue permanently half slave, half free. This convinced southerners that his goal was total abolition of slavery in America.

The national Democratic party had previously been able to attract both southerners and northerners. In the 1860 election, however, the party split. Southern Democrats nominated for president John Breckinridge of Kentucky. Northern Democrats backed Stephen Douglas of Illinois, with Georgia governor Herschel Johnson for vice-president. Further dividing voters, a third party, called the Constitutional Union, organized; it nominated John Bell of Tennessee. Counting Lincoln, there were four candidates running for president.

The presidential election was held on November 6, 1860. The split among Democrats assured the election of Republican challenger Abraham Lincoln.

Reaction in Georgia

Lincoln's election sent shock waves through Georgia. On November 16, 1860, the General Assembly voted $1 million

Above: The "Oglethorpe Infantry," an Augusta militia unit, April 1861. After the firing on Fort Sumter, local militia units from across the state volunteered for duty.

Page 184: On November 8, 1860, the day after hearing that Lincoln had been elected, Savannah citizens demonstrated for southern independence.

Abraham Lincoln, president of the United States, 1861–1865.

Georgia governor Joseph E. Brown.

to defend the state. Two days later, lawmakers authorized the governor to raise 10,000 state troops. On November 21, Georgia lawmakers called for a special statewide convention of delegates from every county to meet in January to decide what Georgia should do next.

In the weeks that followed, prominent Georgians began asking Gov. Joseph Brown what actions he thought the convention should take. Specifically, was Lincoln's election sufficient cause for Georgia and other southern states to secede from the Union? On December 7, Governor Brown wrote an open letter to the people of Georgia. In it, he stated that the rights of the South and the institution of slavery were not endangered by Lincoln the man, but they were in great danger from the Republicans and abolitionists who had elected him. As president, Lincoln likely would appoint Republican supreme court justices who tended to agree with abolitionist views. In the West, as new free states were created from the territories, Congress would soon be controlled by pro-Northern, anti-slavery representatives. The result, Brown concluded, would be that all three branches of the national government soon would be in the hands of the enemies of the South. In less than 25 years, Brown predicted, slavery in America would be totally abolished and the South would be in utter ruin.

So what should Georgia do? Brown predicted that South Carolina was on the verge of seceding and would be followed by Florida, Alabama, and Mississippi. If this happened, Brown believed Georgia had no choice but to join her sister states in leaving the Union. If enough southern states seceded before Lincoln's inauguration in January, a constitutional convention might be called. If that happened, the result could be a new form of union—one giving southern states the constitutional guarantees they sought. No matter what happened, however, Brown doubted that secession would lead to war.

As it turned out, Governor Brown was right when he predicted South Carolina's secession, which came on December 20, 1860. Two weeks later, elections were held in each of Georgia's 132 counties to choose delegates to Georgia's secession convention. On January 16, 1861, delegates met in Milledgeville. By then, four states—South Carolina, Mississippi, Florida, and Alabama—had seceded. Would Georgia be the fifth?

Convention delegates were sharply divided over what to do. Many influential leaders argued for immediate secession from the Union. Among these were Governor Brown; former U.S. senator Robert Toombs; former U.S. secretary of the treasury Howell Cobb; and Thomas R.R. Cobb (Howell's brother).

Other Georgians asked delegates to wait and see what Lincoln did as president before making a final decision. Alexander Stephens, who had served in Congress and knew Lincoln well, argued that his election by itself could not harm Georgia. Stephens's views were supported by the former governor, Herschel Johnson, and by Benjamin Hill, who had run against Governor Brown.

For three days a lively debate went on. A preliminary vote was taken, and it was close—164 delegates voted for immediate secession and 133 preferred to stay with the Union for the time being. The final vote was taken on January 19. By a vote of 208 to 89, the convention adopted an Ordinance of Secession. (A formal action or declaration taken by a special convention is sometimes called an ordinance, rather than a law.) In a show of unity two days later, 286 delegates signed the document. Of those present, six signed a protest, though agreeing to accept the majority's decision.

The Ordinance of Secession was Georgia's own declaration of independence. In it, the new "Republic of Georgia" proclaimed three things:

Confederate president Jefferson Davis.

- Georgia's 1788 ratification of the U.S. Constitution was repealed.
- Georgia's membership in the union of states known as the United States of America was now dissolved.
- Henceforth, Georgia would enjoy all rights that belong to any free and independent nation.

The Ordinance of Secession did not explain why Georgia was withdrawing from the Union. These reasons were listed in a Declaration of the Causes of Secession adopted on January 29. According to that document, Georgia was seceding because Lincoln's election clearly signaled the victory of "abolitionists and their allies in the Northern States" whose guiding principles were "prohibition of slavery in the Territories, hostility to it everywhere, the equality of the black and white races, [and] disregard of constitutional guarantees [to southern states and to owners of escaped slaves]." The Declaration concluded that "we...will seek new safeguards for our liberty, equality, security, and tranquility."

Most political leaders in Georgia and other southern states felt the Union was a compact among states. Just as states voluntarily entered the Union, they could voluntarily leave—especially since there was nothing in the Constitution saying otherwise.

This view, however, was not accepted by President Lincoln and many others outside the South. In his inaugural address, Lincoln countered:

- The Union is older than the Constitution, tracing to the Declaration of Independence and even earlier.
- The Union is a *contract* between two parties—the states and the national government. To break that contract requires the approval of both.
- Secession is illegal and unconstitutional.

Great seal of the Confederate States of America.

▶ **Locating the Main Ideas**

1. Identify: fundamental causes, immediate causes, John Fremont, Abraham Lincoln, ordinance

2. What policies did the Republican party support in 1854?

3. What did southerners fear would happen if Abraham Lincoln were elected president?

4. In which area of Georgia was support for secession the weakest?

• Acts of violence within any state against the United States authorities would be considered acts of rebellion.

Despite Lincoln's warning, Georgia was committed to secession. For decades, southerners had threatened to leave the Union. Now, at long last, they had done it.

Throughout the state, celebrations were held. Secession was the topic of conversation everywhere. Most Georgians serving in the federal government in Washington, D.C., resigned and returned to Georgia. U.S. military officers from Georgia did the same.

Not all white Georgians welcomed secession, however. Many were still loyal to the Union, especially residents of the mountain areas of north Georgia. Some kept quiet in public lest they appear disloyal to their state. Others, however, spoke out. One such Union supporter was Judge Garnett Andrews of Wilkes County. He warned, "Poor fools! They may ring their bells now, but they will wring their hands—yes, and their hearts, too—before they are done with it."

To Georgia's African American people—both free and slave—secession made no difference in their lives. Changes would come later. ◀

A New Nation Is Formed

Now that Georgia was out of the Union, what next? For almost two months, Georgia considered itself a sovereign state, that is, subject to no higher government than itself. Acting as head of a new nation, Governor Brown named a Georgia commissioner to Britain, France, and Belgium.

Soon it became clear that Georgia and the other seceded states were going to have to band together. President Lincoln had announced he would do whatever necessary to preserve the Union. Thus, the seceded states prepared to unite. But under what type of government? Several months earlier, Georgia's General Assembly had recommended that seceding states should form a **confederacy**. (A confederacy is a loose union of sovereign states in which a cen-

Confederate $20 bill featured Georgia's Alexander Stephens, who was vice-president of the Confederacy.

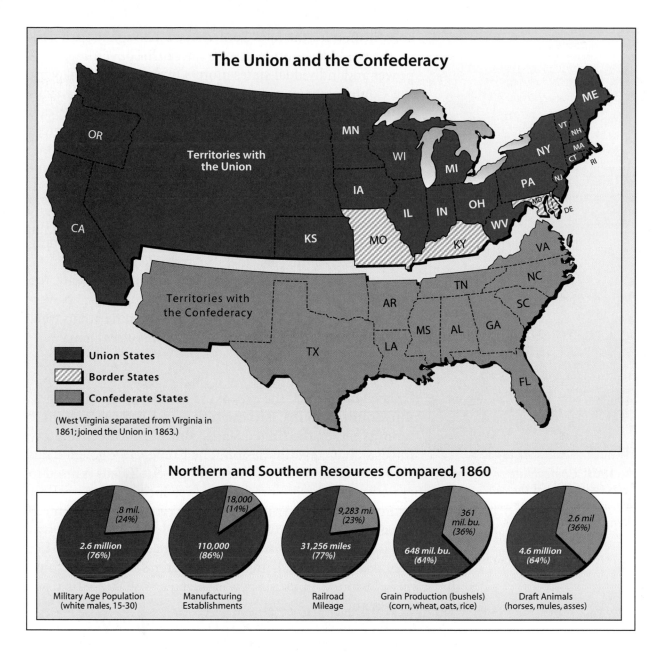

The Union and the Confederacy

Territories with the Union

Territories with the Confederacy

- Union States
- Border States
- Confederate States

(West Virginia separated from Virginia in 1861; joined the Union in 1863.)

Northern and Southern Resources Compared, 1860

.8 mil. (24%)	
2.6 million (76%)	

Military Age Population (white males, 15-30)

18,000 (14%)	
110,000 (86%)	

Manufacturing Establishments

9,283 mi. (23%)	
31,256 miles (77%)	

Railroad Mileage

361 mil. bu. (36%)	
648 mil. bu. (64%)	

Grain Production (bushels) (corn, wheat, oats, rice)

2.6 mil (36%)	
4.6 million (64%)	

Draft Animals (horses, mules, asses)

tral government is given limited powers. This is the type of government America had from 1781 to 1789 under the Articles of Confederation.)

On February 4, 1861, delegates from Georgia, South Carolina, Alabama, Florida, Mississippi, and Louisiana met in Montgomery, Alabama. Texas delegates arrived later. There, they voted to form a new nation. Its official name was the Confederate States of America, though many people simply called it the Confederacy. Jefferson Davis was elected as its first president. He was a former military officer, U.S. senator from Mississippi, and U.S. secretary of war. Georgia's Alexander Stephens was picked to be the Confederacy's vice-president.

Thomas R.R. Cobb, a noted Athens lawyer and University of Georgia law professor, was principally responsible for drafting a

On April 12, 1861, Confederate troops fired the first shots of the Civil War at Union troops stationed at Fort Sumter.

constitution for the new Confederacy. Though modeled after the U.S. Constitution, it gave the central government less power and individual states more. On the matter of slavery, the Confederate Constitution prohibited importing blacks from any foreign country. At the same time, it eased the fears of slaveholders by prohibiting the Confederate Congress from passing any law to abolish slavery.

On March 11, the constitution was adopted. At Montgomery, the Confederacy's first capital, the new government began work, raising money and preparing for a *short* war.

Although seven states had declared themselves out of the Union, Lincoln was determined not to let them go. Hoping to persuade southern leaders to rethink their actions, he announced that he was not inclined "to interfere with the institution of slavery in the States where it exists." Nevertheless, he warned them he had taken a solemn oath to "preserve, protect, and defend" the national government.

Fighting Begins

By late March 1861, the eyes of the nation turned to Charleston, South Carolina. Although the state had seceded three months earlier, the United States continued to keep military forces stationed at Charleston. The Confederate government prepared to take control of these bases, but U.S. officials refused to turn them over. One base, Fort Sumter, was located on a small island guarding the harbor. Twice, its U.S. garrison rejected Confederate demands to withdraw. On April 12, 1861, a final message was sent to the fort. Confederate forces opened fire an hour later. After two days of bombardment, Union forces surrendered. Down came the Stars and Stripes. In its place was raised a new flag—the Confederate Stars and Bars.

Church bells rang out across the city, and Charleston's streets were a scene of glorious celebration and rejoicing. Back in Georgia, news of Fort Sumter's fall brought additional cheering. One 10-year-old girl in Macon wrote in her diary: "Sumter is taken and the stars and bars wave over it, Hurrah! Unto God be the praise."

Most people believed that Lincoln would now back down on his determination to hold the Union together. Little did they know what lay ahead for the South.

News of Sumter's fall was telegraphed to Washington, D.C. The next day, President Lincoln took action. He called for 75,000 volunteers to enlist for three months to put down the "rebellion." Within a month, the call was raised to 500,000 volunteers willing to serve three years. Across the North, young men answered the president's call.

Lincoln also declared a naval **blockade** of the South. The U.S. Navy would prevent all ships from entering or leaving southern ports.

Other southern states now were forced to choose sides. Virginia, Arkansas, North Carolina, and Tennessee picked the Confederacy. Because of Virginia's size, location, and resources, the Confederate government moved its capital to Richmond, Virginia.

Four other slaveholding states—Delaware, Kentucky, Maryland, and Missouri—stayed in the Union. These four were known as **border states** because they bordered free states. Though divided, most residents did not favor secession. Also staying with the Union were the non-slaveholding counties in western Virginia. In 1863, they seceded from Virginia and joined the Union as the new state of West Virginia.

Both Sides Square Off

In the early months of 1861, neither southern nor northern leaders expected that war, if it came at all, would last very long. Southerners tended to believe that the people of the North would have no stomach for fighting and wouldn't support Lincoln. For their part, northerners felt their huge advantages in resources would mean swift military defeat of the South. Both sides were wrong. The Civil War would last four years. Its cost would be staggering: over 600,000 southern and northern soldiers killed and another 400,000 wounded. ▶

Georgians in the War

Within days of Lincoln's call for 75,000 volunteers in the North, Governor Brown called on the young men of his state to rally to the defense of Georgia. By October 1861, more than 25,000 Georgians had volunteered. Unfortunately, there weren't enough weapons, uniforms, and supplies to equip them. **Arsenals**—facilities where weapons and ammunition are manufactured or stored—were built in Augusta, Atlanta, Savannah, Macon, Columbus, and other cities.

To the sound of music and cheering home crowds, young recruits in both the North and South marched off to war. Soon, "Johnny Reb" would face "Billy Yank" on the battlefield.*

At first, superior military leadership gave the South an advantage. Yet, its soldiers were vastly outnumbered by the North, forcing the Confederate government to begin a **draft** —a law requiring civilians to join the army. Georgia's Governor Brown strongly opposed the Confederate draft. As a strong believer in states' rights, he felt only individual states had this power. On this and other issues, Brown

---

*Confederate soldiers were often called "Rebels" (or "Rebs") by northerners, who considered the South in rebellion. Union soldiers were known as "Yankees" (or "Yanks") and "Federals." Popular names for the common soldier on the opposing sides were "Johnny Reb" and "Billy Yank."

▶ **Locating the Main Ideas**

1. Define: confederacy, blockade, border states
2. Identify: Confederate States of America, Thomas R.R. Cobb, Stars and Stripes, Stars and Bars
3. How were the Articles of Confederation and the Confederate Constitution similar?
4. What reasons did the North and the South each give for believing it would be a short, victorious war for their side?

Many Confederate soldiers were barely old enough—16—to serve. Some young boys would write "16" on the soles of their shoes so they could swear to the army recruiter that they were "over 16."

soon became a thorn in the side of the Confederate government, and particularly its president, Jefferson Davis. Although loyal to the cause, Brown tended to think of Georgia first, and the Confederacy second.

The first major battle of the Civil War was at Virginia's Manassas Junction, near Bull Run Creek. There, Confederate forces won a stunning upset. There were other early southern victories, but the superior numbers and equipment of the North soon began to make a difference.

Both sides realized it was going to be a long conflict, and the glamour of war began to fade. On battlefields in Virginia and other states, thousands of Georgians were being killed and wounded. One was Gen. T.R.R. Cobb, killed at the battle of Fredricksburg in 1862. Soon, caskets and disabled soldiers were returning to Georgia in a steady flow. Of the 120,000 Georgians who fought for the South, about 25,000 lost their lives.

Life in Georgia during the Civil War

For two years, most of the fighting was far from Georgia's soil. Nevertheless, the people of Georgia felt its effects in several ways.

First, the Union's naval blockade of southern ports prevented the export of cotton, the South's main source of income. Unable to sell cotton to Great Britain and other countries, the Confederacy had

Confederate general Joseph E. Johnston rallies Georgia troops to a victory at Bull Run near Manassas Junction, Virginia, in July 1861. Note the sergeant carrying the Georgia flag, which had the state coat of arms on a solid background.

During the war, women helped to care for sick and wounded soldiers in hospitals and sometimes on the battlefields.

little money to buy military supplies and food. As the blockade tightened, Georgians faced food shortages and sky-high prices.

The women of the state rose to the occasion, finding substitutes for such necessities as coffee, sugar, and tea. With medicine in short supply, they learned to use native-grown roots, herbs, and other plants to care for the sick. Old clothes were dyed and tailored into uniforms. Many women also took over the responsibility of running farms and plantations. As the war waged on, women helped care for the wounded soldiers returning to Georgia.

During the first three years of the war, most slaves lived much as they did before. Some, however, were assigned to build forts and prisons, and to repair railroads in the state. Others worked behind the lines in Confederate army units, sometimes as cooks, wagon drivers, and blacksmiths. Throughout the war, Confederate leaders considered arming slaves to fight in return for their freedom. Some, however, worried that having slaves fight would put them on equal footing with white soldiers and contradict arguments in defense of slavery. Also, some whites feared that armed slaves might be tempted to turn their guns on Confederates rather than aim at Yankee soldiers.

With many of Georgia's slave owners off to war, the number of slave runaways increased. By spring 1862, Union forces had captured all of Georgia's coastal islands, making them a popular destination for escaped slaves.

Meanwhile, in September 1862, President Lincoln issued his **Emancipation Proclamation**. This historic document stated that on January 1, 1863, all persons held as slaves in any state of the Confederacy "shall be thence forward, and forever free." The war was no longer just a fight to preserve the Union. It was now a war to free southern slaves. Despite Lincoln's declaration, slavery continued in Georgia as before.

Substitute for Coffee

Take sound ripe acorns, wash them while in the shell, dry them, and parch until they open, take the shell off, roast with a little bacon fat, and you will have a splendid cup of coffee.

(Recipe printed in a southern newspaper during the Civil War.)

Half of the African American soldiers who served in the Union Army were former slaves from the South.

Lincoln's Emancipation Proclamation had a second provision: "[S]uch persons of suitable condition, will be received into the armed service of the United States to garrison forts, positions, stations, and other places, and to man vessels of all sorts in said service." Not only was Lincoln freeing southern slaves, he was welcoming them to come join the Union army. Many did. Of the 186,000 African Americans who enlisted as Union soldiers and sailors, 93,000—half—came from Confederate states, plus an additional 40,000 from the border states. Of all who enlisted, 38,000 African Americans died during the Civil War.

Georgia Supplies the Confederacy

While Georgia soldiers fought elsewhere, the state became one of the Confederacy's most important sources of supplies. Farmers were told to switch from growing cotton to raising corn and other foodstuffs needed by the southern soldiers.

Georgia, with more industry than any other southern state, supplied the Confederacy with military equipment. Confederate troops depended on Georgia to provide rifles, cannons, gunpowder, sabers, wagons, railroad cars, tools, saddles and harnesses, and clothing. Atlanta, Augusta, Columbus, Macon, and Savannah were the main manufacturing centers. Also, thousands of small operations, some in private homes, turned out uniforms, shoes, bandages, and other supplies.

Georgia had over 1,400 miles of railroad, the best system in the Deep South. This system, with Atlanta as its hub, was vital in supplying and transporting Confederate troops. Georgia's strategic location, its rail network, and its ability to supply southern armies with sorely needed food and equipment, made it the "heart of the Confederacy." Therefore, destruction of Georgia's resources would be fatal to the Confederate war effort. ◀

The Tide Turns

The first two years of the Civil War brought many Confederate victories—largely due to superior military leaders. In 1863, however, the course of the war began to change. For one thing, the South could not match the North in number of soldiers, arms, and economic resources. Second, more capable generals were now commanding Union armies. Third, Lincoln's Emancipation Proclamation had given the people of the North a new reason to continue the war. What had begun as a war to save the Union was now also a war to free the slaves.

In May 1863, Gen. Thomas "Stonewall" Jackson was accidentally shot and fatally wounded by one of his own soldiers. The Confed-

▶ Locating the Main Ideas

1. Define: arsenal, draft, Emancipation Proclamation

2. Name two contributions women in the South made to the war effort.

3. What were two provisions of the Emancipation Proclamation?

4. What factors made Georgia an attractive military target?

The Great Locomotive Chase

During the Civil War, Georgia's railroads were vital to the Confederacy. In 1862, James Andrews, a Union spy from Kentucky, planned a secret mission to disrupt one of the most important rail lines in Georgia. This was the 138-mile Western & Atlantic Railroad, which connected Atlanta with Chattanooga.

On April 12, 1862, Andrews and 19 Union soldiers dressed as civilians arrived at Marietta. Here, they boarded an early-morning northbound train pulled by the locomotive *General*. At Big Shanty (today's Kennesaw), the train stopped so that the passengers and crew could eat breakfast. Andrews and his men used this opportunity to steal the train. Calmly, they uncoupled the passenger cars and sped off with their prize—the *General*, a fuel car, and three boxcars. Their objective now was to tear up track and burn railroad bridges during their journey northward.

William Fuller, conductor of the *General,* looked through the dining room window with disbelief as his train chugged away. Off he ran to try to catch his stolen train. Running with him were two W & A employees, Anthony Murphy and Jefferson Cain. For over two miles, they followed the train on foot. Finding a work crew, they borrowed a handcar to continue the chase. At last, they came upon a small locomotive used to haul coal to a local ironworks. Rather than let the Yankee spies escape, its conductor let them borrow his locomotive.

Meanwhile, Andrews and his men pulled into Kingston. Because they had cut telegraph wires along the way, no one at the station knew the *General* had been stolen. But there was bad news. Ahead on the single track were three southbound trains. Andrews was directed to pull his train off onto a siding and wait. Two trains passed. Suddenly, from the south came the whistle of Fuller's borrowed locomotive. Andrews now knew they were being pursued. He had no choice. Despite a third train ahead, the *General* pulled back out on the main track.

At Kingston, Fuller and his party boarded a larger locomotive. But north of the station, damaged rails forced them to stop. For three miles, he and Murphy continued the chase on foot. At last, they encountered a southbound train pulled by the *Texas*. Fuller waved the train to a stop and quickly told his story. They backed the train onto a siding, uncoupled the freight cars, and steamed off—in reverse—after the *General*. For the first time, Fuller and Murphy had a locomotive of comparable size and power.

In Calhoun, Fuller and Murphy were joined by Confederate soldiers. The chase was on again. A few miles north of Calhoun, Fuller came in sight of Andrews's men trying to tear up the track. There was not enough time to disrupt the track, so the raiders jumped back on the *General* and sped northward.

Knowing the penalty for spying could be death, Andrews's men were now desperate. They dropped railroad ties from the rear boxcar onto the track, but these were pushed aside. Then, they began unhooking box cars, one by one, to block the track. Fuller, however, simply coupled them to his train and continued the chase.

Near Ringgold, the *General* ran out of fuel. Andrews and his men scattered to the woods. Within days, however, all were captured. Their mission had been a failure. The damaged track was easily repaired. Rainy weather also spoiled several efforts to burn bridges along the route.

Seven raiders—including Andrews—were subsequently hanged as spies. The rest were spared but sent to prison. Some escaped. Six were exchanged for Confederate prisoners the next year. In March, these six were summoned to Washington, D.C., to become the first recipients of the new Medal of Honor. Eventually, other members of the raid, or their survivors, received the award also. Interestingly, the man who had planned and led the raid, James Andrews, was not included. According to Congress, recipients of the Medal of Honor had to be members of the military. Andrews—though a Union spy—had never enlisted.

Primary Source

A Georgia Soldier's View

Written correspondence (letters) is one of the best sources of information about the past. Letters provide clues to the private thoughts and attitudes of people who lived long ago.

John W. Hagen was a sergeant in the Twenty-ninth Georgia Volunteer Infantry. The following letter, written to his wife, Amanda, at home in Lowndes County, is an example of private correspondence. That is, the writer did not intend for it to be published.

Mrs. John W. Hagen
Cat Creek
Lowndes County
Georgia

In Line of Battle, Georgia,
July the 4th, 1864

My Dear Wife,

…We have given up our works & fell back 3 or 4 miles from Marietta, leaving it to the mercy of the Yanks….

We thought this morning being the 4th of July we would have a hopping time with them, but they seem to keep their proper distance. Our men was up on the look out & on the march all night. When we got here we went to work in an open field & worked all day & all night & is yet at work & is about ready to receive them. Our skirmishers are now having a plenty to do & if we stay here we may have something to do in the way of fighting from our works.

We are in the breastworks [ditches] now in an open field & they are in line of battle in a hill in another old field about one mile off, but we can see all they do. I do not know whether they will attack us or not, but I hope they will for I am wore out marching and building breastworks.

The reason we had to leave Kennesaw mountain was because the Yanks was flanking [going around the side] us on the left & we was forced to fall back. The Yankees' army is so much stronger than ours that they can put a force in our front to compete with ours & then they have a corps or two which they can send on either flank & then we have to fall back to prevent them getting in our rear….

Our generals say when we reach the river 8 miles from Atlanta that they will then be forced to fight us in our works. They say the Yanks can not flank us any further, but I do not know. It seems we have a strong position here, but I feel doubtful about their attacking us. But they will roll up their artillery & keep up an incessant shelling.

The Yankees seems to be in fine spirits playing their bands and hallowing. I am now sitting in full view of their line of battle & their wagon trains bringing supplies. They seem so cheerful and full of fun. Some of our troops grow despondent, but it is only those who are always despondent. All good soldiers will fight harder the harder he is pressed, but a coward is always ready to want an excuse to run or to say they or we are whipped….

You must not think strange at this scribbled letter for I am writing in a hurry for I never know how soon a shell may order men to the breast-works, etc.…

Tell James to think of us when he is eating but-ter & drinking buttermilk & eating many good things. We get tolerable plenty of meat & bread now, but we want something in the way of veg-etables. You must send us something if you get a chance to send it safely.

I must close for the shells is bursting too near me. Give my love to all.…

I am as Ever your affectionate husband

J.W.H.

Interpreting the Source

1. What does Hagen's letter tell you about his spirit or morale? the morale of Confederate troops in gen-eral? of Union troops?

2. What was Hagen doing just before he wrote his wife?

3. What evidence is there that Hagen feels the Confed-erates are badly outnumbered?

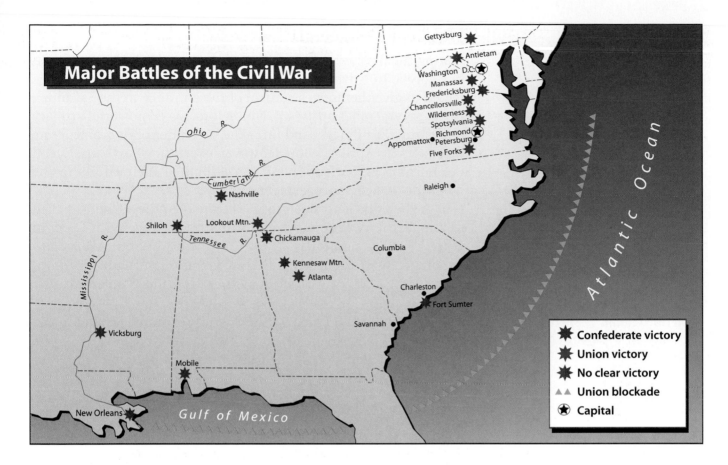

Major Battles of the Civil War

Gettysburg

Antietam

Washington D.C.

Manassas

Fredericksburg

Chancellorsville

Wilderness

Spotsylvania

Richmond

Appomattox • Petersburg

Five Forks

Raleigh •

Ohio R.

Cumberland R.

Nashville

Shiloh

Lookout Mtn.

Tennessee R.

Chickamauga

Columbia •

Kennesaw Mtn.

Atlanta

Charleston

Fort Sumter

Savannah •

Mississippi R.

Vicksburg

Mobile

New Orleans

Gulf of Mexico

Atlantic Ocean

★ Confederate victory
★ Union victory
★ No clear victory
▲▲ Union blockade
⊛ Capital

eracy thus lost one of its greatest military minds. In June, Gen. Robert E. Lee decided to take the war to the North. If the Confederate Army could win some battles in the northland and capture Philadelphia or Washington, the North might agree to a political settlement to end the war. With this in mind, Lee led his Army of Northern Virginia (which included many Georgia soldiers and officers) into Pennsylvania. By chance, at the little town of Gettysburg, Confederate forces looking for supplies ran into a Union cavalry unit of Gen. George Meade's Army of the Potomac.

Lee had 75,000 men, while Meade had 97,000. Still, Lee decided to fight, and the two sides squared off for battle. Of the more than 2,000 land battles of the Civil War, the Battle of Gettysburg would prove to be the most important. Here, on July 1, 1863, the greatest battle ever fought on the continent of North America began.

During three days of terrible fighting, both sides fought bravely. By July 3, Confederate losses were 28,000 killed, wounded, or captured. Union casualties numbered 23,000. Unable to dislodge Meade's army, Lee decided to retreat to Virginia.

The South suffered another setback on July 4. That day, Union forces under Gen. Ulysses S. Grant captured Vicksburg, Mississippi, giving the North control of the Mississippi River and splitting the Confederacy in two. In late November, Chattanooga, Tennessee, fell to Union forces. Except for a few victories, 1863 was not a good year for the Confederacy. The tide of war had now changed.

General William T. Sherman led the Union Army through the heart of Georgia in 1864.

Union forces advance on *Confederate troops at the Battle of Atlanta, July 22, 1864.*

War Comes to Georgia

During the first two years of the war, few battles had been fought in Georgia. In November 1861, federal forces had occupied Tybee Island to give themselves control of the entrance to the Savannah River. Several miles upstream, Union forces used powerful artillery to destroy Fort Pulaski and force the surrender of its Confederate defenders on April 1, 1862. However, except for Fort Pulaski and the burning of Darien, Union forces limited their efforts to the blockade of Georgia's coastal waters.

Elsewhere in Georgia, a group known as Andrews' raiders tried to cripple the W & A Railroad north of Atlanta in 1862. Then, in 1863, a large Union force, 1,500 strong, rode in from Alabama to cut off the W & A. Near Rome, Confederate Gen. Nathan Bedford Forrest with a 500-man cavalry force tricked the much larger force into surrendering.

In September 1863, the Union Army captured Chattanooga, Tennessee, which is several miles north of the Georgia border. Two weeks later, federal forces advanced into Georgia, where the Confederate Army turned them back in a bloody battle at Chickamauga.

The Civil War had come to Georgia. Now, all eyes were on Atlanta. Atlanta wasn't the largest city in Georgia, nor was it the state capital. But, with its industrial and transportation resources, Atlanta was the most important military target in Georgia.

Sherman Invades Georgia

The story of Atlanta's destruction began in early 1864. A Union army of 99,000 men, commanded by Gen. William T. Sherman, was at Chattanooga, Tennessee. Thirty miles south at Dalton, 62,000 Confederates, commanded by Gen. Joseph E. Johnston, had dug into defensive trenches.

On April 4, from Washington, D.C., the commander of U.S. armies, Gen. Ulysses S. Grant, wrote to General Sherman:

> You I propose to move against Johnston's army, to break it up, and get into the interior of the enemy's country as far as you can, inflicting all the damage you can against their war resources.

In the late spring, the armies of Sherman and Johnston battled at Dalton, Resaca, and New Hope Church. Sherman relentlessly pushed south toward Atlanta. Greatly outnumbered, Johnston would dig in and then retreat south, following the W & A railroad line, not allowing Sherman to break up or encircle his army.

On June 27, at Kennesaw Mountain, Sherman recklessly attacked head on. Johnston taught him a lesson: 3,000 Federals were killed while only 500 Confederates were lost. But again, Johnston's men had to fall back and dig their trenches—this time to defend Atlanta.

Unhappy with General Johnston's retreat, the Confederate government in Richmond replaced him with Gen. John B. Hood. As expected, Hood attacked Sherman's army, but he was thrown back several times.

For 40 days, Sherman's artillery pounded Atlanta. Hood, fearing his army would be trapped, evacuated the city on September 1. The next day, the mayor of Atlanta rode out under a white flag to surrender the city. Within a week, Sherman ordered all civilians to leave.

Sherman's army occupied Atlanta until mid November. Then, still following Grant's original plan, he gave orders for the city's destruction. A Union soldier described it this way:

> On the night of November 15th, the torch was applied to the railroad shops, foundries, and every one of the many buildings that had been used in fitting out the armies of the enemy in this vast "workshop of the confederacy," as Atlanta was called. The flames spread rapidly, and when morning came, it is doubtful whether there were a score of buildings remaining in the city, except in the very outskirts.

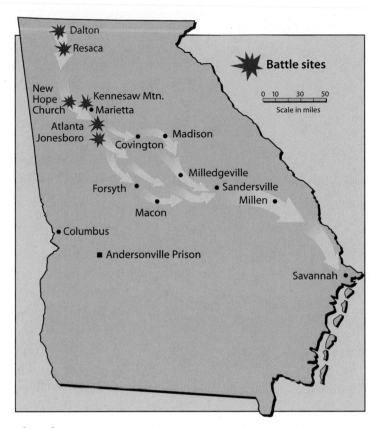

The March to the Sea. Sherman's army moved over a 60-mile–wide path between Atlanta and Savannah. Which areas escaped destruction?

Sherman's March to the Sea

On November 16, after sending part of his army north after Hood, Sherman began his "march to the sea." On this march, the Union forces were to live off the land and destroy Georgia's resources, particularly railroads and supplies on which the Confederate armies depended. To accomplish this, Sherman divided his troops into different columns. As they moved through Macon, the southernmost column passed within 50 miles of the Confederacy's dreaded Andersonville Prison.

In addition to destroying legitimate targets, Sherman's troops frequently plundered private property, despite orders to the contrary. The Union commander later reported that during the march, his army destroyed $100 million worth of food and other resources. Sherman defended the destruction as a way of bringing "the sad realities of war" to the heart of Georgia. Neither Georgia nor the Confederacy would recover in time to change the outcome of the war.

On December 21, 1864, Sherman's army entered Savannah. Along the way they had been joined by about 14,000 African Americans, although because of age and health, only about half completed the march. The general telegraphed President Lincoln: "I beg to present you as a Christmas gift the city of Savannah, with 150 guns and plenty of ammunition, also about 25,000 bales of cotton."

On April 9, 1865, at Appomattox Courthouse in Virginia, Gen. Robert E. Lee surrendered the small force he still commanded. Other Confederate generals across the South followed his action.

On their march through Georgia, Sherman's forces seized or destroyed millions of dollars worth of food and property.

About 10 miles from Americus, Georgia, you will find the site of one of the great tragedies of the Civil War. Today, it is a National Historic Site operated by the National Park Service. During the war, it was the home of Andersonville Prison, a name that came to be associated with horror and death.

In November 1863, the Confederacy was faced with growing numbers of Union prisoners and no place to put them. The War Department picked southwest Georgia, far from the battle front, to build its largest prison. In the small village of Andersonville, work on the prison began. Though officially called Fort Sumter, it was more commonly known as Andersonville Prison.

Andersonville consisted of a double stockade of tree trunks surrounding a 27-acre open area in which 10,000 prisoners would be kept. Originally, barracks were planned for the camp. Before they could be built, however, the War Department began sending prisoners of war.

In February 1864, 600 Union prisoners were transferred to Andersonville. In less than two months, the prison population increased to 12,000! By May, there were 19,000 prisoners, and by June, 23,000. The camp reached its peak population of more than 33,000 Union prisoners in August 1864.

Conditions at Andersonville were horrible. The sanitary conditions were unspeakable. What water was available was polluted. Food supplies were so inadequate that some prisoners starved. Clothing and medical supplies were always scarce. The only shelter in the cold and rain were crude tents, and not everyone had them. During the summer of 1864, more than 100 Union prisoners died each day at Andersonville. Most died of dysentery and other diseases.

Capt. Henry Wirz, camp commander, was faced with an impossible situation. The number of Union soldiers far exceeded Andersonville's capacity, but the government kept sending more and more prisoners. As the tide of war turned against the South, the Confederacy had difficulty even feeding and clothing its soldiers in the field, let alone sending provisions to prison camps. Also, at the time of Andersonville's greatest overcrowding, many of its staff were transferred north to protect Atlanta from Sherman's advance. The camp was left with a small crew of poorly trained guards.

Conditions improved in September 1864, when many of Andersonville's prisoners were shipped to other camps. When the war ended in April 1865, the prison was closed. It had been in operation just 14 months. During this time, over 45,000 Union soldiers were imprisoned there. Almost 13,000 died.

After the war, Captain Wirz was arrested and sent to Washington, D.C., for trial by a military commission. In his defense, Wirz presented a wide variety of evidence to show that he had done all he could to improve conditions at Andersonville. For instance, he showed copies of numerous letters he had written to the Confederate government pleading for food, clothing, medicine, and shelter for his prisoners. However, Lincoln had just been assassinated, and the mood in Washington was not one of sympathy for the South. The military commission found Wirz guilty of "murder in violation of the laws and customs of war." On November 10, 1865, he was hanged.

Gen. Robert E. Lee surrendered to Gen. Ulysses S. Grant on April 9, 1865, at Appomattox Court House in Virginia. Within weeks most other Confederate commanders did likewise, thus ending this nation's most deadly war.

▶ **Locating the Main Ideas**

1. Identify: Andrews' raiders, workshop of the Confederacy, March to the Sea

2. What did General Lee hope to accomplish by moving the Confederate Army north to attack Union troops?

3. Describe General Grant's plan for the Union attack on Georgia.

4. What did General Sherman do to Atlanta after the city surrendered?

5. What was the purpose of Sherman's destructive march to the sea?

Georgia troops were under the command of Gen. Joseph E. Johnston, who was in North Carolina preparing to surrender to Sherman. In Washington, Georgia, 25-year-old Eliza Frances Andrews, daughter of Judge Garnett Andrews, recorded these words in her diary:

> *April 21, Friday*....Confirmation of Lee's surrender, and of the armistice [truce] between Johnston and Sherman. Alas, we all know only too well what the armistice means! It is all over with us now, and there is nothing to do but bow our heads in the dust and let the hateful conquerors trample us under their feet. There is a complete revulsion in public feeling. No more talk about fighting to the last ditch; the last ditch has already been reached....

For Georgia, the Civil War officially came to an end on April 26, 1865, when Johnston's formal surrender was accepted by Sherman. In later years, Georgia's General Assembly would make this date—April 26—a state holiday known as Confederate Memorial Day.

Holding its last official meeting in Washington, Georgia, the Confederate government collapsed. On May 10, Union forces captured Jefferson Davis near Irwinville in south Georgia. The long war was over. The South's "second war of independence" had ended in defeat, with dreams of a southern nation now painful memories. It was time to prepare for an uncertain future. ◀

CHAPTER ACTIVITIES

Reviewing the Main Ideas

1. How did the split in the Democratic party in 1860 allow Lincoln's election?

2. What reasons did Georgians opposed to leaving the Union give for delaying a vote on secession?

3. What three things did Georgia's Ordinance of Secession proclaim?

4. What did Lincoln mean when he said the Union was older than the Constitution?

5. In what way did Lincoln try to persuade southern leaders to rethink their actions and return to the Union?

6. For what reason did Confederate forces attack Fort Sumter in April 1861?

7. How did Lincoln's Emancipation Proclamation change the nature of the war from a battle over the Constitution to a war of abolition?

8. How did Georgia earn the nickname "the heart of the Confederacy" during the Civil War?

9. List three factors that contributed to an increasing number of Union victories after 1863.

10. Name two factors that contributed to the horrible conditions at Andersonville.

11. What was General Sherman's Christmas present to President Lincoln in 1864?

Give It Some Extra Thought

1. **Put It in Your Own Words.** Put Judge Andrews's quote in your own words. "Poor fools! They may ring their bells now, but they will wring their hands—yes, and their hearts, too—before they are done with it."

2. **Analyzing Relationships.** Why would there be difficulties for a national government based on states' rights? Give an example of a problem such a government might have.

3. **Explaining.** Why do you think support for secession was weak in the mountain regions of Georgia?

Sharpen Your Skills

1. **Making Bar Graphs.** Using percentages, convert the information comparing northern and southern resources from the circle graphs to bar graphs. In which resource were the differences between the North and the South the greatest? In what two resources was the South closest to the North in 1860?

2. **Analyze the Artifact.** Numerous artifacts exist from this period of history. If possible, locate or find a photo of a Civil War period artifact such as a household item, a military object, money, photograph, letter, or diary. Share it with the class and analyze its use or significance to the period.

3. **Following Events on a Map.** Name at least five cities that Sherman's army passed through on his march to the sea. In what general direction was the army traveling?

Going Further

1. **Putting Events in Chronological Order.** Put the dates for the following events in chronological order on a time line. Lincoln is inaugurated, Sherman marches his troops to the sea, Emancipation Proclamation is issued, John Brown raids Harpers Ferry, Lincoln is assassinated, Civil War begins with attack at Fort Sumter, Georgia secedes from the Union, Battle of Atlanta takes place, first Union prisoners transferred to Andersonville.

2. **Considering Other Viewpoints.** Georgia civilians held different views of events during the war based on their backgrounds and positions. Choose and assume one of the following identities: a cotton planter, non-slaveholder yeoman farmer, free black laborer, wife and mother, a Union sympathizer, or a hospital nurse. Like diarist Eliza Andrews did, write entries for the days on which you hear about the following: Georgia's secession, the fall of Fort Sumter, the beginning of the blockade, the battles of Chickamauga and Gettysburg, the Emancipation Proclamation, Sherman's capture of Atlanta, the end of the war, and Lincoln's assassination. Read some of the entries aloud and compare them to others written about the same event but from different points of view.

Coming Up Next!

- Economic reconstruction
- Political reconstruction
- Blacks in Georgia politics
- The end of Reconstruction

Reconstruction Comes to Georgia

The spring of 1865 was a time of despair for most white southerners and of short-lived joy for most black southerners. For either race, it was a time of uncertainty about the future. The South was now a conquered land. The vision of an independent Confederacy was a painful memory.

That spring, war-weary Georgia soldiers returned home, leaving behind about 25,000 dead and missing. Upon returning home, Confederate veterans often found ruin and great confusion. From Chattanooga to Savannah, blackened chimneys—"Sherman's sentinels"—marked the locations of once prosperous plantations. "Sherman's neckties" (rails twisted around trees) and burned depots and bridges were all that remained of the state's railroads. Cotton gins, mills, factories—all lay in ruin.

Georgia businesses faced a bleak future. They had no stock, no supplies, no equipment, no money, and few customers. For many farmers and plantation owners, the situation was equally bleak, for now there were no slaves to work the fields. Most planters' wealth had been tied up in slaves. Now, that wealth—possibly the entire southern way of life—seemed "gone with the wind."

At first, many whites hoped that their former slaves would stay on and work for wages. Some did, but most soon walked away.

Typical was John Banks, a 68-year-old Columbus planter at the time of the war's end. He had seven sons who served in the Confederate army, three of whom were killed in battle. Shortly after the South's surrender, Banks wrote in his diary details of the effect of emancipation on his Georgia plantation:

> Emancipation has been proclaimed by Lincoln and partially carried out.... I owned about two hundred negroes, in which my property mostly consisted. This leaves me poor.

Back at work, 1865. As soon as the fighting ended, Georgians began rebuilding. In Atlanta, tracks were relaid amid the ruins of this locomotive roundhouse to get the trains running again.

Today many of my negroes left me. Celia, who has cooked for me more than forty years, left me. I made no opposition to it. Am now satisfied it [emancipation] will be carried out. George, my body servant, has left me. All the negroes about the yard are gone.... All have left me but such as are of expense to me. Wesley is about ten years old and drove me in the buggy to town today. Windsor, who came in the buggy with me (a good boy) this morning, when I called for him found he was gone. The negroes at the plantation are still there but so demoralized that they work but little.

In rural areas, bands of ex-slaves or army deserters roamed about taking what little there was from unprotected farms. Thousands of former slaves flocked to the cities, seeking food and a place to live. Finding neither, many became homeless. In the months after the war, whites also experienced terrible conditions—with no money, few clothes, and little food. As one Georgia woman wrote in her diary on May 27, 1865: "We are a poverty-stricken nation."

By the spring of 1865, state government had broken down. U.S. military authorities took control of Georgia and other southern states. The federal government planned to change the makeup of southern government, politics, and society. Its intent was to change —or *reconstruct*—Confederate states before allowing them back into the Union. Thus began an era known as **Reconstruction**.

After the Civil War, Atlanta adopted a new city seal. It showed the phoenix—a mythical bird—rising out of flames. The seal suggested that like the phoenix, Atlanta would rise up from its destruction of the war to a new life.

Sidney Lanier, a famous Georgia poet, was also a Confederate soldier, teacher, law clerk, novelist, and a flutist with the Baltimore Symphony Orchestra.

Economic Reconstruction

The Civil War destroyed much of Georgia's agriculture and industry. This destruction forced changes in the social and economic patterns of the people. Antebellum economy had been based on three main resources: land, labor, and **capital** (money). In **postbellum** Georgia (the period after the war), the typical planter had plenty of land, but no slave labor to work it. The freed African Americans had their own labor, but most had no land. Neither had any money. Now, whites and blacks had to find new ways of working together to survive.

Land

After the war, many plantation owners had to sell off some of their land to raise cash. They needed money to pay taxes and buy equipment, livestock, seed, fertilizer, and the labor needed to rebuild.

So much land was available and landowners were so desperate for cash that land sold for a fraction of its pre-war value. It became "dirt cheap." As a result, many more small farms came into being in Georgia. In some cases, blacks as well as whites became landowners through aid from the federal government. Still, the majority of Georgians of both races could not afford to own their own land.

Labor

After the Civil War, Georgia and other southern states faced a serious shortage of workers—particularly on farms and plantations. One reason was the great number of white males killed or disabled during the war. Also, after the war many Georgians left to start life over in such faraway places as Texas, Mexico, and even Brazil.

In 1869, Georgia's best-known poet, Sidney Lanier, wrote a poem about Georgians migrating to the west after the Civil War. In "Thar's More in the Man than Thar Is in the Land," Lanier writes about a Georgian named Jones, who "lived pretty much by gittin' of loans, and his mules was nuthin' but skin and bones." Jones has trouble making ends meet. He finally sells his land—

> And Jones he bought him a waggin and tents,
> And loaded his corn, and his wimmin, and truck,
> And moved to Texas, which it tuck
> His entire pile, with the best of luck,
> To git thar and git him a little land.

An even more important reason for the South's labor shortage was the loss of its large pool of slave labor. After emancipation, some blacks stayed with their former masters and agreed to work for wages. But most left their old plantations. They wanted to leave behind their former way of life—no matter how uncertain the future.

Atlanta, 1865. The remains of a burned out bank stand on the corner. Despite great destruction by Sherman's forces, Atlanta rebuilt quickly. A New York reporter wrote that from morning until night, Atlanta's streets were alive with workers and wagons, loaded with lumber and brick.

Now that they were free, ex-slaves needed to find ways to make a living. They could sell their labor—but they had little experience working for money. Most white landowners needed workers, but were short of cash.

Devising a new working arrangement between whites and blacks was not easy. Because of a shortage of money to pay workers, several approaches came into general use. Black Georgians seeking work would either work for wages, rent land, or sharecrop with a landowner. (See Chapter 16 for a discussion of sharecropping.)

Capital

There's an old saying that "it takes money to make money." To make money growing cotton, a planter needed capital—money available for spending—to buy work animals, plows, seed, fertilizer, and labor.

With emancipation and the war's end, capital that had been tied up in slaves was lost. Remaining capital in the form of Confederate money and bonds was worthless. Very few farmers in the South had any U.S. money. Other than by selling off land, the only way to get money was to borrow it. But many Georgia banks had collapsed with the Confederacy, and little credit was available. The shortage of capital would make Georgia a poor state for decades. ▶

Rebuilding Begins

Not every aspect of economic life in Georgia was bleak. Even though it would take Georgia a long time to rebuild, some bright

▶ **Locating the Main Ideas**

1. Define: Reconstruction, capital, postbellum

2. Identify: Sherman's sentinels, Sherman's neckties

3. Why was land "dirt cheap" after the war? What was one result of land being so low priced?

4. Give two reasons for the labor shortage after the war.

spots marked the start of new growth. For example, in the parts of the state that had escaped war damage—the northeast and the southwest—farm production had resumed. In 1865 and 1866, a worldwide shortage of cotton helped the South revive. Demand for cotton by New England and European manufacturers was so great that Georgia farmers growing cotton could sell it at a high price. Some northern banks, and a few new Georgia banks, began lending money to cotton producers. Slowly Georgia agriculture improved, but as ever, it remained tied to the white fiber plant.

Other parts of the economy received a boost when northern bankers and businessmen began making investments in the South. Money from the North helped get Georgia's mills going, the trains running again, and new companies started.

Carpetbaggers and Scalawags

Along with northern money came northern opportunists, people looking for a way to take advantage of the South's economic and political turmoil. Some gained control of businesses or bought land cheaply to sell later at a profit. Others used their money and influence with federal authorities to gain high positions in Reconstruction governments. Because these persons often carried traveling bags made of carpet material, they were called **carpetbaggers** by white southerners. The carpetbaggers were likened to vultures preying on southerners' misfortune.

Likewise, white southerners who worked with the carpetbaggers received their own nickname—**scalawags**. The scalawags, often looked upon as traitors, were despised by most of their white neighbors.

Help for the People

In March 1865, the United States government set up the Bureau of Refugees, Freedmen, and Abandoned Lands. Popularly known as the **Freedmen's Bureau**, this federal agency issued food, clothing, fuel, and other supplies to needy white refugees and black freedmen.

At first the Freedmen's Bureau helped thousands of poor whites. Soon, however, it became an agency mainly to help blacks function as free persons. Under slavery, blacks had been denied any education, given few responsibilities, and prevented from making decisions for themselves. Suddenly they were free and responsible for their own lives.

Many blacks were unsure about going back to work on plantations. They feared that white landowners would treat them badly. To overcome these fears, the bureau helped blacks and white landowners draw up labor contracts. Written contracts were designed to guarantee the workers a fair wage and job security and the employers a stable work force.

A Freedmen's School, 1866. Why would adults as well as children be in this school?

Because most blacks could neither read nor write, education was a primary concern of the Freedmen's Bureau. The bureau set up schools and assisted charity groups in doing the same. It also helped blacks set up their own churches. And the bureau sometimes acted for blacks in legal matters and encouraged them to take part in politics.

Help for blacks also came from northern missionary and charitable groups, sponsored mainly by the Congregationalist, Methodist, and Baptist churches. Between 1865 and 1873, these groups sent 367 teachers—80 percent of them women—to Georgia. These teachers set up schools across the state and taught both children and adults to read and write. They also stressed the virtues of hard work and good citizenship.

Such groups helped start the first colleges for African American students in Georgia. In 1867, Atlanta University, sponsored by the American Missionary Association, was established. In Augusta, the American Baptist Home Missionary Society founded Morehouse College (later relocated in Atlanta). The northern Methodist Episcopal Church founded Clark College.

Negative Reactions

White Georgians did not always appreciate the activities of the Freedmen's Bureau. At the time, many whites were suffering the same poverty as blacks, but receiving little help from the agency. To

▶ **Locating the Main Ideas**

1. Define: carpetbagger, scalawag, Freedmen's Bureau

2. Why was it easier for northeast and southwest Georgia to recover from the war?

3. How did carpetbaggers take advantage of Georgia in the post-bellum period?

4. What was the purpose of the Freedmen's Bureau? How did its clients (the people who used it) change over time?

them, bureau staff often seemed more concerned with helping the Republican party in state politics than with helping people in need.

Other people not always welcomed were northern missionaries and teachers who came south during Reconstruction. To many white southerners, the message they brought was one of raising former slaves to a position of social equality with whites. ◀

Political Reconstruction

In late 1863, President Lincoln had begun planning for reuniting the nation once the fighting ended. Lincoln saw reconstruction as a healing, not a punishing, process. In March 1865, in his second inaugural address, he had expressed this view:

> With malice toward none, with charity for all,...let us strive to finish the work we are in, to bind up the nation's wounds....

Presidential Reconstruction

Lincoln's plan for reconstructing the South was to bring seceded states back into the Union as quickly as possible. He would name a provisional (acting) governor for each state. Except for former Confederate leaders, southerners would be pardoned and granted full citizenship rights if they took an oath of allegiance to the United States. Qualified voters would then elect delegates to write a new state constitution. If this document did three things—declared secession null and void, abolished slavery, and canceled all war debts—the state would be restored to the Union.

But, on April 15, 1865—only six days after Lee's surrender—Abraham Lincoln was dead, the victim of an assassin's bullet. His vice-president, Andrew Johnson of Tennessee, had been the only south-

Gen. John B. Gordon. In September 1865, Georgia's best known soldier took the oath of allegiance to the United States. What is the probable reason Gordon took this oath?

ern U.S. senator not to resign his seat in 1861. He assumed the presidency, determined to carry out Lincoln's program.

In June 1865, President Johnson named James Johnson, a Columbus attorney who had opposed secession, as Georgia's provisional governor. Governor Johnson called for an election to select delegates to a constitutional convention. That body met in October, and within a month had drafted a document that satisfied President Johnson. State voters approved the new constitution, and elected a new governor and General Assembly. From the old state capitol in Milledgeville, Georgia's state government began operating much as it had before the Civil War.

In December 1865, Georgia's General Assembly ratified the Thirteenth Amendment to the U.S. Constitution outlawing slavery in America. It also adopted legislation recognizing certain rights of freed blacks. For the first time, blacks would be allowed to make legal contracts, sue, and hold and sell personal property. Still, there were many rights blacks did not have. The new constitution, for instance, only allowed white male citizens to vote (which meant that only white males served on juries). The constitution also prohibited the marriage of whites and "persons of African descent." Lawmakers further prohibited blacks from testifying against whites in court.

Certain that Georgia would be restored to the Union, the General Assembly chose the state's two U.S. senators—Alexander Stephens and Herschel Johnson.

Congressional Reconstruction

Not everyone was happy with the manner and speed of the South's "reconstruction." Some Congressmen, known as Radical Republicans, had strongly opposed Lincoln's plan for Reconstruction. Now with Andrew Johnson as president, they were even more upset. The Radicals distrusted Johnson, a former Democrat from Tennessee. Also, Johnson had gone beyond Lincoln's original plan and had pardoned many former Confederate officials and military officers.

Rather than welcoming southern states back into the Union, Radical Republicans felt the South should be punished. They especially wanted to keep Democrats who had been political leaders before the war from regaining political power. If southern states were allowed quick entry back into the Union, Radical Republicans feared Democrats would win control of Congress.

By 1866, Radicals observed that southern states had met President Johnson's conditions for Reconstruction, but they were dissatisfied. Except for Texas, new state governments were functioning in each of the former Confederate states. These new governments, however, were run by white Democrats—most of whom were ex-Confederate officers or officials. Though freeing the slaves, many of the southern legislatures had passed **Black Codes**—laws limiting the political and civil rights of former slaves.

Radical Republicans were furious. They decided to seize control of Reconstruction from President Johnson. In Congress, they refused to approve the new state governments or to seat their representatives. In the congressional elections of 1866, Republicans won a majority in both the U.S. House and Senate. President Johnson, lacking Lincoln's political skill, was unable to prevent the Radicals from taking charge of Reconstruction. His relationship with Congress became so bad that the House later **impeached** him (filed charges to remove from office). By a single vote in his Senate trial, the president was saved from removal.

The Fourteenth Amendment

In reaction to the Black Codes, Congress in 1866 proposed a new amendment to the U.S. Constitution. The Fourteenth Amendment made it clear that blacks were citizens of the United States and of the state in which they lived. All citizens, regardless of race, were to be guaranteed "equal protection of the law." The amendment also made the federal government protector of all citizens' rights, regardless of where they lived.

The Fourteenth Amendment did not expressly give blacks the right to vote. (At the time, only six states in the nation—all in the North—allowed blacks to vote.) It did provide, however, that if a state denied any portion of its citizens their rights, it would lose a similar portion of its representation in Congress. Georgia and the

The 13th, 14th, and 15th Amendments

Amendment 13: Passed by Congress January 31, 1865. Ratified December 6, 1865.

Neither slavery nor involuntary servitude...shall exist within the United States, or any place subject to their jurisdiction.

Amendment 14: Passed by Congress June 13, 1866. Ratified July 9, 1868.

No State shall make or enforce any law which shall abridge [limit] the privileges or immunities [or rights] of citizens of the United States; nor shall any State deprive any person of life, liberty, or property, without due process of law; nor deny to any person within its jurisdiction the equal protection of the laws.

Amendment 15: Passed by Congress February 26, 1869. Ratified February 3, 1870.

The right of citizens of the United States to vote shall not be denied or abridged by the United States or by any State on account of race, color, or previous condition of servitude.

Georgians in History

Alexander Stephens

Like many other southerners, Alexander Hamilton Stephens felt it was his duty to support the Confederacy. His native Georia had, after all, voted to break away from the Union. He is best remembered as vice-president of the Confederacy, but that role was not his most important one. His 28 years of service in the U.S. Congress both before and after the Civil War made Stephens the most prominent Georgian of the nineteenth century.

Born on a Wilkes County farm in 1812, Aleck, an orphan at 14, was educated at the University of Georgia. There he proved himself to be a gifted student and outstanding speaker. Frail and slight, weighing about 100 pounds, Stephens suffered aches, illnesses, and depression throughout his life.

After setting up a law practice in Crawfordville, Stephens was elected to Georgia's state legislature in 1836 and to Congress in 1843. With a reputation for independent thinking, Stephens had generally opposed slavery until 1850. In Congress, he was widely respected for his skills as a speaker and was one of the South's most influential spokesmen. Stephens was not in favor of secession, but not even his great speaking ability could persuade his fellow Georgians to stay in the Union. Once that decision was made, Stephens supported it by helping to draft the Confederate constitution and serving as vice-president.

He spent most of the war at his Crawfordville home, opposing many practices of Jefferson Davis's government. Imprisoned in Boston briefly after the

Alexander Stephens and his servant, Aleck Kent Stephens. The former Confederate vice-president, although in poor health and often confined to a wheelchair, worked hard to get Georgia back in the Union. In this 1882 photo, he is on his way to be sworn in as governor of Georgia.

war, Stephens was never charged with "Confederate crimes" and was allowed to return to Georgia. He once again was elected to Congress in 1872, where he served 10 years before retiring at age 70 with severe health problems. Georgia's badly divided Democratic party immediately urged him to run for governor. Elected in 1882, Stephens was in office for only 119 days before he died, serving the state he had loved all his life.

---

other former Confederate states, except Tennessee, refused to ratify the amendment.

Military Occupation Again

Early in 1867, Radical Republicans pushed an act through Congress to place the 10 southern states refusing to ratify the Fourteenth Amendment under military occupation. The states were divided into five military districts. (Georgia, Florida, and Alabama were in the Third District.) In charge of each district was a U.S. Army general, backed by federal troops.

Under this new setup, the first task was to register voters. All adult males, black as well as white, who took the oath of allegiance to the United States could register. Certain categories of ex-Confederates, however, were denied this right.

1. Define: Black Codes, impeach

2. Identify: Andrew Johnson, Thirteenth Amendment, Alexander Stephens, Herschel Johnson, Radical Republicans, Fourteenth Amendment

3. Why were the Radical Republicans unhappy with President Johnson's reconstruction of the South?

4. What did the Radical Republicans do about states refusing to ratify the Fourteenth Amendment to the U.S. Constitution?

In each state, the new voters were to elect delegates to write a new state constitution (which had to be approved by Congress). When new legislatures were elected, they had to ratify the Fourteenth Amendment. Only after the southern states had done these things would they be free of military occupation and readmitted to the Union.

In April 1868, Georgia voters ratified a new state constitution. In it, race was removed as a qualification for voting. A provision was added that "The State of Georgia shall ever remain a member of the American Union." All married women were guaranteed control of their own property. Imprisonment for debt was abolished. And, for the first time, Georgia was to have a free public school system for all children. This provision was not carried out until 1871.

In the summer of 1868, Georgia's General Assembly finally ratified the Fourteenth Amendment. Nine days after that action, federal troops were withdrawn. But Reconstruction was not over. Federal troops would return and occupy the state a year later. ◀

Blacks in Georgia Politics

In 1867, African Americans voted for the first time in Georgia, selecting delegates to a convention to draft a new state constitution. Of 169 convention delegates elected, 37 were black. When the black delegates were denied rooms in Milledgeville hotels, U.S. Gen. John Pope, who commanded the Third District, ordered the convention moved to Atlanta. This move helped Atlanta in its longstanding bid to become Georgia's state capital, a move voters approved the following year.

In 1868, Georgia blacks voted on a new state constitution and cast their first ballots for state and federal offices. The Constitution of 1868, which they helped ratify, gave more rights to more citizens than previous Georgia constitutions. Black males gained full civil rights, including the vote. In the election that followed, 32 black Republicans were elected to Georgia's General Assembly. Of 172 state representatives, 29 were black; of 44 senators, 3 were black. In the same election, a white Republican, Rufus Bullock, defeated a popular hero, ex-Confederate general John B. Gordon, to become governor.

The participation by blacks in politics was not easily accepted by most whites. While the newly elected General Assembly ratified the Fourteenth Amendment, many of its white members looked for ways to remove the black members. Over the protests of the black members, the white majority, in September 1868, voted to expel 28 blacks. The

The First Vote. Freedmen go to the ballot box supervised by federal officials. This event was carried on the front page of the national news magazine, Harper's Weekly, *November 16, 1867.*

argument for doing this was that the state constitution did not grant blacks the right to hold public office. Four mulatto members (persons of mixed black and white ancestry), however, were allowed to retain their seats.

The Rise of Terrorist Groups

The summer and fall of 1868 also witnessed the rise of the Ku Klux Klan (KKK) in Georgia. This secret organization, founded in Tennessee in 1866, began as an effort by southern white Democrats to regain control of their governments from Republicans.

Disguised in hoods and robes, Klan members used terror and threats of violence in their attempts to restore southern Democrats to power. This meant attacking the base of Republican strength in the South—the large number of freed slaves. But the Klan was interested in more than political parties. It sought to control the social and economic activities of blacks. Klan sympathizers—and there were many—argued that the KKK was necessary for white self-protection, particularly in areas where whites were a minority.

To achieve its goals, the Klan and other similar organizations attempted to **intimidate** (frighten) blacks into submitting to control by whites. Blacks who did not submit, and others who stood by them, faced having their houses burned, whippings, or even death. The Klan encouraged lynching (illegal killing, usually by hanging, by violent mobs) of blacks. In one month in 1868, the Freedmen's Bureau reported 142 terroristic acts against blacks, including 31 murders, 48 attempted murders, and 63 beatings in the South.

One way that the Klan intimidated blacks was at the polls. At the time, Georgia did not use the secret ballot. During elections, Klan observers would often watch to see which ballot—Republican or Democrat—a black voter would take. If the voter did not take the Democratic ticket, he risked being the target of KKK violence.

The activities of the KKK and other such organizations alarmed the Radical Republicans in Congress. In 1868, 1869, and again in 1871, Congress set up committees to investigate the Klan and other secret organizations.

The End of Reconstruction

The activities of the Klan, the expelling of black legislators from the General Assembly, and other problems led Governor Bullock to ask Congress for help. In December 1869, Georgia was placed under federal military control for a third time. An army commander ordered the General Assembly to reseat the expelled black mem-

Members of the Ku Klux Klan dressed in robes and hoods to disguise themselves and to make their appearance more frightening.

Jefferson Long, a Macon tailor, became Georgia's first black congressman. After a short term, he resumed his business and remained active in Republican party politics.

▶ **Locating the Main Ideas**

1. Define: intimidate, amnesty
2. Identify: Rufus Bullock, John B. Gordon, Jefferson Long, Fifteenth Amendment
3. What event helped Atlanta to become the capital of the state?
4. What was the Ku Klux Klan attempting to do through its terroristic activities? How did Klan members justify their activities?
5. Why did Governor Bullock ask federal soldiers to return to Georgia? What happened to Bullock when the soldiers left?

bers. In south Georgia, seven counties were placed under military occupation because of Klan terrorism. Various laws were enacted to protect Republican voters.

Now Georgia had to satisfy additional requirements before becoming part of the union. Congress ordered Georgia to ratify a new constitutional amendment—the Fifteenth—to protect the voting rights of blacks. In February 1870, the General Assembly ratified the Fifteenth and reapproved the Fourteenth amendments. In October, it authorized the statewide system of public schools. The schools were to be "for the instruction of white and colored youth of the district in separate schools."

Federal troops left the state, and in July 1870 Georgia was again one of the United States. That year, Jefferson Long, a former slave, became the first black Georgian elected to Congress. After the Civil War, Long had become active in the Republican party. He successfully ran for a seat in the U.S. House of Representatives and became the first black ever to make a speech in that body. Long called for an end to lynching and other violence and spoke out in Congress against a bill that would make it easier for ex-Confederates to hold public office.

Once federal troops withdrew, the administration of Rufus Bullock, the Republican governor, was doomed. During his term in office, he and his aides had recklessly spent public funds. Newspaper editorials charged that Bullock's friends were filling their pockets with much of this money. The state also had run up a large debt in an effort to rebuild railroads.

As proof of corruption mounted, Georgians elected a solidly Democratic legislature that began looking into the financial dealings of the "carpetbagger" government. Facing impeachment, Governor Bullock resigned and returned to his hometown in New York. In a special election to fill the governor's office, Democrat James M. Smith was elected.

Meanwhile, in Washington, D.C., Radical Republicans were losing their strength and their interest in punishing the South and helping southern blacks. In 1872, Congress granted **amnesty** (forgiveness) to all but 500 former Confederates, making them eligible to hold public office. The Freedmen's Bureau was abolished the same year.

In 1872, Governor Smith was easily reelected. Only four blacks were elected to the General Assembly. With the state firmly controlled by white Democrats, the *Atlanta Constitution* noted the passing of "the long night of Radical rule." The newspaper concluded, "Thank God Georgia is redeemed." ◀

CHAPTER ACTIVITIES

Reviewing the Main Ideas

1. How did Georgians continue to feel the effects of Sherman's March to the Sea after the war had ended?

2. Explain why capital in the South had almost vanished as a result of the Civil War.

3. Discuss land, labor, and capital in terms of who had them, and how that affected the rebuilding of the South after the war.

4. How did the Freedmen's Bureau help blacks and white landowners work together?

5. Why was education an immediate concern of the Freedmen's Bureau? How did colleges for black students get started in Georgia?

6. Why did white Georgians react negatively to the Freedmen's Bureau as well as other groups who had come south to help former slaves?

7. Describe the different views of Reconstruction as held by President Lincoln, President Johnson, and the Radical Republicans.

8. How did Georgia's Constitution of 1868 benefit women and children in the state?

9. Summarize the meaning of the Thirteenth, Fourteenth, and Fifteenth amendments to the U.S. Constitution.

10. What became of the Radical Republicans in the 1870s?

Give It Some Extra Thought

1. **Identifying Problems.** As a result of the Civil War, Georgia's slave population was freed. Discuss how the system of slavery left blacks unprepared for freedom. What kind of help did they receive?

2. **Comparing and Analyzing.** What were the main differences between the reconstruction plans of Lincoln and the Radical Republicans? What parts of the radical reconstruction do you think were good or helpful? What parts do you think were bad or harmful? Explain your conclusions.

Sharpen Your Skills

1. **Pie Charts.** Make three pie charts showing the black and white makeup of the 1868 General Assembly as a whole and of each house. Look up the 1860 black and white population figures for the state on page 163. Were blacks represented in the General

The Kimball Opera House served as the state capitol from 1869 to 1889.

Assembly in proportion to their numbers in the population?

2. **Analyzing Visual Evidence.** Carefully examine the picture of "The First Vote" (page 214). What does the fact that it was on the front page of a national news magazine tell you about the importance of the event? Look at the way the first two men in line are dressed and guess what their occupations might be. What is the man in uniform doing? How does the artist show the voting being conducted? Is it a secret ballot?

3. **Demonstrating the Need for Rules in Society.** Give examples of how the Ku Klux Klan operated outside the law. How do its activities demonstrate the need for rules and laws in society?

Going Further

1. **Imagining.** Imagine that you visited Atlanta in the summer of 1865. Write a letter to your parents describing what you see and how you feel about it. You may want to look at some photographs taken of Atlanta during that time to help you imagine what your visit would be like.

2. **Collecting Evidence.** Find evidence in this chapter of Democratic and Republican activities to support the following statement. "In many ways the political reconstruction of the South was a struggle for control between the Democrats and the Republicans."

UNIT 6

Georgia Centennial	Constitution of 1877 adopted	Edison invents electric light	Coca Cola developed in Atlanta	New state capitol building opens	Tom Watson elected to Congress	General Assembly passes first "Jim Crow" laws	Cotton States and International Exposition held in Atlanta		Democratic party begins holding primary elections	First white primary elections held
1876	**1877**	**1879**	**1886**	**1889**	**1890**	**1891**	**1895**	**1896**	**1898**	**1900**
United States Centennial	Thomas A. Edison invents phonograph	Edison invents electric light	Statue of Liberty dedicated	North and South Dakota, Montana, and Washington admitted to Union	Idaho and Wyoming admitted to Union	Populist party formed	Babe Ruth born	Supreme Court upholds "separate but equal" doctrine; rural free delivery begins	Spanish-American War; United States annexes Hawaii	

Georgia Enters the Second Century of Statehood

1876–1917

1903	1905	1906	1907	1908	1910	1912	1913	1914	1915	1916
		Atlanta race riot; Georgia's first child labor law	Alcohol prohibition begins	Literacy test required for voters; "grandfather clause" adopted	State regulation of automobiles begins	Girl Scouts first meet in Savannah	Leo Frank trial	Carl Vinson elected to U.S. House of Representatives	First juvenile courts created	First compulsory school attendance law; state highway department created
Wright brothers' first successful flight	W.E.B. DuBois organizes Niagara Movement	San Francisco earthquake		Henry Ford introduces Model T	NAACP established	Arizona and New Mexico admitted to Union	Sixteenth Amendment (federal income tax) adopted	World War I begins in Europe; Panama Canal opens	First long distance telephone call, New York to San Francisco	Federal-Aid Road Act passed by Congress

15

Coming Up Next!
• Redeemers gain control
• The Progressive movement

Political and Social Change in the New South

In many ways, 1876 was a notable year. It was the 100th anniversary of the nation and of Georgia's statehood. In the West, Colorado joined the Union as the 38th state. In Montana, Gen. George Armstrong Custer and his entire force of 265 cavalry soldiers were killed by Sioux Indians at the Battle of Little Big Horn. Back east, Alexander Graham Bell obtained a patent for a new invention, the telephone.

This nation's centennial year also witnessed one of the most controversial presidential elections in American history. Samuel Tilden, a Democrat from New York, won the popular vote against an Ohio Republican, Rutherford B. Hayes. But, by one vote, Tilden failed to win a majority of the electoral votes. By law, Congress then had to determine the winner. Southern Democrats in Congress made a deal. If Hayes would promise to pull out all federal troops remaining in the South, thus ending Reconstruction, they would vote for the Republican.

Redeemers Gain Control

Four years earlier, in 1872, Democrats had regained Georgia's governorship. The Republican party in the state was rapidly losing strength as a political force. Because of threats and other forms of pressure, Georgia's black citizens no longer turned out in great numbers to support Republican candidates. Across the state, the number of black officeholders dropped dramatically. Of the 32 blacks elected to the General Assembly in 1868, only 4 returned four years later.

After Reconstruction, Georgia Democrats continued their efforts to "redeem," that is, to win back, their state from Republican influence. Known as Redeemers, the Democrats worked to undo the changes imposed during Reconstruction. This meant restoring Democrats to public office and making clear that control of society was in the hands of the white race, an idea known as **white supremacy**.

Constitution of 1877

Although the federal troops were gone and most Republicans removed from office, Georgia still had one holdover from Reconstruction—the Constitution of 1868. Many Democrats considered it a document written by the enemy. Robert Toombs, known as the "unreconstructed rebel," began a campaign to replace it.

Atlanta rail depot, 1887. Atlanta rebuilt so quickly after the Civil War that it became the symbol of the New South.

In 1877, the General Assembly called for a convention to rewrite Georgia's 1868 constitution. Toombs quickly took charge of the proceedings. He reminded members of the large state debt and other abuses that occurred during Reconstruction. Now, he argued, was the time to weaken state government and limit its role in economic development.

The resulting Constitution of 1877 was the most restrictive constitution in Georgia history. This new document made it almost impossible for state government to borrow money. Tax money could be spent only for purposes spelled out in the constitution—and these were few. Terms of office for the governor and state senators were reduced from four years to two.

Bourbon Redeemers

Many of the new constitution's supporters wanted Georgia to return to the cotton-based economy of antebellum days. Another Redeemer faction, however, soon gained the upper hand. These Democrats believed that the South's prosperity depended on manufacturing and other industry, not cotton. Often referred to as Bourbons,* they wanted the state to become more self-sufficient.

---

*The name "Bourbon" referred to an old French ruling family that returned to power after the French Revolution. During Reconstruction, Radical Republicans gave this title to southern Democrats, who appeared to want to return to the days of old. In reality, Bourbon Democrats came to oppose many aspects of Georgia's antebellum economy.

Georgia Gets a Capitol

When Atlanta became Georgia's capital in 1868, state government met temporarily in an over-crowded building that served as both Atlanta's city hall and Fulton County's courthouse. State officials soon decided that Georgia needed a new **capitol** (central government building). Atlanta agreed to complete an unfinished building downtown known as the Kimball Opera House for use by the state. In 1869, the building was ready and lawmakers moved in.

With the end of Reconstruction, some politicians began calling for the General Assembly to move Georgia's capital back to Milledgeville. The matter came before the constitutional convention that met in 1877. Atlanta's city council, however, didn't want to lose the capital. They proposed to the convention that Atlanta be designated permanent capital of Georgia. In return, the city would build and give to the state a new capitol "as good as the old Capitol building in Milledgeville."

Convention delegates decided to place the question of Georgia's state capital on the ballot. Speeches were made across the state. Milledgeville supporters associated Atlanta with Reconstruction abuses. They argued that big city temptations were too great for members of the legislature. Atlanta supporters pointed to Atlanta's growing importance to the state, especially noting its superior rail facilities. In December 1877, by a vote of 99,147 to

Georgia's newly completed state capitol, 1889.

55,201, Georgians voted to keep Atlanta as state capital.

Rather than have Atlanta build a new capitol, the General Assembly accepted a payment of $115,625 from the city. The state would be responsible for the remaining costs and would oversee construction. Lack of funds kept the state from acting until 1883, when the General Assembly agreed to spend $1,000,000 to build the new capitol.

On September 2, 1885, the cornerstone of the new capitol was set before a crowd of 10,000 onlookers. Construction was completed in March 1889 and the keys delivered to state officials. On July 4, formal dedication of the capitol took place. At the ceremonies, Gov. John B. Gordon praised the building as a symbol of Georgia's redemption from Reconstruction.

This meant attracting investors from the North to build mills and factories in Georgia. It also meant farmers needed to **diversify** (give variety to) their crops. They could do this by growing less cotton and more of the foods and grains usually purchased from other parts of the country. Diversifying agriculture would allow Georgians to buy from Georgians. It would keep badly needed capital from leaving the state.

The Bourbon call for a New South referred to modernizing the economy. It was not a proposal for social or political change. White supremacy, one-party politics, low taxes, and a limited role for state government were still at the heart of the Bourbon program.

Recognized as the three political leaders in the New South movement were ex-Confederate generals John B. Gordon and Alfred E. Colquitt, and ex-governor Joseph E. Brown. They were referred to as the Bourbon Triumvirate. A strong supporter was *Atlanta Con-*

stitution editor Henry Grady, who frequently wrote praises of an industrialized South. ▶

Challenges to the Democratic Party

From 1865 to 1900, the nation suffered from a depressed economy. During the 1870s, the slowdown was particularly bad in the South. Georgia Democrats in public office feared voters might hold them responsible for the hard times.

Bourbon Democrats in Georgia and other southern states looked for ways to strengthen their support among white voters. One strategy was to ignite white fears of "black rule" and social equality. Without a unified Democratic party, whites were warned, the balance of power was in the hands of black voters. White supremacy became a frequent and effective rallying cry in Democratic campaigns for most of the next century.

Farmers and Politics

The Bourbons had made it clear that they believed the future of the South lay in industry and manufacturing, not in growing cotton. Yet, most Georgians were cotton farmers. They believed state government was more concerned with recruiting industry than helping them. Small farmers always seemed to be in debt and they believed that Bourbon favoritism toward industry was partly responsible for their situation.

In 1874, northwest Georgia farmers organized a challenge to the regular Democratic party. Their leaders were Dr. William H. Felton of Cartersville and his wife, Rebecca Latimer Felton. As an Independent Democrat, Dr. Felton was elected three times to the U.S. Congress on a campaign to help the farmer. Mrs. Felton made speeches, wrote articles, and sent letters to the newspapers about the injustices that farmers and other "little people" were suffering.

The Independent movement reached its peak in 1878, when Georgians elected three Independents to Congress. Despite these successes, the movement died out after 1882, forcing farmers to find another way to challenge the Bourbons.

The next challenge came from a self-help organization known as the Farmers' Alliance, which came to Georgia in 1887. It attracted farmers rapidly and by 1890 had a membership in the state of 100,000.

The Alliance called for better schools, better roads, and changes in state tax laws to ease the burden of farmers. The Alliance also confronted the railroads. Farmers had no choice of transportation facilities. They had to pay whatever rate the railroad charged to transport their produce to market. Often, the railroad charged the small farmer higher rates than the large shipper. The rates changed frequently and from place to place. The Farmers' Alliance fought for laws requiring railroads to post their rates in the railroad stations and charge the same rates per mile for all shippers.

▶ **Locating the Main Ideas**

1. Define: white supremacy, diversify, capitol
2. Identify: Redeemers, Robert Toombs, Bourbon Triumvirate
3. The Democratic party had two Redeemer factions. What was the aim of each?
4. Who made the final decision to keep Atlanta the capital of the state after Reconstruction ended?

Georgians in History

Henry Grady

He held no political office, but he helped place others in positions of power. He made no new inventions, but he helped the war-torn South create a new image after the Civil War. Although bitterness about the war lingered, he traveled the country in the late 1800s, spreading a message of reconciliation. And when in 1889, Henry Woodfin Grady died at age 39, the *Atlanta Constitution* lost its most distinguished editor and the state of Georgia one of its most admired citizens.

Born in Athens in 1850, Henry Grady attended the University of Georgia, where he excelled in academics and public speaking. After graduation, he studied briefly at the University of Virginia before returning to Georgia and writing letters to the *Atlanta Constitution*. In the days before electronic media, newspapers were especially important, and the publication of his letters sparked Grady's interest in journalism.

For 10 years, Grady worked for various Georgia newspapers before buying, in 1880, one-fourth of the *Atlanta Constitution*. He hired respected journalists, broadened the paper's coverage, and increased its circulation and reputation. Its 122,000 weekly sales made the *Constitution* the region's most influential newspaper—and Grady equally important. He continued to write for national publications, and his August 1886 reports of the Charleston earthquake were carried worldwide.

Grady was the first Southerner to address the annual meeting of the New England Society of New York City, a group of prominent industrialists. On December 22, 1886, he delivered his now-famous "New South" speech in which he described a region rebuilding itself and looking forward to a bright economic future. He used the *Atlanta Constitution* to deliver a similar message. He also used his considerable influence to plan the International Cotton Exhibition and the Piedmont Exposition, both symbols of the South's strong economic potential, and to organize Atlanta's first baseball club.

In 1889, Grady traveled to Boston to speak on race relations. Already ill, he weakened on the return trip, dying of pneumonia at his Peachtree Street home on December 23. A public hospital, a county, a national highway, and the journalism college at the University of Georgia all bear his name.

Democratic candidates for the General Assembly noted the strength of the Alliance and agreed to support its demands. For two years, a "farmer's legislature" passed laws to help farmers.

Tom Watson

One Alliance leader soon became a champion of Georgia's farmers. He was Thomas E. Watson from Thomson, Georgia. In 1882, McDuffie County's small farmers—black and white—joined forces to send this dynamic 26-year-old lawyer to the General Assembly.

Watson did not share Henry Grady's dream of an industrialized Georgia. He argued that industry would do little to help the majority of Georgians who toiled in the cotton fields. He lashed out at those he saw as the farmers' enemies: bankers who charged high interest rates, railroads with their high freight rates, and politicians who supported the banks and railroads.

In 1890, with Alliance support, Tom Watson was elected to the U.S. Congress. There, he won a big victory for farming people. He sponsored and pushed through a law providing for RFD—rural free delivery. No longer would farm families have to travel miles to town to pick up their mail.

About this time, a new political movement, the People's party, was growing in the United States. Many Democrats, including Tom Watson, joined it. The **Populists** (as they were commonly known) were for political equality and called on all farmers, black and white, to unite.

In the election of 1892, Tom Watson ran for Congress as a Populist. Most Georgians were farmers, but Watson felt that political and economic power was in the hands of merchants, bankers, and lawyers who lived in the cities. Bourbon Democrats, he argued, had allowed business and financial interests in the North to get rich at the expense of the farmer.

The Democrats fought back fiercely. They charged that voting for Watson, a Populist, would split the white vote, allowing blacks to hold political office once again. Many white voters began to have second thoughts. Some voters were paid to vote Democratic. In Richmond County, 2,000 more votes were cast than there were registered voters. In an election filled with fraud, Watson was defeated.

Tom Watson, Populist leader.

Tom Watson ran again and again as a Populist, but never won. Later, he became well known and wealthy from publishing magazines and books. But Watson wound up a bitter, hateful man, turning in particular against African Americans, Catholics, and Jews. ▶

The Progressive Movement

By the late nineteenth century, the Bourbons were no longer the guiding force in state politics. Despite some success in attracting northern industry and capital, Georgia was still a cotton state. Attempts to diversify agriculture had failed. Yet, even though planters and small farmers could not be convinced to grow different crops, another type of diversification was occurring—the breakup of plantations.

As urban populations grew, new concerns developed about social conditions. An informal group of Democrats known as "Progressives" had some plans for improving conditions in the state. The most influential leader of the movement, Hoke Smith, became governor in 1906.

Like the Bourbons, Progressive Democrats believed in keeping Georgia a one-party state. They also opposed any laws or programs that would promote social equality or competition between the races. Progressives differed from the Bourbons, though. Their attempts to improve society focused on legislating moral behavior (especially with respect to alcoholic beverages), improving education, and helping those in need.

▶ **Locating the Main Ideas**

1. Define: Populists
2. Identify: Dr. William H. Felton, Rebecca Latimer Felton, Farmers' Alliance, RFD
3. Why did farmers feel they were being neglected by the policies of the Bourbon Democrats?
4. How did Democrats use the issue of race to defeat Tom Watson in the congressional election of 1892?

Progressive Era advertisement, 1906. How does this soft drink ad reflect the movement for social reform?

Disfranchisement

Progressive Democrats across the South stressed the importance of white supremacy. But they went further, openly supporting a policy of taking away the **franchise** (the right to vote) from blacks. Some politicians felt **disfranchisement** (taking away the right to vote) should apply to poor whites as well. One Alabama politician expressed that view when he said that restricting voting would place the power of government in the hands of "the intelligent and virtuous."

Because the Fifteenth Amendment guaranteed blacks the right to vote, state legislatures could not disfranchise blacks outright. Instead, they passed laws which technically applied to everyone, but had the consequence of making it harder for blacks (and many poor whites) to register and vote.

Since 1798, paying property and other taxes had been a condition for voting in Georgia, but the rule only applied to the previous year's taxes. The Constitution of 1877 had changed this. Thereafter, in addition to the previous year's taxes, *all* unpaid taxes from 1877 on had to be paid in order to vote. Payment was due at least six months before the election.

Among the taxes voters had to pay was the **poll tax**. First enacted in 1866, Georgia's poll tax was an annual $1 tax levied on each male in Georgia between the ages of 21 and 60. (This did not apply to women until 1922, when women gained the right to vote.) Money raised by the tax was earmarked, or reserved, for education. Citizens could not vote until they paid their poll tax. Although the amount was quite small, it was just one more obstacle to discourage poor people from voting.

A second way to disfranchise blacks was to keep them from participating in Democratic party affairs. Until 1898, party leaders from each county had selected candidates for statewide office at a state convention. That year, however, the Democratic party opened the process up to rank-and-file members by holding a **primary election**. This is a statewide election held by a political party to allow its members to decide who will be their party's candidate for each race in the **general election**. The winner of the general election (the official election conducted by the state) then becomes the officeholder.

Few Georgia blacks considered themselves Democrats in 1898, and it is not clear whether any voted in the first Democratic primary. Before the next primary, however, the party's state committee stepped in. In 1900, the committee ruled that only white Democrats would be allowed to vote in its primaries. Thus was born the **white primary**.

Those in favor of the white primary recognized that the Fifteenth Amendment kept states from excluding blacks from voting in the general election. But party primaries, Democrats argued, were different. First, they said, each political party is a private organization. Its primaries are private affairs—for members only. Second, party primaries are not real elections; rather, they simply select those who will represent that party in the general election.

By 1900, however, the South was overwhelmingly Democratic. In the general election, there was usually one candidate for each race—a white Democrat. This meant that political races were decided in the Democratic primary, not the general election. Four decades would pass before the U.S. Supreme Court would put an end to the white primary, ruling that it violated the Fifteenth Amendment.

In 1906, Hoke Smith used a band to rally a crowd in front of the Aldine Hotel in Fitzgerald. Later, as a U.S. senator, Smith became nationally known for his work on passing laws to create the Agricultural Extension Service and provide for vocational education.

In 1906, Progressive candidate Hoke Smith ran for governor on a platform that included black disfranchisement. At his urging, Georgia lawmakers proposed a constitutional amendment to impose a **literacy test** on voters. To many Georgia voters, the amendment seemed reasonable: those who select the state's leaders and amend its constitution should be able to read and write. In 1908, they approved it.

Why did this action disfranchise blacks? Under slavery it had been against the law to teach blacks to read or write. Efforts to provide schooling for blacks since emancipation had been limited. Thus, most Georgia blacks could not qualify to register to vote.

Because many whites were also illiterate, the law provided exemptions from the literacy test. For example, all persons of "good character" and who "understand the duties and obligations of citizenship under a republican form of government" were exempted from the test. Voter registrars in each county decided on who met these qualifications. Generally, the rule was applied to exempt illiterate whites but not illiterate blacks.

Another exemption was for any person who owned at least 40 acres of land in Georgia, or who had other taxable property worth at least $500. Few blacks owned this much land or taxable property.

A third exception to the literacy test went to any person who had served during wartime in the United States or Confederate armies or navies, or who was a descendant of such a veteran. Because many white Georgians had grandfathers who had fought in the Civil War, this provision became known as a **grandfather clause**. ▶

Preventing Social Equality

The Civil War forced the end of slavery, but it did not erase racial attitudes and customs that had grown up over 200 years in America.

▶ **Locating the Main Ideas**

1. Define: franchise, disfranchisement, poll tax, primary election, general election, white primary, literacy test, grandfather clause

2. What were three ways illiterate whites could exempt the literacy test and register to vote?

During Reconstruction, many whites became convinced that the radical Republicans were trying to force black social equality on the South. A central theme first of the Bourbons and later of the Progressives was to uphold white supremacy in all areas of society. This meant almost total **segregation** (keeping apart) of blacks and whites in public places. In general, whites refused to associate with blacks as equals.

In 1891, the General Assembly passed the first of a series of laws known as **Jim Crow laws**. The term "Jim Crow" was taken from an old minstrel song called "Jump, Jim Crow." It referred to written laws and unwritten customs which kept members of the two races apart. Georgia's first Jim Crow law required railroads to provide separate passenger cars for blacks and whites. Another law stated that black and white prisoners were to be segregated in convict camps.

Gradually, local governments joined the state in enforcing segregation. Atlanta and Savannah segregated streetcars. Soon Georgia cities had by law segregated theaters, elevators, and park benches. "White" and "Colored" signs appeared in train station waiting rooms, restaurants, and other public facilities.

Blacks protested strongly. But in the 1890s and early 1900s, black boycotts against segregated streetcars gained little reaction from white Georgians. Segregation became an accepted way of life.

In the North as well as throughout the South, attitudes of white supremacy took hold. "De facto" segregation (segregation existing *in fact*) if not "de jure" segregation (segregation existing *by law*) became commonplace. Certain areas such as neighborhoods, parks, and beaches became "off limits" to blacks. Certain jobs were closed to them.

Even the federal government accepted segregation as lawful and proper. It continued to maintain separate military units for black and white soldiers after the Civil War.

In 1896, the U.S. Supreme Court delivered a stunning blow to the struggle for black equality. In the case of *Plessy v. Ferguson*, the Court upheld the Louisiana conviction of a black man who tried to ride in a train car reserved for whites. This ruling put the federal courts in support of the so-called **separate but equal doctrine**. If equal public facilities were provided for both races, the Court ruled, then they could be legally separate.

Blacks had no power, however, to make sure facilities such as schools and parks were equal. In fact, black facilities (if they existed at all) were usually far inferior to those provided for whites. ◀

Social Reform

Progressive Democrats were known primarily for their efforts to make life better—especially for some of those less fortunate. They were part of a social reform movement that crossed the United

▶ **Locating the Main Ideas**

1. Define: segregation, Jim Crow laws, separate but equal doctrine
2. Identify: *Plessy v. Ferguson*
3. Explain the difference between de facto segregation and de jure segregation.

States from 1890 to 1910. Their special targets were evils related to the growth of industries and cities.

As a result of this reform movement, federal, state, and local governments passed laws on subjects they had never before considered. They began to regulate child labor, health and safety standards, and the working conditions of mill and factory workers.

Georgia's first compulsory (required) school attendance law came in 1916. Not everyone agreed with it or with the child labor laws. Some parents insisted they had a right to work their children as they saw fit, without any interference from government. For many years child labor and school attendance laws lacked public support, so they were difficult to enforce.

Young workers at the Enterprise Manufacturing Company in Augusta, 1909. Many of these children had already been employed for years. Note the way they are dressed and the lint on their clothing.

At a time when fewer Americans were producing their own food, reformers urged lawmakers to protect the public from unwholesome practices in the food industry. Governments passed laws setting standards of cleanliness and providing for inspection of packing houses, bakeries, and canneries. Other laws were passed to protect against products containing narcotics, alcohol, and other potentially harmful ingredients that were being sold as medicines.

Many kinds of reform laws were enacted in the Progressive Era, as it is often called. They covered not only labor and health, but also education, business, moral conduct, and even government itself. Child labor, prison reform, **prohibition** (forbidding the manufacture and sale of alcoholic beverages), and giving women the right to vote are areas that received attention in Georgia.

Child Labor

With the growth of industry—particularly textile mills—Georgia's children became an important source of labor. Working youngsters were deprived of an education and subjected to conditions which would be considered unthinkable today. In some cases, children under age 10 were forced to work 12 hours a day for as little as four cents an hour.

In 1906, Georgia Progressives finally moved state government to take a first step toward getting children out of the factories. That year, the General Assembly passed a child labor law prohibiting any boy or girl under 10 years of age from working in a factory. Children under 12 were also excluded, unless the child was an orphan

Young textile workers stand outside the mill houses in Augusta near the John P. King Manufacturing Company, 1909.

The Georgia Cracker in the Cotton Mills

The following account of working conditions for children is from an 1891 article by Clare de Graffenried, a Macon-born investigator for the U.S. Department of Labor:

The name coined to specify the native folk that spin or weave in the villages and towns is—"Crackers." The term embraces hundreds of thousands of non-slaveholding whites in antebellum days and their present descendants.

No colored people are employed in textile industries. Their labor market is limited to the cotton fields and farms of the country....

Around country mills the provision for housing the wage-earners is often inadequate. It is at serious risk to life and health that the operatives in remote settlements are forced to lodge in rotting, neglected habitations, even though they be rent free.

The choicest of these rickety abodes [dwelling places] was described by a girl whose only home it had been for fourteen years: "I reckin hit'll set up thar a right smart while yit, but hit's pow'ful cold en leaky...."

...Not a clock or watch is owned in the settlement. Life is regulated by the sun and the factory bell, which rings for rising, breakfast, and work. The hours of labor vary from seventy to seventy-two a week.

The workers were "borned in the country," and seldom visit even the neighboring town. Now and then a traveling minister enlivens the little church on the hilltop. At intervals a Sunday-school furnishes the only religious instruction. There is no regular school.

All purchases are made on the order system at the "company's store." Though it is not compulsory to deal there, there is no competition. Women often work a lifetime without touching a cent of their pay. One forlorn old maid lamented: "I hain't seed er dollar sence Confed [Confederate] money gave out. Hit 'u'd be good fur sore eyes ter see er genewine dollar...."

The hardships everywhere disastrous to textile workers fail to account for the wrecked health of so many of the Southern workers. Malaria, lurking about the stream, invades the houses close to the bank. Draining is neglected and epidemics are common.

The use of snuff is a withering curse. Habitual users smoke and chew tobacco, and dip snuff and "lip" the powder. Excessive use of this stimulant

or was helping support a needy parent. Children under 14 could work if they could write their name and a simple sentence, and if they had attended school for 12 weeks the previous year.

But these laws and other similar ones were hard to enforce. By 1920, Georgia led the nation in number of working children between ages 10 and 15. Not until the Fair Labor Standards Act of 1938 would the federal government set basic standards for the employment of children. ◀

Prison Reform

In 1866, Georgia's Reconstruction government had faced a growing problem: how to handle persons convicted of serious crimes.

▶ **Locating the Main Ideas**

1. Define: prohibition
2. How effective were the child labor law of 1906 and the compulsory school attendance law of 1916 in improving the lives of working children?

often creates the desire for a stronger one, and among the older women drunkenness is not uncommon.

The weakness and sickness of the operatives also stems from the early age at which work in the mills is begun. When five or six years old the juveniles follow the mothers to the mills, where they are incarcerated till premature old age. Unmarried women of thirty are wrinkled, bent, and haggard.

Take a little maid whose face is buried in her sunbonnet, and who, when asked her age, responds, "I'm er-gwine on ten." Push back her bonnet, hoping to find a face of vigor and joy. A sad spectacle reveals itself. Out of unkempt hair look glassy eyes ringed with black circles reaching far down her yellow cheeks. Her nose is pinched, the yellow lips furrowed with snuff stains. The skin is cadaverous [like that of a dead body].

"When do you go to school, my child?"

"Hain't never been thar," she responds.

"Never at school! Can't you read?"

"No,'m; but Lizy kin."

"Who is Lizy?"

"Me 'n Lizy's sisters."

"Where is your father?"

"Him done dade."

"And your mother?"

A backward motion of the thumb toward the mill is the only response.

"What is your name?"

"Georgy Alybamy Missippy Kicklighter."

"What do you do all day, Georgy?"

"Wuks." The same backward turn of the thumb.

Asked to state at what age work began, she guessed:

"Seven year."

"What do you do in the mill?"

"Pieces ainds." Then she recollects, "But I hain't been nowhar 'cep'n' in mill he'pen maw since I was five year ole."

"And were you never put at school?"

"Teacher done sont fur us, but me 'n' Lizy nary one didn't git thar, fur hit broke [quit]."

"You look sallow. Does anything ail you?"

"I be pow'ful weak."

"What does the doctor give you?"

"Don' give me nothin'. Maw, she gimme groun' pease. She 'low them's better'n doctor's truck."

This is the product of three generations of mill workers, the grandmother, mother, and child drudging side by side. None of them could read or write, none had ever been four miles from their shanty and the factory. "Lizy" was the freak of nature, the genius of the family, having learned her letters at Sunday-school.

Though the public are indifferent, mill officials as a rule oppose child labor as utilized in the South. Often a wholesale dismissal takes place, quickened by protests of labor unions. But, under various pretexts, the gnome-like toilers creep back, because of the scarcity of hands. A most powerful factor in this abuse is that the fathers will not work and the little ones must. Year after year bills to prevent the employment of children under ten and twelve are defeated in the legislature.

The government had little money to spend on the care of prisoners. Also, the state prison had been almost completely destroyed by Sherman's troops.

To solve this problem, Georgia adopted an approach in use in some other states—the convict lease system. For a fee, state government would lease persons convicted of serious crimes to railroads and other private companies.

This system moved the cost of caring for prisoners from the government to businesses. At the same time, businesses had a source of cheap labor. Across the state, convicts were put to work laying railroad track, mining coal, sawing lumber, making bricks, and distilling turpentine.

As the number of convicts increased in Georgia, the lease system became big business. In 1876, three companies arranged a 20-year lease of almost all the state's prisoners for $25,000 a year. Some of the state's top leaders became involved in it. Ex-governor Joseph E. Brown headed one company, and John B. Gordon owned part of another. In 1879, when the lease began, 1,196 convicts were turned over to them. In 1899, when it ran out, the three companies had 2,201 convicts.

Under the lease system, boys as young as 10, women, old men in their 70s, and those who were sick or insane were all treated alike. It soon became clear that the system was a monstrous evil.

The state had regulations that private companies were supposed to follow, but many abuses occurred. For example, it was against regulations to work leased convicts on the Sabbath and longer than sunrise to sunset. Yet, some worked as long as 15 hours a day, seven days a week. By day, prisoners usually worked in chains, overseen by "whipping bosses" ready to punish them. At night, some convicts slept chained together or locked in outdoor cages.

In the late 1800s, Georgia's courts were run by whites only. A black person's testimony seldom counted. Georgia's convict population was 90 percent black. The families and friends of black convicts had little influence, so the brutal system continued.

Some well-known Georgians did speak out against the system. The Feltons and Tom Watson fought to have it abolished. Ten years after he himself had leased convicts, John B. Gordon, as governor, spoke out against the lease system. He told the General Assembly that it "makes possible the infliction of greater punishment than the law and the courts have imposed...[and] it reduces to minimum the chances for reformation."

However, it would be another decade before the efforts of reformers would bring change. They published articles, made speeches, and held mass meetings to arouse the public.

In 1897, Gov. William Atkinson and the General Assembly took the first steps toward prison reform. They set up a state-run prison farm for all female prisoners, and for male prisoners either under 15 years old or too sick or weak to work.

Finally, in 1908, reacting to harsh criticism from newspapers and the public, the General Assembly thoroughly investigated the convict lease camps. Its findings were shocking. The system was abolished.

Thereafter, prisoners were kept on state prison farms or assigned to county prison camps to work on public roads. Although this change meant better living conditions for many prisoners, the chains and brutal treatment lasted for many years.

Agitation for reform continued. In 1915, the General Assembly, recognizing that young people in trouble should not be treated like adults, created the state's first juvenile courts. More reforms were to come in the 1930s and 1940s.

African American leader and teacher, Selena Sloan Butler was interested in many social reforms. As a member of the National Association of Colored Women, she supported prison reform in an 1897 speech, excerpted here.

The Chain Gang System

It is those convicts leased to private corporations who suffer miseries which [only] their poor miserable selves and God know. The chain-gang bosses, as a rule, are selected from the lowest element of the white race, and rather glory in their office and the freedom of dealing out misery and cruelty to helpless convicts for small offences, and often for no offence at all. Many of the chain-gang camps are situated in places remote from settlements and public roads, where no one can interfere with the inhuman treatment these poor, helpless creatures receive from beings who would be a disgrace to the brute kingdom. Many of the prisoners have scarcely enough clothing on their uncared for bodies to protect them from the gaze of others, or from winter's cold or summer's heat . . . .The majority of the prisoners in these private camps are poorly fed. . . .

In one camp sixty-one men were found sleeping in a room not more than nineteen feet square and seven feet from floor to ceiling. . . .Many of these convicts know not the comfort of sleeping upon even a cheap mattress or heap of straw, but must wrap about their tired and neglected bodies a blanket much worn and filled with dirt and vermin, and lie down, not upon a wood floor, but the dirt floor of a tent. . . .

. . .Little or no provision is made for the care of the sick; some have been forced to work till they fell upon the ground, dead.

Prohibition

Several Progressive reforms were designed to enforce "proper" moral behavior. One of these was prohibition.

After the Civil War, the Methodist and Baptist churches, and organizations such as the Woman's Christian Temperance Union (W.C.T.U.) and the Anti-Saloon League tried to stop the sale of liquor in Georgia. At first, a county wanting to go "dry" had to get the General Assembly to pass a law. So many bills were being introduced that in 1885, the General Assembly passed a **local option** prohibition law, allowing the citizens of each county to vote on the question. The "wet" forces fought back and some counties reversed their vote, but by 1906 over 100 had voted out liquor.

In 1906, Atlanta was the scene of a terrible race riot, which some whites blamed unfairly on drunkenness among black residents. Georgia's "dry" forces used the riot to push for statewide prohibition. In 1907, they succeeded. The General Assembly made it illegal to manufacture or sell alcoholic beverages in the state. In 1916, lawmakers went further by also making it a crime for citizens to possess liquor. Three years later, the nation voted in prohibition with ratification of the Eighteenth Amendment.

Voting Rights for Women

"Woman suffrage had its inception [beginning] in the fight against Saloons." These words were spoken by Rebecca Latimer Felton, a

In the following reading, Rebecca Latimer Felton, in a speech in 1915, responds to some of the arguments against woman suffrage.

Votes for Women

It is claimed that a woman should not vote, because she does not pay her husband's debts, while he is obliged to pay hers. That is not correct. He can put a little "ad" in the newspaper and nobody will give her credit who sells dry goods or provisions.

It is said that women are represented by their husbands at the ballot box. This is not true of the ten millions of unmarried women who have nobody to vote for them. (But there are eight or nine millions of unmarried men, who vote for nobody but themselves. *And, nobody votes for the drunkard's wife!*)

There are as many widows in this country as widowers. As a rule they manage well their business affairs....They deserve the ballot because their property is taxed to the limit and beyond, and they are not allowed to protest.

Women make fine teachers. But, a callow youth can vote at 21, while his capable teacher, a woman, is forbidden to vote. Women are the mainstays in public schools. They are not only forbidden the vote, but their pay is reduced because of their sex.

They make superior stenographers, but while their pay may reach $50 a month; the young man in trousers gets from $75 to $100, with no better work—and according to common report, not so reliable as to fidelity and regular work habits.

The more I think about these inequalities and this manifest injustice, the more I am tempted to eulogize [praise] the heathen who lived on the Ganges river, and who drowned the girl babies, because they were unfit to live!

leader in the prohibition movement and in the struggle for **suffrage**—the right to vote—for women.

For many years, Mrs. Felton had fought political battles along with her husband, Dr. William Felton, against the Democrats, liquor candidates, and "big interests." She saw these groups as working against the hopes of ordinary people. Unlike her husband, however, she could neither vote nor hold political office.

The struggle for woman suffrage was a national one. In the years following the Civil War, Susan B. Anthony and Elizabeth Cady Stanton tried unsuccessfully to get the Fifteenth Amendment applied to all women as well as all men.

However, at the state level, women were meeting with some success. In 1869, the territory of Wyoming granted voting rights to women. By 1900, Colorado, Idaho, and Utah had done likewise. In Georgia and most other states, however, strong opposition to giving the vote to women persisted.

Mrs. Felton and other Georgia "suffragettes" were not successful at the state level. In 1920, the Nineteenth Amendment to the U.S. Constitution was ratified, granting women the right to vote. The following year, Georgia complied. ◀

▶ Locating the Main Ideas

1. Define: local option, suffrage
2. Identify: Eighteenth Amendment, Nineteenth Amendment
3. What was the convict lease system?
4. What reasons did Rebecca Felton use in her speech for giving women the right to vote?

CHAPTER ACTIVITIES

Reviewing the Main Ideas

1. List three features in the Constitution of 1877 that made it more restrictive than previous ones.

2. What were the four goals of the Bourbon Democrats' program?

3. Discuss two of the political aims of the Farmers' Alliance and how accomplishing them would help farmers.

4. Explain why in Georgia after 1900, the person selected in the Democratic primary election almost automatically became the winner of the general election.

5. How did segregation in both the North and the South gradually become an accepted way of life?

6. On the surface, the doctrine of separate but equal sounds as if everyone gets treated fairly. Why was this not so for blacks?

7. What was the reason some parents opposed compulsory school laws?

8. Based on Georgia's national ranking in 1920 for number of working children, how successful were its child labor laws?

9. How did post–Civil War conditions in Georgia make the convict lease system attractive to state government leaders? to businessmen?

10. How would you restate the Fifteenth Amendment on page 212 to include women, giving them the right to vote?

Give It Some Extra Thought

1. **Expressing Viewpoints.** Write a statement expressing the point of view a rural farmer might have about Tom Watson's 1890 campaign. Write another statement about his campaign from the viewpoint of an urban banker.

2. **Identifying Problems.** Clare de Graffenried wrote of "cracker" families who traded life on the farm for life in the mill as Georgia became more industrialized. Make a list of the new problems mill families faced.

Sharpen Your Skills

1. **Doing Research.** Find out why Robert Toombs was called the "unreconstructed rebel."

2. **Making Comparisons.** Make a chart with three columns labeled Reform Topics, Problems, and Results. In the first column, list the four reform topics discussed in this chapter. In the second column, write the problem reformers were trying to solve, and in the last column, describe the results. Then, write a sentence describing how successful the reformers were in each case.

Going Further

1. **Using the News Media.** Women no longer need to campaign for the right to vote in America. Scan through newspapers or news magazines, or watch news reports and identify the issues women are likely to be campaigning for today.

2. **Making National Connections.** Report on either the woman suffrage or prohibition movement in the United States. What part did Georgia play in those efforts?

Rural free delivery, championed by Tom Watson, brought farm families daily delivery of newspapers, catalogs, magazines, advertisements, and letters. This new service brought rural southerners into closer contact with the rest of the nation.

Coming Up Next!
- Industrializing Georgia • Agriculture
- Growth of towns and cities
- Strains on Georgia society
- Public education • Leisure time activities

16

Life of the People in a Changing Society

Work crews install the first water and sewer lines in LaGrange, 1900.

As the twentieth century approached, most Georgians had to struggle just to make a living. The state's heavy dependence on cotton and its lack of factory jobs continued to hold its people back. Two out of every three Georgia workers were engaged in farming. With an average income of $259 a year in 1900, Georgia farmers were among the poorest people in the nation.

At the same time, towns and cities were growing in numbers. There, residents not only enjoyed better incomes but even had such luxuries as electric lights, indoor plumbing, streetcars, and paved streets.

Determined to rise from the ashes of the Civil War, thousands of Georgians, natives and newcomers alike, looked for ways to improve their way of life.

Industrializing Georgia

The New South concept—one based on manufacturing and industry, not just agriculture—appealed to many Georgia leaders. Henry Grady, its most enthusiastic booster, thought that Georgia and other southern states were serving as little more than economic colonies of the North. Southern cotton was shipped north, where it was made into clothing and then shipped back south to be sold at a handsome profit.

To illustrate Georgia's dependency on the North, Grady liked to tell the story of a funeral in which the only thing from Georgia was the body and the hole in the ground:

> A few years ago I told, in a speech, of a burial in Pickens County, Georgia. The grave was dug through solid marble, but the marble headstone came from Vermont. It was in a pine wilderness, but

236

the pine coffin came from Cincinnati. An iron mountain over-shadowed it, but the coffin nails and screws and the shovels came from Pittsburgh. With hard woods and metals abounding, the corpse was hauled on a wagon from South Bend, Indiana. A hickory grove grew near by, but the pick and shovel handles came from New York. The cotton shirt on the dead man came from Cincinnati, the coat and breeches from Chicago, the shoes from Boston; the folded hands were encased in white gloves from New York, and round the poor neck, that had worn all its living days the bondage of lost opportunity, was twisted a cheap cravat [necktie] from Philadelphia. That county, so rich in undeveloped resources, furnished nothing for the funeral except the corpse and the hole in the ground, and would probably have imported both of those if it could have done so.

Grady believed that the key to breaking the South's dependency and poverty was industrialization. Yet, the South did not have the capital to build new factories and mills. During the 1870s and 1880s, Grady traveled throughout the North urging businessmen there to invest their money in the South. In his eagerness to industrialize, Grady took the message that all was forgiven and northerners were now welcome in the South. From his desk at the *Atlanta Constitution*, he fired off articles painting the bright future of an industrialized South.

To a degree, the New South message was successful. The rise in manufacturing in Georgia between 1870 and 1910 was dramatic. In 1870 only about $14 million was invested in manufacturing establishments. By 1890, that figure had risen to almost $57 million, and by 1910 it would exceed $202 million.

Textile Manufacturing

Cotton mills had existed in Georgia since 1829. Before the Civil War they were small mills, located mainly along the Fall Line where water power was plentiful. Even then, Georgians had to buy almost all their manufactured goods, including cotton cloth, from outside the state.

The Hillside Cotton Mill in LaGrange, built around 1915, was typical of the textile mills springing up across the state.

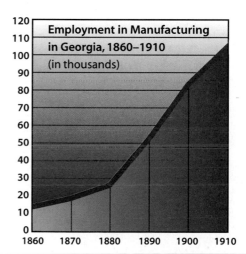

Employment in Manufacturing in Georgia, 1860–1910 (in thousands)

Value of Manufactured Goods in Georgia, 1860–1910 (in millions of dollars)

BIRD'S-EYE VIEW OF THE COTTON STATES AND INTERNATIONAL EXPOSITION==ATLANTA, GA., U.S.A.
OPENS SEPTEMBER 18th. CLOSES DECEMBER 31st
1895.

The Cotton States and International Exposition, 1895. Attended by 800,000 people, the exposition did more than promote industry and trade. It tried to portray the progress made by the South—especially Atlanta. Exhibits ranged from displays of the latest in horse-drawn fire-fighting equipment to a model library. Buffalo Bill's Wild West Show entertained visitors.

But Georgia had the potential to manufacture cotton goods on a large scale. Many Georgia business and government leaders thought it would be a way to industrialize the state. After all, Georgia had lots of cotton. It had enough available labor. All that was needed was heavy investment in large textile plants.

In 1881, Atlanta staged the World's Fair and Great International Cotton Exposition. The idea was to bring people to Georgia and show them why they should invest in industry in the state. In one popular feature at the exposition, cotton growing in a field was picked in the morning, ginned, woven, and tailored into a suit all in the same day. Governor Colquitt put on the cotton suit and then made a speech and toured the fairgrounds in it.

The 1881 fair was such a success that Atlanta held another, the Piedmont Exposition, in 1887. The president of the United States, Grover Cleveland, attended. The fairgrounds later became Piedmont Park.

Then, in 1895, the city put on its biggest show, the Cotton States and International Exposition. On display were the resources and achievements of Georgia and the other cotton-producing states. Booker T. Washington, a black educator, spoke on the role of black people in the South's economic life as he saw it.

As a result of these and other efforts to attract industry, textile manufacturing was Georgia's leading industry by 1900. Textile mills sprang up across the state, many financed or owned by northern companies. They came for many reasons. The mills were closer to cotton fields, cutting down transportation costs. Taxes were lower, and the climate milder. But the main reason was the availability of cheap labor in the South.

Other Industry

Georgians and investors from other states put their money into many kinds of industries. Iron, coal, gold, and clay were mined. Granite and marble quarries were developed. New factories and mills, steam-powered as well as water-powered, turned out a variety of products, such as cotton-seed oil, fertilizer, construction materials, and furniture. Wherever the resources and the railroads were available, manufacturing plants might spring up. In time, new towns grew up around the mills and factories. ▶

Agriculture\

Although industry became more important to Georgia's economy in the late 1800s, the state remained mainly rural and agricultural. Some Georgia farmers attempted to diversify. A few tried growing fresh vegetables for nearby markets. Others experimented with raising peaches, pecans, corn, cattle, and hogs. Cotton, however, remained king. In fact, more cotton was now produced than in the antebellum years. Georgia's **Black Belt** region, so named for its high percentage of black residents, continued to form the heart of cotton country. (See maps, page 163.)

Tenant Farming

Across the South, planters were in dire need of laborers to work their fields. They turned to poor whites and blacks who had no land of their own, but who were willing to live on and work someone else's land. These were known as **tenant farmers**.

Landowners would divide their plantations into small sections, constructing on each a simple (and often crude) dwelling place for the tenant farmer to live in. Each family then worked its part of the land as if it were a separate farm.

Some tenant farmers were renters. They agreed to farm a section of land, providing their own seed and supplies. At the end of the season, when they sold their crops, they were to pay the landowner an agreed upon amount, in cash. In some cases, the rent was a portion of the crop harvested.

But some Georgians were too poor even to rent. All they had was a willingness to work. For these poor people, and

▶ **Locating the Main Ideas**

1. What point was Henry Grady trying to make in his story about the Pickens County burial?

2. Use the graphs on page 237 to determine when employment in manufacturing and value of goods manufactured in Georgia began to rise sharply. How many people were employed in manufacturing in 1860? in 1900?

3. What do you think was the main purpose of Georgia's great cotton expositions in the 1880s and 1890s?

A tenant shack, Lowndes County, 1905. Not all sharecroppers lived in houses this run-down, but thousands did.

Tenant farmers in Gwinnett County around 1910. Children often worked alongside parents and grandparents.

for landowners in need of labor, a new system of tenant farming emerged—**sharecropping**. This was an arrangement where a landowner provided land to farm, a house, plows, mules, seed, and other supplies to a family. In return, the owner received a share of the crop raised on the land. Various kinds of deals were worked out between landlords and sharecroppers (known as "croppers") for dividing up the costs of raising a crop and the income from selling it.

Advantages and Risks of Renting

Renters were not under an owner's direct supervision. This meant that a renter was responsible for managing his part of the owner's land. This kind of independence appealed to many tenants, black and white.

However, there were drawbacks to renting. The renter had to know how to farm. He had to make his own decisions about buying seed, using fertilizer, and raising and selling his crop. He took all the risks, not the landowner. If the renter mismanaged his farm or lost his crop because of bad weather, he suffered all the loss—not the owner who still was due the rent.

The renter who made no money off one year's work soon found himself in debt. To pay off what he owed, the renter might have to sell his mules, plows, and other tools. Next year, he would likely be a sharecropper.

Credit

To make money, a farmer had to have money. Unless he could sell something, the only way the Georgia farmer could get money was to borrow it. It was usually difficult for poor farmers to borrow from the bank. This meant buying goods "on credit" from local merchants.

Whether they borrowed money from a bank or bought on credit from a merchant, farmers had to put up security. That is, they had to possess something of value the lender could have in case farmers couldn't pay off their debt. The loan security that bankers and merchants demanded was a **crop lien**—a legal claim—on the farmer's cotton crop. The crop always had more value than anything else a Georgia farmer might possess. To protect lenders, Georgia law required that the merchant or bank be paid off first, once the farmer sold his cotton.

What happened if farmers raised a crop too small to pay off their debts? Or, if the price they got for their cotton was too low? Obviously, merchants could easily fall into debt as well. They too borrowed money—sometimes from northern banks—to set up their businesses. They also bought on credit the supplies they sold to farmers. They had bills to pay.

Often a merchant had to take the owner's land or the tenant's work stock and sell it to pay off his own debts. Usually, however, he chose to carry the farmer's debts another year. He would often

An 1890s hardware store in Americus. How many different items can you identify in this photo?

extend more credit and hope that next year's crop would bring enough to pay off two years' worth of debt.

Help for the Farmer \

Georgia's system of agriculture involved thousands of families sharecropping or renting small farms and living on a local merchant's credit. It meant years of poverty and debt for these Georgians. Dissatisfied, many of them organized to improve the situation.

The Grange, a nationwide "self-help" farmer organization, came to Georgia in 1872. It set up cooperative stores—stores run by and for farmers—where members could buy supplies directly from producers. Its aim was to cut out the merchant's markup and get supplies at lower cost. By 1876, about 18,000 Georgia farmers had joined the Grange.

In 1874, Georgia Grangers and other farmers pressed the General Assembly to create a Department of Agriculture (the first of its kind in the nation). The department's purpose was to improve agriculture by distributing information about new seed, and how to use fertilizer, control insects, and market crops.

About the same time, the University of Georgia established a College of Agriculture. The state also set up agricultural experiment stations to determine what plants and animals could be most profitably raised on Georgia farms.

Grange membership dropped after 1880, but help came to the farmer in 1887 from another self-help group—the Farmers' Alliance (see page 223). Farmers joining the Alliance could borrow money at lower interest rates. The Alliance also set up farmer "co-ops" and organized boycotts of suppliers who charged too much. ▶

▶ **Locating the Main Ideas**

1. Define: Black Belt, tenant farmers, sharecropping, crop lien
2. Why was credit so important to farmers? In order to get a loan, what possession did a farmer have to put up as security?
3. How were farmers helped by the Grange? the General Assembly? the University of Georgia?

Rabun County sawmill, around 1900. Lumbering was important in north Georgia as well as in south Georgia. What kind of power did these men have to help them in their work?

Alonzo Herndon (center), president of the Atlanta Life Insurance Company office located on Auburn Avenue. Born into slavery, Herndon became a very successful and wealthy businessman. At his death in 1927, his insurance company had expanded into seven other states.

Growth of Towns and Cities

Although most of Georgia's people were rural farmers, the main population growth was in the state's towns, villages, and cities. Tenant farming and the arrival of new industries in Georgia were two reasons for this development.

Tenant farmers needed seed, tools, and supplies to start crops. At the end of the season, they needed a place to trade and to gin and press their cotton. Planters, recognizing the opportunity to add to their incomes, began operating cotton gins, general stores, and other businesses to supply their tenants. Soon, with the addition of a church, a small school, and a blacksmith shop, a small village was created.

The movement to attract new industries to Georgia gave its cities a boost. Sometimes the industry would be the reason a city or town developed. A ginning operation or a sawmill might draw workers to an area. As more workers were needed, stores and schools would appear. Similarly, new industries locating in established cities needed factory hands and workers for their operation. As a result, the populations in those cities increased.

Although Georgia's rural population continued to grow, many people chose to leave the countryside for the city. By 1910, one out of every three residents lived in a village, town, or city. That year, Georgia had 45 cities and towns with at least 2,500 residents, and an additional 500 villages and small communities.

Atlanta: Gate City of the South

Atlanta was a city developed around a rail line. A prospering city before the war, it was destroyed by General Sherman. Of about 3,600 homes in the city, 400 were left standing when he departed.

But, like the mythical phoenix bird, reborn from the ashes of its own destruction, Atlanta rose with amazing speed from the ashes left by Sherman's torch. By 1910, its population was more than four times greater than in 1880, growing from about 37,000 to nearly 155,000. Largely responsible for this growth was the railroad. Fifteen different rail lines served Atlanta, making it the warehouse distribution center for the Southeast. Atlanta's transportation advantage and its New South philosophy influenced numerous businesses from the North and Midwest to open regional headquarters and branch offices there. Atlantans began to enjoy their city's reputation as "Gate City of the South."

Atlanta's growing prosperity and the lure of jobs attracted many people. As Georgia's capital city, Atlanta was temporary home to many politicians as well as home to government workers. Sales representatives found Atlanta a convenient and exciting place to stay while they traveled the Southeast doing business. Unsuccessful tenant farmers came to the city looking for day jobs. Ambitious entrepreneurs (people who take the risk of establishing businesses) saw opportunities there. They recognized that a growing urban population needed grocery stores, drug stores, general stores, transportation, and many other services to survive in the city. All this activity increased the rate of growth of Georgia's largest city.

By the early 1920s, Coca Cola was being bottled and sold nationwide. Many bottlers, like this one in Cobb County, still used horse-drawn delivery wagons.

Black Georgians moved to Atlanta where they found freedoms and opportunities they did not have in the countryside. Black-owned and -operated businesses were established to serve Atlanta's growing population. The area around Auburn Avenue soon developed into a social and commercial center for African Americans that became known throughout the country.

One very successful business on Auburn Avenue, the Atlanta Life Insurance Company, was owned by Alonzo Herndon, a former slave from Walton County. At the time of his death in 1927, his company was worth over $1 million. Before buying the insurance business, Herndon operated several barbershops. The largest and most elegant, on Peachtree Street, had 25 chairs and served, because of segregation, an all-white clientele. Herndon gave generously to worthy causes and made many contributions that improved life in Atlanta's black community.

Two other Atlanta "institutions" came into existence during this period. Rich's, later thought of as "Atlanta's department store," was established in 1867 through the hard work and perseverance of Morris Rich, an immigrant from Hungary. Rich, after working as a store clerk and peddler in Ohio and Tennessee, chose Atlanta as the place to open a small dry goods* store. After several moves to accommodate an expanding inventory, Morris was joined by his two brothers. Known as "M. Rich & Bros.," the store continued to grow and flourish. Rich's success reflected Atlanta's progress.

Coca Cola, the most famous product Georgia has ever produced, was developed in Atlanta in 1886. Originally sold in drug stores as a headache remedy, it was created by John Pemberton, a druggist.

---

*"Dry goods" included textiles, ready-made clothing, and notions rather than hardware and grocery items.

Up from Slavery

[This exposition] will awaken among us a new era of industrial progress. Ignorant and inexperienced, it is not strange that in the first years of our new life we began at the top instead of at the bottom; that a seat in Congress or the State Legislature was more sought than real estate or industrial skill; the political convention or stump-speaking [campaigning] had more attraction than starting a dairy farm or truck garden....

Our greatest danger is that in the great leap from slavery to freedom we may overlook the fact that the masses of us are to live by the productions of our hands, and fail to keep in mind that we shall prosper in proportion as we learn to dignify and glorify common labor, and put brains and skill into the common occupations of life....

No race can prosper till it learns that there is as much dignity in tilling a field as in writing a poem. It is at the bottom of life we must begin, and not at the top. Nor should we permit our grievances [complaints] to overshadow our opportunities....

The wisest among my race understand that the agitation of [fighting over] questions of social equality is the extremest folly, and that progress in the enjoyment of all privileges that will come to us

Atlanta University, 1890s. How would this sewing class fit Booker T. Washington's view of vocational education?

must be the result of severe and constant struggle rather than of artificial forcing....

It is important and right that all privileges of the law be ours, but it is vastly more important that we be prepared for the exercise of these privileges. The opportunity to earn a dollar in a factory just now is worth infinitely [much] more than the opportunity to spend a dollar in an opera house....

—Booker T. Washington, 1895.

▶ **Locating the Main Ideas**

1. How could a new industry help a town develop and grow?
2. Why was Atlanta known as the "Gate City of the South?"
3. What were the advantages of living in a city or town? Can you think of any disadvantages?

When a soda fountain operator at Jacob's Drug Store mixed the remedy with carbonated water rather than tap water to provide quick headache relief to a customer, the result made history. Frail health forced Dr. Pemberton to sell his interests in the remedy. Asa G. Candler eventually acquired total ownership of the product for $2,300 and a few items in trade. Candler emphasized the refreshing qualities of the drink rather than its medicinal values, and by 1895 it was sold in every state in the union. In 1919, Candler sold Coca Cola for $25 million to the Trust Company of Georgia, headed by Ernest Woodruff. His son, Robert W. Woodruff, became president of the corporation in 1923. Under his leadership, Coke became an international product before the start of World War II. ◀

Strains on Georgia Society

In the years following Reconstruction, there was a great effort by whites throughout the South—and indeed in much of the rest of the nation—to keep blacks "in their place."

Many white people felt that the "place" of black people was in the countryside, working as tenant farmers. Some whites, such as the Populists, were willing to grant blacks political equality, but very few were willing to consider social equality. At the same time, black leaders expressed different ideas about accepting the place whites thought they should occupy.

Black Leaders Differ

Probably the best known African American leader in the 1890s and early 1900s was Booker T. Washington. Washington built Tuskegee Institute in Alabama into a leading center of education for blacks. There he stressed technical training, learning a trade, and agriculture. Washington made many speeches around the country, calling on whites to support this kind of education for blacks.

In 1895, Booker T. Washington came to Atlanta to speak at the Cotton States and International Exposition. There he gave one of his most famous speeches, calling on fellow blacks to accept their status for the time being, and forget about social equality and political action. Rather, Washington advised, learn a skill, become self-sufficient, and acquire a home. Eventually, full rights and privileges would come, but in the meantime, blacks first should prepare themselves to exercise these rights.

Many whites liked Washington's message, which quickly became known as the "Atlanta Compromise." While some blacks followed his line of thinking, others did not. Among black leaders not agreeing with Washington were John Hope and William E.B. DuBois.

For many years, Dr. John Hope was one of the nation's leading educators. He was president of Morehouse College in Atlanta and later president of Atlanta University. In 1896, a year after Booker T. Washington had presented his views, Hope challenged them.

William E.B. DuBois was born in 1868 in Massachusetts. In the same year that Washington spoke at the Atlanta exposition, DuBois became the first African American student to earn a Doctor of Philosophy degree at Harvard University.

Like Dr. Hope, Dr. DuBois was associated with Atlanta University, teaching and studying the problems of black people living in America. He was an outspoken, controversial leader in the fight for black civil rights. In 1903, his book *The Souls of Black Folk* made it clear that all black leaders did not agree with Washington's views.

In 1905, in New York, DuBois organized the Niagara Movement, the first national effort to end Jim Crow laws. Four years later, he

W.E.B. DuBois

Niagara Movement Aims

These are the things we as black men must do:

Stop the curtailment of our political rights.

Urge Negroes to vote intelligently and effectively.

Push the matter of civil rights.

Organize business co-operation.

Build school houses and increase the interest in education.

Open up new avenues of employment....

Distribute...information in regard to laws of health.

Bring Negroes and labor unions into mutual understanding.

Study Negro history.

Increase the circulation of honest newspapers and periodicals.

Attack crime among us by all civilized methods....

—W.E.B. DuBois, 1905.

helped found the National Association for the Advancement of Colored People (NAACP) and edited its magazine, *The Crisis*.

Violence and Lawlessness

A year after DuBois launched the Niagara movement in New York, race relations in Georgia were getting worse. In a bitter campaign for the governorship, one candidate for the Democratic party nomination called for taking the vote away from blacks. A month after the primary election, a race riot in Atlanta left 25 blacks and 1 white dead.

The 1906 Atlanta race riot was not an isolated incident of racial violence. By then, Georgia had gained an unwanted reputation for lynching. The victims of this form of murder—carried out by unruly mobs—were mostly blacks. In the worst year, 1899, 27 African American men were lynched for alleged crimes ranging from "inflammatory language" and "resisting arrest" to "robbery and murder."

As Jim Crow laws were passed and blacks were denied the vote, racial hatred became more intense. Tom Watson, the man who had spoken up for blacks in the 1880s, now preached racial hatred and violence. He had learned that the votes of poorer, less-educated whites could be won by playing on their fears of black social equality. Eventually Watson told the readers of his newspaper that Jews and Catholics were also their enemies.

In 1913, Leo M. Frank, a white factory manager who was a Jew, was tried for the murder of a 14-year-old girl at the pencil factory he managed. In a disorderly trial dominated by loud and abusive spectators, Frank was found guilty and sentenced to hang. The evidence used to convict Frank was highly suspect, but appeals to the Georgia and U.S. Supreme Courts were unsuccessful. Reviewing the trial record, Gov. John Slaton was so troubled that he reduced the sentence to life imprisonment. In 1915, urged on by anti-Jewish editorials written by Tom Watson, a lynch mob took Frank from state prison and hanged him. His lynching gained national attention. That year, the Ku Klux Klan was reborn at Stone Mountain. ▶

▶ Locating the Main Ideas

1. Identify: Booker T. Washington, John Hope, William E.B. DuBois, Niagara Movement

2. Why do you think Booker T. Washington's speech became known as the "Atlanta Compromise?"

3. According to Dr. John Hope, what does the phrase "social equality" mean?

Public Education

The Constitution of 1868 set the stage for Georgia's public school system. It provided for a "thorough system of general education to be forever free to all children of the state." Two years later, the schools got their real start. The General Assembly created the office of state school commissioner and the board of education. In 1871, with an appropriation of $174,000 from the legislature, the public schools of Georgia enrolled about 31,000 children. Schools were to be open three months of each year.

At first, public support for the schools was meager. Some whites disapproved of public education for blacks, even though black and white pupils were to be segregated.

Then, in 1872, Gustavus J. Orr was appointed school commissioner. Almost single-handedly he built a permanent system of public education for Georgia. For 15 years he traveled through the state, often at his own expense, pointing out the benefits of schooling. He encouraged citizens to tax themselves to pay for schools.

In 1902, Martha Berry began a school near Rome, Georgia, allowing underprivileged children to work and earn an education. She worked tirelessly, using her own money and enlisting the generous support of others, to bring quality education to her students. Berry College, founded in 1926, continues today in the same tradition.

He helped county school boards make the most of the little money available for education. Commissioner Orr is remembered as the "father of the common school system" in Georgia.

Attitudes toward Schools

Into the early 1900s, public education was mostly a local—not a state—effort. Local property taxes furnished most of the money for the schools. Georgia was a poor state, so these funds were not easy to raise.

According to the Constitution of 1877, state funds could be used for elementary grades and for the state university, but not for high schools. Teenagers were needed to work on the farms or in the textile mills. Besides, some delegates who wrote the 1877 constitution worried that a high school education would only make youngsters unhappy with their station in life. Thus, if a community wanted to have a high school, it would have to pay for it on its own.

In 1912, Georgia voters approved amendments to the state constitution that included high schools in state funding. They also gave counties the authority to levy taxes for their support. As a result, by 1920 Georgia had 169 high schools.

Meanwhile, Georgia's General Assembly had recognized that all children needed some education. In 1916 it passed the state's first compulsory school attendance law. The law said that all children ages 8 to 14 had to attend school for at least four months of the year. However, if a child lived more than three miles from the nearest school, he or she could be excused from attending. A child could also be excused for seasonal labor in agriculture.

In rural areas, schools usually had only one room with no electricity or water. They were often run-down. In the cities and larger towns, schools had several rooms and were in better condition.

Georgia Schools Segregated

The Georgia Constitution of 1877 specified segregated education. It stated, "separate schools shall be provided for white and colored

EDUCATIONAL FACILITIES IN 1908				
	White	Percent	Black	Percent
Total school population	386,227	53	349,244	47
Number pupils enrolled	306,891	60	201,512	40
Number pupils in high school	17,253	91	1,697	9
Value of school furniture, etc.	$590,336.00	85	$101,385.00	15
Value of school libraries	77,528.00	99	940.00	1
Average teacher's monthly salary	44.29	59	20.23	31

Source: Dorothy Orr, *A History of Education in Georgia,* 1950.

children." For nearly a century, Georgia public schools separated students by race.

Black Georgians challenged laws providing for segregated schools. But the courts upheld the separate but equal doctrine. As long as blacks were furnished school facilities equal to those of whites, schools could by law be separate.

Under this doctrine, Georgia operated a dual education system: one for whites, one for blacks. This practice applied to state colleges as well as public schools.

Although it was supposed to be equal, the education furnished black children was quite different from that offered to white children. Figures taken from the 1908 Georgia Department of Education's Annual Report tell part of the story. (See chart on page 248.)

Clearly, more state and local tax money went to educate white children than black children. As a result, white students had finer school buildings; more books, supplies, and equipment; and better-prepared and better-paid teachers.

The Siloam baseball team in 1902. What evidence is there that baseball was important in this small Greene County town?

Leisure Time Activities

Life in Georgia was not all problems and hard work. Like people everywhere, Georgians found time for fun and entertainment.

For many Georgians, both black and white, the church was the center of social as well as spiritual life. Revivals, singing conventions, camp meetings, Sunday school picnics, and church suppers were special events.

More of Georgia's people were living in villages, towns, and cities, where community activities provided opportunities for enjoying life. Often, there were town parks where band concerts were held on the weekend. Also popular were traveling shows, stage plays, and circuses. Baseball, first played in 1845, quickly became a favorite public pastime. Some of Georgia's larger cities had symphonies and opera companies.

Other popular forms of entertainment were music boxes, player pianos, cameras, and a new invention—the phonograph.

In Athens, Mary Lumpkin started the first garden club in 1891, an idea that spread throughout America. In 1912, another type of club was formed in Savannah. There, Juliette Gordon Low organized a group of girls into a "troop" and called them Girl Guides. This idea spread quickly through the nation, though its name changed to the Girl Scouts of America.

Much like traveling fairs today, this 1901 carnival troupe entertained the citizens of Wilkes County with rides and exhibits in the downtown square.

Juliette Gordon Low

If you haven't been a member of the Girl Scouts, chances are that you know someone who has, be it your sister, mother, classmate, or neighbor. With more than three million members coast to coast, the Girl Scouts has become a familiar feature of American life since it was founded early this century by Georgia native Juliette Gordon Low.

Born in 1860, Juliette Gordon grew up in Savannah during the Civil War, later attending boarding schools in Virginia and a French "finishing school" in New York. After her debut into Savannah society, the adventurous, energetic Miss Gordon began traveling, first in America and then abroad. On a trip to Great Britain, she met—and later married—William Mackay Low, a wealthy Englishman.

The couple settled in Warwickshire, England. There they enjoyed a glamourous and privileged life, moving easily in social circles with British nobility and royalty. Mrs. Low pursued her artistic interests by studying oil painting, wood carving, and ironworking—and even forged the wrought iron gates of the Low estate.

After her husband died in 1905, Mrs. Low resumed her extensive travels. She journeyed to Egypt and India, and also returned to her art work, relocating in Paris to study sculpting. There, she met Robert Baden-Powell, founder of the Boy Scouts, and his sister, who was organizing a parallel group, the Girl Guides.

Baden-Powell encouraged Mrs. Low to form a Girl Guide group in Scotland. Her efforts there

Juliette Low

proved so successful that she returned to America, intent on establishing a similar program to help girls and young women become productive and self-sufficient.

Mrs. Low held the first Girl Scouts meeting at her Savannah home in 1912, attracting 18 girls. For the next five years, she funded the fledgling organization with her own money and used her extensive social contacts to generate more support. In 1920, she resigned as president of Girl Scouts of the USA and devoted the rest of her life to the worldwide organization.

When Juliette Gordon Low died in Savannah in 1927, the Girl Scouts of the United States of America had 148,000 members, financial security, and a constitution and bylaws.

▶ Locating the Main Ideas

1. Identify: Gustavus J. Orr, Martha Berry, Mary Lumpkin, Juliette Gordon Low, Joel Chandler Harris
2. Why is Gustavus J. Orr known as the "father of the common school system" in Georgia?
3. Describe Georgia's dual education system.
4. What were the main sources of news for turn-of-the-century Georgians?

Before the days of radio and television, newspapers and magazines were the main news sources. From them, Georgians learned about local and world events. Newspapers and magazines were also entertainment. One of the most popular writers of the day was Joel Chandler Harris.

Joel Chandler Harris, creator of the fictional storyteller Uncle Remus, was born in Eatonton in 1848. In his early teens he decided to become a journalist. He worked for several newspapers before joining the *Atlanta Constitution* in 1873. There he became an associate editor, along with Henry W. Grady.

Harris used his evenings to write short stories based on African folklore brought to America by slaves. In the 1880s and 1890s, his "Uncle Remus" stories made him world famous. Later, Harris started his own magazine, called *Uncle Remus's Magazine*. ◀

Reviewing the Main Ideas

1. How did Henry Grady and business and government leaders try to make the New South concept a reality?

2. What resources did Georgia have that were necessary for large-scale textile manufacturing? What resources were lacking?

3. Describe the arrangements that renters had with landowners concerning (a) what the owner furnished, (b) what the tenant furnished, (c) what the owner received, and (d) what the tenant received. Describe the arrangements that sharecroppers had for the same four categories. Compare the two.

4. What were two reasons for population growth in Georgia's towns, villages, and cities?

5. Often a city is identified by famous places, establishments, or products. Discuss the importance of Auburn Avenue, Rich's Department Store, and Coca Cola to Atlanta.

6. What was the message in Dr. John Hope's speech on equality?

7. How were the positions of Dr. Hope and Dr. DuBois different from those of Booker T. Washington?

8. Why were the framers of Georgia's Constitution of 1877 reluctant to support high schools in the state?

9. What data from the chart of 1908 Educational Facilities on page 248 show that black students were not likely to receive as good an education as white students?

10. List at least three leisure activities Georgians enjoyed at the turn of the century still popular today. List three leisure activities we enjoy today that were not available then.

Give It Some Extra Thought

1. **Writing a Speech**. Write a second paragraph for Grady's speech describing the changed and industrialized South that he sees. Use the following two sentences to begin your para-graph: Today, that burial in Pickens County, Georgia, would be different. Georgia would be the source of many products and services.

2. **Analyzing Differences.** Imagine going back in time to the early 1900s. How would the length of the school year, financial support for schools, ages of children required to attend school, and racial segregation compare with those of today?

Sharpen Your Skills

1. **Using a Map.** On a map of the United States, locate the cities Henry Grady mentioned in his speech on pages 236-37. Make a list of the cities and the states they are located in. What region of the country are those states in?

2. **Graphing.** Make a graph titled "Investments in Manufacturing in Georgia, 1870–1910" to accompany the two graphs in the text. Use the data on page 237 to create the graph. Based on your graph and the other two graphs, write a general statement about the success of the industrial development of the New South.

3. **Following a Historical Trend.** Life for black Georgians worsened between 1870 and 1915. Gradually, the political rights they had obtained during Reconstruction slipped away. What caused this to happen? Using dates from this chapter and Chapter 15, construct a time line of events affecting the relationship between black and white Georgians.

Going Further

1. **Making Local Connections.** Investigate the industries in or near your community. Did any of them get their start between 1880 and 1915? Find out more about them and report to the class.

2. **Interviewing for Information.** As a class, invite your local Cooperative Extension agent to meet with you. Prepare questions to ask about the history of the extension service and the services the state provides the farmer today.

TROLLEY CAR

UNIT 7

17 | Boom and Bust

18 | The New Deal and World War II

GEORGIA EVENTS

1917	1918	1919	1920	1921	1922	1925	1926	1929	1930	1931
General Assembly enacts county unit system	Female students gain full admission to UGA		Tom Watson elected to U.S. Senate	Boll weevil ravages cotton fields	Rebecca Felton first woman in U.S. Senate	Franklin D. Roosevelt first visits Warm Springs	Air mail service begins from Atlanta	Air passenger service begins	Richard B. Russell elected governor; Bobby Jones wins "Grand Slam"	Number of counties reduced to 159; state government reorganized
United States enters World War I	World War I ends	Eighteenth Amendment establishes prohibition	Nineteenth Amendment gives women right to vote		Stock market boom begins	Florida land boom hits peak	Theo "Tiger" Flowers of Camilla becomes world middleweight boxing champ	Stock market crash; Great Depression begins		

EVENTS ELSEWHERE

Rise of Modern Georgia
1917–1945

Richard Russell elected to U.S. Senate; Eugene Talmadge elected governor	Eugene Talmadge becomes governor; Georgia celebrates bicentennial of founding		*Gone with the Wind* published	Governor Rivers promotes "little New Deal"; free textbooks for schools	First four-lane highway links Atlanta and Marietta	World premier of *Gone with the Wind* in Atlanta	University System colleges lose accreditation	Ellis Arnall elected governor; Bell Aircraft plans B-29 plant in Marietta	Georgia first state in nation to allow 18-year-olds to vote	New state constitution adopted
1932	**1933**	**1935**	**1936**	**1937**	**1938**	**1939**	**1941**	**1942**	**1943**	**1945**
Low point of depression; FDR elected president	Prohibition repealed; New Deal begins	Social Security, WPA, and REA created	FDR re-elected	First worldwide radio broadcast	Germany annexes Austria	World War II begins in Europe	Bombing of Pearl Harbor; United States enters war	Benjamin Mays files lawsuit that ends segregated dining cars on trains	War turns in favor of Allies	Atomic bomb dropped; World War II ends

17

Coming Up Next!

• The coming of world war
• The twenties in Georgia
• The Great Depression

Boom and Bust

The first two decades of the twentieth century were a period of great change in America. New technology was revolutionizing the way people lived, worked, and traveled. In December 1903, Orville and Wilbur Wright made the first successful airplane flight at Kitty Hawk, North Carolina. Years later, Georgians would see the powerful effect of this new form of transportation on the growth of their state.

Even more significant was the new "horseless carriage." Invented in the late nineteenth century, the automobile was getting better and better. Still, many Americans considered it an oddity and were sure it would never replace the horse. Slowly, people began accepting it.

By 1900, there were 8,000 automobiles in the nation. The following year, autos made their first appearance in Georgia. A steam-driven car made a 9-mile journey through Atlanta, at times reaching the amazing speed of 20 miles per hour!

In 1908, Henry Ford introduced the first edition of the car that would make him famous (and wealthy). During the next year, he produced over 19,000 Model T Fords. He set up the world's first automobile assembly line in Detroit, Michigan. Ford expanded into the South in 1915, building a factory in Atlanta. His assembly line could turn out 1,000 cars a day. The efficiency of this new approach to building cars allowed Ford to sell the Model T for just $360, making it affordable to many Americans.

The popularity of automobiles was just one more thing adding to the excitement of urban life. The city was the place to be to experience the newest technology, fashions, and fads. Atlanta, Savannah, Macon, and other Georgia cities could now boast of electric streetlights and trolleys. Buildings 12 stories or higher were beginning to appear. In Atlanta, viaducts (elevated roadways) were built

College Avenue in Athens, 1923. The thriving city of Athens showed all the signs of progress that went with urban living. How many of them can you spot?

over the many railroads that ran into the city. Left at ground level were the bottom floors of buildings, shops, and stores. This shadowy world would fade from most people's view, only to become famous one day as "Underground Atlanta."

In rural areas of Georgia, life moved at a slower pace. There, tenant farmers lived and worked pretty much the way they had for decades. This meant no running water, electricity, refrigerators, telephones, or other modern luxuries. Like their parents and grandparents, most rural families used wood stoves for cooking and heating, oil lamps for lighting, and outdoor toilets. Farmers continued to work fields of cotton with mule-drawn plows, more often than not ending the year deeper in debt than they started. If they were lucky, once or twice a month families would board a horse-drawn wagon for a trip into town.

As you can see, the early years of the twentieth century brought great change, but not for everyone. It depended on where you lived —in the city or the countryside.

The Coming of World War

In 1912, the year New Mexico and Arizona were admitted to the Union, Woodrow Wilson was elected president of the United States. Wilson had many ties to Georgia. He had lived in Augusta as a boy, practiced law in Atlanta, and married a young woman from Rome.

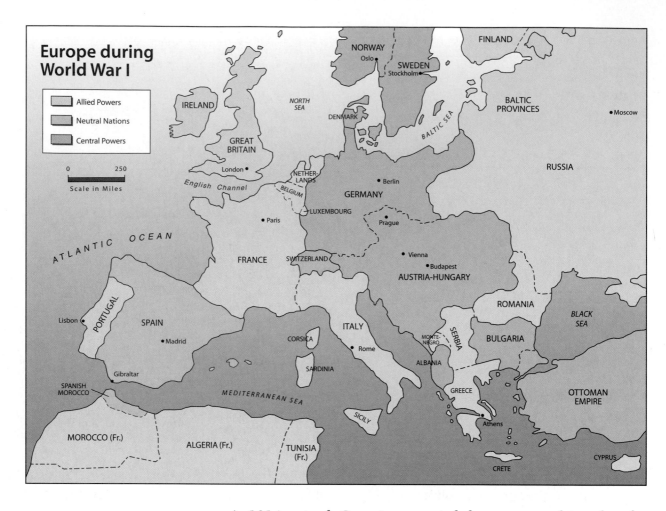

Europe during World War I

Allied Powers
Neutral Nations
Central Powers

0   250
Scale in Miles

NORWAY
Oslo
SWEDEN
Stockholm
FINLAND
IRELAND
NORTH SEA
DENMARK
BALTIC SEA
BALTIC PROVINCES
Moscow
GREAT BRITAIN
London
English Channel
NETHER-LANDS
BELGIUM
LUXEMBOURG
Berlin
GERMANY
Prague
RUSSIA
ATLANTIC OCEAN
Paris
FRANCE
SWITZERLAND
Vienna
Budapest
AUSTRIA-HUNGARY
ROMANIA
BLACK SEA
PORTUGAL
Lisbon
SPAIN
Madrid
CORSICA
ITALY
Rome
MONTE NEGRO
SERBIA
BULGARIA
Gibraltar
SARDINIA
ALBANIA
GREECE
OTTOMAN EMPIRE
SPANISH MOROCCO
MEDITERRANEAN SEA
SICILY
Athens
MOROCCO (Fr.)
ALGERIA (Fr.)
TUNISIA (Fr.)
CRETE
CYPRUS

Fort McPherson, 1917. During World War I, Atlanta's Fort McPherson served as an officer's training camp and a hospital for the wounded. It also housed over 1,000 German prisoners of war.

As 1914 arrived, Georgians worried about events taking place far across the Atlantic Ocean. With talk of war, European powers began forming **alliances**. These were agreements between countries to come to each other's aid in case of war. One alliance was between Germany, Austria-Hungary, and Italy. In another, Britain, France, and Russia promised to support one another.

In the summer of 1914, the archduke and archduchess of Austria-Hungary were assassinated by a young Serbian. Austria-Hungary then declared war on Serbia. Germany joined Austria-Hungary, while Russia came to the aid of Serbia. Soon, other alliance members honored their agreements, and Europe was at war.

At first, the United States followed a policy of **neutrality** (not taking sides in a conflict). Most Americans believed the war was strictly a European affair. In 1916, President Wilson won reelection on a promise to keep the United States out of war. But as the conflict progressed, staying neutral became more and more difficult.

America Enters the War

In 1917, American officials found out about a telegram sent by a German official, Arthur Zimmermann, to Mexico. Zimmermann's telegram suggested that if Mexico would go to war against the United States, it might be able to get back lands ceded to the United

States in 1847. In March, several American cargo ships in the Atlantic Ocean were sunk by German submarines. President Wilson asked Congress for a declaration of war, which came in April.

In May 1917, Congress passed a law to begin drafting young men into the armed forces. Even with the draft, about half of this nation's fighting men had volunteered for duty. Of the 4,000,000 Americans who served in World War I, some 100,000 were from Georgia.

Georgia's Role in World War I

Georgia contributed to the war effort in other ways. Atlanta's Fort McPherson, created in 1889, became a center for training recruits and draftees, as well as housing German prisoners of war. Atlanta's climate and excellent rail access prompted military authorities to build another training facility, Camp Gordon. Over 230,000 American soldiers would train there before the war's end.

Other Georgia sites were selected for military installations as well. Columbus became the home of Camp Benning, which later was made permanent home of the U.S. Army's Infantry School. In Augusta, Camp Hancock was temporary home to thousands of soldiers training at its military supply and weapons school.

In the process of learning to be soldiers, many Georgia farm boys got their first real look at city life and all the exciting things it had to offer. There were telephones, motion pictures, streetcars, electric lights, indoor toilets, and even hot and cold running water. Many young Georgians had never been far from home. They had their world expanded even more upon arrival in Europe.

By late spring of 1918, an average of 200,000 American soldiers were arriving in France each month. The United States and its allies took the offensive and began to push the Germans back. By October 1918, Germany was ready to surrender. On November 11, what President Wilson had called "the war to end all wars" officially ended.

Meanwhile, back at home, the war was helping to change the role of women. With many men gone to war, women stepped in to fill all types of jobs. At the University of Georgia, female students gained full admission to undergraduate programs in September 1918. President Andrew Soule argued that women trained in nutrition and extension work were needed for the war effort. He convinced the board of trustees to admit them. ▶

U.S. troops march in a parade through Five Points in downtown Atlanta, 1918. The Liberty Bond sign lists the names of soldiers from Fulton County fighting in France.

▶ **Locating the Main Ideas**

1. Define: alliance, neutrality
2. Identify: Henry Ford, Woodrow Wilson, Zimmermann telegram
3. What events caused the United States to go to war in Europe?
4. How did the war create new opportunities for Georgia women?

The Poppy Lady

Maybe you've seen people on street corners collecting money for the American Legion and giving passers-by red silk poppies in return. Money raised through the sale of poppies is used to help disabled veterans of all wars and their families. Remembering those in the armed forces with flowers was the idea of Georgian Moina Belle Michael, a Walton County native known today as "The Poppy Lady."

Born in the Good Hope Community in 1869, Miss Michael grew up in a family devastated by the Civil War. She attended various schools, including Georgia State Teachers College and Columbia University, and began teaching before she was 16. She held different teaching jobs and directed an orphanage before going abroad in 1914 with the YMCA to help Americans stranded by World War I.

In 1918, Miss Michael accepted a job at Columbia University's YMCA training center, helping to prepare YMCA employees heading overseas. While there, she read "In Flanders Fields," a poem by Canadian John McCrae, which begins, "In Flanders fields the poppies blow/Between the crosses, row on row...."

Inspired, Miss Michael began wearing a red poppy to commemorate the fallen soldiers. When she was later asked to select flowers for the 1918 YMCA and YWCA overseas conference, she bought red silk poppies. Her idea continued to spread even though she left New York and returned to her job with the Georgia State Teachers College in Athens. In 1920, the Georgia American Legion state convention adopted the red poppy as its official memorial flower, and the national convention also endorsed it. Miss Michael started another tradition in 1918, that of launching an anchor-shaped wreath of poppies in honor of servicemen killed at sea.

Despite holding down a fulltime job and caring for her parents, Miss Michael devoted the last 26 years of her life to the cause of raising money for veterans. By the time of her death in 1944, about 200 million dollars had been received from the sale of poppies. A U.S. warship, a U.S. stamp, an Athens park, and a stretch of U.S. 78 all bore her name, honoring the woman who "planted the memorial poppy in the heart of the English-speaking world."

The Twenties in Georgia

World War I had created a huge demand for agricultural products to feed America's expanding military force. This brought sudden prosperity to farmers who were willing to grow wheat, corn, potatoes, peanuts, and other food crops.

But soldiers also needed to be clothed. The war created a great demand for cotton. As a result, cotton prices skyrocketed. By 1916, cotton farmers were being paid three times what a pound of cotton had brought in 1900. Many Georgia farmers were prospering. It was like a dream—once again, cotton was "king" in Georgia.

Hard Times for Farmers

The prosperity did not last long. With the end of the war, cotton dropped from 35 cents per pound to 17 cents. At the same time, farmers were hit by another disaster. A small insect known as the boll weevil was leaving a path of destruction across the cotton fields of the South. First detected in Georgia in 1913, the weevil's larvae

Viola Ross Napier

While Georgia women secured the right to vote in 1921, it was the elections in the following year that gave them the opportunity to exercise that right. In 1922, women voted for the first time in Georgia. That year, voters elected the first women to serve in the House of Representatives of the General Assembly. They were Viola Ross Napier from Bibb County and Bessie Kempton of Fulton County. Mrs. Napier was sworn into office first (since Bibb County alphabetically comes before Fulton County) and served from 1923 to 1926. She sponsored bills to improve conditions for women and children and a bill requiring that the state and federal constitutions be taught in Georgia schools. Napier, a lawyer, was also the first woman to argue a murder case and to argue before both the Georgia Supreme Court and the Georgia Court of Appeals.

The death of U.S. Sen. Tom Watson in 1922 resulted in another first for women. In October, Gov. Thomas Hardwick appointed Rebecca Latimer Felton to Watson's seat until a special election could be held for a successor. In doing so, Hard wick wanted to recognize Mrs. Felton for her work in Georgia politics and her role in securing women's suffrage. At the time of her appointment, she could not be officially sworn in because the U.S. Senate was not in session.

In November, a special election was held to fill Watson's unexpired term. Walter F. George won the election. When the Senate convened in late November, George arranged for Felton to be officially sworn in for one day. On November 22, the spunky 87-year-old lady took the oath and became the first woman to serve in the U.S. Senate.

Rebecca Latimer Felton

could destroy fields of healthy cotton almost overnight. Within 10 years, cotton harvests fell to less than a third of what they would be in a normal year.

On top of the plunge in cotton prices and the boll weevil, Georgia farmers suffered through one of the worst droughts of the century in 1925. Across the state, farmers abandoned their fields. Between 1920 and 1925, Georgia's farm population fell by 375,000, resulting in the loss of 60,000 farms. Desperate for some type of income, departing farm families headed for Atlanta, or to Chicago, Detroit, and other large cities up north.

Then, when it appeared that things couldn't get worse, America entered the worst depression in its history. Over a three-year period, cotton prices fell by 60 percent to only 5 cents per pound!

If it wasn't the boll weevil, it was probably the drought or the depression that forced Georgia farmers off the land. They left, searching for a better life somewhere else.

Yet, as bad as things were, most farmers had always had a tough life. They were survivors. Those who refused to leave began turning to other crops. Tobacco became Georgia's second most important crop. By 1930, Georgia led the nation in peanut production, and a decade later was the leading pecan producer. Farmers also became more involved in growing vegetables, dairies, livestock, and poultry—particularly broilers (chickens produced for eating, rather than for egg production).

The Brighter Side

Even though the 1920s was a period of hard times, there were positive things happening within the state. More and more paved roads were being built, helping farmers get their crops and produce to market. Thanks to the Federal Aid to Highways Act of 1916, great improvements were made. By 1920, Georgia had 170 miles of paved road, 673 miles of sand and clay roads, 34 miles of graded dirt roads, and 28 bridges.

These Greensboro couples celebrated Valentine's Day by dancing to the latest hits at the Richland Hotel.

In 1920, the nation's first regular radio station began broadcasting in Pittsburgh, Pennsylvania. Two years later, the South's first radio station, WSB, began operation in Atlanta. The "Voice of the South" broadcast weather and cotton market reports and special music programs and story hours for children. On Sundays, Georgians could listen to church services in the morning and baseball games in the afternoon.

Every Georgia town of any size soon had a motion picture theater. Larger cities had fancy movie palaces, the grandest of all being the Fox in Atlanta. The invention of air conditioning made these one of the most popular sources of entertainment during the hot days of summer.

Georgia had its share of national heroes. In baseball, Ty Cobb from Royston, Georgia, batted over .400 more seasons than any other major league player and was one of the game's all-time greats. In 1926, Theo "Tiger" Flowers, a boxer from Camilla, became the world middleweight boxing champion and first African American to hold that title. Several years later, Atlanta native Bobby Jones was winning one golf championship after another. Recognized as the world's greatest amateur golfer, Jones helped to make the game a popular sport in the United States. Football grew more popular as the teams from Georgia Tech and the University of Georgia defeated such opponents as Notre Dame and Yale.

WSB, Georgia's first radio station, went on the air in 1922. Operated by the Atlanta Journal, *it was one of the first radio stations in America to feature programs of country music. People liked to say that WSB's call letters stood for "Welcome South, Brother!"*

Boosting Atlanta

In the 1920s, stories began circulating about investors who had become rich by buying cheap land in Florida and then reselling it for a small fortune. Suddenly, Florida was the center of a great land boom in America. In Atlanta, bankers, business leaders, and real estate agents debated on what could be done to stop the loss of people and capital to Florida. They wanted to turn some attention toward Georgia's capital city.

In late 1925, Atlanta leaders came up with a new strategy to promote the growth of Atlanta. A "Forward Atlanta Commission" was organized, chaired by Atlanta business leader Ivan Allen. Over the next three years, almost $1 million was spent telling the nation about Atlanta's location, transportation, climate, resources, and workforce. The results were amazing! Between 1926 and 1929, 700 new firms—mostly branches or assembly plants of national companies—were attracted to Atlanta. As a result, more than 17,000 new jobs were created, and annual payrolls totaled $30 million.

Atlanta added a new transportation dimension in 1926, when the first regular air mail service in the region began from Candler Field. In 1929, Delta Air Lines (then based in Louisiana) began passenger

An Augusta movie theater. Even when times were hard, movie theaters often did a good business. Why do you think this was true?

service between Atlanta and Dallas. The next year, Eastern Air Lines began serving Atlanta with passenger service to and from New York.

Wanting to do even better, the city of Atlanta bought Candler Field in 1930 and began building hangars and lengthening runways. The city's goal was to build a first class airfield. By the end of the year, the airfield was serving 16 regular flights per day, a figure exceeded only by New York and Chicago. The next year, Atlanta's airport became the first in the nation to have a passenger terminal. Many years later, it was named the William B. Hartsfield International Airport. The name honored a former mayor of Atlanta who had been one of the earliest and strongest supporters of the airport. ◄

The Great Depression

For this nation's middle and upper classes, the 1920s in the United States had been a time of excitement, and for many, prosperity. The decade known as the "roaring 20s," however, ended with a crash in the fall of 1929.

The United States had suffered business depressions before. Cycles of ups and downs—prosperity and depression—were common in industrialized nations in the 1800s. Typically during a depression, sales, profits, and investments fall, forcing factories to produce less and lay off some of their workers. As unemployment rises, causing demand for new goods to fall, another cycle of unemployment and falling sales begins.

▶ **Locating the Main Ideas**

1. Identify: Moina Michael, Viola Ross Napier, Rebecca Latimer Felton

2. How did World War I bring prosperity to Georgia farmers? What happened to farmers when the war ended?

3. What were some of the things that made life more enjoyable for Georgians living in the 1920s?

4. Why was the "Forward Atlanta Commission" created?

Depressions were not unusual. Always before, the economy had been able to bounce back without any long-term effects on American society. Then, in 1929, a decade-long depression hit America. It was unlike anything ever experienced before or since. Its effects were far-reaching, changing the federal government's relationship with the states, with the people, and with business. Before the **Great Depression** was over, the federal government would play a greater role in setting *national* requirements for states to follow. It would assume greater power in regulating American business and take on greater responsibility for the welfare of the people. Americans, too, would change. Many abandoned old beliefs that government should not interfere with business or get involved with charity or welfare for the needy.

The Crash of '29

The beginning of the nationwide depression dates from the "stock market crash"—an enormous drop in stock prices—in late October 1929.

During the late 1920s, America's economy was booming. A growing number of people invested their money in stocks (ownership shares in a business or corporation). Everyone wanted to make a fortune, some in a hurry through **speculating**.

Speculating involves buying stock, real estate, or any other valuable item at a low price with a plan to sell it soon at a higher price. In the 1920s, stock prices kept climbing as the economy boomed, so to many Americans, speculating seemed like a good idea. The favored stocks were in the new and rapidly growing industries, such as automobiles, aviation, radio, telephone, and motion pictures.

As more and more speculators jumped into the market, hoping to get rich quick, the prices of stocks continued to zoom upwards. The future looked so bright that more and more people jumped on the bandwagon. To buy stock, they used their savings and borrowed money from banks. Buying stock on borrowed money was risky, but many Americans expected to make their profits in the market before the loans became due.

Flaws in the Prosperity

The prosperity of the 1920s was flawed. For example, agriculture had remained depressed since the end of World War I. Farmers had been producing more than consumers demanded, so their crop prices stayed down. Farmers had little money to spend on the goods other Americans were enjoying.

Certain industries, such as textiles and mining, were not prospering. Workers in these industries got low wages and had little to spend. Then too, as transportation of goods and people shifted to trucks and cars, the railroads began to suffer.

Poverty in Atlanta, 1936. During the depression, eight families shared one bathroom in the apartment house shown here.

Americans themselves were going heavily into debt with big mortgages on new houses and installment loans for cars and luxuries. Credit was easy to obtain, and there were so many new inventions to make life easier, such as refrigerators and washing machines.

Some economists and government leaders pointed out that questionable business and banking practices were leading to trouble. However, the national government in the 1920s believed that business was the backbone of this country. President Calvin Coolidge expressed this feeling in 1927 when he observed, "The business of America is business." In fact, many Americans believed in government following a **laissez-faire** policy toward business. This means that government should adopt a "hands off" policy with respect to business.

With little regulation from government, American corporations and banks were free to operate as they pleased. Sometimes their practices were unsound or unfair; sometimes they were downright dishonest. For example, certain corporations were set up that sold stock but produced nothing. Unsuspecting investors were stuck with worthless stock, while the sellers got away with the money. Bankers sometimes took foolish risks with their depositors' money, making loans with little or no security to back them. They, too, sometimes bought worthless stock.

In 1929, many industries found themselves with surplus goods on hand. They had overproduced. To get rid of their huge inventories, they cut prices and cut back on production. Investors realized that stock prices might not continue to rise. Expecting that prices would drop, they then began selling off their stocks. More stockholders joined in the selling. Soon, buyers could not be found for all the stocks that were up for sale. Stock prices started dropping. Then, investors became frightened. Panic selling set in, and stock prices plummeted.

Suddenly, investors were selling their stocks for less than they had paid for them. They were unable to pay back the loans they had made to buy the stock in the first place. Banks collapsed. People with deposits at those banks lost their savings, including many Americans who had not been involved in the stock market.

In 1930 and 1931, thousands of businesses cut back production or went bankrupt. Millions of their employees were laid off. Unemployed, and often without any savings, these people had no way to pay off their debts or even to buy necessities. Many families lost their homes, farms, and cars. By 1932, about one of every four American workers was without a job. Local governments and private organizations, such as the Salvation Army, set up shelters for the homeless and distributed food to the hungry. Everywhere, there was a feeling of hopelessness and despair. ▶

The Depression Continues

Americans continued to ask why the Great Depression was so much worse than earlier depressions? How could this be happening in the richest and most powerful country in the world?

Back when American society was more agrarian and less industrial, the majority of the people were not affected by business cycles. They provided for most of their own needs—working on their own farms, raising their own food, building their own shelters. But by 1930, the American people had become far more *interdependent*. That is, they depended upon one another for food, clothing, tools, appliances, homes, cars, roads, water, electricity, protection, and other services.

Moreover, practically all parts of the United States economy had become linked together. A change in any one part affected other parts. For example, the mining industry was tied to the steel industry, which was tied to the auto industry, which was tied to the tire industry, and so on. When the Great Depression set in, it quickly spread to all parts of the economy and affected almost every American. It also greatly affected federal, state, and local governments, which depended on tax revenue from the citizens. As the economy weakened, governments began running short of money. Governmental services were cut, and sometimes public employees were not paid on time.

▶ **Locating the Main Ideas**

1. Define: Great Depression, speculating, laissez-faire
2. Describe what happens during a business depression.
3. What was the crash of '29? What brought it on?

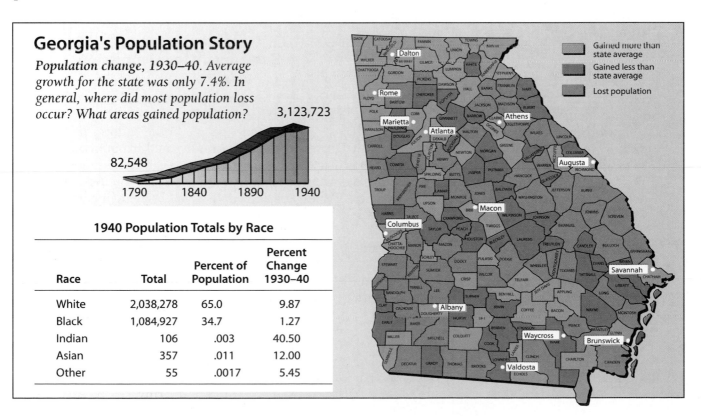

Georgia's Population Story

Population change, 1930–40. Average growth for the state was only 7.4%. In general, where did most population loss occur? What areas gained population?

3,123,723

82,548

1790   1840   1890   1940

Gained more than state average

Gained less than state average

Lost population

1940 Population Totals by Race

Race	Total	Percent of Population	Percent Change 1930–40
White	2,038,278	65.0	9.87
Black	1,084,927	34.7	1.27
Indian	106	.003	40.50
Asian	357	.011	12.00
Other	55	.0017	5.45

Using Interviews for Information

In 1981, **several people** living in northeast Georgia were asked to remember what life was like growing up. Their interviews recall life in the 1920s and during the Great Depression. Interviews and personal recollections are primary sources that give historians firsthand accounts of events. They are valuable for learning about the past—but memories are not always 100 percent correct.

Interviews are often a mixture of facts and opinion. It is important to be able to recognize and separate facts from opinions. A **fact** is a piece of information about something or someone that has been observed or proven true. An **opinion** is a view or conclusion a person holds about some matter or thing, which the person assumes to be true. Opinions are based on what people know as well as on their values; that is, beliefs about what is right or wrong.

As you read the interviews, try to separate facts from opinions. Also keep in mind that these people were asked to remember events 50 or 60 years past.

Emory Hurt Remembers the 1920s

My daddy was a school teacher. Didn't have money —that was one of the poorest paying jobs I know of. He worked for $35-40 a month. Taught 10 grades in school. One or two months out of the year sometimes, the trustees didn't have the money to pay him.

Entertainment? Well, somebody played the fiddle, somebody played the banjo, somebody played the guitar, and just moved everything out of one big room—we loved to go to a dance. We had a good time—and maybe somebody'd have a cake, parched peanuts, somebody'd have a good bunch of apples, and have a good time.

Times were hard, wasn't any money. We had a period [1916-1921] when cotton went way up, you know. That was where it broke so many people that had money and big farms, that were holding it [cotton] for the 50-cent margin. The bankers told 'em to hold it, "it was going there." And, it never went there. I sold my little bit I made,...and I come out all right doing that. But the others held theirs when they could have got 30-40 cents. They were holding for 50 cents—and some of 'em finally took 6 cents and 8 cents.

Lot of 'em lost their farms. Hard, sho' nuff, hard. The boll weevil hit 'em then, hit along in 1921. The dry years got us in 1925—that's when I thought I had a nice crop. But it didn't rain on it from the time it come up to the time I gathered the first bale of cotton and ginned it—and that's all I made.

So, I lit out for Florida the next day to try to make a livin' and pay my debts, too. I was willing to work. I couldn't find work here, an' everybody said, "go to Florida, there's a gold mine in the sky down there." It wasn't quite that way, but I found a job anyway. Put my shirt and britches in an old Dodge car I had and four other men went with me. We all went down there and got jobs. Stayed 20 years, met my wife, raised my family—and then, I decided to come back here.

Many people left. Yes, sir—just as fast as they could get the money to leave. Some of 'em in my town went to Gary, Indiana, to work in the steel factories up there. There was boys leavin' every which way. [Lexington, 1981]

Sidney Thurmond Remembers the Depression

I worked in a grocery store and ran a corn mill. I believe I worked for 50 cents a day, and a lot of people worked for 35. You'd work all week for $3.

At that time, people in the country had their own cows and corn. You could go out in the country and find something to eat. Course you didn't find steak and pork chops, but you found something to eat. People would bring their corn to the mill and sell it and buy coffee or something.

Different from the '20s to the '30s? I tell you the truth. For black people it was hard all the way through. Black people didn't have something to give up, 'cause they didn't have nuthin' to start with. A day's work, that's all they had.

Nobody got no checks, nobody got no handouts or nuthin'! During the last Hoover days, they would ship carloads of flour to each county and they would give that. That's the first I knew of a handout.

Country grocery store near White Plains, Georgia.

But you didn't find nobody robbin' nobody and they didn't bother nobody. I don't remember anybody robbin' or breakin' in. People didn't harm you. They'd come by and beg you for something. You give it to 'em and they'd take it and go on. If you didn't they'd just go on down the road. No, it wasn't like it is today.

Gas was 15-16 cents a gallon, [but] a lot of people just parked their cars. Had no money. Had to get mules and horses and buggies again. I seen a lot of big men park their car and went to drivin' a horse. People had to change.

People worked for anything—clothes, bread, food. I know a lot of women worked all day and bring home some old suit of clothes they didn't want. What they had left over from dinner, or some milk and butter—that's all she'd get. They didn't have nuthin' to pay 'em with.

My family didn't feel the depression. We saw it, but we were lucky. I always had a job. I could buy a heap with the little money I was making. [Athens, 1981]

Dorsey Crowe
Remembers the Depression

That's what we called "Hoover days" because he was president and everybody had to blame somebody for the hard times. So, they blamed Hoover. I think it would a been a depression regardless of who was president.

We had old Ford automobiles, weren't able to buy gas for 'em. We'd taken the motors out, taken the body off and made a wagon out of the frame and pulled it with the horses and mules. With them ball bearings, it pulled real easy. We called them "Hoover buggies."

Every little town around here had a bank—was one at Statham, Bogart, Eastville, and Watkinsville. When they went broke, the people lost their money. A few of the banks paid 'em maybe 10 percent or something like that. It was a great loss. For years after that, country people would hide their money—instead of puttin' it in a bank. They were afraid it would go broke again. They put it in jars and buried it around their homes.

I was around 15 years old then. We'd pick a sack of cotton every morning before we'd go to school and when we'd get in from school, we'd go to pickin' cotton. We were out there by daylight—and then pick until dark. Cotton back then, at one time, got down to 5 and 6 cents a pound, [but] cotton was the money crop, only way to make a livin'.

Daddy also had a store, built it in '24. I guess we was better off than the average person 'cause of the store he run. People would bring eggs to the store and he'd pay 'em. Every Saturday, he'd go to town [Athens] and take those eggs and sell 'em to a store. Then he'd buy groceries from the store at wholesale price to bring back to his store. He had to give a lot of credit until fall when people sold their cotton. Back then people would pay you—they paid off their debts. [Bogart, 1981]

Practice Your Skills

1. What is the difference between fact and opinion?
2. Choose one of the interviews and write out the questions you think the interviewer was asking.

Gov. Eugene Talmadge makes a point to listeners in a Telfair County store. His rural supporters would often drive long distances to hear him speak at political rallies.

▶ **Locating the Main Ideas**

1. How did America's interdependent economy cause the depression to spread quickly and affect almost everyone?

2. How did the depression affect Georgia state government in 1930?

3. What appeal did Eugene Talmadge have to rural voters in 1932?

Depression Politics in Georgia

For many Georgians, the depression began long before the stock market crash of 1929. Many Georgians, not just farmers, barely scraped by. It is said that some rural families lived in such poverty anyway that they hardly noticed there was a depression going on.

In the late 1920s, the General Assembly spent more money than was available from taxes. By 1930, state government couldn't pay its bills. It owed public school teachers alone about $4 million in back pay. City and county governments were also having a hard time. So hard, in fact, that voters of two Georgia counties short on funds—Milton and Campbell—agreed in 1931 to become part of neighboring Fulton County. This merger left the state with 159 counties (its present number).

In 1930, Richard B. Russell, Jr., was elected governor on a promise to reorganize state government and straighten out its finances. With the cooperation of the General Assembly, Russell provided Georgia with a more efficient government. Under Russell, the office of governor gained more power—especially over the spending of state money.

In 1932, in the depths of the depression, Governor Russell was elected to the U.S. Senate. At the same time, Georgia voters chose Eugene Talmadge to be governor.

Talmadge had been Georgia's commissioner of agriculture. He championed the small farmers and preached the ideals of thrift, hard work, and self-reliance. Talmadge was popular with rural white Georgians. He knew the hardships farmers were suffering and promised to help them as governor. Like Tom Watson, whom he admired, Talmadge was a speaker who could move his audience. He pledged to cut the auto tag fee, reduce property taxes, lower utility rates, and cut state spending. During the rough times of the depression, many voters liked what they heard from Talmadge. He won easily.

When Eugene Talmadge took office, he found the General Assembly and other state officials opposed to the changes he had called for in his campaign. To Talmadge, however, a promise to the voters was sacred, so he took several steps to carry through. He pressured some officials, threatened to withhold the salaries of others, and suspended still others. He even imposed martial law and had the National Guard remove certain officials from their offices.

Talmadge used the powers of the governor—especially his control of finances—as no one before him had done. Many Georgians were outraged by the governor's open use of rewards and punishments. Newspapers attacked him, but many voters applauded his strong actions. For more than a decade to come, Eugene Talmadge would influence Georgia politics. ◀

Reviewing the Main Ideas

1. How did Henry Ford change the lives of many Americans?

2. What contributions did Georgia make to the war effort?

3. Why was World War I a time of prosperity for Georgia farmers?

4. What three events put many Georgia farmers out of business in the 1920s? How did some farmers recover?

5. What were some of the ways Georgians entertained themselves in the twenties?

6. How successful was the "Forward Atlanta Commission"?

7. Many Americans appeared to be prospering in the 1920s. What were some of the problems in the prosperity?

8. How did the government's laissez-faire policy result in many investors losing their money? How did banks and depositors lose their money?

9. What problems did Richard Russell face as governor in 1930 and how did he go about solving them?

10. What tactics did Governor Talmadge use to carry out his campaign promises? What was the reaction of Georgians to those tactics?

Give It Some Extra Thought

1. **Drawing Conclusions.** Why would Georgia farmers be attracted to northern cities after their farms went bust in the twenties?

2. **Defend a Position.** Before the Great Depression, government had a laissez-faire policy toward business. Explain why you would defend or object to this policy.

Sharpen Your Skills

1. **Using a Map.** Using the scale of miles on a map of the United States, determine how far farm families living in Sandersville, Georgia, had to travel if they moved to Atlanta, to Chicago, or to Detroit.

2. **Verifying Facts.** Choose one of the interviews on pages 266-67 and find two references in the chapter to events the person being interviewed talked about.

These smartly attired young women show off *dresses made in styles that were popular in the* twenties and thirties.

3. **Identifying Opinions.** Choose a different interview from the one you used above and identify an opinion expressed by the person who was interviewed.

Going Further

1. **Conducting an Interview.** Using the interview questions you developed in the skill activity, interview a person who lived during one of those same time periods. Write their responses so they can be shared with the class.

2. **Write a letter.** Imagine you are head of the "Forward (your town) Commission." Write a letter to the editor of the *New York Times* describing the resources in your town. Be sure to include the things that make it a good place to live and work.

18

Coming Up Next!

- The New Deal
- Reaction and reform
- The coming of World War II

The New Deal and World War II

The United States had never experienced anything like the Great Depression. Everyone, including governmental leaders, began asking the question, "What should be done?" Americans began to wonder what responsibility the government had, if any, to end the crisis.

Herbert Hoover was president of the United States when the Great Depression set in. He felt that America's economy was basically sound. Hoover, a Republican, believed strongly that government should not interfere with the economy. Business could take care of itself. In this belief, he was supported by most business leaders.

As the depression worsened, pressures mounted to do something. President Hoover and Congress set up government programs to lend money to keep banks and businesses going, and to buy surplus farm products.

By the time of the presidential election of 1932, many Americans were blaming Hoover for the depression. His Democratic opponent, Franklin D. Roosevelt, governor of New York, won by a landslide.

In his campaign, Roosevelt—nicknamed FDR—promised the people a **New Deal**. Government, he pledged, would become directly involved in ending the depression and in preventing another one. As soon as he took office in March 1933, Roosevelt began a series of actions that eventually would change the role of the national government in American society.

The New Deal

Roosevelt's New Deal programs were aimed at "Relief, Recovery, and Reform." Because there were so many new government agencies set

up to administer these programs, they were usually known by their initials rather than their names.

Relief programs were aimed at providing help to the millions of unemployed and their families, many of whom were near starvation. Although some relief programs gave direct handouts of food, clothing, and cash, most programs involved work.

- Civilian Conservation Corps (CCC): Put young men to work in rural and forest areas, planting trees and terracing fields to prevent soil erosion. These men also worked on dams, roads, and forest fire prevention and mosquito control projects. They lived in army-type camps. The government paid them $30 a month—$22 of which was sent to their parents.
- Public Works Administration (PWA): Put about a half-million men to work on public construction projects, such as school buildings, community auditoriums, hospitals, dams, roads and bridges, airports for the military, and ships for the navy.
- Works Progress Administration (WPA): The biggest and most controversial work relief program. From 1935 to 1941, the WPA gave work to almost 8 million unemployed men and women, ranging from construction workers to artists, musicians, and writers. Its 250,000 projects included such widely varying activities as clearing slums, building power plants, and providing free plays and concerts.

The WPA spent over $11 billion on its projects. Many citizens criticized these projects as a waste of the taxpayers' money. Others defended the WPA, pointing out that work relief did more than provide people with income, which when spent stimulated business recovery. It also boosted their pride in

WPA road crew, Bibb County, 1936. Works Progress Administration road projects such as this one employed many Georgians.

Left: Presidential candidate Franklin D. Roosevelt (waving his hat) visited Atlanta in October 1932. Governor Russell is sitting on the back seat, left.

Below: Emblem for the National Recovery Administration.

Primary Source

Lina Belle McCommons Remembers the New Deal

Lina Belle McCommons lived in Greene County during the 1930s. She was interviewed at Greensboro in 1981.

I came directly from college to Greensboro to teach in the high school in 1928.

I well remember when President Roosevelt came into office and how everybody sat by the radio to listen to his fireside chats. They thought he was just wonderful. I didn't hear a single person in this area criticize him. No, he wasn't that popular everywhere else, but in most small towns and rural areas, they thought he had really come to turn the country around. He would tell us over the radio that things were getting better all the time and that all we had to fear was fear itself. He would say not to be uneasy about the future, that it was going to get better all the time.

We benefited in this area because it was chosen for a number of the CCC camps—the army of young workers, who worked in forests and fields, stop-ping erosion. Some people said it was a waste of money. But it kept a lot of young fellows employed. And it resulted in newly planted forest areas that of course led into the sawmill and pulpwood business still flourishing today.

The business people thought it was a good thing because the young men spent money with the local merchants. They not only kept themselves going, but helped their families, their parents, survive those hard years.

Another thing they did was to build beautiful parks. So, it had many fringe benefits besides giving young unemployed men jobs. The benefits of those programs were far-reaching.

Interpreting the Source

1. According to McCommons, how did Roosevelt assure citizens that everything would be all right?
2. How did Greene County benefit from New Deal programs?

themselves and gave them hope at a time when the morale of millions was at a low point.

Recovery programs were aimed at helping the economy get back on its feet. One of the main problems was low farm prices because of overproduction.

- Agricultural Adjustment Administration (AAA): Aimed to bring farm income back up to World War I levels. It paid farmers to produce less cotton, corn, wheat, rice, and milk, and fewer hogs. It also bought farm products to distribute to people on relief. The effect was to raise farm prices and thus enable farmers to buy manufactured goods.
- Farm Security Administration (FSA): To relieve rural poverty. Provided loans to almost a million sharecroppers, renters, and farm laborers to buy land, tools, and livestock. It also assisted farmers in trying new crops and taught them soil conservation, livestock raising, and farm management.
- National Recovery Administration (NRA): To help business, industry, and their employees. Attempted to have business operate according to strict codes of conduct. The codes specified how much certain businesses would produce, the prices they would charge, and the wages they would pay. Their goal was

to control production and raise prices. The codes outlawed such practices as unfair advertising and price discrimination. The codes also set minimum wages and maximum working hours for each industry. Child labor was prohibited.

- Federal Deposit Insurance Corporation (FDIC): A recovery program to help restore confidence in the nation's banks. Deposits in an insured bank (which had to meet certain federal regulations) were protected against loss up to $5,000.

Reform programs were aimed at making changes in the way Americans worked and did business so as to prevent future hardships like the ones they suffered in the 1930s.

- Securities and Exchange Commission (SEC): Set up to oversee the buying and selling of stocks. To protect investors, and the corporations themselves, the SEC set rules against the wild speculation and shady dealings that had led to the 1929 crash.
- National Labor Relations Board (NLRB): To protect workers who wanted to organize unions. Under the NLRB, employees were guaranteed the right to choose representatives to bargain collectively with employers over wages and working conditions.
- Rural Electrification Administration (REA): A major reform effort to provide electrical power to rural areas of the country.
- Tennessee Valley Authority (TVA): Built dams and operated power plants to provide low-cost electricity to people in seven states. Brought power to millions of farm families through cooperatives.
- Social Security Act: Began to provide government pensions, or retirement pay, to older citizens. It also provided federal money to state governments for helping people who were unemployed or unable to work. ▶

Posters like this in 1936 told citizens how to sign up for the new Social Security program. According to the poster, who was not eligible to participate?

Eugene Talmadge and the New Deal

At first, Governor Talmadge supported Roosevelt's efforts to combat the depression. Then, he began to fear the New Deal as threatening "Georgia's way of life." For example, he opposed new minimum wage requirements, saying:

Some of the opposition want the state of Georgia to pay a boy who drives a truck, or a negro who rolls a wheelbarrow, a minimum

▶ Locating the Main Ideas

1. Define: New Deal
2. How did presidents Hoover and Roosevelt differ on the proper role of government in fighting the Great Depression?
3. Discuss the three aims of the New Deal.

Franklin D. Roosevelt, took a personal interest in his neighbors when he visited the Little White House at Warm Springs, Georgia. Some of his New Deal programs were conceived because of what he saw and heard in Georgia.

of 40 cents per hour, when a hardworking white woman in the cotton field, right beside the road where they are, is picking cotton from sunup to sundown. If you put a minimum of 40 cents per hour on picking cotton this year in Georgia, the present price of lint and seed would not pay the pick[ing] bill.

Governor Talmadge had other arguments against minimum wage laws. He said that they would hurt private enterprise by paying too high a wage. He said that they would threaten white supremacy by giving blacks equal pay with whites.

When the General Assembly passed laws to enable Georgia to participate in other New Deal programs, the governor vetoed them. For instance, he vetoed social security retirement benefits and unemployment insurance for Georgia.

By 1936, Governor Talmadge was openly calling President Roosevelt a **socialist** (someone who believes in government ownership of major services and the means of production). In fact, since Georgia's constitution prohibited him from running again for governor, Talmadge prepared to challenge Roosevelt for the presidency of the United States.

Georgia voters had mixed feelings. They believed in many of the values that Talmadge preached, but they also appreciated the help Roosevelt was giving them. Furthermore, since the late 1920s, FDR, a victim of polio, had come regularly to Warm Springs, Georgia, for treatment. As president, it was there he established his "Little White House," which made him special in the eyes of many Georgians.

The New Deal produced great change in America, both immediately and in the decades that followed. Monuments to the great rescue program still stand today. Across Georgia are courthouses and other public buildings, low-income housing projects, roads and bridges, dams, and numerous other public works projects from the 1930s. New Deal changes, however, were not always visible. New programs were launched—such as social security, unemployment assistance, and bank regulations—to improve the social and economic life of Americans in need.

When President Roosevelt took office, almost 13 million Americans were out of work—about 25 percent of the nation's labor force. By 1940, over 8 million were still unemployed, almost 15 percent.

The New Deal, then, was not successful in ending the Great Depression. Its programs were experiments. Some worked; some didn't. Still, many people in the 1930s saw that their government was trying. The New Deal gave them hope and helped them get through the hard times.

What were the long-term effects of the New Deal? According to the U.S. Constitution, one purpose of government is "to promote the general welfare." The New Deal gave that phrase a new meaning: government has the duty to protect all its citizens.

Since the 1930s, citizens have come to expect various kinds of government protection. They deposit their money in banks without fear of losing it. They approach old age expecting to have an income even when they can no longer work. Working people expect to be paid a minimum wage. They also expect government to support their right to organize a union and bargain with employers. By law, persons who are handicapped, unemployed, or otherwise needy are entitled to certain kinds of government protection.

Americans also pay for these protections. Government is far bigger, costs much more, and is tied into the daily lives of citizens far more than before the New Deal. Of course, many questions remain about the role of government in American society. But the New Deal resulted in general acceptance—if not expectation—that government will take an active role in attempting to better the life of citizens in this country.

Georgia's "Little New Deal"

In 1936, Georgians got a chance to vote on the New Deal. An overwhelming 87 percent gave their support to Roosevelt for president. In the governor's race, Georgia voters elected E.D. Rivers—a Talmadge foe who supported Roosevelt's New Deal. At the same time, they re-elected Richard Russell to the U.S. Senate over Eugene Talmadge, who ran for the Senate instead of the presidency.

Georgia now joined the New Deal fully. Roads, bridges, courthouses, school buildings, and other public works were constructed across the state with federal money. Georgians began to participate in such programs as social security retirement, unemployment benefits, slum clearance, and soil conservation. Rivers even hoped to lead his own "little New Deal" to do more for Georgia's needy. Working with federal programs, he tried to bring health care and basic welfare programs to rural citizens.

At the same time, the General Assembly upgraded public education by providing funds for free textbooks and a seven-month school year. In response to the growing number of highway deaths, lawmakers created a state highway patrol and required all drivers to be licensed. By 1938, Georgia got its first four-lane highway, link-

Gov. Eugene Talmadge, wearing the red suspenders that became his trademark, had an electrifying speaking style.

ing Atlanta with nearby Marietta. That same year, prohibition ended in Georgia when a law was passed allowing each community to vote on the sale of alcoholic beverages.

Many of the programs Rivers envisioned—such as new hospitals, schools, and highways—were very costly. State government needed a way to borrow money to build these projects, and then pay off the loans over a period of years. At that time, however, Georgia's constitution prohibited state debt.

Using Roosevelt's Tennessee Valley Authority as a model, Rivers proposed creating special state authorities. An **authority** is a public corporation created by government to perform a special service or function. As a corporation, an authority can be given special powers (such as borrowing money) that regular government agencies do not have. In 1939, Rivers successfully pushed legislation to create a State Hospital Authority with power to borrow money to build new hospital facilities.

Despite his successes and good intentions, Governor Rivers's "little New Deal" ended on a sour note. Refusing to raise taxes to cover all the new expenses, he juggled the state finances. State government was again in debt. As Rivers's term ended, New Deal opponent Eugene Talmadge was back, running again for governor. Nationally, FDR was running for an unprecedented third term as president. Both won. ◀

Reaction and Reform

Since the election of Richard Russell in 1930, state politics had been dominated by strong governors. However, as Georgians anxiously followed the events of World War II overseas, events occurred at home that would bring big changes to state government—especially in the office of the governor.

Talmadge Re-elected

In 1940, with Europe on the brink of war, Talmadge ran a successful race for governor by attacking many of the New Deal programs. He criticized them as unnecessary, costly, and a dangerous threat to American federalism. Moreover, he warned white voters, the New Deal's real aim was to end segregation in the South. The strategy worked.

▶ **Locating the Main Ideas**

1. Define: socialist, authority

2. What was Governor Talmadge's attitude toward the New Deal's program of minimum wages?

3. How did Georgians express their support for the New Deal in the 1936 elections?

4. Once Georgia began to participate in the New Deal, what changes came about?

Once back in office, Talmadge objected to what he called "ultra-liberals" everywhere, but particularly in Georgia's colleges and universities. He warned of "foreign professors trying to destroy the sacred traditions of the South." By "foreign," Talmadge meant from other parts of the country. He even went so far as to propose dismissing university professors and administrators who were not native Georgians. He backed off, though, when told that 700 educators fell into this category. Still, he promised to rid Georgia's colleges of any professor who favored "communism or racial equality."

Soon after taking office in 1941, Governor Talmadge received word that certain professors in Georgia's university system supported school **integration**—educating white and black students in the same schools. Among the leading integrationists, he was told, were two administrators—the dean of the College of Education at the University of Georgia and the president of Georgia Teachers College at Statesboro. Talmadge brought the issue before the Board of Regents—the governing body of Georgia's university system. The governor not only appointed members of the board, but also served as a member. After replacing three board members who wouldn't agree, Talmadge and the board voted to fire the two professors.

This and other interference by Talmadge caused the Southern Association of Colleges and Secondary Schools in 1941 to remove its accreditation (official approval) of the University of Georgia and other white public colleges in the state. This meant the credits and degrees of students going to these schools would not be recognized outside Georgia.

The University of Georgia's loss of accreditation gained national attention. Many Georgians were outraged, and students began protest demonstrations against Talmadge's interference.

At this point, Ellis Arnall, Georgia's attorney general, announced that he would run against Talmadge for governor. In the spring and summer of 1942, college students by the hundreds traveled across the state campaigning for Arnall. It was the only race for governor that Eugene Talmadge would lose.

Ellis Arnall and Reform

Ellis Arnall had promised voters that he would reform state government if elected. They approved, and change came quickly.

First, Arnall asked the General Assembly to propose a series of constitutional amendments and adopt new laws that would reduce the power of the governor. This legislation particularly affected education. The governor was removed from the boards that ran the state's public schools and the university system. He lost the power to remove certain elected officials from office or to strike salaries from the budget, as Eugene Talmadge had done. Another law took away the governor's power to pardon convicted criminals, instead giving this power to a board of pardons and paroles. Because the

During the 1942 campaign for governor, Ellis Arnall spoke to a crowd in front of the University of Georgia campus. Why would Arnall have been popular in Athens?

former governor had often blocked changing the state constitution, the governor's power to veto constitutional amendments was revoked.

During his term in office, Governor Arnall called for prison reform. The chain gangs, with their striped clothes and leg irons, were finally abolished.

There were changes in voting, too. Arnall argued that any person "old enough to fight for us in the deserts of North Africa or the swamps of New Guinea is old enough to take part in our government." In 1943, he pushed for a constitutional amendment to lower the voting age to 18. Lawmakers approved the change, and voters then passed the amendment. Georgia became the first state in the nation to allow 18-year-olds to vote. Eighteen-year-olds would not have this right nationwide until 1971, when the Twenty-sixth Amendment to the U.S. Constitution was approved.

By 1943, Georgia's "redeemer" Constitution of 1877 had been amended over 300 times. It was confusing because of all the changes upon changes. Arnall called on the General Assembly to assemble a special commission to draft a new state constitution. In March, lawmakers named a 23-member body, with Arnall as chairman. During 1943 and 1944, committee members labored over revising the old constitution. Finally, in January 1945, the new constitution was presented to the General Assembly, where several changes were made. In August, Georgia voters approved what became known as the Constitution of 1945.

Other changes took place under Arnall's leadership. In 1945, Georgia became the fourth southern state to drop the poll tax. That year, a federal district court ruled that Georgia's white primary was unconstitutional. Arnall urged Georgians to accept the ruling rather than come up with a new strategy for keeping blacks from voting in the Democratic primary. In 1946, the party voted to abandon the white primary. Blacks could now vote in its primaries. ◀

The Coming of World War II

As the country emerged from the Great Depression, thoughts turned to prosperity and better times at home. Yet, increasingly, Georgians were hearing troubling news from abroad. Japan had invaded China in the early thirties. By 1938, Japan was in command

▶ Locating the Main Ideas

1. Define: integration
2. Why did the University of Georgia and other white public colleges in Georgia lose their accreditation in 1941?
3. In what ways did Governor Arnall reduce the powers of the office of the governor?
4. Why was Georgia's constitution rewritten?

Margaret Mitchell

Perhaps no book has shaped the world's perception of Atlanta and the South more than *Gone with the Wind*, Margaret Mitchell's epic novel of power and passion set in mid-nineteenth century Georgia and published in 1936. Visitors to modern Atlanta routinely ask for directions to Tara, a plantation in Mitchell's book, and search in vain for the graves of characters who existed only on paper.

Margaret "Peggy" Mitchell was born in 1900, a sixth-generation Atlantan who grew up listening to old Confederate veterans telling stories of Civil War battles. She was graduated from Washington Seminary and attended Smith College. Her mother's unexpected death ended her college career. She returned to Atlanta to tend house for her father, a prominent attorney.

After a debut into Atlanta society and a brief marriage, Mitchell landed a job as a reporter for the *Atlanta Journal Sunday Magazine*. Her co-workers, writers Frances Newman and Erskine Caldwell among them, praised the quality of her interviews, profiles, and features.

Mitchell married again, this time to Georgia Power advertising executive John Marsh. When a severe ankle injury forced her to leave the *Journal*, Mr. Marsh urged his wife to fill her time by writing a novel. His support and encouragement continued through Mitchell's 10 years of researching, writing, and editing her lengthy manuscript.

Once her project was completed, Mitchell was reluctant to let it go, but a Macmillan Company editor—and her husband—knew she had created a bestselling novel. They convinced her to allow its publication. *Gone with the Wind* was an instant success, winning the 1936 Pulitzer Prize and spawning an Academy Award–winning movie classic.

Constantly beseiged by reporters during the 1940s, Mitchell fought to maintain her privacy and modest lifestyle. She was active with the Red Cross during World War II and nursed both her father and husband. On August 16, 1949, Mitchell died from injuries received a few days earlier when she was hit by a taxi while crossing Peachtree Street with her husband.

---

of the major cities in eastern China—including the capital city of Beijing. In the fall of 1935, Italy invaded Ethiopia, a historic kingdom of northeastern Africa.

America's Great Depression had contributed to a worldwide economic slowdown, and many nations began to turn to strong leaders to take control and solve their problems. Many of these new leaders became **dictators** (rulers with few limits on their authority). To them, order was more important than freedom, and the nation more important than the individual. By appealing to **nationalism** (strong feelings for one's nation and its traditions), these new leaders diverted their people's concern away from democracy and human rights.

German Expansion and the Outbreak of War

Many Germans had never forgiven the victorious Allies for a peace settlement forced on them at the end of World War I. Germany had been forced to disarm and told to make huge payments to the victors for having started the war. It also had to give up many of its overseas colonies and much of the land it held in Europe. America's Great Depression made Germany's situation even worse, as Americans began withdrawing funds deposited in German banks. Factories closed and unemployment shot up. Unable to pay its war debts, Germany resorted to printing more and more paper money, which became worthless. Soon, Germany's economy was near collapse.

During these hard times, many Germans began listening to a group of extremists known as National Socialists (or Nazis). Their leader, Adolph Hitler, set out to take over Germany's government. Once the Nazis were in power, no one was allowed to oppose them. Anyone who did could be imprisoned or executed. All political parties—except the Nazi party—ceased to exist. Minorities—particularly Jews—were viewed as "inferior" and blamed for many of Germany's problems. What began as Nazi discrimination against and persecution of German Jews became a policy of eliminating all Jewish people. Eventually, millions of innocent men, women, and children were sent to their deaths.

Though the treaty ending World War I had prohibited Germany from rearming itself, Hitler launched a vast program of military

Europe during World War II

Neutral Nations
Area held by Allies
Axis Powers
Germany's maximum expansion

U.S. Navy ships ablaze after the Japanese bombing of Pearl Harbor on December 7, 1941.

arms buildup. He also directed the beginning of a military draft so he could have an army.

In 1936, Germany and Italy signed a treaty of alliance. Soon, Hitler was ready to move. In April 1938, he announced that Germany was annexing (adding) Austria to Germany. Next, he prepared to annex the Sudetenland, an area of Czechoslovakia where many people of German ancestry lived. Britain, France, and Italy stood by, saying little and doing nothing. The next year, Russia signed a pact with Germany, allowing Hitler to take what was left of Czechoslovakia.

On September 1, 1939, Hitler's forces marched into Poland. Two days later, Britain and France declared war on Germany. Shortly thereafter, Germany launched a three-month "lightning war" on its European neighbors. Denmark, Norway, Belgium, Luxembourg, Holland, and finally France fell to the German forces. In 1940, Hitler launched a massive air attack on Great Britain. For months, German bombers dropped thousands of explosives on London in nightly raids. Nearly 13,000 residents were killed during the bombings, but the city refused to give up. After the loss of thousands of planes, Germany gave up what came to be known as the Battle of Britain.

In 1941, Hitler turned his attention to the east. After taking over Yugoslavia and Greece, Hitler now turned his sights on Russia. Disregarding the former treaty, the Germans invaded Russia, a move that resulted in millions of deaths.

America Enters the War

Despite strong political and cultural ties to Great Britain and France, the United States at first tried to stay neutral in the war. Germany's

During World War II, black and white Americans trained and fought in segregated units. An MP stationed at Fort Benning in Columbus, Georgia, is pictured here.

military successes, particularly its capture of France, helped change the mood of the American people. At first, President Roosevelt hoped that providing military arms and supplies to its allies would be enough. But soon it became clear that Germany and Italy were unstoppable without U.S. troops being sent to Europe. Thus, in September 1940, Congress enacted a military draft law.

Japan, which had an alliance with Germany, then proceeded with an act that assured the entry of the United States into World War II. Early on the morning of December 7, 1941, Japan conducted a massive bombing raid on the giant American naval base at Pearl Harbor, Hawaii. The attack was unexpected by the United States. As the Japanese planes flew back to their aircraft carriers, they left behind 2,330 Americans killed, 1,145 wounded, and hundreds of destroyed ships and planes.

On December 8, President Roosevelt went before a joint session of Congress. Calling December 7 "a day that will live in infamy," he called for a declaration of war against Japan. Congress granted that declaration with only one dissenting vote—that of Montana congresswoman Jeannette Rankin.* Rankin was a **pacifist**—a believer in nonviolence—who had lived in Georgia prior to her election in 1940 and maintained a residence in the state for many years.

Earlier, Japan had signed a treaty of alliance with Germany and Italy. Three days after the United States had declared war against Japan, Germany and Italy declared war on the United States. Before the end of the second World War, some 50 nations would be involved, either on the side of the Allies (a term for the United States, Great Britain, and their allies) or the Axis (a term for Germany, Italy, Japan, and their allies). ◀

Georgia's Role in World War II

Georgia contributed in many ways to America's war effort. Over 320,000 Georgians volunteered or were drafted into the military between 1941 and 1945. One of Georgia's most well-known native sons in World War II was Gen. Lucius D. Clay. He gained fame for his ability to keep a steady stream of vital supplies and equipment reaching American troops in Europe. Other military officers from Georgia serving in World War II included future governors Marvin Griffin, Herman Talmadge, Ernest Vandiver, and Carl Sanders.

Georgia had another role during the war. It provided places for training soldiers. Only Texas had more military bases than Georgia.

▶ **Locating the Main Ideas**

1. Define: dictator, nationalism, pacifist

2. Identify: Margaret Mitchell, Pearl Harbor, Jeannette Rankin, Allies, Axis

3. Why was the German economy near collapse in the 1930s?

4. How did President Roosevelt attempt to avoid sending U.S. troops to help Britain and France win the war against the Axis powers?

---

*The first woman elected to Congress, Rankin voted against the war in 1917. She is the only representative in history to vote against both world wars.

This was in part due to Georgia's climate, cheap land, extensive rail network, deepwater ports, and numerous farms and mills to feed and clothe soldiers.

The number of military bases in Georgia also reflected the influence in the national government of two Georgia congressmen—Rep. Carl Vinson and Sen. Richard Russell. Both became widely respected for their knowledge and commitment to military preparedness. First elected to the U.S. House in 1914, Vinson served in Congress for more than 50 years. While there, he sponsored legislation creating the U.S. Army Air Corps (which later became the U.S. Air Force). Believing a navy was a country's first line of defense, he also was the driving force in Congress for building a naval fleet in the Pacific Ocean. In the Senate, Russell developed a similar reputation for helping build America's military strength during World War II.

Fort Benning, 1941. U.S. infantry soldiers engage in a bayonet drill. In the background are jump towers used for paratrooper training.

When war broke out in Europe in 1939, the U.S. Army consisted of only 174,000 soldiers. By the end of the war, this figure jumped to 6,000,000 men and women. For many of these young Americans, their first visit to Georgia was spent in "boot camp" at one of the many military training facilities in the state.

Georgia's most famous base was Fort Benning, outside of Columbus. Known as "home of the U.S. Infantry," Fort Benning was the largest infantry training school in the world. Other important facilities were Warner Robins Air Service Command south of Macon, Camp Gordon near Augusta, Hunter Field near Savannah, and Atlanta's Fort McPherson.

Georgia industries soon became an essential part of the war effort. Factories and mills switched to production of military equipment and supplies. Car makers changed to building tanks, jeeps, and other military vehicles.

In early 1942, Bell Aircraft Corporation announced plans to locate a plant to build B-29 bombers—then America's largest military plane—in Marietta. By fall of 1943, the huge facility was in full operation, employing 20,000 civilian workers. Among other Georgia war production facilities were shipyards for building naval vessels at Savannah and Brunswick, and weapon plants at Macon and Milledgeville.

Peace at Last

America's entry into World War II helped turn the tide of war in Europe. On May 7, 1945, Germany surrendered to the Allies. But Japan continued to fight, despite great losses. When it appeared that an invasion of Japan would be necessary to end the war, President Truman gave the order to use a new, secret weapon—the atomic bomb. On August 6, 1945, a B-29 dropped the first atomic bomb on Hiroshima, Japan, leveling the center of the city and instantly killing 70,000 to 80,000 civilians. Three days later, a second bomb was dropped on Nagasaki, killing about half that number. On August 15, Japan agreed to surrender to the Allies.

Women welders at the Brunswick Shipyard, 1943. Nicknamed "Rosie the Riveter," women workers were hired to do jobs during World War II that previously had been considered men's work only.

The most deadly world war in history was over. According to some estimates, as many as 50 million people died during the conflict. United States losses were 405,000 dead and 671,000 wounded. About 7,000 Georgians never returned from the war.

World War II also was the most expensive war until that time. But as Georgia and the rest of the nation turned to military production, thousands of new jobs were generated. During the war, the annual income for the average Georgian doubled. By the end of the war, more Georgians were employed in manufacturing than in agriculture, a trend that would continue in the decades that followed.

The end of the war marked the beginning of a period of rapid social and economic change for the state. Hundreds of thousands of Georgia GIs* had served in such far-off places as Europe, Africa, Asia, and the Pacific. Their view of the world had been changed. As the war ended, the United States was now promising to send former GIs to college. Many young Georgians now had a chance for a better life. Postwar Georgia would never be quite the same. ◀

▶ Locating the Main Ideas

1. Identify: Carl Vinson, Richard Russell
2. What were Georgia's contributions to the war effort?
3. How did World War II boost Georgia's economy?
4. What events forced Japan to surrender, thus ending World War II?

---

*The term "GI" (an abbreviation for *government issue*) was a common term used for American military personnel.

CHAPTER ACTIVITIES

Reviewing the Main Ideas

1. What events contributed to FDR's landslide victory in the presidential election of 1932?
2. Identify two programs in the New Deal that specifically helped farmers, and explain how they did.
3. Which reform program was aimed at preventing a recurrence of conditions that had led to the stock market crash of 1929? How did it work?
4. Why did Gov. E.D. Rivers's "little New Deal" run into problems?
5. How did Governor Talmadge use the issue of segregation to attack university professors and administrators?
6. What was Governor Arnall's reason for giving voting rights to 18-year-olds?
7. What advances were made during Arnall's administration that benefited African American voters?
8. What actions of Adolph Hitler caused Britain and France to declare war on Germany?
9. What event brought the United States directly into World War II?
10. When World War II ended, more Georgians were employed in industry than in agriculture. Why?

Give It Some Extra Thought

1. **Explaining Change.** Write a paragraph describing how the role of government changed because of Franklin D. Roosevelt's presidency and the New Deal program.
2. **Relating Past to the Present.** What protections do Americans still have today that were started during the New Deal?

Sharpen Your Skills

1. **Using a Globe.** Use a globe or a map of the world and calculate the distance from Tokyo, Japan, to the Hawaiian Islands. Is it further than the distance from the Hawaiian Islands to Los Angeles, California?
2. **Critiquing.** Critique the success of the Works Progress Administration during the New Deal. Be sure to cover why some citizens opposed its projects and why others defended them.
3. **Analyzing the Outcome.** Give the main reason why you think Georgia voters rejected Gov. Eugene Talmadge in his race for re-election in 1942.

Going Further

1. **Doing Research.** Choose one of the programs of the New Deal and locate more information about that program. Write one paragraph describing the facts about the program and another paragraph evaluating its effectiveness.
2. **Write a Slogan.** Write a campaign slogan that Ellis Arnall could have used in his 1942 race against Eugene Talmadge.

At its peak, the Brunswick facility employed 16,000 men and women to produce huge military supply vessels, known as "Liberty Ships." During the war, 99 of the ships, which were 416 feet long, were produced in Brunswick.

UNIT 8

GEORGIA EVENTS

1946	1947	1948	1950	1951	1954	1956	1961	1962	1964
Three Governors Affair	12th grade added to public schools	WSB-TV broadcasts as first TV station in Georgia		Georgia's first sales tax (3%) enacted	Marvin Griffin elected governor; massive resistance to integration begins	General Assembly approves new state flag	School integration begins	County unit system abolished; Leroy Johnson elected as first black legislator since 1906	Georgia votes Republican in presidential election
Cold War begins	Jackie Robinson integrates baseball	Berlin crisis	Korean War begins	First commercial computers available; first commercial color TV broadcast	Supreme Court rules against segregation in public schools	Congress decides to build interstate highway system	American soldiers begin training South Vietnamese forces	Cuban missile crisis	Congress passes Civil Rights Act; Martin Luther King, Jr., wins Nobel Peace Prize

EVENTS ELSEWHERE

Modern Georgia
1945–1990s

	Maynard Jackson elected mayor of Atlanta	Hank Aaron breaks Babe Ruth's record	State constitution revised	Constitution of 1983 becomes effective; 250th anniversary of Georgia's founding	State sales tax raised from 3 to 4 percent	U.S. census results in 11th congressional seat for Georgia	Georgia lottery begins	Atlanta hosts Summer Olympics	
1968	**1973**	**1974**	**1976**	**1983**	**1989**	**1991**	**1993**	**1996**	**1998**
Martin Luther King, Jr., and Robert Kennedy assassinated	Arab oil embargo begins; ceasefire in Vietnam War signed; Watergate affair	President Nixon resigns	United States bicentennial; Jimmy Carter elected president	Congress establishes MLK's birthday as federal holiday		U.S. and allies defeat Iraq in Persian Gulf War; Soviet Union breaks up	Georgia sends first majority Republican delegation to Congress	Bill Clinton wins second term as president	Troops from Fort Stewart sent to Middle East during crisis in Iraq

19

Georgia Moves into the Modern Era

In the fall of 1945, war-weary Americans looked forward to the return of a peacetime economy. People were hungry for consumer goods that they could not get during the war. Factories that once turned out guns, tanks, and uniforms now began producing tools, trucks, and clothing.

One consumer item in great demand was the automobile. With the war over and gasoline no longer scarce, owning a car was a dream come true for many Georgians. Drive-in restaurants, drive-in movies, and even drive-in banking became popular. Paved highways replaced dirt roads, allowing people who worked in the city to live in the countryside. Soon, housing subdivisions and shopping centers covered what once was farmland. Suburban growth skyrocketed, particularly in the Atlanta region.

To ease the GI's return to civilian life, Congress provided several important benefits in legislation known as the GI Bill of Rights. Among these were four years of college education and low-interest loans to buy a home, farm, or business. GIs were also entitled to $20 a week in unemployment benefits (for up to a year) and help in finding a new job. These benefits were extremely popular with ex-servicemen, giving them the security to marry, buy a home, and start a family. In fact, so many births took place in the years right after the war that people described the period as a "baby boom."

For many, the GI Bill changed their lives. By the thousands, veterans enrolled in Georgia's colleges and universities. At the University of Georgia, enrollment jumped from 1,836 students in 1944 to 6,643 students in the fall of 1946. Of these, more than 4,000—some 60 percent of the student body—were veterans.

Like the rest of the country, Georgia experienced a baby boom.

The Disappearing Farmer

Between 1945 and 1950, almost 28,000 Georgia families—mostly tenant farmers—left agriculture. Altogether, between 1920 and 1950, the number of Georgia farms decreased by more than 100,000.

The number of farmers in Georgia decreased for many reasons. Thanks to the GI Bill, young men who had farmed before the war now had new opportunities. Also, agriculture was undergoing great changes in the state. Big improvements had been made in seed technology, fertilizer, and pesticides. Farmers were being encouraged to practice crop rotation, terracing, and erosion control to preserve top soil and land fertility. Agricultural extension agents from the University of Georgia informed farmers of new technology and research. Also, more and more farmers were able to afford tractors and harvesters.

The days of mule-drawn plows and hand-picked cotton were not entirely over, but they were fast coming to an end. As farming efficiency improved, two important things happened. Crop yield per acre increased. At the same time, tractors and other motorized implements allowed a single farmer to work larger plots of land. Farmers were becoming so efficient that they were producing too much. This further reduced the need for farmers. In an effort to keep food prices from falling, the federal government began paying farmers *not* to plant on some of their land.

Harvesting turnips in Colquitt County. After World War II, how did tractors and other mechanized farm equipment reduce the need for farm laborers?

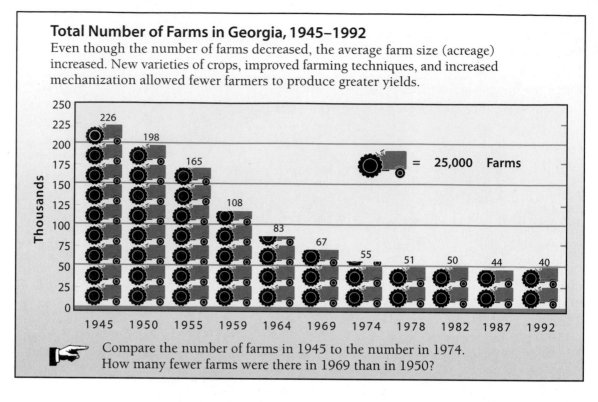

Total Number of Farms in Georgia, 1945–1992

Even though the number of farms decreased, the average farm size (acreage) increased. New varieties of crops, improved farming techniques, and increased mechanization allowed fewer farmers to produce greater yields.

= 25,000 Farms

Compare the number of farms in 1945 to the number in 1974. How many fewer farms were there in 1969 than in 1950?

Also contributing to the decline of farming was the clothing industry's growing use of synthetic fibers instead of cotton. The peak year for cotton had been 1911, when 2,769,000 bales were produced. During the five years after World War II, the harvest fell from 669,000 bales in 1945 to 490,000 bales in 1950. Farmers turned to such crops as peanuts, soybeans, tobacco, corn, and wheat, as well as to non-crops, such as poultry and livestock. Also replacing cotton was another "crop"—pine trees. The demand for pine wood to produce pulp for paper, as well as lumber and plywood, encouraged landowners to become tree farmers. As a result, thousands of acres of what once had been cotton land were now covered with pine trees. Forestry was becoming an important part of Georgia's economy.

Population Shifts

As tenant farming declined after World War II, 91 of Georgia's 159 counties—all rural—*lost* population. Where were rural Georgians going? Many moved to other states. The 1950 census showed that 1.2 million people born in Georgia now lived in other states. Many of these were black Georgians who had migrated to the large cities of the North in search of jobs and greater opportunities. This trend of black migration had begun in the 1880s, resulting in a continuing drop in the percentage of African Americans in Georgia's total population up until the 1970s.

However, not all rural migrants moved out of state. Many moved to the city. Helping account for Georgia's city growth was the very thing Henry Grady had dreamed about 60 years earlier—new business and industry. For example, in 1947, General Motors opened a new assembly plant at Doraville. Ford responded with a new plant at Hapeville. Other factories came to Georgia as well. In the decade after World War II, the Atlanta region became home to 800 new industries and 1,200 regional offices for out-of-town companies.

Other urban areas in Georgia also benefited from postwar industrial growth. During the 1940s and 1950s, almost every Georgia city with at least 10,000 residents gained population. Older cities such as Atlanta, Macon, and Savannah were growing at healthy rates, but the most dramatic increase was in the newer cities of Atlanta's suburbs. During the 1940s, the city of Atlanta grew by 10 percent, but nearby College Park grew by 77 percent, Marietta by 139 percent, and Forest Park by 360 percent.

What accounted for the rush of business and industry to the state? There were many reasons. Atlanta continued to develop as the transportation hub of the Southeast. Except for summer Georgia had a favorable climate, and the growing use of air conditioning after the war made even the summer heat bearable. For the most part, Georgia workers were not unionized, and thus labor was cheap compared to other parts of the country. Low state and local taxes in Georgia also meant higher profits than in the North or Midwest.

The two decades after World War II brought more change to Georgia than the previous two centuries. Accepting that change was another matter. As rural populations decreased, urban politicians looked forward to a greater voice in state political affairs. Rural politicians, however, prepared to defend Georgia's traditional way of life. ▶

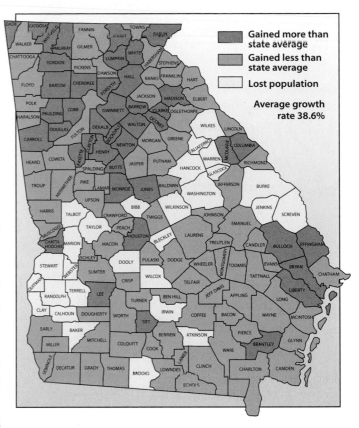

Population change, 1960–1980. Which parts of the state grew at a greater rate?

America in the Cold War

Americans had entered the post–World War II era with new hopes for world peace. For the time being, the United States was the only nation with the atomic bomb. Also, a new international organization—the United Nations—had been created to prevent aggression and resolve disputes among nations.

But by 1946, the United States was at war again. This time, it was not a fighting war. It was a political war in which the two most powerful nations in the world—the United States and the Soviet Union—competed for the loyalty of other nations. Nations aligned with the Soviet Union were known as the "East," while America and its allies were known as the "West." In this **Cold War**, as it was called, tensions were high, but no direct fighting occurred between the two superpowers.

▶ **Locating the Main Ideas**

1. Identify: GI Bill of Rights, baby boom
2. What are some changes automobiles made in how and where Georgians lived after the war?
3. What effect did new agricultural technology have on Georgia farmers?
4. What were some of the crops Georgia farmers switched to after the war? Why?
5. What conditions made Georgia attractive to new businesses and industry?

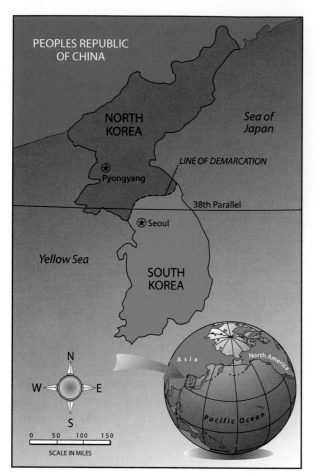

The Cold War began soon after the end of World War II. The Soviet Union took political control of several countries of eastern Europe. As the Soviets attempted to spread their influence into other countries, the United States adopted a policy of containing (preventing the spread of) **communism**—the political system of the Soviet Union. Communism is a system in which goods, property, and capital are controlled by the central government rather than the individual.

At home, there was increasing concern that agents of the Communist party were actively at work in the United States. Watching as the Soviets took over eastern Europe, some Americans began to wonder if this country would be the next target. That fear was reinforced by some politicians who charged that Communist agents, or those who sided with them, were everywhere. Many people who worked in government, labor unions, civil rights organizations, colleges, and the entertainment industry found themselves being suspected of having Communist ties.

In 1948, the Cold War almost became a shooting war over the issue of Berlin. After World War II, Germany had been divided into four zones. Each of the four major victors—the United States, Great Britain, France, and the Soviet Union—was given one of the zones to control. Berlin, the capital of Germany, was also divided into the four zones.

Berlin lay far within the zone of Germany that was controlled by the Soviet Union. The Soviets had promised the other three powers highway access to the city. In 1948, however, the Soviet Union changed its policy, blocking roads to western access. When food and supplies began to run out in Berlin's western zones, the United States began a massive air lift. Gen. Lucius Clay, a Georgian, commanded the relief operation. For 11 months, U.S. planes flew in more than two million tons of needed food and supplies. Eventually, the Soviets were forced to lift their blockade.

Within two years of the Berlin crisis, the Cold War began to heat up in the Asian country of Korea. In 1910, Japan had seized control of Korea, holding it until the end of World War II. After Japan's defeat, the United Nations temporarily divided Korea into two parts. Until the country was reunited, North Korea would be aided by the Soviet Union, and South Korea by the United States.

In June 1950, North Korean soldiers, supplied by the Soviets, invaded the south. The United Nations voted to help defend South Korea, but could not assemble a military force quickly. When it appeared that South Korea would fall, President Truman sent U.S. troops to defend its ally. A three-year war followed, in the end involving Chinese Communist forces. At times, people feared that the fighting would escalate into another world war. Although both sides

Symbol of the United Nations.

suffered numerous casualties, the conflict finally ended in 1953 with neither side claiming a victory.

During the Korean War, Marietta's Bell Aircraft plant, which had closed in 1946, was reopened by the Lockheed Aircraft Corporation. There, Georgians built and modified B-29 bombers, still America's largest bomber. After the war, Lockheed continued operating its huge facility as a producer of military aircraft. ▶

Georgia Politics in Action

While the Cold War was changing the course of world affairs, an old era was about to end in Georgia. Although old-style Georgia politics were alive and well, power was shifting away from the rural areas of the state. In addition to the growth of cities, events were taking place that would change the nature of state politics.

During World War II, Gov. Ellis Arnall had worked hard to modernize Georgia, changing the way state government operated. By the end of the war, he was speaking out for political equality for black Georgians. Though not opposing segregation, Arnall argued that blacks were entitled to equal opportunities. He believed that one way to improve race relations in Georgia was to attack poverty. In fact, if economic growth could eliminate poverty, he suggested, everyone's lot would be improved.

Both black and white workers in Georgia and other southern states were poorly paid compared to workers in other regions of the country. In 1940, for example, the average income for a Georgian was only about half the national average. One reason for low wages was a lack of **labor unions** (organizations of workers who bargain as a group with employers over salaries and working conditions). Governor Arnall was among those urging Georgia workers to unite and join labor unions. Many black leaders agreed.

Generally, labor unions had never been popular in the South. Higher wages meant less profits for mill and factory owners, who sometimes threatened to close their plants if workers unionized. Union organizers from the North were often viewed as "outside agitators." Also, union organization was hurt during the Cold War era by charges that

▶ **Locating the Main Ideas**

1. Define: Cold War, communism
2. Identify: East, West, Berlin airlift
3. Why were Americans concerned about Communist agents at work within the United States?
4. How did the Korean War start?

A merchant in Barrow County gives cigars to the first group of Georgia men leaving to serve in the Korean War.

In 1946, a record number of black citizens in Fulton County registered to vote. The line of people waiting to register circles the courthouse.

Communists were involved in the labor movement. The effort to expand labor unions in the South had only limited success.

After World War II, black Americans looked for ways to improve their lives. Increasingly they adopted political and legal strategies to fight the **discrimination**—deliberate unequal treatment—they faced. One strategy was to mobilize black voters. In large cities, to which more and more African American families were moving, voter registration drives met with some success. By 1946, Georgia's white primary and poll tax had been eliminated, and over 100,000 blacks across the state were registered to vote. That year, black voters in Georgia had their first chance to influence an election since Reconstruction. When a vacancy occurred in the congressional seat representing Atlanta, Helen Mankin, a white woman, ran to fill the remainder of the term. Actively seeking black support, she won, becoming the first Georgia woman *elected* to Congress.

Despite the success of black voter registration in Atlanta, statewide the picture was far different. Out of every 100 Georgia blacks of voting age, fewer than 5 were registered to vote. In rural areas, this figure was even lower. Even though some legal barriers had been eliminated, others remained. For example, blacks attempting to register to vote still faced a literacy test requiring them to read and interpret a section of the state constitution. Also discouraging blacks from voting were threats and various other pressures by whites, especially in rural areas.

The 1946 Governor's Race

Former governor Eugene Talmadge was shocked that Atlanta's black voters had been able to swing the election to Mankin. Deciding it was time to act, Talmadge announced he would run again for the office of governor. His campaign called for bringing back the white primary, maintaining white supremacy, and protecting Georgia from Communists and other outside agitators.

This platform was not particularly popular in Atlanta and other large cities. But Talmadge was not campaigning for the urban vote. He was appealing to white voters who lived in rural counties. Talmadge was able to ignore city voters because of the **county unit system**. (See page 297.)

In 1946, Georgia's constitution prohibited a governor from running for re-election. Arnall gave his support to James Carmichael, head of Bell Aircraft at Marietta, in that year's Democratic primary. With no white primary to exclude them, thousands of black Georgians participated, helping give Carmichael a victory in the popular election. But Talmadge pulled ahead in the county unit vote and claimed victory.

The primary victory assured Talmadge's election as governor. At the time, only the Democratic party nominated candidates in Georgia.

The Three Governors Controversy

Eugene Talmadge's primary win came at a cost. In ill health before the race, his condition worsened during the hectic campaign. Some of his supporters now feared that Talmadge was dying. Even though no Republican was running against him in the general election, what would happen if he were to die before being sworn in?

Georgia's constitution provided that if no candidate for governor received a majority of the votes in the general election, legislators should choose from the two candidates with the highest number of votes. But, in 1946, only one candidate's name was on the ballot—Talmadge. Some of Talmadge's supporters decided to write in the name of his son, Herman Talmadge, on their election ballots. Write-in votes were cast for other names as well.

In the November 1946 general election, Eugene Talmadge won the uncontested race for governor, though several thousand write-in votes were cast for other candidates. Among these were 669 votes for James Carmichael, 637 votes for Republican D. Talmadge Bowers, and 617 votes for Herman Talmadge. Voters in 1946 also elected M.E. Thompson to the newly created post of lieutenant governor.

A month later, before either could be sworn in, Eugene Talmadge died. No one was sure who was to be governor. Talmadge supporters said that the General Assembly had to choose the write-in candidate with the most votes. Suddenly, 58 uncounted write-in votes were "discovered" in Telfair County—Talmadge's home county. All were for Herman Talmadge, giving him 675 total votes. The General Assembly then declared Herman Talmadge the next governor.

Atlanta Congresswoman Helen Mankin. What was special about her election?

Citizens in Hartwell follow the local vote count in the 1948 governor's race. Acting Gov. M.E. Thompson lost to Herman Talmadge. How would voters get this information today?

Georgia went into an uproar. M.E. Thompson, the newly elected lieutenant governor, claimed he should be governor. Governor Arnall agreed with Thompson and refused to give up the office to Talmadge until the issue was settled in court.

One night, Talmadge forces seized the governor's office in the state capitol and changed the locks. Arnall set up in another office, while Thompson was in another. Georgia had three governors! Secretary of State Ben Fortson refused to let any of the three use the official state seal on government documents. Thus, little official action could be taken.

After two months of confusion, Georgia's Supreme Court ruled that Lt. Gov. M.E. Thompson should be acting governor until the next general election in 1948. Arnall then resigned, and Thompson was sworn in. Herman Talmadge gave up the governor's office, but promised to take the case "to the court of last resort...the people of Georgia." ◀

Governors at Mid-Century

Herman Talmadge did come back, defeating Governor Thompson in 1948 in a special election to fill the remaining two years of his father's term. In the campaign, civil rights emerged as the main issue. Talmadge, like his father, promised the return of the white primary. Once elected, Talmadge fought hard to preserve segregation of the races, but he was unable to restore the white primary. At the same time, he sponsored programs to develop Georgia and improve the life of its people.

One of Talmadge's greatest achievements was passage of the Minimum Foundation Program for Education Act in 1949. After his reelection in 1950, Talmadge also pushed through Georgia's first sales tax. The 3 percent tax was needed, he argued, to improve public schools. Just one year after the tax went into effect, state funding of public education increased by an amazing 74 percent! Black and white schools were still unequally funded, but state support for teacher salaries no longer differed by race.

In 1956, the popular ex-governor decided to run for the U.S. Senate seat of Walter George. George was widely recognized as one of the most powerful members of the Senate, having served there for 34 years. Failing health, however, forced him out of the race, and Talmadge won the election easily.

Following Talmadge as Georgia's chief executive were Marvin Griffin and Ernest Vandiver. These three governors served during a time of great social, political, and legal changes in America. Blacks,

▶ Locating the Main Ideas

1. Define: labor unions, discrimination, county unit system

2. Why did Governor Arnall want labor unions in Georgia?

3. How did the election of Helen Mankin help bring Eugene Talmadge back on the political scene?

4. How did Georgia have three governors at one time?

Georgia's County Unit System

The county unit system was a special formula for counting votes in primary elections of the Democratic party. It applied only for statewide races, such as governor and U.S. senator. Enacted by the General Assembly in 1917, the county unit system was intended to keep political power from shifting from rural areas to the growing urban centers.

Under the system, the candidate who won the most popular votes in a county won that county's "unit" votes. These unit votes, rather than the total statewide vote of the people, determined the winner of the Democratic primary.

Under the county unit system, a county's vote in statewide races depended on the number of members it had in the state House of Representatives. State law provided that the eight most populated counties were entitled to three representatives. The 30 next largest counties had two each, and all the remaining counties had one representative. For each representative, a county could cast two unit votes. Here's how the breakdown looked:

Counties According to Population	Unit Votes per County	Total Unit Votes for Group of Counties
8 largest counties	6	48
30 next largest counties	4	120
121 remaining counties	2	242

In races for governor and U.S. senator, a majority of county unit votes was needed. This meant at least 206 of the total 410 county unit votes. For other statewide races, a **plurality** (more votes than any other candidate) was needed.

How did the county unit system help rural counties and hurt larger, urban counties? Two out of every three voters in Georgia lived in the 38 largest counties. Yet, these counties were entitled to only 168 county unit votes. The 121 remaining counties, however, got 242 unit votes. This meant that one-third of the voters controlled 60 percent of the total county unit vote in the state.

Defenders of Georgia's county unit system pointed out that the system protected the small rural counties from being controlled by the large cities, particularly Atlanta. Opponents, however, pointed out that the system violated the voting rights of Georgians who lived in urban counties. For example, in 1940, Fulton County had 392,886 residents but was entitled to just 6 unit votes in statewide races. In contrast, Quitman, Echols, Towns, Long, Glascock, and Dawson counties had total populations of 23,966 residents, but got 12 unit votes—twice as many as Fulton. In the case of the smallest county, Echols County got one county unit vote for each 1,247 residents. Fulton, in contrast, got one unit vote for each 65,481 residents.

Another problem of the county unit system was that it was possible—as had happened in 1946—for a candidate for governor to receive a majority of the popular vote in Georgia but lose the election. This could happen if another candidate won a majority of the county unit votes.

In April 1962, a federal district court struck down Georgia's county unit system, saying it violated the Fourteenth Amendment of the U.S. Constitution. The case was appealed to the U.S. Supreme Court, which in 1963 confirmed the lower court's decision. In so ruling, the high court established its famous "one person, one vote" rule. No matter where you live, one person's vote cannot count any more than any other person's vote.

Interpreting the Source

1. Define: plurality
2. What was the purpose of the county unit system?
3. Why was the county unit system unfair to the individual voter? to urban areas?

increasingly supported by the federal government, began the movement for civil rights. In the South, many white political leaders responded with a policy of "massive resistance." Candidates expecting to be elected had to publicly pledge their support of segregation. They also had to oppose federal interference in state affairs. State legislatures across the South passed laws to keep the races separate, especially in the public schools.

In Royston, Georgia, supporters lift Herman Talmadge to their shoulders at a campaign rally in the 1948 special election. Talmadge was elected as governor to finish the last two years of the four-year term to which his father had been elected in 1946. He went on to serve another full term as governor before being elected to the U.S. Senate.

Rural/Urban Power Struggles

Not all Georgians defended segregation. Support for civil rights was greater in the rapidly growing urban areas than in rural areas. By the mid 1950s, a majority of Georgians lived in urban areas, but rural Georgia continued to control state politics into the 1960s. This was possible because of the county unit system, which allowed rural counties to control the election of the governor and other statewide officials. Also, election to the House of Representatives in the General Assembly was based mainly on counties, not population. Every county in the state—no matter how small—had at least one representative. No county—no matter how large—could have more than three.

A federal district court issued a ruling in 1962 declaring the county unit system unconstitutional. The decision said that the votes of rural citizens could not count more than those of urban citizens. According to the ruling, the Fourteenth Amendment to the U.S. Constitution is clear in requiring "one person, one vote."

Politics in the New Era

In 1962, the death of the county unit system changed Georgia's political scene. In the Democratic primary, former governor Marvin Griffin opposed Carl Sanders of Augusta. While Griffin campaigned in the old way, appearing at county courthouses or barbecues in rural areas, Sanders went on television to appeal to urban voters. Sanders easily won the election, becoming the first resident of a large city to be elected governor of Georgia. For the first time, Georgia's rural counties had not determined the outcome of the governor's race.

In 1964, another court ruling led to more change. Rural control of the General Assembly had continued because the state constitution guaranteed each of the state's 159 counties at least one state representative. The U.S. Supreme Court, however, ruled that the practice violated the rights of voters in more populous counties. The Court said that legislative districts must be drawn solely on the basis of population. This decision forced Georgia's General Assembly to **reapportion** (redraw) election districts so that each consisted of similar numbers of people. Since more Georgians lived in cities, urban areas gained and rural areas lost representatives.

Reapportionment not only affected rural-urban political power. It increased the variety of people elected to the General Assembly. No longer would state legislators be all male, all white, and all Democrat. In 1962, Atlanta voters elected Leroy Johnson, the first black legislator since 1906. In a few years, other black legislators were elected from urban areas. Women and Republicans also gained additional representation in the chambers of the state capitol.

Carl Sanders had campaigned for governor on the idea of a "new Georgia." Once elected, he tried to avoid the open appeals to racism that had been part of Georgia's politics since Reconstruction. His stress was on the need for progress in Georgia. To move the state ahead, he encouraged business and industry from other states to invest in Georgia. Governor Sanders worked to improve the state's public colleges and universities. He also tried to improve Georgia's relations with the federal government. But presidents Kennedy and Johnson, Congress, and the federal courts took actions in support of civil rights that angered many white Georgia citizens. As a result, in the 1964 presidential election, a majority of Georgia voters supported Republican Barry Goldwater in his failed bid to defeat Pres. Lyndon Johnson.

Two years later, federal support of civil rights was still on the minds of many Georgia voters. Governor Sanders was prohibited by the state constitution from running for re-election. Democratic contenders included ex-governor Ellis Arnall, Atlanta businessman Lester Maddox, and state legislator Jimmy Carter from Plains. In the primary, voters chose outspoken segregationist Lester Maddox, who had closed his restaurant rather than serve black customers.

In the general election, for the first time in almost a century the Republican Party had a serious candidate for governor—Howard "Bo" Callaway. In 1964, Callaway had been elected Georgia's first Republican congressman since Reconstruction. Like Maddox, he defended segregation and opposed federal attempts to enforce civil rights.

In the 1966 general election, Callaway got more votes than Maddox. But because 7 percent of the voters had written in Ellis Arnall's name on their ballots, Callaway did not receive a majority of the total vote. According to the state constitution, the General Assembly had to choose between the two highest vote-getters. Even though Callaway had received the most popular votes, the Democratic legislature chose Maddox.

The 1966 election proved to be an important turning point in the relationship between the governor and General Assembly. Until then, a newly elected governor got to name the speaker of the House of Representatives and the committee chairmen. As a result, the legislature tended to be a "rubber stamp" for the governor. But when the General Assembly met after the 1966 general election to choose a governor, for the first time they were free to name their own officers. After that, no governor would dominate the legislature as before. ▶

Carl Sanders was Georgia's first governor to use television extensively in his campaign.

▶ **Locating the Main Ideas**

1. Define: reapportion
2. What were the benefits from the new sales tax that began during Gov. Herman Talmadge's administration?
3. How did the end of the county unit system change Georgia's political scene?
4. What was Carl Sanders's idea of a "new Georgia"?

Lester Maddox, Georgia's governor from 1967 to 1971, ran for office promising voters a program of "truth, patriotism, and Americanism."

Growth and Change in Metropolitan Atlanta

Just as politics had changed, life for Georgia's people went through great changes in the decades after World War II. One big change was Atlanta's rapid growth. Helping contribute to this growth was the decision by Congress in 1956 to build a 41,000-mile national network of interstate highways. Atlanta was chosen as the southeastern hub on which the national interstate system would be built. It would become one of only five cities in America served by three separate interstate highways—I-75, I-85, and I-20. The addition of I-285 (a perimeter freeway around the city) further attracted business, industrial, and transportation facilities to Atlanta. Then came new industrial parks, warehouses, office complexes, shopping centers, and a boom in housing and apartment construction.

During the 1950s and 1960s, the Atlanta metropolitan region—an area consisting of Fulton, DeKalb, Cobb, Gwinnett, and Clayton counties—grew rapidly. Easy access to Atlanta by train, truck, or plane was a major reason for that growth. Railroads and super highways extended out in every direction from the city. About one in five Americans lived within overnight delivery of goods shipped from Atlanta by truck. In 1961, a new $20 million terminal helped make Atlanta's airport one of the busiest in the nation. Led by Delta, Eastern, and Southern Airways, Atlanta was the heart of air transportation in the Southeast.

Atlanta was enjoying a diversified economy, with a good mix of manufacturing and industry, banking, business, and services. A healthy industrial sector included such transportation giants as Lockheed, Ford, and General Motors. Atlanta was recognized as the most important business and financial center of the Southeast. By the 1960s, a majority of the nation's 500 largest corporations had offices in Atlanta, and 8—including Coca Cola and Delta Airlines—had their headquarters there. Metropolitan Atlanta also was strong in the service industry. Law, insurance, real estate, accounting, and other professional firms prospered. Other services were provided by hotels, restaurants, wholesale and retail businesses, and the communications, transportation, utilities, and entertainment industries.

In the public sector, Atlanta was home to a very large city government, as well as the governments of Fulton County and the state of Georgia. Also important to the economy were several independent authorities, notably those to build and operate Grady Hospital, the Atlanta-Fulton County Stadium, and Atlanta's public housing. Many federal agencies chose to locate their southeastern regional offices in Atlanta, too. Other important federal facilities in Atlanta included Fort McPherson, the Federal Reserve Bank, the Centers for Disease Control, and the Atlanta Federal Penitentiary. The fed-

Benjamin Elijah Mays

Atlanta's Morehouse College is today one of the most respected institutions in the country. The school's rise to prominence is credited to Benjamin Elijah Mays, who served as its president from 1940 to 1967. Though known primarily as an educator, Dr. Mays was also a great humanitarian, public servant, author, and civil rights advocate—as well as the spiritual mentor of Dr. Martin Luther King, Jr.

Little in Mays's background hinted at his future accomplishments. He was born in 1895 in rural, impoverished South Carolina. His parents were former slaves turned tenant farmers. As an adult, he would tell a story about praying while he plowed. In his prayers, he would ask God to help him receive an education during a time when most blacks couldn't read.

At 22, Mays was graduated first in his class at the high school department of South Carolina State College. He enrolled in an all-black Virginia college, then transferred a year later to previously all-white Bates College in Maine, graduating with honors in 1920. He went on to the University of Chicago for further study. When his funding ran out, he left the school and held a variety of jobs—including teaching and pastoring—before earning his doctorate from Chicago in 1935.

Mays served as dean of Howard University's School of Religion for six years before moving to Morehouse. While he was president, Morehouse's enrollment doubled and its endowment quadrupled. It was at Morehouse that he first met a bright eleventh grader who would become one of America's greatest leaders—Martin Luther King, Jr. He became his friend and mentor, and suggested that King study the nonviolent teachings of Gandhi.

Mays was also involved in unraveling segregation. He filed a lawsuit in 1942 that ended the practice of separated dining cars on Pullman trains. In 1954, he told the American Baptist Convention that the Christian church was America's most segregated institution. In 1960, Mays encouraged students to hold sit-ins at public establishments across Atlanta to protest segregated conditions.

At age 72, two years after retiring from Morehouse, Mays was elected to the Atlanta Board of Education, serving 12 years as its president. During that time, he was instrumental in gaining support for a compromise desegregation plan and averting a strike by teachers and employees.

Mays was recognized widely for his contributions, receiving 49 honorary doctorate degrees from 1945 to 1981. An Atlanta street and a public high school are both named for him. He died in 1984, at the age of 89.

---

eral district court for Georgia's northern district was also located in Atlanta.

Atlanta public and private colleges and universities also helped contribute to the growth of the region. By the 1950s and 1960s, several had attained national reputations. The Georgia Institute of Technology was recognized for its engineering and technology programs. Emory University was known for its liberal arts and theology programs, medical school, and hospital. The Atlanta University Center (which included seven associated colleges) was famous as the leading center for African American higher education in the United States.

During this era, the Atlanta Division of the University of Georgia, created in 1949, became the Georgia State College of Business Administration in 1955, and Georgia State College in 1961. The college was elevated to university status in 1969. Several Atlanta-area junior colleges were also created in the 1960s.

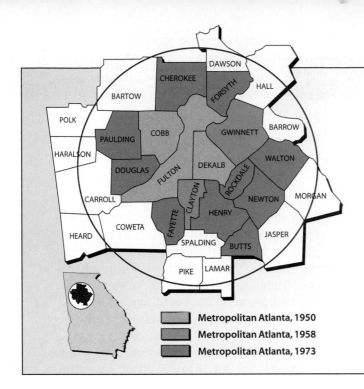

Atlanta's Population, 1940–1970

	Metropolitan Atlanta		City Limits	
Year	Total Population	Percent Black	Total Population	Percent Black
1940	442,294	29.3	302,288	34.6
1950	671,797	24.7	331,314	36.6
1960	1,017,188	22.8	487,455	38.3
1970	1,390,164	22.6	496,973	51.6

Atlanta's metropolitan region grew dramatically every decade. In contrast, the population actually living within Atlanta's city limits grew more slowly, with much of the growth during the 1950s due to annexing new land to the city. The largest annexation came in 1952, when 92 square miles were added. This not only tripled the land area of Atlanta, but gave the city 100,000 new residents.

Metropolitan Atlanta, 1950
Metropolitan Atlanta, 1958
Metropolitan Atlanta, 1973

In part, Atlanta's success was due to the efforts of its business and political leaders to promote the city's future. In 1961, for example, Mayor Ivan Allen, Jr., launched a "Forward Atlanta" program (similar to that led by his father in the 1920s). Atlanta's ability to attract new business and industry, Allen believed, depended on achieving these goals:

- completion of the interstate highways that served the city
- a new sports stadium
- professional baseball and football teams for the city
- rapid rail as part of the public transportation system
- keeping the public schools open at a time when some politicians were calling for closing schools rather than integrating them

During the first three years of Forward Atlanta, 173 new plants and 323 branch offices opened in Atlanta, creating an estimated 70,000 new jobs. By the end of the decade, the city had professional baseball, football, basketball, and hockey teams. Atlanta also had a perimeter expressway around the city, six four-lane highways to enter and leave downtown, and a new Metropolitan Atlanta Rapid Transit Authority (MARTA).

At the same time, Atlanta was undergoing a major change in the makeup of its population. Large cities such as Atlanta, Savannah, and Augusta provided African Americans with more opportunities than they had found in rural areas, including a growing number of jobs that came with new businesses. As a result, during the 1960s, some 70,000 blacks moved into the city. During the same period, 60,000 whites left the city, often settling in the suburbs to the north and east of downtown. By the late 1960s, blacks were a majority of Atlanta's population. ◄

▶ Locating the Main Ideas

1. What decision by Congress helped make Atlanta a transportation hub in the Southeast?

2. Were the goals of Ivan Allen, Jr.'s, Forward Atlanta program met?

3. How did the population makeup of Atlanta change during the 1960s?

CHAPTER ACTIVITIES

Reviewing the Main Ideas

1. How did the GI Bill of Rights help ex-servicemen?
2. Give three reasons why the number of farmers in Georgia decreased after World War II.
3. Where did the most dramatic growth occur in Georgia in the 1940s and 1950s?
4. What actions by the Soviet Union after World War II caused Americans to become concerned? As a result, what was America's policy toward communism?
5. What hurt the effort to bring labor unions to the South?
6. Why were Eugene Talmadge's promises more popular in rural areas than in Georgia cities in his 1946 campaign for governor?
7. How did Secretary of State Ben Fortson prevent official business from being conducted during the three governors controversy?
8. What were two effects of the 1964 U.S. Supreme Court decision that forced Georgia to reapportion its legislative districts?
9. What changes resulted in the relationship between the governor and the General Assembly after the 1966 election?
10. How did the population shift in the state result in a power shift In Georgia politics?

Give It Some Extra Thought

1. **Give Reasons.** As tenant farming decreased, rural counties in Georgia lost population. In addition to the decline in tenant farming, what are some other reasons that Georgia's rural counties lost population?

2. **Making Connections.** What statement would Henry Grady likely make if he had observed Georgia in the 1950s?
3. **Identifying Trends.** After World War II, Georgia changed more rapidly than at any other time in its past history. Name two trends that were changing the state.

Sharpen Your Skills

1. **Classifying Information.** Make two lists of the accomplishments of Dr. Benjamin Mays—one in the area of education and one in civil rights. Some accomplishments may belong in both categories.
2. **Using Data.** Choose a Georgia farm product mentioned in this chapter and locate data on its production during this century. Use information from as many decades as you can. Present the information in a chart or graph to explain the product's importance to the state. The *Georgia Statistical Abstract* is one source for this information.

Going Further

1. **Investigate.** Find information about Charles Herty, a chemist whose work resulted in the establishment of the paper industry in Georgia. In a brief report, explain his significance to Georgia's forest and paper industry.
2. **Fact Finding.** The United Nations has played an important role in international affairs. Develop a fact sheet on the United Nations and include when it was established, its purpose, where it is located, and how many countries are members. What Georgian served as a U.S. ambassador to the United Nations in the mid 1970s?

During the 1960s, Atlanta's skyline underwent dramatic changes.

20

The Civil Rights Movement

At the time America entered World War II, segregation of the races was still a way of life in most of the United States. This was particularly true in the South, the region of the nation with the highest percentage of African Americans. Reminders of America's dual society were common, especially in public places. Signs reading "White" and "Colored" marked water fountains, restrooms, movie theater entrances, and places to sit on the bus and train.

In Georgia, blacks had organized early to protest laws that discriminated against them. Resistance to segregation dated back to the late 1890s and early 1900s. Black leaders in Atlanta, Augusta, Rome, and Savannah had organized boycotts to protest new laws requiring segregation on streetcars. But their efforts were unsuccessful, and blacks were forced to ride in the back of the streetcars.

World War II was a turning point for race relations in the United States. During the war, many young Americans of both races served in the armed forces. Though assigned to segregated units, black soldiers fought and died just like white soldiers. After the war, some black war veterans began to challenge the segregated society back home. Also, many black workers were not willing to accept lower pay for doing the same jobs as whites.

During the Cold War era, the United States presented itself to the world as the defender of freedom and democracy. Yet, how could a country make this claim and still practice racial discrimination at home? In 1947, President Truman appointed a civil rights commission to recommend ways to ensure equality for all Americans. The next year, he issued an order to end segregation in the armed forces.

Most white southerners feared ending the only way of life they had ever known. But by the 1950s, black Americans, and some whites, were showing a new determination to break down the bar-

The March on Washington, 1963, was led by civil rights groups with the support of religious organizations and labor unions.

riers to equal opportunity in America. Their determination became the force behind the civil rights movement of the 1950s and 1960s.

Civil Rights and the Law

Segregation laws during the first half of the twentieth century were possible because of the 1896 U.S. Supreme Court ruling in the case of *Plessy v. Ferguson*. This ruling (described in Chapter 15) said that segregation was legal as long as blacks had access to facilities equal to those for whites. Under this separate but equal doctrine, however, facilities for blacks were seldom comparable to those for whites.

In the decades that followed, black leaders debated the best approach for gaining social and political equality. In 1910, the National Association for the Advancement of Colored People (NAACP) was established. Its approach was to secure **civil rights**—the protections and privileges given to all citizens by the Constitution—for blacks through the nation's courts. The NAACP frequently filed lawsuits against discriminatory laws and practices. ▶

School Desegregation

In the late 1940s, lawyers for the NAACP and other civil rights groups went to court. Their targets were the dual school systems

▶ **Locating the Main Ideas**

1. Define: civil rights
2. Why was World War II a turning point in race relations in the United States?
3. How were segregation laws in the first half of the twentieth century influenced by an 1896 Supreme Court decision?

The Civil Rights Movement / 305

Separate schools for blacks and whites, like these in Chatham County and Camden County (opposite page), existed in Georgia for many years after the 1954 Brown v. Board of Education decision.

set up by law in Georgia and other states. They argued that although black people paid taxes just like white people, they did not receive the same services from government. In Georgia, for example, state government spent over four times as much to educate a white student as it spent to educate a black student. White teachers' salaries were more than double those paid to black teachers.

With black and white schools so clearly unequal, the legal basis for separate but equal began to crumble. Courts began ruling that educational opportunities for blacks had to be improved.

Even segregationists began to approve of spending more money on black schools. Perhaps in that way, they thought, separate schools could be maintained. In Georgia, more money was pumped into public education for blacks and whites. However, inequalities still existed. In 1954, Georgia spent $190 to educate each white child, $132 on each black child. Through an order of the U.S. Supreme Court, those conditions were about to change.

On May 17, 1954, the U.S. Supreme Court handed down a historic decision. The case, *Brown v. Board of Education*, wiped out the legal basis for racial segregation in public education. According to the Court, segregation laws were unconstitutional; they violated the Fourteenth Amendment, which guarantees all citizens equal protection (or treatment) under the law. Said the Court, "We conclude that in the field of public education the doctrine of 'separate but equal' has no place. Separate educational facilities are inherently [by nature] unequal." The ruling threw the weight of the nation's highest court behind the movement to give all citizens equal rights. In time, the entire federal government would uphold this principle.

The *Brown* ruling did not set a date for achieving the integration of public schools. In the South, most government and school offi-

cials opposed it. Georgia's Governor Talmadge denounced the Supreme Court's decision, saying it had reduced the Constitution to "a mere scrap of paper." An *Atlanta Constitution* editorial advised that this was no time to encourage agitators on either side "or those who are always ready to incite violence or hatred.... It is time for Georgians to think clearly."

In May 1955, the U.S. Supreme Court issued a second ruling in the *Brown* case. The court now ordered that segregated schools be ended "with all deliberate speed." Public schools had to take immediate steps to **desegregate** (enroll black and white students in the same schools).

Across the South, reaction was immediate. Most white politicians and newspaper editors expressed outrage with the Supreme Court, calling its action unconstitutional. Georgia's new governor, Marvin Griffin, spent most of his four years in office (1955–59) pushing a program of "massive resistance" to the two *Brown* decisions. Officials thought that a massive effort to avoid enforcing the Court's decision would result in the federal government changing its position on segregation. The General Assembly even went so far as to pass laws that would abolish Georgia's public schools if need be. It voted to support private schools, to close schools that desegregated, and to prosecute local school officials who permitted desegregation. These laws were never enforced.

Eventually, change did come. As the 1960s began, some Georgia political leaders, including Gov. Ernest Vandiver, recognized that the schools had to be kept open, even in the face of desegregation. In 1961, token integration of Atlanta public schools began. In Athens, Charlayne Hunter and Hamilton Holmes became the first black students to be admitted to the University of Georgia.

Rosa Strickland

In 1981, a black woman who had been a teacher and a school principal, was interviewed in Athens, Georgia. In the following passage, Rosa Strickland describes her school of the 1940s.

The particular school where I was, was fair. But getting fuel was bad. We had a pot-bellied stove in each room—we had three rooms, three teachers. In the winter, the boys spent most of the time going to the woods and picking up trash to burn in the stoves. They couldn't study for going to get wood, because the county did not furnish wood to us.

Most of our books were used, second-hand books; some were too old to really be used in school.

We had outdoor toilets—the boys' was pretty bad. The principal was very old and she didn't feel like askin' the superintendent—you know how some black people were afraid to ask white people to do anything—she thought it was an imposition to ask the superintendent to do anything. I would ask her, "Why don't you ask him to fix that floor in the boys' toilet?" But she wouldn't do it.

And we didn't have any water on the place—we had to walk about four blocks or more to a neighbor's house to get water. The children would bring buckets of water from that distance to pour in a big barrel. That's the way they got drinking water. [Of course, many white pupils in Georgia in the 1940s went to schools that had no indoor plumbing.]

Then, I became principal and I went to the [main] office more and looked around and saw how we were cheated out of books. I saw the many nice readers that they had on the shelves and I asked the superintendent for them and why he hadn't given us any. He said, "Well, Ah didn't know yuh needed 'um," or something. So, in fact I got the readers, and workbooks along with 'em, and other books—new editions we should have been gettin' all the while.

After that, I asked him about fixing the boys' toilet. He said, "Well, ah am." So, finally, one day, the floor fell through. And that day I got hot. I went by the office and said to the superintendent, "The county could get sued." So, then he sent somebody out to put a new floor in.

Then, after that, I said, "We really need some water on the grounds. It's dangerous; the building could catch on fire. It's not healthy for the children to bring water in the dust all up and down that way, their little dresses getting in the water. It's bad." So, I found somebody to come out and dig a well, and the county paid for it.

Then, after that, I said, "I feel the county should furnish us some fuel." He said, "Well, we just don't have the money for fuel." So, I called the parents together and told 'em the conditions we had and I said if we pledged $2 each, I believed we could buy enough coal and wood to supply us for a time. And we did—enough to keep the boys in the classroom.

Later, I got a blacksmith to make us swings and seesaws for the playground. He came out and put them up.

We even had lights in the building. I told the superintendent we wanted to have some programs out there at night. He said the county didn't have the money. I asked him if we, the parents, raised $10 would he do it? We raised the money and the county sent the folks out to wire the building. Then we had lights.

Desegregation of Public Facilities

The schools were only one type of public, or tax-supported, facility segregated by law. After the *Brown* ruling, civil rights lawyers challenged segregation in other areas, such as public transportation, libraries, auditoriums, parks, and beaches. In a series of rulings, federal judges struck down segregation of these facilities, too.

While the courts were considering these cases, blacks—and whites who supported their cause—began using other methods to arouse public support. In 1955, Rosa Parks, a department store seamstress in Montgomery, Alabama, tired from a long day at work, refused to give up her seat on the bus to a white passenger. She said she had paid the same fare as everyone else, and had a right to a seat. Following her arrest, the black community, led by Dr. Martin Luther King, Jr., organized a boycott of the Montgomery bus system.

King, who was born and raised in Atlanta, was the new pastor of the Dexter Avenue Baptist Church in Montgomery. His role in the bus boycott established him as a national civil rights leader. He advanced the cause of civil rights through the use of a technique called non-violence. His followers might choose to disobey laws they felt unjust, and fill up a community's jails by doing so. They might resist—and take abuse—when ordered to move on. But, they would be peaceful. There would be no violence on their part.

For over a year, black residents of Montgomery stayed off city buses. They walked or organized car pools as their means of transportation. Some whites reacted harshly, trying to prevent the changes that appeared to be coming. There were bombings of churches and homes, threats, and beatings. In the end, however, Montgomery buses were integrated.

Hamilton Holmes and Charlayne Hunter graduated from the University of Georgia in 1963. They went on to successful careers, Holmes as an Atlanta physician and Hunter—now Charlayne Hunter-Gault—as a reporter on national television and radio.

Attitudes toward Civil Rights Progress

Many white Georgians, as well as other southerners, were outraged at what was happening. Some blamed the racial unrest on outsiders—whites and blacks from the North. Many accused the federal government of tampering with southern customs. Candidates for public office and leaders in state and local governments spoke out against federal government attempts to enforce civil rights laws.

Other voices among white southerners attacked the unfair treatment of black southerners. One such voice belonged to Ralph McGill. Born in Tennessee in 1898, McGill went to work for the *Atlanta Constitution* in 1929 as a sports writer. Later he wrote about politics, economics, and life in the South. He was concerned about the plight of the poor—black and white—and worked to bring help to them.

In his writing, he attacked the white supremacy policies of Gov. Eugene Talmadge. In 1942, McGill managed Ellis Arnall's successful campaign for governor. That same year he became editor of the *Atlanta Constitution*.

Brotherhood in the South

One night I was asked to talk to the men's Bible class of a smalltown church. I tried to speak casually, yet seriously, noting that we Southerners have a reputation for being Bible-oriented, for quoting from it, and for using it in our politics. I said that somehow along the way we had managed to exclude the Negro from our concept of the Fatherhood of God and the brotherhood of man....

Our basic national problem, but more especially ours in the South, was to accept the Negro as one with us in human brotherhood. We need him in the South, and in the nation, as an educated, trained, participating citizen. This did not mean, I insisted, that anyone's privacy would be disturbed. It was only necessary for us to grant the full rights of citizenship and to see the Negro as just another human being....

There was polite applause. Later, when the meeting was concluded, an old man came up to me. "I just want you to know," he said, and there was no heat in his voice, "that I believe in white supremacy. Even the Bible says as much. I hold with our traditions."

I patted him on the shoulder and said, "Well, the Bible is interpreted in many ways."

He was old and troubled and on the defensive. Also, there was a genuine pathos [sorrowful quality] in him. There are many like him, young and old. If they cannot hold on to the concept of their superiority, their small universe will crumble....

There was an impulse to put my arms about his frail shoulders, showing so beneath his worn,

Ralph McGill won a Pulitzer prize in 1959 for a column he wrote about the bombing of the Atlanta Jewish temple and the burning of a black school.

clean, church-supper coat, and to say to him, Everything will be all right. Don't you try to change. You go right on clinging to what gives you strength.

I put out my hand and he took it. I went away thinking about all the cynical and bitter men, in politics and out, of this generation and of those of the past who have had a part in making that old man (and the thousands like him) what he was....

[This excerpt by Ralph McGill was adapted from *The South and the Southerner*, published by Little, Brown and Company, 1959, 1963.]

▶ Locating the Main Ideas

1. Define: desegregate

2. What was the argument used by NAACP lawyers to challenge the dual school systems in Georgia and other states?

3. What was the importance of the U.S. Supreme Court case, *Brown v. Board of Education*?

4. How were the black residents of Montgomery able to make the bus boycott a success?

In the 1950s, McGill called on his fellow southerners to tear down the barriers that prevented blacks from participating fully in community life. He said not to wait for the federal government to step in. His opinions gained national attention. By 1958 he was being called the "conscience of the South." Not all readers, however, liked what Ralph McGill wrote. In some places in Georgia, the *Atlanta Constitution* vanished from newsstands. He was threatened by the Ku Klux Klan and others.

Ralph McGill tried to see all sides of the issues surrounding race relations in the South—and tried to explain what he saw to his readers. He also tried to explain to Americans in other parts of the country what was happening in the South in the 1950s and early 1960s. ◀

Civil Rights Movement Grows

In 1957, Martin Luther King, Jr., helped create a new civil rights organization, the Southern Christian Leadership Conference (SCLC). The headquarters of the SCLC were in Atlanta. King became its first president, and his friend and fellow pastor from Montgomery, Ralph Abernathy, became the treasurer. Andrew Young, who had worked as a minister in Thomasville, Georgia, left a job with the National Council of Churches to direct a voter registration project for the SCLC. Young, like Abernathy, became one of King's top aides. The SCLC developed into one of the dominant civil rights organizations in the country. The organization's strategy to end segregation was based on non-violence. Its work included peaceful marches and protests, boycotts, and sit-ins. Sit-ins are organized protests in which participants sit peaceably in a racially segregated place, such as a restaurant or a movie theater, to integrate it.

Students Join the Movement

Early in 1960, four black students in Greensboro, North Carolina, sat at the Woolworth's lunch counter and asked to be served. When they were refused, they stated that they would remain and keep coming back until they were served. Joined by black and white students from nearby colleges, the sit-in continued for months. Eventually, the lunch counter was integrated.

Following their example, other students started sit-ins throughout the South. In Atlanta, Lonnie C. King (no relation to Dr. King) and Julian Bond became student leaders. They announced their goal was to use legal and non-violent means to obtain their full rights as citizens. Boycotts and sit-ins were organized. Dr. King joined the students at a sit-in to integrate the lunch counter at Rich's department store.

To better organize and plan their activities, students formed the Student Nonviolent Coordinating Committee, SNCC (pronounced snick), in 1960. Headquartered in Atlanta, SNCC worked closely with the SCLC to end segregation.

Increasing Violence

Under the leadership of James Farmer, another civil rights organization, the Congress of Racial Equality (CORE) prepared to challenge segregated southern bus terminals. The Supreme Court had outlawed segregation on interstate buses and trains in 1946, and in terminals in 1960. In reality, however, segregated terminals remained. In 1961, trips on interstate buses, known as "freedom rides," were organized. Black and white members of CORE and SNCC volunteered as freedom riders. On the first trip, the riders were beaten and one bus was burned in Alabama. Angry mobs attacked the riders at some stops, and riders were arrested as they tried to enter segregated terminals. Despite the violence, freedom

Letter from Birmingham Jail

...For years now I have heard the word "wait." It rings in the ear of every Negro with piercing familiarity. This "wait" has always meant "never." We must come to see...that "justice too long delayed is justice denied."

We have waited for more than 340 years for our constitutional and God-given rights...but we still creep at horse-and-buggy pace toward gaining a cup of coffee at a lunch counter. Perhaps it is easy for those who have never felt the stinging darts of segregation to say, "wait." But, when you have seen vicious mobs lynch your mother and father,... when you see the vast majority of your twenty million Negro brothers smothering in an air-tight cage of poverty in the midst of an affluent society; when you suddenly find your tongue twisted and your speech stammering as you seek to explain to your six-year old daughter why she can't go to the public amusement park that has just been advertised on television, and see tears welling up in her eyes when she is told Funtown is closed to colored children;...when you take a cross-country drive and find it necessary to sleep night after night in the uncomfortable corners of your automobile because no motel will accept you; when you are humiliated day in and day out by nagging signs reading "white" and "colored,"...then you will understand why it is difficult to wait.

—April 16, 1963

[This excerpt from a letter by Martin Luther King, Jr., appeared in 1963 in *Why We Can't Wait*, published by Harper & Row Publishers.]

rides continued throughout the summer. In November, new regulations were issued by the Interstate Commerce Commission to put an end to segregated terminals.

In 1963, SCLC leaders targeted the city of Birmingham, Alabama, for their next effort to integrate public facilities. Eugene "Bull" Connor, Birmingham's police commissioner, vowed to stop integration no matter what it took. King, Abernathy, and others were arrested and jailed as they began a protest march. By then, King was getting a lot of criticism, not only from segregationists but also from white moderates, even members of the clergy. He was causing too much turmoil by trying to move too fast, they said. He should be patient. In response, King, while being held in solitary confinement, penned a "Letter from Birmingham Jail," explaining his actions.

After his release, more marches were planned. As promised, Bull Connor tried to stop the marchers. He used police dogs to attack and intimidate them. He ordered that powerful fire hoses, strong enough to knock mortar off bricks, be turned on the marchers to drive them back. Hundreds were arrested, but more and more marchers came. All the while, the rest of the nation watched the violence and brutality on the evening news. Finally, Birmingham business owners agreed to integrate. Angered, white supremacists bombed local black churches, homes, and businesses.

By now, racial unrest was rocking America. Protesters in Maryland, Virginia, Florida, and other states were beaten and jailed. On national television, President Kennedy asked "whether all Americans are to be afforded equal rights and equal opportunities,

Martin Luther King, Jr.

Few who grew up in the Auburn Avenue area of Atlanta during the 1930s could have predicted that Martin Luther King, Jr., would become Georgia's most famous native son. King was born in Atlanta in 1929. His father, Martin Luther King, Sr., was pastor of Ebenezer Baptist Church, and his grandfather, A.D. Williams, founded Ebenezer. The bright "M.L." (as he was called then) finished Morehouse College at age 16, and entered Crozer Theological Seminary in Chester, Pennsylvania. That was when he began to emerge as the brilliant thinker and speaker who would later help found the Southern Christian Leadership Conference, work to end segregation, and win the 1964 Nobel Peace Prize.

Dr. Martin Luther King, Jr., on the steps of his boyhood home in Atlanta in 1967. The house is located only a few blocks from Ebenezer Baptist Church where Dr. King preached.

At Crozer, King was exposed to ideas such as pacifism, social activism, and non-violent civil disobedience. He would continue to refine and practice them his entire life, both at Boston University, where he earned a Ph.D., and in the pulpits of Montgomery's Dexter Avenue Baptist Church and Ebenezer Baptist in Atlanta. Dr. King urged those in the civil rights struggle to put New Testament teachings into practice, to meet violence with passive resistance and prayer as they staged sit-ins, voter registration projects, and marches during the changing 1960s. After the passage of the Civil Rights and Voting Rights acts, King turned his attention to fighting poverty and discrimination in housing and jobs. For him, the issue wasn't white against black; it was justice against injustice.

While holding fast to his belief that all people, of all colors, are created equal and should be treated equally, Dr. King endured threats, beatings, and imprisonment. He was assassinated in 1968 while visiting Memphis, Tennessee, to support a city garbage workers' strike.

As news of the assassination spread, riots broke out in Washington, D.C., and in dozens of other cities. But Atlanta, Dr. King's home, was relatively quiet as the city prepared for his funeral. Thousands of mourners poured into Atlanta from all over the country. Watching television, millions of Americans saw Dr. King's casket borne through the streets on a mule-drawn wagon. They also saw the nation's leaders gather at Ebenezer Baptist Church to pay tribute to King.

The Martin Luther King, Jr., Center for Nonviolent Social Change in Atlanta continues his work today. In 1986, Congress and the president designated the third Monday in January as a national holiday, to honor Dr. King's January 15 birthdate.

I Have a Dream

...I have a dream that one day this nation will rise up and live out the true meaning of its creed, "We hold these truths to be self-evident, that all men are created equal." I have a dream that one day on the red hills of Georgia, sons of former slaves and the sons of former slave owners will be able to sit down together at the table of brotherhood. I have a dream that one day even the state of Mississippi, a desert state sweltering with the heat of injustice, sweltering with the heat of oppression, will be transformed into an oasis of freedom and justice. I have a dream that my four little children will one day live in a nation where they will not be judged by the color of their skin, but by the content of their character....

[From a speech by Martin Luther King, Jr., delivered on August 28, 1963.]

whether we are going to treat our fellow Americans as we want to be treated." He went on to outline his plans for civil rights legislation. That same night in Mississippi, NAACP leader Medgar Evers was shot and killed in his driveway as he returned from a meeting. In the 10 weeks after the Birmingham agreement, 186 American cities experienced racial demonstrations. A total of 14,733 arrests were made, and the number of demonstrations reached 758.

The March on Washington

The time was right. Leaders of the nation's civil rights organizations met in New York to plan the March on Washington. Its purpose would be to demonstrate the tremendous support behind the civil rights movement. Present at the July meeting were Roy Wilkins of the NAACP, Martin Luther King, Jr., of the SCLC, John Lewis with SNCC, James Farmer of CORE, Whitney Young of the National Urban League, and A. Philip Randolph of the Brotherhood of Sleeping Car Porters. It was agreed that Randolph would lead the march.

In August 1963, more than 250,000 citizens blacks, whites, Indians, Hispanics, and others—gathered and marched in Washington, D.C. The highlight of the gathering was a speech by King, from the steps of the Lincoln Memorial. "I have a dream," King said. In a speech that would become a part of history, he described his vision of racial equality. The March on Washington generated support for civil rights. The next year, 101 years after the Emancipation Proclamation had been issued, Congress passed far-reaching civil rights legislation. ◄

The Federal Government Acts

The legislative and executive branches of the national government followed the lead of the federal courts. In 1957, Congress passed a law giving the U.S. Department of Justice new powers to investigate violations of civil rights. That same year, Pres. Dwight Eisenhower used federal troops to enforce court-ordered school desegregation in Little Rock, Arkansas.

In the early 1960s, Pres. John Kennedy used the power of the federal government to enforce desegregation of schools and colleges in Alabama and Mississippi. After President Kennedy's assassination in 1963, Pres. Lyndon Johnson pushed for passage of more laws to protect civil rights. Congress passed the **Civil Rights Act of 1964**. The act prohibited racial discrimination in employment and labor unions and in public facilities, such as swimming pools and play-

▶ **Locating the Main Ideas**

1. What strategy did the Southern Christian Leadership Conference use to end segregation?

2. What was the purpose of the freedom rides?

3. Why was Dr. King criticized after his arrest in Birmingham in 1963?

4. What was the purpose of the March on Washington?

A civil rights protest, 1962. In front of a segregated Atlanta hotel, one man pickets for an end to discrimination while another hands out KKK leaflets.

grounds. The Civil Rights Act allowed the government to withhold federal funds from school systems that refused to desegregate.

One of the first court cases to challenge the Civil Rights Act originated in Atlanta. In *Heart of Atlanta Motel v. United States*, the Court ruled that discrimination by race in privately owned public accommodations, such as motels, was illegal. Hotels, restaurants, theaters, amusement parks, and sports stadiums could no longer turn away black customers or force them to sit in separate sections.

In 1968, the Fair Housing Act outlawed racial discrimination in the buying, selling, renting, and leasing of real estate. This law made it possible for blacks to choose where they wanted to live. Property owners and managers and real estate agents could no longer refuse to allow blacks access to housing.

Voting Rights

By 1960, most blacks in Georgia and other southern states still were disfranchised. Voter registration drives were conducted throughout the South but with only limited success. Some whites fiercely opposed registration of black voters. They wanted to keep blacks from gaining political power even if they committed murder to do it. In June 1964, two white civil rights workers, Andrew Goodman and Michael Schwerner, went to Mississippi to work in a voter registration drive. They both disappeared along with James Chaney, a local CORE member. Their bodies were found two months later. But even murder did not stop people from continuing to work for black voter registration.

The Civil Rights Act of 1964 required state election officials to treat white and black voting applicants the same way. Still there

As a young lawyer, Maynard Jackson won election as vice-mayor of Atlanta in 1969. Four years later, Atlanta voters elected him mayor, making him the first African American to head a major southern city.

Civil rights activist, educator, and state legislator Grace Hamilton was the first African American woman elected to the Georgia General Assembly, in 1965.

were problems. In order to focus attention on obstacles to voter registration in the South, King and Abernathy planned a march in Alabama from Selma to the state capitol in Montgomery. Gov. George Wallace of Alabama objected to the march. He sent mounted state troopers to stop the marchers. Troopers met them at the Edmund Pettus Bridge and used cattle prods and whips to disperse the crowd. The marchers persisted. With the help of federal troops sent in by President Johnson, thousands of people of all occupations, ages, and races continued the march from Selma to Montgomery in support of voting rights for all Americans.

That fall, Congress passed the **Voting Rights Act of 1965**. Under this act, the federal government, rather than state government, had the power to register voters in certain states. It could also send federal examiners into counties where local election officials might be discriminating against blacks. Finally, no new law that affected voting in any way could be passed without the approval of the U.S. Justice Department. This was to make sure that election laws were not unfair to blacks.

Following passage of the Voting Rights Act, hundreds of thousands of black citizens registered to vote in Georgia and six other southern states. As a result, black candidates were elected to public office. In 1965, eight black candidates were elected to the Georgia House of Representatives. Among the eight were Grace Hamilton, the first black woman to hold that office, and 25-year-old Julian Bond, who gained national attention when the House refused to seat him because of his opposition to the draft during the Vietnam War. Andrew Young, after losing his first race, was elected to Congress in 1972, becoming the first black congressman from Georgia in the twentieth century. In 1973, Maynard Jackson became the first black mayor of Atlanta.

Efforts Continue

Nationally, and in Georgia, the civil rights movement was changing. There were growing disagreements among its leaders. Even though the civil rights and voting rights acts had been passed, continuing white resistance to change was discouraging. Many new, young leaders felt resentment and anger. Not all agreed with Dr. King's tactics of non-violence as the way to bring about change. Militant groups were forming that rejected even working with sympathetic whites. Rather, they appealed to black pride and called on fellow blacks to take control of their own destiny. This was the beginning of what was being called the Black Power movement. African dress and natural hairstyles called Afros became popular. Such phrases as "Black Is Beautiful" and "Black Power" came into use.

One of the most radical new leaders was Malcolm X. Born Malcolm Little, he changed his last name when he joined the religious organization known as the Nation of Islam. Popularly known as the Black Muslims, the group had strict rules of no alcohol, drugs, or tobacco. Black culture and family life were emphasized. Malcolm X preached separation and economic independence from whites as a means of power. He criticized the civil rights movement for its slow progress. In 1965, he was assassinated by members of the Nation of Islam—a year after he had broken away from the group.

In 1961, Stokely Carmichael joined the Student Nonviolent Coordinating Committee. Five years later he became its head. After years of practicing non-violent techniques, Carmichael was frustrated with the results. He urged black militants to act now. The next head of SNCC, H. Rap Brown, was even more radical. He and other militant African American leaders told blacks it was time to take over America. On the West Coast, the Black Panther Party preached against whites and frequently clashed with police. They urged their followers to use force and strike back when they met with resistance.

By the mid-1960s, many urban blacks rejected peaceful solutions to their problems. In the large cities of the North and West, black residents began striking out against police brutality, high unemployment, residential segregation, poor schools, and other problems. They were no longer willing to accept peaceful solutions to the problems. Moreover, people of both races were frustrated over what to do next.

In a climate of hopelessness and anger, massive rioting broke out in the black neighborhoods of some large cities. The worst was in 1965, in an area of Los Angeles known as Watts. Detroit, New York, Chicago, and other cities faced similar outbursts. Most of the people killed in the riots were black. Estimates of property destruction were in millions of dollars. After the assassination of Martin Luther King, Jr., in 1968, yet another round of rioting spread across the nation. It was evident that racial problems were not exclusive to the South.

W. W. Law has been a leader in Savannah's civil rights movement since the 1940s. In more recent years, he became involved in saving the last surviving black neighborhood in Savannah's downtown historic district.

After serving in the U.S. Congress and as U.S. Ambassador to the United Nations, Andrew Young became mayor of Atlanta in 1982. Known internationally, Young helped Atlanta win the bid for the 1996 Summer Olympics.

The Focus Changes

At the same time, something else was happening. By the late 1960s, public attention began shifting away from civil rights to America's involvement in the Vietnam War. Antiwar protest marches and free speech demonstrations made the nightly news. Much of the criticism was directed against President Johnson, who had increased U.S. involvement in Vietnam. To many Americans, ending the war was more urgent than ending discrimination.

President Johnson was a powerful advocate of the civil rights movement. Before leaving office, he could claim major civil rights accomplishments—in particular, the Civil Rights Act (1964), the Voting Rights Act (1965), and the Fair Housing Act (1968). In addition, Johnson appointed Thurgood Marshall to the U.S. Supreme Court, making him the first black justice to serve on the Court.

Civil rights victories brought hope for better lives to many black Americans. The civil rights movement began to expand as other groups identified with it. New gains were made for blacks as well as newly identified minority groups of Hispanics, Native Americans, women, and the handicapped. All were seeking fair treatment under the law. The Equal Employment Opportunity Act passed by Congress in 1972 helped eliminate employment discrimination for minorities. Georgia state and local governments began taking steps to end minority discrimination in employment. Efforts were made to hire minorities for positions in police, fire, and other departments of government.

As a result of the civil rights movement, blacks and other minority groups gained opportunities and rights they had been earlier denied. For the most part, *de jure* (legal) discrimination has ended. Moreover, the idea of equal treatment for all citizens has become an accepted belief for the great majority of Americans. In this sense, the movement has achieved many of its original goals.

After the early '70s, the movement shifted to attack *de facto* (actual) discrimination as well as the legacy of past discrimination. Affirmative action—government policy intended to increase minority opportunities—became a new focus. Another objective was the reapportioning of legislative districts to increase the number of black elected officials. Many of those who marched with Martin Luther King, Jr., at Selma or Washington—such men and women as Ralph Abernathy, Coretta Scott King, Andrew Young, Joseph Lowery, John Lewis, and Jesse Jackson—would continue the work of the civil rights movement. ◄

▶ **Locating the Main Ideas**

1. Define: Civil Rights Act of 1964, Voting Rights Act of 1965

2. What resulted from the Voting Rights Act of 1965?

3. Why did the Black Power movement begin?

4. What were some of the reasons for the urban riots in the mid 1960s?

CHAPTER ACTIVITIES

Reviewing the Main Ideas

1. How did the practice of racial discrimination in America during the Cold War make U.S. actions abroad seem a contradiction?

2. What was the flaw in the doctrine of separate but equal?

3. What method did the NAACP use to end discriminatory laws?

4. What efforts were made by politicians before the *Brown* decision to improve the schools for blacks?

5. How did political officials practice massive resistance to desegregation?

6. Why was Ralph McGill called the "conscience of the South"?

7. Describe Dr. King's technique of using non-violence as a means of accomplishing change.

8. According to Dr. King's "I have a dream" speech, what was his dream for the future of his children?

9. Give an example of an action taken by the legislative branch of the federal government, and one taken by the executive branch, that furthered the progress of the civil rights movement.

10. What other groups benefited from the expansion of the civil rights movement?

Give It Some Extra Thought

1. **Interpreting the Meaning.** What did the phrases "dual society" and "dual school systems" mean in American society before the 1950s?

2. **Evaluating.** What was the significance of the Montgomery bus boycott to the civil rights movement?

Sharpen Your Skills

1. **Role Play.** Divide the class into two groups and use information from Rosa Strickland's description of her school to present evidence to support or oppose the segregated school system that existed at the time. One group should speak from Rosa Strickland's point of view and the other from the point of view of the school superintendent.

2. **Analyze a Primary Source.** Restate, in your own words, three reasons Dr. King gave in his "Letter from Birmingham Jail" why it was difficult for black Americans to wait for changes to take place.

Until 1947, professional baseball, like other aspects of American life, was segregated, with black and white ballplayers in separate leagues. On April 15, 1947, Georgia-born Jackie Robinson, wearing a Brooklyn Dodgers uniform, took his position at first base—breaking baseball's so-called color barrier forever. His courage in the face of intense racism, as much as his athletic ability, distinguished him throughout his baseball career and life. Why were people like Jackie Robinson important to black Americans? to white Americans?

Going Further

1. **Time Line.** Develop a time line of significant events in the civil rights movement. Use information from earlier chapters in this book as well as information from other sources.

2. **Field Trip.** Plan a class field trip to Atlanta to visit the Martin Luther King, Jr., National Historic Site that includes his childhood home, Ebenezer Baptist Church, The King Center, and the National Park Service Visitor Center.

21

Georgia's New Place in the Sun

By the end of the 1960s, much of the nation's attention turned to a far-off country called Vietnam. American troops were fighting and dying there, in what had already become this nation's longest war.

On the nation's college campuses, students (and some professors) held sit-ins, marches, and other types of demonstrations, sometimes openly defying police and campus authorities. For the most part, they protested against the war and the draft (compulsory military service). They also showed support for such causes as student rights, free speech, and social justice. The late sixties also marked the first time illegal drug use became widespread in America. At Georgia's colleges and universities, students took part in a variety of protests and demonstrations. Most were peaceful, although that was not always true in other states.

A variety of factors accounted for the social change and political unrest in this country. Foremost was the long and deadly war in Vietnam, a conflict which increasingly divided Americans.

The Vietnam War

Since the 1800s, France had controlled an area of Southeast Asia known as Indochina. After World War II, revolutionary forces led by communists began fighting for the independence of a region known as Vietnam. By 1954, France had lost the fight to hold on to its former colony. That year an international conference of major world powers met and divided Vietnam into two parts. North Vietnam would be led by a communist government with ties to Communist China and the Soviet Union. South Vietnam's new government would be allied with the West.

President Jimmy Carter and Rosalynn Carter. A few minutes after being sworn in, the president and Mrs. Carter broke with tradition and walked the mile from the inaugural stand at the Capitol to the White House.

Elections to reunify Vietnam were scheduled, but South Vietnam officials cancelled them when they feared the communists would win. Thereafter, South Vietnamese communists—known as Vietcong—began a **guerrilla war** with support from North Vietnam. In this type of war, small groups of armed revolutionaries conduct surprise attacks on government forces, then quickly retreat into the jungle or countryside.

In 1961, President Kennedy sent units of American soldiers to train South Vietnamese forces to fight the Vietcong. By 1964, however, South Vietnam's army was losing control of the countryside. President Johnson's military experts warned that without U.S. help, South Vietnam would fall to the communists.

As yet, American soldiers had not been directly involved in the fighting in Vietnam. The president now had a critical decision to make.

Among those whom Johnson consulted were two influential Georgians in the national government. One was Secretary of State Dean Rusk, who had also served in that post under President Kennedy. Rusk joined some of Johnson's other advisors in recommending greater U.S. involvement. In particular, Rusk argued that under a 1954 treaty, America had a legal duty to defend South Vietnam from **aggression** (attack by another country).

The other Georgian consulted was Sen. Richard Russell, chairman of the Senate Armed Services Committee. Russell, one of the most powerful men in Congress, opposed U.S. military involvement and advised caution.

Sen. Richard Russell displays a model of the Lockheed C-5A Galaxy, produced in Marietta.

(Right) Georgia's Dean Rusk served as U.S. Secretary of State under Presidents Kennedy and Johnson.

In August of 1964, the U.S. Navy reported that two of its ships had been fired on by North Vietnamese torpedo boats in the Gulf of Tonkin. Johnson asked Congress for new authority to deal with the crisis. Though still troubled, Senator Russell believed our national honor was at stake and that we had a responsibility to protect American men and women serving in South Vietnam.

Under the U.S. Constitution, only Congress can declare war. However, the Constitution also makes the president commander-in-chief of the nation's armed forces. So in that role, Johnson sought congressional approval to protect American troops in South Vietnam.

In Congress, Russell worked for approval of what came to be called the **Gulf of Tonkin Resolution**. Under it, the president was given authority to resist aggression by North Vietnam "by any means necessary, including the use of arms." From this point on, Russell no longer publicly questioned the U.S. presence. As he explained, "The flag is there. U.S. honor and prestige are there. And most important of all, U.S. soldiers are there."

In early 1965, the Vietcong attacked a camp of American military advisors. President Johnson then ordered the bombing of North Vietnam, which was supplying the guerrillas with arms and supplies. When Vietcong forces struck an American air base, Johnson ordered U.S. ground forces to be sent in.

North Vietnam responded by sending regular army units into the south. Soon, U.S. and North Vietnamese units were battling each other. By 1967, almost half a million American troops were involved.

As Democrats in Congress began to question whether the war should continue, Georgia's delegation stood with President Johnson. The state was tied to the war effort in other ways, due in part to Senator Russell's long service on the Senate Armed Forces Committee.

As in previous wars, thousands of U.S. soldiers received their training in Georgia. About 100,000 military personnel and 33,000 civilians were employed at the state's 15 military bases. Thus, many Georgians were directly or indirectly connected with the war. Georgia also was among the top 10 states receiving U.S. defense contracts during the war. One of the most important contracts was for Lockheed's C-5A Galaxy —the world's largest aircraft.

By 1968, as the war continued to expand, Americans were deeply divided over President Johnson's policies in Vietnam. Hundreds of U.S. soldiers were dying each week, with no end to the war in sight. That spring, President Johnson announced that he would not run for re-election.

Richard Nixon, Johnson's successor, adopted a policy of slowly pulling U.S. troops out and letting South Vietnamese forces do more of the fighting.

Still, the war lingered on. Finally, in January 1973, a ceasefire was signed. By April, all U.S. troops were out of South Vietnam. It was now only a matter of time before that country's government and army would shut down. Many South Vietnamese began fleeing their country. By 1975, there was only one Vietnam, and it was under a communist government.

It had been a long, painful war for all sides. During the nine-year war, some 56,000 American soldiers—1,700 from Georgia—had died and more than 300,000 had been wounded. The loss of soldiers and civilians in the two Vietnams was even greater. The cost of the war to America's economy was staggering and would be felt for decades. Socially and politically, this nation had been torn apart. But, in time, the wounds began to heal. ▶

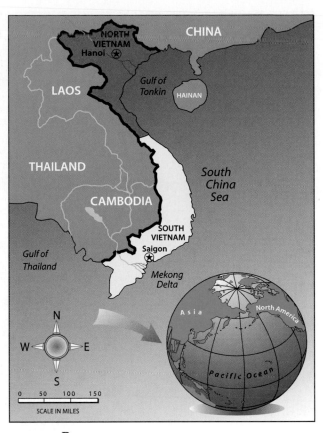

Georgia's Image in Transition

Although great changes had taken place, Georgia entered the 1970s still suffering a problem with its national image. Some Americans who had never been to Georgia had a mental picture of the state based on what they had read in novels or seen in movies. Often, this meant a land of cotton fields, dirt roads, chain gangs, and Klan meetings. Southerners of both races were frequently portrayed as poor, backward, and illiterate. Because of such views, national businesses sometimes had difficulty getting their workers to transfer to new jobs in Georgia.

In fairness, Georgia did have many problems. On such measures as income and education, Georgians historically have trailed the national average. Even today, rural and inner-city poverty remains

▶ **Locating the Main Ideas**

1. Define: guerrilla war, aggression, Gulf of Tonkin Resolution

2. What was the main reason for demonstrations by Americans in the 1960s?

3. At what point did Richard Russell change his position on the involvement of American military in Vietnam?

Georgia's New Place in the Sun / 323

Julian Bond in 1966, the year after his election to the Georgia House of Representatives.

a real problem facing the state. It is also true that efforts to achieve racial equality had long been resisted throughout the South. Forms of racial discrimination still remained, although other parts of the country could not be considered free of discrimination either.

Additionally, there was the sensitive matter of Georgia's flag. In 1956, the General Assembly had approved a new state flag—one that included the Confederate battle flag. At the time, some Georgians were beginning to make plans for the Civil War centennial, and supporters of the new flag said that it better marked Georgia's southern heritage. The change, however, also came on the heels of the *Brown v. Board of Education* desegration case. Thus, some people saw a different message behind the new flag—one of protest against the federal government and desegregation.

Yet, much of Georgia's national image was out-of-date, inaccurate, or exaggerated. By 1970, most Georgians lived in urban areas, with incomes moving toward the national average. The state's economy was principally based on manufacturing and services, not farming. For those who did farm, cotton was no longer a major crop. Georgia's highway system was now one of the best in the South. Extensive prison reforms had taken place, and chain gangs were a thing of the past. Except for an occasional speech or small demonstration, the Klan had all but disappeared.

Georgia's struggle to be recognized as a modern and progressive southern state was set back by several highly publicized events. In 1965, black civil rights activist Julian Bond had been elected to the Georgia General Assembly. Bond opposed the Vietnam War and was particularly critical of the draft. Because of his views, the House refused to seat him for two years. He finally got his seat after the U.S. Supreme Court ruled that lawmakers had deprived him of his constitutional rights to freedom of speech.

While Bond was fighting for his seat, another Georgian was making national news. Atlanta restaurant owner Lester Maddox openly defied the Civil Rights Act of 1964. That law prohibited restaurants and other public accommodations from discriminating because of race. Maddox, however, refused to serve blacks. Rather than comply with the law, he sold his restaurant. In 1966, he entered the race for governor.

Lester Maddox Supports Segregation

In 1967, Lester Maddox, an outspoken segregationist, became Georgia's governor. He strongly opposed forced integration and even encouraged parents to put their children in private academies rather than send them to integrated schools. As governor, he fought federal efforts to enforce federal civil rights and voting rights laws. Yet, Maddox denied being a racist. Rather, he claimed his views were based on his belief in states' rights, free enterprise, the Bible, and fighting communism. Though believing in segregation, he appointed blacks to some boards and commissions in state government. He also supported many programs that helped Georgians of all colors, especially the poor.

Despite many accomplishments during his four years as governor, Maddox is remembered most for his segregationist stand and criticism of the federal government. Frequently, to state and national audiences, he charged that the civil rights movement was made up of liberals, socialists, and—worst of all—communists. Maddox made similar attacks against the president and other officials in the federal government. To many Americans, the fact that this message was coming from the governor of Georgia suggested that a deep racism lingered in the state. ▶

Jimmy Carter's Term as Governor

Among the candidates in the 1966 race for governor was a peanut farmer from the rural community of Plains. His name was Jimmy Carter. When he lost, the former naval officer and state senator decided that the next election would be different. For four years, Carter and his wife, Rosalynn, traveled throughout the state to talk with voters about what was on their minds.

Based on what he heard, and his own beliefs, Carter's 1970 campaign platform called for racial equality. He said that Georgians should no longer resist integration or fight the federal government. Also, he promised to modernize state government, operate it more economically, and better serve the people of the state.

At the time, Georgia's constitution said that governors could not serve consecutive terms, so Governor Maddox ran instead for the office of lieutenant governor, and won. In the Democratic primary **runoff** (an election between the top two candidates when no one has received a majority of votes), Jimmy Carter defeated former governor Carl Sanders. In November, Carter went on to beat Republican candidate Hal Suit, an Atlanta television news personality.

In January 1971, Governor Carter announced to a joint session of the General Assembly, "I say to you quite frankly that the time for racial discrimination is over." This was not just a message to legislators. Aware of the state's sagging image, Carter promised that at the end of his four-year term, "We shall be able to stand up anywhere in the world—in New York, California, or Florida and say 'I'm a Georgian'—and be proud of it."

When Carter took office, he found 250 departments, boards, commissions, and other agencies. Many had similar functions, with no one having overall responsibility. For example, 36 different agen-

▶ **Locating the Main Ideas**

1. How did the image of the state affect the willingness of some Americans to move to Georgia?

2. Even though Gov. Lester Maddox was a segregationist, he did some things to help black Georgians. What were they?

Jimmy Carter's first priority as governor was to reorganize and modernize Georgia's state government.

cies were involved in natural resources. Citizens didn't know which agency to go to for help.

As governor, Carter moved to reorganize the executive branch of Georgia's state government. He believed that reorganization would save money while improving services for citizens.

Governor Carter also pushed for a constitutional amendment to allow state government to borrow money. As a result of Reconstruction abuses, state debt had been prohibited since 1877. However, state agencies sometimes had difficulty paying for expensive buildings and highways in a single year's budget. To get around the constitution, the General Assembly began creating public corporations—called *authorities*—to do the borrowing. But this was proving costly and inefficient. It also resulted in an ever-growing list of authorities. In 1972, Georgia voters approved a constitutional amendment to allow the state to borrow money.

Carter's term contributed to an improved image of Georgia in the nation. His reorganization was being called one of the most ambitious of any state in recent history.

Sun Belt Growth

Several other events were occurring at the same time that would change Georgia's image. In October 1973, citizens of Atlanta elected Maynard Jackson as the first black mayor of a major southern city. That same month, an Arab **embargo** (ban) on exporting oil to the United States started a series of events that would bring more people and businesses to Georgia.

The oil embargo was a reaction to U.S. support of Israel during that country's conflict with Arab nations in the Middle East. America was heavily dependent on foreign oil, and the embargo caused oil prices to shoot up almost overnight. The price of a gallon of gas quickly rose from 35 cents to 50 cents, then to a dollar and higher. Where would it stop? Gas was not only expensive—it was in short supply. Customers faced long lines at service stations, as well as limits on how much gas they could buy.

In many ways, directly or indirectly, America runs on oil, and rising oil prices caused severe damage to the national economy. The price of almost everything was affected, which led to high rates of inflation—a period of rapidly rising prices and interest rates. Inflation had a double impact on American manufacturing firms trying to compete with cheaper imports from foreign mills and factories. Although the entire nation was affected, older businesses and industries in the Northeast and Midwest suffered the most. Many closed or had to lay off workers.

For years, mild winters in the South—especially in Florida—had attracted northerners who could afford to move there upon retirement. The jump in heating oil prices and the economic downturn after 1974, however, helped convince many families in the North not to wait until retirement. This was especially true since the economy in southern states was not as severely affected as in the Northeast and Midwest.

During the 1970s, Americans in large numbers packed their belongings and headed southward and westward into an area nicknamed the **Sun Belt**. They came in search of jobs, warmer climates, and cheaper costs of living. Over the decade, states such as New York, Pennsylvania, and Michigan actually lost population, while states such as Georgia, Florida, Texas, Arizona, and California grew at healthy rates. ▶

▶ **Locating the Main Ideas**

1. Define: runoff, embargo, inflation, Sun Belt
2. What one point in Jimmy Carter's 1970 campaign platform best showed that he had different views from Lester Maddox?
3. What were two purposes of Governor Carter's reorganization of the executive branch of state government?
4. Why was the Sun Belt a popular place to move to in the 1970s?

George Busbee Takes a Business Approach

The leading contender to replace Carter as governor was George Busbee, an Albany lawyer who had served 18 years in the Georgia House of Representatives. He was convinced that he could govern the state with no new taxes. His businesslike manner appealed to Georgia voters, who elected him in 1974.

Busbee singled out education as his first priority. In particular, he pushed for teacher pay raises and state-funded kindergarten in public school.

Also, Governor Busbee was a great supporter of a new constitution for Georgia. When he took office, Georgia had one of the longest and most confusing state constitutions in the nation. To change this, the long Constitution of 1945 was reorganized and presented to voters in 1976.

Also on the ballot in 1976 was a constitutional amendment to allow a governor to have two successive terms in office. Both the amendment and the revised constitution were approved. Two years later, Busbee ran for re-election—again pledging not to raise taxes—and won easily.

During Busbee's second term, a commission of experts and citizens was appointed to write a new, modern state constitution for Georgia. The study lasted over five years, but finally a draft document was ready. In November 1982, Georgia voters approved the rewritten and shortened constitution. Because it became effective the following July 1, it is known as the Constitution of 1983.

Gov. George Busbee welcomes a trade delegation from Japan.

In addition to pushing for a constitutional change, Busbee promoted Georgia as a progressive state for business and industry. State officials encouraged American business and industry to come south to Georgia. The governor also was successful in convincing companies already operating in the state to expand. He traveled extensively abroad trying to encourage foreign investment in Georgia. Finding foreign markets for Georgia-made products was another goal of his administration.

Joe Frank Harris Leads the State

The next governor, Joe Frank Harris, campaigned on a pledge of no new taxes during his term of office. Harris, a businessman from Cartersville, had served in the House 18 years and was chairman of the House Appropriations Committee before his election. He was probably the most knowledgeable of all governors in budgetary matters. He took office in 1983, a time when prices for everything were going up. Teachers and state employees needed raises, and new highways and prisons had to be built. Could Georgia survive four more years without a tax increase?

Harris's promise of no new taxes did not mean that each person's taxes would remain the same. It meant that no new *types* of taxes would be passed, and that existing tax *rates* would not increase. Harris believed Georgia's healthy economy would produce new jobs, which would attract new residents to the state. New residents meant more income and sales tax revenue for the state.

Governor Harris signed the Quality Basic Education Act in public ceremonies at the capitol in 1985.

By the mid 1980s, however, the nation's economy had slowed. In his successful re-election campaign in 1986, Harris was no longer willing to pledge no new taxes. During his second term, Georgia's economy began to stumble. Unemployment rose, as more and more manufacturing jobs were lost to overseas competition. In 1989, with Georgia facing a federal lawsuit over prison overcrowding, the governor and legislature agreed to raise the state sales tax from 3 cents to 4 cents on the dollar.

During his eight years in office, Governor Harris, like Busbee, stressed economic development. He worked to bring more industry and investment into the state, helping to account for 850,000 new jobs in Georgia.

Through Harris's efforts, the General Assembly passed a massive educational reform bill in 1985.

Known as the Quality Basic Education Act, or QBE, the bill created statewide standards—including a core curriculum that applied to every school system.

Like governors Carter and Busbee before him, Harris represented a quiet, efficient, businesslike style of leadership. None were fiery speakers in the style of Eugene Talmadge. On the other hand, they could effectively use the formal and informal powers of their office when needed. They contributed to Georgia's image as a modern, progressive state. ▶

Georgians in National Politics

For many years, such Georgians as Carl Vinson, Walter George, Richard Russell, and Herman Talmadge had a good deal of influence in the national government. This was particularly true in the area of military affairs. In 1965, Vinson retired from the House of Representatives after serving 50 years—at the time, the longest term of service in the history of Congress. In 1971, Russell died while in his 38th year as U.S. senator.

After Senator Russell died, Governor Carter named David Gambrell to serve as senator until the next election. In the 1972 election, a young Georgia state representative named Sam Nunn won a surprise victory. Nunn, the great-nephew of Carl Vinson, went on to become chairman of the Senate Armed Services Committee. In this role, he gained a national reputation as an expert on military matters.

Georgia's senior senator at the time was Herman Talmadge, who was first elected in 1956. The former governor was chairman of the Senate Agriculture and Forestry Committee. As an expert on agri-

▶ **Locating the Main Ideas**

1. What were some criticisms of Georgia's state constitution when George Busbee became governor?

2. How was the governor's term of office changed by constitutional amendment during Busbee's term?

3. What jobs and past positions made Gov. Joe Frank Harris especially knowledgeable about budgetary matters?

4. What led to the increase in the state sales tax in 1989?

Sam Nunn, after his election to the U.S. Senate, frequently sought the advice of his well-known great uncle, Carl Vinson, on military matters.

cultural and tax affairs, Talmadge became Georgia's most important voice in Washington, D.C., after the Russell years. He became widely known for his contribution to the Senate investigation of the Watergate controversy in 1973. But improper handling of his own financial affairs led the Senate to denounce his personal conduct. The highly publicized action hurt Talmadge in Georgia, and the veteran senator lost the 1980 election to Mack Mattingly.

A Georgian in the White House

By the mid 1970s, no Georgian had ever served as president of the United States. This was about to change. Shortly after leaving the governor's office, Jimmy Carter began to think seriously about the presidency.

At that time, many Americans had lost confidence in national politics. In 1974, because of a scandal known as Watergate, Pres. Richard Nixon had been forced to resign from office, something no president had ever done before. Some of his closest aides even went to prison over Watergate.

When Jimmy Carter began his campaign, most Americans had no idea who he was. Few people recognized the name. But he and a group of supporters known as the "Peanut Brigade" crisscrossed the nation in 1975 and 1976, stressing the need for honesty and for restoring confidence in government. In one campaign speech, he told voters:

> I intend to win. Being elected president is very important to me. But it is not the most important thing in my life. I don't have to be president. There are a lot of things that I would not do to be elected. I would never tell a lie. I would never make a misleading statement. I would never betray your trust in me....

What Carter had to say appealed to a majority of the nation's voters. In 1976, he became the first candidate from the Deep South to be elected president of the United States. Suddenly, there was a new fascination in America with peanuts, grits, and other southern foods and customs. After the election, reporters from national TV networks, news magazines, and newspapers flocked to Georgia to find out more about the new president's home state. For the most part, the message they reported showed a modern and progressive state. More than any single event, Carter's election changed the national image of Georgia.

Jimmy Carter's presidency faced difficult domestic and foreign problems. At home, the oil embargo had made the nation realize it faced an energy crisis. Inflation caused by rising oil prices resulted in higher prices for almost everything. Interest rates went up, too, making it more difficult for Americans to buy homes. The president and Congress tried to solve these problems, but they couldn't.

President Carter's foreign policy stressed peace and human rights. He won praise for working out a peace agreement between Israel and Egypt. But in November 1979, 52 Americans were taken hostage at the U.S. Embassy in Iran. The next month, the Soviet Union invaded Afghanistan. Carter tried to free the hostages and get the Soviet Union to withdraw from Afghanistan, but without success.

In 1980, President Carter ran for re-election, but the nation was ready for a change. In the November election, Republican Ronald Reagan polled 51 percent of the popular vote, compared to 41 percent for Carter. However, in terms of electoral votes, Reagan won overwhelmingly with 91 percent of the votes. Of southern states, only Georgia, Maryland, and West Virginia voted for Carter.

On January 20, 1981, President Carter's work to release the American hostages in Iran finally was rewarded. As the 52 freed hostages flew home to the United States, Jimmy Carter flew home to Plains. Since then, he has devoted his time to a variety of causes on behalf of peace, human rights, health, and improved living conditions for the world's poor.

Since leaving the White House, the former president has continued to be active, nationally and internationally. Working side by side with other Habitat for Humanity volunteers, he has helped build houses for low-income Americans in communities across America. He is involved in the programs of the Carter Presidential Center, established in Atlanta in 1982, and occasionally teaches at Emory University. In addition, Jimmy Carter frequently travels abroad, meeting with political leaders, and remains a champion of human rights and peaceful resolution of conflicts. ▶

Georgia's Exploding Growth Rate

With release of the 1980 census, Georgia boosters had reason to celebrate. During the 1970s, Georgia's population had grown by 19.1 percent—the highest since 1900 and almost twice the national average. Measured in another way, in 1980 Georgia had 876,000 more citizens than it did in 1970. Just over half of this gain came from residents of other states moving to Georgia. Only California, Texas, Florida, and Arizona had larger increases.

Also significant was the fact that for the first time in almost a century, the percentage of blacks in Georgia rose instead of falling. Helping account for this were job opportunities and an improving civil rights picture.

The high growth rate in the 1970s continued into the 1980s. The 1990 census revealed a 10-year growth rate of 18.6 percent, again almost twice the national average. Census figures showed a continuing migration of residents into Georgia. By the 1980s, more than one in three Georgians had been born in another state.

Yet, this impressive population growth was not spread across the entire state. It was concentrated mostly in regions known as Metropolitan Statistical Areas (MSAs).

▶ **Locating the Main Ideas**

1. What national event had occurred that made Jimmy Carter's campaign pledge of honesty in government appealing to the voters?

2. How did Carter's election as president help change Georgia's national image?

3. What were some of the problems President Carter faced during his term in office?

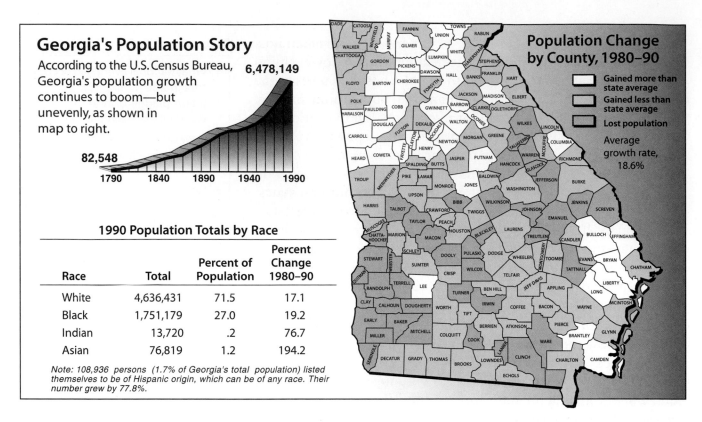

Georgia's Population Story

According to the U.S. Census Bureau, Georgia's population growth continues to boom—but unevenly, as shown in map to right.

6,478,149

82,548

1790   1840   1890   1940   1990

1990 Population Totals by Race

Race	Total	Percent of Population	Percent Change 1980-90
White	4,636,431	71.5	17.1
Black	1,751,179	27.0	19.2
Indian	13,720	.2	76.7
Asian	76,819	1.2	194.2

Note: 108,936 persons (1.7% of Georgia's total population) listed themselves to be of Hispanic origin, which can be of any race. Their number grew by 77.8%.

Population Change by County, 1980-90

- Gained more than state average
- Gained less than state average
- Lost population

Average growth rate, 18.6%

In the 1980s, 8 out of every 10 new Georgia residents moved to a metropolitan region. Most settled in the Atlanta MSA, which was home to almost half of all Georgians. In contrast, during the same period, a total of 43 counties—more than one in four—*lost* population. Most of these were rural counties south of the Fall Line.

A Booming Decade

Georgia's 19 percent population growth in the 1970s and 1980s dramatically changed the state and its image. Would this fast pace continue into the 1990s? Although the official answer won't come until results of the 2000 census are reported in 2001, yearly U.S. Census Bureau estimates suggest that the growth rate of the 1990s will be even higher than in the two previous decades.

Georgia today ranks as one of the fastest growing states in the nation. Here is how Georgia stacks up on three measures of population growth.

- *Rate* (expressed in terms of percent). Georgia is the third fastest growing state in the nation, the fastest growing state in the South, and the fastest growing state east of the Mississippi. In the decade of the 1990s, Georgia grew by over 2 percent a year —twice the national average.

- *Number of residents*. With a net increase of over 150,000 residents each year, Georgia is the fifth fastest growing state in the country.

- *Population size*. In the mid 1990s, Georgia became the ninth most populous state in the nation.

What accounts for this growth? Some of it occurs because more Georgians are born than die each year. But the majority of Georgia's growth is a result of people from other states and countries moving to Georgia. Many factors account for this in-migration. Job opportunities, cost of living, quality of life, location, physiographic diversity, and mild climate are key reasons. One consequence of this growth is that almost 40 percent of today's Georgia residents were born in another state or country.

In the 1990s, Georgia's population grew more rapidly than in any other decade of the twentieth century—but the growth was uneven. Although every racial group grew in number, Georgia's composition changed. Continuing a trend since the 1960s, the percentage of Georgians who are white is falling slowly. At the same time, the numbers of both African Americans and Asians are increasing as a percentage of the state's population. The fastest growing segment in Georgia is the Hispanic population, whose number may double during the 1990s.

Another way population increase has been uneven is in the way it is spread across the state. It would be one thing if growth occurred uniformly throughout the state—every county would gain new residents. But that's not what happens. In the 1990s, eight out of every ten new residents moved to one of Georgia's eight metropolitan areas. Even then, growth was uneven—at least six of those eight new residents moved to the Atlanta metropolitan area. By the end of the twentieth century, almost 60 percent of all Georgians will live within a 60-mile radius of downtown Atlanta. Outside the Atlanta area, growth has been much slower. With all the growth, the number of counties losing population dropped in the 1990s. However, some Georgia counties do not have as many residents as they did a century ago. ▶

Growth Brings Change

In the 1970s, some people began talking about there being *two* Georgias—Atlanta and the rest of the state. By the 1980s and 1990s, however, some people observed that there might be four different Georgias: large central cities with little growth, growing suburban areas, growing rural areas, and declining rural areas.

What that means is that Georgia has become a land of contrasts. Over half the state's population lives within 60 miles of Atlanta. In the city once burned by Sherman, you can find skyscrapers, professional sports, rapid rail transit, and one of the nation's busiest airports. You can see shopping malls, crowded interstates, and other indicators of a large, modern city. Yet only an hour away are communities that don't have a single fast-food franchise, shopping mall, or office complex, and where the tallest structure in town is often a church steeple. As you travel even farther away from Atlanta, par-

▶ **Locating the Main Ideas**

1. In which metropolitan region do most people moving to Georgia choose to live?

2. Within the United States in the 1990s, how does Georgia rank in rate of growth? in net increase? in population size?

3. What reason accounts for the majority of Georgia's growth?

Atlanta's skyline is constantly changing as new skyscrapers are built.

ticularly in areas of eastern and southwestern Georgia, you find areas with few jobs or opportunities to attract or keep residents. Populations in these areas are small, and the people tend to be older and poorer—quite a contrast to the image of one of the fastest growing states in the nation.

Changing Political Alignment

Traditionally, Georgia has been a one-party state. The reality was that almost anyone serious about running for political office in Georgia ran as a Democrat. This began to change in the 1964 presidential election, when a majority of Georgia voters supported Barry Goldwater—a conservative Republican—over Pres. Lyndon Johnson—a liberal Democrat. Across the South, some Democrats even changed their party affiliation. More common, however, was voting Republican in the presidential election every four years—while voting Democrat in state and local races. The real growth of the Republican Party in state and local politics, however, did not occur until the 1980s and 1990s. As late as 1977, out of 236 total members of the Georgia General Assembly only 31 were Republican. By 1997, this number had more than tripled to 101.

Excluding Reconstruction, Georgia's congressional delegation historically had been all-Democrat and, with a few exceptions, all-white and all-male. Change came in 1966, when voters in Atlanta's fifth congressional district elected Fletcher Thompson—Georgia's first Republican congressman since Reconstruction. Andrew Young, a black Democrat, won the seat in the 1972 election, once again giving Georgia an all-Democrat congressional delegation.

In 1977, Young resigned from Congress to become America's ambassador to the United Nations, and Democrat Wyche Fowler won the fifth congressional district seat. The next year, Republican Newt Gingrich won election to the House of Representatives. Two years later, Mack Mattingly defeated Herman Talmadge to become Georgia's first Republican in the U.S. Senate. After one term, in 1986 Mattingly was defeated in his bid for re-election by Congressman Fowler. That same year, Atlanta city councilman John Lewis won the fifth congressional district seat.

In 1992, Senator Fowler lost to Republican challenger Paul Coverdell, former head of the U.S. Peace Corps. But it was in the 1992 elections for the U.S. House of Representatives that Georgia Republicans won the most dramatic victories. Newt Gingrich won re-election in the sixth district, while fellow Republicans were elected in the first, third, fourth, seventh, eighth, and tenth districts. Black Democrats won the second and fifth districts, and in the new eleventh district Cynthia McKinney became the first African American woman elected to Congress from Georgia. In the ninth district, Congressman Nathan Deal, a Democrat, won re-election. Three years later, he switched parties. This meant that in 1995, of Georgia's 13-member congressional delegation, only one—Sen. Sam Nunn —was white, male, and a Democrat. In 1996, former Georgia Secretary of State Max Cleland, a white Democrat, won that Senate seat.

Republican congressman Newt Gingrich became Speaker of the U.S. House in 1995—the first Georgian to hold the post in more than 140 years.

Thus, in only a few decades, Georgia went from being a one-party state to being a two-party state. By 1995, Republicans held a majority of Georgia's seats in Congress—and a majority in both houses of Congress. That year members of the U.S. House of Representatives elected a Georgian, Newt Gingrich, as speaker, and they re-elected him two years later.

Zell Miller—A Governor Makes Changes

In 1990 and again in 1994, Georgia voters elected Zell Miller as governor. In his campaign, he promised many changes and reforms— but most important was a state lottery for education. Miller came to office with a wide variety of experiences—including service as a Marine, history professor, state legislator, state board member, and lieutenant governor. Miller believed that Georgia voters had elected him to make some fundamental changes in state government. Therefore, he was determined to use all of the formal and informal powers of his office to achieve his campaign promises.

Soon after his election, Miller pushed through legislation that, with the voters' approval, created a state lottery. What made Georgia's lottery different from any other in the nation was the requirement that all proceeds, except prizes and administrative costs, had to be used for new educational programs, not previously existing

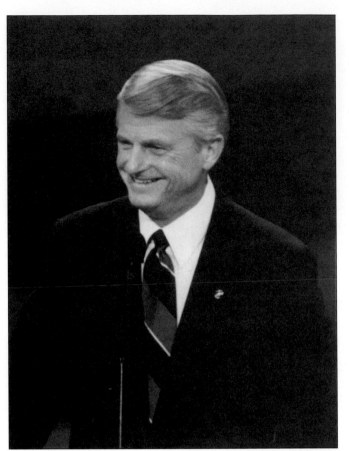

Because of the HOPE scholarship program and his work on behalf of the National Democratic Party, Zell Miller was recognized nationally during his two terms as Georgia's governor.

ones. Lottery revenues funded new programs, such as pre-kindergarten and the purchase of school computers. But no program was more popular with Georgians than the HOPE (Helping Outstanding Pupils Educationally) scholarship program—which gained considerable national publicity.

During Miller's eight years as governor, salaries for public school teachers increased significantly. When he took office in 1991, teacher salaries in Georgia were among the lowest in the South. At the end of his second term, they would be among the highest.

In addition to education, Miller had other important priorities during his administration. Laws were passed to reduce drunk driving, reform the welfare program, eliminate state sales tax on food, reduce the state income tax, privatize (turn over to the private sector) certain governmental functions, and redirect spending by state agencies. ◀

Important Events Involving Georgia

The final decade of the twentieth century was an eventful period for Georgia. Iraqi invasion of Kuwait in 1990 led Pres. George Bush to mobilize U.S. forces. Several Georgia military bases, especially Fort Stewart, played an important role in what was initially called "Desert Shield" but became "Desert Storm" when U.S. and allied forces attacked Iraqi soldiers and locations. In 1998, units from Fort Stewart were again deployed to the Middle East to force Iraq to allow United Nations inspectors in to search for chemical and biological weapons.

In July 1991, President Bush announced his nomination of Clarence Thomas as associate justice on the U.S. Supreme Court. Thomas, who was born in 1948 near Savannah, became the second African American and the fifth Georgia-born jurist to sit on the nation's highest court.

In 1992, Georgia voters approved a constitutional amendment to allow a state lottery for education, which went into operation the following year. Proceeds from the lottery funded the HOPE scholarship program, which had a dramatic impact on enrollment at Georgia colleges and universities. So many graduating high school seniors with HOPE scholarships began applying to the University of Georgia that officials had to impose various measures to limit the size of the incoming freshman class.

Along with its dramatic growth, Atlanta has become a major convention and sports center. The Democratic National Convention chose to meet in Atlanta in 1988 (a first-time event for Georgia). Then, a partnership between state government, the city of Atlanta,

▶ Locating the Main Ideas

1. Prior to the 1990s, what was the make up of Georgia's congressional delegation, excluding the period of Reconstruction?

2. What makes Georgia's lottery different from any other in the nation?

3. List at least three priorities, other than education, of Governor Miller's administration.

and Fulton County paved the way to building a domed stadium in Atlanta. Completed in 1993, the Georgia Dome has hosted the 1994 Super Bowl, as well as numerous other events.

In other sports events during the 1990s, baseball fans enjoyed many thrilling moments provided by the Atlanta Braves. Between 1990 and 1997, the Braves played in four World Series—and in 1995 beat the Cleveland Indians to become world champions of baseball.

No sporting event in the decade—or in the history of Georgia— would compare to the 1996 Summer Olympics. Having won the bid in 1991, the Atlanta Committee for the Olympic Games (ACOG) spent five years preparing to host the games. Under the leadership of Billy Payne, Olympic organizers prepared the city of Atlanta for this international event. With financial help from the Braves, a new Olympic Stadium was built just south of the existing Atlanta-Fulton County Stadium. On the campus of Georgia Tech, the Olympic Village was constructed as home for athletes from around the world during the 17-day event. Finally, everything was ready. On the night of July 19, 1996, opening ceremonies were held in the new stadium. For 17 days, the eyes of the world were on Atlanta—especially after a bomb was ignited in Centennial Park, killing one bystander and injuring many others. Another death was later blamed on the bombing. When the Olympics ended, the Olympic flag was passed by Atlanta mayor Bill Campbell to the mayor of Sydney, Australia, host city of the 2000 Olympics.

In the 1990s, Atlanta continued to attract major corporations. Although Georgia had expected an economic decline following the

The Chattahoochee River is the principal source of drinking water for the Atlanta region. Increasing use and pollution problems, however, threaten downstream users of the Chattahoochee in Georgia, Alabama, and Florida. As a result, the Atlanta region one day may have to impose limits on future growth.

1996 Summer Olympics, Georgia's economy proved more resilient than had been predicted. In fact, even with the elimination of the sales tax on food, the governor and General Assembly were still able to cut state income taxes in 1998.

Looking to the Future

Because of many factors—including a diverse economy, mild climate, low cost of living, highways and other transportation facilities, and strategic location—Georgia is expected to continue as one of the leading growth states in the nation.

Its successes, however, have not been without problems. Crime and drug abuse exist not only in urban communities but throughout the state. No matter how many new beds are added, prisons seem to stay permanently overcrowded. Numerous health-related problems confront the state, including the AIDS epidemic, rising medical costs, and a shortage of rural doctors and hospitals. Teenage pregnancy and infant mortality are continuing health problems. Reducing Georgia's high rate of school dropout is a major priority.

Population growth has been a mixed blessing for Georgia. New residents mean new taxpayers and a growing economy. But they also force local governments to expand many services, including schools, streets, water and sewer facilities, trash disposal, police and fire protection, parks, and animal control. New residents also put a strain on Georgia's environment, particularly with regard to air and water quality.

Yet, today's problems can be tomorrow's opportunities. Georgia is a big state, a diverse state, and a growing state. An exciting future lies ahead as Georgia enters the twenty-first century. ◀

▶ **Locating the Main Ideas**

1. What was Georgia's contribution to military efforts in Iraq?
2. What major sporting event took place in Atlanta in 1996?
3. Name three factors that contribute to Georgia continuing as a growth state.

CHAPTER ACTIVITIES

Reviewing the Main Ideas

1. Compare the positions of Dean Rusk and Richard Russell before 1964 on using U.S. troops to defend South Vietnam.

2. How was President Johnson able to commit U.S. troops to fight in Vietnam without Congress actually declaring war?

3. What led some people to conclude in the late 1960s that racism continued in Georgia?

4. What actions by Gov. Jimmy Carter helped to improve Georgia's image in the eyes of the world?

5. What efforts did Governor Busbee undertake to help the economy of the state?

6. How was it possible for the state of Georgia to go 12 years, under the administration of two governors, without a tax increase?

7. How does former President Carter continue to demonstrate a commitment to the objectives of his foreign policy while in office?

8. Describe how the composition of Georgia's population has been changing since the 1960s.

9. List three ways Governor Miller has attempted to improve education in Georgia.

10. How has population growth been a mixed blessing for Georgia?

Give It Some Extra Thought

1. **Give Your Opinion.** In your opinion, how did Gov. Lester Maddox affect Georgia's national image in the 1960s and 1970s?

2. **Making National and International Connections.** How can events such as Atlanta's hosting the Democratic National Convention, the Superbowl, and the 1996 Summer Olympics help the economy and image of the state?

3. **Speculate about the Future.** What are some reasons that account for Georgia's population growth? Based on those reasons, do you think Georgia will continue to experience similar growth in the twenty-first century?

Sharpen Your Skills

1. **Cause and Effect.** Explain how the 1973 Arab oil embargo that started nearly halfway around the world could affect Georgia as it did.

2. **Analyzing Changes.** Since 1777, Georgia has had 10 constitutions. Using your textbook or other sources, list the date for each constitution and give a reason why it was adopted by the state.

3. **Interpreting the Source.** Reread the excerpt from Jimmy Carter's campaign speech on page 330. What does the speech tell you about him?

Going Further

1. **Interviewing for Information.** Interview a person who lived during one of the decades covered in this chapter. Compare his or her memories to the events discussed in the chapter.

2. **Making Community Connections.** Identify something being built in or near your community today. It might be an office building, an apartment complex, a shopping center, a public park, or someone's new home. Describe what is being built, the purpose it will serve, and speculate about its effect—both positive and negative—on the community.

22

Coming Up Next

• A multi-cultural society
• Georgians' cultural achievements
• Support for the arts
• Preserving culture

Georgia's Cultural Heritage

In the summer of 1996, worldwide attention focused on Georgia. Atlanta was the site of the 1996 Summer Olympics. For two weeks, Georgians had an opportunity to greet and mingle with thousands of people from around the world who came for the Olympics. This event provided Georgians with a chance to learn, firsthand, about people from many different cultures. At the same time, having the Olympics confirmed Atlanta's reputation as an international city.

What does being an international city mean? For Atlanta, it means that the city is recognized throughout the world. It is connected to the rest of the world by transportation facilities, business ties, cultural exchanges, and communications. People from other countries visit and live there. Many foreign governments have offices and trade missions in the city.

Throughout history, people with different backgrounds have contributed to Georgia's culture in many ways. Anthropologists tell us about the cultures of prehistoric mound builders and other Indian groups who lived here long ago. Later, their descendants, the Creeks and Cherokees, developed distinctive cultures. With the arrival of Europeans and Africans, Georgia became a **multi-cultural** society—a society with many cultures.

Though forced from the state, Georgia's Native Americans left something that daily reminds us of their presence. You may know what it is. Hundreds of geographical features across the state still bear Creek and Cherokee names. These include rivers, such as the Chattahoochee, Amicalola, Etowah, Oostanaula, and Tugaloo. Oconee and Chattooga counties have Indian names. The Okefenokee Swamp is named for an Indian word "o-wa-qua-phenoga," which means "land of the trembling earth." In some cases, towns such as

A 1921 family reunion birthday celebration in Tattnall County.

Talking Rock bear the English translation of the original native name. And the city of Ball Ground in Cherokee County got its name because long ago Cherokees played a ball game much like lacrosse.

Georgia's first people left another legacy. They developed paths and trailways that crisscrossed the state. Today, many of those pathways, originally developed by Georgia's native inhabitants, are covered with asphalt and used by motorists.

A Multi-cultural Society

After thousands of years, Georgia's native population was replaced by Europeans, Africans, and others. As each new **ethnic group**—people with shared customs, languages, or background—arrived, they brought with them their unique or special way of doing things. That included their food, dress, skills, occupations, customs for occasions such as weddings or funerals, and ways of expressing themselves in art, music, story, and dance.

Not only did these newcomers have to adapt to Georgia's physical environment, they had to adapt to its larger cultural environment. At the same time, they contributed to the existing culture. As a result, cultural change became a two-way process and a continuing one.

While adapting to new environments, ethnic groups often attempt to recognize and hold on to important aspects of their culture. For example, in recognition of their African heritage, many black Americans have chosen to call themselves African Americans.

Shops and restaurants often accompany a growing ethnic community. Pictured in 1930 are workers at a Chinese restaurant in Augusta.

Also mindful of their heritage are those who prefer to be known as Hispanic Americans and Native Americans. Ethnic groups also try to maintain their cultures by creating networks of churches, businesses, and social organizations.

Today, Georgia has a multi-cultural society. This means that its population is made up of people of many cultures, living and working together. The majority—71 percent in 1990—are white, mostly descendants of immigrants from Great Britain and other European countries. Blacks, or African Americans, make up the largest minority in the state, accounting for 27 percent of all Georgians. But there are other cultures as well.

With nearly 3 percent of the population, Hispanics are Georgia's second largest minority. Historically, traveling migrant workers from Mexico came to Georgia to harvest farm crops. But today, many Hispanics are moving to the state to become residents. Georgia's manufacturing, food processing, and service industries offer jobs that are scarce in Mexico, Central and South America, Cuba, and Puerto Rico.

Asians form Georgia's fastest-growing cultural group, tripling in number during the 1980s and nearly doubling that number by the mid 1990s. Represented are a variety of ethnic groups, including Chinese, Koreans, Vietnamese, Thai, and Hmong (mung), a people from the mountains of northern Laos. Although most of the newcomers have settled in the Atlanta area, for over 100 years there has been a sizeable Chinese community in Augusta.

Georgia's ethnic groups observe their traditions in different ways. They may celebrate holidays or other special events unique to their culture. Atlanta's Greek community, for example, holds an annual festival that has become a popular event. Through food, music, dance, costumes, and programs, visitors learn of their traditions. Every Mother's Day in Brunswick, Portuguese shrimpers participate in a religious tradition known as Blessing of the Fleet. Atlanta's growing Hispanic population holds an annual festival to renew cultural ties and to share their customs with the community. Each fall, people of Scottish descent gather at Stone Mountain for a festival and to compete in an event called the Highland Games.

These festive occasions give visitors an opportunity to learn more about each culture by tasting the foods that are considered special, seeing the costumes and crafts of a particular group, and enjoying other unique features such as singing and dancing.

All these many cultures—living, working, and playing together—create the culture of Georgia, and America. Some aspects of Georgia culture are shared with neighboring southern states. For example, foods such as grits and boiled peanuts are not usually found outside the South. They are a southern tradition.

These men, from Savannah's Greek community, took part in the 1907 St. Patrick's Day parade. Today, the parade has become an international event, attracting entrants and thousands of visitors from around the country and the world.

Festivals are a popular way to celebrate Georgia culture. They recognize Georgia's history, products, music, hobbies, even pests! Georgia Week each February in Savannah marks the arrival of James Oglethorpe and the first colonists. In Dahlonega, annual "Gold Rush Days" commemorate the time when gold was first discovered. There is a Taste of the South celebration at Stone Mountain and an Andersonville Historic Fair at the former Confederate prison. Camilla is the home of the annual Gnat Days. The state sponsors the Georgia National Fair in Perry with livestock shows, exhibits, and carnival rides. Some celebrations recognize well-known Georgia products such as cotton, seafood, Vidalia onions, blueberries, mayhaws, peanuts, peaches, and marble. These products are a part of the state's culture and represent how some Georgians make a living. At various times of the year, you can hear bluegrass, beach music, or jazz at festival gatherings. You can also attend or participate in arts festivals, crafts shows, road races, horse shows, and hot air balloon races. All these events help people to come together, learn about our culture, appreciate differences, and have a good time. ▶

Georgians' Cultural Achievements

Over the years, many Georgians—both native-born and those who have adopted the state—have excelled in many areas, ranging from sports and entertainment to art and literature. Their achievements have been a source of pride and enjoyment not only to Georgians, but to other Americans as well.

▶ **Locating the Main Ideas**

1. Define: multi-cultural, ethnic group
2. What are some distinguishing characteristics of an international city?
3. What are some features by which an ethnic group might be identified?
4. Grits and boiled peanuts are common in Georgia. Why are they considered a part of our southern culture?

Achievements in Sports

Teresa Edwards, Olympic gold medal winner, holds the University of Georgia Lady Bulldogs record as the all-time leader in assists and steals.

Competing with one another, ourselves, or nature has become an important part of the American culture. This is true in Georgia, where such sports as football, basketball, baseball, golf, hunting and fishing, and auto racing are enjoyed by so many people—either as participants or observers. Sports and recreation are popular in our culture for several reasons, including tradition, school pride, desire for physical fitness, and need for relaxation.

Georgians not only compete for fun; many have become national, and even international, champions. Atlanta golfer Bobby Jones is recognized as one of the game's greatest players. After retiring from the game, Jones spearheaded the effort to build the Augusta National Golf Course. The Masters Tournament, one of the premier golf tournaments in the world, is held there every spring. Three Georgians have won the Masters—Claude Harmon from Savannah in 1948, Tommy Aaron from Gainesville in 1973, and Augusta-born Larry Mize in 1987. Another golfer from Georgia is Louise Suggs, known as "Little Toughie." One of the greatest female golfers of all times, she was the leading winner on the ladies professional circuit from 1953 to 1960.

Georgia has produced a number of Olympic gold medalists. The earliest was sprinter Ralph Metcalf, who was on the 400-meter relay team at the 1932 Olympics. University of Georgia track star Forrest "Spec" Towns won first place in the 110-meter high hurdles at the 1936 games. In 1948, Albany's Alice Coachman Davis won the women's high jump. Weightlifter Paul Anderson won a gold in 1956, going on to be recognized as the "strongest man in the world." Sprinters Martha Hudson Pennyman (1960), Edith McGuire Duvall (1964), Wyomia Tyus (1964), and Mel Pender (1968) also brought home Olympic gold medals.

Edwin Moses, who attended Morehouse College in the 1970s, became the premier 400-meter hurdler of his day. He won the event at the 1976 and 1984 Olympics and set the world record in 1983. Another Georgian participating in the 1984 games was swimmer Steve Lundquist, who won two gold medals and set two world records. Georgia swimmer Angel Martino, who lives in Americus, won a gold medal at the 1992 Olympics in Barcelona. The only U.S. basketball player—male or female—to participate in four Olympic games is Teresa Edwards. Born in Cairo, she was a gold medalist in 1984, 1988, and 1996, and a bronze medalist in 1992.

Georgia has produced other world champions. Camilla's Theo (Tiger) Flowers was world middleweight boxing champion in 1926—the first African American to hold the title. Sidney Walker, once a shoeshine boy at the Augusta National Golf Course, became the lightweight boxing champion in the early 1940s. In 1951, Georgian Ezzard Charles held the world heavyweight title. More recently, in 1996, Atlanta's Evander Holyfield became the second boxer to win the world heavyweight boxing championship three times. Working as Holyfield's strength coach was another Atlanta champion, body builder Lee Haney. In 1991, Haney won his eighth "Mr. Olympia" title, setting the record for the most consecutive wins.

In 1942, University of Georgia running back Frank Sinkwich became the first Georgian to win the Heisman Trophy, symbol of the best college football player in America. The trophy is named for John Heisman, an innovative football coach who was at Georgia Tech from 1904 to 1919. He developed the forward pass and the snap from center. Also, he was the first to put numbers on players' jerseys. In 1961, University of Georgia quarterback Fran Tarkenton was drafted by the Minnesota Vikings football team. There, the "scrambling quarterback" achieved career passing records for touchdowns, completions, and yardage. Georgia's second Heisman trophy winner came from Wrightsville. Running back Herschel Walker had a spectacular career at the University of Georgia, winning the nation's top football honor in 1982. He went on to a professional career with the New Jersey Generals, Dallas Cowboys, and Minnesota Vikings.

In other professional sports, Ty Cobb of Royston was considered to be one of the all-time best baseball players. His lifetime batting average (.367) is the highest in history. Another baseball great was Hank Aaron of the Atlanta Braves, who in 1974 set the all-time major league record for home runs. With 755 home runs, he broke the lifetime record of 714 long held by Babe Ruth. The Atlanta Braves were the winningest team in major league baseball in the 1990s. They won the World Series in 1995. The Braves won the National League championship in 1991, 1992, and 1996, and they were division champs in 1993 and 1997. In basketball, University of Georgia standout Dominique Wilkins went on to play with the Atlanta Hawks, where he became one of the league's top scorers. In stock car racing, Dawsonville's Bill Elliot has won numerous national championships.

In addition to individual sports greats, Georgia colleges and universities have won many team championships in different sports, including several national titles.

University of Georgia bulldog, Uga, was named the number one mascot in the country in 1997 by Sports Illustrated *magazine. He played himself in the movie,* Midnight in the Garden of Good and Evil.

Music in Georgia

Many musicians, some known around the world, claim Georgia as their home. They represent a wide variety of musical styles.

Some of those styles, such as blues, jazz, gospel, bluegrass, and country music, had their origin in the South. Blues and jazz became

Albany native Ray Charles, one of America's most popular rhythm and blues singers.

(below) With Yoel Levi as conductor, the Atlanta Symphony Orchestra became one of America's greatest orchestras.

popular, appealing to both black and white audiences in the United States and abroad. Songwriter and singer Thomas Dorsey, born in Villa Rica in 1899, earned the title of "father of gospel music" with his many blues arrangements of gospel hymns. Gertrude "Ma" Rainey of Columbus was known as the "Mother of the Blues." Fletcher Henderson, Jr., of Cuthbert, recognized as one of America's great jazz musicians, helped the careers of young jazz instrumentalists who played in his orchestra. He became known to white audiences when he worked as an arranger for Benny Goodman. Joe Williams, a jazz vocalist from Cordele, and Albany-born trumpeter Harry James made names for themselves during the "Big Band Era." In 1987, blues singer Robert Cray won a Grammy award for his work.

The Sea Island Singers and the McIntosh County Shouters are groups nationally known for continuing coastal music traditions. They have performed at the National Black Arts Festival in Atlanta and the National Folk Festival in Virginia, presenting songs, narratives, and dances as handed down by black Georgians along the coast.

In classical music, Roland Hayes, an African American tenor from Calhoun, sang for British royalty in 1921. James Melton of Moultrie performed as an opera tenor, recording artist, and actor during the mid century. Mattiwilda Dobbs of Atlanta (an aunt of Atlanta mayor Maynard Jackson) and Jessye Norman of Augusta are internationally recognized opera singers. Both have performed with the New York Metropolitan Opera.

Several Georgia cities have symphony orchestras, including Atlanta, Augusta, Columbus, and Savannah. The Atlanta Symphony Orchestra began in 1947 and rose to prominence under the direction of Robert Shaw. The orchestra performed for the inauguration of President Carter in 1977. Under director Yoel Levi, the Atlanta Symphony's reputation has reached new heights.

Songwriter Johnny Mercer of Savannah published 701 songs between 1933 and 1974. Among them are "Moon River" and "I'm an Old Cowhand." He wrote music for movies, radio, and recordings, and won four Academy awards. Georgia has an abundance of famous performers of popular music. Ray Charles of Albany popularized "Georgia on My Mind," now our state song. Soul singer James Brown from Augusta has a long list of hit records over a career that began in the 1950s and influenced many other artists. The city of Macon produced many musicians, including Otis Redding (soul), "Little Richard" Penniman (rock

and roll), and the Allman Brothers Band (rock)
Atlanta rhythm and blues singers Gladys Knight
and the Pips have recorded several gold albums
and won Grammys for their music. Amy Grant,
a singer of Christian and popular music, has won
five Grammy awards and continues to make recordings. The works of many rhythm and blues
artists were recorded and produced in Atlanta
during the 1990s.

Fiddlin' John Carson was the first person to
broadcast and record country music. In 1922, he
performed live on WSB radio, and a year later recorded "Little Old Log Cabin" and "The Old Hen
Cackled and the Rooster's Going to Crow." Other
well-known country singers from the state include Brenda Lee, Bill Anderson, Ronnie Milsap,
Travis Tritt, and John Berry. Songwriters who
also perform include Ray Stevens, Jerry Reed, T. Graham Brown,
Joe South, and Billy Joe Royal. Recognized as male and female
country vocal entertainers of the year, respectively, were Alan Jackson from Newnan (1995) and Trisha Yearwood of Monticello
(1997). Both entertainers have gold records, and Yearwood won two
Grammys in 1998.

In the 1980s, the city of Athens developed a reputation as a home
for alternative music. Athens bands such as the B-52s and R.E.M.
and the Indigo Girls of Atlanta went on to become nationally famous, and continue to perform.

*The Grammy-winning band R.E.M.
has sold more than 30 million
albums and has an international
following.*

Literature

Georgia writers have received national recognition for their poems,
short stories, and novels. Often, their works have been based on
fictional accounts of life in Georgia or the South. Most noteworthy
in the nineteenth century were poet Sidney Lanier and folktale
author Joel Chandler Harris. Popular when it was published in
1910, Corra Harris's *The Circuit Rider's Wife* was based on her life
as a traveling Methodist minister's wife.

In 1925, poet and Atlanta journalist Frank Stanton was named
as Georgia's first poet laureate—an honorary title given by the governor. Byron Herbert Reece, who grew up in Union County in the
1920s, wrote poetry and novels that reflected the isolation of his
north Georgia mountain home.

Three Georgians won Pulitzer prizes in the 1930s for their liter-
ary works. In 1930, Conrad Aiken from Savannah won the award
for his *Selected Poems*. Later, in 1973, Governor Carter named him
poet laureate of Georgia. Waycross native Caroline Miller won the
1934 Pulitzer prize for *Lamb in His Bosom,* a fictional account of
frontier life before the Civil War. Margaret Mitchell of Atlanta won
the 1936 Pulitzer prize for her novel, *Gone with the Wind.*

Flannery O'Connor at an autograph party for her book, Wise Blood.

Another famous Georgia author of the 1930s was Erskine Caldwell, who grew up in Wrens. Caldwell painted a harsh picture about the lifestyles of poor Georgia sharecroppers. His best-known books were *Tobacco Road*, which became a long-running Broadway play, and *God's Little Acre*.

Three important women writers who published in the 1940s and 1950s were Carson McCullers of Columbus, Flannery O'Connor of Milledgeville, and Lillian Smith of Clayton.

McCullers wrote about the lonely side of contemporary life in the South. Her best-known works are *The Heart Is a Lonely Hunter* and *The Member of the Wedding*. Flannery O'Connor is recognized as one of America's best short story authors. Her stories and novels often use violent and shocking events to describe southern culture. Lillian Smith wrote about racism and its crippling effect on the South.

James Dickey was a well-known Atlanta-born poet. His work includes a popular book called *Deliverance*, a violent tale of three city men canoeing through the wilds of north Georgia. Pat Conroy, from Atlanta, has written novels based on his experiences at The Citadel, a military school in South Carolina, and as a school teacher on one of that state's barrier islands. Harry Crews draws on his childhood in Bacon County for many of his stories and novels.

Olive Ann Burns of Banks County became famous for *Cold Sassy Tree*, an account of turn-of-the-century life in a small Georgia town. Eugenia Price, who lived on St. Simons Island, is best known for her historical novels about coastal Georgians. Ferrol Sams, from Fayette County, has written best-selling novels about a young boy growing up in Georgia before World War II.

Midnight in the Garden of Good and Evil by John Berendt, a book about a murder in Savannah, has brought fame to the city. A national best seller for several years, the popular book was made into a movie filmed in Savannah, and many tourists have visited the city because of it.

Several black Georgia authors have achieved national recognition. Raymond Andrews, son of a Madison-area sharecropper, wrote several novels about life for black people in the segregated South of the 1940s and 1950s. Frank Yerby, an African American writer from Augusta, published popular, action-packed historical fiction. He wrote many novels and won a short story award in 1944. Poet and author Alice Walker is from Eatonton. For her best-known novel, *The Color Purple*, she won the Pulitzer prize in 1983. The book, written as a series of letters, tells the story of a black woman growing up in Georgia. It was later made into a movie.

The Performing Arts

Atlanta is the home of several professional theatre companies. Among them is the Alliance Theatre at the Woodruff Arts Center. The Alliance, besides its regular play season, also has a children's theatre and a theatre school. Jomandi Productions is an African American theatre company that performs in Atlanta and nationally. The Center for Puppetry Arts not only presents performances but also has a museum and offers classes in the art of puppetry. Touring theatre companies also stage productions, often in the restored Fox Theatre or the Atlanta Civic Center. The Atlanta Ballet, created in 1929, is the oldest continuously operating ballet company in America.

Throughout the state, numerous community theatre groups stage and present plays, giving local residents the opportunity to see performances or to perform. In Columbus the Springer Opera House, established in 1871, is the setting for many types of productions. Governor Carter named it the State Theatre of Georgia in 1971.

Today, many Georgia actors and actresses perform on stage and in movies and television programs. Ossie Davis (Cogdell) has had a long career in movies and television as an actor, director, and screenwriter. The original Star Trek television series featured DeForest Kelley (Atlanta) as Dr. "Bones" McCoy. Other faces seen on television are Demond Wilson (Valdosta) in *Sanford and Son*; Claude Akins (Nelson), *Sheriff Lobo*; Pernell Roberts (Waycross), *Trapper John, M.D.*; Alvin "Junior" Samples (Cumming), *Hee Haw*; and Jeff Foxworthy (Atlanta).

Long-established stars include the character actor Charles Coburn (Savannah); Oliver Hardy (Harlem) of the comedy team Laurel and Hardy, popular in the 1930s; Melvyn Douglas (Macon), who was in *Hud* and *Hotel*; and Joanne Woodward (Thomasville), famous for her role in *The Three Faces of Eve*. Thelma "Butterfly" McQueen who grew up in and later retired to Augusta had an unforgettable supporting role in the movie *Gone with the Wind*. Burt Reynolds (Waycross) popularized the good old boy image in such movies as *Smokey and the Bandit*. Recently, Holly Hunter (Conyers), Julia Roberts (Smyrna), Kim Basinger (Athens), and Laurence Fishburne (Augusta) have appeared in popular movies. Spike Lee (Atlanta) has produced and directed many movies that examine race relations in America.

In recent decades, Georgia officials have promoted the state as a setting for movies and television shows. Movies such as *Glory* and *Driving Miss Daisy* were made in Georgia, as were *Deliverance*, *Smokey and the Bandit*, and *Fried Green Tomatoes at the Whistle Stop Cafe*. Television series filmed in the state include *The Dukes of Hazzard*, *In the Heat of the Night*, *I'll Fly Away*, and *Savannah*.

Kim Basinger won the 1998 Academy Award for best supporting actress for her role in the movie L.A. Confidential.

Dr. Strangepork and Link Hogthrob, stars of "Pigs in Space" from television's The Muppet Show, *are part of the permanent museum collection at the Center for Puppetry Arts.*

▶ **Locating the Main Ideas**

1. Why are sports a part of a people's culture?

2. Name four types of music that had their origin in the South.

3. Like the historian, writers and authors have a frame of reference. How do the Georgia authors mentioned in this section show a Georgia frame of reference in their work?

4. How have Georgians been active in the performing arts?

Georgia has another tie to motion pictures and television—the Turner Broadcasting System, which merged with Time Warner in 1997. Formerly owner of an outdoor advertising firm, business entrepreneur Ted Turner purchased an Atlanta UHF television station in 1970. By bouncing its signal off a satellite, Turner transformed the operation into SuperStation WTBS. Today, through satellite broadcasting, the TBS network reaches a national television audience, and in the case of its cable news network, CNN International, a global audience. ◀

The Visual Arts

Georgia has a rich variety of artists, from painters to potters. Some Georgia artists have exhibited their work in national and international settings.

At the beginning of the twentieth century, Lucy May Stanton of Atlanta and Athens received international recognition for her miniatures painted on ivory. Some of her works are in the Smithsonian's National Portrait Gallery and at Emory University. Lamar Dodd was a well-known Georgia painter. Space missions and open heart surgery are among the subjects of his later works. Benny Andrews, an artist and illustrator, illustrated the books of his brother Raymond Andrews. His work is in the collections of major museums around the country. Athens resident Beverly Buchanan is known for her drawings and sculptures, often accompanied by a story. Her work, which appears in major museums, celebrates the spirit of shack dwellers in the rural South.

Along with many other Americans, you may already have seen the work of two Georgia sculptors. University of Georgia professor William J. Thompson did the *Prisoners of War* sculpture of three figures—humanity, suffering, and death—at Andersonville National Historic Site. His sculpture of Sen. Richard B. Russell can be seen at the state capitol. Frederick Hart of Atlanta designed and sculpted a biblical scene for one of the main entrances to the National Cathedral in Washington, D.C. More widely known is Hart's bronze statue of three soldiers at the Vietnam War Memorial in the nation's capital.

Prisoners of War memorial at Andersonville National Historic Site near Americus, by sculptor Bill Thompson.

Folk Art

Folk arts and crafts are items made by hand using skills that are generally self-taught or learned at home. These skills are often passed along through generations. It is not uncommon to find families who are known for a particular craft or style. In the past, folk objects were usually functional and served a useful purpose, such as a quilt to keep a bed warm. Because of changing times and modern inventions, the functional value of some objects may be lost, but those same objects are prized for their decorative value. Popular folk arts and crafts today include pottery, quilts, baskets, and wood carvings.

Locally produced clay pottery items such as butter churns, milk pans, and jugs were once practical containers for holding every product in the Georgia kitchen. After the introduction of glass and metal containers in the twentieth century, folk potters found new uses for their products. The Meaders family of Mossy Creek is known for face jugs. The Hewell and the Merritt families produce flowerpots and other garden pottery items. Members of the D.X. Gordy family produce figurines, along with more traditional pottery items.

Howard Finster of Summerville is a folk artist known for his religiously inspired visions and art. He has completed over 7,000 paintings, drawings, and sculptures, and constructed a multi-storied chapel of art. A self-

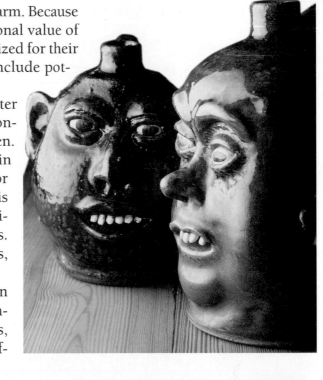

Robert Smalls Road *by Beverly Buchanan.* *(above) These face jugs have been produced by three generations of the Meaders family. Collectors now pay up to $10,000 for an original.*

Folk artist Howard Finster explains his Chapel of Art, located in Summerville.

ordained preacher, he uses wood, concrete, car parts, and other discarded items in his work. His art often contains messages, Bible verses, warnings, and prophecies. Nellie Mae Rowe was a visionary folk artist from Fayette County who became well known for her small sculptures and drawings. Her work has been shown in major exhibitions, including an exhibit of black folk art 1930–1980, and is in the collections of the High Museum of Art in Atlanta and the Library of Congress. Mattie Lou O'Kelley, a self-taught folk artist from Maysville, became nationally known for her colorful primitive style paintings. She did not start painting regularly until she was nearly 60 years old. Her paintings are in folk art collections in many museums.

Support for the Arts

The arts in Georgia have been helped by people who recognize their importance to the community. One way people have helped is by encouraging the development of cultural centers—places where artists can work or display their works to the public. Many cities have cultural centers that offer studio, performance, and gallery space to artists. Some may also have museum space. The Nexus Contemporary Arts Center in Atlanta, the Madison-Morgan Cultural Center, the Sacred Heart Cultural Center in Augusta, and the Arts Experiment Station in Tifton are among the many centers throughout Georgia supported by a combination of individuals, businesses, and different levels of government.

Some institutions have been started or continued through the actions of **philanthropists**, people willing to contribute money for causes they feel are worthy. Mary Telfair of Savannah left most of her estate for the establishment of the Telfair Academy of Arts and Sciences. In 1886, the Academy became an art gallery open to the public. The High Museum of Art and the Atlanta College of Art are memorials to Harriet Wilson High. The donation of her home and art collection to the Atlanta Art Association was the seed that started the museum and school.

Associated with the High Museum is the Robert W. Woodruff Arts Center. Formerly known as the Memorial Arts Center, it was renamed as a birthday tribute to the generosity of Woodruff. The center was built in memory of 122 Atlantans who were killed in a

The Georgia Farm. *For her paintings, artist Mattie Lou O'Kelley drew on childhood memories of growing up in Banks County, Georgia. Which season of the year has she painted?*

plane crash at Orly Field near Paris in June 1962. Financed almost solely by private donations, the center includes the Alliance Theatre, the Atlanta Symphony, the Atlanta College of Art, and the High Museum.

Alfred H. Holbrook, a New York attorney, collected paintings by American artists as a tribute to the memory of his wife. In 1945, he presented the Eva Underhill Holbrook Memorial Collection of American Art to the University of Georgia with the stipulation that a museum be established on campus. As a result, the Georgia Museum of Art got its start and houses the collection along with many other holdings.

Philanthropy can be used to encourage distinguished achievements in a particular area. George Foster Peabody, a Columbus financier and talented businessman, used his fortune to endow the Peabody Awards. The awards, established in 1939, recognize achievements by radio and television networks, cable organizations, and individuals. These prestigious awards are given every spring in a ceremony in New York, but the program is administered by the University of Georgia.

The Seney-Stovall Chapel in Athens, dedicated in 1885, was constructed with a donation from philanthropist George Seney. Part of the Lucy Cobb Institute, the chapel deteriorated after the girls' school closed in 1931. Community members—including many former students—rallied and rescued the chapel. It is now used by the community and university groups.

Preserving Culture

Knowing about the past is important to preserving a people's culture. Of course, reading books is one way to learn about that past. Another way is seeing actual artifacts from history. This is one reason museums are so important. Through exhibits and displays, museums tell us about our past.

Although Georgia does not have a state museum of history, a variety of smaller, specialized museums across the state explore Georgia's past. Museums dedicated to Native American history and prehistory can be found at New Echota and at the Etowah, Ocmulgee, and Kolomoki Indian mounds. Interpretive exhibits and displays tell the story of Atlanta's past at the Atlanta History Center. The history of agriculture in the state is told at the Georgia Agrirama in Tifton. Museums and state historic sites associated with the Civil War are found in such cities as Columbus, Savannah, and Crawfordville. Additionally, the National Park Service operates two Civil War national battlefields at Kennesaw Mountain and Chickamauga, and the National Prisoner of War Museum at Andersonville.

Not all museums are called museums. For example, Atlanta's APEX (African-American Panoramic Experience) displays artifacts from black history as well as contemporary exhibits. The birth home of Martin Luther King, Jr., part of a national historic site, is a type of museum. Historic exhibits can be found at the Carter Presidential Center and Library in Atlanta.

Historic buildings and structures in your community are a type of museum. But sometimes, distinctive old buildings are lost in the rush to build new office buildings and parking lots. Out of a desire to protect these structures from the past came a movement known as **historic preservation**.

Savannah was one of the first cities to take advantage of its standing historic structures. Run-down shops, factories, residences, churches, and public buildings were restored, and the historic areas attracted many tourists. The idea caught on in cities throughout the state. Sometimes, a historic structure has been saved by adapting it for a different use. Traveling around the state, you will find many offices in antebellum homes, museums in former schools, or art galleries in old factories. Historic preservation allows Georgians of all ages and cultures an eyewitness view of the past. ◀

▶ Locating the Main Ideas

1. Define: philanthropist, historic preservation
2. What are folk arts and crafts?
3. What purpose do community cultural centers serve?
4. How did an interest in historic preservation benefit Savannah?

CHAPTER ACTIVITIES

Reviewing the Main Ideas

1. Explain how Georgia became and continues to be a multi-cultural society.

2. Why might the customs of an ethnic group change following a move to a new environment? Name two ways an ethnic group might resist change.

3. How is cultural change a two-way process?

4. Thanksgiving Day in November is a traditional holiday in American culture that is not celebrated in foreign countries. Can you think of other holidays that would be part of American culture only?

5. Look back at the pictures of people in this book and notice what they are wearing. If you wanted to, you could dress up in a "costume" so you would look like one of them. Write a description of what you are wearing today so a student 100 years from now could dress in your costume.

6. How could novels written by authors from different ethnic groups give you information about their culture?

7. Many well-known actors and actresses have come from Georgia. How else has Georgia contributed to television and motion pictures?

8. How has Ted Turner been able to affect national and international communications?

9. What are some items that may be considered as folk arts or crafts?

10. What is one way individuals, businesses, and governments have supported the arts?

Give It Some Extra Thought

1. **Seeing Cultural Contributions**. Look at the map of Georgia rivers and Native American paths (page 131). Along what geographic feature does the Lower Creek Path run? What interstate highway does the Hightower Trail follow (approximately)?

2. **Understanding Relationships**. Explain how the state's climate helps make certain outdoor sports a popular form of recreation in Georgia.

3. **Making International Connections**. What do you think would most surprise a visitor from a foreign country about your culture?

Sharpen Your Skills

1. **Map Study**. On a Georgia highway map, identify five features with Native American names.

Artist Benny Andrews painted A Soul *in 1974.*

2. **Cultural Artifacts**. Bring a cultural artifact to class. It may be an album; a book; ticket stubs; a folk craft item; a program from a concert, sports, or other event; a photograph of a cultural event; an invitation; or some other artifact. Describe the artifact to the class.

3. **Examining Changes in Data over Time**. Look in the *Yellow Pages* of the telephone directory and count the total number of restaurants listed. Count and categorize by type the number of ethnic restaurants listed. Following the same procedure, collect the same data from a telephone book from a previous year. Compare the two sets of data. Can you explain the differences?

4. **Reading the Newspaper**. Read about sports events in the newspaper. Make up a special sports page featuring well-known Georgia athletes from this century. Write articles and headlines, and put information, pictures, drawings, or sports statistics on the sports page. Include Georgians mentioned in this chapter, as well as others you might discover or know about.

Going Further

1. **Hosting a Visitor**. Invite someone from another country to your classroom to talk about how they observe weddings, birthdays, and holidays. After the talk, discuss similarities and differences in the way different cultures observe the same events.

2. **Make Nominations**. Many more Georgians have contributed to sports, music, literature, theater, movies, television, and art than are in this chapter. Nominate Georgians who should be recognized by writing a short explanation of their achievements and naming the category in which they belong. Display the nominations in your classroom.

UNIT 9

1775	1776	1781	1787	1788	1830	1848	1854	1861	1865	1893
Georgia delegates attend the Second Continental Congress	Declaration of Independence signed by Georgia representatives	Colonies win independence, become the United States under the Articles of Confederation	Georgia delegates help draft the Constitution of the United States	Georgia becomes the fourth state to ratify the U.S. Constitution	Congress passes the Indian Removal Act	Women declare their rights as citizens at Seneca Falls, New York	The Republican Party is formed	Georgia secedes from the U.S.; Confederate States of America organized	Civil War ends; Thirteenth Amendment ratified	Tom Watson introduces bill in Congress creating rural free mail delivery

American Government and Citizenship

1896	1913	1920	1924	1933	1954	1963	1964	1965	1991	1995
U.S. Supreme Court rules in *Plessy v. Ferguson* that separate facilities for blacks are legal	U.S. Constitution amended to allow federal tax on income	Nineteenth Amendment gives women the right to vote	Congress grants all Native Americans citizenship	Congress enacts New Deal programs to provide relief, reform, and recovery	U.S. Supreme Court rules against segregation in public schools	U.S. Supreme Court upholds lower court ruling that county unit system is unconstitutional	Civil Rights Act passed	Voting Rights Act passed guaranteeing voting access for all eligible citizens	Georgia gets eleventh Congressional seat	Newt Gingrich elected Speaker of the U.S. House of Representatives

23

Coming Up Next!
- Some big questions
- Finding the answers

Let's Talk Government

Why study government? Government gives us the framework for solving public problems. Our government provides opportunities for us to participate in many different ways. So, if we understand how government functions, we have a better chance of making it work for us.

The work and results of government are visible all around us—highways, streets, parks, the city bus system, schools, post offices, and courthouses. Governments also provide services to protect the well-being of the public. It's government that is responsible for inspection of food, safety codes for building construction, and health regulations to protect against the spread of disease. And government sets speed limits for autos, school graduation requirements, and safety regulations for work places.

Learning about government will enable you to share in the democratic process and look out for your interests as a citizen. It will help you to understand more about services to the public—what they are, who provides them, how much they cost, and how to access them. You will have a better idea of how government services affect you and other citizens. You will be able to think about the role of government in addressing public issues.

Government is the framework—the organization—for promoting the common interests of society. There are many issues to think about, discuss, argue over, and finally resolve through decisions for action. Rarely does everyone agree totally on how to solve problems, and often we must reach our solutions through compromise. In American government, elected officials debate the issues, compromise when there is disagreement, and then reach solutions. This constant process occurs at the federal, state, and local levels of government.

Some Big Questions

As our state grows and prospers, we as citizens will have to answer many hard questions about what kind of state we want Georgia to be. These questions involve such issues as increasing prosperity, protecting natural resources, restoring infrastructure, fighting crime, providing health care, and improving education. Now could be a good time to begin thinking about some of these questions. How they are answered will affect you, your family, and your future.

Population and Prosperity

Georgia's population has been growing for several decades as people move in from the north and the west. Our state has been in a prosperous period in the 1990s. The **per capita income** (average annual income per person) in Georgia increased from 84 percent of the national average in 1980 to nearly 94 percent in 1996. But the good effects of growth and prosperity have not spread evenly across the state. Some areas have done very well, like the Atlanta area where annual per capita income is about $26,000. But some other parts of Georgia that are rural and less developed average around $13,000 to $14,000 per person. Even in the most populated areas, some have not shared in the success story. Officials in state and local governments in Georgia must continue to address the question, "How can government help to increase prosperity and spread it throughout the state?"

Natural Resources

As the population has multiplied in and around the largest cities, both water pollution and air pollution have increased. That can have a negative effect on forests and wetlands, as well as on the air we breathe and the water we consume. Georgia state and local governments are working together to respond to the question, "For the health and safety of Georgia citizens, how can we clean up the water and air and prevent any further damage to the environment?"

Infrastructure

The buildings and other construction of state and local governments are referred to as the **infrastructure**. Everything government builds—from highways, water lines, and sewers to jails, courthouses, and public swimming pools—begins to weaken and wear away the moment the public starts using it. Water and sewer pipes go slowly, while streets and roads develop cracks and potholes quickly. Repairing the infrastructure is an ongoing problem. If these public facilities are not kept up, they become damaged and unsafe. Maintenance and repair of all of these structures relies on the allocation of tax money. State or local governments must answer this question: "What can we do to restore these public facilities and prevent the decay of the infrastructure?"

Crime

About 89 percent of the crimes in Georgia are property crimes, such as burglary, motor vehicle theft, and larceny. Millions of dollars worth of funds and goods are stolen in the state. About 11 percent of crimes in Georgia are violent, involving aggravated assaults, murder, armed robbery, or rape. Some crimes, such as the sale and use of illegal drugs, can involve both property and persons. One crime that has received attention in recent years is drunk driving.

State government is trying to build and operate more prisons and pass laws that will prevent criminal acts. At the same time, local governments are working to discourage crime and to capture and convict criminals. Both levels of government must respond to the question, "How can we protect people in Georgia from all types of crimes?"

Health and Welfare

The cost of hospital care, doctors, nursing homes, and medicines continues to increase. Many people who have no health insurance must rely on public health facilities funded by governments. Certain health problems require special attention, such as the state's high rates of infant deaths and AIDS.

People also turn to state and local government for other types of public welfare programs—assistance for the homeless, help for the elderly and the disabled, and services for poor children and families. Georgia also has programs for treatment of mental health problems, mental retardation, and substance abuse. The cost of many of these programs is shared by the federal government. State and local government officials are faced with another important question: "How can Georgia respond to people's needs for health and welfare assistance?"

Education for a Global Age

At the time of the 1990 census, about 29 percent of Georgians did not have a high school diploma, and only 41 percent had any education beyond high school. In recent years, policies of the state government and efforts of local school districts have improved education in Georgia. But more improvements are needed. Lawmakers must deal with the question, "How can governments in Georgia continue to improve education in schools and colleges so that Georgians are better able to be full participants in the world society and economy?"

Finding the Answers

These are some of the issues that people serving in government in Georgia must consider. Learning about government and public issues will serve you well—as a citizen, as a future voter, and as an individual preparing for life in the twenty-first century.

CHAPTER ACTIVITIES

Reviewing the Main Ideas

1. Define: per capita income, infrastructure
2. Why do citizens need to understand how government functions?
3. Using the examples of government services at the beginning of the chapter, describe how you benefitted from or used one of them.
4. How is government an organization that allows us to solve problems?

Give It Some Extra Thought

1. **Making Connections.** Choose one of the six issues on page 359-60 and write a paragraph describing how questions and answers about it might shape the future of Georgia.
2. **Comprehending.** Explain in your own words why we should study government.

Sharpen Your Skills

1. **Cause and Effect.** The government decides it is too costly to regulate and monitor air and water pollution, so it repeals all previous laws on those subjects. What do you think could be some of the likely effects?

Going Further

1. **Identifying Sources.** Choose one of the six issues discussed in this chapter and list the sources where you could get more information about it. For your list, think of printed materials, electronic materials, and people. Be specific and include at least three different types of sources.
2. **Presenting Information.** Design a poster or public service ad for TV to inform people about where they can get information on one of the six issues.

24

Coming Up Next!
- A nation of many governments
- A government of the people
- A government of law

A Government of People

What is government? If you ask people, many will say that government is a mystery to them. They don't understand it. Some will define it by naming persons in government, like the president or governor. Others will mention government activities, like police and fire protection. Others, when they hear the word "government," will gripe about the taxes they have to pay. But putting one's finger on government itself is not so easy.

Some people think of government as a kind of machine with many impersonal moving parts and enormous power over us. For the great masses of European people in past centuries, it was natural to think of the governments of kings and queens as being all powerful. After all, European monarchs often claimed that they ruled by "divine right." That is, they said they received their authority from God. All the king's ministers, governors, sheriffs, and soldiers made sure the masses stayed in line. Quite correctly, our ancestors saw government as being a power over which they had no control.

Do these images of an all-powerful force fit American government? No, they do not now and have not for a very long time. Since the United States became an independent nation, the American people themselves have been the powerful force that governs our country.

Think about these events you read about in earlier chapters:

- In 1776, the Second Continental Congress adopted the Declaration of Independence which stated that if the people no longer approve of a government, they can do away with it.

- In 1795, outraged by the Yazoo Land Fraud, Georgia citizens chased corrupt legislators out of office.

- In 1920, responding to the national woman suffrage movement, state legislatures ratified the Nineteenth Amendment giving women the right to vote.

In each instance, the people changed the government to fit what they believed. If a government is shaped by what the people believe and what the people do, what does that tell us? It tells us that *government is the people themselves.* This idea, called **popular sovereignty**, is discussed in Chapter 8.

Need for Rules

Why do we have government? What human needs does it serve? To answer these questions, think back to some events in earlier chapters:

- In 1803, the General Assembly of Georgia devised a lottery system to distribute public land to persons who would settle and develop it.
- From 1935 to 1941, the Works Progress Administration (WPA) of the federal government gave jobs to almost 8 million unemployed Americans.
- In 1965, Pres. Lyndon Johnson ordered federal troops, FBI agents, and the national guard to protect civil rights marchers in Selma, Alabama, against violence.

Public meetings, such as this one, are a feature of democratic government. Attending them is a form of political participation. Here, a citizen tells government officials his views on a community problem.

Pedestrians and motorists meet at an intersection. In what ways does government try to manage conflict in this situation?

What did government do in these examples? It encouraged economic development. It helped men and women who were out of work. It protected the public against violence. We have government for all these reasons and more. But above all, we have government because we have to live with other human beings.

The 269 million people who make up America's huge society share many common needs, interests, and goals. But they do not have exactly the same needs or interests. Even people who live together in a small community won't all have the same goals. Some conflict is sure to arise.

Government is a **social institution**. A social institution is a group of people organized to manage conflict and establish common behaviors. It does this by having rules about the way individuals and groups relate to one another.

Every day, we live by rules. Some rules tell us the duties we have. To feed the dog every morning is an example of a family duty you might have. Other rules tell us our rights. As a church member you may have the right to participate in certain church activities. Some rules regulate behavior, such as a school rule prohibiting weapons. Enforcing rules is necessary so people can get along together—fairly and safely.

We are all members of a society. Society's rules generally apply to everyone. These rules may be divided into two categories. In one category are *informal rules*. These are self-enforced or enforced by social pressure from other people. For example, we learn a sense of fair play and respect for others. So, we learn that we should not cut in line to buy movie tickets or get on a bus. Our own conscience or other people's reactions help enforce the rule.

In the second category are *formal rules*. These rules are enforced by our governments and we call them *laws*. Examples are laws prohibiting the sale of cigarettes to minors, or requiring students to stay in school until age 16. Or, another rule by law is that children have access to free public schooling. These are *legal* rights or requirements that can be enforced by government. Also enforced by government are duties, such as paying taxes that pay for the fire department and for building and operating schools. Paying taxes is a *legal* duty or obligation.

What is **government**? It is a social institution created to hold society together. It is composed of people who serve everyone. Other social institutions—like the family, church, and school—are responsible for informal controls on social relations. Government is the social institution responsible for formal controls. It makes and enforces the rules that people must obey. ▶

▶ **Locating the Main Ideas**

1. Define: popular sovereignty, social institution, government
2. How did the idea of government as a power *over* the people develop?
3. Where does the power come from in U.S. government?
4. Why is it necessary to have government?
5. How are informal rules enforced? How are formal rules enforced?

A Nation of Many Governments

Commonly we speak of *the* government, as if there were only one. Actually, that is not the case in the United States. We are a nation of many governments.

Suppose you are a resident of Decatur, Georgia. That means you would be living within the **jurisdiction** (area of legal control or authority) of at least seven government areas:

United States of America
State of Georgia
DeKalb County
City of Decatur
City of Decatur School System
Metropolitan Atlanta Rapid Transit Authority (MARTA)
Fulton-DeKalb Hospital Authority

To live in and pay taxes to so many governments is not unusual. Most citizens of the United States live within four or more governments. In 1992, the United States had 85,006 governments.

All these governments, except school districts and special districts, are general-purpose governments. That is, they provide many services to the people. School districts and special districts (such as MARTA) are special-purpose governments. Usually, they are created to provide a single or special service, such as education or transportation.

These governments are all parts of one system of government. The system is based on two powerful ideas of a good government. Ours is a government *of the people* and a government of *law*.

U.S. Governments in 1992	
Type of Government	**Number of Governments**
National Government	1
State Governments	50
Local Governments	84,955
Counties	3,043
Municipalities (Cities)	19,279
Townships	16,656
School Districts	14,422
Special Districts	31,555

I am a CITIZEN of-

City
County
State
Nation

A Government of the People

We are proud to say that we have a government "of the people, by the people, and for the people." Pres. Abraham Lincoln spoke these words in the Gettysburg Address in 1863, but the idea is much older. You can find the idea in Georgia's 1776 Rules and Regulations (see page 108) where it says that all power "originates" from the people.

Of the people means that all government authority comes from the people themselves. Authority does not come from a king's claim of "divine right" to rule. It does not come from an army's conquest of the land. It means that people have given their consent to the governing officials to run the government.

By the people refers to the means by which the people control their government. Generally, our government operates according to the choices made by a majority of the people. Who do the majority of citizens want to run the government? What does the majority want the government to do? These questions are decided by voting. Also, political parties, campaign activities, and public opinion polls let elected representatives know what the majority of the people want.

For the people announces that the government exists only for the good of *all* the people. It is not intended to serve one person, a privileged class of individuals, or one religion. We can judge if a government is for the people by looking at the *policies* it pursues. A policy consists of a goal and the plan or strategy to reach the goal. These policies should serve all Americans.

Georgia senators vote by hand on many questions.

Citizens and Citizenship

The phrase "as a citizen of" is frequently found in letters written to the newspaper about some event in government. Why? What is the letter-writer's reason for saying "as a citizen"? The writer is announcing to all who read the letter, "You should listen to me because of who I am—a citizen."

What is a **citizen**? A citizen is any member of a political system—be it a nation, state, county, or city—in which the people have a voice in their government. The status of being a citizen is called **citizenship**. Not everyone who lives in the United States is a citizen.

The U.S. Constitution provides that a person may acquire citizenship in two ways: by birth and by **naturalization**.

By birth. Children born in the United States are citizens. Children born abroad of parents who are U.S. citizens are also citizens.

By naturalization. Persons who are not U.S. citizens by birth and who seek to become citizens must follow a legal process called naturalization. They must meet certain requirements, including lawful entry to the United States and good moral character. They must also learn the principles of American government.

Just as there are several levels of government in America, there are several levels of citizenship. Citizens of the United States are also citizens of the state and county in which they reside. That means a family from Iowa who become residents of Cobb County, Georgia, become citizens of Georgia and Cobb County. If they live in a city, they also become citizens of that city.

Does having citizenship make a difference in a person's life? It can make a big difference. All residents—whether they are citizens or not—must obey the laws of the United States and the state in which they live. They must pay federal and state taxes. But only citizens have a say in deciding what those laws and taxes will be. Only citizens have the right to vote in federal, state, and local elections. Only citizens of Georgia can be elected to public office in this state. Only citizens can serve on juries.

To the editor:

As a citizen of Cobb County and the State of Georgia, I would like to express my disapproval of the recent government decision to

To many Americans, citizenship means much more than the *right* to do something. It means actually doing it. It can mean, for example, writing a letter to the editor.

Citizens take part in the affairs of their nation, state, city, or county in many ways. Here are a few ways to participate:

- learn about candidates and issues
- vote in every election
- work with others to solve some community problems
- serve on school boards and city councils
- join a local volunteer fire department
- gather signatures on petitions to express public opinion
- contribute money to political parties or candidates
- contact state officials about some issue
- join a political club or organized interest group
- volunteer for military duty in wartime
- respond when called for jury duty
- report information about crime to the police

Most of the time, Americans meet their citizenship obligations *voluntarily*. That's what makes self-government work.

Majority and Plurality

In democratic decision making, a **majority** vote is generally used to determine the outcome.

A majority is any number greater than one-half of the total vote. Ordinarily, a *simple majority*, consisting of 50 percent plus one of the total persons participating in the vote, is used to decide the outcome. In special cases, however, a government may require a specific majority—such as two-thirds of the total persons voting.

Even though allowing the majority to make political decisions is an important principle, there are exceptions to it. When there are more than two candidates, some states allow the one who gets more votes than anyone else to be the winner, even if it is not a majority. This is called a **plurality**. Georgia is one of these states.

The other exception is that in a democracy there are certain rights of the minority that the majority cannot take away. For example, the majority cannot vote to prohibit criticism by the minority. Thus we have majority rule but minority rights.

Government *of, by,* and *for* the people is a **democracy** or democratic government. The word democracy is from the ancient Greek words *demos*, meaning the people, and *kratia*, meaning authority.

A Government of Law

In the United States we have a "government of law." What does this mean? It means that the government's authority is limited by laws. The limits are set forth in the U.S. and state constitutions and laws passed by legislative bodies. This idea is sometimes expressed by the terms "limited government" and "due process of law."

In our government, officials can only do what the law specifically says they can do. They may not do whatever they please. Even if the majority of the people back them, and even if they are the highest officials in government, they may not operate outside the law. Also, the people we choose to make the laws must obey them just like everyone else.

So, we have a government that is both "of the people" and "of law." The powers that it has come from the people, but those powers are limited by law. How can we know the powers and limits of our government? The answers are found in its constitution. The next chapter tells you more about the written constitutional basis for national and state government in America. ◀

▶ Locating the Main Ideas

1. Define: jurisdiction, democracy, citizen, citizenship, naturalization, majority, plurality

2. What are two ways people may acquire citizenship in the United States?

3. Explain how a general-purpose government is different from a special-purpose government.

CHAPTER ACTIVITIES

Reviewing the Main Ideas

1. Why is it not correct to think of American government as an institution that is *over* the people?

2. Give an example of a social institution and explain how it manages conflict and helps establish common behaviors.

3. Why do we have rules in our society?

4. What is the difference between legal rights and legal obligations?

5. Explain why government is created, what it is composed of, and what its purpose is.

6. What political institutions exist that allow us to have a "government by the people"?

7. What is one way to tell if a government exists for the good of the people?

8. Explain how the Greek words *demos* and *kratia* describe the type of government in the United States.

9. How can we have a government both of the people and of law?

10. Explain the meaning of "limited government."

Give It Some Extra Thought

1. **Understanding Civic Participation.** How do elections allow people to change their government to fit their own attitudes and values?

2. **Applying Democratic Principles.** Why do democracies use majority rule as a way of deciding issues and making policies? How does majority rule differ from rule by a king or queen?

Sharpen Your Skills

1. **Identifying Citizen Participation.** For each level of government—national, state, and local—identify an activity that allows the citizen to participate in that particular level. (Some examples are listed in "Citizens and Citizenship," page 367.) Of the activities you chose, can any be done at more than one level of government? If so, explain.

2. **Put It in Your Own Words.** Explain what the phrase "of the people, by the people, and for the people" means.

3. **Knowing How Many.** The Georgia Senate has 56 members and the Georgia House of Representatives has 180 members. For each body, calculate the number for a simple majority and for a two-thirds majority.

Going Further

1. **Working Democratically with Others.** Divide the class into small groups for the purpose of choosing new school colors. Each group should choose two colors and designate a group representative to make a presentation (not longer than one minute) to the class. Presenters should try to convince other class members to vote for their colors. At the end of the presentations, the floor can be opened for discussion before voting. Decide by majority vote what the new school colors will be.

   After the class has reached a decision, answer the following questions: (a) Did everyone have an opportunity to participate? (b) How was disagreement about the choice resolved? (c) Did the process result in a decision by the majority? (d) Was the process democratic?

25

Coming Up Next!
- The Constitution of the United States
- The changing shape of federalism
- The Constitution of the State of Georgia

Constitutional Government

The government of the United States of America is based on a written **constitution**. The U.S. Constitution states the basic principles of our government. It spells out the powers of government, the limits of those powers, and how the government is to be organized. It guarantees certain rights to the people. The 50 states also have constitutions, but the U.S. Constitution is the highest law—"the supreme law of the land."

The Constitution of the United States

The U.S. Constitution was not the first written law of the country. After the American Revolution, the new nation of 13 states was first governed under the Articles of Confederation. This document established a central government that had little power and could not deal with national problems. States were taxing goods from other states. Some printed their own money. Some made agreements with foreign governments. Public debt went unpaid. Serious conflicts occurred in several states. By the mid 1780s, the nation was in political and economic turmoil. Many leaders believed that the central government should have more power.

A convention of delegates from every state except Rhode Island met in Philadelphia from May until September, 1787, to strengthen the Articles of Confederation. However, they soon decided to draft a new constitution. This is how it began:

> We the People of the United States, in Order to form a more perfect Union, establish Justice, insure domestic Tranquility [peace], provide for the common defence, promote the general Welfare, and secure the Blessings of Liberty to ourselves and our Poster-

ity [future generations], do ordain and establish this Constitution for the United States of America.

The "Preamble," as this introduction is called, assures the public that the new constitution bases the authority of government on the support of the people—the principle known as popular sovereignty. The Preamble also makes it clear that the framers wanted to give the nation a good chance to survive.

In shaping the new government, the framers faced two complex problems. First, they had to construct a national government strong enough to rule and hold the country together. They had to do this and still protect the liberties the people had won in the Revolutionary War. Second, they had to persuade the states to give up some powers they had under the Articles of Confederation. This action would strengthen the national government so it could better deal with national problems. At the same time, they had to respect the special interests of each state to control its internal affairs.

With these concerns in mind, the framers of the Constitution laid out a plan of shared powers. Power would be shared in two ways. First, a national government would be divided into three branches —an arrangement commonly called **separation of powers**. Each branch would have various checks on the other branches to balance power. Second, the national government would share power with

Scene at the Signing of the Constitution of the United States, a painting by Howard Chandler Christy. In September 1787, four months after they began work, delegates to the Constitutional Convention sign the new constitution. George Washington stands at the front.

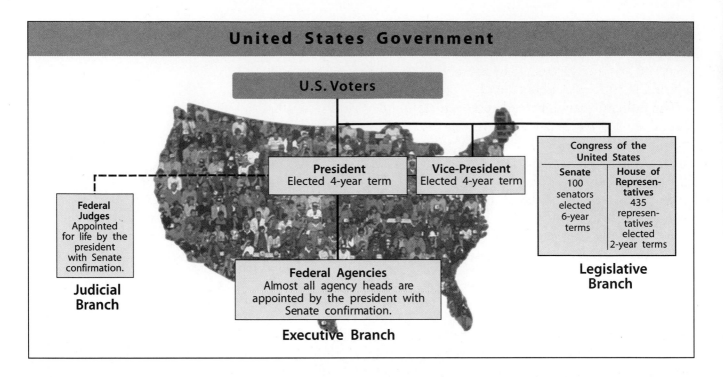

United States Government

U.S. Voters

President
Elected 4-year term

Vice-President
Elected 4-year term

Congress of the United States

Senate	House of Representatives
100 senators elected 6-year terms	435 representatives elected 2-year terms

Legislative Branch

Federal Judges
Appointed for life by the president with Senate confirmation.

Judicial Branch

Federal Agencies
Almost all agency heads are appointed by the president with Senate confirmation.

Executive Branch

state governments, though in certain areas the national government would be supreme. This arrangement is called **federalism**. These arrangements became two of the most important principles of the new American government.

Separation of Powers

The framers wanted to strengthen the national government but prevent the concentration of power in the hands of any individual or small group. To do this, they designed a government with three main divisions or "branches." This principle, the separation of powers, provided for

1. a legislative branch to make laws;
2. an executive branch to carry out, enforce, and administer laws; and
3. a judicial branch to interpret the law and make judgments in legal disputes.

The legislative branch is the U.S. Congress, which is **bicameral** (with two houses). This lawmaking branch consists of members of the U.S. Senate and the U.S. House of Representatives and their staffs. Senators serve six-year terms. Two senators are elected from each state, for a total of 100. There are 435 U.S. Representatives. They serve two-year terms and are elected from districts in each state. The number of districts is based on the state's population, but each state is guaranteed at least one representative.

The executive branch is headed by the president. The president and the vice-president are the only elected officials in the executive branch. It is the largest branch because it takes many thousands of employees to carry out the laws. The executive branch includes the army, navy, and air force and numerous departments organized to carry out specific services. The president has the power to appoint top officials for each department.

The judicial branch is made up of the Supreme Court and other federal courts. They review and interpret U.S. laws in cases that are brought before them. Voters do not elect any officials in the judicial branch of the national government.

State governments today have a three-branch organization similar to the national government. Titles are different, however. The state chief executive is called "governor." The state legislature is not called "Congress" but is the "assembly," "general assembly," or "state legislature." The state judicial branch is often called the "state court system."

Checks and Balances

The powers of each of the three branches are not completely and neatly separated from one another. Through a system called **checks and balances**, each branch can curb the powers of the other two branches. The power of one branch to check another prevents any single branch from taking full control. Because of this relationship, the three branches must work together to make the government function effectively.

The presidential power to **veto** (refuse to approve) a bill passed by Congress is one example of a check. Congress, in turn, has the power to override a veto by a two-thirds vote. The U.S. Supreme Court has the power to overturn a law passed by Congress and approved by the president if it determines the law is unconstitutional.

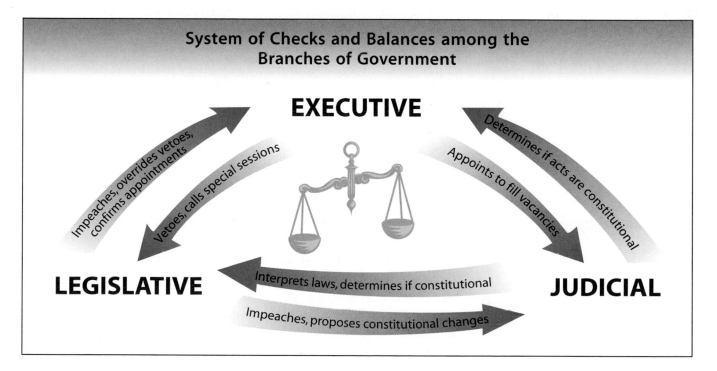

System of Checks and Balances among the Branches of Government

EXECUTIVE

Impeaches, overrides vetoes, confirms appointments

Vetoes, calls special sessions

Appoints to fill vacancies

Determines if acts are constitutional

LEGISLATIVE

Interprets laws, determines if constitutional

Impeaches, proposes constitutional changes

JUDICIAL

▶ **Locating the Main Ideas**

1. Define: constitution, separation of powers, federalism, bicameral, checks and balances, veto

2. What was the main weakness of the central government under the Articles of Confederation?

3. How were the framers of the Constitution able to keep governmental power from being concentrated in the hands of a few powerful people?

4. Give an example of how one branch of government can check the power of another branch of government.

By checking power with power, the framers aimed to achieve a balance among all three branches of the national government. Likewise, authors of state constitutions sought a balance among the branches of state governments. This system of sharing power is found not only within the national government but also within the state governments. The result is that each branch can get involved in activities that are the primary responsibilities of another branch. ◀

Federalism

Remember that the framers of the Constitution faced a difficult problem. They wanted to make the national government stronger, but they were committed to assuring that the states would retain certain powers. Their solution was to devise a federal system that distributes power between the national government and the states, with the national government supreme in matters of national interest. In matters of concern to both national and state government, they share power. In some matters, the states are free to govern without national interference.

The United States was the first government to have divided powers in a dual (double) federal-state system. Federalism was a new idea in 1787—very different from systems of other nations at that time. Most nations then had unitary (single) governments with power concentrated in the central government. Local governments, such as counties, were arms of the national government in those countries. But in the United States, local governments became arms of the state. States were allowed to develop many laws based on local culture and local traditions.

For citizens of the United States, federalism means that they live as citizens of two governments at the same time. Authority over certain matters (coining money, for example) is given to the national government. Authority over other matters (such as child custody) is reserved for the states. Other powers belong to both levels of government. Both can impose taxes on citizens. Both can enforce penalties on citizens who don't obey the law. In contrast, under unitary governments citizens live under the authority of only one central government.

Distribution of Power

Both the national and state governments have lawmaking powers under the U.S. Constitution, but neither has unlimited powers. Rather, the Constitution distributes some powers solely to the national government. These include authority to issue coins and paper money, declare war, set up a post office, and establish rules for citizenship. The national government also has the power to regulate business between states, make treaties with other nations, and maintain an army and navy.

U.S. Capitol.

In addition to specific grants of power, the Constitution also says Congress has the power "to make all Laws which shall be necessary and proper for carrying into Execution the foregoing Powers, and all other Powers vested by this Constitution in the Government of the United States...." This statement is sometimes called the "necessary and proper" clause. It is also known

Today, most bridges and highways are built with a combination of state and federal funds.

as the "elastic" clause because it allows Congress to stretch its powers and to make laws on subjects not actually listed in the Constitution.

The U.S. Constitution prohibits states from doing some things, such as printing money, but it does not spell out what they can do. When it was sent around to the 13 states for ratification (approval), there were demands for some **amendments** (additions or changes). These demands resulted in 10 amendments, popularly known as the **Bill of Rights**. One of these amendments, the 10th, reads:

> The powers not delegated to the United States by the Constitution, nor prohibited by it to the States, are reserved to the States respectively, or to the people.

This statement means that the states can make and enforce laws on subjects not mentioned in the Constitution.

Here are some of the things states do under their "reserved" powers: create local governments, regulate marriage and divorce, operate public schools and colleges, license occupations and businesses, conduct elections, regulate political parties, protect persons and property, and regulate traffic on public roads.

In some areas, the national government and the state governments exercise power concurrently (at the same time). These include the power to **levy** (set) and collect taxes, establish courts, regulate public utilities, take property for public use, build highways, and define crimes.

Police Power

The general reserved power under which states protect the public, consumers, or the environment is sometimes referred to as its **police power**. A state government may pass laws to protect public health, morals, safety, or welfare, as long as such laws do not violate U.S. or state constitutions.

▶ **Locating the Main Ideas**

1. Define: amendment, Bill of Rights, levy, police power
2. Identify: necessary and proper clause
3. Describe how powers are distributed between the national and state governments under federalism.
4. Why would a driver who moves from Tennessee to Georgia have to apply for a new driver's license?
5. List three guaranties made to states by the U.S. Constitution.

Guaranties to the States

In addition to distributing powers between the national government and the states, the U.S. Constitution makes several guaranties to the states. It also provides for relations between the states.

The Constitution guarantees that the national government will protect each state from foreign invasion and, if requested, from domestic violence (violence at home). Also, citizens of one state cannot be denied any of their rights by moving to another state.

The Constitution provides for the admission of new states to the Union. It also guarantees that no new state will be carved out of an existing state without the agreement of that state's legislature.

Perhaps the most important guarantee is the following: "The United States shall guarantee to every State in this Union a Republican Form of Government...." This statement means that no state can set up a monarchy or a dictatorship. The people are guaranteed representative government, a government of the people. Beyond this statement, however, the U.S. Constitution leaves it up to the people of each state to shape their state government.

Amending the Constitution

The Constitution includes a process for making changes to that document, but it is a difficult process. Over the past 200 years, it has been amended fewer than 30 times. Two-thirds of each house of Congress must propose an amendment (or call a convention to propose it). Three-fourths of the states must then ratify the proposed amendment for it to become effective. ◀

The Changing Shape of Federalism

In the 1990s, federalism is not quite what the framers of the Constitution planned in 1787. Over the past 200 years, technological, social, and economic changes and several big events—including the Civil War and the Depression of the 1930s—altered the relationship between the national government and the states.

Until the Civil War, Americans generally thought of their state and the nation as two distinct supreme authorities. They saw two equal partners acting separately in different areas of life. In those days, neither government had a very big influence on the daily life of most Americans. Generally, though, the state played a bigger role than the national government in everyday life.

As a result of the Civil War, the national and state governments were no longer equal powers. Instead, national supremacy was recognized. The war had settled the question of whether states could withdraw from the Union. They could not. The Fourteenth Amendment to the U.S. Constitution, added in 1868, prohibited the states from violating specific rights of citizens. The effect of this amendment was to make the national government the protector of personal rights against state action.

In the late nineteenth and early twentieth centuries, problems arose that forced government to take on new functions with respect to the economy. Railroads and other giant corporations that engaged in interstate commerce were driving competition out of business. Public health was threatened by unsanitary practices in food industries and by impure and dangerous drugs. Forests and other natural resources were being depleted. Georgia and other states tried to curb unfair and dangerous business practices but were generally not effective. Farmers, merchants, and other citizens clamored for national action.

Congress responded with laws that outlawed unfair business practices, regulated interstate commerce, and protected resources. By 1920, the national government had also established the Federal Reserve System (a nationwide banking system) and federal funding for vocational education and highway construction.

One of the biggest shifts of power within the federal system—away from the states and to the national government—came with the Great Depression that began in 1929. States were unable to deal with the crisis, and the national government stepped in. Its New Deal activities involved cooperation with state and local governments and grants of funds to those governments. Together, they provided jobs and welfare assistance; built roads, bridges, health clinics, and schools; and aided agriculture and manufacturing.

However, when the states accepted federal funds, they usually had to accept federal regulations that came with them. As a result of the New Deal, policies of the national government affected not

Techwood Homes in Atlanta was built in 1934–35 by a New Deal program to replace city slums with modern apartments for low-income tenants. The 600-unit complex, built just south of Georgia Tech, was the first public housing project in America.

▶ **Locating the Main Ideas**

1. Describe how Americans viewed the authority of their state and the nation before the Civil War.

2. In the late nineteenth and early twentieth centuries, why did the federal government rather than state governments need to solve problems in the economy?

3. How did the Great Depression trigger a shift of power in the federal system?

only the lives of individual citizens but also the operations of state government more than ever before.

The 1950s and 1960s brought another shift of power to the national government. This shift was linked to the civil rights movement, the Cold War with the Soviet Union, and urban problems. The civil rights movement had the greatest effect on the relationship between the national government and the states. Beginning with the U.S. Supreme Court ruling in *Brown v. Board of Education* in 1954, the national government stood more firmly on the side of civil rights. New federal laws, such as the Civil Rights Act of 1964 and the Voting Rights Act of 1965, increased federal authority over activities traditionally handled by states. These included schools, public accommodations, and voting. Massive federal aid to education came after the Soviet Union orbited the satellite, Sputnik, in 1957. If America was going to win the space race, it had to have more scientists and engineers. Finally, as more federal funds were applied to the problems of the nation's older cities and its poor people, federal influence on local government grew.

In recent years, Congress has shifted more responsibility back to the states. Still, in many cases, the activities of the national government and the states are closely intertwined. This means that when the states—and their local governments—act, they are often carrying out federal policies. ◀

The Constitution of the State of Georgia

When on January 2, 1788, Georgia became the fourth state to ratify the U.S. Constitution, it already had a state government operating under a constitution written in 1777. This constitution was rather short and sketchy and provided for a small government run completely by a one-house legislature.

The next year, Georgians wrote a new state constitution, one more in line with the new national constitution. The Constitution of 1789 was longer, more detailed, and provided for a larger state government and a bicameral legislature. It had true sharing of powers among the three branches.

Generally, state constitutions—including Georgia's—have been longer than the U.S. Constitution. They contained more details and placed more restrictions on government action. As social and economic conditions in the country changed, they became outdated, but the U.S. Constitution did not. Therefore, most state constitutions have had to be amended thousands of times and have been replaced in many states several times. Georgia, for example, has had 10 constitutions: those of 1777, 1789, 1798, 1861, 1865, 1868, 1877, 1945, 1976, and 1983.

Georgia's 1983 constitution is in many ways like the U.S. Constitution. It includes a preamble that says why the constitution was written:

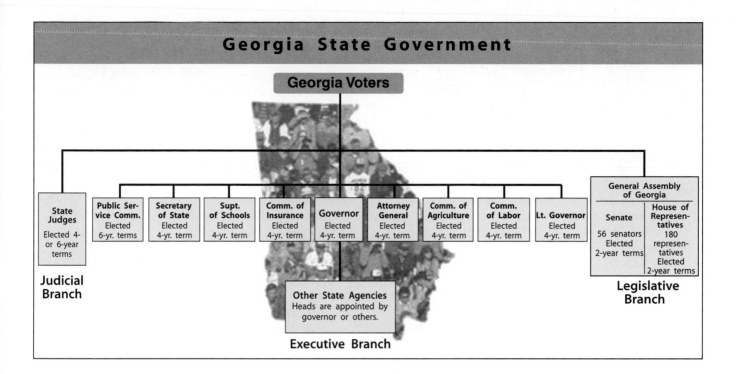

Georgia State Government

Georgia Voters

Judicial Branch

State Judges
Elected 4- or 6-year terms

Executive Branch

Public Service Comm.	Secretary of State	Supt. of Schools	Comm. of Insurance	Governor	Attorney General	Comm. of Agriculture	Comm. of Labor	Lt. Governor
Elected 6-yr. terms	Elected 4-yr. term	Elected 4-yr. term	Elected 4-yr. term	Elected 4-yr. term	Elected 4-yr. term	Elected 4-yr. term	Elected 4-yr. term	Elected 4-yr. term

Other State Agencies Heads are appointed by governor or others.

Legislative Branch

General Assembly of Georgia

Senate	House of Representatives
56 senators Elected 2-year terms	180 representatives Elected 2-year terms

To perpetuate the principles of free government, insure justice to all, preserve peace, promote the interest and happiness of the citizen and of the family, and transmit to posterity the enjoyment of liberty, we the people of Georgia, relying upon the protection and guidance of Almighty God, do ordain and establish this Constitution.

It has a Bill of Rights, articles that concern how state government will work, and a process for amending the constitution.

Georgia's constitution, however, is much longer than the national Constitution. It has more details on the powers of government and limits on power. It is more specific about the qualifications and duties of officials, and about taxation. Also, it includes the basic law on several matters that are not covered in the U.S. Constitution. These include city and county government, and public schools and colleges.

Three Branches of State Government

Georgia's government is organized into three branches. It is slightly different from the national government structure. It took the state governments many years to work out the power-sharing arrangement among their three branches. Today, the balance differs slightly from one state to the next.

Generally, state governors have less power *within* the executive branch than the president of the United States. The president does not have to share power with other elected executive officials. But many governors do. Also, governors may have less influence over the judicial branch than the president has. Most state judges are elected by the voters, but federal judges are appointed by the presi-

Bill of Rights

"No person shall be deprived of life, liberty, or property except by due process of law."

This statement is from the Bill of Rights in the Constitution of the State of Georgia. Many citizens are aware that the first 10 amendments to the U.S. Constitution are called the U.S. Bill of Rights. But did you know that every state constitution also has a bill of rights—a list of freedoms or liberties protected by law? In most cases, the rights listed in state constitutions are much like those set forth in the U.S. Constitution.

What is in the U.S. Bill of Rights? It spells out two kinds of rights that Americans in the late 1700s believed were their traditional rights: rights of individual liberty and rights of persons accused of crimes.

Rights of individual liberty include freedom of religion, speech, and the press; the right to assemble peaceably and to petition the government; and the right to keep and bear arms.

Rights of persons accused of crimes include the right to trial by jury and to a lawyer; protection against unreasonable searches and seizures; against self-incrimination; against deprivation of life, liberty, or property without due process of law; against excessive bail and fines; and against cruel and unusual punishments.

Originally, the U.S. Bill of Rights protected citizens only from actions of the national government. State bills of rights protected citizens from actions of their state governments. Then, in 1868, the Fourteenth Amendment to the U.S. Constitution extended the protection of the U.S. Bill of Rights to cover actions by the state governments.

Today, state constitutions guarantee all the rights listed in the U.S. Constitution. For example, they specify that no citizen will be deprived of life, liberty, or property without due process of law. Also, state constitutions may guarantee additional rights not mentioned in the U.S. Constitution. Some state constitutions, for example, guarantee a right to privacy, which is not specifically listed in the U.S. Constitution.

---

dent. On the other hand, many governors have relatively more power in their state legislatures than the president has in Congress.

A Third Level of Government

Although the Constitution establishes just two levels of government, within the states there is a third level—local governments. Local governments are created by the states and work as arms of the states, carrying out state functions. The authority they have comes from the state constitution and state laws. The state may also abolish local governments. In Georgia there are three types of local governments—counties, cities, and special districts.

Local governments are very important in the federal system of government because they directly serve the people. They carry out national and state law. They also enact and enforce their own laws, called **ordinances**, on traffic, local taxes, land use, and other community matters. However, local governments are not full partners with national and state government. Their power comes from and may be taken back by the state.

Because each level of government has lawmaking powers, conflict is possible. If there is a conflict, then the higher level of government prevails. ◀

▶ **Locating the Main Ideas**

1. Define: ordinance
2. In what ways is Georgia's constitution like the U.S. Constitution? How does it differ?
3. What two kinds of rights are guaranteed in the U.S. Bill of Rights?
4. What is the third level of government in the United States?

Reviewing the Main Ideas

1. What two ways of sharing power were devised by the framers of the U.S. Constitution?

2. Why is the executive branch of government the largest branch?

3. How are citizens protected by having governmental power distributed among three branches of government?

4. How did the delegates to the Constitutional Convention in 1787 solve the problem of how to create a strong national government without weakening the state governments?

5. What does the Tenth Amendment to the U.S. Constitution mean?

6. Give an example of state and national governments exercising concurrent powers.

7. In the U.S. Constitution, what is the meaning of the guarantee to every state of a republican form of government?

8. How did the Georgia Constitution of 1789 differ from the Georgia Constitution of 1777?

9. As a rule, how do state constitutions compare in length to the U.S. Constitution? What accounts for the difference?

10. What is the supreme law of the land?

Give It Some Extra Thought

1. **Giving Reasons.** Why should the authority to issue coins and paper money be restricted to the national government?

2. **Demonstrating Understanding.** How do state governments fit into the American system of federalism? How about local governments?

Sharpen Your Skills

1. **Analyze and Compare.** Make a chart of four columns with these headings: *Branch of Government, National, State, Comparison.* In the first column, write executive, legislative, judicial. Use the second and third columns to give the titles or names given to each branch. In the fourth column, compare the levels of government by writing either a similarity or a difference between the two.

2. **Make a Time Line.** Describe the changing shape of federalism in a time line by choosing at least one state or national event from each of the following time periods: 1787–1860, 1861–1917, 1918–1950, 1950–present. Put the date and the event on the time line and explain how the event affected federalism.

Going Further

1. **Reading a Newspaper or News Magazine.** Find an example of an action by government in a newspaper or news magazine. Identify which branch of government performed the action and at what level of government it occurred.

2. **Making National Connections.** Who are Georgia's two U.S. senators and how many terms have they served? Who is the U.S. representative from the congressional district in which you live?

3. **Doing Research.** Report on the amendments to the U.S. Constitution. Find out how many times the document has been amended and when the amendments were ratified. Briefly summarize each amendment. Find out if any amendments were proposed but not ratified.

26

Coming Up Next!

- Politics in a democracy
- Political organizations
- Election year

Citizens and Government

Our democracy is a government by the people. American citizens elect the president, vice-president, and members of Congress. Citizens of Georgia elect the Georgia governor and General Assembly as well as city and county officials. Every two years in November, more than one million Georgians and millions of other Americans cast their votes. They are choosing leaders and decision makers for local, state, and national communities. Voting is an important way in which Americans participate in democracy.

News reports often describe state and national election campaigns in much the same way that a horse race is announced. Public opinion polls project who is in the lead. Observers comment on the image and appeal of each candidate. Speculation about the winners and losers runs high. But in political campaigns, voters also need to know the interests and capabilities of the candidates and their views on public issues. Public officials who are elected will be making decisions that affect everyone.

Politics in a Democracy

Elections are just one part of politics in a democracy. **Politics** is the process of deciding about public issues. It is all of the public activity that revolves around two general questions:

1. Who will represent us in government?
2. What decisions or public **policies** will government representatives make?

Politics is a necessary part of democracy because people have differing ideas about what is important and what should be done about

it. All groups in our democracy have the freedom to express their political opinions. In politics, groups and individuals compete for the power to decide which actions government should take. Think about students in your class trying to make a decision about rules in the lunchroom. Most likely, there will be several different ideas about what the rules should be. To come to a decision, students would speak up for their views and campaign to convince others to be on their side. They might even have to compromise to get a majority vote and a final decision. These are activities of democratic politics.

In some ways, politics is like a public game. It has rules and players, winners and losers. It has goals and strategies for reaching those goals. The rules are the federal and state laws aimed at keeping the game fair. The players are all the people who care enough about their government to take part in it. Most of the players are average citizens who are part-time players. These people get involved because they care about certain public issues such as crime, roads, education, or health care. There are some full-time players who are professional politicians. Politics is their job. They may be political party officials, campaign directors, lobbyists, or people who have been elected to public office.

Participation in Politics

Americans may get involved in politics in many ways. Some join political parties and become active in local and state political organizations. Some participate by contributing money to a candidate or

At the state capitol, citizens express their views on a legislative issue. The constitutions of Georgia and the United States guarantee the people the right to assemble peaceably.

political organization. Others campaign for individuals or become candidates for public office themselves. Citizens join associations that are interested in specific public questions and work to influence certain outcomes. For example, desired outcomes might be improving public parks, strengthening drunk-driving laws, or setting higher standards for drinking water.

There are many ways in which people can have a say in politics, but the first step is for the citizen to become informed. Citizen political participation in a democratic society requires keeping up with what's happening in government. Newspapers, news magazines, and television news all help the people monitor policy arguments and decisions.

Many people get information and participate in politics from their homes. They learn about public problems through television and other news sources and then contact their elected representatives to voice their opinions. People who follow the news and political debates can form opinions about a proposed government decision on what would be best for the state or nation. Armed with information, citizens of all ages can influence government policies.

Voting

An election is the most visible kind of political activity in our democratic government. Election activities include nominating candidates, developing party platforms and election strategies, raising campaign funds, getting the candidates and their position on the issues before the public, and urging voters to go to the polls. Finally, election day comes, and the votes are cast.

Voting is probably the most significant form of citizen participation. Voting is how we choose our representatives. Since these officials make government decisions for us, voting is an important

Registering to vote is easy, but many citizens neglect to do so. How is democracy weakened when many citizens fail to vote?

At their college campus, Georgia students register to vote. In 1943, Georgia was the first state to allow persons as young as 18 to vote.

way to influence government. Voting rights are protected by both state and federal laws. Every U.S. citizen who is at least 18 years old has the right to vote freely and in secret. Each is entitled to have his or her vote counted the same as every other citizen's vote.

When voters elect their political representatives they are participating in the American form of democracy, *representative democracy*. This means they elect officials to make policy decisions for them. This is different from *direct democracy* where people themselves—not elected representatives—make policy decisions.

The Election Process

Under the U.S. Constitution, each state is responsible for holding elections. In Georgia, elections are conducted by the government according to two sets of laws. The Georgia Election Code is for federal, state, and county elections. The Georgia Municipal Election Code is for city elections.

State and local election officials prepare a ballot that lists the names of candidates for office. On election day, qualified citizens go to designated voting places, or **polls**, in firehouses, courthouses, and schools to vote in the privacy of a voting booth. Some counties use voting machines, some use a vote recorder, and others use paper ballots. In the evening after the polls close, local elections officers count the votes. They send the totals to Georgia's secretary of state, who serves as the chief elections officer for the state. The state totals are then compiled and the official results are sent out immediately on the Internet and to newspapers and radio and television stations.

How Many Elected Officials Are There?

In 1992, there were 511,039 elected officials in the United States, with 6,556 in Georgia. Of this total, 542 held federal offices and 18,828 state offices. The remainder—491,669—were elected to local government offices.

Elected Officials

The top officials of each level of government—national, state, and local—are elected. These elected officials appoint and oversee the work of additional people who work in government.

For what offices may Georgia citizens vote? In the national government, they participate with other Americans in electing the president and vice-president. To represent the people of Georgia in the U.S. Congress, they vote for 2 U.S. senators and 11 U.S. representatives.

The greatest number of races in which a citizen may vote is at the state level. For some state offices, such as the governor, candidates run statewide. All Georgia voters may participate in these elections. For other state offices, such as state representative, candidates run within a district. Only the voters living within the district may participate in these elections. Here are the state-level elective offices in Georgia:

> **Legislative Branch: elected by district**
> State Senator
> State Representative
>
> **Executive Branch: elected statewide**
> Governor
> Lieutenant Governor
> Secretary of State
> Attorney General
> State School Superintendent
> Commissioner of Insurance
> Commissioner of Agriculture
> Commissioner of Labor
> Public Service Commissioner (5 positions)
>
> **Judicial Branch: elected statewide or by district**
> Supreme Court Justice (7 positions, statewide)
> Appeals Court Judge (10 positions, statewide)
> Superior Court Judge (district)
> District Attorney (district)

At the local level, voters elect a sheriff, judge of the probate court, clerk of the superior court, and other local officials. The number varies from place to place. ◄

Voting Opportunities

The average citizen has many opportunities to vote. In addition to the **general election** for national, state, and county offices held on the Tuesday after the first Monday every November in even-numbered years, there are special elections and primaries.

Special elections may be held almost any time. They are used to fill elective positions that become vacant when an officeholder

▶ **Locating the Main Ideas**

1. Define: politics, policy, polls
2. Why are politics necessary in our democracy?
3. List three ways citizens can participate in politics.
4. What is the difference between a representative democracy and a direct democracy?
5. For which national offices can Georgia citizens vote?

(called an **incumbent**) resigns or dies. A special election called a **recall** is sometimes held to remove a person from office before the end of his or her term. If the person is removed, another special election may be held to fill the vacant position.

Another type of election is called a **primary**. In the primary, voters **nominate** (name) party candidates to run in the November general election.

Besides voting for persons to fill government offices, citizens may vote on questions. A vote on a question, at either the general election or a special election, is called a **referendum**. In a referendum, the people make a decision directly rather than through their representatives.

Voters are regularly called on to approve constitutional amendments. They also vote on the issuing of local government bonds to raise money for constructing public projects. To be adopted, amendments to the Georgia constitution have to be approved by a majority of those voting in the general election. Similarly, in special "bond" elections, voters decide whether local governments should borrow money for building such projects as a stadium, civic center, or new high school. ▶

BALLOT
STATE OF GEORGIA
HENRY COUNTY
GENERAL ELECTION

November 5, 1996

―――――――――――――――――――――――――――――――――― ELECTION DISTRICT

If you desire to vote YES for a proposed constitutional amendment, place a cross (X) or check (✔) mark in the square beside the word YES. If you desire to vote NO for a proposed constitutional amendment place a cross (X) or check (✔) mark in the square beside the word NO.

☐ YES Shall the Constitution be amended so as to authorize the boards of education of county school districts and independent school districts to impose, levy, and col-

☐ NO lect a 1 percent sales and use tax for certain educational purposes subject to approval in a local referendum?

This constitutional amendment was on the general election ballot in every county of the state. In this case, a majority of voters statewide voted "yes."

Political Organizations

Politics is played not only by individuals, but also by organizations. Many citizens recognize that they can have more influence on government through a political organization than on their own. There are two general types of political organizations: interest groups and political parties.

Interest Groups

An **interest group** is a group of people or organizations who share a special interest and attempt to satisfy that interest through politics. Their special interest may be higher wages for police, lower property taxes on forest land, or opposition to building a hazardous waste facility. Or, it may be better housing for the poor, less regulation of business, or increased pension checks. Hundreds of interest groups try to influence specific government policy. They include such groups as retired workers, textile manufacturers, labor unions, doctors, government employees, real estate developers, tobacco growers, churches, and insurance agents.

By joining with people who have the same interests, members of interest groups can have more influence on elections and policy making than they could as individuals. Interest groups advertise and contribute money to candidates. They organize their members, or

▶ **Locating the Main Ideas**

1. Define: general election, incumbent, recall, primary, nominate, referendum

2. In addition to electing politicians, what other decisions do voters make?

What Is a Lobbyist?

Persons who contact lawmakers in an attempt to influence legislation on behalf of others are called "lobbyists." They got this name years ago because of their habit of gathering in the lobbies of hotels where legislators were staying. Today, they still contact legislators in lobbies or halls of state capitols. Georgia law requires lobbyists to register each year with the secretary of state. Currently, more than 1,000 lobbyists register during a session of the General Assembly.

hire professional agents, to personally contact policy-making officials.

Political Parties

The goals of a political party are much broader than those of a special interest group. **Political parties** are political organizations that seek to elect their members to public office in order to organize government and determine public policy. A political party includes a number of interest groups.

To control government, the party has to win elections. To win elections, it has to appeal to a majority of voters. Therefore, unlike the special interest group, a political party attempts to bring together people with many interests. Party members may agree on only a few major issues, such as spending on welfare and regulating business.

While parties sometimes take sides on specific issues and work to get specific laws passed, they play their biggest role in elections. Political parties nominate candidates to run for election to local, state, and national offices. Then, they work to get their candidates elected.

The United States has a two-party system. The Democratic party and the Republican party are the only major national parties. Since the Civil War, only the candidates of these two political parties have been elected president of the United States. Only a few candidates from third, or minor, parties have been elected to other top offices.

The two major parties operate on the local and state levels in every state as well as on the national level. Because the parties' role in elections is so important to having government by the people, their operations are regulated by state and federal laws. ▶

Election Year

The process of electing persons to office begins long before that November day on which the general election is held. The process generally involves the two-party system, with candidates identified by political party, or **partisan**, label. Exceptions include election to certain judicial offices such as judges of the superior court and court of appeals, and state supreme court justices. Candidates for these offices, as well as some local government offices, run in **nonpartisan** elections—that is, without a party label.

Primaries

During the late spring in election years, campaigning begins for the primary elections, which are held in July and August. A primary election gives voters a chance to participate in nominating the parties' candidates who will compete in the November general election.*

A primary is a party's election to choose its candidates for a coming election. In the Democratic primary, Democrats run against each other. Democratic voters choose one person for each contest in the general election. Meanwhile, in the Republican primary, Republican voters choose their candidates.

Georgia's primaries are "open" primaries. This means that both the Democratic and Republican primaries are open to any registered voter. One does not have to be a member of a party organization to vote in a primary.

However, if a voter decides to vote, let's say, in the Republican primary in a certain year, that voter cannot also vote in the Democratic primary. Also, if no candidate wins a majority vote in the primary and a *runoff* is necessary, the voter has to stick with the same party. (A voter can switch parties from year to year.)

What if no one runs for a certain office in the primary of one of the parties? The person nominated in the other party's primary would be unopposed for that office in the general election. He or she would win automatically.

---

*Every four years, most states, including Georgia, also hold a separate presidential preference primary.

▶ **Locating the Main Ideas**

1. Define: interest group, political party
2. Why would a person join an interest group?
3. How did lobbyists get their name?
4. What are the two major political parties in the United States and how are they involved in elections?

To use the voting machine, voters usually operate a key or handle. However, a voter may choose to vote for a person whose name does not appear on the machine by writing in the name.

Other Methods of Nominating

A party may nominate its candidates in other ways. In the past, candidates were often chosen at state conventions or at a **caucus** (meeting of party leaders). Today, the primary is the method most often used.

A candidate may also use a **petition** to get on the general election ballot. If the candidate seeks an office voted upon statewide, the petition must be signed by a number of voters equal to 1 percent of the total number of voters eligible to vote in the last election for the office the candidate is seeking. For other offices, the number is 5 percent. Generally, the petition method is used by an **independent**, a person who is not affiliated with a political party, to get his or her name on the ballot.

General Election

In the November general election, the names of all candidates for state offices, opposed or unopposed, nominated in primaries or by petition, appear on the ballot. Names of candidates for local and federal offices are also listed.

In the general election, there are no rules governing party voting. A voter may choose all Democrats or all Republicans, some from each party, and any independents on the ballot. The voter may even write in the names of persons not listed on the ballot.

In order to be elected, a candidate must receive at least 45 percent of the votes cast. If no one receives 45 percent, a runoff is held between the two candidates with the highest vote totals. Runoffs are scheduled three weeks after the election. A runoff is seldom needed, though, because usually only two candidates compete for each position in a general election.

The winners in the general election take office the following January. ◀

▶ **Locating the Main Ideas**

1. Define: partisan, nonpartisan, caucus, petition, independent
2. How is a party primary different from a general election?
3. How could a candidate be unopposed in the general election?
4. In a general election, are voters in one party allowed to vote for candidates of the other party or for independents?

CHAPTER ACTIVITIES

Reviewing the Main Ideas

1. What two questions are at the center of all the public activities of politics?
2. List three ways citizens can participate in politics.
3. Why must citizens have an understanding of the issues in order to influence public policy?
4. What does it mean to elect a person "statewide?"
5. How do general elections differ from special elections?
6. What is the difference between an interest group and a political party?
7. Why does a political party need to bring people with different interests together?
8. What is an "open" primary?
9. Why are runoff elections held?
10. Beginning with the preparation of a ballot by state and local election officials, what are the remaining steps for holding an election in Georgia?

Give It Some Extra Thought

1. **Examine the Role of State Government.** Why are there more elective races at the state level than at the federal level?
2. **Explaining Relationships.** Explain why a member of a political party could also be a member of an interest group. Why would a person be a member of several interest groups?
3. **Understanding Politics.** Who do you think would be more effective at playing politics—an individual or an organization? Tell why.

Sharpen Your Skills

1. **Participating in Civic Affairs.** Imagine the school board wants to eliminate some of your school holidays to try to improve national test scores in the school. Working in small groups review the school board's stated purpose and decide if you agree. If not, develop a plan to persuade board members to change their minds. Decide what steps to take to

have an effective plan. Present the group plan to the rest of the class and be prepared to explain it. As a class, decide which plan or combination of plans would be most effective.

2. **Making Local Connections.** Along with more than 6,000 elected officials in Georgia, there are many other people who work in government. Government is one of the largest employers in the state. Most likely, you know someone who works in government. If you do, write their job title or a brief job description, and the level of government where they work, on a card. Display the cards on the bulletin board to show how many people who work in government are known by members of the class.

Going Further

1. **Citizen Awareness.** What kinds of issues do you think each of the following interest groups would take a position on? Business Council of Georgia, Georgia Association of Educators, Fraternal Order of Police, Georgia Farm Bureau, Mothers Against Drunk Driving.
2. **Investigating.** What is the Australian ballot? Find out what it is, when it was first used in this country, and why it was used.
3. **Researching.** What third parties have put up candidates in past Georgia elections?

UNIT 10

1732	1752	1758	1777	1789	1824	1845	1868	1874	1915
Charter of the colony of Georgia granted by King George II	Georgia becomes a royal colony	Georgia divided into eight parishes	First state constitution ratified; parishes replaced by counties; legislature names first governor	New state constitution adopted creating a bicameral legislature called the General Assembly	Georgia Constitution amended to allow popular election of the governor by voters	General Assembly enacts legislation creating the Georgia Supreme Court	Atlanta becomes the capital of Georgia; office of state school commissioner established	Georgia Department of Agriculture, oldest in the nation, established	Counties with population of 60,000 or more given authority to establish juvenile courts

State and Local Government

1931	1943	1945	1953	1964	1971	1972	1973	1983	1992	1998
Milton and Campbell counties merged into Fulton County, leaving Georgia with 159 counties	Georgia first state to allow 18-year-olds to vote	Office of Lieutenant Governor created in new state constitution	Jury duty opened to women in Georgia	Ten congressional districts reapportioned by act of General Assembly	Columbus and Muscogee County join to become the first consolidated local government	State government reorganized by Gov. Jimmy Carter; constitution amended to allow state debt	Maynard Jackson, Jr., elected first black mayor of a large southern city	New constitution for Georgia goes into effect	First African American woman from Georgia elected to Congress	Georgia sales tax on groceries completely eliminated

27

Coming Up Next!

- Representation in the Georgia legislature
- Organization
- The lawmaking process

State Government— The Legislature

All activities of state government are based on laws. Before a state hospital can treat a patient or a GBI agent can investigate a crime, there must first be a law to authorize such activities. Before a judge can conduct a trial or a highway crew can repair a bridge, there must first be a law. Also, laws must be passed to **appropriate** (set aside) public funds—money the state has received from taxes and other sources—to pay for the activities.

Where do these laws come from? Who decides exactly what the laws will say? Laws come from ideas. Anyone can have an idea for a new law. But, the task of turning the idea into a law belongs to persons elected to do the job.

All three branches of government share power and they all influence lawmaking. But the main responsibility for lawmaking belongs to the state legislature.

Representation in the Georgia Legislature

Our state legislature—officially known as the **General Assembly**— is an example of a representative body. So is a city council, a county commission, and the U.S. Congress. Representative bodies are composed of persons elected by the people to represent them. The people rule indirectly through their elected representatives.

The authority of Georgia's legislature to make laws is set forth in the state constitution: "The legislative power of the state shall be vested in a General Assembly which shall consist of a Senate and a House of Representatives." The state constitution leaves it up to the General Assembly to set the size of the legislature, but requires that there be "not fewer than 180 representatives" and "not more than

56 senators." Lawmakers have set the size of the House at 180 members and the size of the Senate at 56 members.

Election Districts

Each of the 236 members of the legislature is elected by voters in a district. Why? Early in the history of the United States, Americans adopted the practice of electing representatives from geographic districts. The thinking behind this practice was that people living in different communities could have different interests which needed to be represented. For example, in the days of steamboats, the state spent tax money to remove obstructions to river traffic. Where you lived probably affected how you felt about the state doing this. If you lived along the Altamaha or the lower reaches of the Savannah or Chattahoochee rivers, your community would be served because rivers there would become navigable. However, if you lived in the mountains, your community would be affected much less, if at all, by improved navigation on these rivers.

The capitol dome in Atlanta.

Often, the interests of people in different parts of the state clashed over matters such as promoting and regulating business, or spending to improve transportation. Electing state legislators from districts proved useful not only for serving the different local interests people had but also for finding the common interest that all the people had. For example, farmers, merchants, and industrial workers alike had a common interest in fair treatment by banks and other businesses that lent money. Residents of all communities had a common interest in protection from crimes such as arson, burglary, and assault. When their legislators came together at the state capitol, those common interests were brought to light and laws were made that served those interests.

On the floor of the legislature. This is where all the influences of constituents, interest groups, and political parties come together in working out policies for the "common good." This is where representatives of the people make the laws.

Apportionment

State legislators represent people, not cities or counties. The people in each legislator's election district are called **constituents**. To ensure that all people are represented fairly, election districts of both houses of the legislature are redrawn every 10 years on the basis of equal population. In other words,

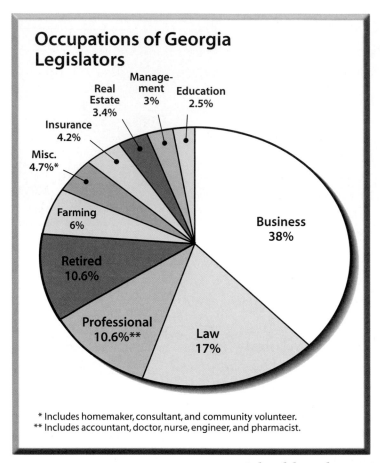

Occupations of Georgia Legislators

- Business 38%
- Law 17%
- Professional 10.6%**
- Retired 10.6%
- Farming 6%
- Misc. 4.7%*
- Insurance 4.2%
- Real Estate 3.4%
- Management 3%
- Education 2.5%

* Includes homemaker, consultant, and community volunteer.
** Includes accountant, doctor, nurse, engineer, and pharmacist.

each legislative seat (or position) in the House or Senate represents approximately the same number of people as any other House or Senate seat. It is based on the principle of "one person, one vote." This means that no matter where you live in the state, your vote counts no more, no less, than any other person's vote.

Since people move and populations change, the U.S. and Georgia constitutions require that boundaries of election districts be redrawn after every U.S. census. This redistricting—commonly called **reapportionment**—is to make sure that the size of their populations remains approximately equal. Generally, population changes over the past 50 years have resulted in more legislative districts in urban and suburban areas and fewer rural districts.

Membership

Who gets elected to the Georgia General Assembly? The legislator's job is not a full-time job, although many legislators end up working year-round. The work of the 236 legislators is concentrated in the 40 legislative days each year when they meet in Atlanta to make the laws. This part-time legislature was designed to allow ordinary citizens to serve in it. More and more, however, legislators are being called on to attend committee meetings, help constituents, and perform other legislative business year-round. Thus, time demands plus the relatively small salary—just over $10,000 each year—limits the types of people who can serve. ◀

Organization

Each year, the General Assembly meets for a 40-day session beginning the second Monday of January. Because of recesses, the actual length of the session can extend into April. The governor can call legislators back into special sessions to handle emergency situations.

For a group of 236 persons to get anything done, they have to be organized. There are two houses, and legislators of both are elected for two-year terms. After each election, each house of the General Assembly organizes itself for the coming two years. Leadership and the committee system are important in the organization process.

▶ **Locating the Main Ideas**

1. Define: appropriate, General Assembly, constituent, reapportionment

2. How do the people rule indirectly in American government?

3. Why are election districts redrawn every 10 years?

Leadership

Each house has leaders who organize the work of the members. The presiding officers hold the top two positions in the legislature. The Speaker of the House and the President of the Senate (an office filled by the lieutenant governor) preside over (or conduct) meetings of their houses. They also appoint members to other leadership positions. They decide which committee will consider a bill. Their actions often determine whether or not a law is passed. After the governor, the speaker and the lieutenant governor are the two most powerful offices in state government.

Following elections every two years, legislators organize into party caucuses. Each house has both a Democratic and a Republican caucus. These are set up to keep party members together on legislative issues. Each caucus chooses a party leader, a party whip (so called because this legislator's job is to "whip" party members into line), and other officers.

Administration floor leaders are legislators who help the governor participate in lawmaking. They introduce proposals for new laws that the governor favors and work to convince other legislators to make those proposals into law. Their role illustrates power-sharing between the executive and legislative branches.

The committee chairmen are especially powerful because most of the real work of lawmaking takes place in committees.

Leadership In the General Assembly	
Position	**How Filled**
Presiding Officers	
☆ Speaker of the House	a member elected by the House
☆ President of the Senate	lt. governor, designated by state constitution
Party Leaders	
☆ Majority Leader	a member elected by majority party caucus in each house
☆ Majority Whip	a member elected by majority party caucus in each house
☆ Minority Leader	a member elected by minority party caucus in each house
☆ Minority Whip	a member elected by minority party caucus in each house
Governor's Leaders	
☆ Administration Floor Leaders	a member in each house appointed by governor
Committees	
☆ Committee Chairmen	members appointed by presiding officer of each house

Committee System

Each year, the General Assembly responds to more than 1,000 proposals to **enact** (formally create), amend (change), or **repeal** (abolish) laws. How can it carefully study and decide on so many proposals in 40 days? The answer is the committee system. In each house, the work of considering bills is divided among committees of legislators. Then these committees recommend to all the members of the House or Senate whether or not to pass those bills.

Each house decides what kinds of committees it will have. Generally, committees are organized to work on bills dealing with specific subjects. For example, both houses have a committee on education to study bills dealing with the public schools. Other committees specialize in subjects such as agriculture, industry, transportation, natural resources, and criminal justice.

A legislator cannot be an expert on every subject, but he or she can become a specialist in several subjects. Each senator and representative serves on two or three committees. ▶

▶ **Locating the Main Ideas**

1. Define: enact, repeal
2. Who presides over the Georgia House? the Georgia Senate?
3. How do the governor's floor leaders contribute to power-sharing by two branches of state government?
4. What is the purpose of the committee system in the General Assembly?

State law regulates the games of the Georgia lottery, as well as the use of its proceeds.

Laws provide for the funding of education, the length of the school year, and mandatory school attendance.

The Lawmaking Process

The lawmaking process begins with an idea. Perhaps someone sees a problem—maybe drunk driving, water pollution, or high property taxes—and decides to solve it by passing a law. Most ideas for laws come not from legislators but from individual citizens and interest groups. Also, the governor and other executive branch officers, judges, and local governments may ask for new laws or changes in existing state laws. Sometimes the national government requires changes.

Subject Matter

Except for those subjects prohibited by the U.S. and Georgia constitutions, the General Assembly may enact laws on practically any subject. Generally, these laws fall into four subject categories.

1. *Laws which provide for state agencies and services.* Examples are laws which establish the state highway system, parks, hospitals, and colleges. Under such laws, social workers, state troopers, health inspectors, and other state employees provide services to the public.

2. *Laws which regulate conduct of individuals, groups, or businesses.* Examples are laws against drunk driving, burglary, and other criminal acts. Also, numerous laws regulate interest rates, advertising, and the practice of certain occupations.

3. *Laws which allow the state to raise and spend money.* Examples are laws which set up the 4 percent general sales tax and the state income tax. These laws allow the state to collect money from the people. Other laws tell how much the state can spend each year on transportation, education, health, welfare, conservation, and other activities.

4. *Laws which provide for local government.* Examples are laws that enable counties to collect property taxes, cities to provide water and sewerage services, and school districts to operate elementary and high schools. Local governments get their general power to act from the General Assembly.

Application

Who is affected by the laws? Laws passed by the General Assembly are either of *general* or of *local* application. General laws apply throughout the state of Georgia. For example, the law requiring a license to drive a car on public roads applies everywhere in the state. A local law, however, applies only to a specific city or county. An example is a law setting the number of members on the Oconee County Commission.

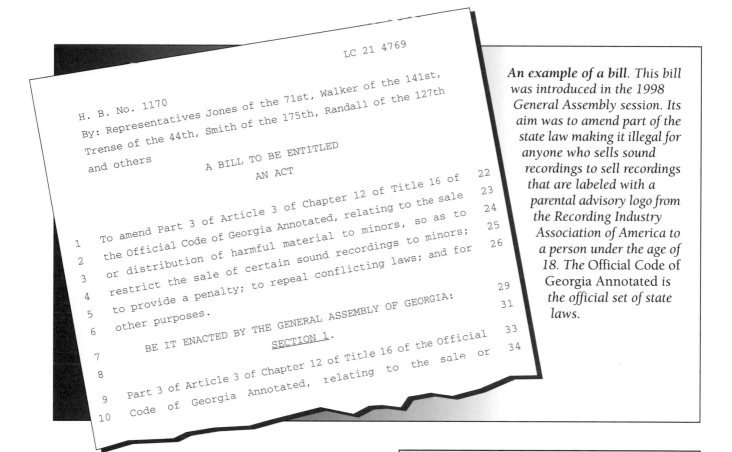

H. B. No. 1170
By: Representatives Jones of the 71st, Walker of the 141st,
Trense of the 44th, Smith of the 175th, Randall of the 127th
and others

A BILL TO BE ENTITLED
AN ACT

1   To amend Part 3 of Article 3 of Chapter 12 of Title 16 of   22
2   the Official Code of Georgia Annotated, relating to the sale   23
3   or distribution of harmful material to minors, so as to   24
4   restrict the sale of certain sound recordings to minors;   25
5   to provide a penalty; to repeal conflicting laws; and for   26
6   other purposes.

    BE IT ENACTED BY THE GENERAL ASSEMBLY OF GEORGIA: 29
                        SECTION 1.   31

7   Part 3 of Article 3 of Chapter 12 of Title 16 of the Official 33
8
9   Code of Georgia Annotated, relating to the sale or   34
10

An example of a bill. This bill was introduced in the 1998 General Assembly session. Its aim was to amend part of the state law making it illegal for anyone who sells sound recordings to sell recordings that are labeled with a parental advisory logo from the Recording Industry Association of America to a person under the age of 18. The Official Code of Georgia Annotated is the official set of state laws.

The Bill

The first step in the lawmaking process is to turn an idea into a *bill*. A bill is a written proposal to enact, amend, or repeal a law. Anyone may **draft** (or write) a bill. However, to be considered by the legislature, the bill must be written in a specific form. It must be introduced (formally presented to the legislature) by a legislator. By examining the bill's title (the formal summary), you can usually tell its purpose and subject.

In each 40-day session, more than 1,000 bills are introduced. Some of them will focus on important problems, and will be carefully thought out and well written. Some will not. It is just as important not to pass weak or unneeded bills as it is to pass strong and needed ones. That is why the General Assembly made the procedure for passing a bill very difficult.

The procedure by which a bill becomes a law is outlined in the chart "How a Bill Becomes a Law." It shows a bill originating in the House of Representatives, but bills may also originate in the Senate. However, bills to raise or spend money must originate in the House.

The State's Budget: An Example of Power-Sharing

The governor's power to veto a bill is an example of power-sharing by the legislative and executive branches. One bill in particular, the appropriations bill, clearly illustrates this power-sharing.

Each year, the General Assembly must pass an appropriations bill, sometimes called the "budget bill." It is a proposal to appropriate specific amounts of money for every program of state government.

Although it is introduced by a legislator, this bill is drafted by the governor's staff. The legislature can make changes in the governor's proposal, but if the governor does not approve of spending for specific items in the bill passed by the legislature, he can veto those items. This is called an **item veto**. The legislature, then, has the right to override that veto.

The governor's authority to draft the state's budget bill and exercise the item veto are examples of legislative power exercised by the executive branch.

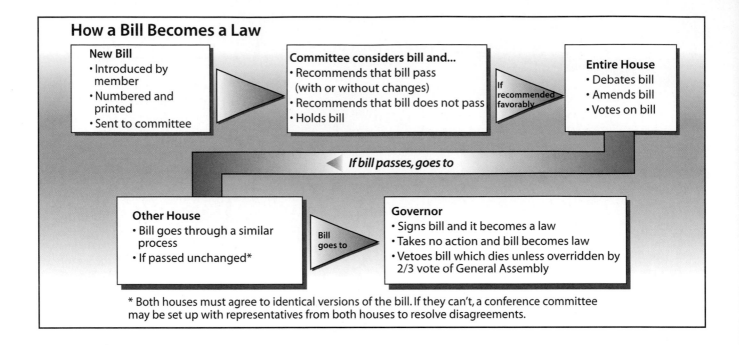

How a Bill Becomes a Law

New Bill
- Introduced by member
- Numbered and printed
- Sent to committee

Committee considers bill and...
- Recommends that bill pass (with or without changes)
- Recommends that bill does not pass
- Holds bill

If recommended favorably

Entire House
- Debates bill
- Amends bill
- Votes on bill

If bill passes, goes to

Other House
- Bill goes through a similar process
- If passed unchanged*

Bill goes to

Governor
- Signs bill and it becomes a law
- Takes no action and bill becomes law
- Vetoes bill which dies unless overridden by 2/3 vote of General Assembly

* Both houses must agree to identical versions of the bill. If they can't, a conference committee may be set up with representatives from both houses to resolve disagreements.

Committee Action

In the House, and again in the Senate, the bill is worked on by a committee. The committee may hold a public hearing and ask citizens for their opinions on the bill. It may pass a bill "as is," change it, or kill it.

Floor Action

On the floor of the House and Senate chambers, the bill passed from the committee is debated and then voted on by all the members. Amendments may also be made at this point. Before the bill can become law, a majority of members in both houses must approve the exact same version of the bill.

Governor's Action

One last hurdle the bill must clear is the governor's office. If the governor vetoes the bill, it does not become law unless both houses vote to override the veto. It takes a two-thirds majority of members in each house to override a governor's veto. However, this rarely happens.

Looking Ahead

What happens after a bill becomes a law? How are the law's words turned into actions that affect the daily lives of Georgians?

The executive branch of state government has the responsibility to **execute** (carry out) the laws. It's a lot simpler to say in a law "roads shall be built" than it is to build them. It takes thousands of employees to carry out all the activities that state laws require. The next chapter describes how the largest branch of government is organized to carry out the laws. It explains the major services that state government provides, and how these services are financed. ◄

▶ **Locating the Main Ideas**

1. Define: draft, execute, item veto
2. Where do ideas for laws come from?
3. On what subjects is the General Assembly not allowed to enact laws?
4. Explain why a bill must go through the same steps twice before it becomes a law in Georgia.

CHAPTER ACTIVITIES

Reviewing the Main Ideas

1. How is Georgia's General Assembly part of our representative democracy?

2. What purpose is served by electing representatives from geographic districts?

3. How is the principle of "one person, one vote" maintained through reapportionment?

4. What areas of Georgia have the greatest number of legislative districts?

5. To be the majority party, how many seats would a political party need in the 180-member house?

6. Most laws passed by the General Assembly are on four general topics. What are they?

7. What are laws of general application? of local application?

8. Why do legislators tend to rely on the committee's recommendation in deciding how to vote on a bill?

9. At what point in a bill's progress through the legislative process do all members of the House or Senate get to debate it?

10. Give two examples of how the governor and legislature share power in the state budget process.

Give It Some Extra Thought

1. **Examining Relationships.** The main responsibility for lawmaking belongs to the state legislature. How do the other two branches influence lawmaking?

2. **Applying Principles.** Why would using each county as an election district for state legislators violate the principle of "one person, one vote"?

3. **Defend a Position.** Choose one of the following endings to the statement and identify reasons why you believe it is the proper one. "If I were a legislator, the most important factor in deciding how to vote would be (a) my conscience—what I think is right for my constituents, or (b) the opinion of my constituents—regardless of how I personally felt."

Sharpen Your Skills

1. **Translating Data to a Pie Chart.** Make a list of the occupations of the parents or guardians of class members. Put the information into the same categories that are on the pie chart of occupations of Georgia legislators. Transfer this class data to a pie

chart and compare it with the legislative pie chart. How closely do the two charts compare? Can you explain the differences?

2. **Reading the Newspaper.** Look in the newspaper for an article about a law passed by the General Assembly. Report on the purpose of the law, and whether it is of general or local application.

Going Further

1. **Draft a Bill.** Using a topic that is subject to state law, such as education, health, highways, criminal law, or the environment, finish the following sentence. "There ought to be a law that . . . ." Write up your idea, explaining the problem it would solve. How would your law work? Where would the money come from to enforce it?

2. **Understanding Effects.** Divide into small groups and list as many specific examples as you can of the ways the General Assembly affects your lives.

3. **Observing.** View "The Lawmakers" on television or videotape one evening and list the procedures that you observed. What topics were lawmakers speaking about?

28

Gov. Zell Miller signs a bill into law.

Coming Up Next!

- People in government
- State government at work
- Financing state government

State Government— The Executive Branch

The executive branch has the responsibility of providing government services to the people. This is an enormous task. About 99 of every 100 state employees work in the executive branch. Its activities account for about 99 percent of the state's budget. This chapter focuses on how the executive branch serves Georgia citizens and how these services are paid for by the people.

People in Government

Just as a successful business depends on having the right persons in the right jobs, so does a successful government. There are many kinds of jobs in state government. The term *official* usually refers to a person in government who makes important decisions that affect his or her agency or the public. Officials, who make up only a small part of government, organize and direct the work of many other state workers. An *employee* is someone who is hired to work at a specific task. Most government workers—also called personnel—are employees.

"The Government Service Pyramid" (on the next page) tells you two things. First, it takes many kinds of personnel to carry out the laws passed by the legislature. Second, a few persons at the top make the big decisions, but many at the base of the pyramid deliver services directly to the people.

The Governor

The governor is Georgia's chief official. The person who holds this office has more authority over government operations and more influence in state politics than anyone else in government. The gover-

The Government Service Pyramid

Policy-making Officials
governor
secretary of state
state revenue commissioner

Executive Managers
prison warden
state patrol major
state college president
state hospital director
head of division within state agency

Government Employees
accountant, auto mechanic, biologist, carpenter, chemist, child-care worker, clerk, college professor, computer programmer, corrections officer, counselor, data processor, dentist, electrician, employment interviewer, food service worker, geologist, health inspector, highway maintenance worker, laboratory technician, lawyer, librarian, mathematician, nurse, office supervisor, painter, physician, pilot, social worker, state trooper, secretary, therapist, typist, veterinarian, welder, writer, etc.

This pyramid contains examples of jobs in state government. At the top are officials who help decide policy. Their decisions must fit within laws passed by the General Assembly.

The governor is elected by the people, as are several other officials who head departments. They are sometimes called **constitutional officers** because their positions are provided for in the Georgia constitution. Other department heads are appointed, either by the governor or a board of citizens. Some departments have their policies set by a board of citizens appointed by the governor.

In the middle are officials who are appointed to manage large state facilities—such as colleges, hospitals, and prisons—or divisions within departments.

At the base of the pyramid are employees. Most of these jobs are filled through the State Merit System of Personnel Administration or the various agencies themselves. Over 78,000 people are employed by state government.

The chart of Georgia state government on page 405 shows whether positions are elected or appointed.

nor heads the executive branch and also has an important role in the legislative branch.

Who can be the governor? The Georgia constitution spells out the term of office, qualifications, and election procedure for the office of governor.

To be eligible for the office of governor, a man or woman must be a U.S. citizen for 15 years and a legal resident of Georgia for the 6 years before the election. He or she must be at least 30 years old before taking office.

The governor has a term of four years. A person may serve two consecutive terms, but after doing so must wait four years before seeking the office again.

The election for governor is held every four years in the November general election. The person elected takes office the following January.

POWERS OF THE GOVERNOR

FORMAL POWERS	INFORMAL POWERS
Chief Executive	**Chief of State**
Appoint executive branch officials and board members	Meet with the president of the United States and other federal officials
Direct executive branch officials in their work	Meet with foreign government and business leaders
Manage the state's budget	Speak officially for the government and un-officially for the people of Georgia
Chief Legislator	**Chief Politician**
Propose laws and state budget	Develop long-range policies for the state
Sign or veto legislation	Meet with interest groups and politicians to develop policies
Present annual messages to the General Assembly	Hold press conferences and speak out on issues and problems
Call special legislative sessions to take up subjects determined by the governor	Serve as honorary leader of state political party
Commander-in-Chief	Head state party delegation to national conventions
Call out national guard in emergencies	
Send state troopers and GBI agents into communities when needed	

What Is an Agency?

Agency is a general term for a division of government. An agency may go by any of several names—such as department, bureau, board, commission, and office. Each agency has its own special concern. Often its name tells you what that concern is: Department of Industry, Trade and Tourism; Georgia Bureau of Investigation; State Forestry Commission.

The chart of "Georgia State Government" shows how the executive branch is divided into agencies. There are about 35 major agencies and dozens of smaller ones. More than 78,000 persons work in these agencies. Note how small the legislative branch and the judicial branch are compared to the executive branch.

Powers of the Governor

The governor is the most powerful official in state government. Some of the governor's powers are formal ones. That is, they are written in the Georgia constitution and in state laws.

Other powers are informal ones. They stem from customs and traditions, from the personal abilities of the governor (such as leadership), and from the expectations of the people.

Most citizens expect the governor to be a leader. When an issue or a problem concerns the public, they expect the governor to speak out and take action. They also expect the governor to take the initiative, to recommend policies, and then work to get those policies enacted into law. They expect the governor to propose legislation and to make changes in government operations when changes are needed.

It is often said that a governor "wears several hats." That is a way of saying that the office of governor has several different kinds of power. In a single day, the governor may act as chief executive, chief legislator, and chief politician.

Georgia's governor is the one state official whom most citizens recognize by name. It is the governor's opinions and actions that are most widely reported in the news-

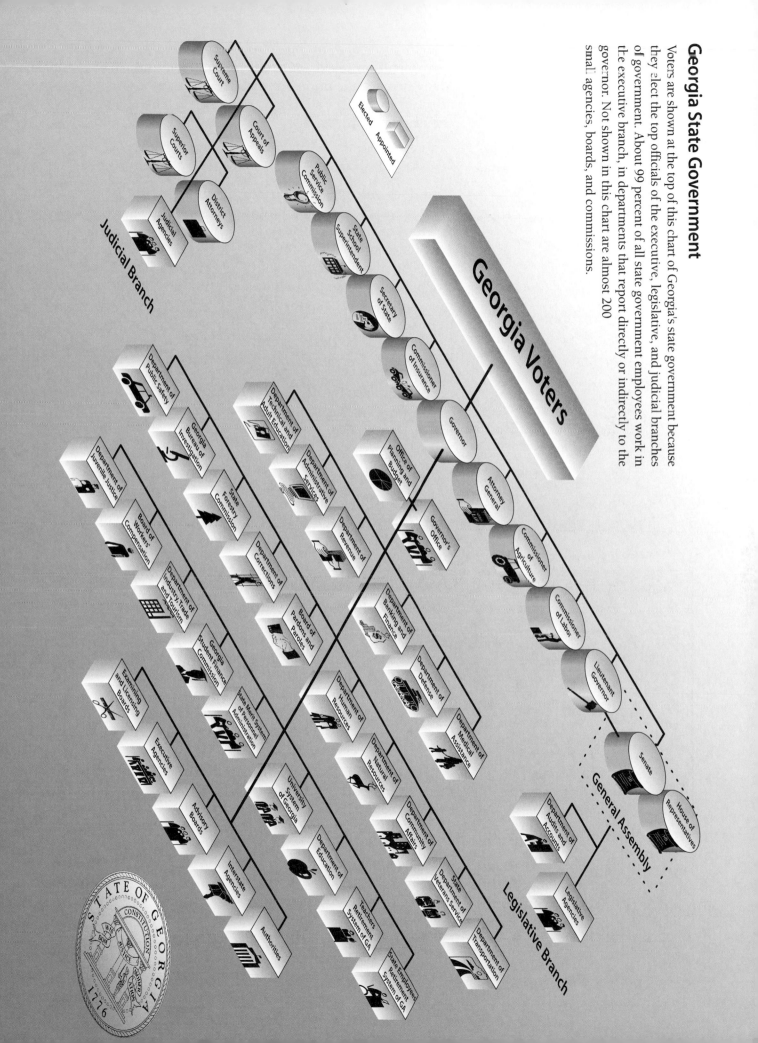

Georgia State Government

Voters are shown at the top of this chart of Georgia's state government because they elect the top officials of the executive, legislative, and judicial branches of government. About 99 percent of all state government employees work in the executive branch, in departments that report directly or indirectly to the governor. Not shown in this chart are almost 200 small agencies, boards, and commissions.

Elected   Appointed

Georgia Voters

Judicial Branch

- Supreme Court
- Superior Courts
- Court of Appeals
- District Attorneys
- Judicial Agencies

Executive Branch

- Public Service Commission
- State School Superintendent
- Secretary of State
- Commissioner of Insurance
- Governor
- Attorney General
- Commissioner of Agriculture
- Commissioner of Labor
- Lieutenant Governor

Governor's departments and offices

- Office of Planning and Budget
- Governor's Office
- Department of Public Safety
- Georgia Bureau of Investigation
- State Forestry Commission
- Department of Corrections
- Board of Pardons and Paroles
- Department of Technical and Adult Education
- Department of Administrative Services
- Department of Revenue
- Department of Banking and Finance
- Department of Defense
- Department of Medical Assistance
- Department of Juvenile Justice
- Board of Workers' Compensation
- Department of Industry, Trade and Tourism
- Georgia Student Finance Commission
- State Merit System of Personnel Administration
- Department of Human Resources
- Department of Natural Resources
- Department of Community Affairs
- State Veterans Service
- Department of Transportation
- Examining and Licensing Boards
- Executive Agencies
- Advisory Boards
- Interstate Agencies
- Authorities
- University System of Georgia
- Department of Education
- Teachers Retirement System of GA
- State Employees Retirement System of GA

General Assembly

- Senate
- House of Representatives

Legislative Branch

- Department of Audits and Accounts
- Legislative Agencies

STATE OF GEORGIA
CONSTITUTION · WISDOM · JUSTICE · MODERATION
1776

▶ **Locating the Main Ideas**

1. Define: constitutional officer, agency
2. Identify: official, employee, department head
3. What is the responsibility of the executive branch of government?
4. What do citizens expect from the governor as the state's leader?

papers and on television, not those of some other state official. Many people take notice. Why? Because a governor's policies can affect every part of state government and, therefore, the lives of thousands of people. ◀

State Government at Work

How does state government provide for the people? State government serves the people in hundreds of ways. You can see that when you look at all the agencies and all the jobs shown in the state government chart and the government service pyramid. But the two charts do not give enough information to answer the question.

One way to understand how state government works is to examine where it puts its money. All executive branch activities fit into these seven major policy categories:

1. educational development
2. human development
3. natural resources
4. transportation
5. economic development
6. protection of persons and property
7. general government

The chart, "Where State Money Goes," shows the percentage of state spending for these seven categories. It also includes spending for the legislative and judicial branches and to pay the state's debts.

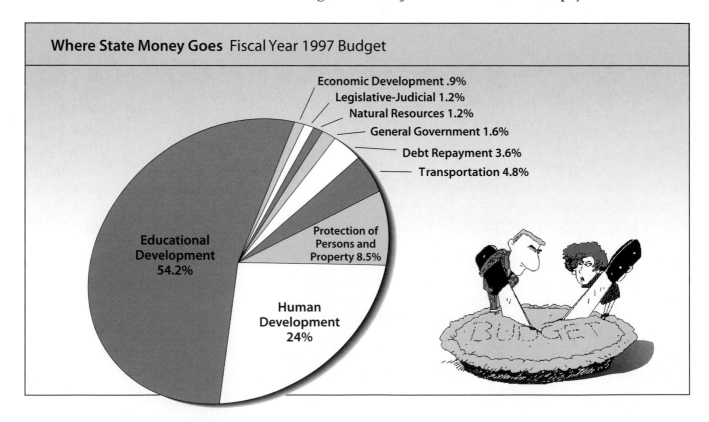

Where State Money Goes Fiscal Year 1997 Budget

Economic Development .9%
Legislative-Judicial 1.2%
Natural Resources 1.2%
General Government 1.6%
Debt Repayment 3.6%
Transportation 4.8%

Educational Development 54.2%

Protection of Persons and Property 8.5%

Human Development 24%

These percentages tell us—in terms of money spent—that the state puts more effort into certain activities than others. Why? Keep in mind that not only state government but also local governments and the national government are there to serve the people.

Educational Development

Education is the biggest responsibility state government has. Why? Successful self-government depends on having all citizens as well-informed as possible. A strong economy depends on having more and more of the labor force trained for highly technical jobs. Long ago, Americans saw in public education the glue that would hold together a nation of immigrants. But the framers of the U.S. Constitution had left the responsibility for education to the states. Today, as a result, more state funds go to education than all other services combined. School teachers, college professors, and other education personnel outnumber all other groups of public employees. Consider this: about 90 percent of all Georgians receive their education in public schools.

Administering Public Education

Elementary and secondary schools are administered separately from "higher education"—colleges and universities. The state directly operates the public colleges and universities. But as the chart, "Georgia's Public School System," illustrates, state and local governments share responsibility for the public schools.

The governor and the legislature are involved in making education policies. Each year, the governor recommends how much of the state budget should go to public schools. The governor may also propose changes in the laws that govern their operations. The General Assembly makes the laws that govern the schools and appropriates the money to pay for them.

To turn these laws into action, the State Board of Education sets specific policies and regulations to cover school operations. Then, the State Superintendent of Schools and personnel in the Department of Education are responsible for seeing that those policies are carried out by the local school districts.

The state's role in Georgia's public colleges and universities is less complicated. One state agency, the University System of Georgia, operates the state's 34 universities and colleges. The system is governed by a Board of Regents, appointed by the governor. In turn, the board appoints a president to manage each of the 34 institutions.

In the 1960s, as more and more citizens wanted a college education, the Board of Regents adopted a policy of locating colleges around the state so that people could get to them easily. Many new colleges were built. The map of the University System of Georgia shows the result of this policy.

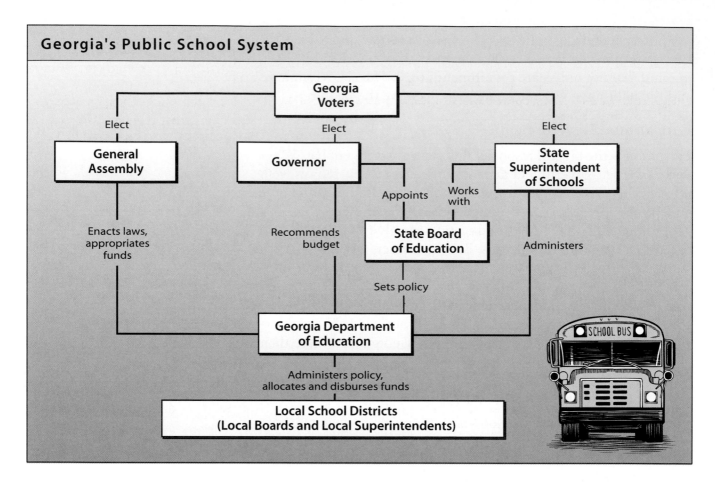

Georgia's Public School System

Georgia Voters

Elect — General Assembly

Elect — Governor

Elect — State Superintendent of Schools

Appoints — State Board of Education

Works with

General Assembly: Enacts laws, appropriates funds

Governor: Recommends budget

State Superintendent of Schools: Administers

State Board of Education: Sets policy

Georgia Department of Education

Administers policy, allocates and disburses funds

Local School Districts (Local Boards and Local Superintendents)

SCHOOL BUS

Human Development

Human development policies are concerned with health and welfare. Spending for human development takes the second largest chunk of the state's budget.

Health and welfare services are provided through the Department of Human Resources (DHR). Some DHR activities—such as disease control, immunization, family planning, and restaurant inspection—serve the general public. Other programs—including health care, child protection, financial assistance, legal assistance, and vocational rehabilitation—serve persons who are poor, retarded, disabled, very young, or very old.

DHR operates hospitals, treatment centers, and training centers for severely ill and retarded adults and children. For persons who can be treated without being placed in a state facility, DHR oversees programs close to where they live. While they are getting help, they can continue to live and hold jobs in their community.

Human assistance activities are good illustrations of how federalism works. One example is Workfirst—a state program funded by federal and state governments. It is designed to provide temporary cash assistance to needy people while helping them to become employed. The program provides assistance for education, finding jobs, training, and child care. Recipients are eligible for only four years of assistance.

The Department of Human Resources, with 23,000 employees, is one of the largest state agencies. These workers carry out over 100 programs throughout Georgia's 159 counties. DHR employees include child-care workers, counselors, nurses, physicians, social workers, therapists, and many others. They all work with people needing help. ▶

Natural Resources

Where should solid waste landfills be located? Should factories be allowed to dump chemical wastes in a river? Should a river be dammed up to make a reservoir to provide electricity, water, and recreation?

▶ **Locating the Main Ideas**

1. Why does so much of the state's budget go to education?

2. What level of government operates colleges and universities? elementary and secondary schools?

3. What was the reason for building so many new colleges in Georgia in the 1960s?

4. Why is the Department of Human Resources such a large agency?

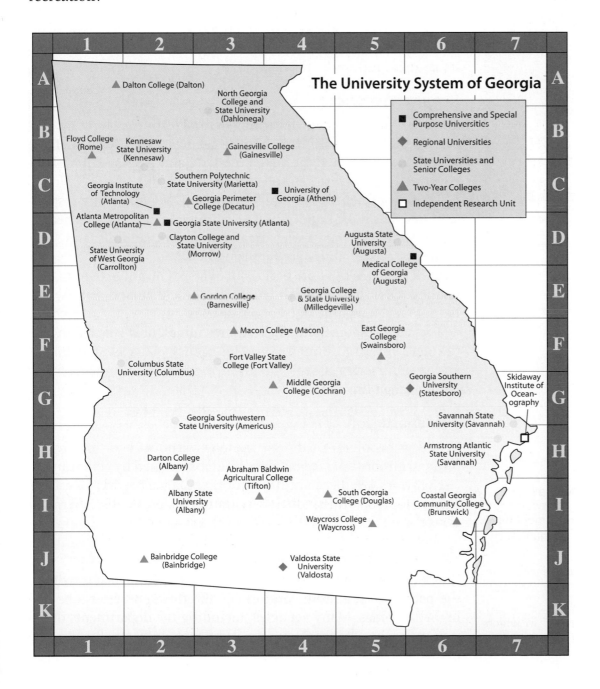

Clean water is everyone's concern.

We all depend on the same limited supply of natural resources for our health and well-being. But we all do not agree on how to use them. Therefore, we have given government the job of seeing that resources are used in the best interests of all people. This responsibility begins with the legislature. At each session of the General Assembly, bills are introduced that affect resource use. They may concern such activities as lumbering, fishing, hunting, waste dumping, land clearing, and road building.

Until the 1960s, the policies of state government tended to favor economic development, even if the environment suffered. But since then, people have become more and more concerned about damage to the environment. Today, policy makers are more likely to consider how development will affect the environment and to attempt to strike a balance between the two. But conflict still arises over such issues as land use, hazardous waste disposal, water quality control, and wetland protection.

Resource Agencies

Once decisions are made regarding natural resources, how are they carried out? Two executive branch agencies, the Department of Natural Resources and the State Forestry Commission, enforce laws covering resources.

The Department of Natural Resources (DNR) has many responsibilities. The most important one is protecting the public's health. Public water systems, sewage treatment plants, landfills, and other waste disposal facilities are regulated by DNR.

DNR operates the state parks and oversees hunting, fishing, and boating. DNR operates fish hatcheries, stocks inland waters, and helps manage wildlife in Georgia's forests.

The main responsibility for forest resources, however, belongs to the State Forestry Commission. This agency manages state forests and tree nurseries, assists the forest industry, and protects forest lands against fire.

Transportation

Very few people get through the day without using the roads, bridges, airports, or seaports built and maintained by government.

Highways are the main item in this policy category. One large agency, the Department of Transportation, plans, builds, and maintains the more than 18,000 miles of the state highway system. ◀

Economic Development

The state's economic development activities are aimed at providing the people with a more comfortable life through better jobs and higher incomes. Many agencies, including the departments of agriculture, labor, transportation, natural resources, and forestry, are involved in economic development.

▶ Locating the Main Ideas

1. Why does state government have policies regarding the natural environment?

2. What two executive agencies have the main responsibility for Georgia's natural resources?

3. What is the main way in which state government is involved in transportation?

One agency, the Department of Industry, Trade and Tourism, focuses specifically on economic development. Its name tells what it does. It works to get new industries to locate in Georgia as well as to encourage existing industries to expand. It promotes trade between Georgia businesses and those in other states and nations. Another big activity is encouraging people from other states and nations to visit and vacation in Georgia.

Protection of Persons and Property

State government protects the public in many ways. One way is by regulating private enterprise.

The state regulates businesses and occupations in order to protect the public's health and safety. For example, the Department of Agriculture inspects dairies, the Department of Human Resources inspects hospitals and nursing homes, and the Department of Labor enforces child labor laws. Examining boards within the Office of the Secretary of State make sure that only qualified persons are allowed to practice medicine, engineering, pharmacy, and other occupations that affect the public's health and safety. Another state agency, the Office of Consumer Affairs, protects consumers against unfair business practices, such as selling used products as new.

The public also expects government to protect persons and property against crime, riots, disasters, and other dangerous situations. This responsibility is shared by federal, state, and local government agencies. Most police officers are employees of local governments, and much of the cost of law enforcement is paid for by city and county taxes. However, several state agencies play big roles in protecting citizens.

The Department of Public Safety's main division, the Georgia State Patrol, focuses on enforcing traffic laws and preventing accidents, injuries, and deaths on public highways. State troopers may also investigate any type of criminal acts committed on the highways. They regularly cooperate with local police. When there is the threat of riot or other civil disturbance, the governor may order the patrol (as well as the GBI and the Georgia National Guard) to be on duty to prevent violence.

The Georgia Bureau of Investigation (GBI) assists local police agencies on many kinds of criminal cases. These cases include stolen autos, burglary, forgery, gambling, arson, controlled substances (drugs), and murder. It can bring to a case trained investigators and special equipment that many local police forces do not have. Usually, the GBI enters a case on the request of a police chief or sheriff. Or, the governor can order the GBI to take action.

Two units within the GBI, the State Crime Laboratory and the Crime Information Center, help other agencies. The crime lab conducts tests on all manner of evidence, from bloodstains to bullets. The information center operates 24 hours a day, seven days a week.

Crime lab worker matches the sole of a shoe with a footprint from a crime scene.

Law officers can, in just a few minutes, find out whether someone they picked up is wanted for committing a crime or if a car they stopped has been stolen.

Protection of persons and property also involves dealing with those convicted of criminal offenses. In some cases, this means the ones convicted are sent to prison. In others, an offender is sentenced to a period of **probation**. During this time, the offender must follow strict rules and report to a probation supervisor. The responsibility for imprisoning convicted criminals and supervising those on probation belongs to the Georgia Department of Corrections. That agency operates correctional institutions for adult offenders. Some are for people convicted of committing violent crimes. Juvenile offenders (persons under the age of 17) are handled by the Department of Juvenile Justice.

What is the purpose of putting criminals behind bars? Four reasons are usually given. One reason is *punishment:* to make the criminal "pay" for his or her crime by serving time. A second reason is *deterrence:* to deter (or discourage) the criminal from more wrongdoing and other persons from committing similar crimes. A third is *protection* of society: to keep a criminal locked up so he or she cannot harm law-abiding citizens. A fourth is *rehabilitation:* to reform the criminal to become a useful member of society.

In addition to the corrections department, a second agency—the State Board of Pardons and Paroles—has responsibility for dealing with convicted criminals. This board has the authority to issue *pardons*—official forgiveness for a crime—but its main function is to grant **paroles**. Parole is a conditional release from prison before the end of a sentence. Like probation, it requires supervision.

General Government

Some agencies have the responsibility to help the rest of state government do its work. Here are three examples. The Office of Secretary of State is in charge of state elections and state records. The Department of Administrative Services operates computer, printing, purchasing, and motor vehicle services for other agencies. The Department of Revenue collects all state taxes, without which there would be no state government. ◄

Financing State Government

To serve the people, state government has to spend money. It must pay salaries to personnel and must purchase goods and services just like a business does. An amount of money spent by government for some purpose is called an **expenditure**.

Also like a business, government must have income. A business's income comes from the sale of goods and services. State government's income comes mainly from taxes (plus smaller amounts from charges such as license fees). The state also receives grants of money

▶ **Locating the Main Ideas**

1. Define: probation, parole
2. Give two examples of how state regulation of business protects the public.
3. How does the Georgia State Patrol serve citizens throughout the state?
4. What are four reasons for putting criminals behind bars?

from the federal government for specific purposes, such as welfare. Money that government receives is called **revenue**.

The size of government expenditures is tied by law to the amount of revenues that will be taken in. Both expenditures and revenues in turn are tied to the amount of services government provides. If many services are demanded by the people, government spending will be high, and so will taxes. Fewer services mean less spending and lower taxes.

The Budget

A budget is a plan for raising and spending money. Without it, state agencies would not know how much money they could spend during the year. Each year, the governor and legislature work out a budget for state government. The state's budget covers a 12-month period called the **fiscal year**. Georgia's fiscal year begins on July 1 and ends on June 30. The governor has the responsibility to predict how much revenue the state will collect during the coming fiscal year. Based on this estimate, the governor then works up a complete budget on how this money will be spent. To help in these difficult decisions, a governor has a staff of budget specialists—known as the Office of Planning and Budget (OPB).

The governor's policies determine the overall shape of the proposed budget. The seven major policy areas of state programs do not change greatly from year to year. However, a governor who feels that certain activities should get more attention may propose more spending in those areas and less in others.

In early January of each year, the governor's budget is introduced into the General Assembly as an *appropriations* bill. The legislature's

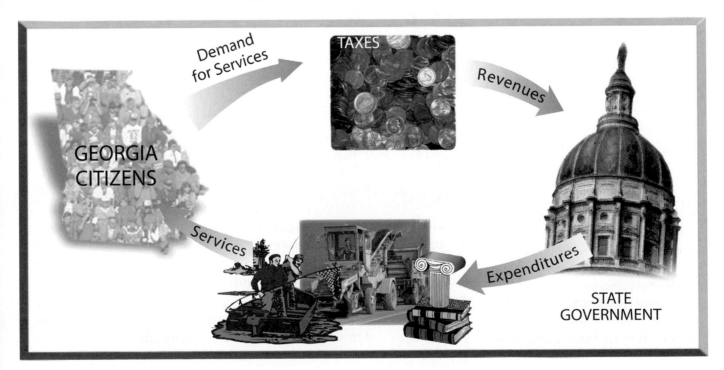

Demand for Services

TAXES

Revenues

GEORGIA CITIZENS

Services

Expenditures

STATE GOVERNMENT

Georgia's Tax Dollar

Source: Georgia Department of Revenue, 1997 *Statistical Report*

50¢
INCOME TAX
Personal 43¢
Corporate 7¢

40¢
SALES TAX

4¢
MOTOR FUEL TAX

6¢
OTHER TAXES

task is to turn the governor's proposal into law. Without such a law, state government could spend no money and would have to shut down. The task of debating and passing the appropriations bill is always long and drawn out. House and Senate appropriations committees may propose to amend the bill to spend more—or less—on certain activities than the governor recommended. Often, there is heated debate over such attempts, but usually the final budget approved is pretty much like that proposed by the governor.

The new budget goes into effect on July 1. The governor's budget staff is responsible for keeping track of the state's expenditures and revenues so that they do not get out of balance. If the amount of revenue the state takes in during the year falls below the level that the governor projected earlier, the governor may have to order cuts in state spending.

Taxes

What kind of taxes does state government depend on? Georgia's personal income tax is the largest source of state revenue. It is imposed on a person's salary or wages, as well as on any profits, rents, interest, dividends, or other sources of taxable income. In addition, there is a corporate income tax imposed on the profits of all corporations doing business in the state. Corporations must also pay this tax on any income gained from property in Georgia.

The general sales tax is the second largest state revenue source. It is imposed on the retail sale, rental, or use of goods and certain services. This tax covers the sale of clothing, automobiles, furniture, building materials, sporting goods, and many other goods. Groceries and prescription drugs are exempt from sales tax.

How is the sales tax paid? The purchaser pays the tax at the time of purchase. The seller in turn sends the tax to the Department of Revenue each month. Special sales taxes on motor fuel, alcohol, and tobacco are collected even before the product is offered for sale to the consumer. The consumer winds up paying them as part of the purchase price. ◄

▶ **Locating the Main Ideas**

1. Define: expenditure, revenue, fiscal year

2. What are the principal sources of revenue for state government?

3. Why is a budget necessary to operate state government?

4. Who has to pay income tax in Georgia? What taxes must Georgia businesses pay?

5. How are sales taxes collected by the Department of Revenue?

CHAPTER ACTIVITIES

Reviewing the Main Ideas

1. What is the basis for the governor's formal powers? informal powers?

2. Give some examples of how the governor "wears several hats."

3. What is the role of each of the following in the operation of public schools? The governor, the legislature, the state board of education, the state superintendent of schools, and the Georgia Department of Education.

4. Describe some of the health and welfare services provided by the Department of Human Resources.

5. How does the Department of Natural Resources protect the public? How does it promote the use of natural resources?

6. Why does the state regulate professions and trades such as doctors, engineers, and pharmacists?

7. In what ways does the Georgia Bureau of Investigation provide assistance to local law enforcement agencies?

8. What kind of help does the Department of Administrative Services provide to other state agencies?

9. Describe how taxes and other revenues affect the expenditures state government makes to provide services to the public. How are revenues and expenditures tied to the amount of services government provides?

10. What is the role of the legislature in financing the activities of state government?

Give It Some Extra Thought

1. **Describing.** Review the discussion of government services in this chapter. List three services and describe how you have benefitted from them.

2. **Justifying Conclusions.** Almost three-quarters of the state's expenditures go to two policy areas, public education and human development. How do these two areas contribute to Georgians' well-being? Are such large expenditures a proper use of state money?

Sharpen Your Skills

1. **Map Skills.** Use the key from the map of The University System of Georgia (page 409) and count the number of universities or colleges in each category. Locate and identify the grid coordinates of the area where you live. Give the coordinates for the grid, outside your own, that contains the college or university that seems closest to where you live. Using cardinal or intermediate directions, describe the direction of that grid in relation to yours.

2. **Converting Data.** Convert the data from "Georgia's Tax Dollar" (opposite) to a pie graph and a bar graph. Which of the two graphs gives you a clearer picture of where Georgia's revenues come from?

3. **Making State and Local Connections.** Look up Georgia State Government in your telephone directory. Try to identify one agency or office for each of the seven policy categories listed in the chapter.

Going Further

1. **Locating Visual Evidence.** Collect photographs of the governor from newspapers, magazines, or other sources. Write a description under the photo, identifying the power of the governor that is illustrated in the photo.

2. **Write a Letter.** Choose one of the executive departments mentioned in this chapter. Imagine you are the department head and write a letter to the governor requesting more funds for your department. Explain what the money could be used for and how the citizens of Georgia would benefit if the department's budget were increased.

29

Coming Up Next!

- The courts and the law
- Court cases: civil and criminal
- Georgia's court system
- The criminal justice process

State Government— The Judicial Branch

In our society, we live by rules. The purpose of rules is to regulate how we interact with one another and thereby manage conflict. Rules establish the rights and duties—or obligations—we have as members of society. Some are *social* rights and duties. They are set down by families, churches, schools, businesses, and other social institutions. They are the rights and duties we have as family and church members, students, and employees. Such obligations as feeding the family dog or attending church are matters for our family and church to settle.

We also have *legal* rights and duties. These are established by the laws of our government. For example, a person has a legal right to own private property such as an automobile. On the highway, that person has a legal duty to obey the traffic laws and a legal duty not to harm other persons. Legal rights and duties are ones that can be enforced by government.

The task of enforcing our legal rights and duties is not an easy one. Disputes over legal rights and duties are part of everyday life. Consider the following situation.

A landowner discovers that a construction company has bulldozed valuable trees on his property. He demands payment from the company. The company claims the landowner's neighbor directed it to clear away the trees for a new building. The neighbor says the company made a mistake and went onto the wrong land.

The landowner has a legal right not to have his property damaged. Has that right been violated? Does he have a legal right to compensation (payment) for the damage? The neighbor has a legal duty not to damage someone else's property. Has he carried out that duty? Does he have a legal obligation to pay for the landowner's

The Judicial Building in Atlanta.

loss of his trees? Does the construction company have legal obligations in this situation?

Because disputes like this one involve legal obligations, government has a role in settling them. That role is filled by the judicial branch at the federal, state, and local levels—the courts.

Making decisions about our legal rights and duties, interpreting our laws—the court's task is an enormous one.

The Courts and the Law

Originally, the court was a government chamber (or room) where a person went to seek justice—or fairness—in settling a dispute. Today, the court is still a place where citizens take legal disputes to be resolved. You may read in the newspaper that so-and-so "appeared in court." But, when the newspaper says "the court ruled," it is referring to a decision made by a judge.

Unlike legislatures and executive agencies, the courts generally do not initiate government action. Instead, the courts wait for cases or issues to be brought to them by private citizens or other government agencies.

There are thousands of courts in the United States. All of them have the same basic function: to interpret and apply the law to settle conflicts. There are four kinds of law:

- constitutional law: written provisions of U.S. and state constitutions
- statutory law: written laws enacted by legislative bodies
- administrative law: written rules and regulations of executive agencies

Entering another person's house with the intent to commit a theft is burglary, which is a felony. Most inmates of Georgia's prison system are imprisoned for burglary.

- case law: court interpretations of written law and *common law* (legal rights and duties that courts have decided exist in situations not covered by written law)

The conflicts may be over

- rights and duties of citizens, businesses, or governments;
- questions of guilt or innocence; or
- constitutionality of laws.

Settling that last type of conflict is a very important power of the court. It is called the power of **judicial review** because it involves reviewing rules or laws (in cases brought to the court) to determine if they violate the Constitution. Sometimes, the court substitutes its judgment of what is lawful policy for that of the legislature or executive. Judicial review is part of the system of checks and balances by which the three branches of government share power.

Not every court in the country has the authority to settle issues of constitutionality. Only higher level state courts and federal courts exercise this power. Neither do all courts have exactly the same authority to settle conflicts over private rights and duties or guilt and innocence. We have different courts to settle different kinds of legal matters.

The federal courts function as an important part of our system of justice. But state courts settle most disputes because most disputes are covered by state law.

In this chapter, we will focus on Georgia's state courts. The work of two of those courts—the superior court and the juvenile court—will get special attention. ◄

Court Cases: Civil and Criminal

State courts handle two general classes of legal disputes: civil and criminal.

In a **civil case**, the court acts as a kind of referee to settle disputes between two or more parties. The parties may be individual citizens or businesses. Sometimes, the government is one of the parties. A typical civil case begins when one party sues (brings legal action against) another. Auto accidents, divorces, and violations of business contracts are common subjects of many civil suits.

The party who brings legal action is called the **plaintiff**. The party against whom the action is brought is called the **defendant**.

▶ **Locating the Main Ideas**

1. Define: judicial review
2. How do courts differ from legislatures and executive agencies in taking action on an issue?
3. What are the four kinds of law that courts may be called on to interpret and apply?

The plaintiff may complain to the court that the defendant failed to meet some legal obligation. An example might be a bank (plaintiff) suing a customer (defendant) who has stopped paying off a loan.

Or, one person may complain that another has violated his or her rights. In an auto accident, for example, the person who caused the accident might be sued for causing harm to the injured person.

Most civil cases do not result in a trial (a formal examination and decision by the court). They are usually settled "out of court" by the two parties reaching an agreement before the trial begins.

If a civil case goes to trial, the court decides whether the evidence presented is stronger on the side of the plaintiff or on the side of the defendant. The court decides which side prevails. A civil court does not find anyone guilty or not guilty.

In a **criminal case**, the state prosecutes (takes legal action against) someone charged with committing a *crime*. A crime is the commission of an act prohibited by law. In some cases, omission of (failure to perform) an act required by law can also be a crime. Stealing a car is a crime of commission. Failing to pay a required tax is a crime of omission.

Not all harmful acts are crimes. For example, a driver may harm another person in an auto accident, but not commit a crime. To be a crime, an act *must* be defined as such by law.

Generally, crimes are considered to violate the public's rights. They offend the whole community, not just the individual victim. Therefore, in a criminal case, one party is the government (sometimes referred to as the state or *the people*). Acting on behalf of the public, the government files charges against a person believed to have committed a crime. The government, not the individual victim of the criminal act, is the **prosecution**. The person arrested and charged with the crime is the defendant.

In a criminal case, the court decides whether the evidence presented by the prosecution proves beyond a reasonable doubt the case against the defendant. It may find the defendant guilty as charged or not guilty.

Felonies and Misdemeanors

Crimes are classified, according to their seriousness, as felonies or misdemeanors.

A **felony** is a very serious crime. A felony is a crime that is punishable by a year or more in prison and/or by a fine of $1,000 or more. Arson, burglary, kidnapping, motor vehicle theft, murder, robbery, rape, and selling certain drugs are examples of felonies under Georgia law. A **capital felony** is a crime punishable by death.

A **misdemeanor** is a less serious crime. A misdemeanor is punishable by one to twelve months in prison and/or a fine of $1,000 or less. Carrying a concealed weapon, criminal trespass, cruelty to

Littering public and private property is a misdemeanor. Throwing garbage onto the right-of-way of a road is a common example of littering.

Georgia Court System

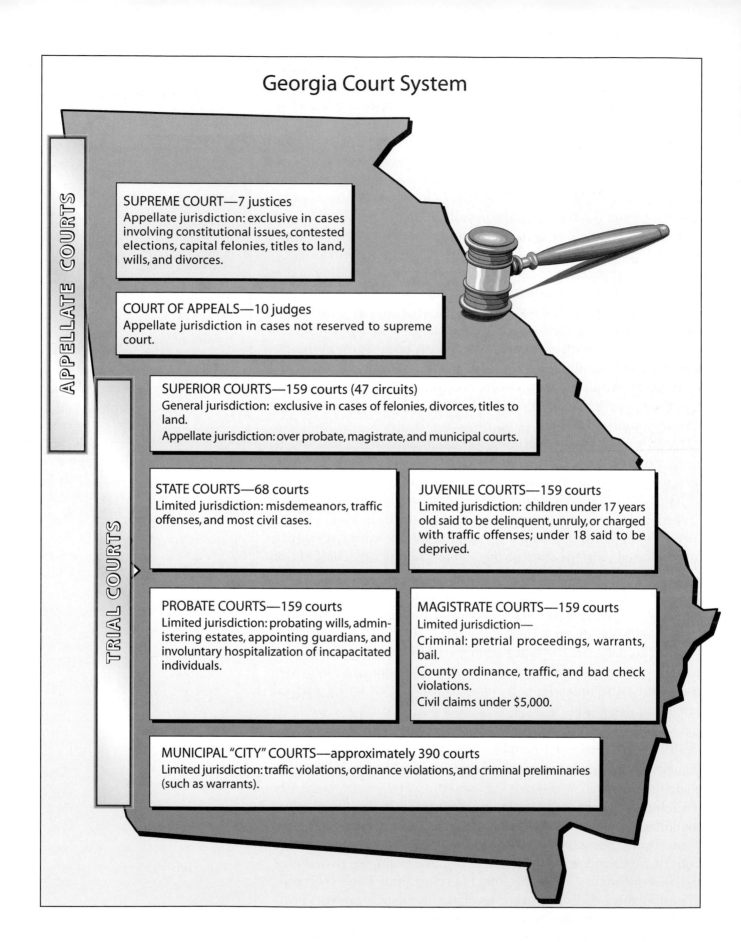

APPELLATE COURTS

SUPREME COURT—7 justices
Appellate jurisdiction: exclusive in cases involving constitutional issues, contested elections, capital felonies, titles to land, wills, and divorces.

COURT OF APPEALS—10 judges
Appellate jurisdiction in cases not reserved to supreme court.

TRIAL COURTS

SUPERIOR COURTS—159 courts (47 circuits)
General jurisdiction: exclusive in cases of felonies, divorces, titles to land.
Appellate jurisdiction: over probate, magistrate, and municipal courts.

STATE COURTS—68 courts
Limited jurisdiction: misdemeanors, traffic offenses, and most civil cases.

JUVENILE COURTS—159 courts
Limited jurisdiction: children under 17 years old said to be delinquent, unruly, or charged with traffic offenses; under 18 said to be deprived.

PROBATE COURTS—159 courts
Limited jurisdiction: probating wills, administering estates, appointing guardians, and involuntary hospitalization of incapacitated individuals.

MAGISTRATE COURTS—159 courts
Limited jurisdiction—
Criminal: pretrial proceedings, warrants, bail.
County ordinance, traffic, and bad check violations.
Civil claims under $5,000.

MUNICIPAL "CITY" COURTS—approximately 390 courts
Limited jurisdiction: traffic violations, ordinance violations, and criminal preliminaries (such as warrants).

animals, and shoplifting are examples of misdemeanors under Georgia law. Most traffic violations are misdemeanors.

Some types of crimes may be treated as felonies or misdemeanors, depending on how severe they are. Assault and battery (threatening and carrying out a physical attack on a person) are examples. ▶

Georgia's Court System

Each of the 50 states has its own court system. These courts resolve legal matters covered by state law. Courts at the local level of government also settle matters covered by local laws (called ordinances).

The Georgia court system is depicted on page 420. The courts are positioned according to the kind of jurisdiction (or authority) they have.

Jurisdiction

Jurisdiction is the power or authority of a court to hear and settle particular kinds of disputes and other legal matters. There are various categories of jurisdiction, but two basic kinds are original and appellate.

Legal actions, such as a lawsuit, originate in a court that has **original jurisdiction**. This is the authority to be the first court to hear a case. Georgia courts that have original jurisdiction are labeled "trial courts" in the chart because they can hold trials.

There are jury trials and non-jury trials for both criminal and civil cases. In a jury trial, a group of citizens, called a **jury**, are selected to decide the outcome of the trial. In a non-jury trial, the judge alone hears the case and makes the decision.

At the bottom of the court system are trial courts of limited jurisdiction. Generally, they settle relatively minor criminal matters such as violations of traffic laws and civil matters involving small amounts of money. However, these courts play an important part in the criminal justice system. They may issue arrest and search warrants. One of these, the magistrate court, regularly handles pretrial proceedings that determine whether a person arrested in a felony case will be tried in superior court.

At the center of the court system is the **superior court**—Georgia's general trial court. It has original jurisdiction over almost every kind of criminal and civil matter covered by Georgia law. It has exclusive authority to try felony cases (except those involving juvenile offenders, in which jurisdiction is shared with the juvenile court). The superior court also has the power to review actions of some lower courts.

Located in each of Georgia's 159 counties, superior courts are organized by judicial circuits—regions of one or more counties. Each of the 47 circuits is made up of one to eight counties. Circuits with

1. Define: civil case, plaintiff, defendant, criminal case, prosecution, felony, capital felony, misdemeanor

2. How are civil cases usually resolved?

3. Why does the state act on behalf of the public in prosecuting a criminal case?

Courts of Limited Jurisdiction

In addition to the superior court, Georgia's court system includes several other trial courts with jurisdiction limited to specific kinds of civil and criminal matters.

In more heavily populated counties, the legislature created a state court to take some of the workload off the superior court. A state court's jurisdiction includes misdemeanor criminal cases, as well as civil matters that are not under the exclusive jurisdiction of the superior court. Trials in this court require only 6 jurors—rather than 12. State court judges are elected to four-year terms in countywide, non-partisan elections.

Every county has a **probate court**. Its name comes from its authority to probate (or prove the validity of) wills and dispose of the estates of deceased persons. Cases involving mentally ill persons who may require a guardian or commitment to a state hospital go to the probate court. In counties that have no state court, the probate court may also hear traffic cases and try violations of state game and fish laws. Probate judges are elected in countywide, partisan elections to a four-year term.

Every county also has a magistrate court. A chief magistrate, who may be assisted by one or more magistrates, presides over each of the 159 courts. The jurisdiction of this court includes trials for traffic violations, violations of county ordinances, and civil trials for claims of $5,000 or less. A magistrate may issue arrest warrants and search warrants, hold preliminary hearings, and set bail in criminal cases that will later go before the superior court. The chief magistrate, who is either appointed or elected in a countywide, partisan election to a four-year term, may appoint other magistrates.

City governments have municipal courts. Their jurisdiction is limited to violations of city ordinances, traffic violations, and preliminaries (such as issuing warrants) in criminal cases. Municipal court judges may be either appointed or elected.

fewer counties are generally located in or near metropolitan areas. The superior court holds sessions in each county in the circuit at least twice a year. Superior court judges are elected to four-year terms in circuitwide, non-partisan elections.

Most cases brought to superior court end there. However, by the process of appeal, a case may be taken to a higher court. A court with the authority to review decisions of lower courts is said to have **appellate jurisdiction**. These courts can decide whether a decision made by a trial court should be upheld or overturned.

Georgia's appellate courts do not hold trials; their function is to hear appeals that errors were made during a trial in a lower court. Unlike trial courts, which have one judge (and often a jury), appellate courts have several judges who hear cases and make decisions as a body.

The Georgia Supreme Court is the highest court in the state. It has *exclusive* appellate jurisdiction for certain kinds of cases. For example, it is the only state court that hears appeals involving felonies punishable by death. Also, it reviews cases that concern state constitutional questions. If a superior court case questioned whether a law passed by the General Assembly was constitutional, the supreme court would make the final decision in the matter.

There are seven judges—called justices—on the Georgia Supreme Court. They are elected to six-year terms in statewide, non-partisan elections.

The justices choose one of their number to be chief justice and preside over the court. Supreme court decisions are determined by a majority vote of the justices.

The Georgia Court of Appeals has appellate jurisdiction over cases in which the supreme court does not have exclusive appellate jurisdiction. There are 10 appeals court judges elected to six-year terms in statewide, non-partisan elections. ▶

The Criminal Justice Process

No State shall…deprive any person of life, liberty, or property, without due process of law.—Fourteenth Amendment, Constitution of the United States of America

What is **due process** of law? It is all the rights and procedures—written in our constitutions and laws, plus those established by the courts—by which we obtain fair treatment under the law.

Examples of rights and procedures guaranteed by due process in criminal matters include the right to

- be notified of charges against you,
- be provided a speedy and public trial,
- be able to confront and cross-examine witnesses,
- be represented by a lawyer,
- have an impartial judge and jury, and
- remain silent (not be a witness against yourself).

How is due process applied in a felony criminal case in Georgia? Because it involves a felony, the case must be tried in superior court—the main trial court in the Georgia court system. Let's look at the persons and procedures involved in making due process work.

▶ **Locating the Main Ideas**

1. Define: original jurisdiction, jury, superior court, appellate jurisdiction, probate court
2. What role do Georgia's courts of limited jurisdiction play in the criminal justice process?
3. Why is it appropriate to call Georgia's superior courts the *main* trial courts in the state?

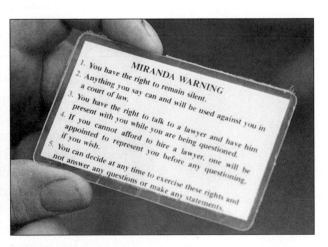

Before questioning him, the officer must read the suspect his rights. This part of due process—the Miranda Warning—is named after a case involving a person named Miranda.

Superior Court Personnel

It takes many persons to make the criminal justice system work. Some of them are employed in executive branch agencies, such as the Georgia Bureau of Investigation and the Department of Corrections. Some work in local police departments. Others are employed in the courts, and some are private citizens. The top official in the superior court is the superior court judge.

Each judicial circuit also has a **district attorney** who represents the state in criminal cases tried in superior court. District attorneys are elected by the voters of the circuit for a term of four years.

Some circuits also employ a public defender. This is an attorney who provides legal assistance to persons charged with crimes who have no money to hire a lawyer. Where there is no public defender, the court arranges for other lawyers to defend such persons.

Other government personnel who serve the superior court are

- a clerk of the court to maintain court records,
- a sheriff to serve court papers on persons who must come before the court,
- a probation officer to investigate the backgrounds of defendants and persons on probation and to collect fines and payments ordered by the court,
- a bailiff to assist in maintaining order in the courtroom, and
- a court reporter to record trial proceedings.

Juries are an important part of the criminal justice system. They are made up of ordinary citizens. Names are selected from a list of registered voters in a county. If called, citizens are required to serve on jury duty unless they have good reason to be excused. Jurors are paid for each day they serve. This pay helps to make up for wages a person may lose while serving on a jury.

In each county, the superior court is served by grand juries and trial juries.

A **grand jury** is made up of 16 to 23 citizens. In criminal matters, it has the responsibility to determine whether or not persons charged with an offense should be indicted (formally accused of the charges) and required to stand trial. The grand jury hears evidence and testimony, presented in secret, by the district attorney, sheriff, and witnesses.

The **trial jury** in a felony case is made up of 12 citizens. As many as 40 potential jurors may be notified to appear for jury duty. The attorneys for the prosecution and for the defense ask questions of those called and then select the members of the jury.

During a criminal trial, the jury's task is to hear evidence presented by the prosecution (the district attorney or assistants) to prove its case. It also hears evidence presented by the defense attorney. It then decides whether the defendant is guilty or not guilty. To convict someone charged with a crime, the jury's decision must be unanimous.

The jury listens as the district attorney questions the witness.

Judicial Procedures

Here are the general procedures in a felony case. Not all cases would follow exactly the same steps.

Pre-Trial Proceedings

These precede a trial.

> *Arrest:* Legal authorities take the suspect into custody.
>
> *Booking:* Authorities make an official record of the arrest and place the suspect in a cell.
>
> *Initial Appearance:* The magistrate sees that the suspect is given due process, including the right to an attorney, bail, and explanation of charges.
>
> *Preliminary Hearing:* Magistrate determines if there is probable cause to believe that a crime has been committed and that the person should be tried.
>
> *Grand Jury Indictment:* Grand jury decides if there is enough evidence to charge the suspect with a crime. If so, the grand jury issues an **indictment** (a formal charge).
>
> *Arraignment* (calling before the court): Superior court judge reads charges and accused pleads guilty or not guilty. (If the plea is guilty, the next step would be sentencing.)
>
> *Plea Bargaining:* Accused agrees to plead guilty to a less serious charge. (If a plea bargain is made, there would be no trial. The next step is sentencing.)

The witness, seated next to the judge, considers the question.

Trial

The judge conducts trial proceedings according to legal rules.

> *Jury Selection:* Twelve jurors are selected to hear the case.
>
> *Opening Statements:* Prosecution and defense state what they expect to prove to the jury.
>
> *Presentation of the Case:* Prosecution presents evidence and witnesses to prove its case. Defense presents evidence and witnesses to discredit prosecution's case.
>
> *Closing Statements:* Defense and prosecution make final arguments to the jury.
>
> *Jury Deliberation and Verdict:* Jury considers evidence and makes a decision. If verdict is not guilty, defendant is freed.
>
> *Sentencing:* If verdict is guilty, judge determines (within limits set by law) what the sentence will be.

Appeal

The defense asks that the verdict be overturned, citing errors in the trial. The district attorney argues that the verdict should stand. The appellate court examines the trial record for errors. If the verdict is

1. Define: due process, district attorney, grand jury, trial jury, indictment

2. What function does the grand jury serve in the criminal justice process?

3. At what two steps in the pre-trial proceedings could the accused agree to be sentenced without a trial?

overturned, the case goes back to superior court. If the verdict is upheld, the sentence is carried out. ◀

Juvenile Justice

Generally, our system of justice treats **juveniles**—persons under the age of 17—differently from adults. A special set of state laws—the juvenile code—covers matters involving children. A special court—the juvenile court—has jurisdiction in cases involving them. However, some cases go directly to the superior court when the juvenile is charged with certain violent offenses such as murder, rape, armed robbery when committed with a firearm, and others.

Treating juveniles differently from adults in the justice system is based on the idea that children may not be fully responsible for their actions. Juveniles may not be able to care for themselves, and they may need to be protected.

Juveniles must obey all laws that adults must obey—including traffic laws. In addition, juveniles have to comply with several laws that do not apply to adults. Juveniles must

- obey reasonable and lawful commands of parents or guardians.
- attend school regularly or have a proper excuse.
- not run away from home.
- not wander or loiter in the streets or in any public places between midnight and 5 a.m.
- not enter any bar where alcoholic beverages are sold without a parent or guardian.
- not possess any alcoholic beverages.

Like adults, juveniles have rights. Among the legal rights of juveniles are these:

- to be notified in writing of the charges against them
- to confront and cross-examine witnesses against them
- to be represented by an attorney
- not to be found guilty solely on the basis of a confession
- not to have their names or photographs made public on a first offense (unless being tried as an adult)

Juvenile Courts

Each of the 159 counties has a juvenile court. The purpose of having separate juvenile courts is to

1. protect the well-being of children,
2. provide guidance and control in the interests of the child as well as of the state, and
3. secure care for any child removed from his or her home.

Who comes under the jurisdiction of the juvenile courts? Generally, any person under the age of 17 who

- has committed a **delinquent act** (any act that would be a criminal offense if committed by an adult),
- has been charged as being "unruly," or
- has committed a traffic offense.

Also, those under 18 who are said to be deprived, abused, or in need of treatment come under its jurisdiction. In some cases, the juvenile court may retain jurisdiction over delinquent youth until they reach the age of 21. The juvenile court also has jurisdiction over cases involving enlistment in the military services and consent to marriage for minors.

Juvenile courts share with the superior courts jurisdiction involving capital offenses, custody, and child support cases. The superior court has authority to preside over adoption proceedings.

Like adult courts, juvenile courts have judges. In some counties, the juvenile court has its own judge who is appointed by the judge of the superior court. In others, the superior court judge also hears juvenile cases in special sessions. Some juvenile courts also have associate judges who are appointed to assist the juvenile or superior court judge in handling cases.

Children who break the law are held accountable by the juvenile court.

Juvenile Cases

Juvenile courts hear cases in which young people are alleged to be delinquent, unruly, or deprived.

Delinquent juveniles are children and youth under 17 who commit acts which would be criminal offenses if committed by an adult. Examples are burglary, robbery, and auto theft.

Unruly juveniles are children who commit acts that would not be offenses if committed by adults. Unruly juveniles include those who refuse to go to school, run away from home, or are otherwise unmanageable by their parents.

Deprived juveniles are children and youth under 18 who are neglected or abused by parents or who have no parents or guardians. They are considered to be in need of some kind of supervision by the court.

Juvenile Procedure

Like other trial courts, juvenile courts must follow a set of rules that governs their procedure. However, because juvenile procedure is intended to protect children, it is somewhat different from adult criminal procedure.

The steps in juvenile procedure are not the same in all cases. However, the following steps would generally apply in cases where a juvenile commits a delinquent act.

Taking into Custody: Legal authorities apprehend juvenile. Parents are notified. Juvenile court officer decides whether to place child temporarily in a juvenile detention center or release the child to parents.

Intake Decision: Juvenile court officer investigates charges and juvenile's family situation. Results of investigation determine the course of action, which will be one of the following:

a. No further action. Case is dropped or juvenile is counseled and released from the juvenile court's jurisdiction.

b. Informal adjustment. Juvenile court requires youth to have counseling, attend school, pay for damages caused, or have other experiences aimed at changing juvenile's behavior. The period of informal adjustment is for three months and can be extended for three more.

c. Filing of petition for formal hearing. Petition requests legal proceedings against juvenile.

Formal Hearing: Juvenile and parents or guardians are issued a summons to appear before the juvenile court to answer the charges in the petition. Witnesses are also notified to appear. A juvenile may be represented by an attorney. A juvenile court judge conducts the hearing. Unlike an adult trial, a juvenile hearing is not open to the public.

The hearing has two separate parts: adjudication (judgment) and disposition. In the first part, if the court finds the juvenile is not delinquent, he or she is released. If it finds the charges to be true, the court—in the second part—looks for a way of treating the delinquent child. It may

- release the juvenile to the custody of parents or guardians, or foster care;
- place the juvenile on probation, allowing the juvenile to live at home and attend school under the supervision of a juvenile probation officer; or
- commit the juvenile to the Department of Juvenile Justice. The goal of this agency is to prevent delinquent juveniles from becoming adult criminals. So, its facilities are more like schools, less like adult prisons.

A Changing Focus

Like other areas of government, the juvenile justice system continually undergoes change. In 1992 responsibility for juvenile justice programs was moved from the Department of Human Resources to a separate state department. This move meant state government was focusing more attention on the needs of at-risk youths and on those already in trouble. In 1997, the department was renamed the Department of Juvenile Justice. It is responsible for detention and rehabilitation programs for juvenile offenders. The department also provides specialized treatment for juveniles with abuse problems and supervises probation and parole if requested by the courts. ◀

▶ **Locating the Main Ideas**

1. Define: juvenile, delinquent act
2. Why are juveniles treated differently from adults by the justice system?
3. What type of problems or offenses are handled by the juvenile court?

CHAPTER ACTIVITIES

Reviewing the Main Ideas

1. How do the courts serve the public?

2. How is judicial review an example of power sharing within the system of checks and balances?

3. What are the differences between civil and criminal cases?

4. How do the penalties for felonies and misdemeanors compare?

5. Why would we call the superior court "the heart" of Georgia's judicial system?

6. In what areas does the Georgia Supreme Court have exclusive jurisdiction to hear appeals and review cases?

7. Give three examples of the ways citizens' due process rights in criminal matters are protected by the U.S. Constitution.

8. Why do we have separate courts for juveniles?

9. Identify three different categories of cases a juvenile court may hear.

10. How does the juvenile hearing differ from an adult trial?

Give It Some Extra Thought

1. **Understanding Differences.** Why is there a federal system of courts in addition to separate court systems in each of the 50 states?

2. **Discussing and Analyzing.** Why do you think our court system was structured so that the highest courts have appellate and not original jurisdiction?

3. **Making Historical Connections.** In what period of American history was the Fourteenth Amendment adopted? What events were taking place that made its guarantee of due process for all citizens necessary?

Sharpen Your Skills

1. **Analyze and Summarize.** Locate a Georgia newspaper article about a court case. Analyze what is happening by identifying whether it is a federal or state case. Which court is handling it? Is it a civil or criminal case? Summarize what the case is about and, if possible, identify the plaintiff or district attorney and the defendant.

2. **Making Local Connections.** Look up your county government in the telephone directory. Write down the names of the courts and any other judicial-related agencies that are listed. Compare your list to the chart of the Georgia court system in this chapter. Which of the courts on the chart are not found in your county?

3. **Making Comparisons.** Watch a television program that involves some aspect of the criminal justice system such as police work, lawyers, or trials. Take notes and summarize important facts about the situation or case. How do the events in the program compare with what you learned in this chapter?

Going Further

1. **Asking Questions for Information.** Help plan for a classroom visit by a law enforcement officer, an attorney, a juvenile court judge, or a court service worker. Prepare a question to ask your visitor about the part of the juvenile justice process in which he or she is involved.

2. **Field Trip.** Participate in planning a visit as a class or on your own to a civil or criminal trial in the county courthouse. Prepare a report on what you saw and learned from your visit.

30

Coming Up Next!
- Three kinds of local government in Georgia
- Working with other governments

Local Governments—
Cities, Counties, and Special Districts

Local government is very close to people. You use it every day. But most of the time you are probably not aware that you are using local government. It serves you personally—in your home, in your school, as you travel through your neighborhood. Local government affects the safety and comfort of your daily life.

Local government comes to you as streets and streetlights, roads and stop signs, and pipelines that carry drinking water. It appears as fire trucks racing to a burning house, storm sewers that drain rainwater off the streets, and tank trucks that spray for mosquitoes. The bulldozers that bury the garbage and the sewer system that takes away wastewater are part of local government, too.

Local government is also the workers who build and maintain streets and roads. It is the people who make decisions about how all the work of local government is to be done. The police and building inspectors who protect people and property and the sanitation crews who take away tons of garbage and trash are all part of local government.

Because local government is so close at hand, it is the level of government that you can easily influence. Knowing about local government can connect you to its people, equipment, and services. It can help you get things done and make life better in your community.

Three Kinds of Local Government in Georgia

In the state of Georgia there are only three kinds of local government: counties, cities, and special districts. Georgia, therefore, is unlike many other states that have additional subdivisions of local government. This makes local government in Georgia easier to understand.

Counties

Everyone living in Georgia lives in a **county**. Counties were created by the state legislature to serve as districts for carrying out state laws and programs. The state named each county and set its boundaries. At the center of county government is the county courthouse. The city in which the county courthouse is located is referred to as the **county seat**.

In 1777, Georgia adopted its first state constitution, which established eight counties. These eight original counties were located on the Atlantic Coast and along the Savannah River, in the populated areas of the state. These early counties had two main responsibilities. They were to carry out the state's justice system by operating courts of law, and they were to build and maintain local roads. As the state grew and developed westward, the legislature created more and more counties. Today, Georgia has 159 counties. That is the maximum number of counties allowed by the Georgia constitution since 1945.

Georgia has more counties than any other state except Texas (which has 254). This state's counties serve relatively small physical areas when compared to counties in other states. The smallest county, Clarke County, is 125 square miles. Ware County, the largest, is 912 square miles but has only half as many people as Clarke County. The majority of Georgia counties have between 10,000 and 50,000 people living in them. Only 12 counties have more than 100,000 people. The more populated counties have larger governments with more employees to help provide services for all of their people.

The county seat was not only the center of local government. It was a gathering place for business and social activity. Here, farmers are selling cotton in the Carroll County courthouse square in 1913.

Randy Turner

Randy Turner, Barrow County commissioner, is pictured here learning to use the Internet, at a class for government officials. In a 1998 interview, he explained why he ran for office and talked about some of his concerns: "Why did I run for the county commission? Honestly, one night on the Internet I came across writings by Jefferson and Lincoln that left a deep impression. The next day I read in the paper that qualifying to run for office was almost over. I stopped in a local barber shop, and a man there told me he was not going to run again. I decided to pay the qualifying fee and run for commissioner.

"Sadly, very few people attend the commission meetings except when a zoning or development issue gets people upset. Our county was once rural but population moving from the Atlanta area is causing growing pains. Along with growth comes the need for more schools and more of other services, and that can require more taxes. When citizens learn the personal side of an issue, they become more active, and then they pack the meeting room."

The County Governing Body

The governing body of a county is its **county commission**, whose members are elected by county voters. The size of the commission varies from one county to another. A majority of counties have a five-member governing body. Some have only 1 commissioner, while other counties elect as many as 11 commissioners.

The commission has a combination of legislative power and executive power. But it does not decide all county policies. The state constitution provides for other county officials who are elected by the people and have specified constitutional powers. They are the sheriff, the judge of probate court, the clerk of superior court, and the tax commissioner. The superior court judge and judge of the magistrate court are also elected. Many counties (60 percent) have a county administrator or county manager who is appointed by the commission to carry out the day-to-day administrative work of government.

County commissions are empowered by Georgia's constitution to enact reasonable laws regarding local property and affairs. These laws, called county ordinances, may establish a new recreation program, a traffic regulation, or other policy of the county. Commissioners can also adopt county **resolutions**, which are informal statements expressing the commission's opinion on a public matter. Examples are a resolution supporting paper recycling in a community, or a resolution to honor the fire department during fire prevention week.

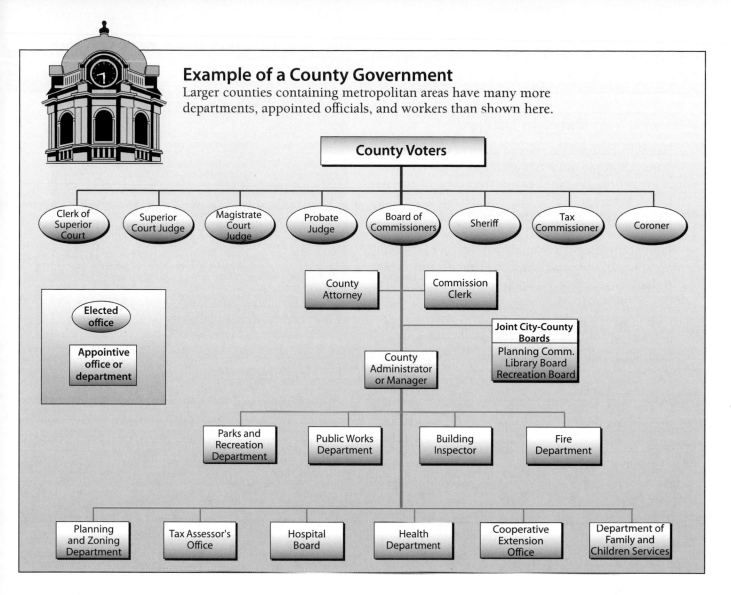

Example of a County Government

Larger counties containing metropolitan areas have many more departments, appointed officials, and workers than shown here.

County Voters

- Clerk of Superior Court
- Superior Court Judge
- Magistrate Court Judge
- Probate Judge
- Board of Commissioners
- Sheriff
- Tax Commissioner
- Coroner

Elected office

Appointive office or department

- County Attorney
- Commission Clerk

Joint City-County Boards
Planning Comm.
Library Board
Recreation Board

County Administrator or Manager

- Parks and Recreation Department
- Public Works Department
- Building Inspector
- Fire Department

- Planning and Zoning Department
- Tax Assessor's Office
- Hospital Board
- Health Department
- Cooperative Extension Office
- Department of Family and Children Services

Powers of County Government

As an "arm" of the state, a county government carries out many basic activities and services for state government. It provides trial courts for the state judicial system, carries out state health and welfare programs, and conducts voter registration and state elections. Counties build and repair their own roads and bridges as well as those that are part of the state highway system. Counties also are responsible for recording important information for the state, such as property ownership, births, deaths, and marriages.

Issuing auto licenses is another way that counties carry out state programs. When you purchase *state* automobile tags, you go to a *county* office. There, you fill out forms to register your car with the Georgia Department of Revenue. But you do so through your county tax commissioner. That office actually records the car and owner, collects the tax, and forwards the record and registration fee to the state.

However, counties do much more than serve as agents of the state. They provide self-government for the people living within

Patsy Jo Hilliard

Patsy Jo Hilliard, Mayor of East Point, is shown here talking to students about local government. A former teacher, she became interested in government years ago when she was elected to an educational post in the South San Francisco school district. Mayor Hilliard feels that her work can contribute to a better quality of life in East Point. "As mayor, I play a role in making decisions that determine the overall well-being of the city. Our decisions must be sound, moral, and when not popular, courageous. We must be willing to put the good of the residents above all else."

their boundaries. Under the Georgia constitution, counties have powers to provide selected local services ordinarily provided by cities to help make life safer and better for county citizens. These services include fire protection, sewer system, public transportation, parks, libraries, police department, recreation facilities, and public health facilities. ◀

Cities

A city is a community that has been **incorporated**—that is, officially created by the state legislature. Once incorporated, a city or town is legally known as a **municipality**. Cities come about because people want certain services not provided by the county. To be eligible for incorporation, a community must (1) have at least 200 people living in the area to be incorporated; (2) be at least three miles from the boundary of any existing city; and (3) be 60 percent developed and divided into tracts designated for residential, commercial, industrial, governmental, or institutional purposes.

If these qualifications are met, the people of a community desiring to be a city must work through the state representatives and senators who represent that community. If the legislators approve the idea, they draw up a proposed **charter** for the city.

The charter is something like a city constitution. It creates the city, gives it an official name, and defines its boundaries. The charter also describes the city's form of government, and defines its powers. Once a charter has been granted, the city can provide various services. Those services might include police protection, garbage pickup, and streetlights.

The final step in becoming a city is to submit the proposed charter to a vote of the General Assembly. If the charter is passed into

▶ Locating the Main Ideas

1. Define: county, county seat, county commission, resolution
2. What powers does the county commission have?
3. Give two examples to show how the county is an "arm" of state government.
4. In addition to serving as an agent of the state, what other purposes does a county serve?

Joan Saliba

Joan Saliba, mayor of Hartwell, with a group representing Hartwell and Hart County, carried a petition with 6,000 signatures to Governor Miller, asking that the state not close Hart State Park. They "won the day," and the park remains open. Mayor Saliba enjoys talking with people, discussing community needs, and trying to figure out whether she can help. "Hartwell is a community with good planning and many volunteers. It was recently selected as *Governor's All Star City.* I enjoy meeting with those who agree with me and those who don't. I look for some common ground where we can work things out." The mayor believes that there *is* a role for young citizens in local govern-

ment. "We have a student government day for 11th and 12th graders. They use our voting machines to elect a student mayor and six city council members. They learn a lot about governing as they meet and make their decisions."

law, the community becomes a municipality, with its own government. Thereafter, the people who live in the new city elect city officials. But they also continue to be citizens of the county in which they live and can vote in county elections, too.

Some cities have grown and developed across county lines. The people in one part of the city may be residents of one county, while people in another part of the city are residents of another county. One example is Atlanta. Most residents of Atlanta live in Fulton County, but those who live in one eastern portion are in DeKalb County.

When we compare cities and counties, we find that cities are an older form of local government. Some cities, such as Savannah and Augusta, were established before there were counties, when Georgia was still a colony. But the great majority of Georgia cities were formed after the counties in which they are located.

Remember that counties are established on the initiative of the state legislature to serve as administrative districts for the state government. Cities, on the other hand, are formed on the initiative of people in a local area so they can have additional local self-government and services.

The great majority of Georgia cities are small. The 1996 population estimates show that the state has 264 cities with less than 1,000 people. Of the 537 cities in Georgia, 52 have populations larger than 10,000, and three of those are cities that are consolidated with the county. The top ten cities in population range from Atlanta with 401,907 to Warner Robins with 45,559 people.

When a city population increases rapidly and its growth spills over into the surrounding unincorporated area, the city government

Alan Reddish

Dougherty County Administrator Alan Reddish explains to local elected officials how the new public safety radio system works. Reddish enjoys his work. "Being a county administrator is a rewarding and exciting job. I'm responsible for the daily operations of Dougherty County. That involves me in decisions relating to law enforcement, budget, street maintenance and construction, solid waste disposal, and various employee issues. I also have the opportunity to assist the county commission in developing policies and responding to requests for services from the public.

may attempt to annex property. **Annexation** is an action to extend a city's boundaries by adding land from adjoining unincorporated areas. There are several ways in which land can be added to a city. One common way is to hold a referendum of the voters in the area to be annexed. If a majority approves the annexation, the land becomes part of the city.

The City Governing Body

A city is governed by an elected **city council** (sometimes called the city commission). The council's legislative powers to adopt ordinances and resolutions for the city are similar to the county commission's powers in the county. Cities also have an elected **mayor**, who is usually the leader of the city and may or may not have much power in that role.

Executive power varies with the form of city government. The three forms found in Georgia are listed here with key features.

1. Mayor-Council Government with a "Strong" Mayor
   - Mayor serves as ceremonial head of government at public functions—public speeches, ribbon cuttings, dedications.
   - City council decides on policies of the city but has no administrative power.
   - Mayor may have a veto over council legislation.
   - Mayor has strong executive power to carry out policies—prepares the budget, makes appointments, and manages the daily operations of the city.
   - Mayor may have an administrative assistant who helps oversee departments that provide city services.
   - City council has limits set on its power.

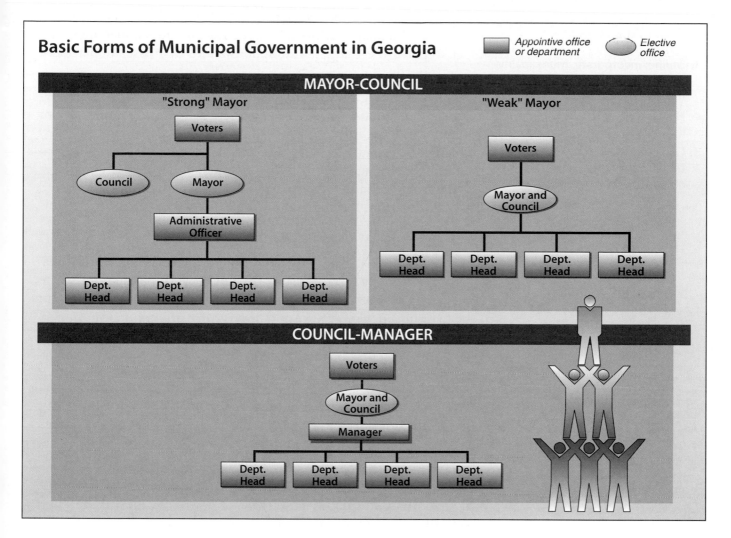

Basic Forms of Municipal Government in Georgia

Appointive office or department

Elective office

MAYOR-COUNCIL

"Strong" Mayor

Voters → Council, Mayor → Administrative Officer → Dept. Head, Dept. Head, Dept. Head, Dept. Head

"Weak" Mayor

Voters → Mayor and Council → Dept. Head, Dept. Head, Dept. Head, Dept. Head

COUNCIL-MANAGER

Voters → Mayor and Council → Manager → Dept. Head, Dept. Head, Dept. Head, Dept. Head

2. Mayor-Council Government with a "Weak" Mayor

- Mayor serves as ceremonial head of government at public functions—public speeches, ribbon cuttings, dedications.

- Mayor appoints department heads with council approval.

- Mayor may preside over council meetings and recommend ordinances.

- City council decides policies and makes laws.

- City council committees review how departments carry out programs.

3. Council-Manager Government

- Mayor serves as ceremonial head of government at public functions—public speeches, ribbon cuttings, dedications.

- Mayor may preside over council meetings but has little or no executive power.

- City council decides policies and makes laws.

- **City manager**—usually a professional trained in conducting the city's business—is appointed by the city council to administer the government and can be removed by it.

1. Define: incorporate, municipality, charter, annexation, city council, mayor, city manager

2. How is a city officially established in Georgia?

3. Compare the "strong" mayor and the "weak" mayor forms of the mayor-council governments.

These are just a few of the hundreds of special-purpose districts and authorities established to give special services to local communities in Georgia. What special purpose governments are operating in your community?

- City manager draws up the agenda for council meetings, prepares the budget, and appoints and dismisses department heads.

Most of Georgia's 533 cities have a mayor-council form of government. But most larger cities also hire a professional manager or administrator. Cities are generally governed by part-time elected councils. The councils of mid-sized and larger cities have found that running a city has become a full-time business. The city manager is there daily to supervise the work of the departments and respond to requests from local citizens. ◀

Special-Purpose Governments

A third type of local government found in Georgia is the **special district** or **authority**. These are mostly small governmental units set up by cities or counties for a single special purpose. The purpose might be to build a new firehouse and provide fire protection for one section of a county. Or, it might be to provide a water system for a city or county. It might be established to provide a bus system for a district that includes a city and a county. The Gwinnett County Airport Authority is an example of a special-purpose government.

Not all special-purpose governments are created by counties or cities. Authorities and districts may also be created by an act of the state legislature. Such action is taken to offer a specific service in a specified part of the state. The Metropolitan Atlanta Rapid Transit Authority (MARTA) is a good example. This authority serves the people living in the city of Atlanta and two counties, Fulton and DeKalb, with a rapid rail and bus system.

Examples of Special-Purpose District Governments and Services They Provide

Airports:
Barrow County Airport Authority,
Washington–Wilkes Airport Authority

Transportation:
Macon–Bibb County Transit Authority,
Metropolitan Atlanta Rapid Transit Authority
(MARTA)

Recreation facilities:
Atlanta–Fulton County
Recreation Authority,
Gainesville Area Park Commission

Fire protection:
West Jackson County Fire District,
Paulding County Fire Protection
Districts

Parking facilities:
Marietta Parking Authority,
East Point Parking Authority

Water plant/Sewer system:
Rockdale County–Conyers Water
Authority, Gwinnett County Water
and Sewerage District, Spalding
County Water District

School districts are also special-purpose governments. They were formed by the state to provide elementary and secondary education. School districts rely on property taxes for most of their local revenue. The state pays more than half the cost of running the districts, including funds for textbooks and teachers' salaries.

Some special-purpose governments are organized with the same boundaries as the county or city. Some are located in a part of a city or county. Others are set up across city or county lines. The boundaries depend on the purpose of the district and the people it is designed to serve.

Few people notice the special-purpose governments. That may be because members of most governing boards are appointed rather than elected. So, any issues that arise may not get much public attention. In fact, these separately governed special districts and authorities are sometimes called "hidden governments."

These apartments are operated by the Athens Housing Authority.

Why do we have special-purpose governments? They have advantages that encourage local governments to create them. One, they offer an efficient way to respond to an urgent problem. Second, the special-purpose government can readily borrow money for its projects. Although the state limits the amount of money cities and counties can borrow, these limits do not apply to the special-purpose government.

A third advantage of special-purpose governments is that they can charge fees to users and in that way raise money to pay back the funds borrowed. This allows the development of a specific service, such as a new water treatment plant, without the city or county needing to borrow more money than state law allows. In addition, by setting up a special-purpose government, the city or county can add a service without doing something that is often unpopular—raising taxes.

There are some disadvantages to these nearly invisible governments. Because they receive little publicity and their governing boards are seldom elected, they may not be responsive to public opinion. Also, if a community has many special-purpose governments, each with its own narrow concern, the result can be a hodgepodge of uncoordinated activities.

Working with Other Governments

Many activities of local governments overlap or are similar. Different counties have some of the same needs. They provide some of the same services and have some of the same expenses. They also

Consolidation of city and county. The outgoing city council of Athens and board of commissioners of Clarke County celebrated unification of the two governments in January 1991. They tied a ribbon linking the county courthouse and the city hall.

levy some of the same taxes. Consequently, counties sometimes find that they can benefit by working together.

Counties often work cooperatively to provide a service on a regional basis. A regional library, hospital, or landfill might be built to serve several counties. These counties then share the bill and all of their citizens benefit from the common service that is provided. Fulton and Cobb counties, for example, share the costs and work of keeping up a bridge over their common boundary, the Chattahoochee River.

County and city governments frequently work together, too. It is not unusual for a city to furnish a service jointly with the county government. Brantley County and the cities of Nahunta and Hoboken share the costs of animal control. Coweta County and the city of Newnan jointly support an airport. Albany and Dougherty County jointly provide many services, with city and county governments sharing the same office building. In all parts of the state, cities and counties work together (intergovernmental cooperation) to furnish ambulance service, develop parks and recreation programs, and build water or sewer systems.

City-County Consolidation

In some cases, the cooperation of a city and a county government has led to **consolidation**, a formal merging of the two governments decided by a vote of the people. When community leaders encourage consolidating city and county governments, they usually want to combine services, eliminate duplication, increase efficiency, and reduce costs.

In Georgia, city-county consolidation has occurred only three times in the 26 years between 1970 and 1996. In 1972, the people of the city of Columbus and Muscogee County voted to combine their governments. In 1990, citizens of Clarke County and the city of Athens voted to unify. In 1995, the people of Augusta and Richmond County voted to consolidate.

There have been other efforts to combine city and county governments, including attempts in Bibb, Candler, Dougherty, Glynn, Lanier, Rockdale, Spalding, Schley, and Ware counties. As yet, these have not been successful. Still, interest in this approach to eliminating duplication and holding down costs continues. ◀

▶ **Locating the Main Ideas**

1. Define: special district, authority, consolidation

2. What are three ways a special-purpose government can be created?

3. Why are special-purpose governments and authorities called "hidden governments"?

4. Give two examples of how counties work together. Give two examples of how a city and county can cooperate.

Reviewing the Main Ideas

1. Give three examples of how local government affects you every day.

2. For what purpose were counties originally created?

3. How does the county administrator or manager assist the county commission?

4. Name three activities or services that counties perform on behalf of the state.

5. What important information is found in a city's charter?

6. On whose initiative and for what purpose were counties established? cities established?

7. Why would large cities be more likely to adopt a council-manager form of government than small cities?

8. What are some reasons for establishing a special district or authority?

9. What are the advantages of special-purpose governments? What are the disadvantages?

10. What are the main reasons given for consolidating city and county governments?

Give It Some Extra Thought

1. **Explaining.** Explain how local government is the level of government citizens can most easily influence.

2. **Connecting Past to Present.** Why is city government one of society's oldest forms of government? Why are cities considered to be the oldest local governments in Georgia?

3. **Making Comparisons.** Which of the three general forms of city government is most like the county commission form of government? Explain your choice.

Sharpen Your Skills

1. **Influencing Local Government.** Write an editorial to persuade local citizens to attend a meeting of the county commission where there will be a final vote on new water rates. Use the editorial to explain how it is easier to influence government at the local level and why it is important for local residents to make their views known.

2. **Locating Information on a Map.** Use the county grid index to locate your county on an official state highway map. Write down the names of the cities in your county. Use the map key to find the population range for each city and identify the county seat. Record population information beside the name of each city. Scan the surrounding counties and their cities. How does your county compare?

3. **Community Investigation.** Look up the county government and the city government entries in the telephone directory. Write down the names of three departments in the county and three departments in the city that have the same name or function. Are there any departments that use both the city and the county names, indicating a joint activity?

Going Further

1. **Citizen Involvement.** Imagine that the street in front of your house is so full of potholes that you are afraid the family car will be damaged from traveling on it. Which government would you contact? What would you do to get your local government to repair the potholes?

2. **Making Local Connections.** Find out the names of the county commissioners in your county. Report on each member's occupation and how many years he or she has served. Is there a county administrator or manager? If you live in a city, do the same thing for the members of the city council. Invite one of these local government leaders to come to your classroom to talk about the biggest concerns of the community today.

31

Coming Up Next!
- The big seven local government services
- Paying the bill for local government

Local Government—
Serving the People Close to Home

Local governments were created to serve the people living within their boundaries. The earliest local governments in Georgia offered only very basic services—courts, law enforcement, and building and maintenance of roads. To pay for these, county and city governments had to collect taxes. The process is the same today, but local government does much more. Since Georgia became a state more than 220 years ago, local governments have expanded their role to provide people with fire protection, garbage collection, recreation, traffic lights, and many other services.

There are many services that counties, cities, and special-purpose districts provide. In some communities, particularly large ones, citizens want numerous public services and are willing to pay for them. In many smaller communities, people want low taxes and are satisfied with only a few basic services. The result is a variation in services from one county to another and from city to city.

The Big Seven Local Government Services

Most local government services can be grouped together into seven categories: public safety, public works, public utilities, planning and development, human services, judicial services, and public record keeping. In your community, specific services may be provided by the county, the city, a special-purpose government, or a combination of these local governments.

Public Safety

The services that we categorize as "public safety" are the government activities that protect people's lives and property. This includes such things as police and fire protection, animal control, traffic regulation, disaster preparations, and building codes.

Probably these are the most visible things that local governments do. We see and hear a fire engine racing to save a blazing building. We hear and recognize a police car or the sheriff rushing to the scene of a crime or pulling a speeder over. While walking or in a car, we are conscious of traffic lights and stop signs. We notice when a siren signals a practice warning for a disaster. Public safety gets the attention of the people.

Protection of people's lives and property is a top priority in local communities. It is also one of the most expensive services of local government. This is because public safety really requires two types of efforts: preventing new problems and dealing with existing ones. For instance, prevention of fires is a main goal of the fire department. Fire inspectors check buildings to see that fire safety regulations are followed. They encourage people to be careful with wood stoves and space heaters, to install smoke detectors, and to consider adding sprinklers. Such fire-prevention education can reduce damage and deaths.

Cops on bikes have become a popular form of community policing.

Special training is required for most public safety workers. Police must be able to respond quickly in cases of crimes and accidents. They must be skilled in keeping peace and order and helping prevent or control situations that lead to crime. Police officers must have basic training of 360 to 440 hours. Then they must take 20 hours of additional training each year.

Fire fighters must pass a course of study approved by the Georgia Fire Academy in Forsyth. Preventing and fighting fires have become more and more demanding. For example, fighting chemical fires, electrical fires, and fires that break out in high-rise buildings requires special training. Paid fire fighters must get at least 120 hours of training each year. Volunteers must meet basic certification requirements of either 60 or 120 hours, as set by their local government.

The inspectors who enforce local building codes (the ordinances that set construction requirements) also must have special training. They must have the skills for checking the safety of construction and the installation of gas lines, plumbing, air conditioning, and electrical wiring. These inspections can help save lives and protect property from fires, building collapse, flooding, and other damage.

Elizabeth Wilson

In this photo, Elizabeth Wilson, mayor of Decatur, swears in Explorers to the city's Police Outreach Program. Mayor Wilson has many opportunities to meet with the people of her city. Here is something she says when she talks to people about government.

"Government is not for me—it's for the people. You know what makes government work? YOU. What you have to do as a citizen is call me. Or call the city manager. We can tell you whom to contact and just what you need to do about that problem. And once YOU (the citizen) get involved, changes will happen. If elected people (like me) and appointed people (like our city manager) do the job well, then government listens and responds to the people—*if the people speak up.*"

Public Works

Public works departments in cities and counties take care of the basic physical facilities of the community. These facilities include roads and streets, water and sewer lines, storm drainage systems, and public buildings. Collection and disposal of solid waste is also a public works activity. In many small counties and cities, public works departments take on additional functions, such as repair and upkeep of parks and other public recreational facilities.

Engineers and road crews work to maintain safe and durable streets and roads. Streets and roads are inspected for cracks, bumps, and other effects of weather and use.

Each person in the United States makes 4.5 pounds of trash per day. Disposing of solid waste has become a big public works problem. Every community has to get rid of its garbage. Homes, factories, restaurants, gas stations, and stores all produce quantities of solid waste. Local governments must determine what to do with food and other garbage, as well as old autos, furniture and appliances, used plastic containers, tree limbs, and grass cuttings. Local governments must also find ways to dispose of hazardous substances, such as oil, caustic chemicals, and radioactive waste material.

The sanitation department of a city or county is often responsible for collecting and disposing of waste material. The most common disposal method is use of a **sanitary landfill**. A landfill is an area of land where solid waste is buried. Landfills must follow standards set by state and federal environmental regulations. But landfills all around Georgia are filling up quickly.

In a landfill, solid waste should be buried using procedures that will prevent air and water pollution.

A method of reducing solid waste is to burn it at high heat in a special furnace. But this burning must be carefully controlled so that it does not pollute the air.

Some materials can be recovered for reuse by recycling. Aluminum cans, newspapers, and glass jars and bottles can be collected, broken down to their basic substances, and used again to make the same or different materials. Through recycling, many communities have greatly reduced the amount of waste that must be carried to the landfill.

Public Utilities

Public utilities are publicly run enterprises that provide utility services for a fee to residents of a local community. Waterworks, sewage treatment plants, and electric power companies are three common examples.

Residents of a community need water that is safe to drink and easily available for bathing, cooking, flushing toilets, and washing clothes. They also need to have wastewater removed from houses and businesses.

Typically, cities have provided water for the people who live there by establishing a water plant or waterworks. Water is pumped from a river or other source, purified, and then pumped to residences and businesses. After water is used, sewage plants receive the wastewater, treat it to remove sludge and disease-causing bacteria, and return it to rivers and streams. Although the laying and repair of water and sewer pipes is usually done by the public works department, public utilities operate the plants that treat the water.

Fifty-one Georgia cities run their own electric power companies, purchasing electricity from large power companies and reselling it to local residents. Also, about 64 cities own natural gas distribution facilities, which function in the same way as electricity utilities. ▶

Planning and Development

To assure that a community grows and develops in an orderly, safe, and healthful manner, planning for the future is an important function for local government. The county commission or city council appoints a committee of citizens to the planning commission to study community needs. The commission reviews the existing conditions of the land and prepares a **land-use plan**. Professional planners are hired to work out the details of a land-use plan for the community. They divide the community into areas known as zones. Each zone has a designated use, such as residential, industrial, commercial, or agricultural. This process is known as **zoning**.

Local officials and professional planners work together to determine land-use regulations that will serve the community. Ordinances are passed that regulate for each zone what types of activity may take place. They specify the kinds of buildings that can be built, how much park area or open space is to be preserved, and the

Water is stored in elevated water tanks where the pull of gravity moves the water through the pipes.

▶ **Locating the Main Ideas**

1. Define: sanitary landfill
2. Identify: public safety, public works, public utilities, solid waste
3. Why is public safety one of the most expensive services of local government?
4. What kinds of jobs are generally performed by the public works department in a community?

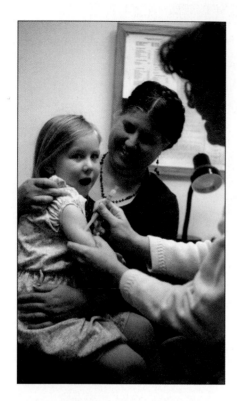

County health nurse Betsy Weisenburg works in the child health program of the Clarke County Health Department. She immunizes children against contagious diseases and screens for lead poisoning. To assure that they are healthy, she checks on the nutrition and development of young children from birth to age 5.

density of population. In addition to local regulation, a number of state and federal standards apply to the use of land (for example, in cases that affect wetlands).

How and where traffic will flow through a city must also be planned and regulated. Traffic engineers determine where stop signs, directions signs, and traffic lights should be placed. They also recommend one-way streets or regulations to help the traffic flow.

After the planning comes the development. Once a community has set aside land for parks, for example, it must develop a plan for park use and maintenance. This plan may include creating recreation programs and building new facilities. The size and extent of a recreation program depends on the size of the community, what it would like to have, and how much it can afford. A community park often includes a meeting hall, rooms for arts and crafts classes, a swimming pool, a baseball diamond, tennis courts, and other facilities.

Human Services

All counties and some cities carry out public health programs and public assistance programs, called human services. These include hearing and eye tests for school children, spraying for mosquitoes, and community immunization to prevent the spread of disease. Every county operates a health department that offers checkups, counseling, and clinics for needy people including newborn babies, children, and pregnant women.

Public assistance programs, sometimes called welfare programs, are designed to promote the well-being of people in need. These programs help neglected children and people who are poor, disabled, or elderly. Assistance may include providing food, job training, child care, and social programs. Help may also be available for heating, electricity, and other needs.

Most local human services are supported by a combination of state and federal funding. These health and welfare programs are guided by an agency of state government, the Georgia Department of Human Resources.

Judicial Services: County and City Courts

A main purpose that state government had for establishing counties was to organize a system of justice throughout the state. Each county built a courthouse in order to hear and try local cases. In fact, the earliest administrators of Georgia counties were judges who presided over court proceedings and also managed county affairs.

Today, local courts still connect the people to the state and national system of justice. The Georgia judicial system described in Chapter 29 includes local courts. Local governments and courthouses bring that judicial system to the people.

People in Local Government

Dyanne Reese

Dyanne Reese leads a busy life as city clerk of Savannah and president of the Georgia Municipal Clerks and Finance Officers Association. What are the responsibilities of a city clerk? Ms. Reese explains that "the city clerk of Savannah or any other city is the official record keeper. And keeping good records of meetings and ordinances is important to the smooth operation of government. Another part of this job that I really enjoy is working with the public. Most people who come to the city hall feel lost. They come to the city clerk to find out where to go for assistance. It's very satisfying to help people and give them information about their government."

Each county has a superior court. It is the trial court for the more serious criminal cases and for certain civil cases. Each county also has a magistrate court to hear cases that involve violations of local ordinances. The probate court of each county is the court that handles wills and cases of guardianship. Many counties also have a local court called the state court. It helps reduce the caseload of the superior court by hearing cases of less serious crimes and civil cases not required by law to go before the superior courts. The sheriff, serving as an officer of the superior court, summons witnesses and runs the county jail.

Georgia cities have additional courts. Municipal courts handle traffic cases and cases related to violations of municipal ordinances. The courtrooms inside the city hall or the county courthouse in your community are links to Georgia's system of justice.

Record Keeping

It rarely makes the news, but careful recording and storage of vital public information is an important service of local government. Records for the community are maintained by the county clerk and the clerk of superior court. City clerks and other officials also file important records.

County records include marriage applications and certificates, voter registration data, and election results for state and county races. The county also records local property ownership including plats (maps of the property), superior court records, probate court records, motor vehicle registrations, and records of the meetings and finances of county government.

Municipalities keep records of municipal elections, meetings and finances of the city council, and records of municipal court. School

▶ **Locating the Main Ideas**

1. Define: land-use plan, zoning
2. What is a major activity of a planning commission?
3. What types of programs are covered by the term "human services"?
4. List four kinds of records kept by counties.

districts and other special-purpose governments likewise must keep records of their governing board meetings, finances, and formal communications.

Year by year, this vital information increases. State law requires each local government to set up a records management system. So, the clerk who must organize and retain the information tries to develop an effective system for storing it and readily retrieving it when needed. Computers, microfilm, and copy machines have greatly improved record-keeping services in recent years. ◀

Paying the Bill for Local Government

As you can see, local governments have many responsibilities to help make life healthy, safe, and orderly. The people living in local communities rely on local government to meet these responsibilities and provide services. But to provide services, someone must pay. Financing services is one of the most demanding tasks of local governing authorities.

Costs of Services

What does it cost local governments to make life healthy, safe, and orderly in local communities? In 1996, Georgia's cities and counties spent $7.9 billion. This money went to pay workers, buy equipment and supplies, and keep offices, clinics, courts, firehouses, jails, and police and sheriff's departments running. The bills for all of these services to residents of local communities had to be paid. Where did the money come from?

Local Government Income

The income that local governments receive to pay for services is called revenue. Local government revenues come mainly from taxes. There are two types of taxes: property taxes and non-property taxes. Local governments levy or assess **property taxes** on

1. *real property* (land and buildings), and
2. *personal property* (items such as cars, boats, airplanes).

In addition, local governments can collect the following non-property taxes:

1. *one percent local option* sales tax*—money can be used for any purpose
2. *one percent special-purpose local option sales tax*—money to be used for a specially designated purpose for a limited time only
3. *alcoholic beverages tax*—charged per bottle, can, or by the drink

---

*"Local option" means that residents of each county have the option, or choice, of voting to impose this tax on themselves.

Planning for parks and playgrounds is an important part of the land-use decisions in any community.

Funding Local Government

Revenues	Expenditures
Taxes	Administration
• Property taxes on— tangible property motor vehicles	Courts
• Taxes on business activities	Education
• Local option sales taxes	Health/Human Services
• Other county taxes	Highways
	Housing/Community Development
Federal and State Aid	Leisure Services
Non-Tax Revenues	Public Safety
• Charges to users for certain services, including utilities	Public Works
• Licenses and permits	Public Utilities
• Fines and penalties	
• Miscellaneous sales	
• Bank interest	
Borrowing	

4. *tax on lodging bills for hotels and motels*—money to be used to promote tourism and conventions for the community

5. *tax on insurance premiums*

6. *occupation taxes* as specified by state law (examples are taxes on plumbing, construction companies, and funeral parlors)

Local governments have other sources of revenue besides taxes. These other sources of revenues include the following:

1. **user fees** paid by users of a service, such as water, parking, recreation, and garbage collection

2. *charges for business licenses* to regulate certain businesses, such as taxi companies, garbage collection companies, and charity collection agencies

3. *fines and penalties* collected from traffic violations and violations of county or city ordinances

4. *grants* (sometimes called intergovernmental revenues) from state government to help pay costs of roads, recreation, forest fire protection, pollution control, and health and welfare services; and from the federal government to help pay costs of community development projects, such as sewer systems or bus systems, and health and public assistance programs

Money collected from parking meters is a user fee.

Residential property is on the tax digest.

Understanding Property Taxes

The largest portion of revenues for Georgia county government comes from property taxes. In 1996, counties relied on property taxes to bring in $1.6 billion, or 38 percent, of the total county revenues. Cities received $416 million, or about 25 percent, of their revenues from property taxes.

How is the tax on real property determined? The county board of tax assessors decides the value of each piece of real estate in the county. This is called the assessed valuation. County assessors follow guidelines set by state laws and court decisions.

According to state law, property is to be given an assessed valuation of 40 percent of the *fair market value* (the price the property would bring if sold on a fair market). The assessed value of each piece of property is important, because the property tax is an **ad valorem tax**. That means that the tax is based on the value of the property. If property owners disagree with the valuation of their property, they can appeal to a special county board called the board of equalization.

Next, county officials must decide on the tax rate. They take into account the total of all assessed property value in the county (the **tax digest**) and the amount of money they will need to pay expenses. From these figures, they determine the tax rate, called the **millage rate**. A mill is the unit used for expressing the property tax rate. Each mill represents a tax of $1 on each $1,000 of assessed valuation. The millage rate is the amount of tax owed for each thousand dollars of assessed valuation. For instance, a millage rate of 32 mills means that the tax will be $32 for every thousand dollars that the property is valued at for tax purposes.

A house and land with a fair market value of $90,000 would have a taxable value of $36,000 (fair market value × 40% = assessed valuation). Taxed at 20 mills (36 × 20), the property would have a property tax of $720. But many pieces of property have exemptions, or reductions, in the taxes.

People who own property and live in a house on that property receive a partial exemption known as the **homestead exemption**. The regular homestead exemption is $2,000. It is subtracted from the assessed valuation of property before the millage rate is figured. If the owners of the property with the assessed valuation of $36,000 live there, they would receive a homestead exemption of $2,000. So their tax (20 mills) would be figured on $34,000. The tax would be 34 × 20 or $680.

Additional homestead exemptions are given to homeowners over age 65 and disabled veterans. Land and structures belonging to re-

Local Government Expenditures in 1996: The Six Largest Categories

Utilities

water plants, sewage systems, and some gas and electric companies. These costs are usually paid by user fees (charges to the people receiving the service) and do not require taxes to pay for them.

Public safety

sheriff's departments, jails, city and county police departments, and fire departments.

Health and human services

disease prevention, testing and treatment programs, drug education, and welfare funds.

Administrative costs

personnel, insurance expenses, equipment, and supplies.

Roads, streets, storm sewers, and bridges

building new ones and maintenance of existing ones.

Court system

trials, juries, and maintenance of the courtroom.

Additional bills for local governments included recreation or leisure services, other public works (garbage and trash collection, landfills, and parking facilities), and public housing and community development costs.

County

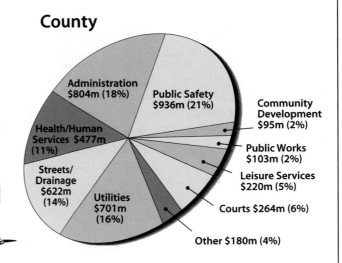

Administration $804m (18%)
Public Safety $936m (21%)
Community Development $95m (2%)
Health/Human Services $477m (11%)
Public Works $103m (2%)
Leisure Services $220m (5%)
Streets/Drainage $622m (14%)
Utilities $701m (16%)
Courts $264m (6%)
Other $180m (4%)

Municipal

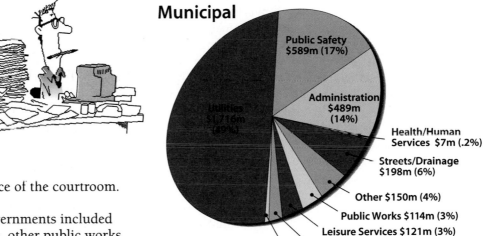

Utilities $1,716m (49%)
Public Safety $589m (17%)
Administration $489m (14%)
Health/Human Services $7m (.2%)
Streets/Drainage $198m (6%)
Other $150m (4%)
Public Works $114m (3%)
Leisure Services $121m (3%)
Community Development $62m (2%)
Courts $22m (.6%)

ligious, educational, and public charity institutions are generally exempt from property tax.

The Cost Crunch

How is the money spent? The pie graphs on this page show how cities and counties spent funds on services in 1996. Georgia counties spent $4.4 billion and cities spent $3.4 billion. A comparison of the pie charts shows the differences between city and county service expenditures.

Save the Courthouse!

Teenagers of Banks County

The students of Banks County High School are credited with saving the historic old courthouse in Homer. The two-story brick building is one of the oldest courthouses in Georgia. Construction on it began in 1859—before the start of the Civil War. Because the old courthouse had become run-down, the county government moved its offices into a new building in 1988. The county commissioners were considering tearing down the old courthouse to make room for a parking lot. The question of whether or not to tear it down was placed on the ballot for the fall 1988 election. Few people seemed to care about it.

Students in the high school, led by a junior, John Clark Hill, campaigned to save the old courthouse. Through a History Day project, Hill had become interested in the old building. With permission of the school principal, the students held a peaceful demonstration in front of the old courthouse to bring community attention to the issue. They also helped raise money to print flyers for the campaign to get out the vote against destroying the courthouse. Then, they helped the Save the Courthouse Committee distribute flyers to every house in the county.

When the votes were counted on election day, people had voted nearly two to one to save the

courthouse. The historic courthouse was repaired and is once again alive with activity in downtown Homer. The building serves as a welcome center and houses a museum with historic photographs, books, and artifacts from Banks County. Community groups use it regularly as a meeting place, and the Superior Court sometimes convenes in the old upstairs courtroom. The courthouse stands not only as a monument to its historic past, but also as a symbol of what young Georgians can accomplish when they take an interest in government.

▶ Locating the Main Ideas

1. Define: property tax, user fee, ad valorem tax, tax digest, millage rate, homestead exemption, privatization

2. Identify: local option tax, fair market value

3. What are three kinds of property that can be taxed by local governments?

4. What are intergovernmental revenues?

The costs of providing services are rising. Requests for local government services are increasing, too. Meanwhile, property owners are generally opposed to raising property taxes. Federal and state grants are declining. As a result, cities and counties are relying more and more on user fees and local sales taxes to help finance services. They are also turning to another option—**privatization**—for providing services while keeping costs down. Privatization is the contracting by a government with a private business to deliver a government service. For example, private companies may contract to perform services such as garbage collection, recycling operations, building maintenance, or the management of jails, civic centers, or parking decks. The services most likely to be privatized are ones a private business can do at a lower cost than the local government.

But providing all the services citizens need and want is still a tight squeeze. Local governments have to try to do more with less. ◀

CHAPTER ACTIVITIES

Reviewing the Main Ideas

1. What kinds of services might citizens in a growing community demand from their government?
2. What examples of public safety services can you see on an ordinary day in your community?
3. How can recycling help solve the problem of landfills that are quickly filling up?
4. How do zoning and land-use regulation help a community achieve orderly growth?
5. What are some ways that local governments take care of the health needs of citizens?
6. What legal matters are handled in magistrate court? in probate court?
7. What are local governments using today to improve local record keeping?
8. What is the main source of local government revenue? What is the largest expenditure for counties? for cities?
9. In addition to property tax, name three other sources of revenue for local governments.
10. What do county officials consider when deciding on property tax rates?

Give It Some Extra Thought

1. **Identifying Problems.** Why should sanitary landfills be subject to state and federal environmental regulations?
2. **Understanding Functions.** Why is record keeping an important and necessary function of local government?
3. **Considering the Consequences.** Why is the property tax rate set at the local level instead of having a statewide property tax?

Sharpen Your Skills

1. **Outline the Steps.** Outline the steps in (1) treatment and distribution of drinking water and (2) treatment of wastewater. You may want to illustrate the steps.
2. **Newspaper Reports.** Summarize a newspaper article reporting on a local government issue or de-

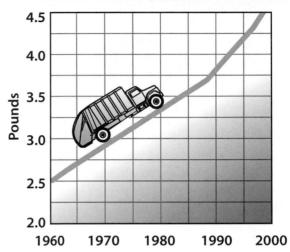

Estimates of Trash Generated per Person per Day in the United States

Use this graph to estimate how many pounds of trash are produced by the students in your class in one day.

cision in your area. The article may be about government officials, meetings, elections, services, or some other government activity. Relate the subject of the article to what you have learned about local government.

3. **Making Comparisons.** Compare the list of seven local government service categories in this chapter with the list of seven state policy categories in Chapter 28. Which ones are the same? At which level of government do the categories seem more specific? Why?

Going Further

1. **Speculate.** Write a brief story about a fictional community that has no planning and zoning regulations. Describe the possible problems of living in such a community.
2. **Research and Report.** Report on the recycling efforts in your community. Find out if there is a program, how long the program has existed, who is responsible for it, and how well it is working. If your community does not have a recycling program, ask how a program could be started.

Appendix

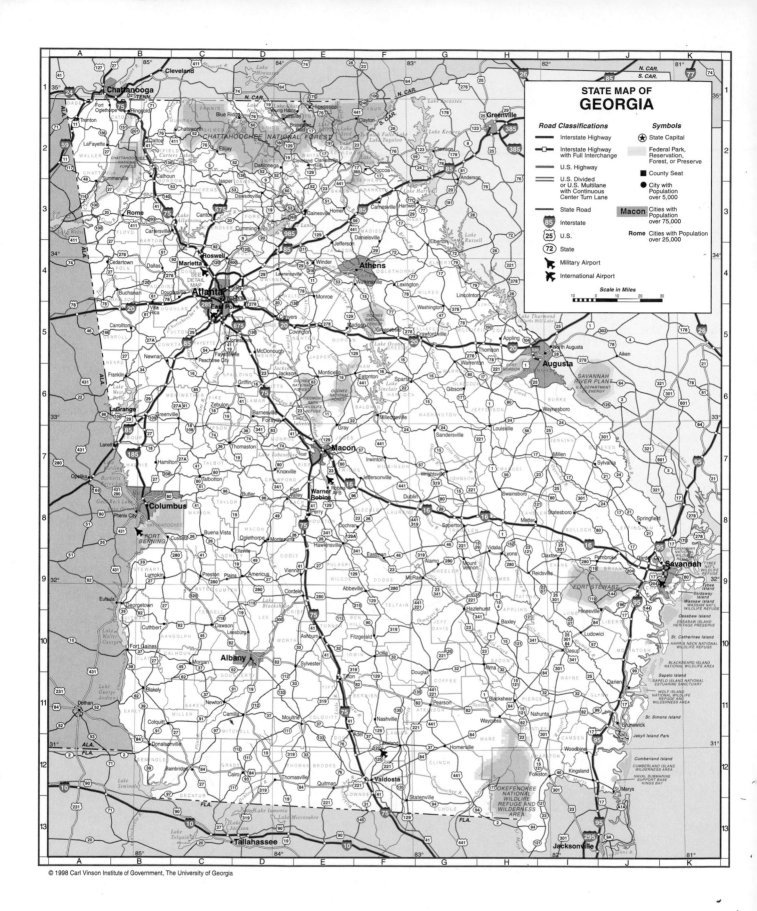

Atlanta Area Detail Map

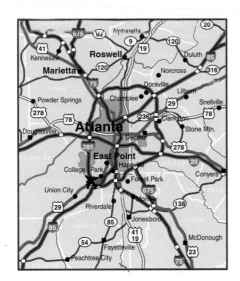

Grid Index to Cities

Physical Regions

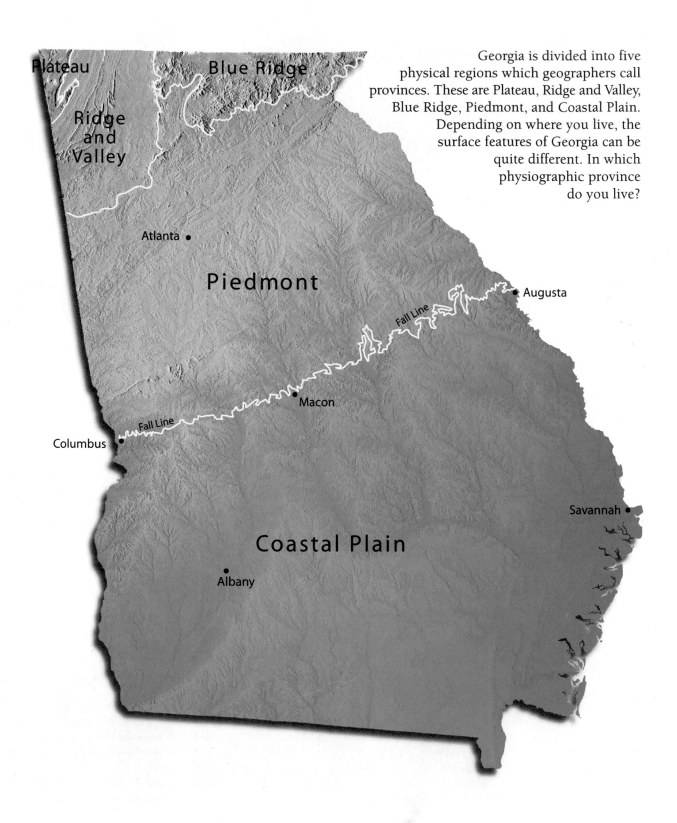

Georgia is divided into five physical regions which geographers call provinces. These are Plateau, Ridge and Valley, Blue Ridge, Piedmont, and Coastal Plain. Depending on where you live, the surface features of Georgia can be quite different. In which physiographic province do you live?

Plateau

Blue Ridge

Ridge and Valley

Atlanta

Piedmont

Augusta

Fall Line

Macon

Fall Line

Columbus

Savannah

Coastal Plain

Albany

Georgia State Symbols

Bird	Brown Thrasher
Butterfly	Tiger Swallowtail
Crop	Peanut
Fish	Largemouth Bass
Flower	Cherokee Rose
Fossil	Shark Tooth
Fruit	Peach
Game Bird	Bobwhite Quail
Gem	Quartz
Insect	Honeybee
Marine Mammal	Right Whale
Mineral	Staurolite
Reptile	Gopher Tortoise
Seashell	Knobbed Whelk
Song	*Georgia on My Mind*
Tree	Live Oak
Vegetable	Vidalia Sweet Onion
Wildflower	Azalea

State Tree– Live Oak

State Flower– Cherokee Rose

State Wild Flower– Azalea

State Fish– Largemouth Bass

State Bird– Brown Thrasher

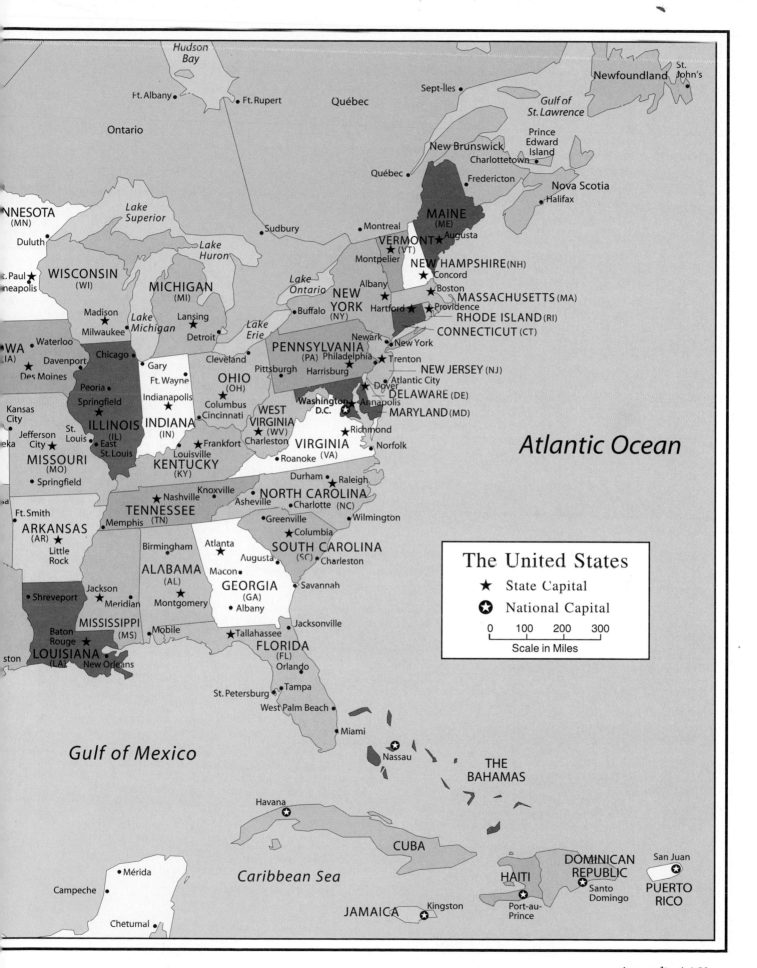

The United States

★ State Capital

⊛ National Capital

0   100   200   300

Scale in Miles

THE WORLD

At right is a political map of the world using the Robinson Projection. Shapes of countries are increasingly distorted as you near the poles, but this projection allows you to see the relative sizes of countries and continents.

Across the bottom of the page are globes showing the seven continents of the earth.

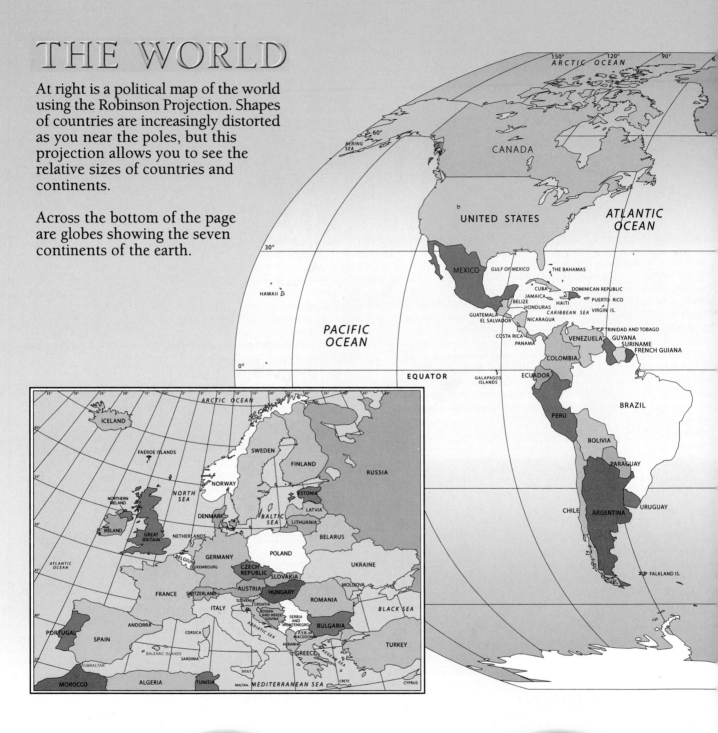

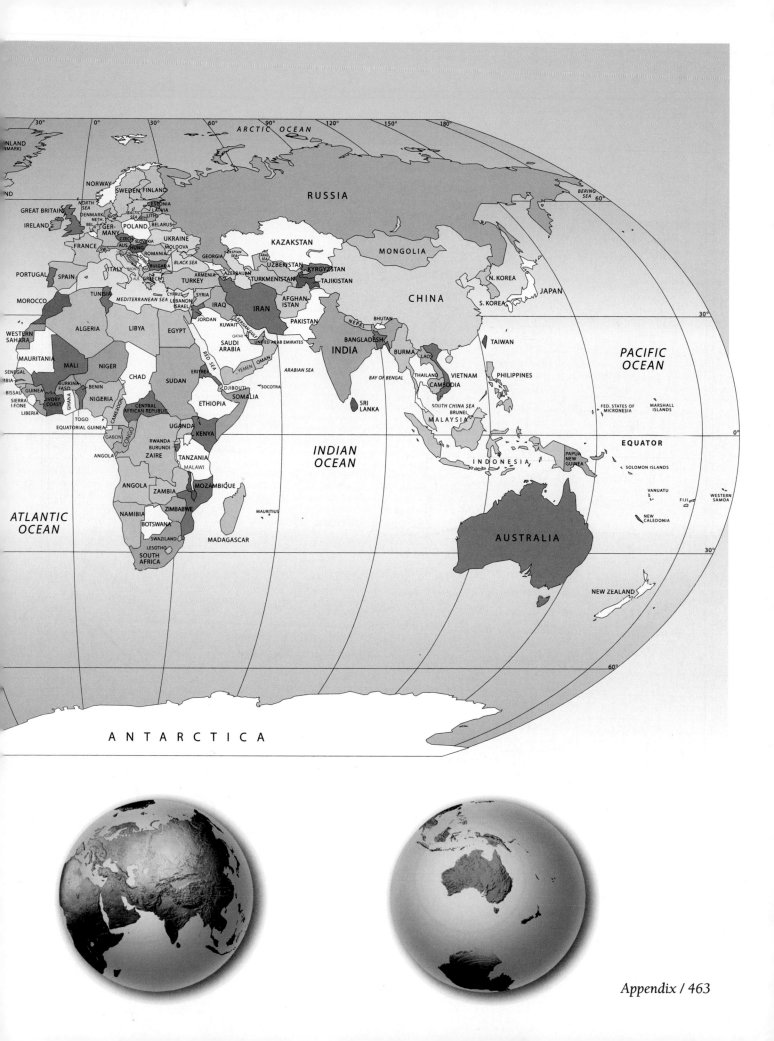

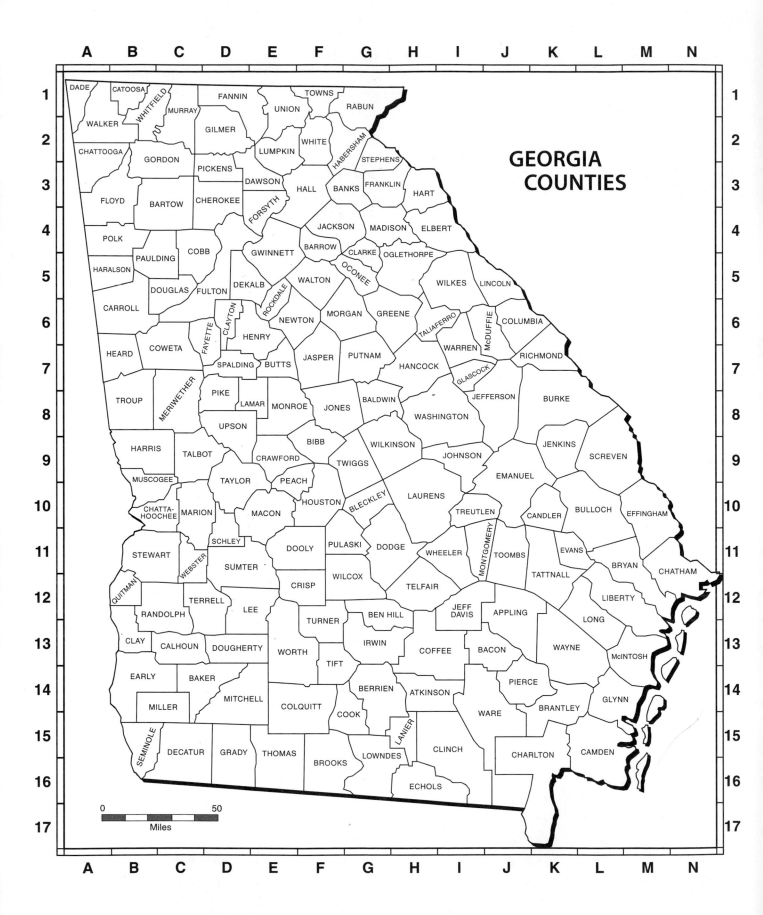

GEORGIA
COUNTIES

0 — 50 Miles

Grid Index to Counties

Georgia County Profiles

County Name	County Seat	Named for	Date Created	Order of Creation*	1980 Population	1990 Population	1990 Population Rank	Area in Square Miles	Area Rank
Appling	Baxley	Col. Daniel Appling	1818	42	15,565	15,744	85	512	23
Atkinson	Pearson	Gov.William Y. Atkinson	1918	153	6,141	6,213	142	344	82
Bacon	Alma	Senator Augustus O. Bacon	1914	151	9,379	9,566	118	286	105
Baker	Newton	Col. John Baker	1825	66	3,808	3,615	152	348	79
Baldwin	Milledgeville	Abraham Baldwin	1803	29	34,686	39,530	37	268	115
Banks	Homer	Dr. Richard Banks	1858	129	8,702	10,308	112	234	129
Barrow	Winder	Chancellor David C. Barrow	1914	149	21,354	29,721	48	163	152
Bartow	Cartersville	Gen. Francis S. Bartow	1832	87	40,760	55,915	25	471	37
Ben Hill	Fitzgerald	Benjamin H. Hill	1906	146	16,000	16,245	83	254	122
Berrien	Nashville	Senator John M. Berrien	1856	116	13,525	14,153	91	458	40
Bibb	Macon	Dr. William Wyatt Bibb	1822	55	150,256	150,137	9	256	121
Bleckley	Cochran	Logan E. Bleckley	1912	147	10,767	10,430	111	219	134
Brantley	Nahunta	William Gordon Brantley	1920	158	8,701	11,077	107	445	47
Brooks	Quitman	Preston S. Brooks	1858	131	15,255	15,398	87	498	29
Bryan	Pembroke	Jonathan Bryan	1793	19	10,175	15,438	86	453	42
Bulloch	Statesboro	Prov. Gov. Archibald Bulloch	1796	21	35,785	43,125	32	689	8
Burke	Waynesboro	Edmund Burke	1777	3	19,349	20,579	64	834	2
Butts	Jackson	Capt. Samuel Butts	1825	70	13,665	15,326	88	190	144
Calhoun	Morgan	Sen. John C. Calhoun	1854	112	5,717	5,013	150	284	107
Camden	Woodbine	Charles Pratt, Earl of Camden	1777	8	13,371	30,167	46	689	7
Candler	Metter	Gov. Allen D. Candler	1914	150	7,518	7,744	134	249	125
Carroll	Carrollton	Charles Carroll	1825	65	56,346	71,422	18	503	27
Catoosa	Ringgold	Catoosa Springs (Indian name)	1853	100	36,991	42,464	33	162	153
Charlton	Folkston	Robert M. Charlton	1854	111	7,343	8,496	128	782	5
Chatham	Savannah	Earl of Chatham, William Pitt	1777	5	202,226	216,774	5	498	28
Chattahoochee	Cusseta	Chattahoochee River	1854	109	21,732	16,934	80	251	123
Chattooga	Summerville	Chattooga River	1838	93	21,856	22,242	59	313	94
Cherokee	Canton	Cherokee Indians	1831	79	51,699	90,204	12	434	51
Clarke	Athens	Gen. Elijah Clarke	1801	26	74,498	87,594	14	122	159
Clay	Fort Gaines	Sen. Henry Clay	1854	110	3,553	3,364	154	217	135
Clayton	Jonesboro	Judge Augustin S. Clayton	1858	127	150,357	181,436	7	149	156
Clinch	Homerville	Gen. Duncan L. Clinch	1850	95	6,660	6,160	144	824	3
Cobb	Marietta	Sen. Thomas W. Cobb	1832	84	297,718	447,745	3	345	81
Coffee	Douglas	Gen. John Coffee	1854	108	26,894	29,592	49	603	13
Colquitt	Moultrie	Walter T. Colquitt	1856	115	35,376	36,645	40	557	15
Columbia	Appling	Christopher Columbus	1790	12	40,118	66,031	20	308	97
Cook	Adel	Gen. Philip Cook	1918	155	13,490	13,456	94	233	130
Coweta	Newnan	Coweta Indians	1825	64	39,268	53,853	29	445	46
Crawford	Knoxville	William H. Crawford	1822	57	7,684	8,991	121	328	91
Crisp	Cordele	Charles F. Crisp	1905	138	19,489	20,011	69	281	110

*Campbell County and Milton County (Georgia's 76th and 121st counties) were merged with Fulton County in 1932, reducing the total number of counties from 161 to 159.

County Name	County Seat	Named for	Date Created	Order of Creation	1980 Population	1990 Population	1990 Population Rank	Area in Square Miles	Area Rank
Dade	Trenton	Maj. Francis L. Dade	1837	92	12,318	13,147	97	176	149
Dawson	Dawsonville	Judge William C. Dawson	1857	119	4,774	9,429	119	214	136
Decatur	Bainbridge	Commodore Stephen Decatur	1823	58	25,495	25,517	54	624	12
DeKalb	Decatur	Baron Johann DeKalb	1822	54	483,024	546,171	2	271	113
Dodge	Eastman	William E. Dodge	1870	136	16,955	17,607	77	506	26
Dooly	Vienna	Col. John Dooly	1821	48	10,826	9,901	115	397	60
Dougherty	Albany	Judge Charles Dougherty	1853	103	100,718	96,321	10	334	87
Douglas	Douglasville	Sen. Stephen A. Douglas	1870	133	54,573	71,120	19	203	138
Early	Blakely	Gov. Peter Early	1818	40	13,158	11,854	104	518	21
Echols	Statenville	Robert M. Echols	1858	132	2,297	2,334	156	421	55
Effingham	Springfield	Lord Effingham (Francis Howard)	1777	4	18,327	25,687	53	482	32
Elbert	Elberton	Gov. Samuel Elbert	1790	13	18,758	18,949	73	374	68
Emanuel	Swainsboro	Gov. David Emanuel	1812	39	20,795	20,546	65	690	6
Evans	Claxton	Gen. Clement A. Evans	1914	152	8,428	8,724	123	187	145
Fannin	Blue Ridge	Col. James W. Fannin	1854	107	14,748	15,992	84	390	63
Fayette	Fayetteville	Gilbert du Motier Lafayette	1821	51	29,043	62,415	22	200	142
Floyd	Rome	Gen. John Floyd	1832	88	79,800	81,251	15	520	20
Forsyth	Cumming	John Forsyth	1832	81	27,958	44,083	31	247	126
Franklin	Carnesville	Benjamin Franklin	1784	9	15,185	16,650	81	267	116
Fulton	Atlanta	Robert Fulton	1853	105	589,904	648,779	1	535	18
Gilmer	Ellijay	Gov. George R. Gilmer	1832	85	11,110	13,368	95	432	52
Glascock	Gibson	Gen. Thomas Glascock	1857	122	2,382	2,357	155	144	157
Glynn	Brunswick	John Glynn	1777	7	54,981	62,496	21	458	41
Gordon	Calhoun	William W. Gordon	1850	94	30,070	35,067	42	355	76
Grady	Cairo	Henry W. Grady	1905	139	19,845	20,279	66	460	39
Greene	Greensboro	Gen. Nathaniel Greene	1786	11	11,391	11,793	105	406	56
Gwinnett	Lawrenceville	Prov. Gov. Button Gwinnett	1818	44	166,903	352,910	4	437	50
Habersham	Clarkesville	Maj. Joseph Habersham	1818	46	25,020	27,622	50	279	112
Hall	Gainesville	Gov. Lyman Hall	1818	45	75,649	95,434	11	428	54
Hancock	Sparta	John Hancock	1793	15	9,466	8,908	122	479	33
Haralson	Buchanan	Gen. Hugh A. Haralson	1856	113	18,422	21,966	60	283	109
Harris	Hamilton	Charles Harris	1827	72	15,464	17,788	74	473	36
Hart	Hartwell	Nancy Morgan Hart	1853	102	18,585	19,712	71	257	119
Heard	Franklin	Gov. Stephen Heard	1830	77	6,520	8,628	127	301	99
Henry	McDonough	Patrick Henry	1821	52	36,309	58,741	23	321	93
Houston	Perry	Gov. John Houstoun	1821	49	77,605	89,208	13	380	66
Irwin	Ocilla	Gov. Jared Irwin	1818	41	8,988	8,649	125	363	72
Jackson	Jefferson	Gov. James Jackson	1796	22	25,343	30,005	47	342	84
Jasper	Monticello	Sgt. William Jasper	1807	31	7,553	8,453	129	374	69
Jeff Davis	Hazlehurst	Jefferson Davis, Confederate pres.	1905	142	11,473	12,032	102	336	86

County Name	County Seat	Named for	Date Created	Order of Creation	1980 Population	1990 Population	1990 Population Rank	Area in Square Miles	Area Rank
Jefferson	Louisville	Pres. Thomas Jefferson	1796	23	18,403	17,408	78	531	19
Jenkins	Millen	Gov. Charles J. Jenkins	1905	140	8,841	8,247	131	353	78
Johnson	Wrightsville	Gov. Herschel V. Johnson	1858	130	8,660	8,329	130	307	98
Jones	Gray	James Jones	1807	32	16,579	20,739	63	394	62
Lamar	Barnesville	Lucius Q.C. Lamar	1920	160	12,215	13,038	99	186	147
Lanier	Lakeland	Sidney Lanier	1920	157	5,654	5,531	149	200	142
Laurens	Dublin	Col. John Laurens	1807	34	36,990	39,988	36	817	4
Lee	Leesburg	Richard H. "Lighthorse Harry" Lee	1825	61	11,684	16,250	82	362	74
Liberty	Hinesville	American Independence	1777	6	37,583	52,745	30	542	17
Lincoln	Lincolnton	Gen. Benjamin Lincoln	1796	24	6,716	7,442	136	258	118
Long	Ludowici	Dr. Crawford W. Long	1920	159	4,524	6,202	143	403	58
Lowndes	Valdosta	William J. Lowndes	1825	68	67,972	75,981	16	511	24
Lumpkin	Dahlonega	Gov. Wilson Lumpkin	1832	82	10,762	14,573	89	288	103
McDuffie	Thomson	George McDuffie	1870	134	18,546	20,119	68	266	117
McIntosh	Darien	McIntosh Family	1793	18	8,046	8,634	126	478	34
Macon	Oglethorpe	Nathaniel Macon	1837	91	14,003	13,114	98	404	57
Madison	Danielsville	Pres. James Madison	1811	38	17,747	21,050	62	286	106
Marion	Buena Vista	Gen. Francis "Swamp Fox" Marion	1827	74	5,297	5,590	148	366	71
Meriwether	Greenville	Gen. David Meriwether	1827	71	21,229	22,411	57	506	25
Miller	Colquitt	Judge Andrew J. Miller	1856	117	7,038	6,280	141	284	108
Mitchell	Camilla	Gen. Henry Mitchell	1857	123	21,114	20,275	67	514	22
Monroe	Forsyth	Pres. James Monroe	1821	50	14,610	17,113	79	397	59
Montgomery	Mount Vernon	Gen. Richard Montgomery	1793	20	7,011	7,379	137	245	127
Morgan	Madison	Gen. Daniel Morgan	1807	30	11,572	12,883	101	355	77
Murray	Chatsworth	Thomas W. Murray	1832	86	19,685	26,147	52	347	80
Muscogee	Columbus	Muscogee Indians	1825	62	170,108	179,280	8	221	132
Newton	Covington	Sgt. John Newton	1821	53	34,489	41,808	34	279	112
Oconee	Watkinsville	Oconee River	1875	137	12,427	17,618	76	187	146
Oglethorpe	Lexington	Gen. James E. Oglethorpe	1793	17	8,929	9,763	117	442	49
Paulding	Dallas	John Paulding	1832	89	26,110	41,611	35	313	95
Peach	Fort Valley	Georgia Peach	1924	161	19,151	21,189	61	152	155
Pickens	Jasper	Gen. Andrew Pickens	1853	101	11,652	14,432	90	232	131
Pierce	Blackshear	Pres. Franklin Pierce	1857	120	11,897	13,328	96	344	83
Pike	Zebulon	Zebulon M. Pike	1822	56	8,937	10,224	114	219	133
Polk	Cedartown	Pres. James K. Polk	1851	96	32,386	33,815	44	312	96
Pulaski	Hawkinsville	Count Casimir Pulaski of Poland	1808	36	8,950	8,108	132	250	124
Putnam	Eatonton	Gen. Israel Putnam	1807	33	10,295	14,137	92	361	75
Quitman	Georgetown	Gen. John A. Quitman	1858	127	2,357	2,210	158	161	154
Rabun	Clayton	Gov. William Rabun	1819	47	10,466	11,648	106	377	67
Randolph	Cuthbert	John Randolph	1828	75	9,599	8,023	133	431	53

County Name	County Seat	Named for	Date Created	Order of Creation	1980 Population	1990 Population	1990 Population Rank	Area in Square Miles	Area Rank
Richmond	Augusta	Duke of Richmond (Charles Lenox)	1777	2	181,629	189,719	6	329	90
Rockdale	Conyers	Rockdale Church	1870	135	36,747	54,091	28	132	158
Schley	Ellaville	Gov. William Schley	1857	124	3,433	3,590	153	169	151
Screven	Sylvania	Gen. James Screven	1793	14	14,043	13,842	93	655	10
Seminole	Donalsonville	Seminole Indians	1920	156	9,057	9,010	120	257	120
Spalding	Griffin	Thomas Spalding	1851	97	47,899	54,457	27	200	140
Stephens	Toccoa	Gov. Alexander H. Stephens	1905	143	21,763	23,436	56	184	148
Stewart	Lumpkin	Gen. Daniel Stewart	1830	78	5,896	5,654	147	463	38
Sumter	Americus	Gen. Thomas Sumter	1831	80	29,360	30,232	45	492	30
Talbot	Talbotton	Gov. Matthew Talbot	1827	73	6,536	6,524	140	395	61
Taliaferro	Crawfordville	Col. Benjamin Taliaferro	1825	69	2,032	1,915	159	196	143
Tattnall	Reidsville	Gov. Josiah Tattnall, Jr.	1801	25	18,134	17,722	75	487	31
Taylor	Butler	Pres. Zachary Taylor	1852	99	7,902	7,642	135	382	65
Telfair	McRae	Gov. Edward Telfair	1807	35	11,445	11,000	108	444	48
Terrell	Dawson	Dr. William Terrell	1856	114	12,017	10,653	109	338	85
Thomas	Thomasville	Gen. Jett Thomas	1825	67	38,098	38,943	38	553	16
Tift	Tifton	Nelson Tift	1905	141	32,862	34,998	43	269	114
Toombs	Lyons	Gen. Robert Toombs	1905	144	22,592	24,072	55	372	70
Towns	Hiawassee	Gov. George W. Towns	1856	118	5,638	6,754	139	171	150
Treutlen	Soperton	Gov. John A. Treutlen	1918	154	6,087	5,994	146	203	139
Troup	LaGrange	Gov. George M. Troup	1825	63	50,003	55,532	26	446	45
Turner	Ashburn	Henry G. Turner	1905	145	9,510	8,703	124	290	102
Twiggs	Jeffersonville	Gen. John Twiggs	1809	37	9,354	9,806	116	363	73
Union	Blairsville	Federal Union	1832	83	9,390	11,993	103	330	89
Upson	Thomaston	Stephen Upson	1824	59	25,998	26,300	51	326	92
Walker	LaFayette	Maj. Freeman Walker	1833	90	56,470	58,340	24	446	44
Walton	Monroe	Gov. George Walton	1818	43	31,211	38,586	39	330	88
Ware	Waycross	Sen. Nicholas Ware	1824	60	37,180	35,471	41	907	1
Warren	Warrenton	Gen. Joseph Warren	1793	16	6,583	6,078	145	286	104
Washington	Sandersville	Pres. George Washington	1784	10	18,842	19,112	72	684	9
Wayne	Jesup	Gen. "Mad Anthony" Wayne	1803	27	20,750	22,356	58	648	11
Webster	Preston	Daniel Webster	1853	104	2,341	2,263	157	210	137
Wheeler	Alamo	Gen. Joseph E. Wheeler	1912	148	5,155	4,903	151	299	100
White	Cleveland	David T. White	1857	125	10,120	13,006	100	242	128
Whitfield	Dalton	Rev. George Whitefield	1851	98	65,789	72,462	17	291	101
Wilcox	Abbeville	Gen. Mark Wilcox	1857	126	7,682	7,008	138	383	64
Wilkes	Washington	John Wilkes	1777	1	10,951	10,597	110	474	35
Wilkinson	Irwinton	Gen. James B. Wilkinson	1803	28	10,368	10,228	113	452	43
Worth	Sylvester	Maj. Gen. William J. Worth	1853	106	18,064	19,744	70	576	14
TOTAL FOR STATE					5,463,105	6,478,149		58,910	

Sources: Association County Commissioners of Georgia, Secretary of State, U.S. Bureau of the Census; The Georgia County Guide.

Decennial Population of Georgia

Year	Total	White	Black	Other*
1790	82,548	52,886	29,662	*
1800	162,686	102,261	60,425	*
1810	252,433	145,414	107,019	*
1820	340,989	189,570	151,419	*
1830	516,823	296,806	220,017	*
1840	691,392	407,695	283,697	*
1850	906,185	521,572	384,613	*
1860	1,057,286	591,550	465,698	38
1870	1,184,109	638,926	545,142	41
1880	1,542,180	816,906	725,133	141
1890	1,837,353	978,357	858,815	181
1900	2,216,331	1,181,294	1,034,813	224
1910	2,609,121	1,431,802	1,176,987	332
1920	2,895,832	1,689,114	1,206,365	353
1930	2,908,506	1,837,021	1,071,125	360
1940	3,123,723	2,038,278	1,084,927	518
1950	3,444,578	2,380,577	1,062,762	1,239
1960	3,943,116	2,817,223	1,122,596	3,297
1970	4,589,575	3,391,242	1,187,149	11,184
1980	5,463,105	3,947,135	1,465,181	50,789
1990	6,478,149	4,636,431	1,751,179	90,539

Source: Data from U.S. Bureau of the Census. *Other ethnic groups were not included in the census until 1860.

Decennial Population of the United States

Year	Total	White	Black	Other*
1790	3,929,214	3,172,006	757,208	*
1800	5,308,483	4,306,446	1,002,087	*
1810	7,239,881	5,862,073	1,377,808	*
1820	9,638,453	7,862,166	1,771,656	*
1830	12,866,020	10,537,378	2,328,642	*
1840	17,069,453	14,195,805	2,873,648	*
1850	23,191,876	19,553,068	3,638,808	*
1860	31,443,321	26,922,537	4,441,830	78,954
1870	39,818,449	34,337,292	5,392,172	88,985
1880	50,155,783	43,402,970	6,580,793	172,020
1890	62,622,250	54,983,890	7,470,040	168,320
1900	75,994,575	66,809,196	8,833,994	351,385
1910	91,972,266	81,731,957	9,827,763	412,546
1920	105,710,620	94,820,915	10,463,131	426,574
1930	122,775,046	110,286,740	11,891,143	597,163
1940	131,669,275	118,214,870	12,865,518	588,887
1950	150,697,361	134,942,028	15,042,286	713,047
1960	179,323,175	158,831,732	18,871,831	1,619,612
1970	203,235,298	177,748,975	22,580,289	2,906,034
1980	226,545,805	188,371,622	26,495,025	11,679,158
1990	248,718,291	208,710,069	30,485,641	9,522,581

Source: Data from U.S. Bureau of the Census. *Other ethnic groups were not included in the census until 1860.

Governors of Georgia

Trustee Period

James Edward Oglethorpe,	
Resident Trustee[1]	1733–1737
Commander in Chief[2]	1737–1743
William Stephens,	
President[3]	1741–1751
Henry Parker,	
President	1751–1752
Patrick Graham,	
President	1752–1754

Royal Period

John Reynolds	1754–1757
Henry Ellis	1757–1760
James Wright[4]	1760–1776

Provisional

Archibald Bulloch,	
President, Council of Safety	1776–1777
Button Gwinnett,	
President, Council of Safety	1777–1777

State

John Adam Treutlen	1777–1778
John Houstoun	1778–1779
John Wereat,	
President, Executive Council[5]	1779–1780
George Walton[5]	1779–1780
Richard Howley[6]	1780–1780
Stephen Heard,	
President, Executive Council[7]	1780–1781
Nathan Brownson[8]	1781–1782
John Martin	1782–1783
Lyman Hall	1783–1784

John Houstoun	1784–1785
Samuel Elbert	1785–1786
Edward Telfair	1786–1787
George Mathews	1787–1788
George Handley	1788–1789
George Walton	1789–1789
Edward Telfair	1789–1793
George Mathews	1793–1796
Jared Irwin	1796–1798
James Jackson	1798–1801
David Emanuel*	1801–1801
Josiah Tattnall, Jr.	1801–1802
John Milledge	1802–1806
Jared Irwin*	1806–1809
David Brydie Mitchell	1809–1813
Peter Early	1813–1815
David Brydie Mitchell	1815–1817
William Rabun*	1817–1819
Matthew Talbot*	1819–1819
John Clark	1819–1823
George Michael Troup	1823–1827
John Forsyth	1827–1829
George Rockingham Gilmer	1829–1831
Wilson Lumpkin	1831–1835
William Schley	1835–1837
George Rockingham Gilmer	1837–1839
Charles James McDonald	1839–1843
George Walker Crawford	1843–1847
George Washington Towns	1847–1851
Howell Cobb	1851–1853
Herschel Vespasian Johnson	1853–1857

* As president of the Senate, became governor upon a vacancy in that office.

1. **Oglethorpe** served as acting governor—though he had no formal title or office.

2. In 1737, the British government commissioned **Oglethorpe** as General and Commander in Chief of all His Majesties Forces in Carolina and Georgia. Also, Oglethorpe served as acting governor of the southern half of the colony of Georgia until 1742.

3. In 1741, the Trustees divided Georgia into two counties—Savannah and Frederica. **Stephens** was named president of Savannah, but no appointment was made for Frederica. In 1742, Stephens was named president of the entire colony.

4. When the revolutionaries took control in 1776, **Wright** fled from Georgia. He returned in 1779 and continued as governor of the British-held part of Georgia until 1782.

5. The patriots were divided into two factions. One elected **Wereat** and the other elected Walton. They came together on January 4, 1780, and elected Richard Howley.

6. **Howley** was elected both governor and representative to the Continental Congress. He chose to go to Congress in February.

7. The office of governor was briefly held by George Wells, President of the Executive Council, who was killed in a duel with James Jackson. For two days, he was replaced by Humphrey Wells before Stephen **Heard** took office.

8. When Stephen Heard moved to North Carolina, he was briefly replaced by Myrick Davies, who was killed. **Brownson** was then chosen by the General Assembly.

Governors of Georgia

Joseph Emerson Brown	1857–1865	John Marshall Slaton	1913–1915
James Johnson[9]	1865–1865	Nathaniel Edwin Harris	1915–1917
Charles Jones Jenkins[10]	1865–1868	Hugh Manson Dorsey	1917–1921
Gen. Thomas Howard Ruger[11]	1868–1868	Thomas William Hardwick	1921–1923
Rufus Brown Bullock[12]	1868–1871	Clifford Walker	1923–1927
Benjamin Conley*	1871–1872	Lamartine Griffin Hardman	1927–1931
James Milton Smith	1872–1877	Richard Brevard Russell, Jr.	1931–1933
Alfred Holt Colquitt	1877–1882	Eugene Talmadge	1933–1937
Alexander Hamilton Stephens	1882–1883	Eurith Dickinson Rivers	1937–1941
James Stoddard Boynton*	1883–1883	Eugene Talmadge	1941–1943
Henry Dickerson McDaniel	1883–1886	Ellis Gibbs Arnall	1943–1947
John Brown Gordon	1886–1890	Melvin E. Thompson[14]	1947–1948
William Jonathan Northen	1890–1894	Herman Eugene Talmadge	1948–1955
William Yates Atkinson	1894–1898	S. Marvin Griffin	1955–1959
Allen Daniel Candler	1898–1902	Samuel Ernest Vandiver, Jr.	1959–1963
Joseph Meriwether Terrell	1902–1907	Carl E. Sanders	1963–1967
Hoke Smith[13]	1907–1909	Lester Maddox	1967–1971
Joseph Mackey Brown	1909–1911	Jimmy Carter	1971–1975
Hoke Smith	1911–1911	George Busbee	1975–1983
John Marshall Slaton*	1911–1912	Joe Frank Harris	1983–1991
Joseph Mackey Brown	1912–1913	Zell Miller	1991–1999

9. President Andrew Johnson appointed **Johnson**.

10. When **Jenkins** refused to pay for the 1867 Constitutional Convention, he was removed from office by General Meade, the U.S. general in charge of Georgia.

11. General Meade named **Ruger** governor to replace Jenkins.

12. Rather than face impeachment, **Bullock** resigned. Conley held office until a special election was held.

13. When **Smith** resigned to serve in the U.S. Senate, Slaton served out his term.

14. Eugene Talmadge won the election but died on December 21, 1946, before taking office. The legislature elected his son, Herman Talmadge, to serve the remainder of the term, but that action was ruled unconstitutional by the Georgia Supreme Court. Lieutenant Governor **Thompson** was acting governor until September 1948, when a special election was held concurrent with the general election.

Glossary

The following words are defined according to their use as geography, history, and government terms in this book. Glossary words appear in **bold type** the first time they are mentioned in the text.

Absolute location. The exact spot on the earth's surface where a place is found.

Abolition. The act of making slavery illegal.

Abolitionist. A person opposed to slavery.

A.D. Anno Domini, or "in the year of our Lord"; used to show that a date falls within the Christian era.

Ad valorem tax. Tax on private property based on its value, commonly called a property tax.

Agency. General term for any department, board, commission, or other unit of government.

Aggression. Action by one country to attack or invade another.

Alliance. Agreement between countries to come to each other's aid in case of attack or war.

Amendment. An addition or change to a bill, law, or constitution.

Amnesty. Pardon granted by the government to a large group of people for something they did.

Annexation. Extending a city's boundaries by adding land from adjoining unincorporated territory.

Antebellum. The period in the South before the Civil War.

Appalachian Plateaus (or **Plateau**). Physiographic province of high plateaus separated by valleys, stretching from northern Alabama to central New York. About 300 square miles of northwest Georgia lie in the Plateau region.

Appellate jurisdiction. A court's authority to review decisions of lower courts.

Appropriate. An action by a legislative body to authorize the spending of public funds.

Aquifers. Water-saturated layers of the earth below the surface.

Archaeologist. A scientist who learns about earlier societies by discovering and studying physical evidence of their lifestyles.

Archaic Indians. Prehistoric Native Americans who lived in the Southeast during the period from about 8000 to 1000 B.C.

Arsenal. A place where weapons are made or stored.

Artesian aquifer. A deep aquifer in which water is trapped and held under great pressure by denser layers of earth above and below the aquifer.

Articles of Confederation. The agreement signed by the 13 original states setting up the first national government for the United States, in force from 1781 to 1789.

Artifact. An object made or shaped by humans, such as projectile points, tools, pottery, and jewelry.

Artisan. A person skilled in a craft, such as woodwork or metalwork.

Atlantic Intracoastal Waterway. The 1,000-mile-long coastal water highway that stretches from New York to Miami, used for navigation by smaller boats.

Atlatl. A spear-throwing tool developed by early prehistoric Indians to increase the speed and distance a spear could be thrown.

Authority. A special-purpose public corporation set up by government to provide a specific function or service, such as hospital care or public housing.

Axis. 1: The imaginary straight line through the earth from pole to pole around which the earth rotates. 2: Name given Germany, Italy, Japan, and their allies in World War II.

Backcountry. The unsettled area of Georgia's frontier far inland from the coast; also called "upcountry."

Band. A group of people.

Barrier islands. Chain of sea islands off Georgia's coast that form a barrier, helping block ocean waves and wind from the mainland.

B.C. Before Christ; used to show that a date falls before the Christian era.

Bedrock. Large areas of solid rock found just below the earth's surface.

Beringia. The exposed land between Alaska and Siberia during the Ice Age that served as a bridge between North America and Asia.

Bicameral. Consisting of two houses or chambers. The legislatures of the United States and Georgia are bicameral, each having a Senate and a House of Representatives.

Bicentennial. Special anniversary that celebrates an event that took place 200 years ago.

Bill of Rights. Fundamental rights and freedoms guaranteed to U.S. citizens by the Constitution's first 10 amendments.

Black Belt. Heart of the cotton-growing region in the South, so named for its high percentage of black residents.

Black Codes. Laws passed by southern legislatures after the Civil War to limit the political and civil rights of former slaves.

Blockade. Use of military forces to isolate enemy territory, such as a harbor, in order to prevent entry of supplies or persons.

Blue Ridge. Physiographic province stretching from northern Georgia to southern Pennsylvania that includes the highest mountains in the Appalachian Highlands.

Border states. Slaveholding states that bordered the free states and did not secede during the Civil War.

Boycott. To refuse to use or buy something as a protest or as a way to force change.

Buffer. A protected area along the frontier to defend more settled areas.

Capital. 1: Money and resources available for spending or producing goods or income. 2: The city that serves as the seat of government for a state or nation.

Capital felony. A crime punishable by death.

Capitol. The principal building where the business of government is conducted.

Carbon 14 dating. Technique used to find the age of plant or animal matter by determining the amount of carbon 14 still in its remains.

Cardinal directions. Four main direction points on a compass: north, south, east, and west.

Carpetbagger. A non-southerner who came to the South during Reconstruction to take advantage of its economic and political situation. Carpetbaggers got the name because many came with travel bags made of carpet material.

Cartographer. A map maker.

Caucus. Meeting of members of a political party or group to choose candidates for office or take a group position on issues.

Cause and effect. A relationship where one event appears to cause or lead to another.

Cede. To give up land, usually for a price. The land given up is known as a cession.

Census. An official count of the population.

Centennial. Special anniversary that marks an event that took place 100 years ago.

Century. A period of 100 years.

Cession. Land given up or ceded.

Charter. 1: A legal document that grants certain rights or privileges. 2: A document passed by the state legislature creating a city and spelling out its boundaries, form of government, and powers.

Checks and balances. A plan built into U.S. and state constitutions to keep the three branches of government from overpowering each other.

Chiefdom. A social and political institution that developed during the Mississippian Indian period. Ruled over by a priest-chief, a chiefdom could consist of from one to many villages.

Chronology. Order in which a series of events occurred.

Citizen. Member of a political system in whose operation the people have a voice.

Citizenship. The rights and responsibilities associated with being a citizen.

City. See **Municipality**.

City council. Governing body of a city.

City manager. An official appointed by the city council to administer such city business as hiring, promotions, purchases, and finances.

Civil case. Any legal dispute involving citizens, groups, businesses, or governments that does not involve a violation of criminal law.

Civil rights. The protections and privileges given to all citizens by federal and state constitutions and laws.

Civil Rights Act of 1964. Federal legislation that prohibited racial discrimination in labor unions, employment, and public facilities.

Climate. Average weather conditions over a time period of at least 25 years.

Coastal Plain. Georgia's largest physiographic province, covering all of Georgia south of the Fall Line (about 60 percent of the state). The low-relief region stretches from Massachusetts to Mexico.

Cold War. The rivalry between the United States and the Soviet Union after World War II for international advantage using diplomatic, undercover, and economic means rather than warfare.

Colonize. To set up a colony.

Colony. A territory on foreign soil claimed, settled, and controlled by another country.

Communism. Political system in which the central government, not the individual, controls goods, property, and capital.

Commute. Travel back and forth in order to go to work or to school.

Confederacy. Name given to the southern states during the Civil War. The official name of the government was "Confederate States of America."

Confederation. A loose union of sovereign states in which the central government is given limited power.

Consolidation. A formal merging of two governments (such as a county and city) that must be approved by the voters of each government.

Constituents. Voters represented by an elected official.

Constitution. The legal document that authorizes a state or national government to exist. A constitution usually outlines fundamental principles, form, major officials, and powers of a government.

Constitutional officer. Any of the elected executive officials in state government whose office is specifically provided for by the Georgia Constitution.

Context. How something relates to its surroundings.

Continental shelf. Large flat underwater ledge from the ocean's shoreline to a major dropoff, about 70 or 80 miles from Georgia's coast.

Coordinates. Letters or numbers used to identify location on a grid.

Corporate colony. Colony established through a grant of land made by the king to a corporation or company.

Cotton gin. A machine that separates the seeds from cotton.

County. A subdivision of the state set up to carry out certain state laws as well as function as a general-purpose unit of local government.

County commission. Governing body of a county.

County seat. City in which a county's government is located.

County unit system. A formula for determining state-wide races in Democratic party primary elections that placed political power in the hands of rural counties. Used from 1917 to 1962, winners were selected by county "unit" votes rather than the state-wide popular vote.

Criminal case. A case in which the state charges that someone has violated the criminal laws of the state.

Crop lien. A legal claim on the crop of the farmer as payment for a loan given to grow that crop.

Cultural features. Features on the earth created by people, such as boundaries, towns, and roads.

Culture. The way of life of a particular group of people at a particular time.

Current. The steady flow or movement of a large body of air or water along a particular path.

Decade. A period of 10 years.

Declaration of Independence. The document adopted by delegates from the 13 American colonies in 1776 proclaiming their independence from Great Britain and their new status as free states.

Defendant. The person or party against whom legal action is brought in a civil or criminal case.

Degrees. The 360 equal divisions of a circle. Degrees are used for measuring latitude and longitude.

Delinquent act. Any act by a juvenile that would be considered a criminal offense if committed by an adult.

Democracy. A form of government whose power comes from the people.

Desegregation. The act of opening once segregated facilities to both races. Also known as integration.

Dictator. A ruler with absolute or near-absolute authority.

Discrimination. Withholding rights, privileges, and equal treatment from minority groups.

Disfranchisement. Taking away the right to vote.

District attorney. The elected official who represents the state in criminal cases tried in superior court.

Diversify. To introduce variety, such as growing crops other than cotton.

Dogtrot. A log cabin with two rooms connected by a covered and floored passageway.

Draft. 1: A law requiring civilians to join the military. 2: To write a proposal for a law or proclamation.

Due process. Rights and procedures guaranteed by the Constitution to ensure that citizens are treated fairly by government.

Duties. Taxes paid on imports.

Ecofacts. Natural objects, such as bones, teeth, and shells, that have survived from earlier cultures.

Ecosystem. Short for ecological system, it refers to a distinct, natural community of living and nonliving things and their environment.

Effigy. An image of a person or an animal.

Elevation. The height of a land formation above sea level.

Emancipate. To set free, especially with respect to slaves.

Emancipation Proclamation. The document issued by Pres. Abraham Lincoln that stated as of January 1, 1863, that all slaves in the Confederacy were considered "forever free."

Embargo. A ban on trade, commerce, and assistance to a particular country.

Enact. Make into law.

Environment. All the things that surround us.

Equator. Imaginary line that circles the earth at its widest part and divides the earth into the northern and southern hemispheres.

Erosion. The wearing away of soil and rock by natural forces such as water or wind.

Estuary. The area around a river's mouth where fresh and salt water mix.

Ethnic group. A group of people who share the same customs, languages, or background.

Excavate. To dig to expose a site and uncover archaeological evidence.

Execute. Carry out a policy, program, or law.

Executive. Refers to the branch of government that carries out the laws.

Expenditure. Money spent by a government for a certain purpose.

Faction. Part of a group united on a major issue.

Fall Line. The line (actually a zone) that marks the farthest inland shoreline of the prehistoric ocean.

Far East. Area of Asia that included India, China, Japan, and southeastern Asia.

Federal. 1: Relating to the national government. 2: Referring to a federal system of government (see Federalism).

Federalism. Political system in which the national government is supreme but shares some powers with state governments, which also have certain independent powers.

Felony. A serious crime punishable by one year or more in prison, a fine of at least $1,000, or both.

Fiscal year. The 12-month period for financial record-keeping. For Georgia state government, the fiscal year runs from July 1 to June 30.

Food chain. A feeding pattern for living organisms whereby one organism serves as food for another, which in turn becomes food for another, and so on.

Founding. The creation and initial settlement of a colony or territory.

Frame of reference. A set of beliefs or attitudes that influences someone's view of events.

Franchise. The right to vote.

Freedmen's Bureau. Federal Reconstruction agency which issued food, clothing, fuel, and other supplies to black freedmen and some needy whites.

French and Indian War. The American name for the war between France and Great Britain (1754–1763), used because many Indians fought on the side of France.

Friars. Catholic missionaries, particularly from Spain, who worked in church missions and outposts in foreign lands.

Garrison. A unit of soldiers.

General Assembly. The official name of Georgia's state legislature.

General election. The election for national, state, and local offices held in November of even-numbered years on the Tuesday after the first Monday.

Generalizations. Broad conclusions.

Geographic region. An area of the earth with shared physical or cultural features.

Geography. The study of the earth's physical features and how they relate to living things.

Government. A social institution set up to promote and protect society through formal rules and services.

Grand jury. A group of 16 to 23 citizens that decides whether or not someone charged with an offense should be formally accused and stand trial.

Grandfather clause. A provision allowing former Confederate soldiers and their male descendants to vote without having to take a literacy test.

Great Depression. The severe economic depression from 1929 to the outbreak of World War II.

Grid. A series of rows placed over a series of columns used to help locate places.

Groundwater. Water that lies underground.

Guale. The name Spain gave to the northern half of Georgia's coast, taken from the name of the Indians who inhabited the area.

Guerilla war. A war of revolution carried on by small, independent bands of fighters often aided by other countries.

Gulf of Tonkin Resolution. Approval from Congress in 1965 for the president to take military action to defend U.S. soldiers in South Vietnam and to resist aggression by North Vietnam.

Gulf Stream. The current of warm ocean water that flows from the Gulf of Mexico northward along the east coast of North America, then northeastward across the Atlantic Ocean.

Headright system. A plan for distributing Indian land ceded to Georgia whereby the head of each family had a right to 100 acres, plus additional land for family members.

Hemisphere. Any half of the earth based on either north and south, or east and west. The Equator divides the earth into northern and southern hemispheres, while the Prime Meridian/International Date Line separates the eastern and western hemispheres.

Hieroglyphics. A form of writing developed by the ancient Egyptians that consisted of symbols and images.

Historian. One who researches and writes about the past.

Historic preservation. A movement that attempts to preserve and restore buildings and other structures of the past.

History. A chronological record and explanation of past events.

Homestead exemption. An exemption for homeowners on a portion of each year's property taxes on their house.

Huguenots. Persecuted French Protestants who fled to North America in the 16th and 17th centuries.

Hypothesis (plural: hypotheses). A preliminary answer given to a research question, based on what one already knows.

Ice Age. A geologic age of the earth when much of the earth's water was frozen into glaciers and polar ice, causing ocean levels to fall.

Impeach. To file charges to remove a politician from office.

Incorporate. To officially bring a city (municipality) into existence through passage of an act in the state legislature.

Incumbent. A person holding office.

Indentured servant. A person agreeing to work for a master for a set period of time without wages in return for passage to the American colonies from Europe.

Independent. A person who has no connection with a political party.

Indictment. The formal charge that a grand jury makes against a criminal suspect so that a trial can be held.

Indies. Another name for the Far East used by Europeans beginning in the 1400s.

Inferior court. A court that handles minor cases.

Inflation. A period of rapidly rising prices and interest rates.

Infrastructure. The physical facilities built, operated, and maintained by government, such as streets, buildings, water and sewer lines, and parks.

Integration. Bringing together people of different races and allowing them equal access to places where they were formerly kept apart.

Interdependent. Being dependent on one another for certain needs.

Interest group. A group of people or organizations who share a particular interest and try to promote that interest through politics.

Intermediate directions. The halfway points between cardinal directions: northwest (NW), northeast (NE), southwest (SW), and southeast (SE).

International Date Line. The 180° meridian half way around the world from the Prime Meridian. It marks the starting point for counting time on earth.

Intimidate. To frighten or threaten persons in order to control their actions.

Item veto. The power of the governor to reject specific spending items in an appropriations bill, while approving others.

Jet stream. A rapid current of air flowing between 30,000 and 40,000 feet above sea level.

Jim Crow laws. Laws that enforced segregation in public places.

Joint-stock company. A business given an exclusive charter by the king to settle a new colony in America. The colony was financed by selling stock to investors.

Judicial. Relating to the branch of government that settles legal arguments, interprets the law, and decides issues of constitutionality.

Judicial review. The power of the court to review the constitutionality of actions by the legislative and executive branches.

Jurisdiction. 1: An area of legal control. 2: The authority of a court to act or hear a matter.

Jury. A group of citizens chosen to decide the outcome of a trial.

Juvenile. Any person under the age of 17.

La Florida. The Spanish name for the Southeast in the 1500s and 1600s.

Labor unions. Organizations of workers who bargain as a group with employers over wages, benefits, and working conditions.

Laissez faire. The policy of government keeping its hands off business, based on a belief that business can perform best without government regulation.

Land speculators. People who buy land cheaply, hold it until the price goes up, and then attempt to sell it for a profit.

Land-use plan. A plan on how land can be used. The plan divides a city or county into zones and specifies the purposes for which land in each zone can be used.

Landform. A land formation found on the earth's surface.

Latitude. The parallel lines that determine location from 0° to 90° north and south of the Equator.

Legislative. Relating to the branch of government that makes the laws.

Legislature. See **General Assembly**.

Levy. To impose or set, as in the case of a government levying taxes.

Line of Demarcation. Line drawn by Pope Alexander in 1493 to divide the rights to the New World between Spain and Portugal.

Literacy test. A test given to persons to prove they can read and write before being allowed to register to vote.

Local option. Allowing citizens of a county or city to vote on whether a particular law or practice will apply in their community.

Longitude. The lines that determine location from 0° to 180° east and west of the Prime Meridian.

Lottery. A drawing for a prize, such as land or money.

Majority. Any number greater than one-half of the total.

Marsh. Another name for saltwater or freshwater wetlands.

Massacre. The brutal killing of a large number of people.

Mayor. Chief executive of a city.

Mercantilism. A trade policy based on the idea that a country should sell more to other countries than it buys from them, in order to increase its wealth.

Meridians. Another name for lines of longitude, which extend around the earth from pole to pole.

Metropolitan. Refers to a large urban area consisting of a central city and communities dependent on that city for jobs, services, shopping, and entertainment.

Metropolitan Statistical Area (MSA). A metropolitan region consisting of a central city of at least 50,000 people and a total population of at least 100,000, including an urbanized area of at least 50,000.

Middens. Garbage heaps of discarded oyster and mussel shells.

Migration. Movement of humans or animals from one place to another.

Militia. A military unit of citizens who are not professional soldiers.

Millage rate. The tax rate as expressed in mills. A mill represents a tax of $1 on each $1,000 of assessed valuation.

Minutes. The 60 equal divisions that make up one degree of a circle.

Misdemeanor. A crime less serious than a felony, carrying a punishment of less than one year in prison, a fine of less than $1,000, or both.

Missions. Church outposts, usually in foreign lands.

Mississippian Indians. The prehistoric Native American culture that first developed along the Mississippi River around 700 to 900 A.D., later spreading to other areas in the Southeast.

Moat. A wide ditch around a village palisade used to provide protection against attack.

Mocama. The Spanish province, in the sixteenth and seventeenth centuries, on the southern half of Georgia's coast between the Altamaha and St. Marys rivers.

Monopoly. Exclusive right to act or conduct business without competition.

Multi-cultural. Made up of many cultures.

Multiple causation. The idea that a number of things cause an event.

Municipality. The legal name in Georgia for a city or town.

Nation. An independent country with its own government.

Nationalism. Strong feelings for one's nation and its culture.

Natural law. A theory that people have natural rights that come from God or nature.

Naturalization. Legal process through which a person who is not a citizen can become one.

Neutrality. Not taking sides in a conflict.

New Deal. Popular title given to the various recovery programs developed during Pres. Franklin D. Roosevelt's administration to end the Great Depression.

New World. Name given in the 15th century by Amerigo Vespucci to the newly discovered continents of South America, North America, and surrounding areas.

Nomads. Wanderers.

Nominate. To formally propose a candidate for appointment or election to an office.

Nonpartisan. Not identified with any political party.

Nullification. Declaring that a law is without force and is not binding.

Ordinance. A law enacted by a city or county affecting local affairs, such as traffic, noise, and animal control.

Organic. Plant or animal matter.

Original jurisdiction. A court's authority to be the first to hear a case.

Pacifist. Someone who does not believe in war.

Paleo-Indians. The first prehistoric Native Americans to live in the Southeast, from approximately 10,000 to 8000 B.C.

Palisade. A wall made of tall posts built around Mississippian Indian villages for protection.

Parallels. Another name for lines of latitude.

Parish. A district set up by the Church of England in the colony of Georgia.

Parliament. The national legislature of Great Britain.

Parole. A release from prison under supervision, after an offender has served part of the sentence.

Partisan. Connected with political parties, as in a partisan election.

Patriots. See **Whigs**.

Per capita income. Average annual income per person, calculated on the basis of total income divided by total number of adults and children.

Petition. 1: A formal written request. 2: A written document signed by a certain number of voters for some purpose, such as listing an independent candidate on the general election ballot.

Philanthropists. People who donate money to causes that they feel are worthy and beneficial to humanity.

Physical features. Natural features on the earth, such as mountains, rivers, and oceans.

Physiographic province. A region defined on the basis of similarities in physical geography, such as land formations, elevation, rocks and minerals, and soils.

Piedmont. Georgia's physiographic province that lies between the Fall Line to the south and the three mountain provinces of north Georgia. This hilly region stretches from central Alabama to southern New York.

Pilgrims. Members of a religious group that chose to separate and break away from the Church of England. Pilgrims settled in America in 1620.

Plaintiff. The person or party filing a suit against another in a civil case.

Plantation. Large-scale farm operation (usually for cotton, tobacco, rice, or sugar cane) in which many workers perform the same simple tasks at the same time.

Planter. An antebellum landholder who owned 20 or more field slaves.

Plat. Map of a land lot's boundaries.

Plateau. See **Appalachian Plateaus**.

Plurality. In elections with three or more candidates, winning more votes than any other candidate, but less than a majority.

Police power. The general power of state government to protect citizens and the environment by passing laws in the interest of public safety and welfare.

Policy. A plan of action to meet a specific goal; also, a position on a specific issue.

Political parties. Political organizations, particularly the Democratic and Republican parties, that regularly compete to win elections in order to control the government and influence its policies.

Political region. An area of land that has legal boundaries and its own government.

Politics. The process by which we determine our governmental policies and choose the officials who will carry them out.

Poll tax. A tax on the right to vote. At one time, Georgians had to pay a yearly tax of $1 to vote.

Polls. 1: Designated voting sites used for elections. 2: Surveys of public opinion.

Popular sovereignty. The idea that government must be based on the will of the people.

Population density. The number of people who live within a unit, such as a square mile, of an area.

Populists. The popular name for members of the People's party, which existed from 1892 to 1912.

Postbellum. Period after the Civil War.

Postmolds. Stains in soil left from wooden posts.

Preamble. An introductory statement to a legal document.

Precipitation. Water which reaches the earth from the atmosphere in either solid or liquid form, such as hail, sleet, mist, rain, or snow.

Prehistory. The period of the past before written records were kept.

Prevailing westerlies. A pattern of winds that blow from the west to the northeast. Important for sailing ships crossing the Atlantic.

Primary election. A statewide election held by a political party to choose its candidates for the general election.

Primary source. A firsthand or original account of a historical event, such as a letter, diary, or old photo.

Primary. A party election in which voters nominate the candidate who will represent that party in the November general election.

Prime Meridian. The meridian (0° longitude) that runs through Greenwich, England, from which all other longitude is measured.

Privatization. The use of a private business to deliver a government service.

Probate court. County court with limited jurisdiction that handles matters such as wills and guardianship, and issues marriage licenses.

Probation. A sentence by a judge allowing a convicted offender to avoid imprisonment if the offender follows certain rules and regularly reports to a supervisor during the probation period.

Proclamation of 1763. Document issued by King George III in which Britain created four new American colonies, extended Georgia's southern boundary, and reserved the land west of the Appalachian Mountains for the Indians.

Prohibition. Forbidding the manufacture, sale, or use of alcoholic beverages.

Projectile points. The general term archaeologists use for the stone points ("heads") of spears and arrows made by Indians.

Property tax. A tax based on the value of real property (a house or land), personal property (car or boat), or other types of property (savings and stocks). Also known as ad valorem tax.

Proprietary colony. Established when the king issued a charter granting ownership of a colony to a person or a group.

Prosecution. The role the government takes in a criminal case, by filing charges against a defendant and then attempting to convict that person in court.

Puritans. Members of a Protestant religious group who were opposed to the Church of England's practices and wanted to change them.

Ratification. Formal approval of a proposed action.

Reapportion. To redraw election districts for representative bodies, such as Congress and the General Assembly.

Reapportionment. The redrawing of election districts every 10 years following the U.S. Census.

Recall. Special election to remove a person from public office before the end of that official's term.

Reconstruction. The period after the Civil War when the federal government took control of the former Confederate states in an attempt to change them before readmitting them to the Union.

Referendum. A direct vote by the public on some question or issue.

Region. A term used by geographers to describe an area of the earth with shared characteristics that make it different from other areas of the earth.

Relative location. The position of one place in relation to another.

Relief. The difference in elevation within a landform from base to top.

Repeal. Abolish, or take back, approval previously given.

Reservoir. An artificial lake built to store and control water for such purposes as public water supply, hydro-electric production, flood control, and recreation.

Resolution. A proposal, similar to a bill, expressing an opinion or the will of a legislative body.

Revenue. Money that government receives from taxes, fees, and other sources.

Ridge and Valley. The physiographic province located in northwest Georgia, noted for long, often parallel ridges, separated by valleys. This province extends from central Alabama northward into Canada.

Royal colony. A colony set up and run directly by the British government in the 17th and 18th centuries.

Run-off. A follow-up election between the two top candidates in an election in which no candidate received a majority of votes.

Rural. Refers to areas of the countryside with a low population density and not considered urban as defined by the U.S. Census Bureau.

Sanitary landfill. The public facility where solid waste is buried under earth.

Scalawag. A southerner who worked with carpetbaggers or Union Army officials during Reconstruction.

Secede. To withdraw voluntarily from a union.

Secession. The action of southern states, in 1860 and 1861, of withdrawing from the Union.

Secondary source. An account of historical events by someone who did not personally witness those events.

Seconds. The 60 equal units that make up a minute of a circle.

Sectionalism. Putting the interests of a particular section or region above those of the nation.

Sediment. Settled deposits of earth and rock caused by water erosion.

Segregation. Keeping blacks and whites apart in public places.

Separate but equal doctrine. The U.S. Supreme Court ruling, in 1897, that separate public facilities for whites and blacks were legal as long as they were equal in character. The doctrine was overturned in 1954.

Separation of powers. A division of governmental power among separate branches, each with distinct roles and powers.

Sharecropping. A system of tenant farming in which the tenant works someone else's land for a share of the crop.

Sherds. Bits of broken pottery left by earlier societies.

Shoals. Shallow river areas where the bottom is made up of sand or layers of rocks.

Site. The location where an archaeological team attempts to locate clues from previous societies.

Slave codes. Laws that governed the ownership, treatment, and behavior of slaves.

Slope. The steepness of a landform, measured in degrees of a circle.

Smuggle. To carry on illegal trade.

Social institutions. Groups of people and their behaviors that have developed over the years to serve particular human needs.

Socialist. One who believes that government should own major services and the means of production.

Sovereign. Independent; subject to no higher authority or government.

Special district. Special-purpose local government set up by government to provide a single service (such as public schools, water, or recreation) within a defined area.

Speculating. Attempting to make money quickly by buying something at a low price and then selling it at a profit as its value increases.

Sphere. A round body, such as the earth, on which every point of the surface is the same distance from its center.

State. One of the 50 political units which make up the United States; the level of government below that of the nation.

States' rights. Belief that American states have certain rights under the Tenth Amendment to the U.S. Constitution that the national government cannot violate.

Suburban. Refers to a heavily populated residential area near a large city.

Suffrage. The right to vote, often used in connection with extending the franchise to women.

Sun Belt. Popular name for the southeastern and southwestern areas of the country, which have attracted many Americans in search of a warmer climate and a lower cost of living.

Superior court. Georgia general trial court with original jurisdiction over most criminal and civil matters.

Surface water. Above-ground water stored in rivers, streams, and lakes.

Syllabary. A set of written characters, or symbols, used to represent spoken syllables.

Tariff. A tax or duty imposed on goods imported from other countries.

Tax digest. The record showing the total taxable value of property in a city or county.

Tenant farmer. A poor farmer who did not own land and had to live on and work the land of others, either for wages or a share of the crop they produced.

Territory. A frontier area belonging to the United States but not yet organized into a state.

Tides. The daily rise and fall of the ocean caused principally by the gravitational pull of the moon.

Time line. A chart that shows the chronology, or time order, of historical events.

Time zone. One of 24 divisions of the earth used for measuring time. Each division marks the approximate distance that the earth rotates in one hour.

Tories. American colonists, also called "loyalists," who supported the British government before and during the American Revolution.

Trade winds. Constant air currents at sea caused by high and low pressure areas attempting to equalize. Important for sailing ships crossing the Atlantic.

Tradition. Another word for Native American cultural periods, such as the Paleo-Indian Tradition.

Trial jury. A group of 12 citizens who hear evidence at a trial and decide whether a defendant is guilty or innocent.

Triangular trade. Trade route used by American colonial merchants that involved Africa, the West Indies, and the colonies in trading rum, slaves, sugar, and molasses.

Trustees. The 21 individuals named by King George II in 1732 to govern the new colony of Georgia. They were to act on behalf of others without personally benefiting.

Turnpike. A road built and maintained by a private company which then charges travelers a fee or toll to use the road.

Underground Railroad. A network of people and places that sheltered slaves as they escaped the South seeking freedom in the North.

Unicameral. Consisting of only one house or chamber, as was the case in Georgia's legislature from 1777 to 1789.

Upcountry. The unsettled area of Georgia's frontier far inland from the coast; also called "backcountry."

Urban. Generally, refers to any city or community with at least 2,500 inhabitants. Urban can also refer to a densely settled area with a combined population of 50,000 or more that is located next to a city.

Urbanized area. Includes a central space and the densely settled urban fringe next to or around it. The combined population must be at least 50,000.

User fee. A charge made to persons for using a governmental service such as water.

Veto. An action by a chief executive to prevent a bill passed by a legislative body from becoming law. Vetoes can be overridden by the legislature.

Voting Rights Act of 1965. Legislation that gave the federal government power to register voters and approve any election law changes in certain states, principally in the South.

Water cycle. The journey of water from ocean to rainfall, its use and reuse on land, and then its return to the sea.

Water table. The upper limit of water-saturated soil.

Wattle and daub. Combination of wood and clay used by the Mississippian Indians for building their houses.

Weather. Conditions in the atmosphere on any given day.

Wetland. Low-lying land covered by water all or part of the time, in which special types of plant and animal life are found. Also known as marshes and swamps.

Whigs. American colonists, also called "patriots," who opposed British government before and during the American Revolution.

White primary. A primary election open to white voters only.

White supremacy. The belief that the white race is superior to others and should control government and society.

Woodland Indians. The prehistoric Native American culture that existed between Archaic and Mississippian periods, lasting roughly from 1000 B.C. to A.D. 1000.

Yazoo Land Fraud. The political scandal in 1795, when Georgia's General Assembly sold millions of acres of Georgia's western territories for just pennies an acre to land speculators who had bribed many of the legislators.

Yeoman farmer. A white middle-class farmer who generally owned fewer than 100 acres.

Zone. 1: A region several miles wide that separates one geographic area from another. 2: An area in a community with a designated use.

Zoning. Dividing a community into zones for different types of uses, such as business, residential subdivisions, and agriculture.

Index

Key: * = glossary word; *c.* = chart, table, or diagram; *m.* = map; *p.* = picture.

Blue Ridge* Mountains, 17, *p.* 17, 20, 21, *p.* 21, 30
Board of Regents, 407
boll weevil, 258–259
Boltzius, John Martin, 90, 91
Bond, Julian, 311, 316, 323, *p.* 324
booking, 425
border states*, 191
Boston, closing of port of, 107
Boston Massacre, 106, *p.* 106
Boston Tea Party, 106, *p.* 107
Boudinot, Elias, 139, 151
Boudinot, John, 151
Bourbon Redeemers, 221–223
Bourbon Triumvirate, 222
Bowers, D. Talmadge, 295
boxing, 261, 344–345
boycott*, 104
Brasstown Bald, 17, *p.* 17, 18, 21
Breckinridge, John, 185
Bridge, Edmund Pettus, 316
Brown, H. Rap, 317
Brown, James, 346
Brown, John (abolitionist), 184
Brown, John (slave), 174
Brown, Joseph E., 186, *p.* 186, 191–192, 232
Brown, T. Graham, 347
Brown v. Board of Education, 306–307, 324, 378
Brunswick Shipyard, 283, *p.* 284
Bryan, Andrew, 100
Buchanan, Beverly, 350–351
budget, 399, *c.* 406, 413–414
buffer* colony, 68
building codes, 443
Bullock, Rufus, 215, 216
Bull Run Creek, 192
Bunker Hill, Battle of, 114
Burns, Olive Ann, 348
Busbee, George, 327–328, *p.* 328
Bush, George, 336
Butler, Selena Sloan, 233

—C—

Cabot, John, 57, 66–67
Caldwell, Erskine, 279, 348
Calhoun, John C., *p.* 172
California, and the slavery issue, 177–178
Callaway, Howard "Bo," 299
Camden County, 30
Camilla, 343
Campbell, Bill, 337
Campbell County, 268
Camp Benning, 257
Camp Gordon, 257, 283
Camp Hancock, 257
canals, 132–133

Canaries, Juan, 91
Candler, Asa G., 244
Candler Field, 262
Cape Cod, 65
capital felony*, 419
capital* (state), *m.* 126, 206, *p.* 383
    in Atlanta, 214, 222, *p.* 222, 242
    in Augusta, 98, 126–127
    in Louisville, 127, 128
    in Milledgeville, 127, 141, 179, 222
    in postbellum period, 207
    in Savannah, 126
capitol*, *p.* 374, 395, *p.* 395
carbon 14 dating*, 45–46
cardinal directions*, 4
Carmichael, James, 295
Carmichael, Stokely, 317
Carolina. *See also* North Carolina; South Carolina
    creation of, *m.* 66, 66–67
carpetbaggers*, 208, 216
Carson, John, 347
Carter, Jimmy, 299, 346, 347
    as governor, 325–327, *p.* 326
    at inauguration, *p.* 321
    as president, 330–331
Carter, Rosalynn, 325
    at inauguration, *p.* 321
Carter Presidential Center and Library, 331, 354
Cartersville, 52
cartographers*, 6
carved shell ornament*, *p.* 43
case law, 418
Catholic Church
    building of missions by, 62–63
    exclusion from Georgia, 73–74
    and settlement, 99
caucus*, 390
cause and effect*, 38
Cave Springs, 166
cede*, 126
census*, 123
    first, 123
census regions, *c.* 11
centennial* celebration, 40
Center for Puppetry Arts, 349
Centers for Disease Control, 300
Central of Georgia Railroad, 135, 136
centuries*, 40
cession*, 141
chain gang system, 233
Chaney, James, 315
Charles, Ezzard, 345
Charles, Ray, 346, *p.* 346
Charles II (King of England), 66
Charles Town (later Charleston), 67, 76
chart*, 124

charter*, 64, 434
Chattahoochee River, 21, 131, 135, 143
    as drinking water source, *p.* 338
    pollution of, *p.* 338
Chattanooga, Battle of, 197, 198
checks and balances*, 118, *c.* 373, 373–374
Cherokee Phoenix newspaper, 146, *p.* 147, 151
Cherokees, 52, 61, 120, 123, 126, 127, 140, *m.* 145, 145–147, *p.* 146, 150–152, 340
Cherokee territory, 29
Chickamauga, 354
Chickamauga, Battle of, 198
Chickasaws, 120, 140
chiefdom*, 51–52, 141
child labor, *p.* 229, 229–231, 273
Choctaws, 140
chronology*, 39, *c.* 39
Church of England, 65
circle graph, 124
circle measurements, 4–5
Circuit Rider's Wife, The (Harris), 347
cities*, 380, 434–438
    growth of, 242
citizen*, 367
citizenship*, 367
city council*, 436
city-county consolidation, 440, *p.* 440
city manager*, 437–438
civil case*, 418–419
Civilian Conservation Corps (CCC), 271
civil rights*
    definition of, 305
Civil Rights Act (1964)*, 314–315, 315–316, 318, 323, 378
civil rights movement, 304–318, 378
    attitudes toward progress in, 309
    change of focus, 318
    continuation of efforts, 317
    desegregation, 324
    growth of, 311
    increased violence in, 311–312, 314
    March on Washington in, 314
    protests in, *p.* 315
    students in, 311
    voting rights for African Americans, 315–316
Civil War (1861–1865), 189–190, 376
    African Americans in, 194, *p.* 194
    battles in, 190–191, 194, *m.* 197, 197–200
    call for volunteers in, 190
    causes of, 184–190
    costs of, 191, 192
    draft in, 191
    economic reconstruction, 206–210
    effects of, 204–205
    end of, 202
    firing at Fort Sumter in, 190, *p.* 190
    Georgians in, 191–194

Sources and Picture Credits

Sources

Page 77. From a letter in the *South Carolina Gazette*, Charles Town, March 22, 1733, reprinted in *Colonial Records of Georgia*, Vol. 3, Allen D. Candler, ed., 1905, p. 406. **90.** February 17, 1736, excerpt from *Georgia Historical Quarterly*, Vol. 53, 1969. All other excerpts from George Fenwick Jones, *Detailed Reports*, Vol. 2, 1734-35; Vol. 3, 1736; Vol. 4, 1737; Vol. 5, 1738 (Athens: University of Georgia Press, 1968, 1972, 1976, 1980). Used by permission. **93.** Adapted from *The Interesting Narrative of the Life of Olaudah Equiano, or Gustavus Vassa, the African, Written by Himself,* Vol. 1, First American Ed. (New York: W. Durrell, 1791). **116-17.** Nancy Hart and Austin Dabney excerpts from George White, *Historical Collections of Georgia* (New York: Pudney & Russell, Publishers, 1854). **132-33.** Excerpt of Gideon Lincecum from extracts reprinted in Ulrich B. Phillips, *Plantation and Frontier Documents: 1649-1863,* Vol. 2 (Cleveland, Ohio: The Arthur H. Clark Company, 1909). **171.** Conversation between Mrs. Lyell and her landlady, excerpted from Mills Lane, ed., *The Rambler in Georgia* (Savannah: Beehive Press, 1973), p. 206. Used by permission. **174.** Adapted from F.N. Boney, ed., *Slave Life in Georgia: A Narrative of the Life, Sufferings, and Escape of John Brown, A Fugitive Slave* (Savannah: Beehive Press, 1972), pp. 158, 165-68. Used by permission. **175.** "A Defense of Slavery," adapted from Thomas R.R. Cobb, *An Historical Sketch of Slavery* (Philadelphia: T&J Johnston & Co., 1858), pp. 217-21. **193.** "Substitute for Coffee," from *Confederate Receipt Book* (Richmond, Va.: West & Johnston, 1863); reprinted by University of Georgia Press, 1960. **196.** "A Georgia Soldier's View," adapted from Bell Irvin Wiley, ed., *Confederate Letters of John W. Hagen* (Athens, Ga.: University of Georgia Press, 1954), pp. 46-48. Used by permission. **199.** Union soldier's description of Atlanta's destruction, from Fenwick Y. Hedley, *Marching through Georgia* (Chicago: R.R. Donnelley & Sons, 1885), p. 257. **202.** An entry in her diary, excerpted from Eliza Frances Andrews, *The War-Time Journal of a Georgia Girl* (New York: D. Appleton and Company, 1908), pp. 171-73. **206.** Quote from "Thar's More in the Man than Thar Is in the Land," from Sidney Lanier, *Poems* (New York: Charles Scribner's Sons, 1901), pp. 180-82. **230-31.** From Clare de Graffenried, "The Georgia Cracker in the Cotton Mills," *Century Magazine,* Vol. 41, No. 4 (February 1891), pp. 483-98. **233.** "The Chain Gang System," was read by Selena S. Butler before the National Association of Colored Women at Nashville, Tenn., September 16, 1897 (Tuskegee, Ala.: Normal School Steam Press Print, 1897). **234.** "Votes for Women," adapted from Mrs. William H. Felton (Rebecca Latimer Felton), *The Subjection of Women and the Enfranchisement of Women* (Cartersville, Ga.: May 14, 1915), pp. 3-8. **236-37.** Story of the Pickens County funeral, adapted from Henry W. Grady, *The New South* (New York: Robert Bonner's Sons, 1890), pp. 188-91. **244.** Speech by Booker T. Washington excerpted from his book *Up from Slavery, An Autobiography* (New York: Doubleday, Page & Co., 1901), pp. 18-25. **245.** "Why Not Equality," quoted in Ridgely Torrance, *The Story of John Hope* (New York: The Macmillan Company, 1948), pp. 114-15. Used by permission. **246.** Niagara Movement adaptation from W.E.B. DuBois, "The Niagara Movement," *The Voice of the Negro,* Vol. 2, No. 9 (September 1905), pp. 619-22. **248.** "What an Eighth Grade Pupil Ought to Know," from *High School Quarterly,* Vol. 3, No. 2 (January 1915), p. 81. In Oscar H. Joiner, gen. ed., *A History of Public Education in Georgia* (Columbia, S.Ca.: R.L. Bryan Company, 1979), p. 263. **248.** Educational facilities in 1908, from Dorothy Orr, *A History of Education in Georgia* (Chapel Hill: University of North Carolina Press, 1950), p. 314. **266-67, 272, 308,** Emory Hurt, Sidney Thurmond, Lina Belle McCommons, and Rosa Strickland interviews with David Lovett; and **267,** Dorsey Crowe interview with author, 1981, all adapted from Lawrence R. Hepburn, *The Georgia History Book* (Athens: Institute of Government, University of Georgia, 1982), pp. 168-69, 173-74, 180, 189-90, 174-75. **310.** "Brotherhood in the South," excerpt adapted from Ralph McGill, *The South and the Southerner* (Boston: Little, Brown, and Company, 1959, 1963), pp. 232-33. **313.** "Letter from Birmingham Jail," excerpt of letter by Martin Luther King, Jr., *Why We Can't Wait* (New York: Harper & Row Publishers, 1963), pp. 83-84.

Picture Credits

Abbeville Press, from *The Great Book of Currier & Ives' America,* 136. Alabama Department of Archives and History, 138, photo courtesy of *Georgia Historical Quarterly.* Bill Allen, 17 (top), 23, 33. Architect of the Capitol, 371. *Athens Banner-Herald,* 309. Athens Newspapers, Inc., 444 (bottom). Courtesy of the Atlanta History Center, 130, 222, 238, 244, 261, 279: photo provided by Hargrett Rare Book and Manuscript Library, University of Georgia Libraries, 310. Atlanta Housing Authority, 377. *Atlanta Journal-Constitution,* 268, 278, 315. *Atlanta Resurgens* (1971), 134. Atlanta Symphony Orchestra, 346 (bottom). Atlanta University Center, Robert W. Woodruff Library: 233, from "Neighborhood Union Papers"; 246, copy of original Carl Van Vechten photo; Special Collections Department, 264, from "Charles Forrest Palmer Papers." Baldwin County land grant, displayed at the Madison-Morgan Cultural Center, 129. Banks County Chamber of Commerce, 452. Nancy C. Bennett, 358, 361. Beverly Buchanan (1991), photo courtesy of Steinbaum-Krauss Gallery, New York City, 351 (bottom). Cahokia Mounds Historic Site, Lloyd K. Townsend, artist, 43 (top), 51. Ruth Carpenter, 442. *Century Magazine* (January 1878), 158, photo provided by University of Georgia Press. Chicago Historical Society, 168 (cropped left and right), 194. Anton Corbijn, 347. Corbis-Bettmann, 295. Hilda Curran, 269. Theodore de Bry, from University of Georgia Libraries: after Le Moyne (1564), 34-35; in de Bry, *America* (1591); 51; 64. Dover Clip Art Series, 104, 107, 108, 203. Davis Factor, 349 (top). Garrow and Associates, 44. Georgia Bureau of Investigation, 411. Georgia Department of Archives and History, 30, 50, 113 (recruitment poster), 185 (top), 195, 205, 227, 232, 234, 235, 236, 237, 239, 240, 241, 242 (top), 243, 249 (both), 254, 256, 257, 260 (bottom), 262, 267, 284, 285, 289, 293, 296, 298, 300, 306, 307, 324, 328 (top), 341, 342, 343, 431. Georgia Department of Industry, Trade and Tourism, 24 (bottom), 53 (top), 346 (top). Georgia Department of Natural Resources, 270, 274. Georgia Department of Transportation, 17 (bottom). Georgia Historical Society, 127; Ayllón Committee, 58, 92. Georgia State University, Special Collections Department,

294, 299, 303. Hargrett Rare Book and Manuscript Library, University of Georgia Libraries, 38, 82, 83, 90, from Oversized Collection: *Harper's Weekly* (January 5, 1867) 97, 102-3, 116, 144, 166, 167, 169, 175, 178, 179, 191, 198 (bottom), 200, 209, 210, 213, 224, 225, 229, 230, 247, 258, 271 (top). *Harper's Magazine* (January 1874), 159. *Harper's Weekly*, January 8, 1878, 160 (bottom); April 27, 1861, 190; November 9, 1872, 208; 214; February 12, 1887, 220, 221. Lawrence R. Hepburn, 350, 362, 363, 364, 384, 385, 419. *Historia general y natural de las Indias, islas y tierra-firma del mar ocèano* (Madrid, 1851-1855), 56. The Herndon Home, 242 (bottom). Collection of the High Museum of Art, Atlanta, Ga., T. Marshall Hahn Jr. Collection, 1996.184, 353. Edwin L. Jackson, 7, 16, 19 (bottom), 20, 22, 23 (both), 28, 40, 45 (both), 56, 80, 81, 89, 110, 112, 114, 121, 142, 153, 286-87, 316 (both), 317, 334, 337, 339, 356-57, 369, 370, 374, 375, 381, 382, 383, 388 (both), 390, 392-93, 394, 395 (both), 398, 401, 410, 415, 416, 417, 423 (both), 424, 425, 430, 432, 440, 445, 446, 447, 449. From the Collection of Edwin L. Jackson, 188 (bottom). Phyllis B. Kandul, Office of the Governor, 328 (bottom), 402. Martin Luther King, Jr., Center for Nonviolent Social Change, 313. Ken Krakow, 351 (top). James E. Kundell, 338. Library of Congress, 181, 182, 184, 201, 204, 207, 216, 252-53, 260 (top), 304, 322 (top right), photo provided by Richard B. Russell Library, University of Georgia Libraries. Allan Lipsett, 335. The Juliette Gordon Low Girl Scout National Center, Girl Scouts of the United States of America, 250. Reid McCallister, 352, 354, 355, 427, 448, 450. Isabel Wier McWilliams, photo provided by Hargrett Rare Book and Manuscript Library, University of Georgia Libraries, 255. Walker Montgomery, 318. Morehouse College Archives, 301. Susan E. Morris, intern, Georgia Department of Corrections, 412. In *Narratives of de Soto* (New York: Bradford Club, 1866), 60. National Archives, 162, 282, 283 (bottom), 305. Courtesy of the National Portrait Gallery, London, 72. National Portrait Gallery, Smithsonian Institution, 185 (bottom), photo of the Alexander Hesler portrait, provided by United States Information Agency. Carol and Harold Norton, Laboratory of Archaeology, University of Georgia, 49. O'Connor Collection, Ina Dillard Russell Library, Georgia College, 348. Ocmulgee National Monument, U.S. Department of the Interior, 53 (bottom). Office of the Governor, 326, 336. Office of the Mayor: Savannah, Ga., 76; East Point, Ga., 434; Hartwell, Ga., 435; Decatur, Ga., 444 (top). Office of the Secretary of State, Georgia Capitol Museum, 29, 259 (both). Old Dartmouth Historical Society, New Bedford Whaling Museum, 165. Rick O'Quinn, Office of Public Information, University of Georgia, 345. Lloyd Ostendorf, 215. Pandora '70, UGA yearbook, 320. Ronald Paulson, William Hogarth engraving, 73. J. Winston Pennock, 288. Walt Petrushka, the *Albany Herald*, 436. Mary Porter, 15, 36, 418. Reader's Digest Association, *America's Fascinating Indian Heritage*, 42, 48. Tom Reed, 31. Regency House Publishing Ltd., 47. Richard B. Russell Library, University of Georgia Libraries, 276, 322 (top left). Schomburg Center for Research in Black Culture, The New York Public Library, 100. Smithsonian Institution, 43 (bottom), 139, 146. David Smoak, 439. Molly Sneed, 329. Southeast Archaeological Center, National Park Service, 52. Southern Railway, 137. Sports Information, University of Georgia, 344. Statuary Hall, U.S. Capitol, 37. Joseph Strickland, 429. The Topps Co., Inc., 319. Juliann Tredwell, 443. U.S. Army Signal Corps, 283 (top), photo provided by Fort Benning, Ga. U.S. Capitol Historical Society, 55, photo provided by National Geographic Society. U.S. Department of the Army, xiv-1. U.S. Department of the Interior, National Park Service, 202. U.S. Department of the Navy, 281, photo provided by U.S.I.A. U.S. Postal Service, stamp designs: 1983 © U.S. Postal Service, half-title page; 1988 © U.S. Postal Service, title page; reproduced with permission. University of Georgia Libraries, 54, 58 (top left), 61, 67, 68, 69, 85, 86, 88 (both), 91, 94, 95, 97 (bottom), 99, 105, 106, 119, 122, 132, 143, 147, 148 (both), 150, 154-55, 156, 160 (top), 161, 170, 172, 174, 180, 183, 186, 187, 188 (top), 192, 193 (top), 198 (top), 206, 217, 218-19, 226, 271 (bottom), 273. The Warner Collection of Gulf States Paper Corporation, Tuscaloosa, Ala., 157, 183 (detail: slaves picking cotton). Wesleyan College, 164. John White (1585 watercolor), 340, from University of Georgia Libraries. White House photo (1977), 321. Courtesy Winterthur Museum, 70-71, 78. Woolaroc Museum, Bartlesville, Oklahoma, 152. Yale University Art Gallery, 109. David Zeiger, 349 (bottom).

Unit Photo Captions

Unit 1 (pp. xiv-1): Carters Dam, Murray County, Georgia. Unit 2 (pp. 34-35): Late Mississippian period Indians in military formation, 1560s. Unit 3 (pp. 70-71): Trustees of Georgia, 1734. Unit 4 (pp. 102-3): Nancy Hart and the Tories. Unit 5 (pp. 154-55): The University of Georgia, Athens, 1840s. Unit 6 (pp. 218-19): Atlanta railroad yards. Unit 7 (pp. 252-53): Hazlehurst, Georgia, 1941. Unit 8 (pp. 286-87): Atlanta skyline, 1991. Unit 9 (pp. 356-57): Demonstration at state capitol, Atlanta, Georgia. Unit 10 (pp. 392-93): State capitol, Atlanta, Georgia.

Georgia State Symbols (p. 459)

Butterfly: Photo by Tom Moreno, Marietta College Department of Biology, Marietta, Ohio

Largemouth bass: Photo by F. Eugene Hester

Peach: Georgia Department of Industry, Trade and Tourism

Peanut: Dothan Area Convention and Visitors Bureau, Dothan, Alabama

All other photos by Edwin L. Jackson

Maps

Except as noted, all maps were created by Reid McCallister (1st ed.) and updated and enhanced by Jessica Mendelson (2d ed.):

pp. 2, 5, 6, 8, 19, 20, 26, 32, 95: Digital images incorporated from Mountain High Maps® copyright © 1993 Digital Wisdom, Inc.

pp. 126, 199: Original work by James D. Ingram, Dolores V. Holt, Cartographic Services, University of Georgia

p. 145: Original work by Edwin L. Jackson

pp. 456-57: Created by Jessica Mendelson, based on Georgia Department of Transportation map.

p. 458: Base map from US Digital Topography copyright © 1994 Chalk Butte Inc.

pp. 460-61, 462-63: Digital maps from MapArt, Cartesia Software, revised and enhanced by Edwin L. Jackson

Cover

Design by Reid McCallister, Jessica Mendelson, and Mary Porter

Stamps from the private collection of Edwin L. Jackson

Stamp designs © 1979–1998 U.S. Postal Service. Reproduced with permission. Stamp images: Permission granted by the family of Bobby Jones; by Zelma Redding; by the United States Olympic Committee; "License granted by Intellectual Properties Management, Atlanta, Georgia, as manager for the King Estate."